La Cañada

San Pascual

San Rafael

Santa Anita

Azusa de Duarte

Azusa Dalton

PUBLIC LAND

Addition to San Jose

San Francisquito

San Jose

1771

Pueblo de Los Angeles

San Gabriel Arcangel

PUBLIC LAND

Potrero Grande

Potrero de Felipe Lugo

Los Nogales

La Merced

Potrero Chico

La Puente

PUBLIC LAND

San Antonio

Paso de Bartolo

PUBLIC LAND

Rincon de La Brea

La Habra

Santa Gertrudes

El Camino Real

Los Coyotes

Los Cerritos

Los Alamitos

Bay of San Pedro

CAL

Scale of English Miles

0   5   10   15

Spanish Leagues

0   1   2   3   4   5

Spanish Varas

0 1000   5000   10000   15000   20000   25000

Santa Clara County Free Library

REFERENCE

584300

Santa Clara Valley Library System
Mountain View Public Library
Santa Clara County Free Library
California

Alum Rock	Milpitas { Calaveras / Community Center / Sunnyhills
Campbell	
Cupertino	Morgan Hill
Gilroy	Saratoga { Quito / Village
Los Altos	Stanford-Escondido

Research Center-Cupertino
For Bookmobile Service, request schedule

LOS ÁNGELES: EPIC OF A CITY

The beautiful Palos Verdes Peninsula on the isolated frontier of New Spain was part of the first rancho granted in Southern California. Beneath these cliffs Indians sped in canoes and sailing vessels anchored when they came to trade. Above rancheros lived and cattle grazed on fields and rolling hills. This stately headland was a leading outpost on the Pacific shore.

(—David Muench)

LOS ANGELES:

EPIC OF A CITY

BY

LYNN BOWMAN

Howell
-North
Books

Printed and bound in the United States of America

Library of Congress Catalog Card No. 74-16723

ISBN 0-8310-7109-5

Endsheet map of the ranchos courtesy of
Title Insurance & Trust Co.

Published by Howell-North Books
1050 Parker Street, Berkeley, California 94710

Contents

Acknowledgments

For historians of the American West, The Bancroft Library is an indispensable center for research. It holds the extraordinary collection of Californiana gathered by Hubert Howe Bancroft during the early years of statehood. His own writings are a basic reference for scholars, and I wish to express utmost appreciation for his great service. He said, "A library is not merely a depository of learning but a society for the promotion of knowledge." This principle is followed by the excellent staff of The Bancroft Library, so that I have been able to do research there which would have been impossible elsewhere.

Certain historians have generously aided my work with suggestions from their own experience and knowledge. Dr. Jacob N. Bowman, historian of the State Archives from 1948 to 1955, described the strange odyssey of the Spanish Archives (records from the period of Spanish and Mexican rule) after American forces invaded California. Thomas Workman Temple II, historian of the San Gabriel Mission and descendant of a pioneer family, gave me special information about Los Alamos and events connected with the beginning of the journey of the colonists to found Los Angeles. W. W. Robinson, author of many books about the history of Southern California, gave me the benefit of his long familiarity with Los Angeles and its background. None of these eminent men are living today, but each of them added to the value of my work.

In addition I wish to thank Edwin A. Beilharz, professor of history at the University of Santa Clara, emeritus, discoverer of the only document which verifies the date of the founding of Los Angeles; Richard L. Reynolds of the Department of Paleontology of the Natural History Museum; and Dr. Gordon B. Oakeshott, former Chief Deputy of the California Division of Mines and Geology and author of *California's Changing Landscape*. I am deeply indebted to them for their kind help.

I am grateful to Adria Locke Langley, author of *A Lion is in the Streets* and a lifelong friend, for her perceptive criticism of my writing.

7

Other people, too numerous to mention, have offered reminiscences as well as specialized information regarding certain aspects of life in the Southland. To them, my sincere appreciation.

I would like to express one regret. There are many pioneer families whose names are not mentioned in these pages, yet to have included them all would have added confusion to this account. As a conclusion to my acknowledgments, I salute them all. Each one had a special part in creating the history of Los Angeles.

Finally, I wish to dedicate this book to my husband, who brought me to this remarkable city.

LYNN BOWMAN

Ventura, California
May 1974

"What is Past is Prologue."

— SHAKESPEARE

I

THE ISOLATED VALLEY

1. *The Locale*

The isolated valley waited. From time to time a slight breeze from the ocean 25 miles away, stirred the dust and grasses briefly, then all was motionless again. Cottonwood, live oak and sycamore trees made silent oases of shade on the sere, faded earth; along a parched riverbed a shallow stream flowed slowly through the valley. It was September 4, 1781, the hottest time of the year as well as the driest.

Toward this scene 11 families, the founders of Los Angeles, moved hopefully. Spaniards, Negroes and Indians, they were at last reaching the end of their long journey from Los Alamos in the province of Sonora, Mexico. The venturesome company included not only adults but also 22 children, almost half of them under five. Huddled on the unstable deck of a small pinnace, they had sailed over the rough waters of the Gulf of California, then followed an arduous trail north across deserts, hills and rock-strewn land. It was February 2, mid-winter, when they had started; at the end of summer, seven months later, they were following a road winding between low foothills until, open to view, their destination lay just ahead.

With no thought that a great city was being born, they gazed at the lonely spot which was to be home. Sloping hills embraced the valley protectively. The stillness gave a feeling of peace. With sudden eagerness the families forded the cool stream and exuberantly plucked wild roses which, growing among the river grasses, bloomed in festive welcome.

2. *Spanish Exploration*

We all know about the early days of the colonies along the East Coast of North America, but how much do we know about the early days in California?

9

The name "California" was coined by a Spanish author in the 16th century for a fabulous land peopled by beautiful sirens. In his romance of chivalry, *The Exploits of Esplandián*, Garcí Ordoñez de Montalvo described an island "close to the Terrestrial Paradise," where precious stones abounded and whose only inhabitants were glamorous dark-skinned Amazons. Although imaginary, the island became a goal for such famous explorers as Cortez and Coronado. An expedition sent out by Cortez in 1533-34 discovered in the Pacific Ocean what the explorers thought was an island, and pearls were found there. Within a few years, the "island" was named California. Old maps show it separated from the mainland by the Vermillion Sea. A century and a half later Father Eusebio Francisco Kino crossed the Colorado River near its mouth in what is now the Gulf of California. He crossed on a log raft propelled by Indians who swam alongside while the intrepid padre remained insulated from the waves, sitting comfortably inside a huge basket on the raft. In 1702 he descended the Colorado River to the gulf. No evidence of a strait could be seen, and this made Kino certain that California was part of the mainland. During the expedition in 1746 of another Jesuit, Father Fernando Consag, up the coast of the peninsula to the mouth of the Colorado, the continuous coastline gave final proof that California was not an island.

In 1542, Juan Rodriguez Cabrillo sailed with two ships along California's Pacific coast, exploring the unknown land in a search for the Northwest Passage. On the shore Indians stared in amazement at the oncoming Spanish vessels which, with what seemed to be wings outspread, were propelled by the wind. They wondered about the colored pennants flying from each mast, and about the flag of Spain rising above the high poop deck, displaying the Towers of Aragon and the Lion of Castile. It was the Indians' first glimpse of the civilization which would destroy their own.

Sixty years later Sebastián Vizcaíno sailed north with three vessels, following the same shore and adding his own careful descriptions of bays, rivers, cliffs and islands.

Spain was busy colonizing Mexico when she realized that if the land along the Pacific Ocean were to be added to her territory there was no time to lose. Russia was already establishing trading posts in the Northwest, reaching ever farther to the south, and England was adding to her colonies in the East, persistently driving farther west. As a result, Spain decided to found a chain of missions and presidios (military garrisons) along the West Coast. California was to be colonized as a joint venture of church and state, soldiers and missionaries marching together into the wilderness.

California as an island. *(—Bancroft Library)*

The land along the West Coast was divided into Baja (Lower) and Alta (Upper) California, called as a whole The Californias. The Jesuit Order was already establishing missions in Baja California, and would have led in the advance north. But King Carlos III became distrustful of the Jesuits' power and decided that they were plotting to depose or kill him. Warned that anything done against them with advance notice might bring about a popular uprising in their support, the king made a secret move, sending sealed orders to leading officials throughout the Spanish empire. In the colonies the envelopes were all to be opened at dawn on the same date, April 2, 1767, but not earlier on pain of death. So on that day the king's edict was disclosed, banishing the Jesuits from Spain and her territories, effective immediately.

Near Mexico City, missionaries of the Franciscan Order received their training at the College of San Fernando. A large number of them eagerly volunteered to take over the relinquished missionary work, and 16 friars were chosen to replace the equal number of Jesuits.

It was on the advice of Don José de Gálvez, Visitador General (Inspector General), that the King of Spain decided to annex Alta California, and he put Gálvez in charge of organizing expeditions by land and by sea. A Pious Fund made up of contributions from wealthy Mexicans would be used toward expenses of the necessary missions, including provisions, clothing, altar equipment and such material for mission work as forges and tools.

For president of the missions the choice fell upon a man of extraordinary ability, Fray Junípero Serra. The learned friar had come to the New World from Mallorca, an island in the Mediterranean off the coast of Spain. There he was professor of philosophy at the friary of San Francisco in the city of Palma. Two of his students, Francisco Palóu and Juan Crespí, followed him to missionary work in Mexico, and years later the same three earnest men labored together in California. Junípero Serra was already 55 when he started north to found missions along the shore of the Pacific, but his undaunted steps took him to a leading role in California history. The military leader of the expedition was Gaspar de Portolá, captain of dragoons in the Spanish army and first Governor of The Californias.

Fray Junípero Serra.
(—*Bancroft Library*)

Spain urged all those in authority, either military or religious, to keep a diary as a record. It is to these diaries that we owe much of our knowledge of the expeditions.

With enthusiasm, Gálvez, Father Serra and Captain Portolá discussed plans. The three men were exceptionally well suited to the need for vigorous, cooperative effort, and there was much to be done. Three ships — the *San Carlos, San Antonio* and *San José* — and two land parties were to leave Baja California for San Diego; in each there would be friars to establish missions and soldiers to establish presidios. Recruits had to be found; ships outfitted and made strong enough for the voyage; clothing and military equipment prepared; religious articles for the missions packed for shipment; cattle, horses and mules rounded up to go to the new frontier; and above all food supplies made ready to keep the expedition from starvation.

Tirelessly Gálvez supervised the work on the ships. Wasting no time on thoughts of his own social eminence, he tossed aside his coat and added his strong hands and shoulders to those of struggling laborers. So deeply involved was he in the project that when the first vessel left for San Diego he jubilantly followed in a smaller bark, watching to see that all was well until finally, when the ship rounded the peninsula into the Pacific Ocean, his eyes could follow it no longer.

It was early in 1769 that the first two ships and a land party started for Upper California. Captain Portolá and Father Serra were due to leave soon after with the second land party. But years earlier, when Serra first arrived in Mexico, an infection from a mosquito bite spread through one leg and never completely healed; during the hurried preparations for departure to the north the leg infection flared up again. The trail ahead would lead across a desolate land of rocky hills and arid deserts, so Portolá urged the friar to send another in his place. Serra refused, undismayed, and after two weeks of rest was ready to start, but about midway on the journey there came a day when he was unable even to stand. In desperation he called in a muleteer and asked for a poultice such as the man used on animals. The pain and swelling lessened, and next morning the indomitable friar continued on his way to San Diego. The incident exemplified Junípero Serra's attitude: although he was lame through the remaining 15 years of his life, nothing ever deterred him from founding and inspecting missions, doing the work to which he was dedicated.

The land parties were still in Baja California, far from their destination, when the *San Antonio* — one of the three vessels which had sailed for Alta California — entered San Diego Bay. The *San Carlos* had been first to leave for the north, yet twenty more days passed with no sign of the ship. Then she made a strangely quiet arrival. The customary salute between ships was exchanged; colors were unfurled, an anchor lowered, but there was no further sign of life. Sailors from the *San Antonio* rowed out and found that all on board the *San Carlos* were sick or dying. During the voyage drinking water had leaked out of the casks; the ship had gone far off course, which meant that the food and water had to last many extra weeks; so scurvy and a contagious illness had taken over the ship. The sick were brought ashore and cared for in an hastily arranged hospital camp just above the water's edge, but of the ship's company all died except five. The crew of the *San Antonio* was likewise stricken: all became ill and eight of the men died. The remaining ship, the *San José*, disappeared at sea.

Two weeks after the *San Carlos* arrived, the first land party, led by Captain Fernando Rivera y Moncada, came upon the tragic scene. Then, a fortnight later on July 1, 1769, Portolá arrived with the second land party. That date, when the expedition as a whole gathered together, is considered the natal day of California. For the 130 pioneers, many of them ill, the day signaled not an end of achievement but time to begin the next stage of exploration.

3. *The Search for Monterey*

The *San Antonio*, with a crew made up of sailors who had recovered enough to be convalescent, sailed to its home port in the Gulf of California to get food and also replacements for both ships. Then a land party was formed in San Diego under Captain Portolá's leadership. The ultimate goal of the trip was Monterey, farther north, a place which the earlier explorer Vizcaíno had described glowingly as a "fine harbor sheltered from all winds," enclosed by land comparable to Castile. (Vizcaíno named the port after the man who had arranged for his voyage of exploration, the Viceroy of New Spain, Gaspar de Zúñiga y Acefedo, Conde de Monte Rey.) That desirable spot was to be made the capital of Alta California and the site of a presidio.

Accompanying Portolá were Capt. Fernando Rivera y Moncada and Lt. Pedro Fages, both later to become military commanders of Alta California. Rivera's "soldados de cuero," or leatherjacket troops, wore sleeveless leather jackets and chaps and carried leather shields as well as leather scabbards for their muskets while on horseback. Of the two friars in the expedition, Francisco Gómez and Juan Crespí, the latter kept an account of the journey. The duty of Ensign Miguel Costansó, engineer, was to map the lands they discovered and to design the presidios.

With a mixture of curiosity and caution, the soldiers and missionaries advanced toward each Indian village. All received them cordially. Father Crespí records that at one village the savages begged them to stay and even wept to see them leave. Most of the Indian men were completely naked, but to the friars' great relief all the women wore knee-length skirts — front and back, two aprons of grass or buckskin.

On August 2, 1769, slightly more than a hundred miles north of San Diego, they came upon what Father Crespí described as "a very

The Indian village of Yang-na. (—*Los Angeles City School District*)

spacious valley, well grown with cottonwoods and sycamores, among which ran a beautiful river from the north-northwest. . . . This plain where the river runs is very extensive. . . . It has good land for planting all kinds of grain and such. It has all the requisites for a large settlement." Indians from a small village called Yang-na, near the present Civic Center of Los Angeles, brought gifts to the explorers — baskets and strings of shells. In return Portolá gave them glass beads and tobacco for their clay pipes.

August first was the important Franciscan jubilee of Our Lady of the Angels of Porciúncula.* Since their arrival was the next day, the river near the Indian village was named the Porciúncula (later the Los Angeles River). Another river nearby, which was dry, was given the name Arroyo Seco (Dry Riverbed). Portolá camped on the east side of the Porciúncula River, near today's North Broadway bridge. The next day's entry in the diary notes appreciatively, "After crossing the river we entered a large vineyard of wild grapes and an infinity of rosebushes in full bloom."

Father Crespí counted nine earthquakes during their stay in the valley. Before that, five quakes occurred when the explorers were near what is now the Santa Ana River. For this reason their name for that river was Jesús de los Temblores (earthquakes). The padre's record describes the most severe as lasting "about half as long as an Ave María." After leaving the village of Yang-na, the party went past "a number of large marshes of a substance like pitch that was boiling

*On that date in 1208, St. Francis of Assisi received the inspiration which led to his founding the Franciscan Order. At that time he lived and worshipped in a chapel on the plain below Assisi, a chapel known as Our Lady of the Angels, but commonly called "Portiuncula" or, by the Spanish Franciscans, "Porciúncula."

and bubbling" (later named La Brea Pits). They decided that the earthquakes had their source in the boiling pools.

When Vizcaíno had sailed along the coast he made rough sketches of the shore, noting bays, capes, estuaries and islands. Portolá tried to use those landmarks as a guide, but upon reaching the place which should have been Monterey he found no resemblance in the wind-swept coast to the lovely sheltered harbor Vizcaíno had described. The explorers continued north for many days, meeting hostile Indians along the way. Their supplies dwindled and landmarks showed that they must have passed their destination. Then scouts sent ahead climbed a hill which overlooked the wide expanse of a great inland sea — San Francisco Bay. The next day everyone in the expedition gazed at the same majestic scene. All explorers of the coast had passed by in rough or foggy weather which kept their sailing ships well off-shore; none of them had caught a glimpse of the bay which lay on the other side of what is now called the Golden Gate. Portolá's scouts exploring along the estuary reported they had seen none of the land-marks which he hoped to find. His mind remained fixed upon only the elusive Monterey, and in what must surely be the greatest under-statement in all history he sadly wrote, "Found nothing."

The explorers retraced their steps to San Diego where Father Serra awaited news. Portolá and several other officers decided that the port of Monterey had probably been filled with sand, washed in by ocean currents since the time Vizcaíno discovered it. At San Diego the rainy season added psychologically to the pervading gloom. Supplies were getting low, because over six months had gone by since the *San Antonio* had left for more provisions. Possibly the ship had suffered the same fate as the *San José* and would never arrive.

The governor was above all a humanitarian. When he was first sent to Baja California with orders to deport the Jesuit missionaries, he had followed the orders efficiently but at the same time showed spe-cial kindness to the men forced to leave work so important to them. He had shown the same understanding when the stricken Father Serra insisted upon starting the long, difficult journey to San Diego. Now, at the end of the fruitless northern expedition, Portolá saw that the lack of food was serious and he was faced with the possible starvation of his followers. Realizing it might be necessary to return to Loreto to avoid such a tragedy, he figured the date when there would remain the minimum provisions necessary for a retreat south. That date was March 20, and he let it be known that if the *San Antonio* did not arrive by then, crucial decisions would have to be made about con-tinuing the expedition in California.

To Father Serra the saving of souls was most important. If the expedition returned to Loreto, it would be many years before another attempt was made to found missions where Indians could be converted to Christianity, and in the meantime hundreds of souls would be lost. Serra and Crespí made a secret agreement with the captain of the *San Carlos*, still in the bay, to remain awhile even if everyone else departed.

As the deadline approached, the scene in San Diego exemplified the religious basis of Spanish colonization. Everyone joined in fervent prayers that the *San Antonio* would arrive with provisions. In modern times we are accustomed to the launching-pad countdown; the friars conducted one of their own on the fringes of the unknown world. Nine days remained, five days, one day. It was at three o'clock on the afternoon of the last day, March 19, that watchers from Presidio Hill saw the white sails of a distant ship come into view. Even at a distance certain characteristics identified the ship as the *San Antonio*. Shouts of joy filled the air until it became evident that the vessel was continuing north instead of turning into the bay.

The mariners had taken it for granted that the expedition would be in Monterey, and when the people on shore realized this, they knew that the voyage north and then the return would take a long time, and so their crisis over food could be postponed no longer. The situation was the more agonizing because of the nearness of relief. Luckily the *San Antonio* entered a small harbor a short distance beyond San Diego in order to replenish her water casks, and from the Indians the sailors learned that the expedition was still in the encampment to the south. Immediately the ship turned around; she entered the bay three days after sailing past. Her arrival meant that plans to colonize California and establish missions could proceed. In gratitude that his prayers had been answered, the devout Father Serra celebrated High Mass on the 19th day of each month as long as he lived.

Gaspar de Portolá led a second expedition north which found the Bay of Monterey and began the scheduled colonization of the coast with the erection of a presidio and mission. On reaching Carmelo Bay (now Carmel) near Monterey, Portolá was surprised to find that a large cross erected on his first journey had been decorated with feathers, arrows, shellfish and meat — offerings by the Indians who recognized the cross as a symbol related to the white explorers' deity.

The San Gabriel Mission, nine miles east of Portolá's first camp by the Porciúncula River, was founded in 1771, the fourth in a growing chain that eventually reached from San Diego to Sonoma. It stood at the western end of the long San Gabriel Valley. The year after its founding, Capt. Juan Bautista de Anza, unheralded, knocked at the mission door. He and his exhausted followers had come down the valley as they ended the first overland trip from Sonora. Anza, believing that the best route to Monterey was to go to the Colorado River and thence cross the Mojave Desert to the Pacific, had formed a party of 34 men to make the hazardous journey. Fortunately for the expedition, they were joined at the beginning by Sebastián Tarabal, a runaway Indian from San Gabriel. When the party's Indian guides abandoned them in the desert, Tarabal was able to lead the way, retracing the route he had taken earlier, until they arrived safely at the San Gabriel Mission.*

All early expeditions included men only, but in 1774 some soldiers with their families came north from Baja California. At the same time Anza, preparing a second expedition across the desert with recruits for the presidio of Monterey and a new presidio at San Francisco, determined to include wives and children. Due to the relaxed discipline of the frontier and the enforced celibacy, troops without families were a constant danger to Indian women living near the missions. (It was for this reason that Tarabal had run away from San Gabriel Mission with his wife and brother. His wife died in the desert after they had been without water for a long time.) To give a measure of protection to the Indians, the padres had carefully located their missions at a distance from the presidios. From every viewpoint the arrival of recruits with their families was an improvement. With Anza's second expedition, which included about 200 people who planned to remain, California crossed an invisible dividing line. What had been considered a frontier for military service and missionary work among savages was henceforth thought of by many as home.

4. *Felipe de Neve Shapes the Future*

It was late winter in 1776 when Felipe de Neve and a small band of soldiers rode north into Alta California. With them the center of government was to move from Loreto in Baja California to Monterey. Neve, who during the previous two years in Loreto had been governor,

----

*An illustration of the extreme remoteness of the West Coast is the fact that New Mexico became a possession of Spain in 1539, over 200 years before plans were made for Portolá's expedition to Alta California. The first Spanish settlement in New Mexico was established in 1598.

though more generally known as *jefe civil* (civil commandant), would be the first governor of The Californias to hold office in the north.

The courtly Spanish aristocrat stoically faced the hardships of life in that remote province and tried to forget that it had been 12 years since he had last seen his family in Seville. He knew the isolation of the frontier. In the thousands of square miles ahead of him there were only three presidios, five missions and no settlements whatever. While holding office in Loreto he had organized the journey north for expeditions of soldiers and missionaries, and he knew that to reach Upper California was a special problem, for there was no easy passage.

One route led up the peninsula of Baja California, over mountains and harsh terrain for more than a thousand miles. A second route, from the Mexican mainland by way of the Colorado River, included weeks of travel across the desert, where for long stretches no water could be found for men or animals. The third route, by sea, was possibly the worst of all: treacherous currents and winds made sailing so difficult that vessels were sometimes delayed weeks or months, blown far off course. On Neve's own voyage from San Blas to Loreto the ship battled its way through storms for fifty days. Occasionally a ship simply disappeared without a trace.

As Neve rode slowly from San Diego to Monterey, thoughts which had been in mind before his arrival began to take a clear shape. Missions were already established; they followed the original intention of converting Indians to Christianity and giving a religious basis to the colonization of California. Presidios were already established; they offered security. But life there was dependent on food and supplies brought by ships from the Mexican mainland. It was time to establish farms to provide food; also, settlements were needed so that the population could steadily increase. If the settlements were made up of farmers, all purposes would be answered.

About a hundred miles north of San Diego he came to the Porciúncula River, which ran through a spacious valley. The wintertime rainy season had brought out a greenness and beauty in the surrounding plains and hills while the river flowed at its fullest. Neve visualized homes, families and farms irrigated by water diverted from the river when necessary. He remembered that when the first explorers rode up the coast, Father Crespí wrote about this valley in his diary: "It has all the requisites for a large settlement."

On February 3, 1777, he reached Monterey and declared it the capital of The Californias. Simultaneously he assumed his role there as governor. The military commandant, Capt. Fernando Rivera y Moncada, moved to Loreto and continued in the same subordinate role.

This is the first paragraph of a letter from Teodoro de Croix, Commandant General of the Interior Provinces, Mexico, to José de Galvéz, Minister of the Indies, in Spain. Edwin Beilharz, who found the document, translates as follows: "The Governor of the Peninsula of the Californias, Don Phelipe de Neve, informed me last November 19 that he completed on September 4 the establishment of the new town of the Queen of the Angels on the bank of the Porciúncula River, with the settlers recruited by the late Captain Fernando de Rivera, who made [part of] their journey by sea."

Exmo or
Exmo S.

El Comte. Gral de Prov Int. de N. E.

Avisa la ereccion de un Pueblo en

la Nueva California.

Muy Señor mio: el Governador de la Peninsula de California Dn Phelipe de Neve me dio cuenta

en 19 de Noviembre del año proximo pasado de

que el dia 4 de septiembre antecedente verificó el

establecimiento del nuevo Pueblo de la Reyna delos

Angeles al margen del Rio de la Porciuncula

con parte de los Pobladores que recluto el difunto

Capitan Dn Fernando de Rivera, y hicieron

su viage por Mar.

For over a century the founding date of Los Angeles was uncertain, as early accounts conflict by as much as several months. In 1961 historian Edwin A. Beilharz, certain that somewhere a report from Governor Neve existed, searched through the Archivo de Indias in Seville, Spain, where ancient reports are still tied in bundles. At last he discovered this one, which proves that Los Angeles was founded on September 4, 1781. (—*Bancroft Library*)

Governor Felipe de Neve was to prove himself one of the great administrators in Spanish colonial history. Although immersed in new duties, Neve eagerly made plans to start a community at the southern end of San Francisco Bay where the Guadalupe River runs through a large valley. Besides its natural advantages, the location would be only about 75 miles from Monterey, and he could observe its progress and test his theories before making another start. There were few families at the presidios of California, but from those of Monterey and San Francisco he recruited 14; over half of the men in those families had had experience in farming. On November 29, 1777, San José de Guadalupe was founded, the first settlement in California.

There was much to be learned. The dam was built too distant from the fields and too late in the growing season; so the first crop was a total loss because of lack of irrigation. The dam was then moved to another site, but a flood washed it away. Also, the pueblo lands were too near the river to be safe in floodtime.

Months after the founding of San José, Teodoro de Croix, Commandant General of Mexico, asked for a report about the country and suggestions of ways in which change might be needed. The Governor was in no haste to reply: he had many ideas in mind and details to study. Finally he was ready, and on June 1, 1779, Governor Felipe de Neve issued his *Reglamento*. In correspondence it had already been decided that a second pueblo should be established, this one by the Porciúncula River, and Neve now recommended the size of the settlement, what inducements should be offered the colonists and what their responsibilities should be.

In response, Teodoro de Croix issued instructions on December 27 of that year for the establishment of a new pueblo "con el título de la Reyna de los Angeles."

5. *Destination: California*

The new step was to be an organized effort on a large scale: three groups were to leave for California at the same time. One would be made up of colonists for the pueblo, and they would be provided with seed, equipment and animals so that their farms and herds could supply the settlers and the presidios. A second group consisting of soldiers and their families would escort the colonists; most of these troops would later be assigned to the proposed new Presidio of Santa Barbara. Both parties were to cross the Gulf of California and go north through Baja California, while a third group of soldiers would go by Anza's land route to the Colorado River and across the Mojave Desert, driving a herd of several hundred animals. For them all, the main destination was the San Gabriel Mission, where Governor Neve would await their arrival.

The entire operation was supervised by Captain Rivera, leader of the first land party to San Diego 12 years earlier. Even today, with the help of modern banking facilities, transportation, communications and food refrigeration, such a project would be complicated enough. In 1780 it was an almost impossible undertaking to coordinate preparations in widely separated places in Mexico for journeys which would last many months. Not only was it necessary to assemble colonists and soldiers in one place, but the travelers must be well enough supplied so that at the end of the voyage they could be self-sufficient in every way, instead of a burden on people already there.

Rivera chose a young officer, Alférez (2nd Lieutenant) Manuel García Ruiz, to search through the Mexican provinces of Sonora and Sinaloa for volunteers to go to California. Ruiz found it a difficult task; he started recruiting in February 1780 but it was May before the first settler enlisted. For one thing, each recruit had to guarantee to remain in the remote outpost for ten years. Rivera hoped to find 24 colonists, but of the 14 who volunteered, 2 had second thoughts and deserted almost immediately. A total of 59 soldiers enlisted to go: 17 of them with their families to escort the colonists, and the remaining 42 (30 of whom took families) to travel by way of the Mojave with Captain Rivera.

The colonists who signed with Ruiz were as heterogeneous as the population itself. Spaniards had settled in all parts of Mexico, and Indians had been drawn into the communities, especially as laborers. In the early 1500s Negroes were first brought from Africa to the Americas, and as their numbers increased they became an important part of colonization. In general they were well treated; any Negro had the right to emancipate himself by purchase. Few Spanish women left their homes in Europe; so Spaniards found wives among the Indians and Negroes. Reflecting an unsegregated society, the men who founded Los Angeles consisted of four Indians, one mestizo (half Indian, half Spaniard), two Spaniards, two Negroes and two mulattoes (half Negro, half Spaniard); all the wives in the colony were mulattoes or Indians. These unassuming farmers and the accompanying soldiers included the ancestors of many future alcaldes (mayors) of Los Angeles and rancheros of extensive lands.

In the mountains about forty miles east of the Gulf of California lay one of the richest mining towns in Mexico, Los Alamos. Founded a century earlier by men seeking gold, it stood instead on a large deposit of silver ore. This town was chosen to be the point of de-

From Los Alamos, most of Captain Rivera's settlers would sail up the gulf and cross the harsh terrain of Baja California at Velicatá en route to Los Angeles.

parture for Alta California, and its merchants, alerted by Rivera, filled their shops with supplies of clothing and equipment for the families approaching the rendezvous.

Each volunteer was to be allowed rations and for three years collected the equivalent of ten pesos per month, mainly payable in clothing and supplies. However, he could draw on his account in advance for current expenses. After reaching his destination he was to be given livestock, farming implements and seed. Their cost and that of the clothing would be repaid gradually, from the sale of surplus farm products.

The first amount advanced to Alejandro Rosas, a young man of 17, was auspicious. He drew 25 pesos for the expense of getting married so that he could take his bride on the journey. In all, five soldiers went through the ceremony of marriage in the little church, and their names are still in the ancient church records.

Men, women and children crowded eagerly into the shops, all of them preparing to be outfitted from head to toe. They bought hats, linen for shirts and blouses, woolen cloth for breeches, cotton cloth for petticoats and skirts, silk handkerchiefs, stockings, shoes and blankets. The men purchased saddles, bridles, spurs and bags to carry water; each woman bought about five yards of ribbon. Children as well as adults delighted in promenading in their new clothes.

Meanwhile, Captain Rivera had appointed Alférez Cayetano Limon to buy the necessary livestock. A veteran of the frontier for over 25 years and a renowned Indian fighter, Limon was an expert judge of animals. Rivera ordered two leading dealers in horses and mules to bring their stock to a huge corral in Los Alamos, and on the appointed day some 500 mules and jennies were brought for inspection. Rivera, Limon, other officers and the vendors went from one animal to another so that their merits and demerits could be judged. Limon, quick to recognize sharp practices, proved his value to Rivera and the expedition. Some of the mules were tame, broken to a saddle or pack rack, but most were wild and still needed training. Afterward, to choose the horses and burros, Limon rode out to view them on the range where certain herds were pastured. He was then placed in charge of all the animals and later supervised the large herd which accompanied Rivera on the overland journey to California.

Commandant General Teodoro de Croix had ordered that 961 horses and mules should be taken to California by the land route, but there is no record of the exact number bought to go across the desert or to accompany the colonists and their escort. All such records were lost during a disaster on the way to California. Croix gave an order that progress should be slow in order to avoid needless fatigue and hardship to the families and to keep the livestock in good condition.

Two young officers were given command of the groups which would go by way of the Gulf of California — Lt. José de Zúñiga to lead the *pobladores* (colonists), Alférez Ramón Laso de la Vega to lead the escorting troops and their families. Because people willing to join the list of settlers were hard to find, extra months went by. But at last, exactly a year after recruiting began, a sufficient number was enlisted and preparations for travel were complete. Saddlebags were ready, filled with dried meat, beans, chick-peas, corn, flour and dried fruits. Barrels and leather bags were filled with water. Muleteers brought horses and saddle and pack mules from the herd destined for Alta California; on them the travelers and their supplies would journey to the coast and embark to cross the gulf, while the muleteers would return to Los Alamos with the animals.

On February 2, 1781, Zúñiga and Laso arranged the colonists and their escort in a long line. Men and women on horses and mules seated their children in front of them or behind. Racks fastened to pack mules were tested to be certain they were secure, and then men and older boys were stationed alongside, ready to keep the mules advancing steadily. An order to start was given, and the line began to move. A shout rang out: *"A California!"* It was echoed by all, *"A California!"* The townspeople who crowded beside the road waved good-bye and called out prayers for God's protection as they watched the disappearing line of travelers. Their journey into history had begun.

6. *The Journey of the Colonists*

Near Los Alamos the Río Mayo curves toward the Gulf of California to empty into the Bahía de Santa Bárbara (Bay of Santa Barbara), and the two groups of the expedition followed a trail along that river. On the eastern shore of the gulf, ships sailed frequently from the large port of Guaymas and also stopped occasionally in the small bay farther south at the mouth of the Río Mayo. It was from there that the families prepared to make the voyage of about 120 miles to Loreto, in Baja California.

The Gulf of California, or Sea of Cortez,* is usually a placid body

---

*In 1533 Hernando Cortez, leader of Spanish exploration in the northwest, sent out ships to search the waters west of the Mexican mainland, and Baja California was discovered. Later Cortez sailed to La Paz and established a short-lived colony. Under the command of Francisco de Ulloa he sent three ships to explore the gulf, which in his honor Ulloa named El Mar de Cortez.

of water. Protected from most ocean winds by the mountains which rise above Baja California, its calm is generally unbroken except during the afternoon when light onshore breezes spring up or when, in extreme contrast, ferocious gales blow in from the Pacific Ocean either through the mouth of the gulf or across the northern part of the peninsula. Such storms, although infrequent, forced sailing vessels off course, as when a ship carrying a friar to a mission in California was blown south as far as Panama.

Lieutenant Zúñiga shepherded his followers onto a small bark called a *lancha*, a vessel of simple construction with only two sails. As the pobladores, unaccustomed to travel, watched their ship draw away from shore they began to realize more completely that they were on their way to a far perimeter of civilization.

It took a week or ten days to cross the gulf, for they arrived in Loreto early in March. *Lanchas* were not built for speed, and in any case ships on those waters often lay becalmed for many hours. During the trip across, Zúñiga learned what an all-encompassing responsibility had been put upon his shoulders. The young man was leader, doctor, counselor, comforter and friend; day or night, family anxieties were brought to him.

Loreto had been capital of The Californias until four years earlier, when the capital was changed to Monterey. The families found that in the large community arrangements had been made for their comfort. But among the colonists a little girl fell ill of smallpox; so she and her father (no mother; just father and daughter had come together) were isolated from the others. Then among the families of the escorting troops a woman gave birth to a son. For everyone else it was a week of rest until on March 12 the escort boarded a pinnace and left the harbor, followed soon after by the pobladores on a similar ship. This time they would sail 350 miles north to the Bahía de San Luis Gonzaga. The smallpox-stricken child and her father were left in Loreto, which meant there were 11 families among the settlers instead of the original 12.

For over forty days the vessels sailed north along the peninsula, a stretch of land made more dramatic by the series of mountain ranges which rose above it like a rugged spine. The ships passed volcanic islands, beaches, coves and shallow reefs. It was a world peopled with marine life including dolphins and sea lions, while overhead flew pelicans, cormorants, terns, gulls and frigate birds.

The ships moved up the gulf, tacking northeast and then northwest to utilize the best winds and also to minimize adverse tides. The Gulf of California is noted among mariners for a special quality: it is dominated by the tidal flow from the Pacific Ocean, with its two high tides within every 25 hours. At the entrance to this large inland sea 150 miles separate the opposing shores, but halfway up, at what is called the Midriff, the shores narrow to 32 miles apart. This compression affects the tidal waters, moving them faster through the Midriff channels; countercurrents form, too, creating maelstromlike whirlpools. In March and early April — exactly the time the pobladores and their escort were on the water — gales from the Pacific often sweep into the gulf. When such adverse winds combine with ebbing tides, a ship trying to make headway against them actually moves backward, and there is no choice but to anchor and wait for a change.

After almost a month and a half the ships came to a place where a long series of low bluffs lined the shore, then the vessels rounded a point into a wide cove, at the northern end of which was the beautiful, sheltered Bahía de San Luis Gonzaga. With relief the families went ashore, glad to change to the rigors of travel by land. From that day it was to be three months until their arrival at San Diego.

Once on land, the groups journeyed together. They made a cavalcade of children, for there were 22 among the colonists, 25 (including the newborn baby) among the escort. From the bay a pass led through low hills for a distance of only 14 miles to the Santa María Mission. Beyond, the route led north to Velicatá and another mission. Time spent at a mission was not only an opportunity to rest but also to renew the travelers' religious faith.

Velicatá, where grass and water were abundant, was the established staging area for departing expeditions to Alta California. There horses, mules and cattle were pastured, available for the missionaries and soldiers who customarily landed at the Bahía de San Luis Gonzaga on their way north. Rations for the weeks ahead were prepared at the mission, and water was poured into barrels and leather bags. From the padres, Zúñiga and Laso were able to receive exact details that might help them on the road ahead. As water was the greatest concern of anyone traversing the arid peninsula, more than anything else the two young leaders needed to know where springs could be found and the distances between them.

After a period of rest, pack mules were made ready and the families mounted horses and saddle mules which had been waiting at the mission. Other livestock followed as the long line started on its way across the barren, monotonous land. Few trees offered shade, but thorned shrubs, mesquite and thirsty vines clung to the dry soil of hills and arroyos. Everywhere cactus grew in countless varieties, some stretching in grotesque shapes which made eerie shadows at night.

North of Velicatá the route they took is unknown, but it can be surmised. Governor Neve planned the journey carefully, and he probably sent the colonists westward from Velicatá, across the peninsula along a main route of travel used by soldiers and missionaries. Seven years earlier El Rosario Mission was established on the west coast, not far beyond the Santa Ursula Mission; near El Rosario a farming and cattle-raising project was begun. These missions would have served as way stations, and the trip would have been less hazardous for the families than along any path directly north.

The travelers came to many Indian villages, where the natives always watched their approach with curiosity, excited to see the procession of families. In the early explorations, soldiers and missionaries had arrived in Alta California accompanied not by women and children but by horses and mules, animals hitherto unknown to the natives. The Indians thus decided that these people didn't procreate in the usual way but probably sprang from mules. Now, however, the children — Indians and newcomers — lost no time in mingling and making friends.

Early in August the party drew near to San Diego, marveling at the trees, flowers and green fields and the beauty of the harbor, just as the first explorers had. Even so the colonists and troops stayed only briefly, because all were impatient to start the last lap of their journey. Finally, on August 18, they reached the San Gabriel Mission where Governor Felipe de Neve awaited their arrival. Overhead the mission bells rang out in welcome. The two young officers, Zúñiga and Laso, reported to the Governor and delivered their charges. During the long journey the only casualties had been the father and daughter left behind in Loreto.

José de Zúñiga had proved himself so competent that he was immediately appointed to the presidio at San Diego as commander. The English navigator George Vancouver, on a voyage of exploration in 1793, named Point Zúñiga on the coast below San Diego in his honor. Ramón Laso de la Vega was made paymaster at the Presidio of San Francisco.

For the colonists, less than ten miles remained before they would reach the valley which was their goal, but several children among the arrivals had just recovered from smallpox. Governor Neve ruled that everyone must be quarantined until danger of spreading the disease was past; so for two and a half weeks the families lived in hastily built shacks one league south of the mission.

About two months after the departure of the first two groups, Captain Rivera, his troops and their families, and the large herd of animals started toward California along the route to the Colorado River near the site of today's city of Yuma.

Rivera can have felt justifiable pride in launching the three parties. Earlier, when he was last in Alta California, jealousy and arrogance had often marked his behavior. He had even had a feud with the great Anza and gone to such fantastic lengths of rudeness that many considered him insane. In spite of the fact that he was military commandant, he had been excommunicated by the friars for invading the San Diego Mission church to arrest an Indian who had taken sanctuary there. Yet no dissensions or complaints marred his work on the colonization project; as he rode away from Los Alamos there was no question but that he had fulfilled an impossible task and done it admirably.

In June the expedition reached the Colorado River where, in Yuma Indian territory on the edge of the Mojave Desert, a small presidio, pueblo and mission had been established half a year earlier with another, similar colony a few miles away. Once the Yumas had been friendly toward the Spaniards, but since the founding of the two settlements the relationship had changed. Soldiers and settlers disregarded Indian rights to land; horses, cows and sheep were allowed to feed on pasture land the Indians prized for their own animals, and any native who protested received corporal punishment. The missionaries tried to befriend the Indians and protect them from injustice, but in vain.

Rivera arrived with his train of soldiers and families when local antagonisms were becoming intense. He brought only insignificant presents with which to influence the Indians toward friendliness, and his followers showed no more understanding than did the settlers already there. The most serious disruption was that Rivera brought a herd of almost a thousand horses and mules for the presidios of California and the new pueblo to be founded by the Porciúncula. Originally there was forage enough for the Yumas, but like a tidal wave the new animals overflowed onto the land as the Indians watched, helpless. Ripening mesquite beans, an important food to the Yumas, were appropriated by the newcomers. After a fortnight the families under Rivera's leadership were sent ahead to California with most of the animals. Rivera himself stayed with five soldiers to rest about 250 horses and mules too weak to start the difficult summer journey across the desert, and an officer and five soldiers from Monterey joined him.

Those of Rivera's company who were sent ahead — 3 officers and 35 soldiers, including all of those with families — reached San Gabriel on July 14, about a month before the colonists arrived. Nine soldiers

from Sonora escorted the group, under the command of Alférez Cayetano Limon. Soon after their arrival at San Gabriel, Limon and the
nine men retraced their steps to join Captain Rivera again.

But during their absence the Indians on the Colorado River had
risen in revolt. First, on the California side of the river they struck
at the two settlements and killed soldiers, male settlers and two friars.
Rivera and his men had camped on the other side of the mile-wide
river, and as its banks were lined with trees, probably little of the
attack could be seen from Rivera's camp. However, word of the revolt had been brought to the Spaniards, because later their hastily
built entrenchments were found where the Indians, using arrows and
clubs, had massacred them all. Then the Yumas returned to the scene
of the day before. Two friars, who had especially befriended the
Indians and therefore were spared in the previous attack, were this
time included in the holocaust of revenge. Only the wives and children of the settlers remained alive, but they were taken captive. The
herds kept by Rivera were driven away, and the records he carried,
noting every detail about the three expeditions to California, all were
lost in the desert sands.

As Cayetano Limon and his men neared the Colorado River on
their return, some Indians warned them to go back because there
had been a massacre. Instead, Limon and seven of the soldiers left
their animals in charge of two men and proceeded ahead to investigate. Where there should have been the sounds of a settlement, there
was silence. They found the buildings burned and bodies of the slain
still lying on the ground. When the Spaniards left the riverside and
returned to the two soldiers who had remained with the livestock,
they discovered that both men had been killed. Later Limon and the
remainder of his troops (one of them his son) were attacked by Yumas;
Limon and his son were wounded, but all survived and were able to
reach San Gabriel.

Governor Neve's thoughts had been concentrated upon the new
pueblo. On August 26 at the San Gabriel Mission — just before receiving news of the tragedy on the Colorado River — he issued his Instrucción para la Fundación de Los Angeles (Instruction for the Founding
of Los Angeles).* In it he ordered that first a site should be chosen
for an irrigation ditch so that it would water the largest possible area

---

*The original document was destroyed in San Francisco during the
fire which followed the earthquake of 1906. The only other copy, one
made by the historian Hubert Howe Bancroft, was at some unknown
time torn from the book of records and stolen.

of land, and after that the pueblo's location was to be chosen near the ditch or the river. He described the layout of the plaza and of the individual pieces of land which would be apportioned by a drawing of lots.

It was then that Limon and his men brought word of the massacre. For many reasons the disaster was overwhelming, and it was possible that news of the attack would incite California Indians to follow suit. Neve gave orders that no one should speak about it to any native.

From Mexico, Teodoro de Croix dispatched Lt. Colonel Pedro Fages with about a hundred soldiers to the scene of the massacre. When they arrived in September, Fages ransomed the captives, taking them back to Mexico, and buried the dead. However, because he failed to search specifically for the bodies of the four friars, Fages later returned and found them all: two were lying on the ground near their half-burned church; two had been buried together by converts, who had marked the grave with a cross. The bodies of the four martyrs were taken to Mexico and interred together in a church. Fernando Rivera y Moncada was buried where he fell. No large-scale campaign was made against the Yumas, nor was there an effort to replace the settlements which had been destroyed.

The disaster closed that route for migration to California. For a long time there was no communication between Mexico and California except by sea or the roundabout route taken by the pobladores. For this reason there never was a firm political connection between Mexico and the distant territory.

At first Neve considered postponing the settlement of the new pueblo but on second thought called the colonists to meet for the last preliminary step. The 11 pobladores, awed by the fact that they were about to become landowners, gathered for the drawing to determine each man's personal piece of ground where he could grow crops for his own use. Because of the Spanish word for luck, "suerte," the plots of land were called suertes.

The Governor appointed Alférez José Darío Argüello, who had accompanied Lt. Governor Rivera from Sonora as far as the Colorado River, to lead the colonists.* They were also escorted by the military guard which Neve assigned to the pueblo — Corporal José Vicente

---

*The appointment of Argüello was not known until 1949, when Mexican historian, José C. Valades, doing research on another subject, reported the chance discovery of an official document in the archives at Mexico City which recorded the fact.

Féliz and Privates Roque Jacinto de Cota, his brother Antonio de Cota and Francisco Salvador Lugo. The presence of Corporal Féliz was appropriate: his ancestors had a century earlier been among the founders of Los Alamos, the starting point of the colonists' expedition. At San José no friars had accompanied what was a civil ceremony, nor did the Governor, who had left details of establishing the pueblo to the soldiers he had appointed. There is no record of the procedure followed during the founding of Los Angeles, but undoubtedly it was similar to that of the other pueblo.

And so, on the morning of September 4, 1781, probably right after early Mass, the pobladores mounted and rode the final distance of about nine miles. A few men and older boys prepared to go on foot to keep the pack animals moving. Most of the cows, sheep, oxen and goats, which along with the horses and mules had been distributed to the settlers as promised, were held at San Gabriel until shelters and corrals were built and the farmers were ready to begin plowing fields to sow corn.

The 44 colonists and their escort followed the well-worn trail the padres used on their journeys to missions farther north.* At first the trail wound between low hills, which after several miles fanned out so that a wide valley was revealed ahead with a river meandering through it. Across that river was the spot chosen by Governor Neve for the pueblo, the destination toward which they had started seven months earlier.

Although the September sun burned fiercely overhead and the land lay faded and parched, wild grapes grew on the opposite shore and rosebushes bloomed. On the bluff over the river, among cottonwood and sycamore trees, Indians — future neighbors — watched in a friendly manner from their village of Yang-Na. Cool waters flowed by the new home. This was the dry season and the river was shallow but wide and inviting. Anticipation surged through the group as they gazed, and the line began to advance. Through the water the hooves of the horses splashed. To the delighted shouts and laughter of children, the journey of the colonists ended.

7. El Pueblo "La Reyna de Los Angeles"

Alférez Argüello led the colonists up a low hillside above the west bank of the river. There he showed each family its homesite, in a lay-

---

*Today's Mission Road replaced the trail. The settlers crossed the river a short distance north of where now the combined San Bernardino-Santa Ana Freeways enter downtown.

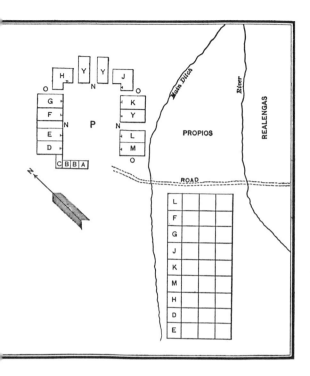

In 1786, when the colonists were granted official ownership, pueblo lands were allotted as follows: A—guardhouse, B—townhouses, C—small granary (pósito), D-M—houselots (solares), Y—vacant. South of the road leading to the San Gabriel Mission were the privately owned suertes. Each man donated his labor on the land marked "Propios" to support the pueblo; similarly, proceeds from the "Realengas" were used by the provincial government—the presidios— as representing the Crown. (—Bancroft Library)

out which followed Governor Neve's Instrucción of ten days earlier. In the pueblo of four square leagues,* each man's house was to face on a common plaza which, surrounded, would give community protection and easy sociability. (The first Plaza was slightly northwest of the present one.) Each colonist — they were all experienced farmers — was given four plots of land near the river for sowing crops, and in another specified area each man was to contribute one-tenth of his labor so that crops grown there could be sold to support the local government. All animals were to be pastured on common land. In five years each colonist would receive an official grant of landownership and a registered branding iron for his cattle.

The settlement followed the same pattern used in other colonies in Florida, Mexico or any part of New Spain. King Ferdinand in 1511 had established the Council of the Indies to supervise the new colonies resulting from Columbus' discovery. Later the council formulated

---

*One Spanish land league equals 2.63 miles; one square league is 4439 acres.

basic rules governing the location, size and layout of every town founded by Spain in the Americas.

The homes of the colonists were at first makeshift huts of willow branches interlaced with tule (reeds from the riverbanks), while a thick coating of the claylike mud was added to the roof. Corrals were made for the animals, and a ditch was built, called the Zanja Madre (Mother Ditch), along which water flowed from the river to the pueblo. Fields were then plowed for the sowing of corn.

Within a month of the pueblo's founding a dispatch from San Gabriel to the Commandant General in Mexico noted: "To this pueblo there arrived but eleven pobladores, and of these eight alone are of any use." On Father Serra's next trip to the mission he ordered the three shirkers to leave with their families, and they departed for the Presidio of Santa Barbara. That it was the duty of the President of the Missions to dismiss the men points up the close relationship between the pueblos and mission authorities.

Another man asked to join the colony, and so on September 4, 1786, nine settlers with their wives and children took part in the official ceremony of ownership. Governor Pedro Fages commissioned Alférez Argüello to give the settlers full title, just as five years earlier he had given them provisional ownership. Corporal José Vicente Féliz and Private Roque de Cota were witnesses, and the head of each family, none of them knowing how to write, proudly marked the document with the "sign of the Holy Cross" in place of his name. Soon after, another family joined the group, making a total of ten families in the new community.

The pueblo was under the jurisdiction of the Presidio of Santa Barbara, founded only six months after Los Angeles. José Darío Argüello was an officer of this presidio and eventually was made governor in 1814-15. His son, Luis Antonio Argüello, was governor in 1822-25, the first to be elected under Mexican rule.

In 1787 Governor Fages appointed Corporal Féliz to be comisionado (commissioner or general manager), responsible to him for the proper handling of pueblo affairs, and the next year the Governor appointed José Vanegas, one of the original settlers, to be the first alcalde (mayor), with a one-year term. The next alcalde was allowed two regidores (councilmen) to share his duties. Appointment of the alcaldes by the Governor was during the first three years only; after that the officers were elected by the people.

During this time ranch land was being set aside for use by special petitioners. In 1784, only three years after the pueblo was founded, three soldiers asked for land near Los Angeles. They received not actual grants but rather cattle-grazing permits for which no payment was asked in return. As a result of the informal allotment of property, there were seven ranchos in the area of Los Angeles (thirty in all California) before the Spanish regime ended in 1821. Mexico, which succeeded Spain, gave formal grants of ownership instead of permits.

Still, the large ranchos had few inhabitants, and the story of the earliest days belongs to El Pueblo itself.

The date of the founding of the pueblo on the western shore of the continent coincided with the end of the American Revolution in the East. There, on September 5, 1781, the British fleet was defeated in Chesapeake Bay, while nearby in Yorktown, Lord Cornwallis prepared for the final battle of the war. Along the Atlantic, cities were already thriving; farms and villages spread across the countryside. But there was scant knowledge of or interest in the wholly different type of civilization three thousand miles away.

The outside world heard little news about the remote village dedicated to The Queen of the Angels. Floods, droughts, earthquakes were faced by a necessarily self-reliant community. Life centered in the small pueblo of only four square leagues, solitary on a shore of the vast Pacific Ocean.

Natural asphalt (brea) coating the surface of the Indian water basket above made it impermeable. (*—Southwest Museum*) Below is a model of an Indian canoe. (*—Los Angeles County Museum of Natural History*)

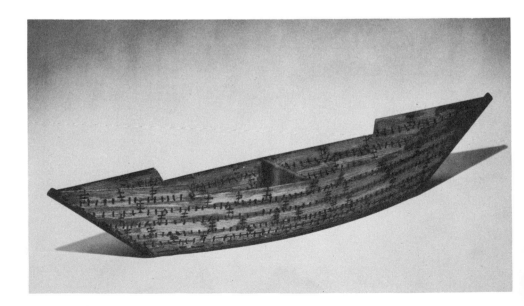

II

THE REMOTE OUTPOST 1781-1848

1. *Earliest Inhabitants*

The remote outpost of Spain was peacefully accepted by its savage neighbors. Natives farther north sometimes faced the Spaniards with hostility, but Indians of the Southland took their disposition from the sunny days, and so the pueblo of foreigners found an easy welcome among them. As farming by the colonists began and one after another their temporary grass huts were replaced with sturdy homes built of adobe bricks (handmade out of the claylike soil), the Indians watched with great curiosity a life style entirely unlike their own.

A decade earlier the leatherjacket soldiers and the missionaries in their long brown robes had first advanced north along the Pacific shore. To the Spaniards the region was remote, but they found it far from uninhabited. In what is now California there was a population of about 150,000 natives — the densest Indian population in North America.

The explorers, eager to know what kind of people lived in Spain's newest territory, found that the Southland Indians were of the Stone Age, had no articles of bronze or iron and, in common with all other North American Indians, did not know of the wheel until the white man came. The explorers found no domestic animal except the dog; it was the Spaniards who brought horses, donkeys, cattle and sheep to the Southwest.

To the eyes of the newcomers an amazingly simple, primitive way of life unfolded. Food was no problem: the Indians ate berries, seeds, roots, cactus apples and green yucca pods. Coastal Indians were skillful at catching fish and seals and gathering clams and mussels. The savages hunted with bow and arrow, and in stalking deer and antelope they wore deer heads fastened on top of their own as camouflage. What most surprised the Spaniards was that the acorn provided the mainstay of diet. Because oak groves flourished on the plains and hills, there was no need to grow corn as other Indians did; instead the natives gathered acorns and converted them into a kind of mush.

The only disadvantage of the acorn meat was its tannic acid, which they removed in an ingenious way: after the husks were taken off, the nuts were ground with a stone pestle into meal which was then spread out; hot water poured over it leached out the acid. When the meal was cooked in water it expanded to become like a porridge.

They cooked in stone vessels. Catalina soapstone, obtained in trade with the island Indians, was best because it could be put directly over a fire, whereas other stoneware cracked. Knives were also made of stone. Until the Spaniards taught them how to make pottery, the Indians used tightly woven baskets for carrying things, storing food or even holding water; occasionally they added brea (natural asphalt) for waterproofing.

In the comfortable, semitropical climate the explorers, encumbered with clothes, noticed with perhaps some envy that the men remained naked most of the year, merely adding a cape of deer hide or fur when days grew cold. Women dressed only in two aprons of grass or buckskin which as separate garments hung knee-length in front and back, and in winter they likewise added a cloak of animal skins. No type of cloth was ever used, because the natives did no weaving. Women ornamented themselves with flowers, shell beads and shell earrings; men sometimes wore earrings made of cane.

The Indians' simple homes were domelike huts covered with tule or grass. A larger hut, the ceremonial lodge or "temescal," was built around a wide, shallow hole so that it could serve also as a sweathouse. When a fire blazed in the hole any man who was tired or sick would sit near the heat, scraping his body with bones as he perspired, afterward bathing in the cold water of a stream or the ocean.

Traditionally Indians used the canoe for transportation over water, but along the Southland coast the canoe was an extraordinary thing made of short planks sewed together. Small boards were split from logs by bone wedges and planed to smoothness by stone scrapers; then holes were bored through the wood with awls of flint, bone or shell. Through those holes the boards were fastened together with cord made of sinew or a strong fiber such as that of the yucca root. Asphalt caulked the holes and seams. Although usually small, of a size to hold four men, some canoes were as long as 15 feet and could hold twenty men. These incredible craft were seaworthy enough for the voyage to Catalina Island, 22 miles south of San Pedro. The small, frail boats, which the men propelled with two-bladed paddles, were able to cover the distance within four or five hours in early morning, when the channel is almost invariably smooth. There was enough advance warning of any coming storm, but when the explorer Vizcaíno

An Indian man is poised with a fish spear. Below is a model of an Indian woman, in typical attire, picking *tunas* or cactus apples.
(*—both, Los Angeles County Museum of Natural History*)

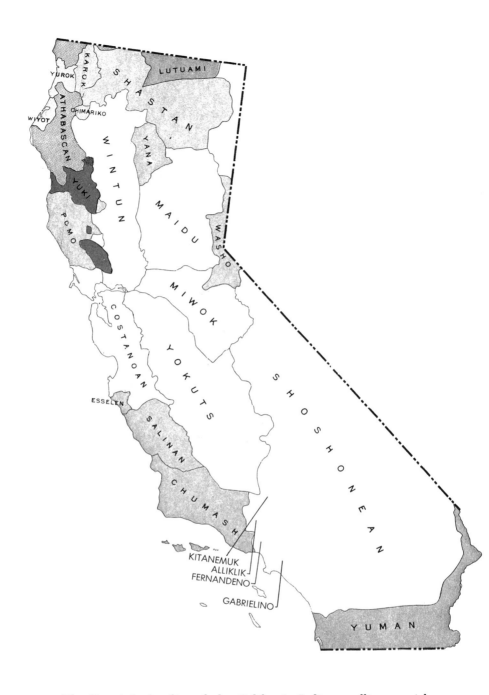

The linguistic families of the California Indians, calling special attention to the four subgroups in the Los Angeles area. (—Adapted from *Bulletin 78, Plate 1, Bureau of American Ethnology*)

spoke of the coastal Indians, he described their putting to sea even in very stormy weather with such speed that they seemed to fly.

As in every aspect of the Indians' lives, the Spaniards found that their religion was simple. They believed in one Giver of Life, who had formed the world out of what was chaos, then created animals and finally men and women. Thereupon He ascended to heaven, where He received the souls of the dead. Except on the island of Santa Catalina, where burial was the custom, the natives cremated their dead until the padres persuaded them otherwise. They had no belief in evil spirits until taught about the devil by the Christians.

The Jimson-weed cult was associated with a deity called Chinigchinich. Used during the initiation ceremony for males when they reached puberty, an intoxicating drink was made from the root of the Jimson weed, which was dried, pounded and then mixed with salt water. The drink induced a stupor, and whatever animal was dreamed of during that time became the boy's guardian spirit. The same potion was supposed to give strength, cure certain diseases, give immunity from snakebites and bestow good luck on a hunter.

Each ranchería (Indian village) had an hereditary chief. Although the other men were allowed only one wife, the chief could have two or three. Of course, when he was converted the padres permitted him to keep but one.

Indians of eastern North America organized themselves into tribes or nations, but those in California had no central government at all. The Indians of the Los Angeles region were Shoshoneans, but only in language roots. This family covered an enormous area and included Indians through most of the Southwest and as far south as Panama. Probably no more than 1500 years ago they came into the Los Angeles Basin, making a wedge between the Chumash Indians on the northwest and the Yumas on the south. As a result, when the explorers and settlers became used to the native tongue in the Los Angeles area, they were amazed to find that the languages spoken by the Indians in the Ventura and San Diego areas were completely different.

Friars named the Indians who lived within the radius of the San Fernando Mission "Fernandeños." Those in the sphere of the San Gabriel Mission they called "Gabrielinos," meaning also the natives on Santa Catalina and San Clemente islands. The languages of the two groups were practically identical, with differences in intonation. When Captain Portolá and his explorers made their first expedition through California there were an estimated 4000 Gabrielino and Fernandeño Indians.

Outside the district of either mission there were two other groups, also Shoshoneans. The Kitanemuk Indians lived in Antelope Valley and its foothills, as well as farther north in the Tehachapi Mountains. They had no permanent rancherías but stayed sometimes in the valley and sometimes in the cooler hills. Still, they always had a place they considered home and thus were not true nomads. The Alliklik Indians lived in the mountains around the Upper Santa Clara Valley. There were only a few, and most of them joined the Indians at the San Buenaventura or the San Fernando Mission. The Allikliks are now extinct, and although it is possible a few Kitanemuks remain, there are none in Los Angeles County.

Because year-round living was easy, the Indians of the Southland failed to reach a high level of achievement, and their culture was among the most primitive in the hemisphere. They were especially happy and friendly, which was an advantage for colonization. But, not appreciating that fact, the newcomers generally felt disdain because the savages were unsophisticated, small and meek. No one was interested in the Indians as they were but only wanted to change them; so for over half a century no study was made of their characteristics, and therefore relatively little was ever known about the Indians of the Southland.

2. *A Contest for Dominance: Military or Church*

Two outstanding men — Portolá and Serra, one a soldier and one a missionary — led the Spaniards into the unknown land of Alta California, but the dual leadership caused serious complications in the years to come. The main dissension was over treatment of the Indians.

From the beginning, the purpose of the missions was to teach the Indians Christianity and the customs of a more modern civilization. Accordingly, self-sufficient feudal communities arose around each mission. For instance, San Gabriel Mission eventually included a large industrial plant with weaving rooms, a flour mill and wine presses; on its lands were four vineyards and thousands of fruit trees as well as livestock numbering 20,000. Converts, called "neophytes" (the unconverted were "gentiles"), lived on the mission grounds — at first in huts, later in adobe buildings. At least twice a year each Indian was given a week off to go away from the mission to his own village or elsewhere, as he chose.

Father Serra, first President of the Missions, was a man totally dedicated to the spread of Christianity. He expected the same dedication from every friar, military leader and Indian convert. Gaspar

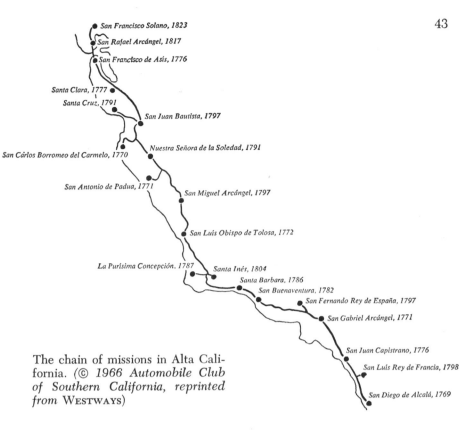

The chain of missions in Alta California. (© 1966 Automobile Club of Southern California, reprinted from WESTWAYS)

de Portolá, the first military leader, worked harmoniously with the missionaries. He was succeeded by two other men who had been in his expeditionary party, Lt. Pedro Fages and Capt. Fernando Rivera y Moncada, and after them Governor Felipe de Neve. Under these men there was constant conflict between the missions and presidios.

For one thing, as part of the mission community, neophytes were expected to do certain work and follow religious rules. Those who disobeyed were punished by imprisonment and extra work, and frequently Indians fled in rebellion. At each mission there were a few soldiers to give protection and bring back fugitive converts, but in time the military leaders urged that it was wholly the duty of the friars to bring them back, and through persuasion instead of force. Meanwhile the friars were protesting the flagrant misbehavior on the part of many soldiers toward the Indians, particularly toward the women. Sometimes in cruel sport the soldiers made advances and then lassoed the women as they fled. The problem was made worse by the fact that among the troops which arrived with each new military leader, a number had been recruited from prisons.

In the earliest years Father Serra won Spain's viceroy to Mexico, Antonio María Bucareli, to sponsor his idea that colonization was above all a religious undertaking. Using Serra's recommendations, he issued a plan of government which remained in effect throughout Spanish rule. But gradually times changed. With the arrival of families for settlements and presidios there was increasing stability. When Pedro Fages returned to California for a second tour of duty, replacing Felipe de Neve as governor, he brought his wife and two children with him, the first time that the family of a commandant had come to the frontier. The missions grew more prosperous and self-reliant. Father Serra was succeeded by Father Fermín Francisco de Lasuén, a man as dedicated and able as Serra had been but at the same time more persuasive and diplomatic, and an easier relationship developed between presidios and missions.

The missions attained a wide scope of practical achievements incredible from the viewpoint of today. The Franciscan college near Mexico City, where the friars studied, gave only religious instruction without technical training. Still, in an undeveloped land the padres installed irrigation systems and organized the necessary communal work: carpentry, masonry, weaving, tanning, care of orchards and gardens as well as animal husbandry. Yet at each mission there were, as a rule, only two friars to pool their understanding. Through more than sixty years, with a final total of 21 missions, only 128 friars took part in the missionary work in Alta California.

Some Indians joined no mission community and took work in the pueblo. As years went on, liquor became their special disaster: they grew accustomed to drinking up their week's pay on Saturday night, and the evening's debauch often included several murders. Every week large numbers of Indian prisoners were brought before the ayuntamiento (town council), and since none of them had any money left, even the smallest fine was too much for them to pay. The cost of feeding so many prisoners became too great; as a result the custom developed of sending them out to work through the week. Owners of vineyards were glad to have these workers, who each Saturday would squander their wages and wind up once more in jail, to be reapprenticed on Monday to work for another week.

As early as 1773, Viceroy Bucareli gave notice that after the missions had converted the Indians to Christianity and aided in settlement of the country, they were to be dissolved and become parish churches instead. The Mexican Government assumed the same policy, and in 1833 the Mexican Congress ordered secularization of the missions. Half of the mission lands were to be distributed to the Indians, to be kept by them but not sold. The remaining property was to be taken care of by administrators, while the padres would continue their religious functions.

Governor José Figueroa ordered ten missions secularized in 1834, the next year six more, and the year after that the five remaining missions were given notice. As a start, the Governor appointed administrators of Mission San Juan Capistrano and assigned to the converts half the land, upon which they were to form a community of their own. The result was a total failure: immediately the Indians sold what they could, and then most of them left for rancherías farther inland; the remainder found work on ranchos or fell into degradation. The administrators were just as irresponsible, laying waste to the buildings and grounds, and allowing fruit trees to be chopped down for firewood. Through neglect of irrigation, the orchards, vineyards and fields fell into useless ruin. Thousands of cattle were killed for the value of their hides and tallow, the only marketable parts.

Other missions at first ignored the Governor's ruling that they must be secularized, but when the order was finally put into effect, the government's purpose was, through its administrators, to sell anything of value to obtain funds to pay state expenses. So many cattle were slaughtered that the land was covered with rotting carcasses. Because of the terrible stench and threat of pestilence, the Ayuntamiento of Los Angeles passed an ordinance requiring cremation of all remains. With the dispersal of the Indians and the destruction of livestock, orchards and gardens, the missionary era came to an end.

Although the government's original intent of giving mission land to the Indians was not carried out, specific pieces of property were granted to 24 Indians. Neophytes of the San Fernando Mission received Rancho El Encino (4460 acres), half of Rancho El Escorpión (about 550 acres) and Rancho Cahuenga (388 acres). A neophyte of the San Gabriel Mission was granted Rancho Potrero Grande (4432 acres); an Indian woman, Victoria — who later married a leading ranchero, Don Hugo Perfecto Reid* — received Rancho Huerta de Cuati (108 acres). Smaller parcels of land were given to 13 other Indians.

The mission Indians, cast adrift from the guidance of the padres, found that their work had made them not self-sufficient but dependent. They were farm laborers rather than farmers. Although before the

---

*Reid was the first person to study the Indians of the Los Angeles region. In 1852 the Los Angeles *Star* published his articles about their language and culture, and much that we know has come from his scholarly efforts.

arrival of the white men the Indians easily made their own living, they now found themselves unable to return to the earlier customs. Furthermore, because the natives were extremely vulnerable to diseases brought by the white men (e.g., measles, venereal diseases) they had a high rate of mortality. In the main, the Indians' contact with civilization was tragic.

Today not one Gabrielino or Fernandeño remains, in the true sense; of the few descendants none can speak the language of his forebears. Approximately 25,000 Indians now live in Los Angeles County, yet they belong to tribes from across the United States — Sioux, Paiute, Chickasaw and others — and almost none comes from a homeland in California.

But what of the village of Yang-na? Historians, trying to locate the site of the village, have placed it near the old bluff which once bordered the wide Los Angeles riverbed. Father Crespí spoke of it as "among the trees on the river," and it is likely that the trees he spoke of lined the bluff. Indian artifacts found during building excavations along Main Street between First and Temple Streets have shown that the huts of Yang-na probably were grouped there. This spot is in accord with Governor Neve's report of the Indian village "adjacent to the Pueblo."

Let us stand on the site of Yang-na and allow the centuries to unroll. Exactly 205 years ago Captain Portolá led his men there and was met by friendly, gift-bearing savages. With the passage of years the grass-covered huts of the Indians were replaced by the Spaniards' adobe buildings. The details which marked that ancient bluff became obliterated. The river below now flows in the distance through a narrow, artificial bed of solid concrete and is lost in a pattern of railroad tracks, both river and tracks going parallel into the distance. But there is a sense of historic brotherhood in the fact that today's City Hall stands on the same spot as the ancient village.

3. *Life in the Outpost*

The earliest days in El Pueblo had a communal quality. Each person's close relationship to everyone else was intensified by the settlement's isolation. Surrounded by the colonists' homes, the Plaza was a focal point where animals could graze, young people promenade and children play; it was a meeting place common to all.

After the location for the Plaza church was chosen, Don José Antonio Carrillo petitioned his brother Anastacio — who was comisionado at that time — for what he considered the choice lot; today the Pico

House stands on the site. Going around the Plaza counterclockwise, the next home was that of Andrés Pico, and, just behind, that of his brother Pío. There was an added closeness in that Don José Antonio married Señorita Estefana, a sister of the Pico brothers, and upon her death married another sister, Señorita Jacinto.

In the Carrillo home was celebrated the most famous wedding in early Los Angeles history, when a fiesta continued for eight days and nights after the marriage of Don Pío Pico and Señorita María Ygnacia Alvarado in February 1834. At the service in the Church of Our Lady of the Angels, Governor José Figueroa was best man. The bride wore a black silk wedding gown; her hair, arranged high on her head, was ornamented by a carved tortoise-shell comb over which a long black lace mantilla was draped, falling almost to the hem of her skirt. After the ceremony, musicians playing violins and guitars led the newly-weds and members of the wedding party in a procession toward the home of Don José Antonio. Bursts of fireworks and the ringing of church bells heightened the celebration. As was customary, the bride changed into a white dress for the wedding breakfast, to which only priests and relatives were invited. From as far away as San Diego and Monterey guests had come, and since the pueblo had no hotel the visitors stayed in neighboring homes. During the afternoon the bridal party and guests danced in the long sala, but for the evening hours tables were set up in the patio, and the entire populace of Los Angeles came in to have food and wine and to dance. Violins and guitars played jotas, fandangos and waltzes, and from time to time especially skilled dancers took over the floor. Toward their flashing feet spectators threw escudos (silver dollars) which the dancers tried to pick up without slackening pace. Dancing continued all night, until at dawn everyone left to get some rest. But each night the dancing was resumed until the ninth day, when the wedding fiesta came to an end and the weary guests went home.

Other homes around the Plaza belonged to people whose names are still familiar in Los Angeles: Francisco O'Campo, Ygnacio del Valle, Vicente Lugo, Juan Sepúlveda and Agustín Olvera.

Always an important center for fiestas, the Plaza was especially so during the festival of Corpus Christi, forty days after Easter. As the number of ranchos increased and families living in ranchhouses made the long journey to town for the festival, they traveled by carreta — a large platform of wood on two enormous wooden wheels turning on wooden axles — and horseback, stopping overnight for the welcome awaiting them at other ranchhouses along the way. In the pueblo every homeowner around the Plaza had an altar out front, decorated

Early Californians, in a rancho scene painted by Carlos Nebel. (—*Los Angeles County Museum of Natural History*) Below is the wooden carreta. (—*Historical Collections, Security Pacific National Bank*)

with family treasures. From the church, as soon as the service ended, churchmen and townsfolk moved around the square in a slow procession which stopped at each of the altars, and the entire town joined in the worship. Christmas was another time when families which lived out of town found an excuse to come in for a long reunion with relatives and old friends.

In 1784 the first pueblo church was completed, a small adobe building at the foot of a hill. This chapel became too crowded, and another was started near the present Aliso Street, although it was abandoned after flooding from the nearby Los Angeles River. A third church was built on the northeast side of the Plaza. (The present Plaza Church, recently enlarged and remodeled, stands at Sunset and Main. The first church was built about 250 yards to the northwest.) To pay for its construction, citizens subscribed 500 cattle, and the friars of San Gabriel Mission contributed seven barrels of brandy. When funds ran short more brandy was contributed by other missions while parishioners donated wine, more cattle and mules. With the proceeds of sale the building was finished in 1822, and the grateful townsfolk filled the church for worship. A bell was loaned by the San Gabriel Mission, and although at first services were held when the church had no flooring or seats, the sound of the bell overhead compensated the worshipers for their dusty knees.

A few years after the church was completed, it acquired another bell, donated by an American, Capt. Henry Fitch, to win forgiveness for carrying off Josefa Carrillo as his bride. The sea captain was a foreigner and a Protestant; so her parents and the Church forbade the marriage, but Pío Pico aided their romance. Sweeping Josefa up onto his saddle, he galloped toward the coast where a boat was ready to carry her to a ship offshore and her waiting beloved. In Valparaiso they were married. The next year they returned to California with their infant son but Fitch was arrested, on charges of forcible abduction, and imprisoned at the San Gabriel Mission. It appears that Governor José María Echeandía refused pardon because he, too, was in love with the fair Josefa and wanted to punish his successful rival. Finally the American captain was freed, with an order to give a large bell to the church in Los Angeles as penance. Later the church acquired two more. For many years the cheerful bells at 6 a.m. and 8 p.m. regulated the daily life of El Pueblo.

Still, few religious services were held in the newly finished church, because there was no pastor. A friar could not be spared from the San Gabriel Mission, where only two were in residence, and none was available elsewhere. The church remained unused except on special occasions, when a padre came from San Gabriel to officiate; for any other service, men and women traveled to the mission.

In the new village the families built sturdy homes of adobe. They made bricks of mud mixed with straw, baked them in the sun and then stacked them together to form stout walls two to four feet thick. The flat roofs were covered with thatch hardened by mud and water-proofed by a coating of brea brought from pools four miles away; the asphalt belonged to all the inhabitants of El Pueblo without charge. The finished earthen homes were comfortably warm in winter and cool in summer.

The pueblo owned all vacant land within its four square leagues. A citizen wanting property on which to build a home petitioned the Ayuntamiento for a certain piece of land. If it were vacant, his request was granted in exactly the size and shape he had stated, without attention as to whether or not the property was on a street. Boundaries were so vaguely described that often ownership overlapped, nor was there any attempt at regularity of streets or alleys. Title to the lots was only given orally, but in 1836 the Ayuntamiento made an effort to bring order into the situation, announcing that all property holders should apply for written titles.

Most of the streets were narrow, and at one time a movement to widen the streets was initiated. However, the authorities found a law (probably coming from Spain long before) reading: "In cold countries the streets shall be wide, and in warm countries narrow." The weather of semitropical Southern California made it obvious that the streets should accordingly remain narrow.

The unpaved roads were perversely changeable with the weather. During summer they lay deep in dust, but in the winter rainy season they turned into troughs of sticky mud. To cross the streets in com-fort, pedestrians carried planks or rented them from boys. When the rains ended, the clay hardened into unyielding ruts which finally dis-integrated into summer dust. There were no collectors of rubbish, and dead animals, old clothing and other trash were often tossed into the road. When the Ayuntamiento passed a regulation that house-holders were to sweep in front of their property on Saturday evenings, the ruling was ignored. Sewers were nonexistent.

At times torrential rains remade the landscape. For instance, in the winter of 1824-25 a flood caused the Los Angeles River (still called the Porciúncula) to overflow its banks. The river normally emptied into Santa Monica Bay, following the present course of La Ballona Creek, but a vast inland sea was formed, after which the stream changed direction to join the San Gabriel River and flow into San Pedro Bay.

About forty years later the San Gabriel itself, at a point much farther north, shifted to a new course, and its riverbed was taken over by the Rio Hondo.

Under the Spanish regime only two ships a year were allowed to visit California, but after September 28, 1821, when Mexico became independent from Spain, all such limits were removed. Trading ships, mostly from New England, came frequently to the Southland and an era of greater luxury began. Families from town, along with those from ranchos, went out to the sailing vessels, where they found everything they might want offered on counters. With great excitement the Californians shopped among the crowded displays of shawls, carpets, watches, hardware, candlesticks, silver and jewelry, furniture, fine rugs to lay over earthen floors, window glass in tiny panes and such luxury foods as tea, sugar and candies. Many customers went to the vessels carrying hides as negotiable currency; otherwise payment was made in drafts, or due bills, and hides and tallow were later delivered to the harbor so the ship could receive what was due.

Now that fine materials were available, the wealthy rancheros and other men of prominence proudly wore jackets and trousers decorated with silver or gold braid. The jackets were short, and the tight-fitting long trousers were made with a sudden flare below the calf. Under the jacket was a white shirt, with a colored sash wound around the waist. Sombreros were wide brimmed with high crowns and worn over a silk kerchief tied around the head. Like the suits, the sombreros were often trimmed with a cord of silver or gold. Boots, rather than shoes, were worn by all the men.

On the ships the women bought velvet or brocade for their skirts and boleros. Combs and lace for mantillas were brought home to decorate the heads of señoras, who piled their hair high in contrast to the custom among señoritas of wearing their hair in braids with flat curls around the face and a rose as ornament. For ordinary dress all wore bright-colored skirts, low-necked camisas and shawls.

Horses, too, were splendidly arrayed. Saddles, bridles and stirrups were made of carved leather inlaid with gold or silver, a tradition carried into today by the ceremonial posses of California, which parade in fancy trappings during a rodeo, fiesta or other special event. Horses which were especially spirited and graceful were kept for the use of the rancheros and called "caballos estimados" (highly-prized horses). The Southland rider, with a flair for drama, prepared himself to mount and then, striking his horse, sprang into the saddle and went off at a gallop. Similarly, when planning to dismount, instead of slowing his horse gradually he reined it into a sudden, rearing halt.

A horse race. (*—California State Library*)

Visitors of those days described their amazement at seeing small children, several on one horse with the youngest sandwiched in between, speeding unafraid across the fields. There were some skilled horsewomen, but not many. When a women rode it was sidesaddle, with a wooden or straw platform on which her feet could rest. A protective male sat just behind her on the crupper, one arm holding her and the other handling the reins. A young woman rode with her sweetheart; an old woman rode with a son or other relative.

The Beau Brummells of the time were Don José Sepúlveda and Don Vicente Lugo, who owned expensively decorated outfits. On fiesta days young men rode into town and paraded down a main street five or six abreast, delighting the onlookers and themselves.

The colloquial word for a ball was a "fandango," the same name as that of a popular dance, and the gaiety at such an affair generally continued all night. Lively seguidillas and fandangos alternated with precise jarabes and intricate contradanzas. However, some dancing was unlike the Spanish style, wherein women always take a spirited part. For instance, in the jota, similar to the Virginia reel in that men and women faced each other in long lines, the women remained almost motionless while the men danced exuberantly around them in circles. The contradanza, a waltz, was danced by only a few and admired as a great accomplishment.

A favorite type of flirtation at these fandangos was with the cascarón — an eggshell pierced at each end so that the insides could be blown out and the shell then filled with confetti or cologne, after which the openings were sealed with wax. Surreptitiously, a caballero approached a señorita and broke the cascarón over her head, then quickly maneuvered to seem guiltless. The object of the game was of course to guess the culprit. The game worked both ways, and if a young lady broke a cascarón on a gentleman's head he gallantly tried to return the compliment.

For many years one of the centers of entertainment in town was a large gambling house by the Plaza, the El Dorado Saloon, whose furnishings were brought from the East around the Horn. Here towns-people and visiting rancheros could play monte; there was a long bar and several "monte banks" were in operation. (Later, renamed the Methodist Chapel, the saloon saw the city's first Protestant services.) More and more gambling places were built until there was an over-abundant supply. In front of Don Francisco O'Campo's adobe, the corner of the Plaza widened into what was called the Plazuela, where cockfights were held.

The favorite sport was horseracing, although a fenced-in bullring in the Plaza allowed extra excitement for the pueblo on Sundays and holidays, with either bullfights or bear-and-bull fights. In the early 19th century many grizzlies preyed on cattle, and the vaqueros cap-tured them and brought them to the Plaza for sport. In the bear-and-bull fights the primitive struggle continued until one of the animals was killed, but bullfights were more like a playful game, with the aim of confusing or enraging the animal. To do this the bullfighter would use such tricks as pulling his tail; often there were several bull-fighters in the ring at once, enjoying an uproarious melee. For the climax, an effort was made to overturn the bull, and when this was successfully done he was allowed to leave the ring and return to pasture. Bullfights were held in the Plaza until the Council announced that the ring was too near the church; so it was moved a few blocks north and the road alongside it named Calle del Toro. Bullfighting and bear-and-bull fighting were outlawed in 1860, and what was once the Calle del Toro is now part of Hill Street.

From the earliest days each cattle owner was required to register his brand with the authorities. He presented a piece of leather branded in the design he wanted registered.* A brand was issued to the owner

---

*In the Los Angeles Hall of Records a large box still holds all the samples which were accepted, and in the Book of Brands (four volumes) are the brand designs and the original authorizations. The last brand was recorded in 1935.

of 150 head of cattle or more; the owner of fewer was given an ear-mark — a simple design to be notched at the end of an ear on each animal.

Andalusian longhorns, a bony but picturesque breed of cattle, wandered freely from rancho to rancho. To keep ownership distinct, round-ups were held every year, at which time all cattle in a certain area were driven together into a large corral. The animals were then divided according to brand, and each calf given the same mark as the cow it followed. Entire families attended these rodeos, everyone in festive dress. Three hectic days were spent in the branding of calves, competition at horsemanship, feasting and dancing.

At each roundup one man was appointed by the ayuntamiento to be Juez del Campo (Judge of the Plains), a position of great honor. The Judge was in charge of settling any disputes among the cattle owners and was given a despotic power over the proceedings and the people involved. Among the Judges of the Plains through the years were members of families whose descendants still live in the neighborhood today: Yorba, Dominguez, Machado, Avila, Sanchez, Cota and many others. Rules concerning this function were continued under California law until declared obsolete in 1933.

On all Spanish and Mexican documents, each signature was followed by a rubric, or flourish. This was characteristic of Spanish countries especially; in other lands which followed the custom a simpler flourish sufficed. The rubric was so much a part of the signature that it was recognized equally with the name itself. Governor Micheltorena found humor in playing a kind of game with his own signature, even on official documents: sometimes he wrote his name out in full, sometimes it was Michelta or Micha, and once he penned the rubric only.

Signatures of Agustín Olvera, Governor Juan B. Alvarado, Ygnacio Coronel and Manuel Dominguez.

4. A Simple Environment

At first El Pueblo was an agricultural community, raising corn, peppers and other foods customary in Mexico. Grapes were grown from cuttings brought from the San Gabriel Mission, whose vineyard therefore was called the "Viña Madre" (Mother Vineyard). In the pueblo the vines made a welcome stretch of green along either side of the river and irrigation ditches; their fruit became the Southland's first agricultural export. A Frenchman with the appropriate name of Jean Louis Vignes (usually called by the Spanish name "Luis") in 1831 started the Aliso vineyard with cuttings of different varieties of grapes imported from France via Boston and then by ship around the Horn. To preserve the moisture of the vines, they were embedded in potato slices throughout the trip. Near the Plaza, alongside the river, the vineyard covered over a hundred acres and included a grape arbor one-quarter of a mile long; the narrow road which once bordered the vineyard is today Vignes Street. A huge sycamore tree (aliso, in California usage) stood at the entrance to Vignes' hacienda, which was a famous gathering place, and the name of Aliso Street is derived from that tree. Two of his nephews, Pierre and Jean Louis Sainsevain, came from France and became vineyardists too. California was a natural place for the wine industry, and by the middle of the 19th century there were over a hundred vineyards thriving in the vicinity of Los Angeles. Most of them cultivated the black Mission grape.

The first oranges were planted at the San Gabriel Mission in 1804 by Padre Tomás Sanchez. Later Don Luis Vignes started a small grove in the pueblo, but it was William Wolfskill who initiated the orange industry when in 1841 he planted a grove of two acres which was later expanded to include 2500 trees — half the orange trees in California and the largest grove in the United States. Wolfskill also brought the first persimmon tree to Los Angeles and is reputed to have imported seeds from Australia for the first eucalyptus trees in California. (Palm trees were not native to California except for the Washingtonia, a tree with a distinctively large, fan-shaped leaf.)

Fish were plentiful, and for meat there was beef and lamb. To keep beef in those days of nonrefrigeration, the meat from cattle was made into jerked beef, or "jerky." After the flesh was cut into strips about an inch thick, five inches wide and one to three feet long, it was dipped into brine and hung in the hot sun on a fence or on leather thongs tied to poles. Within four days the beef became hard and black, whereupon it could be stored or wrapped in bales for shipment. Despite its unappetizing appearance, this well-flavored "carne

seca" was indispensable to all Californians. It could be chewed while
dry, or to make it more tasty it was soaked, pounded until thin and
then cooked in a pan with a little lard and water, a boiled potato, a
chopped onion, red chili and tomato.

From the first days of the pueblo when its location near a river
was chosen, the scarcity of fresh water has been the greatest concern
of Southern California. The pueblo's first contest over water rights
was with the San Fernando Mission, which lay upstream from the
village boundaries. Early in the 1800s the padres dammed the Los
Angeles River in order to store water for the dry season. The Ayuntamiento brought suit against the mission to remove the dam as an
obstruction to Los Angeles' supply of water, and the court ruled that
the town had a right to the total flow, although the mission was
allowed to use enough for irrigation. Later, in a ruling by the Mexican Government, the pueblo was granted a right to all water of the
Los Angeles River from its source until it left the city area.

From the beginning, the Ayuntamiento controlled water distribution, and the people paid for its use. An open ditch lined with brick,
the Zanja Madre, carried river water around the town. The Zanja
Madre started approximately where North Broadway now crosses the
Los Angeles River; there a large water wheel lifted water from the
river into the wide ditch from which minor channels branched off here
and there (no pipes were used). The ditches were watched by the
zanjero, who was responsible for keeping them free of animals or
the washing of clothes, and who directed the supply of water according to the quota assigned to the vineyards and homes. Owners contracted for a specific amount of water and for the time when it was
to be received, and the zanjero diverted it accordingly. This man was
so important to the town that for a while his salary was higher than
that of the mayor.

Today a stretch of brick diagonally across Olvera Street, by the
fountain, follows the line of the ancient ditch, and alongside is a tablet
commemorating the Zanja Madre.

The river water was far from clean in the early years. Cattle,
donkeys and pigs crossed the riverbed at will, stirring up and polluting the water. Eventually it was prohibited to bathe, wash clothes
or allow animals in the zanja or irrigating ditches under penalty of
a steep fine. Repairs were made under a community system whereby
each landowner furnished a quota of Indian laborers, and each coun-
cilman took his turn as overseer of the work for a week's time.

Transportation was primitive in the Southland. Aside from horseback the main method of travel, the carreta pulled by two oxen, was

extremely slow, but the wooden cart could hold a good-sized family and with blankets could provide sleeping accommodations during long, lonely journeys over the ranchos. Some carretas had makeshift awnings to keep off the strong sunlight. The wheels, secured by long wooden pins hammered into a hole in the axle, squeaked hideously, and the only remedy was to carry tallow and lubricate the axles every few miles.

In the early 19th century a journey by sailing vessel to San Pedro from a port in any other country was a long one. Travelers disembarking with relief after the voyage were usually dismayed to find that half-broken broncos waiting in a pasture near the landing were the only means of transport to the town. To westerners they presented no problem, but for most easterners the first encounter with western saddles and wild-eyed horses was too much. Their journey was usually finished afoot.

At first only trails connected missions, presidios, pueblos and the most important ranchos. Gradually the main trails became wagon roads and finally highways. The eminent historian Jacob N. Bowman (no relation to the author) notes that all public roads and highways were called caminos, caminos reales or caminos nacionales. There was no Camino del Rey (King's Highway); "camino real" was derived not from the Latin word meaning "royal," but from the medieval *realis*, meaning "real, actual," therefore signifying a well-established road or public highway. On maps of the old ranchos, a road along the boundary was sometimes labeled camino real or camino nacional. No single road dominated all others: routes changed according to the weather, the establishment of new ranchos and missions, or the travelers who used them — Indians, rancheros, soldiers or friars. It is pointless to argue whether *the* Camino Real to Ventura went north over Frémont Pass to Newhall and down the Santa Clara Valley, or first turned westward through the San Fernando Valley and Santa Monica Mountains. A camino real will have gone along each route.

On the coastline to the north, between today's cities of Ventura and Santa Barbara, many miles were blocked to travelers by mountains which descended steeply into the ocean. There beaches formed part of the camino real, and at high tide riders or mule teams had to make their way through the surf. For stretches where not even a beach existed, a trail led across the mountainside, and during the rainy season it was sometimes impossible for animals to keep their footing on the narrow, slippery path.

With the coming of paved roads and the building of subdivisions, most traces of the old caminos were obliterated. The metamorphosis of these old roads is strikingly illustrated by the route which follows the approximate path of an ancient main thoroughfare between San Diego and Los Angeles. Originally a narrow trail, it became more and more heavily traveled. Eventually it was broadened, given a modern surface, and marked El Camino Real as a reminder of its historical importance; for emphasis, the Automobile Club of Southern California lined the highway with mission bells. Now the route is traversed by several freeways, soaring far above the ground which once knew the familiar tread of the missionaries' sandals, the Indians' bare feet, the heavy wheels of the carretas and the swift hooves of horses.

5. *Foreign Traders and Privateers*

The first Spanish trading vessels in the Pacific were the Manila galleons. In 1565 they began their long voyages between the Philippines and Acapulco, far south on the western coast of Mexico. For two centuries they brought cargoes of silks, spices, china and other things valued by the Spaniards. Their goods were so prized in Mexico that Spanish merchants protested they were losing trade with the New World, and the government limited the galleons to one voyage a year. On each return trip the ships sailed directly toward California, at a point near Monterey, but when the lookout saw seaweed or other indications of a nearby coast the vessels turned south instead of going into a California harbor.

One of the rules of ocean navigation is that the shortest distance between two points is a curve, the great circle. For this reason ships coming from the Atlantic Ocean destined for California seldom sailed directly up the west coast of South America unless for the purpose of stopping at coastal ports. Instead, after rounding Cape Horn they followed the great circle, steering north in a wide arc which led to the Sandwich, or Hawaiian, Islands. The trade winds, prevailing easterlies, blew the ships across the Pacific; from Hawaii the Japan Current swept them east. The current swings in a circle with California at the eastern end, and in places the Japan Current reaches a speed of 75 or more miles per day. Throughout the era of sail this route was taken by most ships, while vessels which went north along the coast found it a long struggle against capricious winds and conflicting currents. It surprised no one when in the middle of the 19th century, just as war was about to break out between California and the United States, a man bringing an urgent message from Washington, D.C., to Monterey hastened to his destination by way of Hawaii.

In 1818 two ships sailed from the Sandwich Islands toward California, both armed to attack Spanish ships and plunder Spanish settlements. Capt. Hippolyte Bouchard was in command, and the ships — the *Argentina* and *Santa Rosa* — carried crews made up of mutineers and men who in the Islands had escaped from other vessels. On the *Santa Rosa* were two Americans, Joseph Chapman and Tom Fisher.

In October of that year the commander of an American brig upon arrival at Santa Barbara told Don José de la Guerra that in the Sandwich Islands two pirate ships were preparing to attack Alta California. De la Guerra sent a warning along the coast and sentinels were posted. Women and children were told to be ready to flee; valuables were buried or sent to inland missions for safekeeping; herds were taken to safe pastures. On November 20, one month after the warning went out, scouts sighted the ships nearing Monterey.

The two vessels were really privateers rather than pirates. In 1816, Argentina declared her independence from Spain and, finding herself successful, encouraged revolts against Spain elsewhere. With this intention she armed the *Argentina* and *Santa Rosa*, commissioning them to fight Spanish ships and try to create a revolt in California. For a ship to be given a "private commission" of that sort was at the time considered legal among nations. Bouchard, however, used them not like privateers but like pirate ships, marauders.

Late at night on November 20 the frigates anchored in the harbor of Monterey, the *Santa Rosa* near shore. At dawn she opened fire on the shore battery. Reports of the battle are confused and statements conflict, but essentially the facts are that the *Santa Rosa* was badly damaged by bombardment, mainly from a small but well-managed battery on the beach south of the fort, commanded by Corporal José de Jesus Vallejo. The *Santa Rosa* lowered several landing boats filled with men, but Corporal Vallejo's accurate fire caused them all to turn back. Thereupon the *Santa Rosa* lowered her flag, signifying surrender. From the fort an order was shouted across the water for the ship's commander to come in person. After a reply that the commander was on the other frigate, the *Santa Rosa*'s second in command, Joseph Chapman, went ashore with two sailors. Governor Sola questioned the three men, but, angered by what he called their "lies and frivolous excuses," he ordered them thrown into the guardhouse. The other frigate moved closer into the harbor, anchoring just beyond reach of the guns, and Bouchard sent a flag of truce. It was refused. Early the next morning nine longboats, four of them carrying cannon, headed for shore and firing recommenced. In a skirmish south of the fort the forces of Corporal Vallejo captured three men who had become separated from the main body of invaders, among them Tom Fisher, a Negro 24 years old. But the Spanish forces were greatly outnumbered;

there was dissension about strategy, and as an outcome the defenders of Monterey retreated inland. An unwary Spaniard who remained behind was imprisoned on one of the ships. Bouchard made efforts to ransom his men who had been taken captive and at the same time urged the Californians to revolt against the Spanish government, but in vain. After repairing the *Santa Rosa*, gathering food from the orchard and vegetable gardens, looting the warehouse as well as the homes of the Governor and Commandant, and setting fire to the presidio and fort, Bouchard and his men left the harbor and sailed southward.

Thirty miles north of Santa Barbara the two frigates anchored near Rancho del Refugio, owned by Don José María Ortega. The rancho was known among smugglers, and possibly it was chosen because the ranchhouse was reputed to contain valuables. The pirates attacked the central buildings, from which the inhabitants had fled. They broke down doors and proceeded to loot the rooms. Meanwhile, horsemen from as far away as Los Angeles rode to aid the defense. Near the ranchhouse several Spaniards stationed themselves in ambush, and after a while three pirates passed by in search of a carreta in which to carry loot to the shore. From the ambush, coiled lariats noiselessly flew through the air and the three plunderers found themselves bound and helpless. They were taken from the rancho and held prisoner. After the ships sailed away Bouchard returned to shore at Santa Barbara and under a flag of truce arranged to exchange his one prisoner (captured at Monterey) for the three who had been waylaid and lassoed while looting.

Fearful colonists kept watch along the coast in dread of the next invasion, but the ships continued without stopping until they came to the beach near San Juan Capistrano. There Bouchard sent to the mission a request for certain supplies, but the soldiers protecting the mission sent back a refusal. The pirates invaded it, but after damaging the mission only slightly they departed. It was then that four deserters came forward. The four men were sent inland and kept under guard. Without stopping elsewhere the vessels sailed back to South America, and California breathed in relief.

Two of the pirates became important to Los Angeles — Joseph Chapman, officer of the *Santa Rosa*, and Tom Fisher, captured by Corporal Vallejo during the invasion of Monterey. After November 21, when Chapman was put into the guardhouse of the fort, there is no record of what happened to him until on December 2 he walked into the Santa Inés Mission (six miles from Rancho del Refugio) and surrendered. The alcalde of El Pueblo, Don Antonio María Lugo, had ridden to Santa Barbara to help defend against the pirates. In reminiscences many years later he claimed that on his return south he brought Chapman with him.

Joseph Chapman, known as "José el Inglés," became the most useful man in Los Angeles. When sent into the mountains to get timber for building the Plaza church, he amazed everyone by his skill in felling trees: it seemed like magic that he always knew which way a tree would fall. A jack-of-all-trades, he not only helped to build the church in Los Angeles and later a gristmill for the San Gabriel Mission but also had a hand in every local enterprise requiring manual skill. In addition, he figured in one of the favorite romances of Los Angeles' early days. Señorita Guadalupe Ortega was daughter of the ranchero whose home had been attacked by Bouchard's pirates. When in 1820 Chapman was loaned to the Santa Inés Mission to build a gristmill, he was introduced to the Ortega family, and a joking flirtation began between the Yankee and dark-eyed Guadalupe. Each Sunday they met when she attended Mass at the mission. The next year the King of Spain declared an amnesty toward all Anglo-American prisoners and Chapman determined to ask for her hand in marriage. To overcome any enmity on her father's part, the influential Don Antonio María Lugo offered to ride to Santa Barbara as Chapman's emissary. Don Antonio spoke eloquently to Ortega about the young man's virtues and intelligence and won his acceptance as a son-in-law. After Chapman was baptized into the Roman Catholic Church, a festive wedding ceremony was held at the Santa Inés Mission, and then the newlyweds went to Los Angeles to live. Later he became a Mexican citizen, and whatever his past the government held no hard feelings, for in 1838 — twenty years after the raid at Monterey — Governor Alvarado granted Chapman ownership of a rancho by the ocean, bounded on the north by the Santa Clara River, near today's city of Ventura.

After Tom Fisher — for some reason called "Norris" at first — was captured, he was taken along with his companions from Monterey to Governor Sola's temporary headquarters twenty miles away, for questioning. The men testified that the purpose of the ships' arrival on the coast of California was to persuade the provincial army to revolt, and they added that Bouchard had expected the provincial officers to be sympathetic to the idea. Sola accepted their explanation and pardoned them, though with an order to leave the Monterey area. Of the three men, only Fisher went far south, becoming a resident of Los Angeles. In the Spanish language there is no "sh" combination; so he was known as "El Negro Fisar." To everyone's relief the privateer was found to be easily likable, but in vain did the padres and their pious flock try to convert him to Roman Catholic beliefs and worship; he remained a firm Protestant. As a result, "Fisar" went down in history books as a man of merit but without religion, and he was equally adamant about remaining a citizen of the United States. It was as an adventurer that he made his first appearance in Los Angeles, and as an adventurer he was to reappear in Los Angeles history thirty years later, when the Americans approached the Southland during the Mexican War.

Until the end of Spanish rule, few explorers except Spaniards came to the shores of Southern California. Sir Francis Drake, sailing from England in 1579 on the *Golden Hind*, approached the California shore only at Drake's Bay, just north of San Francisco. George Vancouver in 1793 sailed with his British sloop *Discovery* as far down the coast as San Diego, stopping there and at Santa Barbara where people ignored the government's ban on foreign visitors and welcomed him enthusiastically. Frenchmen, Russians and Americans visited California, but mainly in the north. Meanwhile, Spain's Captain de Anza made his two expeditions across the Colorado River and the desert by way of Yuma. So eager was he to be allowed the attempt to find a land route to California from the Mexican mainland that he offered to pay the entire cost of the first expedition. We can still see a graphic example of the hardships faced by Anza and his followers in the sand dunes, west of Yuma, through which the first expedition struggled for days and where its members nearly died of thirst.

The first Americans to come overland were fur traders, incredibly heroic men who endured constant danger, thirst and starvation, threats of all kinds. In 1826, Jedediah Strong Smith with 15 fellow trappers made his way from the Great Salt Lake across mountains and the Mojave Desert to the San Gabriel Mission. Governor Echeandía refused to allow him to journey north along the coast; so instead he went north up the San Joaquin Valley and from there through blizzards across the Sierra Nevada back to the Great Salt Lake. Upon returning to California the next year, he found the government more hostile than before. This time he decided to go north along his earlier route but continue to Ft. Vancouver. En route all but Smith and two other men were massacred by Indians as they neared Oregon. Smith was the first to cross the Sierra Nevada, as well as the man who opened a pathway from the Great Salt Lake to California.

While Smith was making his second trip, a group of fur traders set out from Santa Fe under the leadership of Sylvester and John Ohio Pattie, father and son. Trapping as they went — in search of beaver skins especially — they reached the Colorado River. Attacks by the Yuma Indians were the worst hazard, and so the party built canoes from cottonwood trees and embarked on the river. During daytime they floated downstream and at night set their beaver traps. Near the mouth of the Colorado the party abandoned the canoes and started overland toward the Spanish settlements on the Pacific coast, eventually coming to a mission. A few months earlier, Jedediah Smith had reached California the second time, and to Governor Echeandía's alarm word was now brought that more Americans had arrived. Under his orders the latest group was thrown in jail at San Diego. Months went by, and during that time the leader, Sylvester Pattie, became seriously ill. His son "Ohio" begged for at least temporary freedom for his father so that he could have better care, but still in jail the unfortunate man died.

Then an unexpected cause for the group's release appeared: a smallpox epidemic was spreading through Alta California, and by chance young Pattie had the means to check it. From New Mexico he had brought some smallpox vaccine, and he agreed to vaccinate the inhabitants of Alta California if his entire party were freed. The request was granted, and then, adding to his small amount of vaccine by using the virus of inoculated patients, Pattie began an amazing medical service. Starting in San Diego he continued to Los Angeles, Santa Barbara and as far north as San Francisco, inoculating a total of about 20,000 inhabitants, Indian and Mexican, of the presidios, missions and settlements along the way. Later Pattie returned east, but several of his fellow trappers remained in California permanently.

At that time Santa Fe was the center of trade and trapping in the Southwest. Following the example of the Patties, Ewing Young led a party from there to California, passing through Los Angeles in 1830. That same year William Wolfskill led a trapping expedition to Southern California, and his choice of a route marked the beginning of the Santa Fe Trail (also called the Old Spanish Trail), a caravan route from St. Louis to Santa Fe to Los Angeles. Blankets and American merchandise were brought to California and traded for horses and mules as well as for goods from merchant ships on the coast. Among the men who came to Los Angeles by that route were many whose names have become important in Southland history — not only William Wolfskill but John J. Warner, Isaac Williams and Julian Chavez. However, they came primarily as trappers or traders and remained only in the way that other men left ships to stay in California.

The first American overland pioneer settlers — those who came to Southern California for the specific purpose of making it their future home — arrived in 1841 with the Rowland-Workman party by way of the Santa Fe Trail. The group included William Workman, John Rowland, Benjamin D. Wilson and Lemuel Carpenter. Other pioneers arrived on trading vessels: Abel Stearns, John Temple, Juan B. Leandry, Thomas Robbins. All the above mentioned settlers became rancheros.

Travelers grew familiar with the kind of life offered by California, and the word spread. Although no large numbers were involved, the first migration westward had begun.

6. *Frontier Money*

For lack of other currency, the first money used in the area of Los Angeles was the Indian ponko, a string of clamshells (flat and round, about half an inch in diameter) whose value varied with its length. To the early settlers one ponko thirty inches long equaled one Spanish *real*. But it was not long before Spanish coins became the medium of trade. Most of them were minted in the Spanish colonies, where the mines in Mexico and Peru provided a large supply of silver, gold, copper, brass and nickel. These coins made up the principal specie used in the New World, including the English colonies, and their fine quality made them a universal standard of value.

The escudo, known to the English as the Spanish dollar, was an eight-real piece ("piece of eight") made of silver. When U.S. currency was created, the U.S. dollar was designed to be comparable to the Spanish one in size and value. Other Spanish coins were the four-real, two-real, one-real and half-real pieces. In the English colonies the real (worth about 12½ cents) was called a "bit," and the two-real piece called "two bits." Therefore the slang word for the corresponding U.S. 25-cent coin was (and still is) "two bits." The gold doubloon — so named from the Spanish "doblón" (from doblón de ocho or "double eight escudos") — had a value of $16.

On one side of the Spanish dollar the crowned columns represent the Pillars of Hercules (Straits of Gibraltar), with between them the globes of the Old and New Worlds. On the reverse is the name of Philip V and the royal coat of arms.

The silver Mexican dollar, valued at eight reales, was coined after the formation of the Mexican Republic in 1823. The national emblem of the eagle, snake and cactus appear on one side; on the other the traditional revolutionary cap.

Many coins of those days were beautiful, some from Spain having coats of arms or a picture of two globes representing the Old and New Worlds. On most coins made in Mexico after 1823, one side depicted the Mexican national emblem of an eagle, snake and cactus. Since there were no banks in Southern California, the coins in circulation were of fairly indefinite value, depending upon what the buyer and seller would agree to. Occasional strange shapes occurred, as pieces of coins were cut off when only part of the coin was needed.

The cattle hide, Southern California's staple commodity, took on the status of money. It was used for various payments, including government fines (American trappers paid in beaver skins). From Alaska to the far coast of South America, hides were known as "California banknotes" or "leather dollars" — the value per hide for many years being exactly one dollar, whether the hide was large or small. Later the accepted value became two dollars per hide.

Before 1800, no foreign trading vessel had touched at any Southern California port because of severe Spanish restrictions. All colonial commerce had to be handled by Spanish ships, of which only two each year were allowed to go to California, and there could be no trade with other countries. Duties on shipments were heavy; furthermore, for trade carried on with foreigners the penalty was death and forfeiture of property. In spite of this, New England ships ran a contraband trade until 1821. When Mexican rule succeeded Spanish rule commerce was made legal, although there were still restrictions. Under the new government each trading vessel had to sail first to Monterey, which provided the only customhouse on the California coast. There the cargo was listed while a ship's agent rode through the countryside to missions, pueblos and ranchos, announcing the vessel's arrival. The customs fees required in Monterey when ships reached California, and again when they departed, made up the principal revenue out of which official salaries and other expenses were paid.

It was William E. P. Hartnell, an Englishman representing a Peruvian shipping company, who built the foundation of commerce in California. Until his arrival trading was haphazard, but he arranged with most of the mission padres to take their hides and tallow in exchange for goods needed at the missions. To store the hides until his ship's arrival, he built a small adobe office-warehouse. Solitary on San Pedro Bay, it was the only building within leagues. When his firm disbanded and he no longer needed the warehouse, Hartnell gave it to the San Gabriel Mission.

To the problem of trading restrictions and high customs duties, smuggling was a natural solution. The numerous coves along the peninsula of Palos Verdes made smuggling easy, while customs officials were few and at a distance; so it was hard for the government to check such activities. A ship would anchor at Santa Catalina Island or offshore near the peninsula, and small boats would then bring in the contraband. Today anyone driving around the Palos Verdes coast passes the very coves the smugglers used; one of them nestles innocently right below Marineland.

Don Abel Stearns bought Hartnell's warehouse, called La Casa de San Pedro (located within what is now Fort MacArthur, halfway between Point Fermin and the Fisherman's Dock), from the mission so that he could store skins there until a ship would sail into port. The isolation of the warehouse and its nearness to the hidden coves made the setup perfect for contraband trade. The government grew suspicious, and Don Abel was accused of using La Casa de San Pedro for smuggling. However, as far as the public was concerned, that was a perfectly acceptable occupation. As a result of strong support, the charges of smuggling were dropped and Stearns was made administrator of customs for the Los Angeles area.

The main port on the coast for the shipment of hides was San Pedro, called by sailors "The Hell of California." Richard Henry Dana, who came on a ship to California in 1835 and afterward wrote *Two Years Before the Mast*, described the misery of bringing merchandise ashore to be traded for hides. Heavy barrels had to be rolled over kelp-covered, slippery rocks and then up cliffs. During the rainy season, mud on the steep hillsides made it impossible for the men to find footholds. Returning with the heavy dried hides, the sailors usually threw them down the hill, then carried them on their heads over the stones and out to the boats so that they wouldn't get wet. One hide at a time was all that could be handled. Each vessel sailed up and

Juan Temple at left, Abel Stearns at right.
(—both, *Title Insurance & Trust Company*)

down the coast for a year or more, selling merchandise and gathering a shipload of leather dollars.

Dana's book also describes "hide-droghing," or curing. On the ranchos the hides were stretched out to dry, fastened to the ground by stakes to prevent shrinkage. Then the stiff, unwieldy skins were taken to the warehouse at San Pedro Bay. They were bought by ship-masters and usually taken to what is now Dana Point or to San Diego for final curing. There the hides were unloaded once more, tied with ropes and soaked in the ocean for two days. The next two days they were kept in vats of strong salt brine and then stretched in the sun to dry. All remaining grease was scraped off, all dust beaten out with flails, and the hides were ready for the trip east.

The first gold strike in California was made near Los Angeles in Placerita (Little Placer) Canyon. On March 9, 1842, six years before the discovery of gold in the north, Don Francisco Lopez of Rancho San Francisco (just above San Fernando Valley) rode along the canyons with an Indian member of his household, looking for stray horses. His wife had asked him to find wild onions, and at midday while waiting for the Indian to prepare lunch, Don Francisco dug some up under an oak tree by a stream. To his astonishment, small particles of gold were among the onions' roots. Excitedly he gathered more and galloped home with the nuggets; the next day they were assayed in

Los Angeles and found to be true gold. Word of the discovery spread, and eager prospectors rode into the hills. Although one nugget sold for $1928, the total find never amounted to more than about $200,000. Still, it was from Placerita that California sent its first shipment of gold to the U.S. Mint in Philadelphia. Today, in Placerita Canyon State Park,* the same ancient, gnarled tree is known as The Oak of the Golden Dream.

7. *Public Services — or Lack of Them*

During the early years the people of Los Angeles enjoyed few public services. Packets of mail brought by ship or by overland travelers were distributed with no regular system since there was no post office. Mail for sailors on trading vessels was sent in care of La Casa de San Pedro, well known along the coast of South America and equally famed in New England.

For many years there were no doctors; instead, councilmen were a kind of board of health. For instance, during a smallpox epidemic in 1844 a proclamation by the Ayuntamiento was ordered to be read by a guard at each house and Indian hut. Dramatically it said:

> That destructive power of the Almighty, which occasionally pun- ishes man for his numerous faults, destroys not only kingdoms, cities and towns, leaving many persons in orphanages and devoid of protection, but goes forth with an exterminating hand. . . . This terrible plague threatens this unfortunate department of the grand Mexican nation. . . . What would become of her if this eminently philanthropic Ayuntamiento had not provided a remedy partly to counteract these ills?

The hygienic rules which followed, as a protection against smallpox, included advice about abstaining from peppers or spices, bathing once in eight days, and avoiding unripe fruit.

Since the pueblo had no physician, in 1846 several leading citizens signed a petition to Dr. Richard S. Den of Santa Barbara asking him to move to Los Angeles. It was not the same as offering a medical practice today, for many of the homes he would visit were far out in the countryside, but he accepted the request. Memoirs which speak of Dr. Den note that he seemed to be always on horseback.

---

*East of Saugus, the park is two miles south of Highway 14 on Pla- cerita Canyon Road.

In 1841 an adobe building served as the first jail; it consisted of just one room with no cells. However, a long pine log stretched from wall to wall, and chains attached to iron staples in that log were fastened to one leg of each prisoner. Outdoors, the prisoners were chained to smaller logs in the jailyard. The police force was wholly volunteer.

Many former convicts were among the soldiers stationed in the Southland. Because there were few volunteers to the distant Californias, the number of recruits was filled out by men in prison willing to substitute military service for a sentence. In 1787 it was ruled that any prisoner in Mexico could be granted exile in California if the remainder of his prison term were spent in work at a presidio or mission. However, the ruling was canceled because of the strong reaction in California against being used as a penal colony. Forty-five years later a similar decree was issued, and boatloads of criminals were sent to California. The frightened citizens of the Southland refused to allow the convicts to land, although after a great commotion some prisoners were sent to the island of Santa Cruz while others were given employment in Santa Barbara and Los Angeles. In general the criminals proved well-behaved and glad to be law-abiding in the new environment, but the Governor protested to the central government and no more boatloads were sent.

The missions were dedicated to converting and civilizing only the Indians, and the colonies of settlers brought with them no idea of self-education such as inspired the founders of New England. In California, therefore, education was pioneered by the army and navy, retired soldiers and sailors becoming the first schoolmasters in many communities. Even so, as a rule most of the military were also unlettered.

In 1793 the King of Spain issued an order that schools be established in California for the instruction of Spaniards and Indian neophytes as well. Governor Borica made an effort to comply, notifying the missions of the royal order and starting a search for instructors. As a result California's first school was opened in 1794 in San José. Manuel de Vargas, a retired sergeant of infantry, taught in the public granary and the next year held classes in San Diego and later in Santa Barbara, until five schools were in operation by 1796. However, teachers were poorly qualified; people would not voluntarily contribute to the necessary funds; textbooks and paper were hard to obtain; and parents as well as children soon lost interest.

Education languished until 1816, when Governor Sola began his term of office with an effort to open schools. Los Angeles responded by hiring its first schoolmaster, Máximo Piña, who taught in 1817 and

Antonio María Lugo at left, Don Antonio Coronel at right.
(—*both, Los Angeles County Museum of Natural History*)

1818 for a salary equivalent to $140 per year. Governor Sola urged the schools to put learning first, but in spite of his efforts, doctrina cristiana — religious and moral training — was the chief concern. After students learned to read, only religious books were given to them for practice. Los Angeles' enthusiasm was not a permanent thing, because when schoolmaster Piña departed, education was put aside for ten years.

The next governor to be interested in the subject was José María Echeandía, who tried to establish schools at each mission, pueblo and presidio. Ayuntamientos asked what use it would be to spend money on schools if no children were sent by their parents to attend; so the Governor suggested that parents be required by the local authorities to send their children. It was at this time, in 1827, that Luciano Valdez became schoolteacher of 61 Los Angeles students at a monthly salary of $15. He taught off and on for several years, but severity was a rule and the Ayuntamiento fircd him for being too lenient. After Valdez, a succession of four instructors taught for a year each; the salary of $15 per month was the problem, and each resigned when a raise to $20 was refused. The exception among them was Vicente Morago: at the end of a year's teaching he was offered $30 a month as secretary of the Ayuntamiento. Happily he left the schoolroom, but when the term as secretary ended he returned to teach another year at the same low rate as before, until he too resigned. By that time most of the schools in California had ceased to exist.

In 1834, while instruction was still being given in the pueblo, Governor Figueroa found that only three primary schools were in operation in California — at Los Angeles, Santa Barbara and Monterey — all with poorly qualified teachers and few students. No girls attended any school; in line with the general thinking, a former governor had announced that girls should not be taught how to write since they would only use the ability for the writing of love letters. Under Figueroa's urging, California's Legislative Assembly asked the Mexican Government for an annual sum of money which could help support public schools. There was no reply.

When Governor Juan Bautista Alvarado took office in 1836, he tried in his turn to promote the idea of education, but for several reasons the public reaction was negative. The families of most of the rancheros lived far out of town, and it would have been impossible for the children to attend a school in the pueblo. There was a filial basis to society, which meant that the children were content to be as their parents were, with no wish to surpass them in learning. There was a chronic lack of available funds. Furthermore, in the pastoral life no one felt a need to know how to read and write, and education seemed to have no importance whatever.

Don Ygnacio Coronel called a town meeting and offered to teach if a school would be provided, but there was little interest and few people were willing to contribute toward expenses. Nevertheless, in 1836 he formed a school. The average tuition was the equivalent of $15 per month, but parents unable to afford it paid according to their financial means. Sister Soledad, Don Ygnacio's daughter, was the first woman teacher of Los Angeles, and girls were taught for the first time. The school stayed open for two years.

The next effort at education was made by Governor Manuel Micheltorena, who suggested that patience and kindness on the part of teachers would make students more eager to learn. He pressed Los Angeles to open school again, but the Ayuntamiento pleaded a total lack of funds. The capital of Monterey had been given an annual appropriation for education of its children, and the Governor arranged that Los Angeles would be given an appropriation too, with the Mexican equivalent of $500 per year to be paid as salary to a schoolmaster. A schoolmistress was appointed to teach girls, but there is no record that her classes were ever held.

As a result, Ensign Guadalupe Medina, an officer in the Mexican army, took charge of a primary school. To teach his 103 students of

Agustín Olvera. (*—Title Insurance & Trust Company*)

all ages, he figured out a unique system. Medina himself taught the more advanced pupils, who in turn taught the next lower grades and so on all the way down to the most elementary classes; the schoolmaster held examinations and kept records of each student's progress. He gave manual training and object lessons in handling business. As an example of the latter, when his salary arrived from Monterey it was in the form of merchandise, which the oldest students sold in a school assignment, doing the accounting for each transaction. Ensign Medina was an exciting man; so altogether the pupils enjoyed the classes and performed well. Their parents were delighted, and the Ayuntamiento expressed high praise, but still education was not an established thing. Alternately Medina taught and was recalled to service, and then, in 1846, California found itself at war with the United States, and the schoolhouse was needed by the army. The students were dismissed for a vacation — a vacation which lasted five years — and when school started once more, Los Angeles was no longer part of the Mexican nation.

When the United States acquired California in 1848, 71 years after the date of the first settlement, there existed not one public school in the entire province.

8. A Remote Community

In the main, throughout the earliest years Alta California was left to itself in remote self-reliance. Distances were great and communication was difficult; so government ties remained loose whether under Spain or Mexico. Even the missions kept up little correspondence and sent in remarkably few reports.

Mountains and deserts comprise about half of all land in what is today Los Angeles County. With modern instant transportation it is almost impossible to comprehend the depth of isolation of the small pueblo. Only from the bird's-eye view of a plane does the traveler get a true feeling of the impenetrability of barriers surrounding Los Angeles. On the north, in a seemingly endless series of ridges and canyons, the mountains extend on and on and on. Today, lights of occasional cities and villages shine cheerfully from hilltops or from alongside streams, but during the earliest years no settlements existed where a wayfarer could rest in comfort and companionship. On the east, the long stretch of desert was equally unfriendly. To the small community of Los Angeles the barriers isolating it from the rest of the world seemed the very boundaries of the universe.

The missions were the only places which could give lodging until, with the passage of years, more and more ranchhouses arose. The welcome given by the rancheros to all passersby became legendary.

Under these circumstances the pueblo, missions and ranchos of Los Angeles acquired a distinctive character. It included self-reliance and resourcefulness; enjoyment of all church rituals, which gave a touch of glamor to simple, unglamorous lives; and pride in the ways of the Southland. Certain characteristics distinctive of the Spaniards, such as a sense of drama and personal honor, were therefore intensified. These characteristics became most marked when the men of El Pueblo went to war.

Aleuts in bidarkas. *(—Bancroft Library)*

III

WARFARE IN THE SOUTHLAND 1781-1848

1. *Covetous Powers*

Warfare in the Southland had a theatrical quality wherein every battleground became a stage. At one time the characters performed a comic opera with Latin bravado; at another they enacted the tragic avenging of personal honor; and at last, in brief battle with the oncoming American invaders, the Californios rode across the scene, a gallant, poignant remnant of a medieval era.

In the early 1800s Monterey watched with suspicion the Russian attempts to establish Fort Ross, about a hundred miles north of San Francisco, but in the Southland the peaceful scene was unstirred except for occasional forays by bands of foreign hunters. In 1799 the Russian American Fur Company was formed, having headquarters at Kodiak, Alaska. Its operations did include small colonies of Americans in Alaska, but the shareholders were Russian and so was the director, Alexander Baranof. At that time furs were becoming an important trade with China, yet Russia lacked ships in the Pacific whereas there were many Yankee vessels. Accordingly, the company made arrangements to send furs to the Orient on American ships, which then brought back supplies (chiefly food) for Alaska. The best fur on the West Coast came from otters and seals on islands off Southern California, and Jonathan Winship, captain of the *O'Cain,* suggested in 1803 that Baranof send Aleutian hunters to the coast of California on his ship. So on the *O'Cain* — and later on other American ships as well — skillful Aleuts and their bidarkas (boats made of stretched skins) were taken down the California shore, a number of them to the Channel Islands and Santa Catalina. The hunters were left to kill otters and seals, and later the ship would return bringing food and other supplies and take away the skins. In the usual system of otter hunting, an otter skin was tied airtight and fastened to a line. After blowing up the skin and throwing it into the water, the Aleut pulled the decoy slowly toward shore, attracting live animals which could easily be killed with spears. Thousands of otters were taken for the China trade, and by 1820 the animals were almost exterminated.

In spite of government warnings prohibiting foreign ships in California waters, a Russian vessel under an American captain sailed on an illicit trading voyage down the coast in 1815. On board were twenty Aleuts commanded by Boris Tarakanof, and on an expedition to San Pedro the hunters were captured. Comisionado Cota put them under guard in Los Angeles, and then the prisoners were taken to Monterey. In the north the Spaniards foolishly sent the prisoners to catch sea otters, some of the Aleuts choosing that opportunity to escape to the Russian establishment at Fort Ross. A few of the Aleuts remained and later became Catholics and free citizens, but Governor Sola sent Tarakanof as a prisoner to Mexico.

During these years when California was peaceful except for such brief excitement, Europe was torn by the Napoleonic Wars. In 1808 Napoleon deposed the King of Spain, Ferdinand VII, and put a brother, Joseph Bonaparte, on the throne. This started a series of wars for independence in Mexico, which grew eager for self-rule. Napoleon never completely subjugated Spain, and two years after Ferdinand's dethronement he was reinstated, but Spain remained too involved in her own problems to enforce a strong rule again over the distant American colonies. A successful revolt under Agustín de Iturbide led to the Treaty of Córdoba, and on September 28, 1821, the independence of the Mexican Empire was declared.*

Late the next year Europe's Great Alliance (Russia, Austria, Prussia, France and Great Britain) met to discuss French intervention in Spain and the Spanish colonies. Over Great Britain's objections, the powers gave their approval, and the French army crossed the Spanish border. When news reached the United States that the next step might be European aggression in the Western Hemisphere, President Monroe held a conference with former Presidents Jefferson and Madison. To Jefferson it was "the most momentous" situation facing the United States since its founding. As a result of the conference, Monroe announced that the American continents were not subject to future colonization by the European powers. This message (the Monroe Doctrine) related not only to the freedom of Central and South America, but also to the Pacific coast of North America where, for instance, Russian Fort Ross was fortified and a settlement had already been established. After the declaration of the Monroe Doctrine, the Great Alliance dropped any plans it may have had about intervention in the Spanish colonies of the Western Hemisphere.

---

*Two years later the Central American countries separated from the Mexican Empire. South America was never part of the empire.

In the meantime, six months after the establishment of the Mexican Empire word of the change in government reached Monterey. California had taken no part in the revolt, but Governor Pablo Vicente Sola and his council decided to accept the new regime. On April 11, 1822, he and his council and troops gathered in the Plaza at Monterey to swear allegiance to the new government. To the salute of cannons, an appropriate sermon and a gala fiesta, California transferred its loyalty from Spain to Mexico.

For the *Cortes,* or Legislative Assembly in Mexico City, California was asked to elect a deputy. Therefore each presidio and town chose an elector, and together they appointed Sola as deputy. Afterward, to form the Legislative Assembly of California (also called the Departmental Assembly), the same electors were called back and told to elect themselves as representatives. José Palomares represented Los Angeles.

Mexico had won its independence from Spain, but her affairs remained turbulent. In 1823, Iturbide was forced to abdicate as emperor, and the next year Mexico became a republic. But change had become a habit, and presidents were ousted soon after being elected. With interruptions, Antonio López de Santa Anna, an army officer, was made president five different times — and exiled twice — within twenty years. This constant unrest handicapped the economy of Mexico, which became so impoverished that payments to troops in the distant province of California ceased. In their few remaining years the missions helped to provide supplies for the presidios. Duties levied on coastal trade were kept by the provincial government instead of being sent to Mexico City. California made its utmost efforts to be self-supporting.

2. *A Growing Habit of Rebellion*

Not until the arrival of Governor Manuel Victoria in 1830 did an atmosphere of political turmoil reach California. The Governor, a dictatorial martinet although otherwise a man of exceptional ability, wanted all governmental powers to be in his own hands. In order that no civil agency could have power, he abolished all local ayuntamientos and refused to convene the Departmental Assembly of California. Ignoring the legal rights of individuals, he ruthlessly imprisoned all those who opposed him.

In Los Angeles, Governor Victoria found willing cooperation in Alcalde Vicente Sanchez, who put fifty leading citizens in jail and banished Pío Pico, Abel Stearns and José Antonio Carrillo to Baja California. These three, while in San Diego, joined with Juan Bandini and others to organize a revolt. As in every revolt under Mexico, no complaint was made against the government but only against a governor, a tyrant. A pronunciamiento was issued which began by strongly affirming loyalty to Mexico but reminding the people that Victoria was obstructing legal government. For one thing, while the Departmental Assembly failed to meet, no one could become a landowner, because its approval was required by Mexico before a grant of land could be legal. Other examples of Victoria's despotism were listed. Defiantly the Southland rebels signed the paper, fearlessly allowing their identity to be known by the Governor.

Enthusiasm for the cause was contagious, infecting even Captain Pablo de las Portilla, Commandant of the Presidio of San Diego and Governor Victoria's military representative. He joined the rebels along with fifty of his officers and troops. A total of 150 men marched to Los Angeles and released all prisoners.

Governor Victoria came south to put down the rebellion, and at a spot on the pueblo side of Cahuenga Pass the two forces met. Among the citizens who had been imprisoned was Don José María Avila, a proud man; because of what his jailors considered arrogance, he had been put in irons — greater degradation than Avila could endure. Now, as the armies met, Avila galloped lance in hand toward Governor Victoria, intending to run him through. An officer on Victoria's staff, Captain Pacheco, parried the thrust of the lance, saving the Governor's life but losing his own. Then Avila attacked Victoria again, wounding him seriously. Avila was shot from his horse but continued his efforts to kill the Governor until finally he himself was killed by a soldier.

The bodies of Don José María Avila and Captain Pacheco were carried together to Avila's house. Sounds of grief filled the house and the street outside. (One month earlier Pacheco's widow had given birth to a son, Romualdo Pacheco, who became acting-governor of California from February 27 to December 9, 1875.)

Both sides retreated from battle, and Governor Victoria was taken to Mission San Gabriel, where he decided he was dying and abdicated the governorship. At the mission his physician was none other than the versatile Joseph Chapman, the former pirate. Instead of dying, Victoria recovered and was taken to San Diego to embark for Mexico. Don Pío Pico, senior member of the Assembly, became temporary governor until Victoria's official replacement arrived, Brigadier General José Figueroa.

General Figueroa had already proved himself an able governor of other Mexican provinces. Unfortunately, the troops given him were as usual made up of many ex-convicts. After arms and money had been gathered for the trip, and the Governor was busy with final preparations, the men sailed away to join Santa Anna in a revolt, taking the arms and money with them. Again he prepared for the expedition, and after the ship rejoined him with new recruits he reached Monterey in January 1833. Historians generally consider José Figueroa to be one of the best Mexican governors of California — a capable administrator, tactful, generous, fascinating in conversation. Unorthodox too: presumably unmarried (he brought no family to California), he lived with a mistress in the official residence at Monterey. Although this shocked the conservative citizens, it did not detract from his popularity. To everyone's regret he died two years after he took office.

The rebellion which arose under Victoria became habit-forming, and from then on many revolts sprang up, caused mainly by enjoyment of the excitement. José Antonio Carrillo was an especially enthusiastic revolutionary. The Southland found a good excuse when Juan Bautista Alvarado of Monterey became governor. Although most people approved the fact that a native Californian had been appointed, rather than someone from Mexico City, false rumors about his plans, and appeals to local pride, filled the atmosphere of Los Angeles. The strongest emotion was aroused by the rumor that Alvarado intended to allow the marriage of Catholic señoritas to foreigners and Protestants. In terror women begged that their daughters might be saved from marrying heretics; so gallantly the men of the Southland arose in defense of their women.

From the north, shouting that he would shoot the rebels "full of large and irregular holes," Alvarado marched down the coast toward Los Angeles. Quickly San Fernando Mission funds of an amount comparable to $2000 were appropriated to buy arms. Indians and rancheros were enlisted, and Mayor José Sepúlveda led the pueblo troops to prepare for battle. No one actually wanted to fight; so when the northern troops drew near they were allowed to occupy San Fernando Mission. After a meeting there of both sides for arbitration, the Governor solemnly reassured the fearful Angeleños that their women would remain perfectly safe. As the meeting ended, the soldiers disbanded and the revolt was at an end. This was typical of warfare in the Southland: "battles" were always more skirmishes than anything else, and there were few or no casualties.

The uproar had overshadowed the fact that both north and south were on the same side of another rebellion, this one engineered by Alvarado himself, demanding separation of California from Mexico. At first everyone seemed agreed, but Governor Alvarado soon found that too many people were intent on opposing every suggestion, and he dropped the plan entirely.

Meanwhile, José Antonio Carrillo had persuaded authorities in Mexico City that if someone in Southern California were made governor, there would be no revolt against Mexico. As a result, in 1837 Mexico announced the appointment of Don José's brother, Don Carlos, as provisional governor of California. Yet no word was sent to Governor Alvarado in Monterey, who continued to act as though in authority.

In Los Angeles the Carrillo family rented a building as a temporary capitol; Don Carlos took his oath of office before the Ayuntamiento, and the pueblo erupted into a riotous celebration. Soon Alvarado came south to enforce his own position, but conferences between the two leaders were in strong contrast to the warlike attitudes of the opposing factions. The two governors were distantly related, although in customarily polite terms Carrillo was called "Uncle" by Alvarado. Amicably they discussed the problem, and Don Carlos agreed to relinquish his claim. Later Mexico confirmed Alvarado as Governor, but as a reward for "patriotic services" the Carrillo brothers were given the island of Santa Rosa.

In 1842, General Manuel Micheltorena went through Los Angeles en route to the capital. This seemed like a fine opportunity to try to have the capital city located in the south instead of the north, and therefore a week-long fiesta was arranged, including a grand ball. Unfortunately, the large number of ex-convicts in Micheltorena's army did not hesitate to steal chickens, vegetables, fruit or anything else, seemingly with no reprimand from the Governor. The pueblo lost all desire to be the capital and became eager for Micheltorena and his pillaging army to leave for Monterey.

Later, when an uprising took place in Northern California, Los Angeles joined the revolt against the unpopular Governor and his army. Troops came south to enforce allegiance, and Los Angeles gathered an army of about 400 men (approximately the same size as the army coming from the north). The southern forces were led by the Pico brothers, Andrés and Pío. They encamped in San Fernando Valley near Cahuenga Pass to await the enemy's arrival.

The Americans of the pueblo brought forces of their own. Don Benito Wilson (owner of Rancho La Jurupa where the city of Riverside now stands) and Don Guillermo Workman (owner of Rancho La Puente, now the location of Whittier and Puente) knew that several Americans, friends of theirs, had joined Micheltorena's army, and a secret night meeting with them was arranged. During the convivial all-night "conference" in the hills, aguardiente (brandy) flowed freely and the Americans from the north cheerfully decided to transfer alle-

Governor Manuel Micheltorena.
(*—Title Insurance & Trust Company*)

giance to the army of the pueblo. The loss of their support was a hard blow to the morale of Micheltorena's men.

The Battle of Cahuenga on February 20 and 21, 1845, was pure comic opera. When the two armies were still at long range, the cannons of both sides opened fire loudly and furiously. A mountain (now called Cahuenga Peak) rises just east of Cahuenga Pass, majestically overlooking the San Fernando Valley; on its slopes the wives, children, sweethearts, sisters and mothers of the warriors gathered. Praying and weeping, the fond audience watched while the brave armies thundered at each other. Then the battle ended and the dead were counted: on the northern side the losses were — one horse; the southern side lost — one mule.

Nowadays from the same mountain one can gaze down upon several motion picture studios, and the fictitious battle scenes filmed there cannot be more unreal than the "Battle" of Cahuenga.

On February 22, Governor Micheltorena signed a treaty surrendering to the revolutionists and then marched to San Pedro, where he left California by ship. Don Pío Pico had led the junta against him; so he was made temporary governor until Mexico confirmed him in office.

He was the last Mexican governor of California.

3. *Threat of War*

Serious events were developing. By 1842 it had become clear that Mexico would soon lose her distant colony to some foreign power. The lines of communication and control covered too great a distance; the home government was no longer obeyed without question. England, France and the United States were gazing at California covetously.

In England the idea developed that a British company should be formed to control California in the same manner that the British East India Company controlled India. Sir George Simpson, head of the Hudson's Bay Company — which had trading posts in Oregon and San Francisco — announced in March of 1842 that the Californians clearly wished to separate from the Republic of Mexico, and if they were encouraged to put themselves under the protection of Great Britain, California could be a market for British manufactures and an outlet for her surplus population. Warnings reached Washington, D.C., from the U.S. consul in Mexico City and the ambassador in London that Britain was fostering the establishment of a monarchy in Mexico, to be ruled by a European. Monsieur Duflot de Mofras, investigating the Pacific coast for the French Government, urged France to seize California without wasting time.

Commodore Thomas ap Catesby Jones, commanding American naval forces in the Pacific, was in Callao, Peru, when he received a dispatch which gave him the impression that war between the United States and Mexico had begun. English and French warships were also in ports on the west coast of South America, and since in those days there was no way to check a situation, such as by radio or telegram, he waited for no further confirmation but sailed immediately to Monterey to forestall its takeover by any other power. There, on October 19, 1842, he ordered the surrender of the presidio. The fort was manned by few soldiers with practically no ammunition; it surrendered without resistance and the American flag was raised. Two days later, after discovering that there had been no declaration of war, the commodore apologized, took down the flag and sailed away.

This was the year that Manuel Micheltorena became governor. He happened to be in Los Angeles, and Commodore Jones turned his ship in that direction to seek him out. In the residence of Don Abel Stearns, Micheltorena waited with his staff, all in full uniform. (Commodore Jones, describing the visit later, spoke with admiration about their perfect attire, made complete in each case by gloves and a cane.) Flanked by his aides, the commodore explained his mistake and, with many phrases of diplomatic courtesy, gave an apology. Thereupon a grand ball was arranged in honor of the noble visitor. The home of Vicente Sanchez, just off the Plaza on Sanchez Street, was made ready, and in the exuberance of international goodwill the dancers whirled until dawn. When the commodore and his men returned to San Pedro, the pueblo gave no reminder that the guests had come on a humiliating errand: bells rang in their honor, drums beat a farewell salute and cannons were fired. In hospitable unanimity

General Micheltorena, his wife and the pueblo citizens stood at doors and windows and along the streets calling cordial farewells.

In 1843, Thomas Oliver Larkin was appointed first (and only) U.S. consul at Monterey with the express understanding that the United States would be endangered if any European power gained control on the West Coast. Two years later he sent word to President James Knox Polk that the British were urging Californians to revolt against Mexico and offering money and weapons. In response the President sent Lt. Archibald Gillespie, a young Marine who spoke fluent Spanish, to Monterey with dispatches for Larkin and for Major John C. Frémont, who at the time was on the West Coast making topographical surveys. When Gillespie finally reached the major in Oregon and delivered the dispatches, Frémont stayed up all night reading them and then immediately returned with his men to California.

The springboard into war with Mexico was the United States' annexation of Texas in December 1845 and the question of which country owned the land north of the Rio Grande to the Nueces River. The attitude of the United States followed the opinion expressed by a New York editor, James L. O'Sullivan, who declared it was "our manifest destiny to overspread the continent." President Polk sent General Zachary Taylor to the mouth of the Rio Grande, where he established a fort in what Mexico considered its own territory. Mexico promptly attacked and declared war against the United States on May 18, 1846.

Europe, and in particular England, reacted strongly against the U.S. move, even to the point of British newspapers urging their government to declare war on the side of Mexico. In view of this threat, Washington hastened its plans to take California. Not only was it felt that the country's security was endangered, but also Washington coveted the land and the increased opportunities for trade. (Earlier, President Polk had sent Mexico an offer of purchase, but the envoy was not received.)

During the rising emergency Mexico could send no funds to the distant province for military and other expenses; therefore missions were sold as an expedient. Governor Pío Pico asked British Vice-Consul James A. Forbes to arrange with his government to protect the coast against any American aggressors. The Governor offered 2,400,000 acres of land in the San Joaquin Valley for a British colony of 2000 families. But the offer was too late: a U.S. warship was already in Northern California waters.

On July 7, Commodore John D. Sloat called for surrender of the Monterey Presidio and without opposition raised the American flag. Seven days later Commodore Stockton arrived to take command.

Governor Juan Bautista Alvarado. (*—Huntington Library*)
At right, Kit Carson, in a photo taken in 1867 a few months
before his death. (*—Title Insurance & Trust Company*)

This was a confused moment in California history. On June 14,
exactly a month before Stockton's arrival, a group of 33 American
settlers led by William B. Ide moved against what was still, officially,
a friendly nation. Mariano G. Vallejo, leading citizen of Sonoma in
Northern California, was surprised by a loud knocking on his door
shortly after dawn. Vallejo had always been on good terms with the
Americans, but to his amazement he heard them announce they were
capturing the town and arresting him. With his brother and brother-
in-law, Vallejo was taken to headquarters which Frémont had established at Sutter's Fort. Frémont held the prisoners, although he took
no part in the uprising himself. The Bear Flag — a white background
carrying a red star and a grizzly bear, with the words "California
Republic" underneath — was raised over Sonoma, and the episode was
called the Bear Flag Revolt. (The Bear Flag was designed by Abraham
Lincoln's nephew, Will Todd. At the end of the rebellion the flag was
taken down by a grandson of Paul Revere, Lt. Joseph Warren Revere.)

For years a debate raged as to whether or not Frémont caused
the Bear Flag Revolt, taking advantage of the situation to gain personal power, or if he received orders from Washington to aid the
American settlers. It seems likely that he had been given orders, because correspondence and vouchers show that when he reached the
Sacramento Valley the U.S. warship *Portsmouth,* which was in Cali-

fornia waters nearby, sent him money, supplies, ammunition and an offer of assistance. Nevertheless, Frémont's role is a celebrated mystery, never solved. Gillespie had brought dispatches to several persons in California, all of whom were sworn to secrecy regarding the contents. No one ever revealed a word.

The Bear Flag Revolt was in fact short-lived. When Commodore Stockton took command at Monterey on July 14, he declared Northern California conquered, added the Bear Flag group to his army and sailed to San Pedro to overcome any resistance in the Southland. On another vessel Major Frémont and his battalion (temporarily in naval service because there was no American army in California), as well as Gillespie, who had been promoted from lieutenant to captain, sailed to San Diego.

4. *Temporary Conquest of Los Angeles*

When Pío Pico became governor a year earlier, the capital moved to Los Angeles, where his home was. For headquarters he chose the one-story adobe on Main Street which had been a store owned by the ranchero Isaac Williams. (Later the building was enlarged and became the famous Bella Union Hotel.) The army, under José Castro, continued to have its headquarters in the Presidio of Monterey.

Hearing that Monterey had fallen to the Yankee forces and that Los Angeles would soon be invaded, Governor Pico called for an army of volunteers. But the Angeleños were indifferent to the Mexican Government and equally indifferent toward a new one; barely a hundred men were willing to fight. Realizing the inadequacy of the numbers, Pico prepared to flee.

Before he could leave, the government papers had to be hidden. Under Spanish and Mexican rule, official files were kept in no permanent place: pueblo records were stored in the homes of the secretary of the Council and the judges. Some of those documents were now put under guard; some were concealed in the home of a priest who turned them over to Abel Stearns several years later; many of the local records disappeared. (In San Diego the local archives were almost totally lost or destroyed.)

The archives of Alta California were kept wherever the governor was; so Pico had brought many documents with him when he moved the capital from Monterey to Los Angeles. Boxes were brought out, and frantically the Governor's aides put the documents inside. Agustín Olvera, Secretary of the California Departmental Assembly of 1845 and 1846, brought the Assembly records to be added. As many of the boxes as possible were taken to the home of Luis Vignes on Aliso Street and hidden, but there was no time to conceal them all. Of the papers left in government offices under guard, as well as those Pico had left in Monterey, many were never found again.

When Frémont and Gillespie sailed into San Diego, it was their surprise to find themselves welcome. Nor was there any opposition on their trek through the countryside to San Pedro to join Commodore Stockton. The combined troops marched into Los Angeles on August 13, 1846, without resistance. Stockton paroled leaders of the community on their promise to do nothing against the American Government, and thereupon the commodore decided that the conquest of the Southland was successfully finished. The scout Kit Carson, who was among Frémont's men, was sent to intercept Col. Stephen W. Kearny on his way from Kansas with U.S. troops. When Kearny received the news that California had already surrendered, he sent half of his men back east. Stockton returned to San Francisco, and Frémont to the Sacramento Valley, leaving a small garrison of fifty soldiers under the command of Captain Gillespie, who established his headquarters in the building formerly used by Governor Pico.

To the invaders, the lack of resistance was amazing. The most logical explanation seems to be that the Californians expected any change in government to be as easy as the transition from Spain to Mexico 25 years before. However, in Los Angeles the garrison which Commodore Stockton had left under Captain Gillespie to maintain control soon became arrogant, boasting how easy it had been for them, although few, to conquer this large town. As a result, some young men under Sérbulo Varela began to harass the Yankees with a few ancient weapons — flintlock muskets and lances. In retaliation, Gillespie outlawed gatherings of two or more people in the streets and meetings in homes, nor was anyone to gallop through the streets. He sent soldiers to the homes of leading citizens to take them into custody for questioning.

Very shortly he received a present of beautiful California peaches from some Southland ladies, and the thought that they admired him was no surprise to the young captain. Delightedly he showed the garrison the tasty tribute, then chose a peach and took a bite with gusto. Alas, it had been rolled in the almost invisible prickles of the cactus apple, and his mouth was sore for a week.

One morning before dawn Varela and his friends, shooting their muskets into the air and shouting their loudest, galloped up to the Yankee headquarters and banged on the door, then disappeared while the Americans jumped from their beds and fired into the darkness

Commodore Robert F. Stockton.
(*—Huntington Library*)

from the windows. When none of the marauders could be found, Gillespie ordered that the most important citizens be brought from their homes to his headquarters; among them were men who had given their word not to take up arms against the United States. Gillespie assumed they had violated their parole, and the insult was taken by the Angeleños as a signal for renewed hostilities.

At this point José Antonio Carrillo, Andrés Pico and other leaders chose José María Flores as their general for a new rebellion. The entire community resented the affront to the honor of its citizens; so now there were many recruits for the army.

Most of the Americans who had made their home in the Southland had taken out Mexican citizenship and married Californians. To help the Yankee invaders would be to betray friends and relatives. In order to avoid this, a large proportion of the former Americans declared their neutrality and went to stay on ranchos far off, either their own or those of friends. Several of them with their families went to El Rancho del Chino, owned by Isaac Williams, where they were besieged by a company of about fifty horsemen under command of Sérbulo Varela and Diego Sepúlveda. Surrender was demanded, with a promise of protection as prisoners of war. On the road to Los Angeles, Varela fell behind in conversation with Don Benito Wilson, one of the prisoners. Suddenly the two men could see that the Americans ahead had been stopped and several lined up along one side of the road. Varela realized that they were going to be shot, so spurred his horse to a position in front of the prisoners, shouting that he had given his word they would be conducted safely to town. If anyone were to be shot, he therefore should be included. As a result, no one was hurt. (The prisoners never forgot that they owed their lives to Varela. Years later, when he became dissolute and a vagrant, he was often arrested, but always an American paid his fine so that he never went to prison.)

Gillespie knew that the only hope of survival for his garrison lay in sending a scout to Commodore Stockton in San Francisco for reinforcements. There was a call for volunteers, and a thin man stepped forward; it was John Brown, locally called "Juan Flaco" (Lean John). On several pieces of paper the words "Believe the Bearer" were written, and each was put into a packet of cigarettes. These were handed to Juan Flaco, and on September 24 he galloped north.

Soon enemy horsemen began a chase in the darkness. Then suddenly, to his dismay, he found a wide ravine blocking the route ahead. Possible safety lay beyond it, and he spurred his horse to leap across. As he landed on the other side, the horse was shot and killed, but Flaco crawled through the brush and escaped his pursuers, then ran on foot until he reached the ranchhouse of an American in the Santa Monica Mountains. There he was given another horse and galloped on until he reached Santa Barbara the next night. Without stopping for sleep, he took a fresh horse and kept on riding. Several times on the way north he was given another mount or else commandeered one from a rancho. At Monterey he was given a racehorse, and wearily he at last rode into San Francisco at eight o'clock the night of the 28th. In exactly four days, with only the briefest respites for sleep, he had covered about 500 miles through enemy country, over mountains and through rocky canyons, along cliffs and across mesas. The story became legend so quickly that among the details truth no longer could be separated from fiction. The fact remains, however, that Juan Flaco is among the heroes of the West.

In San Francisco, Commodore Stockton realized the urgency of Flaco's message and gave orders for reinforcements to be sent immediately to San Pedro on the frigate *Savannah,* under the command of Capt. William Mervine. Unfortunately the immediacy of the mission was lost on the captain, for in passing Sausalito he anchored the ship in order to buy something ashore. No one ever knew what that "something" was and whether or not it was necessary, but during the stop fog came rapidly into the Bay, and the vessel was unable to leave until three days later. Ironically, the delay meant that Juan Flaco's ride had been completely in vain. In Los Angeles, Captain Gillespie felt convinced that his messenger had been killed or captured and had never reached Commodore Stockton. The supplies of the garrison became exhausted.

A cannon had stood for years in the Plaza in front of the pueblo church and was used to fire salutes on feast days. To some of the citizens it looked like a valuable weapon, and to keep it from being commandeered by the invaders it was taken to the home of Doña Inocencia Reyes and buried nearby. After the Californios began to revolt against Gillespie, the cannon was unearthed, fastened onto the axletrees of an old gun carriage and pulled by reatas (lariats). Called "The Old Woman's Gun," it was the one piece of artillery owned by the Californios. The rebellious Southlanders pulled it onto a hill commanding the pueblo, and at that moment the warfare took on the flavor of opéra bouffe. General Flores ordered a shot fired from the ancient cannon and sent his order to Captain Gillespie to surrender, which he did. The Yankees were given promise of safe-conduct to an American ship in San Pedro and marched off in style, flag flying and drums beating.

The long-delayed Captain Mervine arrived on the *Savannah* with reinforcements while Gillespie and his men were still waiting to leave the harbor. From the hills of El Rancho de los Palos Verdes, horsemen watched the landing of the new regiment and rode to Los Angeles to warn of the coming attack. Carrillo brought fifty men on horseback to meet the Yankees. General Flores followed, the lariats of his men pulling the Old Woman's Gun.

The Old Woman's Gun, the chief piece of artillery owned by the Mexican army, had a 2.77-inch bore and was only 44 inches long. Here it is shown mounted on a naval gun carriage. An inscription on top of the barrel reads: "Used by Mexicans in Calif. against U.S. forces at Domingos Ranch Oct. 1846 Rio San Gabrael [*sic*] and the Plains of the Mesa Jany. 8th & 9th 1847. . . . Surrendered to Commodore R. F. Stockton USN at Los Angeles, Calif. Jan. 16, 1847." Later the gun was employed by U.S. forces at Mazatlán and in Lower California. (*—Courtesy, U.S. Naval Academy Museum, Annapolis*)

Halfway to Los Angeles, Mervine's men stopped for the night at the Dominguez hacienda. Carrillo surrounded the place and kept up a firing of muskets all night in order to disturb the invaders. Around midnight General Flores arrived with the cannon, which he placed on a hillock overlooking the ranchhouse, though he waited patiently until dawn before ordering the gun to be fired. His patience paid off, for the first shot successfully hit the house. The Yankees quickly ran out and gathered at a point beyond range of the cannon. They then started once more toward Los Angeles.

Immediately two horsemen pulled the gun to another hill overlooking the enemy's route. Because the Californios were on horseback they easily moved ahead of the Americans, who were marching in cadence in columns of eight. However, speed could not make up for poor local production: the cannon fired shot, made at the San Gabriel Mission, of such poor quality that the projectiles fell far short of the American force. Again and again the horsemen moved the cannon to new vantage points, yet always the shot fell harmlessly amid jeers and hoots from the oncoming columns. Eventually there was powder left for only one final effort. The Americans by now paid no attention to the cannon and continued to march on, but this time the shot went as it was supposed to, and several Americans were killed. (Probably six, but the number has never been exactly determined.) The Yankees were sobered and discouraged by the tragedy. They picked up their casualties, turned around and marched back to San Pedro as fast as possible, returning to the *Savannah* on which they sailed to San Diego.

Two weeks later Commodore Stockton came to San Pedro with two ships for another effort. While his men landed and made preparations for the invasion, Californios watched as before from the hills of El Rancho de los Palos Verdes. Carrillo arrived with a comparatively small number of horsemen but realized that the commodore would try to gauge the size of the enemy facing him. Therefore Carrillo put horsemen along every ridge, and then, some distance inland but clearly visible to Stockton, horses were driven down a slope in a gap between some hills. The dust that was raised, and the fact that Stockton could not see that the horses were riding in a circle, gave the Yankees the impression that strength was arrayed against them if they tried to reach Los Angeles. (This strategy set the pattern for the handling of extras in motion picture spectaculars at a much later date.)

Carrillo had intended to demonstrate strength in order to reach more favorable terms with Commodore Stockton than otherwise he could. Don Benito Wilson was to start the negotiations, and he waited near the landing for the commodore's arrival. Later he reported that

during Carrillo's maneuvers four boats loaded with marines and ammunition came ashore but soon were signaled to return with the men
and equipment, after which the frigates sailed away to less-hostile San
Diego, where the American forces could regroup. Carrillo ruefully
confessed to Don Benito his disappointment at oversucceeding. He had
so frightened the enemy as to drive them away, and thus there would
be no negotiations at all.

Shortly after this, General Flores was proclaimed provisional governor of the region. But in those volatile times the public turned
easily against any person in authority, and there was the same lack
of an overall unity which still characterizes many Latin American
governments.

5. *Californios vs. Yankees*

From the East, General Stephen W. Kearny and his men marched
confidently toward the Southland after word arrived from Commodore
Stockton that all California had been taken. On the way west Kearny's
commission as brigadier general had reached him, and to his elated
mind there seemed no problems ahead. Then a message arrived that
rebellion in Los Angeles had changed the situation: Southern California would have to be captured all over again. Scouts brought word
that forces were gathering ahead for battle.

On December 6, 1846, the Battle of San Pasqual took place part
way between Los Angeles and San Diego, near present-day Escondido.
This was the greatest battle in the history of Southern California but
one of the strangest in modern warfare.

As yet there were no gunsmiths in the Southland (there was none
until 1855); so the best firearms that could be found were a few horse
pistols, ancient flintlock muskets and blunderbusses. Even for these
there was little ammunition; so instead lances were prepared by blacksmiths, mainly at the San Fernando Mission, which years before had
been secularized. Files and rasps about eight inches long were used
for blades, inserted into the ends of poles made of willow, mountain
laurel or ash. Often at the base of the blade was fastened a pennon
which combined the Mexican colors of red, white and green. Like
knights errant of another age the Californios led by General Andrés
Pico rode to battle, lances in hand. Although the opposing army of
Americans had modern rifles and artillery, their weapons had become
soaked and useless after days of rain; sabres were the only substitute.
Therefore the decisive battle in California during the U.S.-Mexican
campaign was fought not with firearms but with sabres and long-
outdated lances.

General Stephen W. Kearny.
(—Title Insurance & Trust Company)

The army of the Californios was formed almost entirely of men from the families of rancheros. Their names are like a roll call of the leading families of the Southland.

When word reached the pueblo that General Kearny was marching southward to join Commodore Stockton in San Diego, Antonio Franco Coronel undertook to scout the general's route and find what information he could. The conversation about Kearny's arrival was overheard by Tom Fisher, the American Negro who had arrived as a pirate 28 years earlier and currently was with the Coronel household as a carpenter. Fisher had remained an American at heart, and he realized that the American army would need help in the unfamiliar countryside. Unnoticed, he rode away toward Kearny's army, and the Americans delightedly accepted his services as interpreter and guide.

Coronel's memoirs describe his own journey as scout. After riding through a cold downpour he stopped at a farmhouse for rest and warmth. Before long some horses rode up, and when Coronel peered through a window he could see American soldiers in the moonlight. Leaving his boots and serape behind, he raced out a back door and up a hill, where he climbed a tree to watch. To his astonishment he saw Fisher among the Americans.

Reinforcements of 26 volunteers under Capt. Archibald Gillespie rode north from San Diego. Mariquita, sister of Andrés Pico, saw them go by and sent word to her brother. Don Andrés did not know that General Kearny was approaching, and thought it must be that Gillespie was on his way to steal cattle. He decided to wait in the Indian village of San Pasqual, about thirty miles northeast of San Diego along Gillespie's logical route of return.

With increasing weariness Kearny and his men rode south through heavy rain. By a perverse change of weather, the rain on the mountains nearby had become snow, and a cold wind added to the general misery. At night when they finally bivouacked there was little food.

That afternoon Gillespie had arrived with news that a troop of Californios was somewhere nearby, and a conference was held as to the wisdom of sending a scouting party ahead during the night. The officers considered the Californios the best horsemen in the world, and the point was, if possible, to come upon them when they were unmounted. Capt. Benjamin Daviess Moore urged that no scouts be sent forth, as they might warn the Californios of the American advance, but he was overruled. A party was dispatched and came to

Pío Pico, the last Mexican governor of California. *(—Huntington Library)*

Andrés Pico, dressed in his Mexican finery.

the Indian village of San Pasqual, where Andrés Pico and his men slept comfortably in the natives' adobe huts. The barking of a small dog awoke the Californios, who hastened to their horses.

At 2 a.m. General Kearny had his men awakened to start their ride of about six miles. The icy wind from the north was so numbing that the bugler's lips could blow no calls. Kearny ordered Gillespie and his volunteers to stay behind; incredibly, he even insisted that a 2.77-inch gun Gillespie had brought be sent to the rear. That miscalculation was due to cost the Americans many lives.

When they reached San Pasqual it was still dark. The Californios, hardly visible in the obscurity, were ready on the hillside, but the Americans found to their dismay that their paper cartridges, needed for firing, were completely rainsoaked and useless. The one cannon brought by Gillespie wouldn't reach the front lines for some time. Desperately the men pulled out their sabres and charged.

The Californios aimed their few ancient firearms and fired, killing one of the American officers, Captain Johnston. From then on the fighting was hand to hand. Captain Moore spurred his horse, leading his men. He was so intent that he quickly outdistanced them and suddenly found himself facing Andrés Pico, with no Americans nearby to support him in battle. The thrust of a lance knocked him from his horse; another lance struck him, and a pistol shot ended his life. Lt. Thomas C. Hammond rushed to his aid and was pierced by several lances. The two men, married to sisters, fell near each other under a willow tree.

In the darkness the fighting swirled up and down the hillside, around the Indian huts, among the bushes. Then on command the Californios sped to form a line, pennons fluttering as on a medieval jousting field. At a signal they galloped toward the Americans with lances in attack position, a move which demoralized the opposing ranks.

Captain Gillespie and his men arrived on this incredible scene, which to Gillespie suddenly became a nightmare. Increasing daylight made it possible for the Californios to distinguish the new arrivals, and they recognized the arrogant man who had originally awakened their hatred. From all directions his name rang out, and lances were directed against him. One struck him from his horse, a second pierced his back, a third his mouth, the point of a fourth just missed his heart. Left for dead, Gillespie somehow was able to make his way toward his own ranks and by chance came to the cannon, which the men had been frantically trying to fire. Gillespie carried a wick as part of his equipment, and striking a spark with some flint, he lit the wick and fired the gun. One shot was all that was needed. The Californios knew that horses and lances were useless before a cannon; in a moment they wheeled and left the field.

With General Kearny's forces there had been two howitzers, but neither was used in the battle because lancers had charged the gunners as soon as the artillery reached the field. Around one howitzer lay the bodies of its three gunners, two of them dead, one severely wounded. As the horses of the Californios turned and galloped away, the mules of the untended howitzer raced after them, and the Americans watched helplessly as it was delivered to the enemy.

Among the Californios there had been no deaths on the battleground. One of their men had been frightened as time came to fight, and they had allowed him to stay in an Indian hut. There he was found by the Americans and killed. In all there were about 12 Californios wounded. Among the Americans, 19 were killed and 18 wounded, including Kearny who had been struck twice by a lance.

Dr. John Strother Griffin was the only surgeon with the U.S. forces. General Kearny refused help and insisted that the soldiers should be taken care of first, but while Griffin proceeded to obey, Kearny fell unconscious. Finally the doctor finished caring for the wounded and then sent a messenger to the Californios that he would gladly tend to any of their men. General Pico sent back word that no one needed medical attention. The smell of blood had drawn wolves to the scene, and to the frightening accompaniment of their howls, the American soldiers dug a large grave under the willow tree where all their dead could be temporarily buried.* Then the wounded were put on litters and carried between mules, and without food or water the exhausted troops began their retreat to San Diego, thirty miles away.

Always they were aware of surveillance by the mounted Californios watching from hillsides out of range. On what became known as Mule Hill (because mule stew was their only sustenance) Kearny's men made an encampment between boulders for protection. That rocky barricade still remains as a monument to the beleaguered men.

From there Lt. Edward F. Beale (later an important U.S. official in California), the scout Kit Carson and an Indian started toward San Diego to ask Stockton for reinforcements. Because the hill was surrounded they had to go at night, and in order to crawl as quietly as

---

*The dead were later reburied together in Old Town; later yet the remains were moved to Bennington Cemetery on Pt. Loma. Today the hillside where the battle took place looks much as it did then, although a monument stands where once there were Indian huts.

Midshipman Edward F. Beale.
(—Bancroft Library)

possible through the underbrush the three men removed their shoes. As they crept along in the darkness, their feet were cut and bruised by many sharp rocks, but far worse were the prickly pears which covered two miles of open prairie beyond. Years of hard traveling had toughened the feet of Carson and the Indian, but the young lieutenant's feet became swollen and painful. Through that night and the next they pressed on. Toward the end of the journey they separated, to be sure that at least one of them might get through, but all finally reached Stockton's headquarters. As Beale came to the guard post of the encampment he collapsed. Guards carried him the rest of the way, and it was weeks before he could walk again.

At last relief came for the exhausted, starving Yankees when Commodore Stockton sent 170 men and a cannon as well as food and water.

On July 4, 1847, half a year after the Battle of San Pasqual, a military ceremony took place on the heights above Los Angeles, where an earthen fort was built by the Mormon Battalion. (This group of volunteers, recruited in Iowa from Utah-bound wagon trains, arrived in Los Angeles shortly after the fighting ended.) The structure was named Ft. Moore for the brave captain whose heroism was admired as much by the Californios as by the Americans. Today the fort is commemorated by a waterfall and memorial on Hill Street at Temple.

For three weeks Kearny and his men rested in San Diego and then began the march to Los Angeles. Commodore Stockton led as commander-in-chief; General Kearny was chief of battle operations. Captain Gillespie and Kit Carson once more were with the advancing American forces. As they drew near the San Gabriel River and their logical point of crossing could be determined, Californios hid in wild mustard and willow trees beside the shore, preparing an ambush. But Stockton was warned and changed his route to cross instead at a place about a mile farther north.

The Battle of San Gabriel River (also called the Battle of El Paso de Bartolo Viejo, the name of the rancho where the fighting took place) was fought on January 8, 1847. The Californios rushed their artillery to the top of a bluff overlooking the river. This time they had four guns: the howitzer captured from Kearny at San Pasqual, two small guns of uncertain origin and the Old Woman's Gun. But the ammunition was still of the same poor quality, made by volunteers at the San Gabriel Mission, totally inferior and undependable.

Commodore Stockton ordered his men to cross the river. They plunged in and found that the water was only knee deep, but their guns began to sink into the muddy riverbed. As they crossed, the Californios' cannons on the bluff fired desperately, but the poor grade of gunpowder caused most of the shot to fall harmlessly short. On each side, two were killed and eight wounded. As the Americans advanced with their muskets and five pieces of artillery, the Californios — armed with lances and useless cannons — realized that their efforts were hopeless. The guns, pulled by lariats, were dragged from the field; the horsemen wheeled and followed. Clearly they belonged to an era which had passed.

The site of the battle is on Bluff Road about three blocks south of today's Whittier Boulevard. The ford across the river, called El Paso de Bartolo Viejo, was at the same site. Because in winter the waters of the San Gabriel River were high, the only place where troops and guns could possibly get across was at the Paso. The Californios knew this and awaited the enemy from a bluff overlooking the spot. The flood twenty years later changed the river channel; so the bluff where the actual fighting took place now rises above Rio Hondo. A monument at Bluff Road and Washington Boulevard stands at the point where, about a mile south of the battle, the Californios first prepared an ambush for the Americans.

Generals José María Flores and José Antonio Carrillo commanded the troops in their last efforts to repel the oncoming Yankees. Plagued by disunity and lack of military training, they nevertheless determined on a stand about four miles south of the Plaza. There the artillery was placed, hidden from view by the bank of a ravine. It was the last appearance of the Old Woman's Gun.

The Americans advanced across the mesa (open plain) between the San Gabriel and Los Angeles Rivers toward their final engagement of the war, the Battle of La Mesa. The Californios waited behind a low hill. As the Yankees approached there was one last cavalry charge against the invaders, but it was only a token resistance and the American troops continued ahead, entering the pueblo the next day.

Today the site of the Battle of La Mesa, at 4500 S. Downey Road in Vernon, is marked by a memorial of three large boulders, in one of which is embedded a bronze tablet giving a diagram of the action as drawn by Lt. William H. Emory, U.S. Topographical Engineer Officer on General Kearny's staff. It shows the low hillocks nearby, the narrow road leading to the pueblo, and the Los Angeles River about 200 yards away. Now there is no sign that once the spot lay in open countryside, for growing Los Angeles has engulfed the mesa. Landscaped grounds which for a few years surrounded the monument have been removed, and the boulders stand strangely out of place amid railroad tracks, factory plants and warehouses. Comparing the scene with that marked on Lt. Emory's diagram, one sees that the low hillocks and narrow road have disappeared. In the distance the Los Angeles River still winds from the city but with banks sternly girdled in cement.

During the American advance, Commodore Stockton and General Kearny had threatened that if General Flores — in official command of the California army — were captured, he would be shot. All other citizens were guaranteed protection if entry of the Yankees was not resisted.

General Flores joined about a hundred men at Rancho Los Verdugos for a final council, held under a huge oak tree which is still standing. There Flores transferred command to General Andrés Pico and left for Mexico. So by a remarkable coincidence two brothers held the most important official positions in California at the close of Mexican rule: Pío Pico the last governor, and Andrés Pico the last military commander.

Meanwhile, Colonel Frémont was approaching from the north. He arrived at the San Fernando Mission with his California Battalion the day after the Yankees marched into Los Angeles. The council decided that both Stockton and Kearny would probably give harsher terms than Frémont, who had taken part in none of the fighting. Emissaries were sent to him at the mission with an offer to negotiate peace. The next day a peace treaty was written and translated, and Frémont with his troops marched to a place closer to Los Angeles.

The diary of Lt. Edwin Bryant of Frémont's California Battalion describes the army as "encamped near a deserted rancho at the foot of Couenga plain." The California Peace Commissioners, José Antonio

Colonel John Charles Frémont.
(—Bancroft Library)

Carrillo and Agustín Olvera, met Frémont and his aides in the un-inhabited ranchhouse. There the treaty was signed on January 13, 1847, by both John C. Frémont, Colonel U.S. Army and Military Commander of California, and by Andrés Pico, Commandant of Squadron and Chief of the National Forces of California.

Two copies of the treaty were made, one in Spanish which is now in the Bancroft Library, the other in English which was sent to the National Archives in Washington, D.C. The adobe where the copies were signed was owned by Tomás Féliz; it distintegrated with time and not until the 1920s did the Los Angeles City Council vote funds to buy the property. With the aid of students from John C. Frémont High School the foundation was excavated in 1932 and final restoration was completed in 1950. The ranchhouse is located on Lankershim Boulevard opposite Universal Studios and is open to the public.

The Treaty of Cahuenga ended the last resistance in California to the American occupation, but it wasn't until Mexico City capitulated to General Winfield Scott in September of that year, 1847, that all fighting ended. When the Treaty of Guadalupe Hidalgo was signed in Mexico on February 2, 1848, Mexican claims to Texas were relinquished, and the United States acquired nearly half a million square miles of territory — California, Utah, Nevada, Arizona, part of Colorado, Wyoming and New Mexico — an area far larger than that of the original Thirteen Colonies. On May 30, 1848, U.S. and Mexican ratifications of the Treaty of Guadalupe Hidalgo were concluded, but the news would not reach Los Angeles until August 15.

As the Americans advanced toward the pueblo on January 10, 1847, the morning after the Battle of La Mesa, many residents fled to the safety of distant ranchhouses. Yet even after their last hopeless sally against the enemy at La Mesa the Southland's warriors lingered. On every hilltop overlooking Los Angeles the horsemen gathered and silently watched the Yankee troops march in.

Near the Plaza was the home of Doña Encarnación Sepúlveda de Avila, the widow of Don Francisco Avila. She had left a boy in charge of her house with instructions to keep all shutters and doors closed, but when the troops marched in, their band played a stirring tune and, forgetting to close the door, the boy left the Avila house in order to watch the excitement. American officers saw the lovely interior and chose the home to be headquarters for Commodore Stockton while he was in Los Angeles.

The Angeleños, wary of the conquerors, kept at a suspicious distance. What cut the last cord of resistance to make the American victory complete? It was the intangible power of music. The evening the victorious army moved in, its band formed ranks in the Plaza and began a concert. Gradually from all the streets the townspeople were irresistibly drawn until the band was surrounded. From then on there was a concert every evening. Conquest was a pleasure: these were victors who *understood*. Olé!

6. *Dissension Among the Victors*

An incredible turn of events followed the capture of Los Angeles and the arrival in the town of the American commanding officers. Under conflicting orders from Washington, Commodore Stockton, a naval officer, had been given instructions by the Navy Department that he was to occupy and administer the conquered cities of California; General Kearny, an army officer, had been asked by the War Department to establish civil government in California. Now it was indeterminate which officer was the true commander-in-chief. The headquarters of both men were near the Plaza, and soon the mutual animosity was so intense that Stockton and Kearny completely ignored each other when by chance they met.

It was a situation full of ambiguities. Stockton and Kearny were both senior to Frémont, yet the younger officer had signed the Treaty of Cahuenga for the United States without consulting either of his superiors, although he knew they were nearby. In addition, Frémont had taken two months to bring his forces from Northern California, advancing so slowly that he never reinforced the Americans in any battle. In Los Angeles, Frémont used his rank of lieutenant colonel in the Army but, to Kearny's annoyance, insisted he was still commissioned in the Navy as he had been at the beginning of the war, and he would take orders only from Commodore Stockton.

There was an additional irritation for Kearny in the fact that at the Battle of San Pasqual he had used poor tactical judgment. Even though the Americans won the field, all the known casualties were on their side, and afterward it was not a march to San Diego but an agonizing retreat. He was stung by the general opinion that he had been defeated. Kearny was a veteran of the frontier, brave and energetic, considered one of the ablest officers in the U.S. Army. Just before marching to California he had been an excellent military governor of Santa Fe, New Mexico. But in Los Angeles he felt humiliated on every score. At the same time his forces were hopelessly outnumbered by those of Stockton and Frémont: only a small body of men served with him, because en route to California he had turned back half of his strength when dispatches arrived from Stockton saying, prematurely, that California had already been conquered.

Both senior officers wrote to Washington, asking President Polk to clarify the matter as to which was in overall command. Until a reply could be received, Commodore Stockton acted as though he were commander-in-chief, and he appointed Colonel Frémont governor of California, in accordance with a plan which he thought had been approved by authorities in Washington.

Frémont was a favorite among the Southlanders, to whom the good looks and courtly manners of the young colonel were extremely appealing. The soldiers of his battalion presented a more picturesque appearance than the other American troops. Until the war, Frémont's service had been mainly one of exploration, and his California Battalion included not only recent volunteers but also the explorers and trappers who had traveled with him on the long trail to Northern California from the East. In addition there were several Walla Walla Indians from Oregon, and five Delawares had been with Frémont through all his wanderings.

The official interpreter for the Americans was Stephen C. Foster, and Benjamin D. Wilson (known as Don Benito) was personal advisor to both Stockton and Kearny. In his reminiscences, Don Benito said that Kearny, with only a small proportion of troops under his direct command, grew increasingly obsessed with the fear that his life was in danger. Before long he left Los Angeles for San Diego, where he took a ship to Monterey. Establishing that city as the capital, he appointed himself governor.

President Polk's decision, relayed through orders from the General in Chief of the U.S. Army and also from the Secretary of the Navy, declared that all forces in California should be mustered into the Army, whose senior officer (Kearny) was to be civil governor of the province. The orders took over four months to reach California, during which time Frémont had continued in command as governor in Los Angeles, although Kearny held the same office in Monterey. Commodore Stockton had left California. After the official notice reached Monterey the dissension continued unabated, because Kearny sent no notice to Frémont of the orders from Washington. Serious results followed.

One day, with no explanation, Frémont received a dispatch from Monterey: "By order of General Kearny, you are now ex-Governor Frémont and must turn over the governmental archives and public documents of the Territory of California and all other papers and authorities bearing on the official business as Governor of California." In that era there was no fast way to contact Washington, and Frémont had received no word from there countermanding his appointment by Commodore Stockton, nor had he received any notice to that effect from Stockton. So he refused General Kearny's order. Later the Federal Government sent Frémont instructions to leave California for Ft. Leavenworth, Kansas, with a detachment of soldiers under the command of General Kearny, who would go east at the same time. Colonel Richard B. Mason was left in Monterey as military governor of California, taking office on May 3, 1847.

Upon arrival at Ft. Leavenworth, Frémont was notified that he should proceed to Washington, D.C., under arrest, and that he would be court-martialed on charges of mutiny and disobedience toward a superior officer.*

The trial was headlined throughout the country. Frémont's father-in-law, the prominent Senator Thomas Hart Benton, appeared as his chief counsel. Benton was a man of strong feelings and accustomed to speechmaking in the Senate; with a flow of oratory he turned his son-in-law's defense into an offensive against General Kearny. Irrelevant issues were brought in, especially the loss of the howitzer at San Pasqual. Although the gunners assigned to the cannon had been killed or wounded, and were unable to prevent its loss to the enemy, Senator Benton constantly returned to the issue as proof of the General's incompetence.

---

*Los Angeles' pioneer American Negro, Tom Fisher, went east with Frémont and attended the court-martial hearings.

On the witness stand General Kearny was asked if he had communicated to Colonel Frémont the President's instructions sent from Washington. He replied, "I did not. I am not in the habit of communicating to my juniors the instructions I receive from my seniors, unless required to do so in those instructions." Commodore Stockton gave witness that he, too, had failed to notify Frémont of the President's decision. But Senator Thomas Hart Benton's venom was aimed entirely at General Kearny, not at Stockton, and the vendetta continued on and on.

When the court-martial ended at last Frémont was allowed to summarize his defense. His lengthy statement fills 81 pages of the official proceedings. Benton's unrestrained animosity throughout the hearings undoubtedly injured Frémont's cause, for after three days' deliberation the officers of the court found him guilty of mutiny, which meant dismissal from the Army. The President suspended sentence, but in spite of this Frémont resigned, protesting what he felt was an unjust decision.

To his surprise, he found himself not disgraced before the public but instead made a popular hero. After he moved to California, the state sent him to the U.S. Senate in 1851. Five years later he became the first presidential nominee of the new Republican Party, opposing James Buchanan. About the same time Commodore Stockton, who had resigned from the Navy, was elected Senator from New Jersey and then he later became one of the leading Democratic nominees for president.

After the court-martial, General Kearny was sent to Vera Cruz, Mexico, to join the Yankee forces, and for awhile he was in command as military governor of Mexico City. He returned to the United States just as President Polk asked the Senate to confirm Kearny's nomination for brevet major general. The promotion was confirmed in spite of a 13-day diatribe by Senator Benton. The senator could have saved himself the effort. Kearny was at that time seriously ill with yellow fever he had contracted while in Mexico; less than a year after the court-martial, and only one month after his promotion, General Kearny died.*

---

*Colonel Frémont went to California ahead of his wife, who remained in St. Louis until he could make arrangements for a home. General Kearny was in the same city, on his deathbed. One day Mrs. Frémont received a message from the general begging her to see him. However, a son had been born to Mrs. Frémont a few months after the trial ended, and he had died within a short time. She felt that anxiety during the trial had caused the baby's weakness and death, so in bitterness she denied the general's request for a meeting.

7. End of the Spanish-Mexican Era

With the Treaty of Guadalupe Hidalgo, the Spanish-Mexican era of the Far West came to an end. For the next two years California waited, its identity uncertain, while the United States Congress debated whether to keep the new possession as a territory or accept it as a full-fledged state. There was no realization that '49 would transform the character of California when, in one year, 100,000 would-be miners were to stream from the East, from Mexico, Europe, Latin America, the Orient — all of them drawn irresistibly by the desire for gold. The Californios were to find themselves outnumbered more than ten to one by the jostling newcomers.

The gold fields in the north were everyone's goal. Many went through the City of the Angels, paused to admire the hills which rose above the valley and to enjoy the clear air which tinged everything in a sparkling beauty, but then they hurried on. Ships bringing men to Northern California on their way to the gold fields filled San Francisco Bay as crews deserted to join the miners. There was no similarity in 1850 between the bustling city to the north, with its population of 22,500, and the quiet backwater of the Pueblo de Los Angeles with its population of 1610. (A decade later San Francisco would have a population of 156,800 and Los Angeles 4385.)

The small frontier town surrounded by mountain ranges, far stretches of desert and a limitless ocean to the west, had no communication with the outside world except by horseback or sailing vessel. When California became a state in 1850, two-thirds of the population of Los Angeles could neither read nor write. There was not a bank, no newspaper, not one public school.

From the year 1784, when the first rancheros moved onto their huge cattle domains, the little community was dwarfed by the rangeland surrounding it. The early years of Los Angeles revolved around the pueblo, but even when there were involvements with war, many families on the ranchos heard little news of rushing events and were aware only of the details of daily life. When we turn our eyes to outlying homes a curtain seems to rise; voices sound clearly. The families of the Southland come more fully alive, for now we are looking at the ranchos.

IV

RANCHOS 1781-1848

1. *Cattle Range into Ranchos*

Ranchos stretching in isolation across plains and hills were part of an endless cattle range which covered most of the Southland. Deep into the mountains and far out along valleys, rancheros herded their cattle and horses on the land surrounding the Pueblo de Los Angeles. Four times as many people lived on this range as in the town itself.

Each ranchhouse created its own self-sufficient community, functioning not only as home but also as dairy, tannery, winery, blacksmith shop, harness and carpenter shop, and all the other necessary etceteras. There were no local stores, churches or near neighbors.

In those distant homes lived most of the families who combined to create the early history of Los Angeles. Today, above the freeways, Spanish names on route signs ask us to remember that alien heritage. They speak of the former cattle ranches on nearby plains, or point to boulevards which once were dusty trails leading from the pueblo to remote ranchhouses. The mind of the traveler is charmed by a unique symphony within which the hum of traffic finds a melodious counterpoint in the Spanish words: La Brea, La Cienega, La Tijera, La Centinela.

No history of the Southland is complete unless it includes a view of the pioneers who built their solitary homes on the great cattle range where now there are 78 cities with more than 7,000,000 inhabitants. Except in the modern downtown area and a few small sections elsewhere, every resident of Los Angeles County lives on what was once an enormous rancho.

In the earliest days of colonization, small garrisons of troops manned the lonely presidios of Alta California and guarded the missions. Among them, three simple, uneducated soldiers were destined for renown as the first rancheros of the Southland — Juan José Dominguez, José María Verdugo and José Manuel Nieto.

105

Scene at a ranchhouse, painted by A. F. Harmer.
(—Title Insurance & Trust Company)

Dominguez had retired in 1782 and turned his attention to cattle raising in San Diego, where he had served in the presidio, its oldest trooper. While traveling from San Diego to El Pueblo and San Gabriel Mission his eyes were always searching for well-watered land, and the plain alongside the Los Angeles River seemed a perfect cattle range. During years of presidio duty he had gradually accumulated a herd of about 200 cattle as well as many horses. In 1783, Military Commandant Pedro Fages arrived at the presidio for a visit of several months. Dominguez had served under him 15 years earlier, when both arrived in California with the first expedition. Fages listened sympathetically as his old comrade-at-arms asked for use of pasture land in the area he admired. In fact, another soldier upon retirement had already been allowed use of land in Sonoma. Dominguez' petition was granted in early 1784, and he led his cattle north to the huge acreage allotted to him. It included the sites of today's Compton, Redondo, San Pedro, Wilmington and the Palos Verdes Peninsula.

Hearing of the Commandant's generosity toward Dominguez, Corporal Verdugo decided during the same year to ask for the use of grazing land just north of El Pueblo, because he too had accumulated cattle and horses. With the Governor's consent, Verdugo's herds moved onto the plains and rolling hills where Glendale now stands.

A month later, in November of 1784, Manuel Nieto was given the use of 300,000 acres as a reward for long service in the army outposts of California. From Nieto's adobe near present-day Whittier, the land apportioned to him stretched to the ocean where later arose the city of Long Beach.

In general, permission to use the land was given gratis in recognition of service to the government — especially military service. By the time Spain relinquished to Mexico the government of Alta California, a total of seven permits had been issued for grazing land in the district of El Pueblo de Los Angeles and a total of thirty in Alta California. Under Mexico, the permits were changed to official land grants, and the humble cattlemen found themselves important landowners.

Often the person who petitioned for ranch land was unable to write his signature and had to sign with a cross. In those days the mark was intended not to represent an X, but the shape of the cross on which Christ was crucified.

Along with his petition, the would-be ranchero sent a diseño (drawing of a chosen piece of land). Robert H. Becker, in his *Diseños of California Ranchos*, challenges the reader to put himself in the position of a man trying to make such a drawing. As Becker suggests, "With a pad of paper, pencil and magnetic compass, stand somewhere . . . and draw by eye, to scale, the topography of the surrounding 10-15 square miles." Many of the diseños were drawn in exactly this way, after a "vista de ojos" (survey by eye). A number of the drawings were colored, to give a more lifelike idea of the land. Frequently houses were included, and corrals and other landmarks. Certain people with artistic skill sketched diseños of a number of ranchos.

Measurements of boundaries were figured in varas, a unit of measure a little less than three feet (33.37 inches). If the area was large, the prospective owner would ride around it on horseback. For this unofficial measuring he often used a lariat as a yardstick, with no great effort to be exact.

The governor sent each diseño and petition to appropriate officials, to note approval or reasons for disapproval in the margin. If the final decision was to grant the land, the ranchero at first received only provisional ownership, called a "concedo." Within a year he had to build and occupy a house, erect a corral, stock the land with cattle and horses, and begin some cultivation. The governor usually added the requirement that the rights of any Indians living on the land were to have priority over everything else, and that no fence should inter-

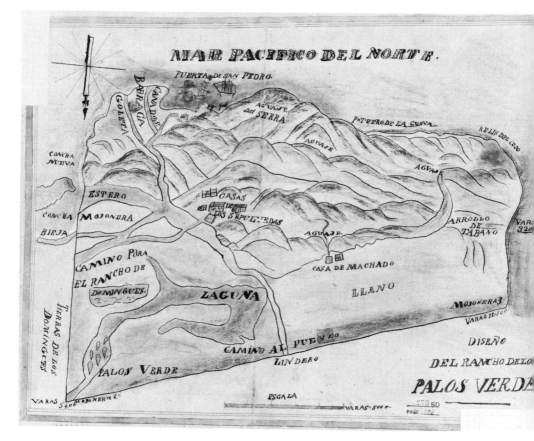

Diseño of Rancho de Los Palos Verdes. (*—Bancroft Library*)

fere with traffic on a public road. If the ranchero met the provisions, the Departmental Assembly approved the grant.

After that only one step remained before he could take possession of the land: the rancho boundaries had to be exactly measured by the pueblo's alcalde or a judge, along with two official witnesses. This simple step often took years to arrange. For one thing, the ranchero himself generally felt no need for haste and sometimes procrastinated twenty years before asking to be granted final title. Then, because the place of office for the pueblo government was usually in an official's home, the address of which changed with new officials, the ranchero's appeal frequently failed to reach the proper authorities. Rancheros at a great distance from El Pueblo — especially those with mountain ranchos — had added problems. Always when boundaries were to be measured a date had to be arranged when the officials

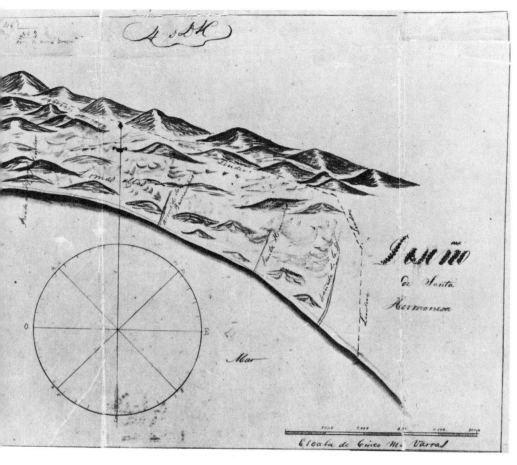

Diseño of Rancho San Vicente y Santa Monica. *(—Bancroft Library)*

could meet the ranchero. Notice also had to be sent in advance to owners of neighboring ranchos so that they could be present and state any objections to the boundary line. In many cases, during actual measuring the officials had to spend hours or days on horseback or afoot climbing tediously over difficult terrain. It is not surprising that there was a tendency to postpone these arduous proceedings.

Two cordbearers measured the boundaries, using a cord of hemp or horsehair, usually fifty varas long with a stake tied to each end. One of the men touched the ground with his stake while the other walked or rode until the cord was stretched full length; he in turn touched the ground with his stake while his partner went ahead. Most of the landmarks chosen for the boundaries were natural objects. For example, those for Rancho Los Cerritos included a sycamore tree, a stone and a dry elderwood stick. The landmarks of Rancho San Antonio included a bullock's skull, a spring surrounded by small willows, a brush hut by the San Gabriel River. The boundaries of Rancho Los Féliz were described as merely: "Commencing at a point in the Los Angeles River, then southerly 3150 varas more or less, thence westerly 6200 varas more or less to a nopalera [cactus patch], thence northerly 5000 varas more or less to a calera [lime kiln], thence easterly 7100 varas more or less to the place of beginning."

After the measurements were written down, juridical possession was given and the title was recorded in Monterey. No report was sent to the supreme government in Mexico; searches there in later years uncovered no records of any California private land grants except for northern offshore islands.

To everyone the process of surveying had appeared businesslike and exact. No one felt a premonition of the painful years ahead when United States courts would wrest ownership from many rancheros because boundaries were not clear.

2. Ranchos South of Los Angeles

South of El Pueblo most of the land was allotted by Governor Pedro Fages in 1784 to two of the first rancheros: Rancho San Pedro to Juan José Dominguez, and Rancho Los Nietos to José Manuel Nieto. Each of these ranchos had the ocean for its southern boundary and stretched far inland over thousands of uninhabited acres. In the face of that immensity, the two men chose to build their ranchhouses not overlooking the sea but by a river and as comfortingly near the pueblo as possible. In time, through conflicting claims and by inheritance, these two ranchos were divided into seven.

Dominguez, first of the rancheros of Southern California, was a bachelor. Unable to bear the loneliness of his isolated home, he spent most of his time in the pueblo and at the San Gabriel Mission until, aging and blind, he was taken into the home of Cristóbal Dominguez, a nephew stationed with troops in San Juan Capistrano. Cristóbal inherited the rancho, and descendants of his still own land from the original grant. When in April 1967 a large block of Rancho San Pedro land owned by Dominguez heirs was put up for sale, it was one of the largest single offerings in recent Southland history.

Before any of Cristóbal's family moved onto the rancho, young José Dolores Sepúlveda — grandson of one of the military guards who escorted the pueblo colonists from Los Alamos — was allowed to pasture his cattle on the unused peninsula in the rancho's southwest corner, now the Palos Verdes Peninsula. A friend, Antonio Machado, accompanied him. Sepúlveda built a small house, planted a garden and erected a corral; in time his sons built homes nearby for their families. Quarrels arose between the Dominguez and Sepúlveda families over use of the coastal land, and finally Governor Figueroa was asked to decide ownership. He decreed that the Rancho de Los Palos Verdes (Green Trees Rancho, originating from the name of a small canyon, La Cañada de Palos* Verdes, found only on the early maps) properly belonged to the Sepúlvedas. His opinion reflected the philosophy underlying all Mexican land grants, that for uninhabited, undeveloped land, use was basic to ownership. Rancho de Los Palos Verdes' 31,629 acres were judged to include the peninsula, San Pedro Bay and what is now the city of San Pedro. Rancho San Pedro, 43,119 acres (five times the area of Manhattan Island), included shoreland which today is the city of Wilmington.

East, adjoining Rancho San Pedro, was the enormous tract where José Manuel Nieto pastured his cattle. The San Gabriel Mission soon claimed part of the land for its own livestock, but that was slight loss to Rancho Los Nietos, whose cattle roamed at will over 167,000 acres.

Across the rancho, endless fields of yellow wild mustard grew with stalks higher than a man's head, so dense that cattle often became lost in the tangled branches. Every springtime rancheros and vaqueros gathered by the colorful jungle for a favorite competition — "runs through the mustard."

Don Manuel divided the land so that his widow and children would inherit it in the form of five smaller ranchos — Los Cerritos, Los Ala-

---

*In Spanish "palo" means stick or log. In California the word was used for tree.

mitos, Santa Gertrudes, Los Coyotes and Las Bolsas. (All the land comprising Rancho Las Bolsas and parts of Ranchos Los Coyotes and Los Alamitos lie in what is now Orange County. See Appendix.) While California was still under Mexican rule, three of the ranchos were acquired by former Yankees, all of them naturalized Mexican citizens and all, by coincidence, from Massachusetts. A fourth rancho was purchased by a former Sardinian.

One of the Americans was Don Juan Temple, originally Jonathan Temple, owner of Rancho Los Cerritos (The Little Hills). On the rancho he kept a large stable, and one of the favorite pastimes of his family was a canter together down the long, empty beach by the harbor, years later named Long Beach. Signal Hill lay half on Rancho Los Cerritos, half on Rancho Los Alamitos; from the foot of that hill many of the Southland's most exciting horseraces started, either to the ocean or toward the pueblo across the plains. The old ranchhouse was restored and landscaped by Llewellyn Bixby in 1930 to re-create early days under both Mexico and the United States. With unusual perception, a weathered section of wall beside the front door has been carefully protected by glass, for upon the worn surface are penciled markings recording the heights of growing children of long ago families.

Another American, Don Abel Stearns, bought Rancho Los Alamitos (The Little Cottonwoods). Governor José Figueroa had purchased it from the Nieto heirs in 1834, but within a few months he died, and his brother Francisco inherited it. At the other end of San Pedro Bay, Don Abel had the warehouse where he handled transactions in hides for the different rancheros. He knew Los Alamitos well, and to him it was the most desirable of all the ranchos. He bought it for his bride, the lovely Arcadia Bandini. Don Abel was 43 years old, and she was only 14; so to avoid public ridicule he offered the padres any sum of money for charity, if they would agree to waive the posting of marriage banns. The church accepted his offer, and no malicious jokes marred the quiet wedding which inaugurated a notably happy marriage. Don Abel restored the Alamitos ranchhouse for his wife, but also kept a house in the pueblo, one block from the Plaza, where a street still bears the name of the beautiful Arcadia. No husband and wife could have been more dissimilar in appearance, for Abel Stearns was an ugly man. A long, disfiguring scar across one cheek remained from an attack upon him by a half-intoxicated sailor in his store, and he was sometimes called "Cara del Caballo" (Horseface). In contrast, his lovely wife's features were painted by many artists, for she was universally admired, and a long list of suitors openly awaited her husband's decease.

Through his business dealings at the warehouse in San Pedro Bay, Don Abel always had plenty of funds to invest. From time to time rancheros turned to him for loans, and in some cases when the money could not be repaid the ranchos securing the loans were forfeited. In this way he acquired Ranchos Los Coyotes and La Bolsa Chica. Some rancheros sold him their land at a low price because they were financially pressed, and thus he acquired Ranchos La Laguna and La Jurupa. Through other dealings as well, he built up the largest land and cattle empire in Southern California. Then in a turnabout of fortune he became financially desperate and lost his own favorite Rancho Los Alamitos when it was sold at sheriff's auction because he could pay neither the interest due on a mortgage nor delinquent taxes of $152.

The third Yankee was Lemuel Carpenter. Rancho Santa Gertrudes, a fertile land watered by two rivers, had every aspect of perfection. Carpenter bought most of the rancho (17,602 acres), planted vineyards and cornfields, and watched his herds of cattle and horses spread over the plains. But after a time the rivers which had brought prosperity raged across the land in destructive floods. The ranchhouse was washed away; vineyards and cornfields were ruined. There followed years of drought when no crops grew and the cattle died of thirst and starvation. Don Lemuel took out a mortgage, but misfortune followed misfortune. Eventually the mortgage was foreclosed and the land was sold at public auction. The loss of his beloved rancho was too great an anguish for Carpenter, and he committed suicide.

A fourth foreign-born landowner of the old Nieto grant was Juan Bautista Leandry of Sardinia. It was because he owned Rancho Los Coyotes but died intestate that a most amazing document arrived in the little pueblo. It came from Nice, in the Kingdom of Sardinia,* announcing that word had been received of Leandry's death while possessed of a large estate. The document stated that standing by as witnesses were three men who swore by the cross and the Scriptures that they knew Leandry's family in Sardinia, where according to law one-third of his estate should go to his mother. There followed pages of legal-sounding, involved, repetitious sentences suggesting appropriate heirs for the other two-thirds of the estate. Family representatives signed the document, each noting his own value in property alongside his name, and then followed signatures of assorted officials such as the Royal Secretary of State for Foreign Affairs, the Prefect

---

*Although now part of France, in the years 1814-1860 Nice was capital of the County of Nice in the Kingdom of Sardinia.

of the Tribunal of Prefecture of Nice, and the Minister of Foreign
Relations of Peru. Official seals, including the Peruvian coat of arms,
were affixed as proof of authority. But Leandry had a widow; she
received half of his property, and after the remaining half was sold
to Don Andrés Pico for $16,000, the money was sent to Leandry's
mother as co-heiress. With obvious relish, Agustín Olvera penned the
accompanying letter. In a style faithful to the one which had been
received, he filled several pages with legal-sounding, involved, repetitious sentences. At the end were eight signatures, stunningly enriched
by flourishes.

Besides the seven ranchos carved from the early grants of Los
Nietos and San Pedro, two other ranchos south of the pueblo belonged
to families of early residents of Los Angeles: Rancho San Antonio,
granted to Antonio María Lugo, whose father stood among the military guard at the founding of the pueblo; and Rancho La Tajauta,
granted to Anastasio Avila, whose father settled in Los Angeles only
two years after its founding.

As a young man, Don Antonio María Lugo was a soldier attached
to the Presidio of Santa Barbara; later he served five terms as alcalde
of the pueblo. Memoirs of those days describe the lean, erect figure of
Don Antonio, who always kept a sword strapped to his saddle and
rode with stiff, military bearing. As early as 1810 he was given permission to take his family to ranchland which lay between the Los
Angeles and San Gabriel rivers and included some low hills and a
beautiful lake. Rancho San Antonio grew to epitomize the qualities
of hospitality and generosity characteristic of the Southland. Yet the
family of the proud ranchero was destined, in 1851, to be the center
of a dramatic criminal trial, when two of Don Antonio's grandsons
were accused of murder in the famous Lugo case.

Unlike the prominent Rancho San Antonio, the neighboring Rancho
La Tajauta never figured in the news. (La Tajauta is the only ranch
name whose meaning is unknown; possibly it was a Gabrielino word
for that area. The rancho sometimes has been called La Tajanta.)
Though bordering the pueblo's public land, its life was wholly private and centered around a patriarch — revered, simple, hard working
and pious.

Don Anastasio Avila was essentially a man of the soil. Use of the
land was granted to him in 1820, but it was 23 years before he was
persuaded that legal ownership was necessary so that he would not
risk losing the land to someone else. When he finally sent an applica-
tion for title, it was signed by a friend "at the request of the party,"
because Avila could not write. He had yet to ask for confirmation of

title when a long illness took his life. It was at the time of his death that every ranchero found he must prove ownership in court. Don Anastasio's eldest son, Enrique, stepped forward to represent the family, and old friends of his father joined him as witnesses — Manuel Dominguez, Julian Chavez, Antonio María Lugo — most of them able to speak only in Spanish. The presiding judge, commenting that he was moved by the rare qualities which unfolded as witnesses gave testimony, acknowledged the claim to be valid, and the Avila title was approved.

During the trial the old ranchero's will was presented as evidence. The document exemplified the piety and simplicity of cattle ranchers who lived remote from the sophistications of civilization. Beginning "In the name of Almighty God, Amen," Avila affirmed his religious beliefs at great length and commended his soul to God. Then, listing the names of his family, he tenderly included those of the deceased along with the living: two Cornelios were mentioned, one having died. In the division of his property he scrupulously noted that he owed one friend a peso, another friend two pesos and a third a gray cow.

The historian, discovering the pastoral innocence of those living on Rancho La Tajauta and the unvarying peace between the Avilas and their neighbors, can only judge that here was a truly Arcadian community. It is the site of today's community of Watts.

The island of Santa Catalina (Saint Catherine), 22 miles south of San Pedro, was the last Mexican land grant to be recognized by the United States.

On October 7, 1542, Rodriguez Cabrillo, earliest explorer of the coast of Alta California, discovered two islands and named the larger for his flagship, *La Victoria*, the smaller for his companion ship, *San Salvador*. Sixty years later another explorer, Sebastián Vizcaíno, sought shelter from a heavy windstorm by the large island. Because he found safety there on the eve of the feast of Santa Catalina, he renamed the island for her. The friendly Indians showed their Spanish visitors everything which might be interesting, such as their canoes and the harpoons with which they fished, and then led them on a tour of the island toward the place where they worshipped an idol with two horns but no head, decorated with colors and with eagle feathers fastened on by tar. Hundreds of otters lived on the island, and they were discovered by fur traders in the late 1700s. As a result, fierce and cruel Aleuts, sent by the Russians, exterminated the otters and victimized the helpless islanders. Afterward the once-happy community on the island gradually disbanded; disease took some lives, and the remaining Indians left for various missions on the mainland.

On July 4, 1846, three days before the date signaling California's annexation to the United States, Governor Pío Pico granted Santa Catalina to Thomas M. Robbins of Santa Barbara. Robbins, formerly a Yankee shipmaster, was a naturalized Mexican citizen. Four years later he sold the island to José María Covarrubias, another naturalized Mexican citizen. Both men, important rancheros of Santa Barbara, found the island too inaccessible and rugged for a cattle range. Covarrubias sold the island for $1000, or about two cents an acre.

3. *Ranchos of Santa Monica Bay*

Santa Monica Bay curves from the hills of Palos Verdes to the Santa Monica Mountains, with forty miles of beach-lined shore.

When, in 1542, Cabrillo's two ships rounded the peninsula from San Pedro Bay, the Spaniards' eyes scanned a graceful sweep of land. They looked curiously at what they named in the ship's log La Bahía de los Fumos (The Bay of Smokes) for the smoke rising above the land in many places. As the Spaniards sailed nearer they discerned Indians on the hillsides, burning brush to force rabbits from hiding. Overhead, in a pattern now familiar, the smoke spread out to make a hazy canopy over the plain. Slowly they sailed past the low-lying shore and the mountains which, at the northern end of the bay, came precipitously down to the sea.

At intervals narrow streams led into the ocean. Early settlers found that those flowing through the lowlands became huge marshes in times of heavy rain. For instance, La Ballona Creek spread over its banks across Rancho La Ballona, covering most of the land between the ocean and today's Culver City. It was there that the Los Angeles River originally emptied into Santa Monica Bay, but during a flood the water which overflowed the land started draining toward San Pedro Bay, creating a new course. The marshland, seared in times of drought, became a breeding ground for grasshoppers, which consumed all vegetation in the area.

Along the ocean, on the southern boundary of Rancho Sausal Redondo, salty springs formed salinas, or salt marshes. (These marshes lay in the area of today's Hermosa Beach.) This water could be boiled in large kettles and the residue of salt removed. The supply was ample.

In time five ranchos lined the bay. Typically, the petition for Rancho La Ballona (a name probably derived from Bayona, on the northern coast of Spain in the Bay of Biscay) did not bear the signatures of Agustín and Ygnacio Machado, brothers, or of Felipe and Tomás Talamantes, father and son. Instead their joint request was

A California rodeo. *(—Bancroft Library)*

signed by a friend. On documents relating to Rancho San Vicente y Santa Monica, a cross marked the signature of Francisco Sepúlveda, and in some places a son wrote his own name "Por mi padre" (for my father).

Rancho Sausal Redondo (Circular Willow Grove) was almost twice as large as the adjoining Rancho La Ballona, which had four owners. One of the four, Ygnacio Machado, petitioned for an unused part of the larger rancho to help him support his family — his wife, mother, four sons and four young nephews. In sympathetic response, he was granted the small Rancho Aguaje de la Centinela (Sentinel Springs) at the farthest point inland of Sausal Redondo. There a hill named La Centinela (The Sentinel) had a commanding view, and the boundaries of the two ranchos met at springs which flowed near the hilltop. Today Centinela Park in Inglewood includes a corner of each rancho, and the springs are commemorated by a granite drinking fountain midway in the park. The water is piped below ground for use by the City of Inglewood, but one can still see the same configuration of land which led Centinela Creek westward on its way to join Ballona Creek. The bed of the stream now crosses under La Cienega Boulevard, and then for a mile and a half follows the same route as the San Diego Freeway going northwest. Perched on a bluff above the freeway, the Machado ranchhouse overlooks the rushing stream of traffic where once the waters of Centinela Creek flowed quietly by. When Don Ygnacio's children were grown, he exchanged his rancho for the townhouse of Bruno Avila, whose brother owned Rancho Sausal Redondo. The 2200 acres of ranch land did not have as much value as a house in town; so Don Ygnacio added two barrels of aguardiente (about forty gallons of brandy) and the deal was made.*

At the beginning of the northern curve of Santa Monica Bay stood Rancho San Vicente, which included not only coastland but the mountains behind, as far as San Fernando Valley. Don Francisco Sepúlveda built his ranchhouse by San Vicente springs, near the present-day intersection of San Vicente and Wilshire Boulevards. At that same place Portolá had rested while sending scouts on an unsuccessful effort to find passage north alongside the ocean.

Tucked into a corner of Rancho San Vicente lay Rancho Santa Monica, a narrow strip of grazing land. Don Francisco felt that it properly belonged with his holdings, and because a year earlier it had been given to another ranchero as a provisional grant only, he asked the courts to annex it to his own property. Through general acceptance that Sepúlveda's request would be granted, it became customary to speak of the two ranchos as one: Rancho San Vicente y Santa Monica. The court denied Sepúlveda's request, but the new name was already common usage. The smaller rancho kept its identity, but the name was changed to Rancho Boca de Santa Monica (Mouth of Santa Monica) after the canyon and stream which formed its southern boundary.

Before making a decision about the two ranchos, the court needed measurements of the smaller one, especially the line dividing San Vicente from Santa Monica. The survey of Rancho "Santa Hermonica" was characteristic of the unbusinesslike attitude of some officials. Together the pueblo's alcalde and Don Francisco Sepúlveda's son, Fernando, marked off length after length of the measuring cord across the ground. Conscientiously they moved down a ravine and along

---

*The Avila family played a leading role in Los Angeles history. Four brothers were rancheros — Antonio Ygnacio of Rancho Sausal Redondo, Anastasio of Rancho La Tajauta, Francisco of Rancho Las Ciénegas, Bruno of Rancho Aguaje de la Centinela. A fifth brother, José María, was killed fighting Governor Victoria.

foothills, but looking at the steep, rough terrain ahead they could see only hard work. In mutual agreement a notation was made ". . . here terminated the survey of these premises."

Rancho Topanga, Malibu y Sequit (the names referred to canyons and Indian villages) lay farthest north along the bay. The mountains of that area were those which Portolá's scouts had seen, falling so so precipitously to the surf that they cut off passage beyond. The mountains were named for a creek which Indians living at its mouth called "Maliwu." In 1804 José Bartolomé Tapia, who arrived in California with Anza's second expedition, was allowed use of that shore land. The rancho extended from Topanga Canyon to what is now Arroyo Sequit, just north of Leo Carrillo Beach State Park, which marks the present boundary of Los Angeles County.

In 1925, of all the ranchos in Los Angeles County, Rancho Topanga, Malibu y Sequit was the only one which remained intact with boundaries the same as in the original grant. In that year the ranch owners were required to cede land to the State of California for a right of way along the coast.

4. Ranchos West of Los Angeles

West of El Pueblo, nearby ranchos took on important roles as the special character of the Southland unfolded. On two of them the spotlight falls most strongly — Ranchos Los Féliz and La Brea.

When the 11 families walked from San Gabriel Mission to found the settlement of Los Angeles, Corporal José Vicente Féliz[*] led their military guard. Six years later he became the pueblo's first comisionado, a combination manager, judge and mother hen of the little village. Before he retired in 1800 he was given the use of land he named El Rancho Nuestra Señora de Refugio de Los Félis (Our Lady of Refuge of the Félis Family), which included the low hills of today's Silverlake area and, beyond, the higher slopes of what is now Griffith Park.

Six years before the founding of the pueblo, Corporal Féliz and his family had come across the desert from Sonora with Capt. Juan Bautista de Anza's historic second expedition, which brought colonists for Northern California. At Tubac, a desert settlement which included a presidio, a waiting group of colonists joined Anza's party and the

[*]Originally the name was spelled Félix, and sometimes Félis. Similarly with other names, Chaves was later spelled Chavez, Abila became Avila, Albarado changed to Alvarado, Ygnacio to Ignacio, Ysabel to Isabel and Yguera to Higuera.

This view of the Mission San Gabriel Arcangel was painted in 1832 by Ferdinand Deppe. (—*Mission San Gabriel*)

complete expedition of about 200 persons started across the desolate waste. Féliz had enlisted with the troops, to be among the colonists of San Francisco with his wife and four children, but Señora Féliz was expecting a fifth child and the arduous journey across the desert was too much for her. The baby was born during the first night's encampment, and she died in childbirth. (Three more babies were born during the journey: one, premature, was stillborn, but there were no problems with the other two. As leader of the expedition, Anza was also its doctor and midwife.) Féliz and his children continued to San Gabriel Mission and from there to Monterey. Later, assigned to the San Gabriel Mission as a guard, he was there to welcome the band of colonists from Sonora at the end of their long journey to found the pueblo.

Another rancho closely related to the new community was Rancho La Brea (Asphalt). The black substance of its endlessly bubbling pits the Indians used in caulking the seams of their canoes, and settlers poured the heavy pitch over tules on the roofs of their adobe homes, making a crude waterproof surface for the rainy season. Even when

the land became a rancho in 1828, the Mexican Government made it
clear that use of the asphalt pits without charge remained an inalien-
able right of the townspeople of Los Angeles.

In 1815 a Portuguese sailor, Antonio José Rocha, deserted from
the English ship *Columbia;* out of 11 deserters he was the only one
who escaped. Later he became a Mexican citizen and was granted
Rancho La Brea, whose boundaries were described casually as: Rancho
Los Féliz on the north, lands of the city of Los Angeles on the east,
Rancho Las Ciénegas on the south and Rancho Rodeo de Las Aguas
on the west. The U.S. Land Commission found the boundaries un-
acceptable and the Rochas lost their claim to the rancho although
they had lived there over twenty years. Then Henry Hancock, lawyer
for the family, took the case to a higher court and led a brilliant
appeal. Ignoring the boundaries, he brought to the court a diseño
which located landmarks on the rancho, and old-time rancheros identified important ones along the boundaries. The result was a triumph
for Hancock and the Rochas. The appeals court decided to use the
diseño rather than the boundary descriptions as a basis for the legal
description of the rancho, and the decision against the Rochas was
reversed. By 1860, Henry Hancock had bought all claims to the land

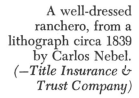

A well-dressed
ranchero, from a
lithograph circa 1839
by Carlos Nebel.
(*—Title Insurance &*
Trust Company)

from Rocha's heirs, and the field in which the famous La Brea Pits are found is today called Hancock Park.

Most of the ranchos were granted to men, but in the group west of Los Angeles there was an exception: Rancho Rodeo de las Aguas (Gathering of the Waters) was granted to a remarkable woman. Doña María Rita Valdez de Villa was the wife of an army sergeant and mother of seven children. To make ends meet she sometimes boarded officers in her home, and near some springs outside the pueblo she planted a garden and pastured a few cattle. One day a relative left for Monterey with petitions to Governor Alvarado for ranch land, and he persuaded Doña Rita, by then a widow, to add her own request. On his way north he met José Castro, a government official who years before had boarded at her home. To plead the case of his former landlady, Castro himself took the petition to Monterey. Governor Alvarado signed his official grant directly on the petition, and within a few hours the relative was on his way south with the paper and the good news. But to qualify as owner of the rancho Doña Rita needed 150 head of cattle. The overseer of the San Gabriel Mission arranged to loan her the necessary number of cattle, and soon she and her children moved to the ranch near a spring formed by waters descending from canyons in the hills above.*

Unfortunately, possession of the rancho was given jointly with a cousin, Luciano Valdez (the pueblo's only schoolteacher in 1830). Although many acres were available for their two homes, he built his house right in front of hers, obstructing the entrance and the view. Valdez drove her cattle away from the one watering place by the springs; so the thirsty animals wandered off the rancho in search of water elsewhere. After she and her children spent months clearing and plowing a piece of land, he claimed it as his. In frustration Doña Rita asked the Ayuntamiento to help by specifying definitely what share of the rancho was his and what was hers. Indignantly she added that Luciano had boasted that she, being a woman, was helpless against him, a man. Gallantly the Ayuntamiento, composed entirely of men, rose in her defense: Luciano was ordered to leave his home

---

*The waters of Coldwater Canyon (La Cañada de las Aguas Frías) and Benedict Canyon (La Cañada de los Encinos) converged at approximately the location of today's Beverly Hills Hotel on Sunset Boulevard; Doña Rita's house was nearby, in the vicinity of Sunset and Alpine. The true "Gathering of the Waters" was in the southern part of the rancho, below Wilshire Boulevard in the Doheny-La Cienega area. There, during the rainy season, a large marsh formed in the low terrain.

and the rancho with no recompense except the equivalent of $17.50.

West of Doña Rita's land were the softly rolling hills of Rancho San José de Buenos Ayres (St. Joseph of the Fine Breezes), which a century later became the site of the University of California at Los Angeles. When Máximo Alanís first arrived in Los Angeles he became a smuggler. Later he joined a revolt which ousted Don Vicente Sanchez as alcalde and was jailed when Don Vicente was reinstated. A tolerant government held none of his escapades against him, however, and with no objections he was granted the exceptionally beautiful ranch land in 1840.

Along the western side of the pueblo, reaching far south, a wide strip was set aside as public land. On it the townspeople kept their cattle in common pasturage. In time, the Ayuntamiento granted some of the acreage to families with large herds, and among the ranchos which resulted were Rincón de los Bueyes (The Oxen's Corner, a rancho where a ravine made a natural corral), Las Ciénegas (The Marshes — the correct Spanish word is "ciénaga," but locally "ciénega" was used) and La Ciénega ó Paso de la Tijera (The Marsh or Scissors Pass, so named for a pass which forked to lead along two valleys in a way resembling open scissors). These ranchos were in the area of today's Baldwin Hills.

Rancho La Ciénega ó Paso de la Tijera belonged to Don Vicente Sanchez, a man involved in more controversy than anyone else in the early days of the Southland. During one of the two times he was alcalde, leading citizens banded together and forced him out of office. When Governor Victoria restored him to the position and then brought his troops south to enforce obedience, embittered townsmen met him in battle, and Victoria was so seriously wounded he abdicated the governorship.

The contentious Don Vicente feuded with his neighbors over their boundary lines. On the west his own rancho was separated from Rancho Rincón de los Bueyes by a deep ravine. Don Vicente claimed the entire ravine and other portions of Rincón for himself and publicly denounced the other ranchero, Don Francisco Higuera, because hogs had strayed across the boundary. The feud became so intense that finally Governor Pío Pico announced that Higuera was in the right regarding every charge. Along the southern boundary of his rancho

Registered brand of Tomás Sanchez.
(*—Los Angeles County Archives, Hall of Records*)

Sanchez claimed marshland on Rancho Las Ciénegas, which had already been granted provisionally to the family of Don Francisco Avila. He lost his case there too. And yet except for his disposition the tempestuous Don Vicente was generally admired for his ability as a leader.

The hills on that group of ranchos became named for Lucky Baldwin, who bought a large area at public auction after several rancheros, because of a bank failure, defaulted on a loan for which the ranch land was security. Baldwin found the land unprofitable, but it brought a fortune to his heirs after it was subdivided. Subsequently a rich oil field was discovered under the hills.

5. Ranchos East of Los Angeles

On September 8, 1771, ten years before El Pueblo was founded, a gathering of padres, soldiers and Indians stood by the banks of the San Gabriel River. The cross was raised and the fourth mission in Alta California was dedicated to San Gabriel Arcangel.

The location of the mission underwent many changes. At first it was to have been established on the Santa Ana River, where several earthquakes shook the first explorers. Therefore the name of the mission was to include "de los Temblores" (of the Earthquakes, or rather, of the Region of Earthquakes), and the brand the padres brought for the mission cattle was shaped with the first and last letters of the word temblores. However, on reaching the proposed site they decided to continue to a more practical location. A spot by the San Gabriel River was chosen and the mission founded. Five years later a flood washed away part of the building, and the mission was rebuilt where it now stands, on Mission Road in the city of San Gabriel. Almost a century later, when the San Gabriel River changed its course, the river alongside the first site became the Rio Hondo. To one standing there now, trying to re-create mentally the day when that important mission was founded, the scene is surrealistic. Pipelines cross the hillsides and riverbanks, and in every direction, even to the water's edge, oil pumps like huge, phantom grasshoppers bend in perpetual motion. (At the corner of N. San Gabriel Boulevard and N. Lincoln Avenue a stone marker commemorates the first building, the Misión Vieja or Old Mission).

The mission was entrusted with lands which spread south from the San Gabriel Mountains. After a few years in its new location, thousands of mission cattle, horses and sheep roamed the unfenced fields. Fruit orchards flourished, and its grove of Valencia orange trees was the first of its kind in California. Cuttings from the "Mother Vines" started most of the Southland's vineyards. The self-sufficient mission included a winery, carpenter shop, weaving room, granary and two gristmills. (One of them, now called The Old Mill, is at 1120 Mill Road, San Marino.) In four enormous vats, chunks of fat were melted in hot water, and the tallow which collected on top was taken off and put into large rawhide bags, later to be used in the making of soap and the very much needed candles.

All the Franciscan missionaries, having been trained in languages and the spiritual life, owed their practical successes to their own pastoral origins, wherein each family had learned to fulfill all roles necessary for basic living. After the first few years a mayordomo was assigned to each mission to help supervise livestock and the fieldwork so that the padres would have more time to teach the Indian men carpentry, leatherwork and masonry, and the women sewing, weaving and cooking.

The San Gabriel Mission was an outpost of civilization and for many years the first habitation that exhausted travelers from across the desert saw at their journey's end. Anza came gratefully to its door, as did other explorers, soldiers, trappers and colonists. At the foot of El Cajón Pass, which leads from the Mojave Desert into the San Gabriel Valley, the padres established the San Bernardino Mission in 1810 as a supply station for travelers in need. But the station had an uneasy history of earthquakes, Indian raids and destruction of the buildings.

When in response to a petition for ranch land in the San Gabriel Valley the governor asked the padres for an opinion, they of course noted special approval of people connected in some way with the mission. Ranchos San Pascual, Huerta de Cuati and Potrero Grande (Large Pasture) were given to a retired lieutenant who lived at the mission, to an Indian woman who lived nearby and to an Indian who was one of the mission's mayordomos. When later the mayordomo transferred possession of Rancho Potrero Grande to Juan Matias San-chez, the Indian continued to occupy his own home and use the land for pasturage or whatever he chose.

South of the mission other would-be landowners asked for Ranchos Potrero Chico (Small Pasture) and Potrero de Felipe Lugo (Felipe Lugo's Pasture). Typically, Don Felipe Lugo used this cattle land for many years, assuming the area would always be recognized as his and therefore not bothering to ask for legal ownership. His rancho was granted to two other men, approvingly noted as "honorable, en-cumbered with family and industrious," but the land continued to be called Don Felipe's pasture.

Below the potreros lay Rancho La Merced (The Grace, or Mercy, of God), also called Rancho Misión Vieja because in its northeast corner the first San Gabriel Mission building once stood. Another of the few ranchos granted to a woman, it was given to María Casilda Soto, widow of a soldier. Under later owners Rancho La Merced and the adjoining Rancho La Puente* (The Bridge) figured in one of the tragedies of Los Angeles history. In 1875 three of the Southland's most respected rancheros pledged their land as security for a loan by Lucky Baldwin to the Temple and Workman Bank: Francis P. F. Temple his part-ownership of Ranchos La Merced and Las Ciénegas; William Workman (Temple's father-in-law) his holdings in Rancho Potrero de Felipe Lugo and Rancho La Puente, and Juan Matias Sanchez his Rancho Potrero Grande and half-ownership of Rancho La Merced. With the bank's failure the ranch land was forfeited. Grief-stricken, William Workman committed suicide; Temple and Sanchez died in poverty. Today the Sanchez ranchhouse still stands, on a knoll near the Rio Hondo; the beautiful old building expresses in every line the hospitable, generous spirit which was the basic fame of the rancheros.

Nearby, Rancho Paso de Bartolo Viejo once belonged to the Los Nietos grant, one of the first three ranchos in the Southland, but was reclaimed by the San Gabriel Mission for its own cattle. The name, Old Bartolo's Crossing, referred to a ford in the San Gabriel River: one Bartolo (nickname for Bartolomé) was allowed to farm on the land and carried his produce to the pueblo by way of the crossing he discovered. The rancho was the site of an important battle in the Mexican War.

After the war Don Pío Pico, last Mexican governor of Alta California, returned from Mexico where he had fled just before the Americans occupied Los Angeles, and in 1850 he arranged to buy the Rancho Paso de Bartolo Viejo. At that time he already owned 133,000 acres of ranch land with his brother Andrés, but this was his favorite rancho. It covered only 9000 acres; so he spoke of it by the affectionate diminutive, El Ranchito. Hard times and many legal battles over his land forced Don Pío to sell his holdings, but he kept El Ranchito until the last. Pico's two-story ranchhouse stood in the midst of orchards and vineyards through which ran a large irrigation ditch. In 1867, when torrential rains caused the San Gabriel River to over-

---

*The Spanish word is "el puente," but it was "la puente" until the 18th century, when the Spanish Academy changed the gender. In early California the change was ignored.

flow throughout its passage across the San Gabriel Valley, the flood-waters filled Pico's ditch to create a new course. Although formerly the San Gabriel River was almost two miles distant from the Pico ranchhouse, after the flood the river remained in its new channel.

In 1887 a colony of Quakers bought land just east of Rancho Paso de Bartolo Viejo to found the community of Whittier, named in honor of the Quaker poet John Greenleaf Whittier. Don Pío's ranchhouse was nearby, and every day the colonists saw the distinguished Californio ride up to watch their construction. Years later the City of Whittier bought land which included the site of the Pico home. At the turn of the century, vehicles still forded the nearby river, but when a bridge was to be built and the low, marshy land filled in, the contractor was given permission to use material from the rancho buildings. He hauled away the adobe bricks of some small houses, a mill and a chapel ornamented by frescoes. Mrs. Harriet Strong, a friend of Don Pío, heard what was happening, and through her efforts the demolition was stopped. Then she enlisted historic organizations in a project to restore the ranchhouse, which was then presented to the State of California as an historic monument. On the adjoining Rancho La Puente, in a Workman-Temple family mausoleum, the remains of Pío Pico and his wife are entombed. They were taken there when the Calvary Cemetery on North Broadway was needed for extensive roadways. In the mausoleum, on marble blocks around the wall, the names of William Workman, Francis P. F. Temple, Thomas Workman Temple and other old friends surround the grave.

When the San Gabriel Mission was founded, Indian huts dotted the plains to the north in small villages grouped near brooks and springs. In 1835 that land was provisionally granted as Rancho San Pascual to Lt. Juan Mariné, a retired army officer living at the mission. Just before sending his request to Governor Figueroa he married Eulalia Perez de Guillen, housekeeper and nurse at the mission. Both bride and groom were in their sixties, and according to dates in her background it is possible that Eulalia was really in her nineties. The celebrated woman long outlived Mariné, and died in 1878 at the age of 104 — or 140. Mexican law required ranch land to be used, otherwise it was "denounced." After Mariné's death in 1838 the rancho was denounced and then granted to new owners; they in turn abandoned the rancho and it was again denounced and regranted.

No foreign-born person could receive a grant of land unless he became a Mexican citizen and a Roman Catholic. Rancho Santa Anita was given to such a man, the Scotsman Hugo Reid. Of the several people who asked for the grant, he was chosen because not only did he change his citizenship and religion but also he married an Indian widow, Victoria, in a ceremony at the San Gabriel Mission. As was customary, the wedding fiesta lasted several days. Reid also adopted Victoria's four children by her previous husband, an Indian. His bride was owner of the small Rancho Huerta de Cuati (Twin Orchard, in reference to the fact that the mission had a similar orchard growing on the other side of the rancho boundary line). At his baptism in the Roman Catholic Church, Reid was asked to choose a name — generally of a patron saint or a virtue — to be added to his own; instead his choice was "Perfecto," in benign self-appraisal. The convert's name therefore became Hugo Perfecto Reid, or "Don Perfecto" as he liked to be called.

Rancho Santa Anita was destined to become one of the best-known in Los Angeles, when it was bought in 1875 by Lucky Baldwin after he sold his controlling interest in a mine in the famous Comstock Lode for $5,000,000. He remodeled Don Perfecto's home, turned the surrounding woods into a deer park and imported peacocks from India and Java. Lucky's flamboyant career included four marriages (the last two with women more than thirty years younger than he), an endless succession of lawsuits over unpaid bills and salaries, two trials for seduction and attempts by two women to kill him — once while he was in the courtroom.

Near the San Gabriel River where it descended from the mountains, the early Spaniards found a small Indian village named Asuksagna. The Indian name, simplified to Asusa by the newcomers, was applied to all the surrounding land. By the middle of the next century the spelling became "Azusa," which gave rise to the saying, "Azusa has everything from A to Z in the U.S.A." When ranchos were granted on each side of the river, they were both named Asusa, but after the one on the east bank came into the possession of Henry Dalton,

Registered brands of Vicente Lugo, Dolores Sepúlveda and Agustín Olvera. (—*Los Angeles County Archives, Hall of Records*)

a former Englishman, his rancho was called Asusa de Dalton, and the other rancho Asusa de Duarte after the name of its owner. Besides Asusa, Dalton acquired part ownership of Ranchos San José and San José Addition, as well as full ownership of Ranchos San Francisquito and Santa Anita.

At the far end of today's Los Angeles County the San José Hills and the Puente Hills were long in being settled. Only Indians lived near the ciénegas and streams while a few mission sheep straggled through the willows, sycamores and oaks upon the hills. When the land was divided into ranchos, the boundaries of Rancho San José included such informal landmarks as dry sticks in the figure of a cross, laid in the branches of a willow tree, and the skull of a bullock placed in an oak.

A route often taken by travelers crossing the desert led past the ranchhouse of Don Ygnacio Palomares. To those wearily following the dusty trail, Don Ygnacio's house surrounded by trees and flowers seemed a paradise, and even more so the welcome found there. Food, water and wine were brought, and each person was given a place to rest. For those who arrived destitute, clothing was found, and money given to the penniless. Hospitality was a characteristic of every rancho, but those which were outposts on roads leading to the pueblo found that welcoming the stranger was their special role.

Most remote in the hills were Ranchos Rincón de la Brea (A Corner, or Small Area, with Pools of Asphalt), La Habra (Pass Through the Mountains, i.e., the Puente Hills) and Los Nogales (Walnut Trees). On all three, cattle grazed deep into arroyos.

When claims for ranch land were presented to the U.S. Land Commission, the court case of Rancho Los Nogales became the most complicated of all those in Los Angeles. The original grant from the Mexican Government specified that the ranch occupied one square league, or 4438 acres. For the commission hearings, three separate surveys of the rancho were made; the one first accepted by the court included only about a tenth of the land claimed while it excluded buildings the ranchero and his family had occupied for many years. The decision centered on a key landmark on the boundary of the rancho, a point called "el monte." Upon the interpretation of this Spanish word hinged the amount of land affirmed to the family of José de la Luz Linares. To the commission, "el monte" meant "the mountain," or "the hill." One witness after another, most of them unable to speak English, testified that in California the word was used to mean "willow grove," whereas the word used for mountain or hill was "sierra" or "loma." (For example, the community of El

Monte received the name because the first homes were built alongside a willow grove.) Witnesses stepped forward who had been present at the boundary survey for juridical possession in 1840. Nevertheless, when finally in 1882 the claimants received their patent to the ranch land, it was for 1003.67 acres, about one-fourth the original grant.

6. Ranchos of San Fernando Valley

San Fernando Valley spread in tranquil beauty before the eyes of Captain Portolá and his explorers as they reached the end of the mountain pass now called Sepulveda Canyon. Live oaks cast their cool shadows on the spacious valley floor, bright in the sunlight. The travelers descended on the feast day of St. Catherine of Bononia; so the wide acres at the foot of the mountains were given the name El Valle de Santa Catalina de Bononia de los Encinos (The Valley of St. Catherine of Bononia of the Live Oaks).

Near the foot of the canyon they could see a large pool of water; around it clustered the huts of an Indian village, huts made of stakes covered with long grasses. The natives, almost naked, stared in wonder at the clothes of the leatherjacket troops, the long robes of the two priests and at the graceful animals which some of the men rode. Slowly the strangers approached, and in mutual friendliness the Indians brought forward gifts of food while the visitors held out beads and ribbons.

The valley, about 20 miles long and 12 miles wide, was surrounded by mountains, but the villagers indicated where a pass to the north could be found. After resting overnight, Portolá and his men followed the steep pass to what is now Newhall and Castaic, then turned west along the Santa Clara Valley to the ocean.

In San Fernando Valley, approximately halfway between the San Gabriel and San Buenaventura missions, the 17th mission was built in the chain of 21. On September 8, 1797, Padre Fermín Lasuén (successor to Father Serra) founded a new mission dedicated to San Fernando Rey — Ferdinand III, a saintly king of 13th-century Spain. Two friars were left in charge, along with a military guard and three Indian families from an older mission who could help instruct Indian converts. During the years since the first mission was built the friars had learned much about architecture and construction, and at San Fernando an especially beautiful building was erected. Along its facade graceful arches framed the view; a bell tower topped the red tiles of the slanting roof.

The restored San Fernando Mission.
(—*Title Insurance & Trust Company*)

The friars and Indians built an excellent irrigation system to bring water to mission gardens, orchards and vineyards. Water from springs four miles north was channeled to a dam and from there to the mission grounds. A huge wine press was erected, where during the wine-making season the grapes were tramped for three days before the juice was drained. Included in the buildings were a tannery and a smokehouse, carpenter and blacksmith shops, granaries, rooms for shoemaking, weaving and the manufacture of olive oil, soap and candles. Increasing herds of horses, cattle and sheep grazed on the surrounding plains. Fernandeño Indians, from small villages such as Tujunga, Pacoima, Cahuenga and Topanga, came to be converted and baptized.

In late spring and early summer the valley offered an exciting vista to riders coming down the San Fernando Pass. Beyond the red-tiled mission buildings which stood amid orchards and vineyards, the long plain was covered with golden, wild mustard. Now and then the tall, strong mustard stalks, many of them thick as a child's wrist, were climbed by ground squirrels seeking vantage points.

The mission's prosperity was soon lost after secularization. Gradually Indians left the community, buildings fell into decay, gardens were untended. In 1845, Andrés Pico and Juan Manso were commissioned to inventory the mission buildings, equipment and other property, and were also given a nine-year lease on all land in the valley which remained ungranted. A year later the bankrupt Mexican army needed funds to fight against the invading Americans, and the Mexican Government authorized Governor Pío Pico to sell the mission to Eulogio de Celís for $14,000. The rancho was called Ex-Mission San Fernando, but the mission building itself was excepted. The resident priest was to be allowed whatever rooms and clothing he might need, and "old Indians" on the mission land were to be taken care of and allowed to plant crops. With Celís' permission, Pico and Manso continued using the rancho for their stock. After California joined the Union, the U.S. Land Commission confirmed Celís' claim to what was the largest grant of land in the state — 116,858.46 acres.

Andrés Pico continued to live in the long mission building, and because of his occupancy the property remained in better condition than other missions. In 1854, for $15,000, he bought a half interest in the rancho, which later he transferred to his brother Pío, who in turn sold the half interest for $115,000 in order to finance his hotel, the famous Pico House on the old Plaza in downtown Los Angeles.

Thirteen years before the San Fernando Mission was founded, the Southland's second rancho was established by the Spanish Government at the eastern end of the valley. In October 1784, Governor Pedro Fages gave permission to Corporal José María Verdugo to take his cattle onto range just north of the pueblo. Verdugo, a leatherjacket trooper of the San Diego Presidio stationed as guard at San Gabriel Mission, was too ill for regular duty but had five daughters and a son to support. So the man whom Spanish documents described as the "Invalid with the Grade of Corporal" was allowed use of Rancho San Rafael, which lay between the two spreading arms of the Los Angeles River and the Arroyo Seco and reached as far north as the hills "where is the Piedra Gorda" (Large Rock, now Eagle Rock).

Verdugo's will divided the ranch land between his one son, Don Julio, and a blind daughter, Catalina. (It was the custom to give a

El Ranchito, Pío Pico's last and most beloved home, was
painted by Herbert Hahn in a scene from the 1880s.
(*—Governor Pico Mansion Society*)

large dowry — usually a substantial number of cattle — when a daughter was married; in a will, property and money were bequeathed to
the widow, sons and unmarried daughters.) In the 1860s hard times
forced Don Julio to mortgage part of the rancho for $3445. Interest
was three percent per month, payable every three months. The first
date for payment arrived, but he was unable to meet the obligation,
so the amount owed was added to the debt, which was then extended for another three months. By the time the property was foreclosed eight years later, the debt had grown from the original $3445
to $58,750. The land was sold at auction, and the new owner quit-
claimed 200 acres to Don Julio, including the ranchhouse. During
that time other acreage on the rancho had been sold or else foreclosed
under mortgages. Part had been transferred to Joseph Lancaster Brent,
lawyer for the Verdugos before the Land Commission, in payment of
his fee. As a result there were many owners yet indefinite boundaries,
and in 1871 the court case known as The Great Partition was held to

decide true ownership and boundaries of the lands which once made up Rancho San Rafael. Eventually the property was divided among 28 different persons, including a few members of the Verdugo family.

The mission system's main purpose had been to convert and civilize Indians, then return the land to them. Remembering the obligation, the Mexican Government approved the grant of ranchos to several natives who seemed most responsible. For instance Rancho Cahuenga (named for the Indian village) was granted to José Miguel Triunfo, a San Fernando Mission Indian. Triunfo built a ranchhouse; the padres loaned him cattle to start a herd, and he was provisionally given "1/4th of a league of land, a little more or less." The southern boundary was marked by a fence which until then had been used as the southern limit of the mission land.

But the rancho had an unusual feature: it stood in the middle of another rancho, Rancho Providencia (Providence, referring to God), which was later granted to Vicente de la Osa. When allowing the grant, the government expressly warned Don Vicente that his claim should not disturb the Indian, and while the boundaries were being officially measured Triunfo stood on his land, an obvious reminder of his prerogative. A few weeks after Rancho Providencia was granted, officials gathered to measure the boundaries of Rancho Cahuenga. Then it was discovered that Triunfo's house stood outside his boundary line. Since the Indian's provisional grant allowed "a little more" than a quarter league of land, the authorities relocated the boundary to include his home. Because he had insufficient pasture for his cattle, "a little more" was later added for that purpose as well. A survey of the rancho made for the U.S. surveyor general in 1868 shows the 388 acres of Rancho Cahuenga in the middle of Rancho Providencia's 4064 acres; on the map the old mission fence at the southern border is clearly marked, as is the site of Triunfo's home.

Across the valley on the northern side, two brothers, Pedro and Francisco Lopez, owned Rancho Tujunga (named for another Indian village). It was 17 times the size of Rancho Cahuenga, but the smaller rancho was nearer town; so in 1845 with mutual satisfaction Triunfo and the brothers exchanged properties.

In the western part of the valley an Indian, Tiburcio, was allowed use of Rancho El Encino (Live Oak). Three other mission Indians joined him — Ramón, Francisco and Roque, two of whom married Tiburcio's daughters.

Rancho El Escorpión (Scorpion) was granted to Joaquin Romero, who was the son of a San Fernando Mission guard, and to three mission Indians — Odon, Urbano and Manuel (Urbano's son).

Of the seven ranchos established in the Southland under Spain, three were in the San Fernando Valley: Rancho San Rafael at the eastern end, and Ranchos Las Virgenes (The Maidens) and El Conejo (The Rabbit) at the far western end. The latter two reached deep into the Santa Monica Mountains and had little in common with the ranchos which more closely surrounded the mission.

When possession of Rancho Las Virgenes was granted, measurement began at an oak marked with a cross on one side. The tree was called "La Cruz de Tapia" (Tapia's Cross) because Don Tiburcio Tapia camped there when he traveled with pack animals from his family's Rancho Topanga, Malibu y Sequit on the other side of the hills. At some time another oak on the same rancho was likewise marked with a cross. When later the United States required proof of rancho ownership and boundaries, the question of which tree was the true landmark became a serious problem in court. For Rancho Las Virgenes thirty years would go by before the case was closed.

In remote, sparsely settled Alta California, relationships were more personal than in today's large communities. If a ranchero felt powerless against some local injustice, it was natural to turn to the governor for help, and usually the governor's response was a paternal one. The story of Rancho El Conejo is a perfect example. In 1802 the Spanish Government allowed two men, José Polanco and Ignacio Rodriguez, to move onto land they had chosen. When Polanco died he left no heirs, but Rodriguez left a widow and children. Before long the land vacated by Polanco was claimed by Don José Antonio de la Guerra y Noriega, who moved his own herds onto El Conejo. Don José was an officer at the Presidio of Santa Barbara and one of the few aristocrats in California, born in Spain of a distinguished family. Although an extremely generous and talented man, the fact that he was accustomed to authority and power sometimes made him insensitive to the feelings of other people. Such was the situation on Rancho El Conejo. For 14 years Doña María del Carmen, a daughter of Ignacio Rodriguez, chafed at Don José's use of land on El Conejo, and when Governor José Figueroa rode south from Monterey to Santa Barbara in 1833 she used that opportunity to make a complaint. In a letter, she explained that neither she nor her brothers had received any notice that possession had been taken from them and transferred to Don José de la Guerra, yet he had been acting like the owner of the rancho, even forbidding her husband to erect a corral for their cattle unless permission was asked first. As soon as Governor Figueroa finished reading her letter, he seized a pen and wrote an order for Don José to report about the matter immediately and to cease dis-

José de la Guerra y Noriega. (—*Title Insurance & Trust Company*)

turbing the Rodriguez family. The reply which arrived three days later did not appease the Governor's anger. It stated that Doña María was the only member of the family who complained and that she and her husband were helped so much by her eldest brother — executor of the Rodriguez estate — that they lived "on the substance of this poor brother." Don José noted that he had been given provisional use of half of the rancho, the part vacated by the death of Rodriguez' partner, and loftily added that he felt it unnecessary to explain this to anyone in the family except the eldest brother, whom he considered should legally be the father's only heir. The indignant Governor granted the Rodriguez family title to the entire rancho, excluding Don José completely, and the grant was affirmed by the Departmental Assembly. But Governor Figueroa had been overly protective: he died at just that time, and his successor, Governor Alvarado, discovered that Don José's claim to half the rancho was valid after all. To stop all dissension, the rancho was divided and all boundaries clearly marked.

7. *Mountain Ranchos*

Mountain ranchos, desired only by venturesome men, lay deep in remote canyons and river valleys, far from pueblo and mission.

The Santa Susana Mountains, rocky and impenetrable, stand at the northwest corner of San Fernando Valley. Before the white man came they were an effective barrier between the Indians of Southern California. Shoshones lived on the south side; beyond, on the north and west, dwelt Chumash Indians, centered along the coast in the area of today's cities of Ventura and Santa Barbara. On different sides of the mountains the natives spoke entirely different languages. The white man looked at the same impenetrable mountains and reacted as the Indians had: ranchos west and north of the Santa Susana Mountains were oriented to Santa Barbara by way of river valleys which led west to the ocean. Not until after the middle of the 19th century was a roadway built through the Santa Susana Pass. Winding and precipitous, this road was often impassable in the rainy season when streams flowing down the canyons washed away the roadbed. Today a direct path has been cut through the mountains, and the distance across is but four miles. The wide, smooth freeway leads easily past rocky slopes and huge boulders that receive hardly a glance from the traveler who, cruising through in less than five minutes, little realizes that these same features were once considered insurmountable.

The first rancho established in the mountainous land was Rancho Simí (named for an Indian village, Simij), which included the Santa Susana Pass. The rancho was one of the seven concessions made under Spanish rule and one of the largest ranchos in California, covering 176 square miles. In 1795 Governor Borica gave use of the rancho to three uncles of Andrés and Pío Pico as a reward for military service: two of them, and probably all three, were soldiers of the garrison in Santa Barbara. José de la Guerra y Noriega bought the land from them in 1822.

At the northern extent of Rancho Simí in the fertile Santa Clara Valley lay Rancho San Francisco. It was granted to Don Antonio del Valle in 1839; after his death the eldest son, Don Ygnacio, built the beautiful ranchhouse named Camulos, which was chosen by Helen Hunt Jackson to be a setting for her book *Ramona*. Rancho San Francisco followed the Santa Clara River far up into the mountains; its pasture around present-day Newhall was rented to a relative, Don Francisco Lopez, and there he discovered the first gold in California, in 1842.

On New Year's Day of 1850 two young men staggered out of the mountains above the rancho. They were William Lewis Manly and John Rogers, who had just come 200 miles from Death Valley seeking help for a party left behind. On their journey they had endured thirst, starvation and injury, and in *Death Valley in '49* Manly describes the moment when he and his companion reached a summit overlooking part of the valley where stood the ranchhouse. "There before us was a beautiful meadow . . . green as a thick carpet of grass could make it . . . and over the broad acres of luxuriant grass was a herd of cattle numbering many hundreds if not thousands. . . . All seemed happy and content, and such a scene of abundance and rich plenty and comfort bursting thus upon our eyes, which for months had seen only the desolation and sadness of the desert, was like getting a glimpse of Paradise, and tears of joy ran down our faces." (The site of the ranchhouse is on a low hill a little over half a mile south of Castaic Junction.) The people they saw were dressed in a manner strange to Manly and Rogers, who realized they were looking at Mexicans, "and if what we had read about them in books was true, we were in a set of land pirates, and bloodthirsty men." Their reception proved otherwise. Although the rancheros themselves were away, the wayfarers were offered rest and hot meals at the rancho. When they started on their return trip to Death Valley they took horses and food, and wanting to pay, the two men spread out all their money. The Mexicans took half, and then a woman came forward with a special gift of oranges for the four children of their party, waiting in the desert. (A plaque in Death Valley commemorates the arrival of help from Rancho San Francisco which saved the lives of the Bennett-Arcane party. The name is mistakenly given as San Francisquito.)

North from Piru, at the edge of the Santa Clara Valley, spreads the harsh terrain of Rancho Temescal (an Indian word for the native ceremonial sweathouse, in this case that of the Indian village of Piru). In 1843 the remote rancho was granted to two friends. They soon discovered that their new property was almost useless as ranch land: most of it lay in narrow canyons and rough hills too rocky and inaccessible for the grazing of cattle. After four disheartening years the two owners decided to sell their rancho. Now thousands of people a day drive along a highway past the land which once seemed remote and useless.

Still farther north, at the border between today's Los Angeles and Kern Counties, the rugged San Gabriel Mountains give way to the gently rolling Tehachapis. Three partners asked for a grant of Rancho Los Alamos y Agua Caliente (Cottonwoods and Hot Springs), although the deserted area was especially vulnerable to Indian raids. One of the partners was Francisco Lopez, who had formerly rented the land on Rancho San Francisco, and only he drove his herds north to Rancho Los Alamos. Several vaqueros went with him, but almost immediately marauding Indians from the San Joaquin and Owens Valleys raided the newly arrived herds. Don Francisco's vaqueros fled; his partners failed to join him, and he found himself completely alone. Then word came that American soldiers under Colonel Frémont were about to invade the Southland and that their path would lead across the rancho. The combined threat of Indians and foreign troops proved too much: the brave but solitary ranchero abandoned Los Alamos and took refuge in Los Angeles. There he died before peace was restored, and Agustín Olvera bought Don Francisco's share of the rancho from his heirs.

Adjoining Rancho Los Alamos, Rancho La Liebre (Jackrabbit) was granted to José María Flores on April 21, 1846. The two ranchos included the Plain of La Liebre (the western tip of Antelope Valley) which formed a wide, fertile cattle range in the mountains. Three months after receiving the rancho grant, Flores was made commanding general of the California forces in the Mexican War. Because of his friendship with Governor Pío Pico, and because the U.S. Land Commission was looking for possible fraud by the Governor and suspected collusion with his friends in the form of land grants which did not legally qualify, Rancho La Liebre became an important case. Flores' claim was denied as fraudulent, but the case was taken before the court of appeals. There the general proved that although his military duties kept him from fulfilling the requirements of ownership personally, he had hired a mayordomo to care for his cattle and horses and construct a house and corral. Other "irregularities" were as easily explained, and Flores' ownership to 11 square leagues was confirmed.

One of General Kearny's officers at the Battle of San Pasqual was Edward Fitzgerald Beale, who in 1852 was named Superintendent of Indian Affairs with headquarters at Fort Tejón. Three years later Beale retired with the rank of brigadier general and bought four ranchos in the area — Los Alamos y Agua Caliente, La Liebre, Castec and Tejón (the last two in Kern County) — forming what he called the Tejón Ranchos.

East of Rancho La Liebre lay the wide expanse of Antelope Valley, part of the Mojave Desert. No cattle ranch was ever established in the valley, which always remained public land. Its only inhabitants were a few Kitanemuk Indians, the nomadic tribe which spent winters in the desert, summers among the foothills. Their homes were mere loosely built wickiups made of branches held together by fibre — often the fibre of a yucca stalk. At one time about 60,000 antelope roamed the valley, but by the end of the 19th century they had disappeared. In springtime, travelers across the high desert of Antelope Valley

(2600-4000 feet above sea level, higher than either the San Fernando or San Gabriel Valley) found it filled with color from blooms of wild-flowers and cactus, while in all seasons the silhouettes of Joshua trees made eerie punctuation marks across the valley floor.

Although modern highways now traverse the northern mountains and Antelope Valley, an aerial view of the long series of peaks and deep canyons makes it clear to any observer why Los Angeles remained so long isolated from the north, while the immense Mojave Desert was equally a barrier on the east.

Running southeast from Tejón Pass to the San Bernardino County line, the great San Andreas Fault leaves marks of ancient upheavals in the earth's crust. Steep, vertical faulting rises alongside the Golden State Freeway south of Gorman. Farther south, alongside the Antelope Valley Freeway, the uptilted slabs of Vasquez Rocks rise like huge vertebrae. In the mountains of the valley's southern rim the Devil's Punchbowl stands, a weird array of massive boulders and rough escarpments just as they were left after a prehistoric cataclysm. In that strange, deep bowl have been found fossil remains of extinct animals of the Ice Age — the three-toed horse, primitive camels and miniature antelope. Standing on the hilltop near the Punchbowl, we feel a sense of timelessness. From that vantage point beside Ice Age formations we can look across the valley toward a Space Age test range, Edwards Air Force Base.

There was no sudden end to the ranchos when California became part of the United States in the middle of the 19th century. Their disappearance was so gradual that when the 20th century began many of them were still included on the maps of Los Angeles. And though the ranch land was sold, to become cities and communities, the Spanish origin has never been forgotten. Today on county maps one can see, clearly marked in the background, the names of the ranchos to which the land once belonged.

Indelibly a part of Los Angeles, the names of the ranchos and their owners remain as names of canyons, creeks, hills, streets, schools, lakes and dams. The Spanish names are a constant reminder of lives which were not in the world's limelight but, rather, were spent in the obscurity of an isolated community. Under a new government the rancheros were forced to fight for their existence. Although many among them lost, each one had already carved his name forever as a founder of the basic heritage of Los Angeles.

V

THE TRANSFER OF ALLEGIANCE 1848-1868

1. *The Pueblo Unchanged*

The transfer of allegiance to the United States was hardly noticed by Los Angeles. Washington, D.C., California's new seat of government, seemed as far off as Mexico City or Madrid had earlier. No head of state crossed the forbidding deserts and mountain ranges to come to the Far West. The small town of only 1610 inhabitants, seemingly untouched by the far-off ruling government, continued its leisurely ways under the bright California sun.

For two hours every midday, shops closed their doors, all work ceased, and the pueblo took an unhurried siesta (a custom which was followed for several more decades). Few newcomers arrived to stay in the Southland, and the close interrelation of ranch families, tied by kinship, continued to be one of the marked characteristics of Southern California.

Life in Los Angeles had focused around the Plaza from the moment that the church was built as a kind of cornerstone. The church stood at the Plaza's head and around it were the townhouses of rancheros. Other homes ranged along the streets leading away. Casually the city fathers took it for granted that everyone knew where everyone else lived, for no numbers were put on the buildings until 1870.

Horseracing, always the favorite sport, reached a climax when, in 1852, the most celebrated of all the races was held between José Sepúlveda's Black Swan and Pío Pico's Sarco. Don José's mare was imported from Australia, and he waited impatiently in San Francisco until the vessel bringing her sailed into the Bay. The race was to be run on San Pedro Road for a league and a half toward Los Angeles and back — a total of about nine miles. Word of the race spread over the state, and as the day drew near people began to arrive from San Diego, Santa Barbara, even from far-off San Francisco. A fever of betting swept everyone — rancheros, vaqueros, townspeople, visitors. At the starting place the two horses got ready, and on each side excited caballeros lined up on the plain to test the speed of their own

Old Glory had 31 stars after the admission of California in 1851.

horses. The starting gun sounded, and off flew Sarco, Black Swan and the unofficial competitors who were soon left far behind. The race went easily to Black Swan, and Don José won fame as well as $50,000 from prize money and bets.

The war had left the coffers of Los Angeles empty. To fill them public land could be sold, but the government in Monterey sent word that first a city map would be needed so that all boundaries could be specific. Lt. Edward O. C. Ord, stationed in Monterey, was suggested for the job of surveyor. At first Ord asked for land and money in payment, but eventually a price of $3000 (with no land) was agreed upon. Even so, Los Angeles had no money with which to pay for the survey and had to borrow the sum from the leading merchant, John Temple.

Lieutenant Ord brought an aide, William Rich Hutton, an artist who sketched local scenes as a sideline to his work. A result of the lieutenant's survey was the numbering of blocks and lots and the straightening of haphazard roads. This realignment placed some houses in the middle of a new thoroughfare or else on no thoroughfare at all, so that access had to be through another man's property. In such cases, right of way to the nearest street could be claimed.

Until the realignment there were no straight streets even around the Plaza. Some houses had encroached on the Plaza land and others were set far back from neighboring homes. The final solution was to move up all the property lines around the square to be even with those farthest forward.

The names of the early streets were, of course, in Spanish. Calle de las Viñas (Street of Vineyards) later became Calle de las Huertas (Street of Orchards), then San Pedro Street because it was the principal road between the pueblo and San Pedro. Calle Zanja Madre, originally the location of part of the Mother Ditch before the zanja was filled in and a road laid out, was later called Los Angeles Street. Calle Principal later became Main Street while Calle Fortín (later Fort Street) is now Broadway. Calle del Toro (Street of the Bull) was named

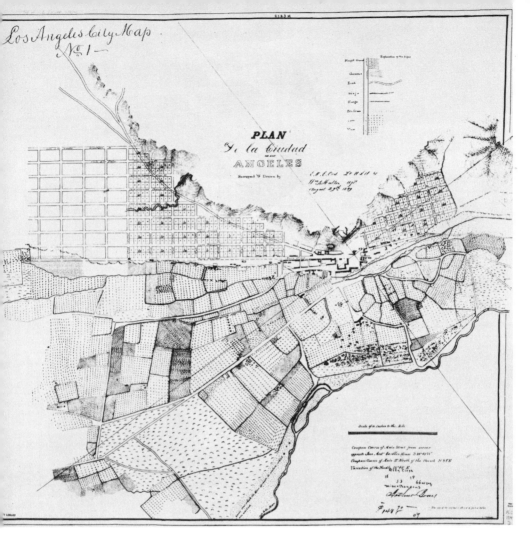

Lieutenant Ord's survey of Los Angeles was completed in 1849. The original Los Angeles City Map No. 1 has disappeared, but a copy of it made for the city in 1872 by surveyor L. Seebold is kept in City Hall; it is the official Map No. 1.

(—Bancroft Library)

for a bullring near where the French Hospital now stands on the corner of College Street; it later became Calle Loma, then Hill Street. Calle Accytuna was eventually anglicized to Olive Street. And Calle de las Chapules (Street of the Grasshoppers), was so named for the inordinate number of grasshoppers which flourished in the land just to the west; later the name was changed to Pearl Street, then to Figueroa Street in honor of the Mexican governor.

At the eastern end of the Plaza was a street one block in length called La Calle de los Negros. (This street figured in much of Los

Los Angeles as seen from the U.S. Hotel at the corner of Main and Market Streets in 1857. (—*Title Insurance & Trust Company*)

Trinidad Ortega, sweetheart of Lt. Edward O. C. Ord, had the nickname "La Primavera." She eventually married Miguel de la Guerra, son of Don José Antonio de la Guerra y Noriega. (—*Title Insurance & Trust Company*)

Angeles' history.) José Antonio Carrillo, responsible for the name, explained that it had no racial significance. In California at that time the word "Negro" referred not to a group of people, whether African or European, but to relative darkness of skin. Along the Calle de los Negros lived several families, and by chance all of them were dark-complexioned. (This use of the word is customary in some countries of South America today.)

At first the burial grounds were near the church, but more space was soon needed. A street named La Calle de la Eternidad led from the church to the hills north of town, where a new campo santo (cemetery) was established. A friar standing in the cemetery gazed up at the slopes rising beyond. "The Elysian Hills," he murmured, referring to the Paradise of mythology where souls of the blest were supposed to go after death, and the citizens of the town made the name permanent. Years later the cemetery was covered when the land was graded. Calle de la Eternidad was extended to the river, and the name was changed to Buena Vista. Finally it received the prosaic name North Broadway, but the Elysian Hills still rise in peaceful majesty above the City of the Angels.

In central Los Angeles few people thought of the land as having much value. In 1859 Andrew A. Boyle, a new arrival, was able to buy a large area on a hill called Paredon Blanco (White Cliff), later Boyle Heights, for 25 cents an acre. All water was laboriously carried up

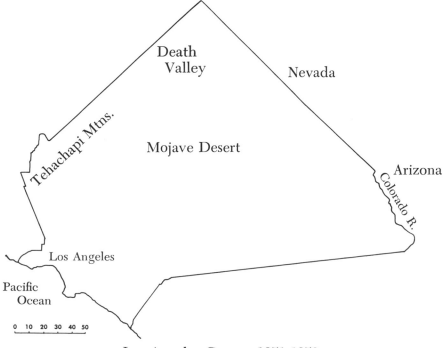

Los Angeles County 1851-1853

the hill from the canal below. Harris Newmark, in his memoirs, tells about a business transaction during the same year: for payment of a debt, a man offered Newmark whichever he preferred — either 110 acres of land, stretching from Washington to Pico and Main to Grand, or two loads of firewood. Newmark chose the firewood.

There are a few interesting stories involving the naming of streets. For instance, when Lieutenant Ord was allowed to suggest the name for one of them, he said "Primavera!" (Spring), which was Ord's pet name for his sweetheart, Trinidad Ortega. The name commemorating that lovely señorita still remains, although now in the English translation.

Three streets bore the Spanish names for Faith, Hope and Charity. In time Faith was changed to Flower, and Charity to Grand when the residents protested that they did not want to "live on charity." Now only Hope remains. Can this be significant?

2. *Statehood*

After California was conquered, it did not immediately become a state. For two years Congress debated what to do about the land newly acquired from Mexico. Should the entire territory be combined into one huge state and later divided into several smaller ones? Should California be divided in half, but extend east to include the Great Salt Lake? Should the southern boundary of California be just north of Santa Barbara? There were many varying proposals. As the debate went on and on, one legislator was inspired with a quick way to end the problem. He jumped to his feet and suggested giving everything back to Mexico — that is, everything except San Francisco Bay — but Congress did not respond. Debate continued until the discovery of gold at Sutter's Mill suddenly made California of such importance that procrastination ended.

Meanwhile the government of California was in chaos, the earlier authority of Mexico having ended without the United States taking its place. California decided to wait no longer before drafting a constitution. Four men important to Los Angeles — Manuel Dominguez, Abel Stearns, Stephen C. Foster and Hugo Perfecto Reid — were elected from that district to meet with representatives of the other districts of California in Monterey, to set up a state government. The meeting was called the Constitutional Convention.

Not only was a constitution prepared and then ratified, but also a general election was held in which the voters elected legislators to

This photograph of the Bella Union Hotel was taken after the building was modernized and enlarged to three stories in the 1850s. During an earlier reconstruction, workers unearthed artifacts indicating that the site was once part of the Indian village of Yang-na. In 1939 the structure was torn down, and today the Los Angeles Mall occupies this land. (*—Title Insurance & Trust Company*)

meet in San José (more central to the population than Monterey) and two representatives to go to Washington. The legislature itself elected California's two senators: on the first ballot John Charles Frémont was chosen, and on the third William N. Gwin. The former was well known in California, but Senator Gwin had just arrived in San Francisco from Mississippi (where earlier he had been a senator). In fact, although California was not yet a state, he had come west for the express purpose of being elected to the very office for which he was chosen. Senator Gwin, a tall man of striking appearance, was a knowledgeable politician: he proposed the Constitutional Convention, presented copies of several state constitutions as samples and helped California take firm steps toward statehood.

For several months both men were only senators-elect, because California was not then part of the Union, but due to certain circumstances Gwin is often called California's first senator. Immediately after their election, they boarded the same ship in Monterey, but Frémont's wife was ill (he carried her onto the vessel in his arms) and when they reached Panama he decided to stay a month so she could have medical care. Gwin, therefore, was the first to present his credentials in Washington.

From the beginning of statehood in California, Americans rather than native Californians held a preponderance of high offices. In a way, Senator Gwin reflected the general attitude when, during deliberations at the Constitutional Convention, he spoke of José Antonio Carrillo as a "foreigner." Frémont championed the native Californians: his popularity among voters at large dwindled, and he was not re-elected.

The fact that a constitution had been drawn was momentous. It was the first time such a thing had been done by a territory waiting for statehood. However, one provision of the State Constitution was controversial: the framers had unanimously voted to prohibit slavery. At that moment the U.S. Senate was composed of 15 free states and 15 slave states. Congress was trying to keep a balance of power between the South and the North, and the anti-slavery stand of California caused Southern states to delay their acceptance. Then Senator Henry Clay of Virginia offered a compromise by which the State of California would be admitted, but the remainder of the territory acquired from Mexico would not prohibit slavery. Finally the United States Senate and House of Representatives, together comprising the 31st Congress, both voted to admit the State of California, and when President Millard Fillmore signed the bill on September 9, 1850, California became the 31st state in the Union.* Toward the end of October, almost six weeks later, the news reached Los Angeles.

While waiting for Congress to make up its mind, the temporary State Legislature formed the County of Los Angeles on February 18, 1850 — at that time much smaller than it is today. The next year the boundaries were redefined by the legislature to contain 34,000 square miles. Los Angeles County extended from the Pacific Ocean to Nevada and Arizona, and from the Funeral Mountains to San Juan Capistrano on the south. Death Valley was part of Los Angeles. Two years later, part of the county land was taken to create San Bernardino County

---

*All the other western lands acquired from Mexico were formed first into territories, afterward into states: Nevada in 1864, Colorado in 1876, Wyoming in 1890, Utah in 1896, and Arizona and New Mexico in 1912.

(today the largest county in the United States): in 1866 five thousand square miles were transferred to Kern County, and in 1889 the southern part of Los Angeles became Orange County. Later there were a few minor changes, and in 1919 the boundaries became defined exactly as they are now, to contain 4083.21 square miles. Originally California was divided into 27 counties; now there are 58.

After the Treaty of Cahuenga on January 13, 1847, local government continued as before, except under military supervision. Twelve years earlier, at the request of the Ayuntamiento, Los Angeles was allowed to have two alcaldes, one to be First Alcalde and President of the Ayuntamiento, the other to be Second Alcalde. At the beginning of 1848 the election of both alcaldes was declared void by the military authorities on the grounds that José Palomares was dangerously anti-American, and José Loreto Sepúlveda "ignorant and vicious." At that time the interpreter for military headquarters in Los Angeles was Stephen C. Foster, the handsome, dashing Yale graduate who had arrived with the Mormon Battalion soon after the Treaty of Cahuenga. He was appointed first alcalde, and José Vicente Guerrero second alcalde. At sight of the two men escorted by soldiers to be sworn into office, the Ayuntamiento was so angered that it unanimously resigned and walked out. Accordingly, Foster and Guerrero were the only city officials for Los Angeles.

On April 4, 1850, the City of Los Angeles was incorporated by an act of the State Legislature. Six weeks later military supervision ceased, and once more officials were elected — although Foster was appointed prefect by Governor Bennett Riley. With First Alcalde Abel Stearns, he gathered and indexed the Los Angeles City and County archives, which had been in complete disorder for several years after the first invasion by U.S. troops. Stearns and Ignacio del Valle, second alcalde, were the last alcaldes of Los Angeles. After the city was incorporated a new government was organized, with Dr. Alpheus P. Hodges elected as the first mayor (July 3, 1850 to May 7, 1851). He was appointed county coroner at the same time, when the man elected refused to serve. Dr. Hodges was a genial Virginian about whom no information remains except that in 1852 he and Dr. James B. Winston owned the Bella Union — the first hotel in Los Angeles and the California capitol during the last months of Mexican rule.

Also in 1850, a census was taken throughout Los Angeles City and County, but the record and its copy were both lost. One day 65 years later, in 1915, an old ranch building in San Fernando Valley was cleared of rubbish for use in a motion picture, and a bonfire was made of the debris. Producer Cecil B. De Mille stood idly watching the fire when he noticed certain papers which looked official. He rescued them and found they were some sort of record with Spanish names. Maurice Newmark, historian and member of an old Los Angeles family, was asked to study the papers; he discovered that they were the only copy of the first census of Los Angeles under U.S. rule. (There had been several under Spain and Mexico.)

Throughout the early years after the change in government there was antagonism between Northern and Southern California, due not to regional quarrelsomeness but to the fact that the areas were entirely dissimilar. Most of the Spanish-speaking legislators came from the Southland, which was still pastoral; most of the wealth was in the north, where commerce and mining flourished. By 1860 there were still fewer than 5000 residents in the City of Los Angeles, whereas San Francisco had become a thriving metropolis with a population of 156,802. Northern California controlled the legislature completely and tax apportionments reflected that control. Taking San Luis Obispo as the median point in the state, at one time the population north of that line was about twenty times that of the southern area, where taxes nevertheless equaled twice the amount levied in the northern part of the state. In 1850, and again the next year, Los Angeles petitioned Congress for a division of California. Finally in 1859 Andrés Pico gave a resolution to the State Assembly authorizing the formation of a "Territory of Colorado," made up of the cities from San Luis Obispo south. This bill was approved by both houses and ratified by the counties which wanted to secede from the State of California. However, the Civil War became predominant in the minds of everyone in Congress, and the bill was never brought to a vote. It is still an issue, sometimes advocated by Northern California, sometimes by the Southland. At this writing, several legislators once again are urging a division of the state.

3. Crime Spreads from the Gold Fields

The Gold Rush in the north completely altered life in California.

The 49ers came by land across mountain ranges and deserts, braving hostile Indians and hostile weather. They came by sea around Cape Horn, enduring three to four months of discomfort on a voyage of 15,000 miles. They came by the Isthmus of Panama or through Nicaragua, leaving the Atlantic behind and risking bandits and tropical fevers as they crossed to the shore of the Pacific, there to wait for the arrival of some ship to take them to El Dorado.

Across northern Mexico the Sonora Trail brought Mexicans to Yuma and then Los Angeles, with the result that "Sonoran" became the term for all would-be gold miners from Mexico. Long before the first wagons of American miners could reach California, the wave of Sonorans appeared. Some few decided to stay in Los Angeles, and they found homes mainly in the section just northwest of the Plaza, giving it the local name of Sonoratown.

Some Angeleños joined the Gold Rush, including Antonio Coronel, Dolores Sepúlveda, Lorenzo Soto and Antonio Machado. At first they worked undisturbed because, already living in California, they had reached the mines early, but as more men arrived by the thousands the competition for diggings became acute. One excuse mobs used for evicting claimholders was that they were "foreigners," which encompassed Spanish-speaking Californios. After months of harassment and danger, the Southlanders turned toward home.

As the Gold Rush continued, gangs of bandits came south, driven to new fields by vigilance committees or wars between Mexicans and Americans. Riffraff and lawbreakers changed Los Angeles into a frontier town of crime and violence. In 1853 a shipload of prostitutes arrived from San Francisco, and more of the women followed. The job of town marshal became so dangerous that his salary was raised to be the same as the mayor's.

After a year when 31 murders were committed in Los Angeles but not one murderer brought to justice, several groups were organized to protect citizens. The California Lancers were under the lead of former General Andrés Pico, and the Los Angeles Rangers were a group half social, half vigilante. As there were only three or four policemen in town and courts of law were often ineffectual, leading citizens assumed positions at the head of vigilance committees as the main protection against outlawry. The first convened in 1852.*

In one case three men were accused of robbing and murdering two American cattle buyers. Of the three men, two came from Sonora

---

*Actually, the first vigilance committee in Los Angeles met in 1836, when the wife of Domingo Féliz, of Rancho Los Féliz, ran off with a vaquero. After authorities apprehended the two lovers, Domingo lifted his wife onto his horse to return to their rancho. On the way home he was stabbed to death by the paramour, who with the runaway wife's help hid the body in a ravine. Several days later it was found. At that time no judge could give a death sentence to a citizen of California, yet the pueblo wanted severe retribution. At the home of Don Juan Temple about fifty leading men of the community met, with Victor Prudon as president. A demand for execution was sent to the alcalde, who refused; so the group took the keys from the jailer, dragged out the murderers and hanged them.

and one from Los Angeles. The ruthlessness of the unprovoked crime so horrified the town that respected leaders offered to serve on a vigilance committee: Abel Stearns was chairman, and among those participating were Andrés Pico, Julian Chavez, Alexander Bell, José Antonio Yorba, Felipe Lugo, Francisco Mellus, Manuel Garfias, Matthew Keller and John G. Downey, as well as lawyers John Randolph Scott and Lewis Granger. A jury was formed and the accused were brought forward to testify. After a trial similar to a legal one, two of the men were convicted and hanged. The third (one of the Sonorans) was set free.

No Black was ever lynched by a vigilance committee.

At one time when by reason of a legal technicality a criminal was about to escape punishment, Stephen C. Foster resigned as mayor in order to lead the vigilantes against him. When Foster again ran for office he was elected by a landslide.

Sarah Bixby, in her memoirs, describes the excitement whenever there was a hanging. Her home overlooked the jail, and during an execution the hillside nearby, as well as the roofs of the chickenhouse and barn, were covered with men wanting a good view of events in the jailhouse courtyard below.

It was in these years that the enduring legend of Joaquin Murieta arose. His name first appeared in an account of an attack against some Chinese, after which scores of Mexicans were killed in retaliation. From then on his name was the one mentioned whenever there was a baffling murder or robbery in the state, no matter where it happened. The last name changed, the spelling changed, but every report referred to the same Joaquin. (An historian going through accounts by old-time residents of California finds "authentic" versions of Joaquin's life, yet all of them differ.) At last, in desperation, the State Legislature ordered a company of rangers to search for him, with a bounty to be paid for his head. They were given three months in which to find him, and just before the time expired the rangers discovered some — to them — doubtful characters in a mountain pass. After a gunfight the head of one of the victims, "identified" as the dreaded Joaquin, was sent to the authorities and the rangers claimed the bounty.

Lawlessness in Los Angeles reached the frightening stage where at times people were besieged in their homes by criminal mobs. During a ball given by Don Abel Stearns in his home on Main Street, one block south of the Plaza, a large group outside tried to force its way in. The heavy doors and strongly barred windows held against them; so they took a cannon from the Plaza and fired it at the house. The raid ended only when some of Stearns' guests shot at the marauders, killing and wounding several.

The problem of crime was compounded by growing antagonism between Yankees and the Spanish-speaking people, with mutual bitterness and lack of understanding. The situation is best illustrated by the story of a significant court trial, one which not only was among the most dramatic in the annals of Los Angeles but which exemplified the city's total change of character.

One day in January of 1851 a band of Ute Indians swept down through Cajón Pass to stampede horses from herds on the ranchos below. Several hundred horses were taken from Rancho San Bernardino, owned by three sons of Don Antonio María Lugo — José María, Vicente and José del Carmen — and Don Diego Sepúlveda. A party of men went in pursuit of the raiders but was unsuccessful. Shortly afterward two men, teamsters, were found murdered in the pass. Accusations focused upon two of Don José María's sons, 18 and 16 years old, named Francisco Lugo, *Mayor* (Senior), and Francisco Lugo, *Menor* (Junior). (The older was called "Chico" and the younger "Menito," an affectionate diminutive for Menor.) A young friend named Mariano Elisalde was also accused. No definite evidence was found against any of them, but two months later Ysidro Higuera, a Sonoran who had been in the pursuit party, said that he had seen the three boys kill the victims, with Chico as ringleader. On his word the boys were taken to jail and put in chains.

Los Angeles found itself divided into two intense camps: the Americans, who immediately had decided the three boys were murderers, and the Californios, who were convinced that the boys were innocent. An American judge, Jonathan R. Scott, presided in court; Scott's partner at law, Benjamin J. Hayes (also an American), was prosecuting attorney.

One morning a young lawyer, Joseph Lancaster Brent, a new arrival in town from the East Coast, looked out of his office window and saw that he was receiving a call. To his amazement they were Californios, horsemen strikingly dressed in clothes ornamented with gold and silver, the horses wearing silver-decorated saddles. His callers were Don José María Lugo and his brother, Don José del Carmen Lugo, who had come to ask him to defend the boys.

After taking the case, Brent discovered that the boys' accuser had at the time of the accusation been in jail for stealing horses. Brent also learned that the jailer was a bitter enemy of the Lugo family, because once they had defended his wife when he was mistreating her. The lawyer felt that quite possibly a false story had been made up by the two men. The same jailer now held the boys in a cell. When the judge refused to let them out on bail, Brent got permission from the judge of the district court. However, bail of $10,000 each had to be paid by two o'clock that afternoon.

With that pronouncement, danger unexpectedly moved closer to the boys. Brent had another caller, this one representing a man called Red Irving, leader of a bandit gang which had recently arrived in town. The man explained that Red Irving had made an offer to the boys' grandfather, Don Antonio María Lugo, to help them escape from jail and from California. Don Antonio had disdainfully refused help from the bandits, and in retaliation Irving sent the message to Brent that unless he was paid $20,000 the boys would be killed as they left the jail.

The streets were thronged with townsfolk, who somehow heard of each new development, when Don José María Lugo arrived with bail shortly before two. As he appeared, some of Irving's gang galloped up the hill to the jail, while Americans in the crowd cheered. (The cheers came not from long-time Los Angeles Yankees but from new arrivals who considered this a foreign, conquered land.) Brent looked toward the jail with frustration. It was useless to ask for a protective police force: there was none. Help must come from the Californios themselves. Only first he must get a day's postponement, which he obtained.

That afternoon, with utmost secrecy, the lawyer sent the rancheros word to come to town immediately and hide near the jail in case Irving's gang should try to break in during the night. With evening a heavy fog moved inland, enshrouding the town. One by one, sixty Californios took their positions unnoticed around the hill. Still, Brent feared what might happen. If fighting broke out between Americans and Californios, many lives would be lost. Real help could come only from Federal troops, but the nearest soldiers were in San Diego.

At eight in the morning Brent sat in his office, puzzling over what move to make next. Then through the window his astonished eyes saw the embodiment of his hopes: a party of fifty U.S. dragoons came marching down the street. Hastening toward them, he explained the emergency, and the troops readily agreed to follow any plan Brent might suggest.

Just before two o'clock the soldiers marched to the jail, formed a hollow square around Sheriff Burrill and the three prisoners for presentment of bail. Irving's men watched, amazed and helpless.

At that time four rooms in the Bella Union Hotel on Main Street were rented to serve as a courthouse. Outside, a large crowd milled around, hopeful that there would be some shooting. Among them, but unsuspected, were Californios ready to protect the prisoners. Inside the courtroom, four former soldiers were stationed to guard the judge and prosecuting attorneys. Behind the prisoners sat a protective wall of relatives. Through the window, Vicente Elisalde, brother of the prisoner Mariano, watched in case Brent waved a key as a signal to send help into the courtroom. Most of the spectators belonged to Irving's armed gang, though Irving himself was still on his way to the courthouse from out of town. Just as the proceedings began, he strode in wearing a six-shooter and a knife. Angrily he looked around the room, then turned to the door to gaze as angrily at the dragoons outside.

When the bail bonds were approved, the families of the prisoners surrounded them to walk toward the door. Outside, the dragoons again formed a hollow square and marched with the prisoners to a place where a large band of Californios waited with horses. The three boys joined them, and all galloped off. Red Irving threatened Brent that he would still have his revenge.

One month later Irving and his gang left Los Angeles, presumably en route to the Colorado River. At each rancho they crossed — Ranchos La Puente, San José and Chino — they rustled horses. Then Red took half of his men and rode in the direction of the Lugos' Rancho San Bernardino. In Los Angeles, word of the raids reached the sheriff, and a posse of fifty men was organized. Brent sent a messenger on a fleet horse to warn the Lugo family that no one should sleep at home and watchmen should be alerted.

Three men were stationed in the ranchhouse. When Irving's band arrived and questioned them, it was answered that the Lugos were away, branding cattle. At that, closets and chests were searched for valuables and the house looted. The instant the thieves rode off, word was taken to a band of Indians Don José kept on the rancho, and they galloped in pursuit. The bandits fled into a deep ravine in the mountains, expecting to find shelter there, but instead the steep sides prevented escape, and Indian arrows killed all except one man who crawled under some bushes.

The boys hid for two months until the threat of lynching was over. Then they returned to Los Angeles. Judge Agustín Olvera presided over the court which gave final judgment: he ordered the case dismissed for lack of evidence. However, Chico Lugo's resentment festered and he turned against the law; eventually he was imprisoned in San Quentin.

The bitter controversy pointed out to the Southland that authority now lay wholly in new hands. The Lugo family was one of the most proud, even autocratic, of any in Los Angeles. Don Antonio María Lugo, patriarch of the family, was one of the city's earliest settlers, and for many years he and his sons had been leaders in the community. It is an interesting coincidence that the young lawyer chosen by the Lugos was from an equally proud family in Maryland. The bond of understanding between the attorney and his clients deepened, and before long Brent became one of the leading defenders of the embattled rancheros of Los Angeles when they appeared before the U.S. Government to prove ownership of their land.

4. *Modernizing a Frontier Town*

With Americanization, Los Angeles had its first experience with a democratic type of government. Yet a special quality was added which democracy did not have elsewhere. For instance, there was no registration, and therefore anyone could vote. Aliens and Indians — ineligible under U.S. law — voted along with everyone else.

The night before elections, newly arrived Mexicans were gathered together by candidates and given free drinks until morning. Then they were taken to the polls, where they voted for their free-spending hosts. Sometimes the same people voted again later in the day, maybe again for the same man but often for someone of the opposite party.

The buying of votes was a practice accepted by all political parties. In one election a hundred people were taken to a corral by a candidate and given all the liquor they wanted through the night. But before they left the corral a politician of another party went in and made such an eloquent speech in Spanish that unanimously the voters changed allegiance. At another time the names on a ship's passenger list were used by people when they made a second trip to the polls. Finally a registration law made such practices as these impossible.

Law courts, too, had an unorthodox quality. Native Californians spoke Spanish almost entirely, understanding little English. Newcomers, on the other hand, spoke English with seldom any understanding of Spanish. Juries were made up of both natives and newcomers; so testimony often had to be translated. Joaquin Carrillo, district judge for 14 years, held proceedings in Spanish. A further problem for the courts in Los Angeles was the lack of law books to be used as reference; for several years the only book available was one volume of Kent's *Commentaries*. Courts were held informally, jurymen wearing no coats or collars in warm weather. Sometimes hearings were violent, with chairs and inkstands thrown in anger; once a judge had to hide behind his platform to avoid being shot.

When in 1849 the Southland settled down to American rule, the City Council searched for a teacher to start the school again. After trying for months only one man could be found — someone who could teach many things, although he knew no English. Just as the decision was made to hire him, word came that the applicant had left for the gold mines in the north. The next year an ex-soldier, Francisco Busta-mente, was hired to teach reading, writing, arithmetic and morals. He was the last to teach in Spanish in the public schools.

In 1851 the first school law of the State of California was passed. After its enactment the government allotted the rent and sale of certain lands for school expenses and teachers' salaries. Then the City Council announced the first school tax, a property tax of 10 cents on $100 evaluation. Under the new regime, Los Angeles County was divided into four districts; in each of them a school year lasted about three months, by which time funds were exhausted. Thomas J. Scully established in a unique way the first uniform course of study: he taught in one district until no funds remained and school was dismissed; then he mounted his horse and moved to another district until the time came to ride on to the next.

During this period many of the rancheros employed instructors for their own children, including sometimes the children of friends and relatives. José Sepúlveda, Manuel Dominguez, William Wolfskill and William Workman followed this practice. The instructor on Rancho La Puente, Henry D. Barrows, later became Los Angeles superintendent of schools.

Vicente Lugo donated his home on the Plaza to the parish priest for use as a boys' school. Later a Protestant, Ozro W. Childs, donated an entire city block (from Sixth to Seventh between Broadway and Hill) to the same school, which became St. Vincent's College, the forerunner of Loyola University.

Still there was no public school building. Not until late in 1854 six years after California became part of the United States, was a public elementary school built, a two-story brick structure on the northwest corner of Spring and Second Streets. The proud achievement was brought about by a group of education-minded citizens led by Stephen C. Foster, superintendent of schools and also mayor.

In 1855 the State Legislature decreed that schools were to be taught in English only. Since in Los Angeles most of the school-age children were Spanish-speaking, they stayed away from public schools. As a result, a church school was organized in 1859, the bilingual Escuela Parroquial de Nuestra Señora de Los Angeles (Parochial School of Our Lady of the Angels) with tuition of two dollars per month. The headmaster, Pioquinto Davila, held classes in Spanish, but English was taught; not only Catholic students enrolled, but also Jewish and Protestant. The 1855 state law was the start of a problem which continues today: among the city's thousands of Mexican-American residents, many of the children have only a slight knowledge of English, which creates a handicap in basic learning and results in a large proportion of dropouts from school among the Spanish-speaking people.

There was no post office in the casually run town of Los Angeles. For many years all letters were taken to a store on Main Street. There the mail was thrown into a big tub at one end of the sales counter, and people sorted through the letters, taking their own away. When Dr. William B. Osburn was appointed postmaster in 1850, he made pigeonholes in a soapbox to arrange letters alphabetically. However, besides his duties as postmaster, Osburn was also a physician, realtor, auctioneer, photographer and (in 1855) superintendent of the Los Angeles city schools; consequently most of the time people searched for their own mail helter-skelter, as before.

News arrived erratically. In times of bad weather the city was cut off from news sources for lengthy periods. Because of such problems, and the illiteracy of the general public, all the early newspapers in Southern California failed. The first successful one was *La Estrella de Los Angeles* (*The Los Angeles Star*), founded in 1851. It was written partly in English, partly in Spanish.

In the early 1850s Los Angeles was still far from modern. Ordinances made an effort to protect the water in the open zanja, since it was needed for drinking as well as household purposes and irrigation, but many people continued to use the zanja for bathing and laundry. There were no sturdy sidewalks to protect pedestrians from thick dust during the dry season and mud during rainy weather. The first effort at improvement was made by John Temple, who in 1860, in front of his Temple Block along Main Street, laid rows of bricks which he covered with asphalt from the Brea pits. At first the sidewalk was a great improvement, but in the heat of summer the asphalt grew soft and gummy, and pedestrians walked in the dusty street by preference.

Because of the small population, one man frequently combined several trades. As an example, Charles L. Ducommun was watchmaker, jeweler, bookseller, stationer, tobacconist and dealer in paints and glass. Itinerant dentists and opticians announced their arrival in the newspaper and stayed in Los Angeles awhile before moving on to other communities and outlying ranchos.

When Mexican rule ended there was not one hotel in California; travelers depended upon the always available hospitality of residents. The first hotel in Los Angeles was the Bella Union, whose site lies at the northern end of today's Los Angeles Mall on Main Street. Erected by Isaac Williams about 1835, it had been chosen by Pío Pico to be the capitol while he was governor. The structure was remodeled into a hotel by Benjamin D. Wilson, who bought it from Williams in 1849; the rooms, mere cubicles, were 6 x 9 feet, and although a few floors were made of wood, most were earthen. Two years later a second story was added. For a decade the Bella Union was the city's only hotel, then the Lafayette was built across the street.

With civic enthusiasm, leading citizens bought the house and vineyards of Benjamin D. Wilson on the corner of Alameda and Macy Streets and established an orphanage to be run by the Sisters of Charity under the direction of Sister Scholastica. Leaders of the large French colony (over 400 persons) built the French Hospital in 1860, the first non-sectarian hospital in Southern California. In that year bullfighting was outlawed, and as the bullring was torn down, the French Hospital was erected on the site adjoining. The hospital is still in operation.

As the townspeople began to want a more dependable supply of water than the variable Los Angeles River, a brick reservoir to store water was built in the center of the Plaza. To distribute water through the downtown area, a pipe system was needed. Metal pipes would be difficult to obtain, however, and no engineer was available for advice; so when Mayor Damien Marchessault and Jean Louis Sainsevain offered to save the day, the city made a contract with them. The "pipes" were pine trees: holes were bored the length of each tree, and the logs were wired together. Not unexpectedly they kept leaking, creating mudholes in the streets which trapped many horses and carriages. The project became a complete failure, but what was a joke to everyone else was no joke to Marchessault. Overwhelmed by weeks of self-blame and humiliation, he committed suicide. After that, iron pipes were procured and a contract made for the construction of a dam and reservoir. The dam was hardly completed when, as had happened several times before, it was washed away during a flood.

The Gold Rush up north, with its sudden influx of 100,000 men, created a tremendous need for food in Northern California. This unforeseen demand resulted in a fantastic increase in the value of West Coast cattle. Until this time the meat of cattle had been considered unmarketable, with only the hides and tallow entering into commerce. Now, however, cattle on the hoof brought from $50 to $200 each in

San Francisco. This caused the beginning of cattle drives up the coast and shipments of other foods by water. Because of the big demand, eggs brought the amazing price of six dollars a dozen in San Francisco, and of course Southern California sent as great a quantity as possible of all kinds of food to the north. Large-scale agriculture began in wheat, barley and beans, although until then there had not been much market for any of them.

With business deals being made between people almost 500 miles apart, some new system of currency was needed. In San Francisco a mass meeting of miners and businessmen agreed on a standard price of $16 per ounce for gold. Coins, however, were needed for ordinary trade, and there developed much private coinage. Diemakers and engravers in San Francisco made gold coins of different shapes — round or many-sided — marked with whatever value the maker decided upon. Some were of an accurate value, but many were false because the coins themselves were not always backed up 100% by the companies issuing them. Currency finally became stabilized in 1854, when the Federal mint opened in San Francisco. To the relief of everyone there was a plentiful coinage of official gold bars, double eagles (gold, $20 in value), eagles ($10), half-eagles, quarter eagles and gold dollars.

Yet there was not one bank in Los Angeles until well after the Civil War. Money sent to San Francisco by express was taken to the agent, who sealed the package and charged a dollar for each hundred he transported safely. In stores, cash was sometimes kept in a small safe, but usually it was held in buckskin bags hidden on a shelf behind merchandise.

5. *Whaling*

Not only was gold greedily taken from the earth in California, but wealth was as greedily taken from the sea. Carelessly the whaling industry decimated the herds offshore.

During springtime each year San Pedro Bay was filled with whales — gray, humpback, finback and right whales — so it became a customary port-of-call for whalers. In the 1850s, Portuguese Bend on the Palos Verdes Peninsula was one of 11 whaling stations along the California coast. Here, in huge kettles set on a circle of rocks within which a fire blazed, the whale blubber was "tried out" (melted). With San Pedro Bay as a rendezvous, the Portuguese Company and the Portuguese American Company transferred cargoes from whalers to merchant ships en route to the East Coast around the Horn.

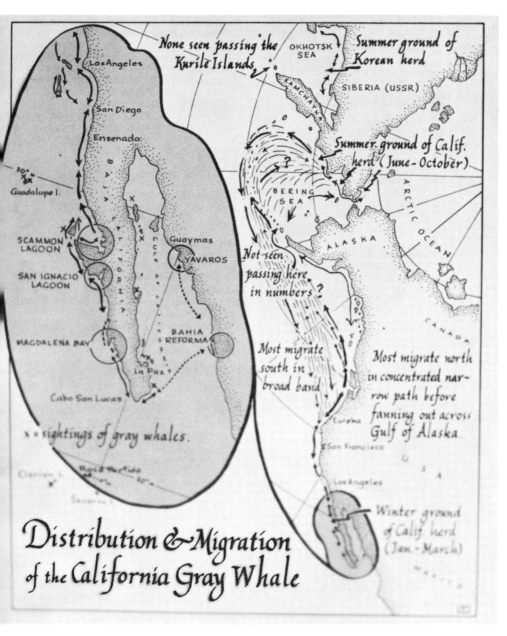

This map outlines the migratory pattern of the California gray whale.
(—*Raymond M. Gilmore, Research Associate, San Diego Museum of
Natural History*)

After 1850 the gray whale began to supersede the others, to the extent that it is now called the California gray whale because it winters off California and Baja California. The black mammal dappled with white (which gives a gray appearance) grows to a length of about 45 feet and a weight of approximately 35 tons.

By 1853 the Americans were establishing whaling shore stations along the California coast from Crescent City to San Diego, as well as allowing New England whaling ships to conduct operations even in bays where the whales calved and mated. Other ships hunted in Alaskan waters. Finally the extermination of so many whales brought an end to the industry. After that, unmolested, the gray whale increased in numbers once more until it was again pursued. Norwegian, American and Russian ships with harpoon cannon searched out the whales from 1924 until 1938, when an international treaty was enacted for the animals' protection. Now the herd increases in number by over ten percent each year. (In 1972 there was an estimated total of 6000-9000 gray whales.)

In summer the herds remain north of Alaska, in the Bering Sea, though some few venture into the Arctic Ocean. Then in November the migration south begins as the herd goes to its winter ground, almost 7000 miles away, for calving and breeding. By the middle of December the first whales pass San Francisco and continue south in a narrow migratory path which brings them close to Santa Barbara, Palos Verdes Peninsula and Point Loma. By an amazingly exact schedule, the leading whales arrive at San Diego every year at Christmastime, between December 22 and 27. Over a period of six weeks the main herd follows in a long line, keeping apart by a distance of one to five miles, cruising at four knots an hour.

Quiet lagoons in Baja California are the migration's destination, and as many as a hundred or more whales gather in a single lagoon. Until 1888 San Diego Bay was one of the chosen waters, but whalers there changed the pattern; also, increasing boat traffic kept them away. San Diego Bay was the point farthest north where any whales mated or calved, and occasionally one still starts into the narrow entrance before it turns and leaves.

Marineland, lying on a cliff 100 feet above the ocean, is a good vantage point for whale watchers. During the months when the huge mammals are offshore, boats from Long Beach, Redondo Beach and other harbors along the coast, as well as from a landing at Marineland, make cruises into the lane of migration. A tall observation tower at Marineland also affords a wider view of the passing cetaceans on their long ocean journey.

6. *Travel*

Travelers usually came to Los Angeles by sailing vessel to San Pedro. Memoirs tell of the startling arrival on shore where two stages waited, each harnessed to six or eight broncos. The instant the last passenger was aboard, the horrified travelers found themselves taking part in a mad race, each stage trying to reach Los Angeles first. Usually the drivers had been drinking heavily while waiting to leave and were cheerfully reckless. On and on over the unpaved road the coaches raced, bouncing through ruts and holes as the drivers lashed their broncos and swore at them in Spanish and English. Appalled, the newly arrived passengers stared at the strange landscape: strings of beef were hung to dry over ranchhouse fences; weird, scrawny birds — roadrunners — scudded over the plains; thousands of ground squirrels ran to their burrows, looking to the unaccustomed eye like huge rats.

At Halfway House the horses were changed, and then the coaches raced along what remained of the twenty-mile trip from the harbor. Reaching the outskirts of town, the competing drivers began to shout (in later years they blew horns, which made more noise) and the excitement mounted. Every dog nearby joined the race, adding barks and howls to the uproar. The coaches rocked and bounced their way to the finish line, the Bella Union and Lafayette Hotels, and the bone-shattering ride ended at last.

North of Los Angeles the steep slopes of hills in Cahuenga Pass left room for only a narrow trail for horses until 1852, when a wagon road was built. Before that year, travel between San Fernando Valley and El Pueblo was around the hills just north of town, near the course of the Los Angeles River. Similarly, only a trail led over the San Fernando Pass through the mountains, a trail too narrow and steep for stagecoaches or wagons to navigate. The earliest explorers thought the mountains impassable, and they went no farther than the Santa Clara Valley, where they turned westward until they reached the coast near present-day Ventura. Later Governor Pedro Fages, in pursuit of deserters from the Spanish army, discovered what became known as Tejón (Badger) Pass, which gave northern access through the mountains. Today's Tejón Pass (twenty miles west of the original Tejón Pass, now Oak Creek Pass) marks the northwest corner of Los Angeles County.

In the early 1850s the pathway leading up from the San Fernando Valley was a hard enough climb but harder and more dangerous to descend. Sometimes mules fell over precipices. The transportation problem seriously held back the development of Los Angeles, but the

State Legislature in Northern California was indifferent to the need for roads in the remote Southland.

Phineas Banning had the enterprise to solve this problem. He arranged with other merchants who would benefit from trade to subscribe to a fund for clearing and leveling a roadway through San Fernando Pass. Chinese were hired to start fixing the worst part of the road, but the project went along slowly because the merchants were reluctant to give the necessary money. Finally, to boost enthusiasm, Banning tried a dramatic stunt: some of the men hardest to convince were invited to drive with him over that pass. The climb was steep, and the passengers went the last part of the way up on foot to make it easier for the horses. From the top there was a sharp drop, and no one dared to enter the coach; so, alone on the driver's seat, Phineas urged the horses forward. Down the winding, rocky, perilous road the carriage lurched, with Banning's foot hard on the brake. All the way he kept the coach under control — something which could never have been done before work on the road had been started. None of the passengers was willing to face such a ride, but they all conceded that the road could become usable at least for mule trains. The men paid into the fund, and many more Chinese were hired for the project. Within a year a wagon train of five 10-mule teams made the trip from Los Angeles to Fort Tejón (75 miles north of the city) in nine days. This gave impetus to more subscriptions toward improving the road and sparked the move toward extending land connections with the rest of the continent.

When it was finished, the United States Government hired John Butterfield (who later organized the American Express Company) to maintain an overland mail route between San Francisco and St. Louis via Los Angeles and El Paso, beginning in 1858. (The southern part of the route was suspended during the Civil War, because Texas was a hostile Confederate state.) The Butterfield Stage Line, carrying mail and passengers, covered its 3000-mile route in about 22 days with both driver and conductor heavily armed. Arrivals and departures were so irregular that often passengers were left behind, and during the rainy season, when the usually dry Los Angeles riverbed became impossible to cross, the coaches were sometimes delayed as much as a week.

The route north avoided crossing mountains as much as possible. It led from the San Fernando Mission over the mountain pass, through the sites of present-day Newhall and Saugus, then along the San Francisquito Canyon to Elizabeth Lake. From there the route skirted Antelope Valley to Fort Tejón.

Freight was carried over the mountain pass in mule-drawn trains of wagons. Some places on the road were so steep that the wagons ascended with the aid of windlasses, and a chock block fastened behind a rear wheel prevented a wagon from rolling back down the hill. Chains and ropes were used to help in descent. It was a welcome day when, in 1863, General Edward F. Beale hacked a narrow pass between two hills and lowered an especially difficult grade by 91 feet.

Phineas Banning established wagon routes to Santa Fe and Salt Lake City. (During winter, Utah's only open roads were in the direction of Southern California.) In 1861 Remi Nadeau, a French Canadian, arrived in Los Angeles with a team of oxen, and Prudent Beaudry, also a French Canadian, loaned him enough money to launch into business as a teamster. Before long he was operating a wagon route to Salt Lake City and Montana, and north in California to the Kern River. But most important, he ran twenty-mule teams between Los Angeles and the Cerro Gordo silver mines in Inyo County, which for six years provided one-fourth of the entire exports of San Pedro harbor.

Today the mountains on the route north have been cut and reshaped so that without steep grades the freeways sweep easily along wide pathways. No hint remains of the problems facing travelers a little over a century ago.

On the road north
to Fort Tejón, Beale's
Cut eased a steeply
plunging grade.
(*—Title Insurance &
Trust Company*)

7. *Fort Tejón and the Camel Trains*

Fort Tejón was established in 1854 to supervise the area near Tejón Pass and try to end the increasing problem of stock rustling; in addition it was a stopping place for troops and travelers. At that time the fort was in Los Angeles County, but with the boundary change in 1866 the site is now about seven miles within Kern County.

The open cattle ranges of the Southland left outlying ranchos almost helpless against rustlers. Outlaws and Indians drove cattle and horses across the Mojave Desert to be sold in Salt Lake City, or led the animals north from mountain ranchos to the San Joaquin Valley. No cattle at all could be kept on Rancho La Liebre, while the San Fernando Mission area, near as it was to Los Angeles, lost over 4000 horses to marauders within four years. As soon as the fort began a patrol of the mountains as well as approaches to the desert, cattle rustling decreased.

On January 9, 1857, the Tejón region, which lies along the San Andreas Fault, was shaken by a great earthquake. For three days violent quakes continued at intervals, and land ruptured along a distance of 200 miles. Fort Tejón itself was mainly unharmed, because the epicenter of the quake was in the almost unpopulated hills nearby, where there was one fatality, a woman killed by the collapse of a building. The intensity of the earthquake was probably the same as that of the San Francisco earthquake of 1906.

Transportation of supplies for the fort across the Mojave Desert from Yuma was difficult, and in 1855 Jefferson Davis, Secretary of War, persuaded Congress to buy camels to supplant the less practicable horses and mules. Camels drink about four or five gallons of water at a time but then need none for three days. They prefer sagebrush and thistles to grass, journey long distances without tiring, need little care and can easily carry loads of 600 pounds. Seventy-five camels were brought from Egypt and Arabia to Texas; 28 were then sent to Fort Tejón, where they arrived in 1857. Not only were the animals used for crossing the desert, but every few weeks a camel caravan from the fort arrived in Los Angeles on its way to buy military provisions in San Pedro. The entire town would gather to watch the strange procession through the streets, and memoirs of townspeople speak of this as being the most fascinating sight in their lives.

In 1861 the Federal Government began to withdraw its troops from the fort. After it was completely abandoned, the buildings fell into ruin; weeds and trees invaded the trim fields. It was not until

Camel at Drum Barracks, San Pedro, during the Civil
War. (—*Courtesy, Robert Kirsch and William S. Murphy*)

1940 that California acquired the central five acres and began to
restore the historic buildings. (The site lies beside the Golden State
Freeway only 77 miles from downtown Los Angeles and is open to
visitors at all hours.)

When withdrawal began, the camels were brought to Los Angeles
to be used for desert transportation between San Pedro and Tucson,
Arizona. At first they were kept in a corral on Main Street between
First and Second, but people were afraid of the ill-natured beasts
who kicked and bit, and within a few months the animals were moved
to Camp Drum in San Pedro. (Drum Barracks, once the officers' quarters at Camp Drum, is at 1053 Cary Avenue in Wilmington.) Two
skilled camel drivers, Greek George and Hi Jolly — an English pronunciation of the Arabic name Hadj Ali — tried to train Mexicans and
Indians to take care of the animals, but unsuccessfully: most of the
camels soon died. When only a few remained they were taken north
to Benicia, near San Francisco, to be sold at auction, and Greek
George and Hi Jolly went with them. The animals were bought for
the purpose of carrying freight, mainly in Nevada, but mules used
by other freighters stampeded whenever a camel approached. Faced
with increasing antagonism, the new owner sold some of the camels
to General Beale, who had bought ranchland near Fort Tejón, and
took the remainder to Fort Yuma to sell, but as he reached Arizona

he died. Stranded, Hi Jolly and Greek George had no way to take care of the camels so turned them loose onto the desert. Later the Silver King mining company caught some and used them for carrying ore to Yuma, but others remained in the desert. For many years travelers in the sparse land told eerie tales of ghostly apparitions — the unexpected vision of a camel in the distance, lumbering clumsily across the plains, homeless and solitary.

8. *The First Towns*

Outside the city of Los Angeles, no towns were founded in the county until 1851, when El Monte became the first American town incorporated in Southern California. At the end of the Santa Fe Trail several willow groves made an inviting camping-place on the banks of the San Gabriel River; because of the green oasis, the spot was called El Monte (Willow Grove in the California idiom). The area was public land and free from any private land grant; so a community arose there, and the many natural springs made farming easy. Ira Thompson built a stage depot with the name Willow Grove, and the first house was built nearby. The "Monte boys" earned a reputation in Los Angeles for being daredevils who liked to stir up excitement.

The same year that El Monte was founded, 150 ox-drawn wagons filed southward from Salt Lake City bringing 437 men, women and children as well as herds of over a thousand oxen, cows, horses, mules and sheep. The people were Mormons, planning to establish a colony in the San Gabriel Valley. They bought part of Rancho San Bernardino, owned by Diego Sepúlveda and three sons of Don Antonio María Lugo, and founded San Bernardino. There they laid out a town similar in plan to Salt Lake City, with right-angled blocks of eight acres and irrigation canals alongside the roadways. The Mormons are famous for their industry, and this community was no exception: they brought lumber from the hills, and Los Angeles benefited from their products such as corn, wheat, vegetables, chickens, eggs and butter. In 1857, however, all Mormons outside of Utah were suddenly recalled to Salt Lake City by Brigham Young, President of the Mormon Church. Washington had received reports of illegal activities in Utah, including the practice of polygamy, and was sending an army of 3000 men to enforce Federal authority. Young wished to strengthen the Mormon home community before the army arrived. About two-thirds of the colonists in San Bernardino prepared to answer Young's call, and in hasty departure they sold their property in the thriving community at low prices.

During that same year, a group of fifty Germans from San Francisco bought 1200 acres of land near the Santa Ana River. They named their settlement Anaheim, blending the river's name and the German word for "home." Around the property about 50,000 willow cuttings were planted, which made a live fence of interlacing branches. Each colonist was assigned a twenty-acre lot, and thousands of grapevines were set out: Anaheim became one large vineyard. Visitors came to gaze at its cool beauty — the immense expanse of dark green grapeleaves framed by the lighter green of graceful willow trees. In 1888 a mysterious blight destroyed the entire vineyard; after that, orange and walnut groves were laid out instead.

At San Pedro Bay, when Phineas Banning stepped ashore in 1851 at the end of a long voyage from Philadelphia, he looked around expecting to find a bustling harbor town such as he had seen in eastern ports. To his amazement there was no town at all. The only structures were a hide warehouse, a corral and a small hut on the beach used as "headquarters" for a company which forwarded cargoes. All commerce was in the town of Los Angeles, about twenty miles distant. The harbor itself was so shallow and filled with submerged sand bars that no ship could go near shore; instead small boats carried goods and people to land — a long expanse of mudflats, since the only beach was a narrow sandy shelf beneath a precipitous cliff.

On the very day he arrived, Banning saw that steps should be taken to make the harbor more serviceable for shipping. He was then 21, and at 28 he decided it was time to start the project. On land he had already bought, he laid out a town named New San Pedro, later changed to Wilmington after his hometown in Delaware. There he built a home, warehouses and corrals, and created a channel along which lighters could bring ships' cargoes to a long wharf on shore. This was not the only project engaged in by the genial, enthusiastic and enterprising young man. When Federal troops were later quartered in Wilmington, at Drum Barracks, a letter from one of the soldiers in 1861 gives some idea of the range of Banning's activities:

Wilmington is a lovely topographical spot. . . . The town consists of Mr. Banning's residence and Mr. Banning's blacksmith shop where Government mules are shod and Government wagons repaired; Banning's soap and tallow factory where Uncle Sam buys soap for us soldiers; Banning's jerked beefery where Uncle Sam buys jerked beef for Drum Barracks . . . ; and Mr. Banning's wharf and warehouses and road; and the whole is covered with Mr. Banning's heavens and rests on Mr. Banning's earth and sea. Banning's steamers crawfish and tote baggage and mules and Sanchos [a term sometimes used for the common soldier in the Southwest] from the steamers, *Senator* and *Wright* to Banning's wharf, a distance of five miles.

He might have added that Banning had built Drum Barracks; that he had constructed a nine-mile flume to bring water there from the San Gabriel River; that, without charge, he handled all the mail which came to Los Angeles by steamer; that, in partnership, he ran a stage line from the port of Wilmington, as well as mule teams banded into wagon trains for large shipments.

Although El Monte, San Bernardino, Anaheim and Wilmington were successfully established, there was as yet no tremendous growth in the population of Los Angeles and no surge to found additional settlements. Wilmington was the last of the new communities for another decade.

9. *Floods and Drought*

When Hugo Reid was in Northern California in 1849 and saw the shortages caused by the influx of miners there, he wrote a letter to Abel Stearns which launched a new era for the Southland. Reid noted the prices in San José and San Francisco for beef and tallow, mentioning that in all Monterey there was not one candle for sale. He suggested to Don Abel that cattle should be killed and sent north on a sailing vessel, but instead the letter signaled the beginning of great cattle drives up the coast. In early spring when the grass was green from winter rains, herds of 700 to 2500 cattle started on the way. Living off the country, they each day covered about 12 of the 430 miles to San Francisco, going circuitously through passes and grassy country. There were few rustlers and few stampedes, although occasionally an entire herd was lost before reaching its destination. An amazing thing is that these colorful drives of enormous herds up the coast have found little mention in annals of the Far West.

By 1856 mines in the north were no longer bringing in the large returns of earlier years. Also, cattle came on trails from the Middle West and New Mexico. The demand for cattle from the Southland fell, and prices followed.

Then weather began to compound a tragedy. After an exceptionally dry year in 1859, when the adobe earth had become hard under the perpetual sun, the December skies suddenly flooded the land with 12 inches of rain within one day and night. The hard ground could not absorb the moisture: the Los Angeles River changed its course by about a quarter mile; walls of buildings caved in; mining equipment in the San Gabriel Mountains was washed away or completely ruined.

In 1861, again beginning just before Christmas, fifty inches of rain fell during a month-long downpour. Thousands of head of cattle perished. For several weeks no mail reached Los Angeles because of impassable floods, and all business ceased. In contrast, the next year was one of drought, which grew even more severe the year after when during the so-called "rainy season" of winter there was no trace of rain until a few drops fell late in March. More heat and harsh, dry winds followed.

At first the horses were slaughtered in order to save the grazing lands for cattle, which had greater cash value, but after a while there was little pasture to be found anywhere. What had once been rich land between Wilmington and Los Angeles was now described by a drover as "a regular mass of dead cattle." The piteous bawling of hungry calves fell achingly on the ears of ranch families at night. How were the animals to be saved from the misery of starvation and thirst? How was the land to be kept free from the stench of rotting carcasses? As one answer, hundreds of cattle, sheep, horses and mules were led to Palos Verdes and driven over the cliffs onto the rocks below. No chapter in the history of the world's cattle ranges can be sadder than that in which anguished vaqueros drove their skeletal herds to mass suicide.

The only oasis was Anaheim. The irrigation system built there by German settlers still kept the land green. So many thousands of despairing cattle tried to force their way through the willow fence to the grass beyond that an armed guard had to keep them out in order to protect the Anaheimers' homes and the grazing land needed by their own cattle.

With summer, which even normally was dry, the drought intensified. Millions of grasshoppers appeared, spreading further devastation. Coyotes, bears and even mountain lions came down from the hills and fell on the listless herds. In the city of Los Angeles no taxes were collected, and merchants stopped giving credit. An example of the widespread hopelessness was the sheriff's auction in 1864 of four corner lots — two at Fifth and Main, one at Fifth and Spring, the other at Fourth and Broadway — to be sold because of delinquent taxes of 63 cents per lot. No buyers came to make a bid.

As the drought continued well into another year, with summer dryness even in winter, there were no buyers for cattle even at $1.50 a head. According to a Los Angeles newspaper, a herd of 5000 cattle in Santa Barbara brought 37 cents each.

To the problems which were already overwhelming, a smallpox plague was added. The epidemic spread almost uncontrollably, because there were many people who could not understand the importance of following government rules: outbreaks of smallpox were concealed from the authorities; quarantine regulations were ignored. Furthermore, there were few doctors in the large towns, and outlying areas had no medical care at all. In self-protection against the epidemic, vaqueros were stationed at approaches to the ranchos, to watch and question anyone coming near.

10. Land Grants in Jeopardy

Unexpectedly, one of the chief causes of financial disaster for the rancheros was the annexation of California to the United States. When Commodore Sloat took possession of Monterey in 1846, he issued a proclamation that "all persons holding titles to real estate or in quiet possession of lands . . . shall have those titles guaranteed to them." The Treaty of Guadalupe Hidalgo reaffirmed the protection of property rights, but shortly after Congress accepted California into the Union it passed a law challenging all the land titles in the new state. Most of the inhabited area of the Southland was covered by Spanish-Mexican grants. (Officially, "private land grants" meant property owned privately, and "public lands" belonged to the pueblos and presidios. In general usage, "land grants" referred to ranchos.) Possession had to be proved before the U.S. Land Board Commission, or the land would be forfeited. Litigation was at the landowner's expense.

It was Senator Gwin of California who, in Washington, proposed the Congressional Act of 1851 which challenged all California titles. Senator Frémont objected, and Senator Thomas Hart Benton protested that in Louisiana — acquired by the Louisiana Purchase of 1803 — and West Florida, where the same system had been put into effect, some claims had remained unsettled for forty years and many claimants were forced into bankruptcy. Benton suggested that it would be better to require a trial only if there were a question of fraud. However, he argued in vain, as Gwin's resolution was passed.

No land which was granted after July 7, 1846, the date when the American flag was raised at Monterey, was accepted as legal by the U.S. Land Board Commission. Annexation of California by the United States was considered by the board to have taken place at that time instead of at the signing of the Treaty of Cahuenga on January 13, 1847. (Because the United States allowed only grants made before the opening of the war instead of the end, Governor Pico was later accused of granting land fraudulently.)

The fact that hearings before the Land Commission were to be held in San Francisco, far from Washington, D.C., was a stumbling block for several months. One after another, competent men refused to serve on the three-member commission. At last, early in 1852, the hearings began. They continued through five years.

It was a government rule that when any case was decided against the United States in favor of a ranchero, it would automatically be appealed to a higher court. This meant that the landowners were put in double jeopardy — if they won they still had to fight for their titles. However, the higher court was impartial: many times a ranchero who had been denied title after hearings by the Land Commission found the decision reversed by the district court when he appealed his case. Some appeals were carried up to the Supreme Court. Between the filing of a claim and receipt of the patent, an average of 17 years went by — almost an entire generation. By 1885, after 33 years, 97% of the cases had been decided.

In 1852, as the hearings began, rancheros frantically started an intensive search for papers which would prove ownership. To their dismay, many of the necessary documents had been lost or destroyed — not only the landowners' personal documents, but also official records among the pueblo archives. The "protocols," or records of juridical possession given by pueblo authorities, had been hidden when the Americans approached Los Angeles during the war, and afterward they were never found.

Also, most of the private land grants with an early origin were difficult to prove. Frequently landmarks casually chosen to define boundaries — such as a large cactus plant, a mound of stones, a tree — all of them completely acceptable at the time of granting, had been destroyed by a flood or drought. Eyewitnesses were no longer alive and able to help prove a claim. Luckily there were a few rancheros from the early days — for example, Antonio María Lugo (76 years old when the hearings opened), José Antonio Carrillo and Manuel Dominguez — who recalled details about some of the ranchos as far back as the beginning of the century. The rancheros, unfamiliar with American laws and procedures, were suddenly involved in a situation strange to them in every way. And they were saddled with the expense of litigation which went on for years, even decades.

Washington was far away, too far away for the Federal Government to understand the different customs of the Southland. Southern ranchers banded together to petition the board, in San Francisco, to meet in Los Angeles, saying they faced the prospect of forfeiting a third of the land in Los Angeles County because expenses were too great. The board members therefore came to Los Angeles but stayed only two days. Their lodgings were at the Bella Union, the "finest hotel south of San Francisco," but by northern standards the building was primitive. The board hastened back to San Francisco and continued to hold hearings at a distance, as before, although at special times it sent representatives south to take the testimony of witnesses in Los Angeles.

As it turned out, forty percent of the land in Los Angeles County whose owners' claims were proven valid was nevertheless lost to them in an effort to meet costs. On some of this land families had lived legally and happily for forty or fifty years. At the time the grants were given, there were no licensed surveyors, no lawyers; the modern, legal appraisal had no relation whatever to the simple, personal transaction that had originally taken place. From the viewpoint of the United States, however, careful investigation was necessary. There was no way to prosecute false claims while leaving legitimate ones unquestioned, and therefore the government had to make a blanket ruling for proof of all titles.

Along with the private landowners, Los Angeles had to present its claim to land. Instructions for the founding of the Pueblo of Los Angeles issued by Felipe de Neve in 1788 were presented. His wording included two contradictory orders: the pueblo was to be to "the extent of four common leagues" and "two [leagues] to each cardinal point," with boundary distances measured from the center of the Plaza. On one hand the size would be four square leagues; on the other hand it would be four leagues square, an area of sixteen square leagues. At first the pueblo settlers accepted the smaller size, but later the town authorities realized that the larger would be just as legal. Of course Los Angeles asked the Land Commission for title to the larger amount. The case hinged upon presentation of evidence that the pueblo's boundaries had ever been so measured, and Agustín Olvera was the crucial witness. He testified that sixteen square leagues was the size intended by the Ayuntamiento; several times that body had ordered the boundaries to be measured accordingly, but not until 1841 was a survey finally begun. A surveyor and two witnesses (one of them Olvera) started from the doors of the Plaza church and measured two leagues to the east. They then returned to the church doors and measured two leagues to the west, and next to the south. At that point the surveyor in charge was taken ill and measurements were halted. They never were finished. The Land Commission rejected the claim for sixteen square leagues, instead accepting a claim for four. And Los Angeles had no one to blame but herself.

The board treated all mission lands as one case, although after the decision each mission received an individual patent. The mission claim was made by Archbishop Joseph S. Alemany, who in 1850 had been sent to California from Baltimore, Maryland, the center of the Roman Catholic Church in the United States. Each "ex-mission" was allowed only the mission site plus the cemeteries and gardens pertaining to it. For San Gabriel this meant 177.78 acres, and for San Fernando 68.02 acres.

When Texas was annexed to the United States at the end of 1845, Governor Pico knew that California was approaching a crisis. No funds were sent from Mexico for military preparedness, and so on March 2, 1846, he explained his problem to the Legislative Assembly, suggesting that money could be obtained by selling the missions. The assembly gave its approval, and in June both San Gabriel and San Fernando were sold. The Land Commission questioned the sales but in the end confirmed Pico's right to sell San Fernando Mission lands. However, on the basis that San Gabriel Mission had not been abandoned, its sale was invalidated.

The government records which would prove ownership of land were called the Spanish Archives and included documents of the Mexican as well as the Spanish regime, written entirely in the Spanish language. Dr. Jacob N. Bowman, for many years Historian in Charge of State Archives in Sacramento, gives an account of the dramatic odyssey of the Spanish Archives in his manuscript, "History of the Provincial Archives of California." After the Battle of La Mesa, when the American forces moved into Los Angeles, Commodore Stockton issued a notice that all archives were to be turned over to him or there would be a severe penalty for the person hiding them. Consequently, Don Luis Vignes sent word that some were in his home. Colonel Frémont had the papers taken from Don Luis' house, wrapped into bales with a protective covering of blankets and sent north to Sutter's Fort by mule. Still later they were taken to Monterey, but by then they were in bad condition and many had been lost. The Americans in Monterey were unfamiliar with Spanish, and to them the battered bales of paper had no significance; they were carelessly stowed in whatever space was available and then forgotten.

After a while Dr. James L. Ord arrived to take charge of the military hospital. On shelves along one side of a hospital room he found piles of Spanish papers. No one knew anything about them, and often they were used as waste paper. Then Lt. H. W. Halleck, Secretary of

State under Governor Richard B. Mason, noticed that a scrap of paper on the floor was an official document. Immediately he deduced that quite probably important records were on the shelves, and he went to the commanding officer to suggest that all the papers be kept in a storeroom. Months later he was put in charge of sorting and indexing them and making a report to Congress about the California land grants. The papers were moved several times from one town to another but eventually were deposited with the U.S. surveyor general in San Francisco. Records of local governments were returned to their places of origin, except those connected with land cases.

The Spanish Archives had not yet finished their strange odyssey. All the expedientes (original documents connected with each land case) were put into a large iron safe in the office of the surveyor general. Then on April 18, 1906, San Francisco was shaken by a devastating earthquake followed by a conflagration; an estimated 28,000 buildings were destroyed, among them the surveyor general's office.

In the building there were two similar iron safes. One was opened too soon, and as oxygen entered, everything in the safe burst into flames. The other safe held the Spanish Archives. Before the fate of the papers could be determined, it was necessary to wait several days until the safe became thoroughly cool. Finally the door was opened, and with great care the irreplaceable documents were brought out. The edges of those nearest the door were badly charred (these included about a fifth of the 21 volumes of expedientes). The Spanish Archives on open shelves were wholly burned, except for a few papers which had been removed for use in current law cases. Fortunately, the expedientes of most of the 848 land grant cases in California (all except for a few which were being used and therefore had been kept outside) were in the iron safe; most of the papers of the Land Commission were in the safe also. Among the documents burned to ashes were the 108 Titulos (Title papers issued by the governor), and the only Toma de Razon (state register of grants and brands) which had been found when the government of California changed hands. (Originally there had been eight. The two Tomas de Razon among the records taken to Luis Vignes' house in Los Angeles were lost or destroyed. Of the eight Tomas, none supposedly remained after the San Francisco fire, but recently Dr. Bowman discovered one which had been thought lost in a fire in 1851. Apparently the valuable book had been taken from the burning building and stored safely elsewhere but then was forgotten and later unrecognized when it was found, until Dr. Bowman identified it about 100 years later. This is the only Toma de Razon still in existence, now in the State Library at Sacramento.)

The documents and ashes were taken to Washington, D.C. All original documents as well as records of the court cases are kept in the National Archives there. An act of the California State Legislature required that copies should be made of the private land grant records, including expedientes: they are held in the State Archives Building at 1020 "O" Street, Sacramento. In 1961 the Federal Government placed other copies, made at the time of the Land Commission hearings and bound in separate dossiers for each rancho, on loan with the Bancroft Library on the University of California campus in Berkeley. All the copies were handwritten.

Fortunately, Hubert Howe Bancroft, a San Francisco book publisher, had devoted his fortune to the preservation of the history of the West, from Alaska to Panama. At his own expense he kept a staff of as many as 50 research assistants at a time, and during one period 15 of them worked solely on abstracting and copying the Spanish Archives (at a cost to Bancroft of $18,000). After the destruction of original papers, his project became invaluable. In 63 volumes, Bancroft's copies were assembled as the California Archives. In addition he sent men to interview pioneers so that their recollections could be written down. Families donated their historical records and manuscripts (such as there were, since few people in the early days of colonization in the Southwest could read or write). Those which were not given, he bought. Some few families, suspecting the purpose of an interview or a request to see old documents, indignantly refused.

Several times Bancroft's collection was threatened by fire, and finally he bought a large San Francisco houselot, in the center of which — so as to be well apart from other buildings — a brick structure was erected with iron shutters at all the windows. The California collection was in that building at the time of the Great Fire of San Francisco. The library had just been sold to the University of California in Berkeley, where it could be more widely used for research, but the books and documents had not yet been moved across the Bay. From Berkeley, people watched in horror as San Francisco went up in flames, and they thought that involved in the tragedy was the irreplaceable historical collection. However, it was undamaged and today is stored in a thoroughly fireproof building.

During the time of litigation the rancheros found their income decimated by the years of drought and the lack of demand for their cattle in markets to the north. To meet expenses they seldom had any ready money. Since there were no banks in the Southland there was no logical place for money to be deposited at the time cattle were sold, and as a result no savings accumulated. Furthermore, when

At the place where now North Broadway crosses the Los Angeles River, this water wheel drew water from the river to start its flow through the Zanja Madre. (*—Los Angeles Department of Water & Power*)

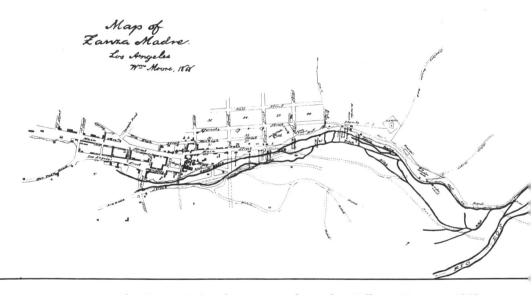

The Zanja Madre, from a map drawn by William Moore in 1868. (—Adapted from *Maps of Los Angeles* by W. W. Robinson. Los Angeles: Dawson's Book Shop, 1966)

it became necessary to mortgage land, the lack of banks meant that loans were made by individuals. Rates varied widely from two to eight percent a month, compounded monthly; sometimes interest equaled the entire amount of the mortgage within one year. Yet the rancheros had scanty new income with which to pay off the debt and little comprehension of the danger they were risking when the mortgage was arranged.

Julio Verdugo lost Rancho San Rafael because of interest on a mortgage. Vicente Lugo lost all his land and cattle; only his wife's inherited property remained. José del Carmen Lugo gave his signature as bond for some friends and later had to sacrifice his house and land to meet the obligation. Don Pío Pico lost all of his property except for a small ranch, and when finally even that was gone he spent his last years entirely dependent on the generosity of relatives and friends.

The Sepúlveda family, after 18 years of uncertainty about ownership of Rancho de los Palos Verdes, was finally given title to the land. During those years there had been a total of 78 lawsuits, including an appeal to the Supreme Court and a great many suits against squatters who tried to take possession. To meet expenses the Sepúlvedas had to borrow on the land, and to repay the debt or meet interest payments land was forfeited. More property was lost through inability to pay taxes.

Henry Dalton, too, had to take his claim for Rancho San Francisquito to the Supreme Court before his ownership was approved, and during that time squatters moved onto the land. To meet expenses he mortgaged Rancho Asusa de Dalton and his part of Ranchos San José and San José Addition; those mortgages were foreclosed. In the court battle for Rancho San Francisquito the squatters declared that for years he had not had possession, to which he replied that the lands had been forcibly held from him. The Secretary of the Interior was the final judge in that case: he decided in favor of the squatters, on the basis that since Dalton had failed to keep the people out he had not held the land in continuous possession for himself.

In 1852 most of the leading landowners were Mexican-Californians, but ten years later those names had almost entirely dropped from the list. Los Angeles County lowered its assessment of range land to 10 cents an acre, and of cattle to about $1.50 a head. Most of the property taxes in the county became delinquent, the list including such proud names as Phineas Banning, Pío Pico, Manuel Dominguez and José Sepúlveda. The home of María Rita Valdez — the valiant woman who owned Rancho Rodeo de las Aguas — was next door to the Bella

Union Hotel, and by 1859 delinquent taxes on the house had accumulated to the sum of five dollars. The home was sold at sheriff's auction.

Don Abel Stearns at one time owned approximately 200,000 acres of ranch land in Los Angeles, besides more land toward San Diego. He built up the largest land-and-cattle empire in Southern California. Thousands of his cattle died during the drought, and he sold most of the remainder to pay off debts. Mortgages which he had taken out in order to tide himself over times of financial trouble became due, although he had no more ready money than earlier. Court expenses continued for years as he tried to prove title claims before the U.S. Land Commission. One after another of his ranchos was advertised to be sold at auction because of incredibly small sums due — $14.07 on Rancho La Habra of 6698 acres, $12.10 on Rancho Cajon de Santa Ana of 21,572 acres. In 1858 his property had been valued at twice that of the next most wealthy landowner, but six years later the list of Stearns' delinquent properties filled two entire pages.

But let no one think that all was disaster. In the property assessment of 1863, Agustín Olvera noted as part of his wealth: "Two fine daughters. No price — value cannot be computed. Great! Great!"

The enormous expanse of ranch land was now an economic problem which Southern California had to solve or become an impoverished back country. The land had proven undependable as a cattle range while large-scale farming was impossible because of lack of irrigation. The heavy interest rates charged by private moneylenders laid a heavy burden on any project to improve the land. Uncertainty of land titles discouraged long-term efforts.

From the shadows of what seemed complete disaster, the Southland made a drastic turn away from the life and customs that had been. The so-called Age of the Dons has been considered glorious by many. It had a quality of singular glamor. But nevertheless a weary, bankrupt Southland stepped with relief into a vibrant, new era.

VI

AMERICANIZATION OF THE SOUTHLAND 1868-1900

1. *Land Boom*

Americanization of the Southland began in 1868. That year marked the beginning of the land boom, the building of a railroad between Los Angeles and San Pedro (which before long became part of a transcontinental line), the founding of the first bank, the digging of the first successful artesian well in Los Angeles — to be followed a few decades later by the incredible aqueduct which brought more water than could be used, from a river 240 miles away. Everything combined to create a totally new type of existence. Yes, 1868 was indeed a magic year!

It was the Stearns Empire that led the way. The ranch land of Don Abel Stearns stretched from Laguna on the south to Pomona on the north, covering 278 square miles of coastland, plain, hills and valleys. The land included the Rancho Los Coyotes (48,825 acres), Rancho La Habra (6698 acres), Rancho San Juan Cajón de Santa Ana (21,572 acres), Rancho Las Bolsas y Paredes (33,509) acres, Rancho La Bolsa Chica (8272 acres), Rancho La Jurupa (41,168 acres) and Rancho La Sierra (17,752 acres).

Bankrupt, Don Abel put his lands into the care of a trust. It advanced him money enough to pay all his debts, and besides his part interest in the trust he was to receive $1.50 per acre of all land which was sold. The remaining profit would be divided among the other members of the trust. The selling agent, the Los Angeles and San Bernardino Land Co., had a map made of the extensive property, dividing it into 640-acre tracts which in turn were subdivided into towns and also farms of 20 to 160 acres. Maps were sent to Europe and throughout the United States, along with advertisements of the marvels of Southern California.

Don Abel failed to live long enough to see the land revolution he had set in motion, but before he died in 1871 he was completely free of debt.

Other ranch land had been subdivided earlier than Don Abel's —
for instance, part of Ranchos San Antonio and Santa Gertrudes — but
sales were not extensive. The subdividing of Stearns' enormous acreage in 1868, however, coincided with the immigration of eastern families seeking new fields after the Civil War. At the same time there
was a surge of migration from the north, where terrible floods in 1867
caused a yearning among people there to seek an easier livelihood in
the Southland.

The farmland offered for sale was low-priced, its advertised advantages fabulous. As yet there were no railroads into Southern California, so canvas-topped prairie schooners brought many of the new
families from Northern California and the East. The migration was
increased by Danish, Swiss, English, German and French settlers — all
drawn by the blandishments of those original "boosters."

Robert M. Widney opened the first real estate office and published
the first paper devoted to the sale of land. He was an all-purpose
agent: in his monthly *Real Estate Advertiser* he announced property
for sale; in his office he sold land to people who arrived in answer to
the ads; as a lawyer he settled disputes over boundaries. Because
he was a man of high reputation, money was trustingly mailed to him
for investment as he thought best.

In "colony" settlements, such as Riverside, development was organized. For instance, advertisements suggested that buyers choose
small farms close to neighbors, in the form of a colony. Townsites
were usually laid out in advance, although others arose naturally at
main crossroads. Irrigation was provided by artesian wells or a canal
linked to some river. Among the colony settlements were Compton,
Los Nietos, Florence, Tustin City, Pasadena, Pomona, Whittier and
Alhambra.

But to make the Southland economically vital, it was necessary to
experiment in various industries. Before this, as a first step, flocks
of sheep had been put to graze on many of the ranchos, and by the
late 1860s the flocks had increased until thousands of the animals
roamed the valleys and plains. Sarah Bixby's reminiscences of days
on Rancho Los Cerritos tell of lonely Basque shepherds isolated on
the range, each tending a flock of about 2000 sheep. Seeing no one
but the driver of the wagon which brought weekly supplies, they were
cut off from human companionship except for twice a year, during the
spring and fall sheepshearing. As that time drew near, the shepherds
guided their separate flocks toward the ranch buildings, and a band
of Mexicans rode up to do the specialized work of shearing. Fifty or
sixty men came dressed as for a fiesta, wearing ruffled white shirts,

black broadcloth suits and sombreros decorated with silver braid. Their spirited horses carried saddles of tooled leather and silver-trimmed bridles. On the day of their arrival all was gaiety and excitement, but the next morning shearing began and the men appeared in brown overalls and red bandanas. When the work was finished the men, once more decked in finery, rode off to another rancho where flocks were waiting. With their departure the shepherds returned to their lonely vigil on the plains.

Basques are sheepmen, and a number of them were sheepowners in the San Fernando Valley. Outstanding among them were three brothers, Eugene, Philippe and Camille Garnier, who raised flocks which had a particularly fine grade of wool. Yet the industry was a most precarious one, subject to drought and to fluctuations in the wool market.

Here and there acreage was sown in grain, but the first large-scale attempt was made by Isaac Lankershim and Isaac Newton Van Nuys in 1876. In the eastern part of the San Fernando Valley, with dry farming, they were able to grow huge fields of wheat so successfully that shipments were sent abroad. Then other landowners planted large stands of wheat and barley. This was the beginning of diversified farming in Los Angeles.

The California Legislature had decided that the southern area was a splendid place for the establishment of a silkworm industry. Bounties were offered for planting mulberry trees where silkworms would breed and grow, but the industry proved to be a mirage. Although thousands of trees were planted, there were no factories for the production of silk thread from the tremendous quantity of silkworms, and the venture collapsed. The mulberry trees were replaced by orange groves.

At that time the citrus industry began to pick up stride. In 1873 the first navel orange trees arrived from Brazil. Although the trees would bear no fruit for five years, and then only two oranges to a tree, they were watched with high expectations. A barbed-wire fence and padlocked gate protected the trees from marauders. When the owner, Luther C. Tibbetts of Riverside, produced oranges 12 inches in circumference, the Southland erupted into a wild boom of orange groves of all types.

William Wolfskill had a grove of several thousand mission-type orange trees. In 1877 he was struck by the bright idea of filling an entire boxcar with the golden fruit and shipping it to St. Louis. The journey took weeks and the car had no refrigeration, but apparently the oranges arrived in good condition because the shipment was an immediate sellout.

In 1884, samples of fruit grown in Southern California were sent to the New Orleans Exposition and won most of the prizes. Later, as an advertisement of the wonders of California, a permanent exhibit of the state's products was sent to each fair throughout the nation.

Success was intoxicating, made more so by Frank Wiggins, a full-time publicity agent. He had arrived ill in Whittier and was carried from the train on a stretcher. The climate was so invigorating, however, that he recovered rapidly. From then on his mission in life was to tell the rest of the country how wonderful Southern California was. The chamber of commerce had been founded in 1873 by Judge Widney and ex-Governor John G. Downey among others, and Wiggins was put in charge of publicity. It was due primarily to the efforts of this one man that the entire nation became familiar with the advantages of living in the Southland.

The greatest boom year was 1887, for by then Los Angeles was linked with the rest of the United States by two railroads — the Southern Pacific and the Atchison, Topeka & Santa Fe. New subdivisions were announced by bands, parades and often elephants and other circus animals. A stirring tune did most to raise the pitch of excitement among the crowds, and at one time it was almost impossible to find enough musicians to fill the constant demand. Amid a fiesta-like atmosphere people were induced to drive out to new subdivisions; transportation and lunch were free. (Times have not changed: today real estate subdivisions are launched with free barbecues, free entertainment by musicians and screen stars, free prizes; airplanes — with free cocktails offered during the trip — bring customers without charge from San Francisco, Sacramento and San Diego.)

In the contagion of optimism, sales were made not only in the offices of real estate agents, but also in suddenly converted shops, in bars, on the curbstone. Promises became more and more extravagant — of theaters to be built, splendid hotels, etc., etc. Property changed hands sometimes twice or three times in a day. One of the most popular methods of sale was through a lottery: a number of chances were sold, equal to the number of lots there were in a tract, and those with lucky numbers got first choice.

Advertisements were flamboyant. For example, when Charles Maclay started a venture in San Fernando Valley, his notices declaimed:

Nature has designed our young queen, sitting by the sunset sea, bathing her feet in its pacific waters, her flowing hair touching our golden hills, her fairy fingers plucking the peach and the lily the year round — as one of the brightest constellations in the galaxy of stars of our never to be ruptured Union. No land so favored; none so promising.

Vernon, near downtown Los Angeles in an area now heavily industrialized, was advertised in 1887 by a poet's rapture:

> Go wing thy flight from star to star
> From world to luminous world as far
> As the universe spreads its flaming wall.
> Take all the pleasure of all the spheres,
> And multiply each through endless years,
> One winter at Vernon is worth them all.

In keeping with the attempt at romance, Alhambra named its main street Boabdil, after the last King of the Moors, who was driven from the Alhambra in Granada by Ferdinand and Isabella. Romance was tossed aside when the exuberance of the citizens wore off, and the name was changed from Boabdil to — Main Street.

In Cahuenga Valley, on the south side of the Hollywood hills, 640 acres were subdivided. One of the first purchasers was Ivar A. Weid. Another buyer was Horace Henderson Wilcox, who in 1887 divided 120 acres of his land into lots, listing the subdivision for sale under the name Hollywood, a word chosen by his wife because of its attractive sound. Later one of his heirs, Mrs. Daeida Wilcox Beveridge, traded three acres of land at Hollywood and Cahuenga Boulevards to Paul de Longpré, a famous artist, for three of his paintings.

A large part of the area now known as Hollywood belonged to Major Henry Hancock, who owned Rancho La Brea and land east as far as present-day Gower Street. When the land grant claim for Rancho La Brea had finally been settled in favor of the rancheros by the U.S. Supreme Court, the landowners were bankrupt. Henry Hancock, lawyer for the claimants, received some of the land in payment of his fee and bought the remainder. For legal assistance in Washington, D.C., Senator Cornelius Cole was given one-tenth of the ranch land. A street which runs through the Senator's area is named for him, and another for his son Willoughby. Other streets, too, have been named for early residents, among them Gower, Whitley and Plummer. A sedate community, Hollywood made its own local regulations, among them the prohibition of poolrooms and sale of liquor. Sheep in flocks of over 2000 were forbidden on Hollywood streets.

In the Midwest one freezing winter, a man named Daniel Berry read Charles Nordhoff's *California for Health, Pleasure and Residence,* which told of the wonders of the West Coast. His sister was ill, and her husband, Dr. Thomas B. Elliott, wanted to take her to live in a gentler climate. Because of the book's rapturous account, and a chance encounter with a Californian who affirmed that what the book said was true, Elliott formed "The California Colony of Indiana," made up of friends who wanted to join him in founding a settlement. That same year, 1873, a committee was sent west to find the best location. Berry was on the committee, and after he had spent several weeks investigating he was invited to visit Judge Benjamin S. Eaton at his home on Rancho San Pascual, a short distance north of downtown Los Angeles. At breakfast Berry greeted his host excitedly, saying he had had the first good night's sleep in three years. He explained that because of asthma he usually slept only a short time before he was forced to sit up for the remainder of the night, but here in the clear atmosphere the problem had disappeared. During that day Berry was shown flourishing orange groves and vineyards on the surrounding plain, and his excitement grew. The nearby mountains made a magnificent backdrop to the fertile land. Enthusiastically he sent a letter to the Indiana Colony saying that he had found a perfect spot. But the letter arrived just as a financial panic gripped eastern money markets, and he received a reply that most of the members could no longer afford to buy land; the move had to be abandoned. Undeterred, Berry formed a new group, the San Gabriel Orange Grove Association, composed mainly of people already living in California, though including his sister and brother-in-law from Indiana.

Rancho San Pascual had two owners: Benjamin D. Wilson, one of the earliest American settlers from the days when California was part of Mexico, and Dr. John Strother Griffin, ranking surgeon with Kearny and Stockton's forces during the Mexican War. Wilson preferred to keep his land, but Dr. Griffin was willing to sell his approximately 4000 acres for $25,000. He gave the settlers extra land free — land he didn't want and which they felt had no particular value but accepted because the taxes had already been paid. (The land bought from Dr. Griffin lay between today's Fair Oaks and Arroyo Seco Boulevards. Benjamin Wilson's land, now part of Pasadena, lay on the east side of Fair Oaks. The land which Dr. Griffin threw in at no cost is part of Altadena.)

On January 27, 1874, the 27 colonists gathered at their new property to choose lots. They arrived in carriages, on horseback and afoot, all bringing lunch baskets. After the picnic a roll call was taken to be sure that everyone was there, and then each family in turn announced its choice of land. In an amazing example of harmonious accord, within twenty minutes each family was assigned the plot it had chosen, with no altercations or counterclaims. Later Dr. Elliott wrote to an eastern friend familiar with Indian lore and asked for an Indian word which might be appropriate for the name of the community. The friend suggested "Pasadena," Chippewa for "valley" (erroneously "key, or crown, of the valley"), and the name was adopted by the colony. The beautiful settlement, with its extensive groves and vineyards, was on the railroad route into Los Angeles, and when a real estate boom was intensified by a rate war between the two transcontinental railroads in 1886, more and more people who arrived chose Pasadena for their home.

A group of expert horsemen living in Pasadena formed the Valley Hunt Club in 1888. That was the year of the Great Blizzard in New York. At a meeting the next fall the club members wished to celebrate New Year's Day in some unusual way, and they decided to emphasize the midwinter abundance of flowers and fruit in California. Someone had just returned from seeing the Festival of Roses in Nice, France, so the club voted to have a parade of decorated horses and carriages on January 1, 1890, at a park in Pasadena. Afterward there was to be a sports tournament with such contests as foot and bicycle races and a tug of war. Each winner would be crowned with a wreath of roses, and the event was called The Tournament of Roses. At the park, as the tournament began, a wagonload of oranges was piled high and people were invited to help themselves.

The parade immediately became famous, and in 1894 several organizations entered flower-covered floats. The first football game took place in 1902, an East-West game between Michigan and Stanford. It was a fiasco. Three times as many spectators arrived in Pasadena as there was seating capacity in Tournament Park (now part of the California Institute of Technology's athletic field). Because of the traffic jam the game started late, at 3 p.m., and ended after dark, with a final score of 49 to 0 in favor of Michigan. After that disaster no more football games were scheduled for 14 years; instead a polo match was held the next year and then chariot races modeled after those described in the bestseller *Ben-Hur*. The first official queen was chosen in 1905, and the parade from then on was a regal affair. The glamor of the annual Pasadena Rose Parade made the city well known across the country.

A new town was sometimes named by its subdivider for himself or for a special landmark; sometimes the name was chosen by vote of the residents. For instance, as today's Glendale developed, the people living there met to consider such suggestions as Verdugo, San Rafael (the town stood on the site of Rancho San Rafael, owned by

One entry in the Rose Parade of 1900 was this carriage decorated by students of Throop Polytechnic Institute. (*—Pasadena Public Library*)

the Verdugos), Portesuelo (colloquial Spanish for "threshhold," or "gateway," referring to the town's location in a portal through the hills between San Fernando Valley and San Gabriel Valley), Riverdale, Etheldean, Minneapolis, Mason, Sepulveda, Tropico and Glendale.

Toward the end of the century San Fernando Valley faced an unwelcome invasion. The Land Settlers League had been formed by certain promoters, and the membership was told that land in the valley was public domain, to be settled on by any homesteaders who so pleased. Squatters swarmed over the land, expecting to take ownership even of property obviously already in use as a farm or grove. The landowners in the northern part of the valley organized, employing cowboys to evict the squatters forcibly. Soon that area was left undisturbed. But in the southern part I. N. Van Nuys took the squatters to court instead of using violence. It cost him ten years, $50,000 and an appeal to the U.S. Supreme Court before he succeeded in ridding the land of the trespassers.

Lack of present-day understanding about road construction led early engineers to build many of the hillside streets straight up. In Echo Park and the Silver Lake area (then called the Ivanhoe Hills), Baxter and Fargo Streets are examples of these precipitous roadways.

Where streets circled the hills, countless permanent rights of way required stairs by which pedestrians might climb to their homes rather than go the long way around. Often a street led directly to a hill, became a stairway (keeping the street name) and, a hundred feet above, continued again as a road. Angelus Street and Landa are examples of this. Micheltorena Street (named for the Mexican governor) above Silver Lake follows the ridge of several hills with a far-reaching view on both sides. After the street descends to cross Sunset Boulevard, it runs into a steep cliff and continues as a stairway up the bluff, until on top it once more becomes a street and resumes its path along another ridge of hills.

In the 1880s a street-naming commission was formed which tried to give historical color and interest to the growing city. It chose names of early Spanish or Mexican families, or else Spanish words significant to the area. There was an angry reaction: new residents petitioned the City Council for Anglo-Saxon street names only, and the change was made. The first pioneer society in Los Angeles was formed in 1896, but there was not one Spanish name among the members; a bylaw of the society stated that "persons born in this state are not eligible to membership."

Prudent Beaudry was the main subdivider of downtown Los Angeles. Among his many projects was the settlement of Bunker Hill,

This chariot race took place in an early Tournament of Roses, about 1908. (*—Title Insurance & Trust Company*)

of which he bought a great portion at sheriff's auction in 1867 for $517. To make the property safe for homes, he built a large retaining wall along the base of the hillside. Then he arranged a system by which water was taken up, and Bunker Hill thereupon became a valued part of the City of Los Angeles. Its establishment as a subdivision took place just before the 100th anniversary of the Battle of Bunker Hill in 1775; so the name was chosen in commemoration.

Several blocks south of the old Plaza was another public park and camping ground (the site now called Pershing Square). Through neglect it had become an untidy eyesore until, in the face of angry complaints, the city allotted $1000 and appointed an "Association of Gentlemen" under Prudent Beaudry to clean up the square. With the help of private contributions, the area was fenced in and landscaped, and a bandstand was built in which concerts were given on Saturdays and Sundays. The park was distant from the center of the business district at that time (mainly in the location of today's Civic Center, around Main, Spring and Temple Streets), but gradually shops and offices began to surround the square. Too many holdups there finally made it seem best to remove the bandstand and make the

San Fernando Valley at harvesttime in the 1890s.
(*—Los Angeles County Museum of Natural History*)

Bicyclists on Cahuenga Pass in1897. (—*Title Insurance & Trust Company*)

plaza more open. In a repetition of history, almost a century later (in 1964) the park was again remodeled for the same reason and made into a completely open square above an enormous, many-storied garage belowground. Through the years it has been variously called La Plaza Abaja (Lower Square), St. Vincent's Park, Sixth Street Park and Central Park; on November 18, 1918, shortly after the Armistice, Pershing's name was finally adopted for the square.

The area which is now MacArthur Park was originally swampland, literally worthless. On the alkali soil nothing grew; in rainy weather it was a mud trap, and at all times it was ugly. When in 1865 the land was offered for sale at 25 cents an acre, there were no buyers. Two decades later an ingenious mayor, William H. Workman, arranged to have topsoil brought in and trees and shrubbery planted. A lake was created by filling a low ravine with water. Because of that lake and the fact that it was in the western part of town, it was called Westlake Park, but the name was later changed in tribute to General Douglas MacArthur. The same Mayor Workman developed Lafayette Park, as well as Echo and Eastlake (now Lincoln) Parks.

In 1885, H. Gaylord Wilshire subdivided what he called the Wilshire Tract. It included the land between Sixth and Seventh Streets from Parkview to Benton Way. Down the center a wide street was created and named Wilshire Boulevard. The first lot sold, at Parkview, went to Colonel Harrison Gray Otis, owner of the Los Angeles

Times. Otis built a home there and later donated the property to Los Angeles County for instruction in the arts, to be operated under the supervision of the Museum of History, Science and Art. Named in honor of the donor, the Otis Art Institute stands there today.

Gaylord Wilshire was a witty, egocentric man who enjoyed dramatic situations. When a law was passed forbidding public speaking in Los Angeles parks, he decided to challenge it, choosing what later became Pershing Square as the place where a test would draw most attention. Standing near a policeman, he began a speech and then urged the policeman to arrest him. The performance continued, enjoyed by the spectators, the policeman and of course by Wilshire himself. He was finally arrested, but in court the decision of the judge was that the Constitution of the United States makes it impossible to outlaw public speaking.

Wilshire became a prominent Socialist and ran for many offices on that ticket. Although never elected, when he ran for Congress he won the largest vote of any Socialist candidate in the country that year. He founded a Socialist newspaper in Los Angeles, *The Weekly Nationalist,* which struggled in vain for a wide circulation. Undaunted, Wilshire dramatically offered fantastic prizes for the sale of subscriptions — a piano, a fruit ranch, a trip around the world. Through investments he made several fortunes but each time spent everything. Through marriage he acquired more wealth and spent it. Through inheritance he received another fortune, but it was almost gone at the time of his death. This gay, humorous, extravagant man did much to enliven Los Angeles.

2. *Renaissance in the Plaza*

For many decades life in Los Angeles revolved around the old Plaza, until it sank into decay and disrepute. Then once more it became a central focus.

Ex-Governor Pío Pico dreamed of the glory and charm of earlier days. In an effort to re-create them, he bought the old José Antonio Carrillo home on the Plaza and in its place built Pico House. The hotel, finished in 1869, was the finest in Southern California. For a decade it was the center for balls and receptions and was host to every distinguished guest in the city. A spacious patio on the ground floor held plants and singing birds; the large dining room and ballroom allowed for luxurious entertaining; a famous chef was brought to supervise the cuisine. All rooms were gas-lit, and the hotel boasted the wonderful innovation of baths on both second and third floors.

Next door (where once the El Dorado Saloon had stood), William Abbott built the Merced Theater, named for his wife Doña Mercedes. She wanted it to seem higher than the Pico House, so an ornamental facade was erected on the roof, rising several inches higher than the roof of the hotel. The theater proper was on the second floor, the family quarters just above, and a store on the street level. With a gay celebration it opened on New Year's Eve 1870. At first the theater shared the success of the hotel, even to the extent that a private entrance was made between the two for hotel guests. But although excellent plays were performed with leading actors brought from across the country, the Merced was poorly managed and soon lost its popularity. After five years as a theater of quality, it drifted through a succession of efforts at variety shows and boxing and wrestling matches. Finally the theater closed its doors. Later, space in the building was used for the first Los Angeles public library.

Actually, Don Pío had envisioned a Plaza which, even as the Pico House was built, existed no longer. The changes in El Pueblo de Los Angeles which began with the Gold Rush were especially noticeable here, because crime and racial turmoil somehow focused on the area. One by one the Spanish-speaking residents sold their houses in town and remained all year on their distant ranchos. They were re-

Pico House, about 1875. (*—Title Insurance & Trust Co.*)

placed by a conglomerate population, and the Plaza became unrecognizable to eyes which once were accustomed to scenes of Mexican fiestas and family reunions.

The many saloons catered to a quarrelsome, often violent, clientele. During the Gold Rush, brothels had opened as women came south in search of wealthy customers. The Plaza became part of the section of town where prostitution was legally authorized. By 1888, on a detailed map of the land and buildings of Los Angeles, the notation "Houses of Ill Fame" occurs along Sanchez Street across from Pico House and for several blocks on nearby Alameda.

The Plaza church with its gazebo bell tower, prior to 1869. (—*Title Insurance & Trust Co.*) Below is a photograph of La Calle de los Negros, where the Chinese Massacre began, taken in 1871 soon after the riot. (—*Title Insurance & Trust Co.*)

3. *The Chinese Massacre*

During the Gold Rush, Chinese sailed across the Pacific Ocean to join the miners. In 1869 about fifty of them came down from San Francisco and settled south of the Plaza, in the adjacent area. As other Chinese arrived they settled alongside the original colony.

Los Angeles was struggling to recover from bankruptcy. The fact that the new arrivals were willing to work for extremely low wages caused deep resentment among other laborers, because there was already strong competition, and in the nonindustrial city relatively few jobs were available. Besides, the Southland was just beginning to emerge from a century of isolation, and people from other countries were suspect. Of them all, the oriental stood out as the most natural target. When by 1870 their numbers had grown to almost 200, a corresponding increase in antagonism culminated in the infamous Chinese Massacre of 1871.

It began with a feud between two tongs, or fraternal organizations. Members of the Hong Chow Tong were accused by members of the Nin Yung Tong of abducting a woman who belonged (according to the custom) to their association. In the Calle de los Negros shooting broke out between the two tongs, and a policeman, Officer Bilderrain, tried to stop it. He followed one of the gunmen into a building — the former adobe residence of Don Ygnacio Coronel, at Arcadia and Los Angeles Streets — but soon reappeared, wounded by a bullet. A passing rancher, Robert Thompson, sprang to join him, but he was killed and two bystanders were wounded. More Chinese appeared with guns, and more townsmen, also armed. On the Plaza at the entrance to the Calle de los Negros a crowd began to gather, and along Los Angeles Street another mob formed, composed mainly of roughnecks wanting an excuse to fight and loot.

Chinese headquarters were located on Sanchez Street behind the Coronel adobe, and most of the block belonged to Chinese merchants. As night fell, Sheriff James F. Burns placed volunteer deputies and the few city police around the Coronel building, stating that in the morning he would arrest the Chinese within but in the meantime the crowd should leave. Instead the crowd grew larger and more threatening. Leaving a marshal in command, Sheriff Burns went to get more help. Before he returned, the besieged Chinese began an attempt to flee to safety. Shots from the mob rang out. One of the Chinese was caught, rescued from the rioters by Emil Harris, a city policeman, but retaken amid howls of "Hang him!" Up Temple Street

Vicente Lugo's home on the Plaza became a Chinese residence and curio store. (*—Title Insurance & Trust Co.*)

two blocks to John J. Tomlinson's corral the hapless man was dragged
and then hanged from a gate beam at the corral's entrance.

At the same time, attempts were being made to drive the Chinese
out of their buildings, especially from the Coronel adobe at the corner. Finally holes were hacked in the roof, through which the attackers
could shoot at the terrified men inside. Those who fled outside were
shot in the streets by the mob. Under the rioters' constant effort the
doors were at last broken down and the frightened victims dragged
to the street. Rooms were immediately looted. One block away, at
Los Angeles and Commercial Streets, were some prairie wagons with
conveniently high frames which the rioters appropriated for gallows.
On a corner of that intersection a courageous man, William Slaney,
owned a shoe store, and several of his employees, Chinese, ran to
him for protection. He locked them inside and stood guard himself.
Men were hanged from the bars of awnings nearby; other victims
were dragged to Tomlinson's corral. The intention of the mob was
to kill all the Chinese in town.

The family of Juan Lanfranco hid their Chinese cook for a week
in their adobe on Requena, one block beyond Commercial, until all
possibility of danger to him had passed. Many men fled to the home
of Judge Wilson Hugh Gray at Broadway and Seventh where he hid
them in his cellar. After that, on every Chinese New Year, Judge

Gray found anonymous presents of silks, porcelain and tea left at his home.

As word spread of the peril facing the Chinese community, most citizens of Los Angeles remained indifferent. Yet some few immediately responded to the urgent need to wrest control from chaotic fury. Judge Robert M. Widney, his younger brother William, Henry T. Hazard and Sheriff Burns plunged determinedly into bands of lynchers, trying to dissuade them and rescue their victims. A courageous law-and-order group formed which included Samuel B. Caswell, Cameron E. Thom and other men willing to brave the tumultuous mob of over 400 rioters. Terrified men seized from the grasp of their captors were taken to the jail at Spring and Franklin (now Court Street) for safety. Under Sheriff Burns' leadership the law-and-order group surrounded the block from which most of the violence stemmed and made it clear that any lynchers would be shot. With this united effort, order began to prevail and the riot ended. A total of 19 Chinese had been killed during the carnage. The long white wall of the Coronel adobe was splattered with bullet holes.

There was a nationwide reaction to the massacre — in fact, a worldwide reaction. In the East, churches considered sending missionaries to Los Angeles. From China a government protest was dispatched, and in response a bill was presented in Congress for payment of a large indemnity. The ten instigators of the riot were brought to trial before a grand jury with Judge Ygnacio Sepúlveda presiding.

During the trial there was an unexpected sidelight of humor, provided by the Chinese themselves. Their witnesses would not swear an oath on the Bible, choosing instead to swear on the severed head of a chicken; so one of the men was asked to write out a proper oath to be used. His response was the following:

> I must speak according the Truth evidents. If I swear lie, God of heaven parnished and binding me like cutting chicken's head, and kill me by thunder, I swear the Truth evidents, God prodest me and gave me good auspicious.

Yet in spite of the rioters' terrible crime, little punishment followed. The list of names of those who were to appear before the grand jury disappeared. Few people had shown concern about the Chinese even when the massacre was at its height, and now many citizens demonstrated outright sympathy toward the accused. Nine men were convicted, but within a year they were freed. Even Congress, though it expressed indignation, failed to pass the bill granting an indemnity.

4. *The Last Bandit*

After the massacre, Los Angeles made intense efforts to erase the "lawless frontier town" label. Vigilance committees ceased, and banditry, too, soon ended.

Tiburcio Vasquez was the last bandit whose audacious raids left authorities fuming but outwitted. Throughout California people were as fascinated as they were frightened by his dramatic exploits. For several years he and his gang robbed stages and lonely outposts so outrageously that in 1874 the California State Legislature offered $3000 for his capture.

In the Southland, Soledad Canyon just north of Los Angeles was Vasquez' favorite hideout. There it was easy to find safety among the boulders and dramatic upthrusts of rock left from some primordial convulsion of the earth.* From there he launched daring holdups and began to concentrate his attention on ranchhouses near town. As the raids of Tiburcio's gang became more and more flagrant, the governor of California increased to $8000 the reward for capturing Vasquez alive.

William R. Rowland, son of an eminent ranchero, had succeeded the courageous Sheriff Burns. Rowland vowed to capture the bandit and several times almost did so, yet always Vasquez was warned that the sheriff was on his way. The large reward for Tiburcio's capture was tempting, and one day someone disclosed that, at a place where now Santa Monica Boulevard passes Kings Road, the outlaw was in the home of Greek George (driver of the Fort Tejón camel train years earlier). Rowland had been tipped off that spies reported his movements to Vasquez; so in order to mislead them the sheriff remained in town but sent out a posse.

Suspecting nothing, the bandit sat in the house unarmed. Suddenly a shout of alarm rang out. Vasquez leaped through the window in the direction of his horse, but before he could mount he was wounded by several shots. Stoically he surrendered. Wild excitement greeted the outlaw when he was driven into town. The streets around the jail were thronged with people eager to see the famous bandido. Even after he was put into a cell, an endless stream of curious visitors came to gaze at him. They all expected to see a wild, uncouth man, but instead they found him to be courtly, educated, genial.

---

*Appropriately, many movie companies today use Vasquez Rocks as the setting for western pictures, and often the rocks are the hideout of a bandit gang.

Tiburcio Vasquez, outlaw. The area shown below to this day is called Vasquez Rocks. (—both, *Title Insurance & Trust Co.*)

Vasquez' desperate career began innocently enough, when at 17 he attended a fandango with two friends. During the evening a constable was called in to stop an argument and was killed by one of the friends. Through association, Tiburcio felt it necessary to go into hiding, and from then on his life became that of a criminal. In a document dictated to George Beers, a reporter who helped the posse with his capture but later became a trusted confidant, Vasquez gave a special warning to young people to avoid vicious companions, saying that his own life exemplified the disaster that could follow.

For a few days excitement over the prisoner filled Los Angeles, then he was taken north by steamer to await trial in San Jose. To many spectators in court he was a hero, and at the death sentence they wept. A large gathering of visitors, with special invitations from the sheriff's office, arrived in the jail on Vasquez' last day there. But the outlaw remained self-possessed even in the face of searching looks and probing questions. The morning of his execution, such a dense throng filled the jailyard that there was scarcely room for the prisoner to be led to the scaffold.

With his death, the era of banditry in Southern California ended.

5. *Progress and Personalities*

In 1867 the first street lights were turned on — 25 lamps which burned gas manufactured from tar. Fifteen years later electric street lights on seven masts, each 150 feet high and intended to illumine an area of several blocks, were inaugurated as part of the city's New Year's Eve celebration.

The Los Angeles post office bore no resemblance to that of the early days, when a box with pigeonholes sufficed for all mail. Similar in most respects to the post offices of other American cities, it had in addition several General Delivery windows. Long lines always stood in front of these windows during the boom years, because a large part of the mail handled was for new arrivals, temporarily with no specific address.

In 1869 the police force ceased to be a volunteer organization, becoming a six-man, paid city department. However, it was almost a decade later that the officers first wore uniforms.

The first horsecar line was a neighborhood project. Judge Robert Maclay Widney and friends who lived in the area of Third Street charged themselves fifty cents per front foot of property, and in 1874 streetcar service began. The horse-drawn cars went between the Plaza and Sixth Street along Main and Spring Streets, and each ride cost ten cents. Thirteen years later the first electric trolley delighted patrons

On New Year's Eve 1882, seven electric arc lights atop 150-foot masts were switched on in Los Angeles. Supposedly each light would illuminate several blocks. (—*Los Angeles Department of Water & Power*)

by going at a faster speed than a horse could pull a car; it also took grades without effort.

Stagecoaches of the Coast Line ran north to Ventura and Santa Barbara by way of the western end of the San Fernando Valley. The line maintained its coaches in unusual style: each was drawn by six matched horses, and all metal parts were kept highly polished. For travelers, the run between Ventura and Santa Barbara held high drama. For a long stretch, notably in the Rincón area, the mountains ended right at the water's edge, and if the passengers were unlucky (though some would have said lucky) and arrived when the tide was high, the roadway was under water. The horses plunged ahead regardless, pulling the stagecoach through the surf. Sometimes when it reached its destination the coach was still trailing seaweed. Travel on this route was popular in the 1870s, but during the following decade the railroads gradually brought about the extinction of the stage lines.

For a long time Los Angeles was dominated by machine politics. Votes were bought for two dollars. The Republican and Democratic tickets were different colors, and therefore at the ballot box the voter could be watched to see how he voted before he was paid.

At high tide a stage drives south toward Los Angeles. Portions of the route between Santa Barbara and San Buenaventura were often under water. (—*Title Insurance & Trust Co.*)

The City of Los Angeles was controlled by acts of the State Legislature until 1887, when cities of over 10,000 population were allowed to elect a committee of 15 members to prepare a charter. Since the previous census (in 1880) showed a population of 11,183 in Los Angeles, a charter was drawn up and went into effect in 1889. It provided for election of a mayor, nine councilmen and the board of education. Unfortunately, the charter was confusing when it came to designating authority: the mayor was charged with "supervision" of the city, while the City Council was made its "governing body." This created a perpetual problem.

Few leading state officials were chosen from the Southland. An exception was John G. Downey, who in Los Angeles led a group of Democrats called the Plug Uglies and through their help was elected lieutenant governor in 1859. During his term of office the governor ran successfully for election to the U.S. Senate and moved to Washington; so Downey took his place for the unfinished term.

In 1897 the Los Angeles Symphony was established, making the city the fifth in the United States to have a symphony orchestra and the first west of the Rockies. (The earliest orchestras were those of Chicago, Boston, New York and Minneapolis.) Tickets to the performances cost 25 cents, and each musician received 50 cents for his work. Harley Hamilton, conductor of the orchestra for 16 years, chose Beethoven's First Symphony for the debut. However, there were problems to overcome which Beethoven could not have foreseen, such as the fact that no player of the oboe or bassoon could be found in the Southland. But the omission meant nothing to the enthusiastic audience.

That same year the Del Conti Opera Company of Italy came to Southern California after a tour in Mexico. At the Los Angeles Theater it gave the American premiere of Puccini's *La Bohème.*

The first Los Angeles high school was built in 1873 at Temple and Broadway. It perched on Pound Cake Hill, but the building was later moved by trestle to a spot nearby, across Temple, and Pound Cake Hill was leveled. In 1917 classes were transferred to a large new high school on Olympic Boulevard, and today the entrance door of the first school is displayed there as a memento. A note about changing times should be added: in early days all janitorial work in schools was done by the teacher and students.

In 1880 a group of Protestants founded the University of Southern California with enthusiastic help from all religions. To pay for construction, 308 lots were donated by a Protestant, Ozro W. Childs; by a Roman Catholic, ex-Governor John G. Downey; and by a Jew, Isaias W. Hellman.* Other people hastened to donate 300 more lots. Judge

---

*The same interdenominational spirit appeared earlier when St. Vincent's College was founded by the Vincentian Fathers of the Roman Catholic Church. The large fair which raised money for the college was suggested and organized by a Jewess, Mrs. Rosa Newmark.

The first high school in Los Angeles perched on Pound Cake Hill. (*—Los Angeles City School District*)

Robert M. Widney gave the university an interest in his Maclay Rancho, in the San Fernando Valley, to a value of approximately $100,000. His brother, Dr. Joseph P. Widney, left his medical practice to become president of the university, guaranteeing the school's debts personally and getting them paid off in four years. Land was given to the school from as far away as Tulare and San Diego. For a while the area was formed into a township called University Place, but except for the university the land was almost unoccupied. Around the buildings rose fields of wild mustard stretching in all directions — an uninterrupted forest of yellow blossoms.

During this period of Los Angeles' history many of the most important colleges in the county were founded, including Occidental, Pomona (first of the group of interrelated Claremont Colleges) and C.I.T., the California Institute of Technology (originally named Throop University).

One Sunday a law professor of the University of Southern California found some of his students in Exposition Park (a nearby area initially used for agricultural shows), watching greyhound races wherein the dogs pursued fleeing jackrabbits until the rabbits were caught and killed. The law professor, William M. Bowen, started a movement to raise money enough to buy the park and change it from use as a racetrack. He found out that really the city itself owned the land. Bowen, who became president of the City Council, persuaded the city and county to landscape the grounds and build a natural history museum and art gallery. A coliseum that could be used for athletic events was added.

Madame Helena Modjeska, the noted actress, came to Los Angeles in 1876 and decided to settle in the German colony of Anaheim because she could speak German but very little English. There her husband, Count Chlapowski, bought an orange ranch, and the barn was made into living quarters for a friend who had traveled with them from Poland, Henryk Sienkiewicz. The charming, elegant foreigners who had no experience at farm labor somehow pictured the trees as taking care of themselves and thought that an easy living could be made by planting one's own vegetable garden. To the Anaheimers, skillful and industrious, the new arrivals were hilarious. They plunged into the planting, fertilizing, watering and trimming which experienced colonists told them was necessary, but then they sat on the veranda in conversation, with no understanding that everything needed day-to-day care. At last they decided to give up the irksome new life, and while the Count sold the ranch Madame Modjeska went to San Francisco and returned to the stage.

Immediately she became a wild success. She learned to speak English, but then she was asked to play Ophelia in *Hamlet*. The language of Shakespeare was not the English she knew; so as the actors came on stage they played their roles in English as usual while Madame Modjeska played hers in Polish. The Count became a naturalized citizen of the United States, and for the remainder of their lives they kept a home in Southern California; in the Santiago Canyon of the Santa Ana Mountains they built a house among live oaks beside a brook. There the pianist Ignace Jan Paderewski visited them while on a triumphal tour of America. Before Madame Modjeska died in 1909 she made a special request, and in response the entire Los Angeles Symphony Orchestra played a movement from Tchaikovsky's Sixth Symphony at her funeral in St. Vibiana's Cathedral. Sienkiewicz, who while here sent accounts of life in California to the Polish press, later wrote the classic *Quo Vadis?*

In 1881 a writer arrived in Los Angeles who, because of her books, would always be associated with the Southland. She was Helen Hunt Jackson. Her visit was for the purpose of studying Mission Indians, and what she learned was to become part of a nonfiction work, *A Century of Dishonor*. During her stay she met Don Antonio Francisco Coronel and his wife, and in conversations with them another book took shape also, a novel. The Coronels drove her to Rancho San Francisco, where in a ranchhouse named Camulos, Doña Ysabel, widow of Don Ygnacio del Valle, lived with her family. At sight of the beautiful rambling home and the tree-shaded gardens, Mrs. Jackson decided to use Camulos as the setting for her novel. She modeled

The Camulos ranchhouse and garden, still lovely today.

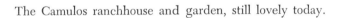

one of the important characters on Doña Ysabel, and made her heroine a composite of two children raised by the del Valles. One day Mrs. Jackson heard the name Ramona. Its musical quality charmed her, and she chose it for her heroine and for the book's title. The hero, Alessandro, was named for a Mission Indian she met, and the character was modeled on the same young man. Two years later the book was published, and so vivid and accurate was the California background that most readers thought it was a true story.

A Century of Dishonor was not published until 1885, the year of her death. Its subject was the treatment of Indians in the United States, and so that she could have official status to interview Indians for the book, Mrs. Jackson was made a special agent for the government, as was a co-worker Abbot Kinney. Again Coronel's help was valuable. He happened to be a friend and confidant of the Mission Indians, and he urged them to withhold nothing from the two investigators, because through this book their story would become known in Washington and something might be done about their problems. Attentively Mrs. Jackson and Abbot Kinney listened to a long list of injustices. In most of the villages no Indian agent had ever appeared, and for years the Indians had been without protection of the law. White settlers had cut down trees on the reservations, seized livestock for payment of fines, used the Indians' pasturage in time of drought at the expense of reservation cattle, moved onto their land and filed claim of ownership for acreage even where Indians' homes and gardens already were, after which the sheriff ordered the Indians to leave. In one case settlers moved onto reservation land at the head of a river and diverted the water so it was unavailable for the Indians' cattle and irrigation. In another case the village had no notice that a claim for the land had been filed until the sheriff ordered the people to leave and to sell enough belongings to pay court costs of the claim against them.

The report sent in by Mrs. Jackson and Abbot Kinney not only spoke of the injustices but included suggestions for steps the government should take to right them. It described land which should be bought, available at a low price and where the Indians could maintain a decent standard of living. It asked the government to survey and mark the land so that the Indians would know where they had a right to pasture cattle and cultivate farms. The government should give the Indians permanent ownership, because it had been proved that while they owned land only under acts of Congress, the land was often restored to the public domain and then sold to influential settlers. There was such a strong popular reaction to the publication

The Fernandeño Indian woman
Espíritu, wife of Miguel Leonis.
(—Leonis Adobe Association)

of *A Century of Dishonor* that Washington followed all the suggestions about the Mission Indians, and in addition a law was passed
by Congress, the Dawes Act, under which the U.S. Government accepted responsibility for the care of Indians throughout the country.

In the meantime, at the far western end of the San Fernando Valley an obscure Indian woman was drawn into an amazing drama of
her own. She was Espíritu, daughter of Odon, one of the three Fernandeño Indians to whom Rancho El Escorpión had been granted.
Espíritu married, bore a son and was widowed; then she became the
wife of Miguel Leonis, a Basque sheepowner. Leonis acquired the
entire Rancho El Escorpión, not only the land but also cattle, horses
and sheep. Because the rancho was isolated, he made his home not
there but alongside the nearby road from Los Angeles to Ventura.

Leonis, six foot four and violent-tempered, bullied his wife and
neighbors. He refused to allow Doña Espíritu's son by her first husband to enter the house, and in a fit of anger he vindictively set fire
to a neighbor's property. He was universally disliked. Yet he pros-
pered and eventually owned about 10,000 acres of ranch land. To
no one's sorrow, he was accidentally killed one night in 1889 when
he got drunk and fell out of his wagon on the way home. His sadistic
nature was expressed even in his will, where, referring to Espíritu
as a housekeeper rather than his wife, he cut her off with a pittance.

As soon as Leonis died, she took her son into her home. Then
she sought a lawyer for help in regaining rights to the property which
had been hers. Stephen M. White took the case, and he was able to

win half of Leonis' estate for her. However, the unworldly woman, despite being educated, was an easy target for charlatans. Unknowingly she gave a power of attorney to one Laurent Etcheparé, who a few months later claimed she owed him $5000. Another man, using a paper she had signed, sold cattle belonging to her and then kept the money. Two others, who owed the Leonis estate about $12,000, used her signature on another paper as proof they had paid her $8000. As a climax, Etcheparé maneuvered so that all her property was conveyed to him, and at last the penniless Espíritu turned again to Stephen White. A complicated court battle followed, going three times to the California Supreme Court. By the time the final verdict was given in Espíritu's favor, Etcheparé had died and so had White, and another lawyer inherited the charge of her case. He had given his best efforts to her protection, and in 1905, after the court verdict was brought in, he jubilantly called for a photographer to take a portrait of his client on that exciting day. It shows her dressed in her best, dignified and at peace. The next year she died at the age of seventy, almost the last of the Fernandeño Indians.

In Santa Monica, a name from the past appeared in the newspapers of 1912 when Arcadia, once the beautiful child bride of Don Abel Stearns, died at the age of 89. A crowd of thousands attended the funeral, and among the escorts and pallbearers were Carrillos, Bandinis and other relatives, as well as friends from half a century before.

Married to Don Abel and later to Col. Robert S. Baker, one of the owners of Rancho San Vicente y Santa Monica, who died in 1894, Arcadia was childless. Family ties remained close between Arcadia and her sisters, brothers, their children and grandchildren. One grandniece was Arcadia's favorite, her namesake Arcadia Bandini Scott. A year after Colonel Baker died, Doña Arcadia asked the blonde, vivacious schoolgirl to visit her. The girl never returned to her parents but assumed the permanent role of the older woman's companion, whether in the handsome Santa Monica house or traveling around California.

She, too, was beautiful and within a few years had many suitors. It seemed likely to Doña Arcadia that the happy arrangement would soon end. One day she asked her grandniece to remain unmarried, promising that her entire fortune of several million dollars would be the recompense, as a bequest in her will. The young girl accepted the offer and lived with her grandaunt for a total of 17 years. Once while on a trip to New York the young Arcadia met a handsome law student of Fordham University, Joseph Brennan. They fell in love, and he followed her to California where they became engaged. Upon graduation he moved to California to begin the practice of law, and eventually he was made a judge. Although they were engaged for years, they did not marry until six weeks after Doña Arcadia's death.

In the meantime, it was discovered that the elderly woman had never made a will. Before an adjudication was finally made, 32 lawsuits were brought against Doña Arcadia's estate and much of the fortune was diverted to legal fees.

Such was the strange end to the life story of the most celebrated beauty of early days in Los Angeles.

One of the city's great men, Charles Fletcher Lummis, arrived in Los Angeles in 1884. Making lengthy detours, he walked alone across the continent from Ohio — 3507 miles in 143 days — traveling on foot just for "fun and study." On the way he sent articles to the Los Angeles *Times* describing his journey. With cheerful self-reliance he met whatever problems occurred along the route, at one point setting his own arm when it was broken during the crossing of an uninhabited region of Arizona, at another successfully escaping from an attack by convicts, and, in the Rocky Mountains, fighting off a wildcat and a mountain lion. On this trek he proved himself an individualist: when crossing one section of the country where mosquitoes were so fierce they even bit through his thick stockings, he bought mosquito netting and sewed it into a long cylinder within which he walked during hours when the mosquitoes swarmed. The day after he showed up in Los Angeles he was made city editor of the paper to which he had been contributing.

Like Helen Hunt Jackson, he too became a champion of the Indians, in particular of 300 Mission Indians who lived on their ances-

Charles F. Lummis.
(—*Title Insurance & Trust Co.*)

tral lands near Warner's Ranch in San Diego County. When in 1851 the U.S. Congress had ruled that all landowners were to file a claim with the Land Commission for title, Indians were included in the ruling. After decades of litigation, the United States Supreme Court decided that because the Indians near Warner's Ranch had failed to file their claim in time (not realizing there was any necessity) they had forfeited ownership. Lummis founded the Sequoya League (named for a famous Cherokee chieftain) to publicize such injustice. The league won the backing of President Theodore Roosevelt, of Commissioner of Indian Affairs W. A. Jones and other influential people. It was as a result of Lummis' efforts as well as Mrs. Jackson's that the government purchased land near San Diego for use solely by the Indians, land which, as Lummis proudly stated, was superior to that from which they were removed.

He led the way to restoration of the missions, which were neglected and decaying. The Landmarks Club, organized by Lummis, received contributions from people throughout the United States and even from Europe. The beautiful San Juan Capistrano Mission was restored, as was the San Fernando Mission and several others. (The restoration of San Fernando, begun in 1898, continued from time to time and was finished in 1948. The San Gabriel Mission was restored by the Claretian Fathers when it was returned to the Roman Catholic Church.)

For many years he published a magazine, *Out West*, and also wrote books on Indians, folklore and Spanish America. After publication of the latter, the King of Spain knighted him for his interpretation of the conquistadors. In his home, El Alisal (The Place of the Sycamores — built by his own hands in a grove of thirty trees), he received visitors from all over the world — statesmen, educators, scientists, actors, musicians, artists, writers. He instigated the founding of a museum about Indians in the U.S. Southwest. (The Southwest Museum and his home may be seen just off the Pasadena Freeway, a short distance from downtown. Both are open to visitors.)

Charles Lummis was an eccentric. In kingly style he kept a minstrel for one purpose only, to provide music for the household. Reversing ordinary hours of work, he began dictating as evening fell and continued until almost midnight. In self-dramatization he wore distinctive clothes — a brown corduroy suit with a red sash around the waist and moccasins or sandals on his feet. Even when invited to the White House this was Lummis' costume.

In 1928, a few months before his death, a characteristic scene took place at the Shrine Auditorium. Wearing his usual corduroy suit, over which he hung the decoration given by the King of Spain, Lummis took his seat in the audience to hear Mary Garden, one of his special friends, sing in the opera *Salomé*. As the curtain fell and then parted for her to step out front, Lummis jumped to his feet, made a dramatic gesture from the heart and shouted "Bravo! Bravo! Bravo!" Other people added their own shouts, but she ignored them all. Turning in his direction she blew kisses to him alone. For the audience it was a memorable tableau.

He was a man suited to the times. His expansiveness fitted the expansion of Los Angeles. His fervent interest in California fitted the enthusiasm of Californians. His energy typified theirs. To many it seemed only the truth when in a poem he exulted, "I am Lummis. I'm the West!"

6. *The Search for Water*

From the beginning, water was the basic need of Southern California, whose dependence upon rivers which disappeared underground most of the year presented problems. A relief from the situation was found when, in 1868, ex-Governor John G. Downey dug an artesian well near present-day Compton, successfully tapping the underground water basin. This inspired the sinking of other artesian wells for a year-round supply of water for irrigation.

Homeowners relied on zanjas which spread like fingers across the city, but in addition many dug wells behind their own homes. Above the wells windmills turned, pumping the water. With the arrival of Yankees, both the spelling and the pronunciation of the Spanish "zanja" changed, becoming instead "sankey." (At the same time the musical-sounding Spanish word for residents of Los Angeles, "Angeleño," became pronounced as though spelled "Anjeleeno.")

Prudent Beaudry built two small reservoirs and pumped their water up Bunker Hill. William Workman built a private reservoir, bringing water to Boyle Heights. When he was mayor, he urged the construction of a large public reservoir, which could mean progress for all Los Angeles. The City Council did not agree because of the expense; so he took each member for a drive, pointing out how it would improve the city if idle acreage could be made usable for homes and cultivation. Near the downtown area there was a canyon between hills where underground springs could be tapped, and he persuaded the Council to put a dam across the canyon so that water could be stored and then piped around the city. The result was Echo

A composite map of the Los Angeles zanja system,
1876. (—Los Angeles Department of Water & Power)

Park Reservoir, now a lake and park. George Hansen was president of the Canal and Reservoir Company which constructed it.

But still irrigation was primitive, and Los Angeles remained very much at the mercy of unpredictable weather. Drought had ruined the cattle industry, and in 1876 and '77 a severe drought was just as ruinous to the sheep industry. On the other hand, in 1884 there was a rainfall of 48 inches with almost no letup: homes, vineyards and crops were washed away and many people and animals perished. Los Angeles had yet to find a system for protection from these extremes and for an adequate supply of water throughout the year.

7. *The Railroads*

The Southland, completely isolated, needed some kind of fast, dependable communication with the rest of the country. The fulfillment of this need is one of the most exciting chapters in the story of Los Angeles. The arrival of the railroads and the development of a harbor are intertwined, and both were necessary before the city could take a strong place in the modern world.

Phineas Banning made the first move. In 1868 he persuaded Los Angeles to build a railroad to Wilmington to connect with ships there. The next step was to persuade the Southern Pacific Railroad to include Los Angeles on its line which would eventually stretch across the continent.

A zanja ran through Pershing Square (at that time known as Sixth Street Park) in the 1880s. (*—Title Insurance & Trust Co.*)

Control of the Southern Pacific was in the hands of the Big Four — Leland Stanford, Mark Hopkins, Collis P. Huntington and Charles F. Crocker. The railroad was willing to include Los Angeles only if the city would pay a large sum of money, but the payment had to be approved by the taxpayers, who objected strongly. During an intense controversy, Judge Widney published a pamphlet at his own expense, explaining the importance to the city of being joined to the rest of the nation by a transcontinental line. Widney mailed this pamphlet to every voter, and as a result the electorate overwhelmingly approved the cost.

Meanwhile, the railroad decided that the road to Los Angeles was too mountainous and a route through Cajon Pass to San Bernardino would be easier. This meant that Los Angeles' only connection would be by a spur track. Finally the railroad returned to its original agreement, but the city was to pay another heavy subsidy and in addition give the Southern Pacific ownership of the existing railroad to Wilmington. Reluctantly the city agreed to the additional terms.

The most difficult part of the route south was a tunnel through the mountains beneath San Fernando Pass. For a year and a half the workmen steadily inched the bore forward. When it was finished the Southern Pacific's final track was quickly laid, completing the north-south tie in 1876. At Lang Station in Soledad Canyon a golden spike made the final connection between the tracks built from San Francisco and those from Los Angeles.

Among the many nationalities comprising the work gangs were Chinese — 9000 coolies. They spoke another language, ate different food and had different ways, but they seemed tireless, accepted low wages and worked in perfect harmony with the other laborers. The Chinese were hired in San Francisco through the Six Companies, a work guild representing six districts of China. The Six Companies arranged for ships to bring the coolies and after their arrival sent them to a work location, helped any who were sick, arbitrated disputes, advanced money for rent or doctors' bills and in general shepherded them. People who attended the celebration at Lang Station when the railroad was finished never forgot the striking scene: along both sides of the track stood lines of oriental figures in blue, baggy trousers and loose-fitting blouses, wearing basket hats under which each man's hair was braided into a long queue. And every man held a shovel in his hand as a mute symbol of his part in the completion of an important task.

The Southland put on a riotous celebration, but the joining of tracks from both San Francisco and Los Angeles did not guarantee a

A Chinese tea carrier prepares to serve oriental laborers on the Southern Pacific Railroad. (—*Southern Pacific Transp. Co.*)

fraternal relationship between the north and south. At a meeting with the Los Angeles City Council, Mr. Crocker, angered by their casual dress and their barbed jokes about monopolies, threatened to "make grass grow in the streets of your city." From then on the railroad tie-in, supposedly so advantageous, brought constant disappointments. The Southern Pacific plus the Wilmington line (which was extended along the water front to San Pedro) soon controlled freight and wharfage charges on all traffic, whether by land or by sea. Rates for freight traffic to Los Angeles by ship were increased so that in some cases they more than tripled. The rate scale for rail shipments from San Pedro to Los Angeles was higher than the shipping rate between San Pedro and Hong Kong. The monopoly lasted for ten years.

Meanwhile another railroad, the Atchison, Topeka & Santa Fe, based in Kansas, was attempting to cross the continent from the Missouri River to the Pacific. In 1883 it reached the Colorado River, and on the other side, at Needles, the line was to continue in California. But at that spot the Santa Fe was confronted by its rival, the Southern Pacific. After intensive power maneuvers, the Santa Fe acquired the Southern Pacific's Mojave Division road, between Needles and Mojave. Then the Santa Fe crossed the Cajon Pass to San Bernardino and from there brought its line to downtown Los Angeles. The city, tired of the pressures employed by the monopolistic Southern Pacific, welcomed the new line by donating land for a Santa Fe depot.

By this time the Southern Pacific had completed its transcontinental connections, and a rate war began between the two great railroads. Los Angeles found itself the object of a tremendous boom. The climax of the rate war came on March 6, 1886, when fares between Kansas City and Los Angeles, which had dropped to $10, then to $5, finally went to a dollar. "Emigrant trains" were put on to carry the influx, and cooking facilities were added to boxcars. People from across the country hurried to come to California while the low fares held, as for nearly a year the rate from Kansas City remained $25 or less. With newcomers crowding into Los Angeles, the saying grew that "a native is one who has resided in the city for 24 hours or more."

Not only were passenger rates slashed, but also freight rates. In memoirs of those days, people recall paying freight rates of 60 cents a ton for a trainload of salt from New York, and one dollar for a ton of coal from Chicago.

Then the rivalry extended to harbor connections. A definite Los Angeles Harbor was needed for the increasing trade. For many years the ships that ran between San Francisco and San Diego had vacillated between the ports of Santa Monica, Redondo and San Pedro for traffic to Los Angeles. A sudden change of mind on the captain's part sometimes caused travelers to arrive at one port while friends waited at another.

The Southern Pacific had bought a small railroad leading to Santa Monica and in addition owned a railroad connection to Redondo. But in order for the Federal Government to help in developing a large harbor, a choice had to be made. The chairman of the Senate Committee on Commerce, Senator William B. Frye of Maine, came out to inspect the different sites and announced that Santa Monica would make the best harbor. At this the Southern Pacific bought property all along the Santa Monica shore and urged Los Angeles to support Senator's Frye's decision. However, the people decided that what would be good for the Southern Pacific would undoubtedly be bad for Los Angeles, and San Pedro became the general choice.

The war shifted to Washington. Collis P. Huntington of the Southern Pacific had strong influence in the Senate; he tried to arrange for the harbor bill to state that only if the location were at Santa Monica would there be government aid. California Senator Stephen M. White, on the other hand, fought to keep Federal aid free of special interests. Climaxing a debate between Frye and White — a debate which lasted three days — the bill was finally passed providing $3,000,000 for the desired harbor at whatever site might be chosen by the Army Board of Engineers.

The gratitude Los Angeles felt toward Senator White was overwhelming. When he returned to California a train covered with banners and flowers met him as he entered the state; crowds lined the track through towns, cheering him as he passed by; a parade awaited him in Los Angeles. A statue of this eminent man still stands at the northwest corner of First and Broadway.

Eventually the Board of Engineers chose San Pedro as the most suitable for a large harbor.

In 1899 the harbor breakwater was begun, but a fight broke out all over again on technicalities. The Southern Pacific controlled most of the shoreline above, below and in San Pedro, except for the bluff to the west. As a first move, the railroad tried to get a provision added to the harbor resolution, specifying that landowners of the East Basin would control any decision as to exactly which part of San Pedro Bay would be the harbor. Interestingly, the East Basin was controlled by the Southern Pacific. When Los Angeles discovered this strategem there was an avalanche of protests to Washington, and the so-called "Joker" provision was rejected.

Then new problems arose, centering around a large area of tidelands (land overflowed with water during floodtide) needed by the harbor but controlled by the Southern Pacific through lease or ownership. On this control hinged the question of whether only one railroad could have access to the harbor, or if it could be a "free harbor" available for use by all railroads. How could Los Angeles obtain a clear right of way?

As a first move, the city went back to the State Admission Act passed when California entered the Union. By this act, all navigable waters within the state boundaries were declared "forever free." The tidelands were therefore the property of the state and could never be leased or sold to San Pedro, a corporation or a person. Yet, with illegal control out of the way, could the city acquire a right of way? The problem was resolved when the State Legislature declared willingness to give its permission.

But the Southern Pacific had found an old law stating that if four or more tracks were laid on a piece of property, no commonwealth could claim right of way. On Labor Day, when the courts were closed and so could not issue an injunction, the Pacific Electric Railway (controlled by the Southern Pacific) sent a large crew of men to part of the strategic land and laid a network of tracks. Another area, the "Huntington fill," had legally been forfeited by the Southern Pacific because the land had not been put to use, yet now, regardless, railroad tracks were laid across it and freight cars hauled in.

When the Los Angeles police chief heard of this maneuver, he hurried to the harbor with forty policemen who shunted the freight cars from the rails, tore up the illegal 2000 feet of track and then remained on guard. After a lawsuit, the court decided in favor of Los Angeles, and the decision was upheld by the Supreme Court. With this crisis over, the way was clear for the state to cede the tidelands to the city for the harbor.

Yet there was another question — how could there be a real "Los Angeles Harbor" when San Pedro was twenty-odd miles away? The ocean certainly could not come to the city. So Los Angeles went to the ocean by annexing a one-mile-wide strip of land between the two — the "Shoestring Strip" — and the city limits included the distant harbor. They still do.

But the story was not quite over, for a new problem arose. Could the harbor be completed in time for the opening of the almost-finished Panama Canal? Delay followed delay, many of them seemingly purposeful, and it appeared likely that when eventually ships came through the canal they would bypass the Southland for the port of San Francisco in the north. Finally all disputes were mediated, and when the Panama Canal opened in 1915 Los Angeles Harbor was ready. Before long it became second only to New York among the important ports in the United States — a sequel to the long, complicated, but engrossing story of power politics.

Early in the 20th century the Union Pacific, through its acquisition of the San Pedro, Los Angeles & Salt Lake Railroad Company, became the third large railroad line to serve the city. The service was established without controversy. The entire transcontinental line was opened to traffic with Los Angeles in May 1905.

8. *Trauma of the First Banks*

Until the great changes which took place along all lines in 1868, the "smalltown" quality of Los Angeles was most evident in her system of banking. A small iron safe kept by the storekeeper was the nearest thing to a bank; good customers were allowed to keep their own cash in it without charge. However, travelers were often robbed, and the transportation of money was difficult. These frontier problems ended when at last, in one year, two banks were opened in Los Angeles.

The first was Hayward and Company. In 1868 John A. Hayward of San Francisco and ex-Governor John G. Downey opened a bank where now the U.S. Courthouse stands.

The same year Hellman, Temple and Company opened its doors. Isaias W. Hellman had been a merchant in the city for ten years, and ranchers had kept their cash in his safe after selling cattle or sheep, hides and tallow. One of his customers, William Workman, suggested that instead of just giving the money safekeeping he should form a bank and put the deposited money to work — paying interest to depositors, with Hellman himself receiving interest when the money was loaned. When Hellman decided to follow his friend's suggestion, he took as partner Francis Temple, brother of pioneer John Temple.

Later the two banks changed names and partners. Downey joined Hellman in management of the Farmers & Merchants Bank (still in existence). Temple and his father-in-law William Workman, also known as "Don Julian," opened the Temple and Workman Bank. These two men had excellent integrity but understood nothing about business. Workman was concerned mostly with his Rancho La Puente, and his partner gave many loans on unsecured notes.

In 1875 a business depression and bank panic started. The Bank of California in San Francisco closed its doors, followed by others all over the state. The only person in either bank in Los Angeles who understood finance, Isaias Hellman, happened to be en route to Europe at the time. Downey and Temple, in charge of the two banks, conferred and decided to close their doors. Since all banking in the city was done through these two houses, business was therefore paralyzed.

Hellman returned from Europe and reopened his bank. Temple tried to borrow money in San Francisco to reopen his as well but found only panic in the northern city. At last Elias J. "Lucky" Baldwin, the Comstock millionaire, agreed to loan the bank $210,000 and accepted ranch land as security for the loan. The bank reopened, but there was such a run on the funds that three weeks later Baldwin was asked for more money. He added another $100,000. For the loan, William Workman mortgaged to Baldwin his half-ownership in the huge Rancho La Puente as well as his Rancho Potrero de Felipe Lugo. Francis P. F. Temple mortgaged his half of Rancho La Merced and part-ownership of Rancho Las Ciénegas, while Juan Matias Sanchez pledged the other half of La Merced and also his Rancho Potrero Grande. In addition, Temple and Workman mortgaged their valuable properties in downtown Los Angeles, including the Temple Block, a large building which housed a number of offices and stores and stood on the site of today's City Hall. The contract included pages concerned particularly with Baldwin's rights, while the multitude of penalties the other parties could be subjected to promised a nightmare for any debtor in default of either interest or principal.

Lucky Baldwin.

Friendship alone caused Sanchez to add his landholdings. The Sanchez and Temple families were exceptionally close and Sanchez felt impelled to join his friend in facing the desperate financial problem. Their efforts were useless: within two weeks the bank was forced to close again. Auditors found to their amazement, when investigating the books, that records had been so carelessly kept that for four years there had been no posting (transfer of entries from the daybooks to the ledger, to bring the overall records up to date). The bank's notes had a face value of $390,000, but they brought only $30 at the public auction. Because Temple and Workman's ranch land had been assigned to Lucky Baldwin as security, the property was not available to help satisfy creditors of the bank. After Baldwin foreclosed the mortgages he bought most of the property at the sheriff's sale.

The shock of having caused his loyal friend, Juan Sanchez, to lose his ranch land, and grief over the loss of his own home, caused William Workman to commit suicide. Francis Temple became seriously ill. The impoverished Sanchez retired to his son's holdings in Whittier. The history of the families of these men was interwoven with that of Los Angeles itself, and the entire city mourned the tragedy which had befallen its three distinguished sons.

9. *Oil in Downtown Los Angeles*

A new industry began when the world's first oil well was drilled in Pennsylvania in 1859. In the 1860s a few wells were developed in California's Humboldt and Ventura Counties, but not until the next decade did Los Angeles enter the field.

A quarter of a century earlier, in 1850, Andrés Pico had taken oil from seeps in Pico Canyon near Newhall and distilled it into a kerosene he called "burning oil" to light the dark rooms of the San Fernando Mission where he lived. In that same canyon a 300-foot well was dug in 1876, and thirty barrels of oil a day were produced. It is considered the first truly commercial oil well in California. Similarly, the refinery built nearby at Newhall (for the production of benzine and kerosene) is considered the state's first true oil refinery. After two years the well's depth was increased, and then 150 barrels of oil per day were produced — an astounding amount at that time.

In 1879 the state's first oil pipeline (approximately five miles of two-inch pipe) was laid between the well and the refinery. Because costs of rail transportation to San Francisco were high, another pipeline was laid between Newhall and the harbor at Ventura so that steamers fitted with steel tanks could take shipments of oil to San Francisco at low rates.

Edward Laurence Doheny, a prospector, arrived in Los Angeles in 1892. Curious about a wagonload of what people told him was "brea," he found out it came from near Westlake Park (now MacArthur Park). Doheny was by nature interested in materials dug from the ground, so he climbed aboard a horse-drawn streetcar and rode out to the source of the brea he had seen. Upon viewing the pools, he realized he was looking at an asphalt formed by the evaporation of petroleum. With a former partner who happened to be in Los Angeles, Charles A. Cannon, he investigated different brea pits and finally bought a lot near the intersection of Patton and Colton Streets with Glendale Boulevard, one block north of present-day Beverly Boulevard. There the two men dug a 4x6-foot mine shaft. Beginning at seven feet down, the walls of the shaft seeped oil, which gave off gas. The deeper they dug the worse the fumes became. Then Doheny remembered a method he had seen used in digging artesian wells. He chose a eucalyptus tree for a drill, sharpening the trunk at the narrow end; it did the work effectively though slowly. For forty days they labored with their drill, and eventually oil began to fill the shaft. Doheny brought it up in buckets, from which the oil was poured into barrels — about seven barrelsful per day.

Doheny's discovery had been made in a residential area. Within eight years there were about 600 wells, most of them in lawns and gardens, and of course each well meant an ugly pump. Often homes were moved to make it possible to dig more wells where they stood.

All the equipment was brought around the Horn (the Panama Canal had not yet been built) from Pennsylvania, where machinery for oil fields was manufactured.

It was a fairy tale for many, including Emma Summers, a piano teacher who became the "Oil Queen of California." She lived near the spot where oil had first been found, and she assumed joint ownership in several ventures besides investing $700 as half interest in a well near her home. When that investment was spent, there was still no sign of oil. In order to pay for continued drilling she gave music lessons at night, borrowed what she could and became her own overseer. Within eight years her name was among those of the wealthiest oil operators.

In 1896 a successful well was dug on the northeast corner of Adobe and College Streets, and soon 270 wells dotted the neighborhood. This was called the Eastern Area of the city field, while the earlier section was known as the Central Area (bounded by Figueroa, First, Union and Temple Streets). Also in the mid-1890s about 300 wells were dug near Westlake Park, called the Western Area. The Los Angeles City Oil Field formed a long, narrow strip less than half a mile wide bordering downtown; at one time there were 1150 wells in operation. Today the Central Area, California's first great oil land, lies cradled in the arms of the Hollywood and Harbor Freeways.

Echo Lake, which had ceased to be used as a reservoir, was larger than it is today and extended much farther toward the central downtown area, especially during the rainy season. The primitive wells in the neighborhood often leaked, and oil was carelessly handled. Not only the brush around the lake but also the water's surface became covered with a thin film of oil. One day some of the weeds caught fire: immediately the flames spread, and soon, incredibly, the entire surface of the lake was ablaze. For three days people gathered to watch the strange sight, until at last the fire was extinguished.

At the turn of the century there was less use than now for petroleum, and before long the market was glutted. The price of crude oil dropped from a high of $1.80 per barrel in 1900 to 15 cents three years later. And then by the time automobiles caused increased demand, most of the earlier wells were used up. Prospectors moved elsewhere. However, the era of oil drilling in the Southland was still in the future.

Edward L. Doheny did not stop with his discovery of the Los Angeles field. In 1897 he discovered the Fullerton Oil Field and, two years later, an oil field in the Kern River Valley. In 1901 Doheny opened an even larger field in Mexico, bringing in that country's first

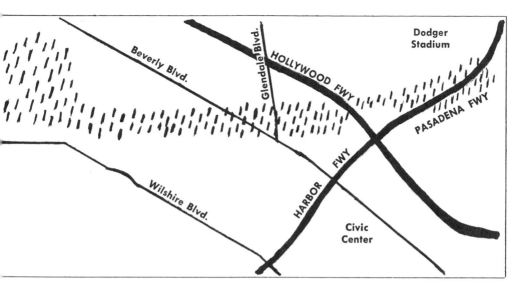

Sketch indicating the downtown Los Angeles City Oil Field.

Los Angeles' backyard oil wells in the 1890s. (—*Title Insurance & Trust Co.*)

commercially successful well. A congressional probe in 1923 questioned the lease of government oil land at Teapot Dome, Wyoming, to Harry Sinclair, and at Elk Hills, California, to Doheny; the contracts had been arranged by Albert B. Fall, Secretary of the Interior. Although the U.S. Supreme Court nullified all contracts, Doheny and Sinclair were acquitted of intent to defraud. Senator Fall was sentenced to prison.

A few of the old Los Angeles wells are still in operation. On Glendale Boulevard at Rockwood, near the spot where Doheny first struck oil, is a scene which once was typical. A house sits in the midst of three wells on a small lot. Using the famous Allen Patent Pumping Unit, the pumps of all three wells are linked by cables so that one activates the others. The grease-covered machines still churn black gold out of the land, and they have been steadily at work since Doheny's eucalyptus drill reached oil and the rush began.

10. *Two Reminiscent Figures*

During this era, frontier Los Angeles stepped into a vital, fast-moving, progressive, enthusiastic life. All things conspired to push her out of the past. Huge acreage was opened up to subdivision as the cattle ranges went out of existence. This shift coincided with a time when people in other parts of the world turned their eyes to Southern California as a land of opportunity. It also coincided with the arrival of railroad transportation, the building of a harbor and the increased availability of water. The fortuitous combination of many advantages set the stage for a city which exuberantly fell in step with other important cities in the United States.

Yet in the midst of change two great men were reminders of the quickly receding past. On Christmas Eve in 1887, John Charles Frémont and his wife came to live in the city which had surrendered to him forty years earlier with the Treaty of Cahuenga. Once wealthy, the Frémonts were now impoverished and disillusioned, and they sought the unsophisticated friendliness to be found in the Southland. Townsfolk became familiar with the sight of the tall, white-bearded, distinguished man in a military cape who, after arising at dawn, took long early-morning walks in a radius from his home on Oak Street, which was 25 blocks from the Plaza where once American headquarters had clustered. The same warm welcome was given to him as when he first marched into Los Angeles. It was during the three years he lived there that Congress raised his rank to major general.

Then, while on a trip east to see a son (also an Army officer) and to arrange for his military pension, Frémont suddenly died. In order to demonstrate the sympathy that the community felt toward Frémont's widow, the women of Los Angeles presented her with a beautiful home (on Hoover Street at 28th) near the campus of the University of Southern California. She lived there for the next twenty years.

In the old Plaza, Pío Pico, the last Mexican governor of California, had also come back to early scenes. It was in 1883, when Don Pío was over eighty, that he received the final blow which cost him his last ranch property and his little remaining wealth. Earlier, because of debts, he had borrowed $62,000 from Bernard Cohn, a Los Angeles businessman. Pico spoke only Spanish and knew almost no English; so during the negotiations and when the papers were signed he used an interpreter, Pancho Johnson, with no one else present. All the property Pico still owned secured the loan. Two months later he went to Cohn with a payment of $65,000 to cover principal and interest, but the money was refused on the grounds that Pico had sold his property outright, that he had signed a deed and not a mortgage. Stunned by the turn of events, Pico took his case to court. During the business transaction there had been one person, the interpreter, who knew Pico's intention. Before the case reached court, Pancho Johnson confirmed with the ex-Governor's lawyers that a loan had been clearly intended, but when he was on the witness stand he insisted it had definitely been a sale. Later it was proved that Pancho had accepted a bribe of $2000 to give false testimony, but even so, a final decision made by the California Supreme Court in 1890 went against Pico and he lost everything.

Juan José Warner, a friend of over sixty years as well as Don Pío's brother-in-law, invited him to live in his home a few blocks from the Plaza. From then on the respected ex-Governor sat for many hours each day in front of Pico House, which had once been his. Usually he wore a short overcoat with velvet collar and cuffs, to which he added the decoration of one or two pieces of heavy jewelry as well as medals given him by Mexico. Love of ornamentation was a deep-seated characteristic. In reminiscences Don Pío confided that when he was twenty years old he met Governor Vicente Sola in Monterey, and for the important occasion he wore the uniform of his father, who had been a sergeant at the Presidio of San Diego. To the Governor he explained that his father had bequeathed the uniform to him; so he was entitled to wear it although not a soldier. The kindly Governor took a liking to the young man, and arranged Pico's appointment as lieutenant of the militia. Don Pío was always pre-eminently Spanish: the first half of his life was spent under the rule of Spain and Mexico, and when, the year after California was conquered, he returned from self-imposed exile in Mexico, he made no effort to learn the language of the invaders. This proud, courtly, beloved man embodied the qualities of a more relaxed era; of mixed ancestry himself (he is known to have been one-eighth Negro), he survived from a time when racial intolerance was not practiced. He could still be seen in his chosen place on the Plaza until shortly before his death in 1894, when he was 93 years old.

But except for an affectionate glance at reminiscent figures, the city kept its eyes resolutely fixed on the future.

Los Angeles was no longer isolated from a progressing world, but was an integral part of life in the United States. It had found reasons to be glad of its location and special qualities. Proudly in step with the rest of the country, Los Angeles moved into the remarkable 20th century.

VII

THE BEGINNING OF THE TWENTIETH CENTURY
1900 - 1932

---

1. *The Movies*

The first years of the 20th century found Los Angeles still a city of less than 300,000 residents. Citrus orchards, walnut groves and vineyards gave an agricultural pattern to the community. As in the century before, a zanjero kept close watch over the city's supply of water.

Weather and scenery were the lures which drew travelers to the Southland — the sparkling air and semitropic comfort, the long, curving shoreline and, always, the mountains to form a background of grandeur.

Los Angeles had grown accustomed to the trains which arrived and left on the mighty transcontinental lines. For an easy interrelationship with the more cosmopolitan San Francisco, two Pullman trains, *The Owl* and *The Lark*, made nightly trips between the two cities, one through the inland mountains and valleys, the other along the Pacific coast. Daylight passenger trains shuttled along the same two routes. The distinctive sound of train whistles was heard, a beckoning voice across the land.

Quickly the 20th century gathered speed, and Los Angeles was propelled into change — change so extreme as to be an explosion. In recurrent waves, millions of newcomers poured into the Southland. Industries crowded out the orange groves; cities multiplied. The continent of North America developed a "westward tilt" as more and more people moved west, especially in the direction of Southern California.

Amazingly, the forerunner of change was the motion picture industry.

It was in the East that a new branch of art began, one destined to turn a spotlight on Los Angeles. Thomas A. Edison collaborated with George Eastman in 1889 to perfect a celluloid strip containing a series of frame-lined pictures. When the pictures were projected one after another onto a screen, they gave a semblance of motion. The first "moving pictures" were shown in penny arcades in New

York and other eastern cities. There a customer would drop a penny in the slot of a machine and look through an aperture. The pictures, lasting hardly a minute, were really just a scene — of a girl climbing an apple tree, a train approaching, a kiss. The first action story, made in 1903, was *The Great Train Robbery*, which lasted less than ten minutes.

As the films improved they were projected onto large screens in vaudeville houses as a type of variety show. Enterprising men made theaters out of storerooms, unused lecture halls and other available space. Their charge of five cents for a performance gave rise to the term "nickelodeon" for the theaters. In the cities most of them were dark and dingy, and this together with the cheapness kept fastidious people away.

Actors of the stage, the so-called "legitimate" theater, looked down on motion pictures as a low form of entertainment comparable to burlesque, until Adolph Zukor through his Famous Players Film Company brought the picture *Queen Elizabeth* to New York. It was made in Paris with Sarah Bernhardt playing the lead and was the first long feature seen in this country. With its presentation, Zukor proved several things. For one, because such a great actress as Bernhardt was willing to take a role, no actor need feel demeaned to work in a motion picture. Also, although *Queen Elizabeth* lasted over an hour the audience showed no sign of restlessness. This disproved the general belief that an audience would not be interested for more than twenty minutes. Nor did the fact that it was a quality picture make it automatically unpopular. Most convincing of all, the audience which would have scorned to go to a nickelodeon paid the higher theater prices for tickets, without murmuring.

For many years the Motion Picture Patents Company, called the Trust, controlled the film industry. It was an alliance of the leading manufacturers of equipment and raw film, as well as operators of processing laboratories. The Trust leased equipment and received royalties from finished pictures. Within the group the most important company was that of Thomas A. Edison, inventor of the kinetoscope (a forerunner of the projector), the most widely used camera and several other types of machinery. Until the Trust was formed, the different companies fought constantly over infringements of patents on the different inventions, but the new alliance created peace among its members. In turn, however, it became a monopoly which ruled the industry: no maker of a moving picture was supposed to buy raw film except with its approval nor use a camera or projector except those leased from the Trust. When Zukor wanted to make a feature

y Pickford, in *Stella Mar-*
played the dual role of
a Maris and the Slavey.
dark line toward the
er indicates where the
n was "split." (*—Robert
man Collection*)

ia Swanson, when she
a Sennett Bathing Beau-
as her hand held by lead-
comedian Mack Swain.
Turpin lurks in the rear.
*ademy of Motion Pic-
Arts and Sciences*)

in the United States, the Trust refused to give him a license to do so for the reason that "The time is not ripe for feature pictures, if it ever will be." Zukor's only choice was to make his picture, *The Prisoner of Zenda,* in a makeshift studio in the top floors of an armory, with guards posted to warn of possible trouble. Companies called Independents, operating on low budgets, used their own cameras and other equipment unauthorized by the Trust. In retaliation their film was often sabotaged during processing or their cameras were stolen. It was not until 1915 that the Sherman Anti-Trust Act was invoked; consequently the Trust, judged guilty of operating in restraint of trade, was dissolved.

Until then California, 3000 miles distant, was a welcome refuge. In addition it offered early producers another advantage — year-round sunshine. In New York and Chicago each year they gloomily faced the dark, stormy days of autumn and winter. Indoor stages were lit, but outdoor scenes depended on daylight, which fluctuated undependably with the weather. One day late in 1907, the Chicago producer Col. William N. Selig was filming a picture, *The Count of Monte Cristo.* Years earlier he had visited California, and nostalgically he thought of the winter sunshine there. Suddenly he made a decision: he ordered everyone working on the film, except for actors, to entrain for California, where all the outdoor scenes would be made. The leading role was played by two different men — one appeared during indoor scenes filmed in Chicago, the other during sequences made in California. When the picture was complete it had a special quality which set it apart from any other. Alas, there is no record of the audience reaction to this extraordinary motion picture.

In wintertime the next year another company from Chicago, Essanay, was the second to turn to the Far West. It filmed a cowboy adventure story in California.

D. W. Griffith was producing films at the Biograph studio in New York City (11 East 14th Street). Early in January 1910 he announced he would leave immediately for Los Angeles with members of the production crew and several actors, including Mary Pickford, who had been working in movies for less than a year. In Los Angeles the "studio" was an open lot without roof or walls but having a wooden platform around which curtains hung from wires. The company stayed only until spring.

Late in 1911, Thomas H. Ince arrived to make some pictures for the New York Motion Picture Company. In Edendale (today's Echo Park area) he found some shabby buildings which he rented and converted into a studio. One day while on his way to a mountain location near Santa Monica Canyon he chanced to see a wild west show wintering nearby. Seizing the opportunity, he hired the show for the season. Among the properties was a covered wagon, which was used in a quickly improvised story. From then on the covered wagon held an accepted place among westerns. In a move from the earlier studio, "Inceville" was built where Sunset Boulevard joins the Pacific Highway. The natural hills were convenient for western backgrounds.

Actors in the earliest movies were not identified by name. However, in 1912, after Mary Pickford had been a leading actress for three years, her full name appeared for the first time on posters and handbills. With that the studio discovered that actors had a name value and people would go to pictures especially to see their favorite stars. The star system evolved, and studios chose films which would enhance the image of a particular actor or actress in the public eye.

Early in 1912 Mack Sennett (real name Michael Sinnott) moved his studio from New York to Los Angeles and brought his actors, Mabel Normand, Ford Sterling and Fred Mace. His was the Keystone Company, so named from the trademark of the Pennsylvania Railroad (Keystone State) which struck Sennett's fancy when he saw it on Pennsylvania Station in New York. In Sennett's memoirs he describes the propitious arrival of his company in California. As they walked out of the Santa Fe depot they saw a Shriners' parade going past along Main Street nearby. Quick to use such an opportunity, he sent an actor to a store to buy a baby doll and ordered the camera set up with a good view of the parade. When Mabel Normand was handed the doll and a shawl to wrap it in, she knew exactly what to do. Stumbling alongside the marchers she held out her baby pathetically, crying that she had been abandoned. The men reacted with dismay, which the camera recorded. When one of the men was especially sympathetic, Ford Sterling began upbraiding him loudly as father of the child. The police ran up, and in a tumultuous scene Ford ran ahead, insulting the police as they chased after him. In the finished picture the police chase was more hilarious than anything else.

From then on Sennett hired a corps of Keystone Cops at $3 each per day, sometimes using off-duty policemen. They dressed in badly fitting uniforms, wore handlebar mustaches and constantly piled into and out of an old Ford. The car, which could hold as many as 15 cops, had a removable steering wheel and often was driven over a road covered with soap to make it slippery and unpredictable. For hair-raising dashes in front of a train, Sennett sat at a crossing with a carload of his cops until a train approached, and then raced across the tracks at the last moment. He kept a close eye on the newspapers to see what good ideas he could fit into local happenings for comedy. A lake to be drained became the essence of a story in which the villain pulled a plug, letting out the water and marooning a boat in which were the hero and heroine. When a tall factory chimney was to be torn down, a comedian climbed on top and the demolition later was part of the story — at no expense to the studio, of course. Auto races were used, and serious fires. He invented false props such as cloth bricks and police clubs that broke. A suction pump held over a man's head just out of camera range made his hair stand on end. After pie throwing became standard in his pictures, the local grocer who supplied the pies developed a lucrative specialty — custard pies, for throwing rather than eating. But Sennett made one terrible mistake: he fired Harold Lloyd because he was not funny.

The Mack Sennett Bathing Beauties, who never went near the water, drew audiences to his pictures as much as the comic plots did. Swimming attire for women at that time included bloomers, tunics with sleeves, and black cotton stockings. The Bathing Beauties changed all that. Their clothes, becomingly abbreviated, shocked some audiences at first, but they led the way to daring new fashions in beachwear. Among the Bathing Beauties who later became stars were Gloria Swanson, Carole Lombard and Phyllis Haver. (The Mack Sennett studio was formerly the Ince studio in Edendale.)

Late in 1913 the Jesse L. Lasky Feature Play Company sent Cecil B. De Mille west to make *The Squaw Man,* but only by accident did he reach Hollywood. Flagstaff was his intended destination. Easterners thought that every place in the West looked alike, but as the train pulled into Flagstaff, De Mille discovered that it looked totally unlike what he had imagined as the picture's background. Besides, it was snowing. The train stopped a few minutes and then continued westward. Before it left the station De Mille was once more on board, this time bound for California.

The Squaw Man was the first long feature made in Los Angeles. To find a studio with enough space, De Mille went out of town. On the eastern side of Vine Street at Selma he found a large barn, the stalls of which could be made into dressing rooms and offices. He decided to rent the barn, but the owner would agree only if, until he was able to make other arrangements, he could keep his carriage and horses there. So for a while the Lasky company shared its quarters. Pictures were filmed on an open stage lit only by sunlight, even for indoor scenes. The stage had no walls except curtains which could be drawn aside to let in extra light. This was typical for all the motion picture companies.

Hollywood as a suburb was considered far out in the country. In fact, when Lasky arrived in Los Angeles to join his company the taxi driver had never even heard of Hollywood. After finding out the location, they drove along dirt roads into open countryside, past farmhouses and orchards. Large homes and shady trees lined sedate Hollywood Boulevard (then Prospect Avenue), and behind them were barns for horses and carriages. At the Hollywood Hotel, a large, quiet country resort at Hollywood and Highland, they were given directions to the Lasky studio barn. Lasky drove by the lacy foliage of rows of pepper trees which gracefully decorated the center of Vine Street until he came to the studio. (The Lasky studio later included all the land between Selma and Sunset from Vine to El Centro. When the company moved to the Paramount lot on Melrose Avenue, the barn was moved too. In 1974 it was still standing, a building which formed part of a western street scene.)

Hollywood itself was not impressed by anyone who wanted to make motion pictures. The residents were prominent and wealthy, and the community stayed aloof from Los Angeles and towns nearby. Show business people were looked at suspiciously as being irresponsible charlatans, moving picture people especially. Accordingly the small bank on the corner of Cahuenga and Hollywood Boulevard refused to accept the deposit of the Lasky company's funds. Instead they were held by the more accommodating owner of a grocery store. North of the Lasky studio, Adolph Zukor rented a farmhouse at Hollywood and Vine, but it was used only in the winter. Headquarters remained in New York, where the company could hire professional actors of the stage.

Charlie Chaplin arrived in Los Angeles in 1913 to work for Mack Sennett. After Ford Sterling quit to strike out on his own, Sennett needed someone to take his place whom he could groom for a leading comedian. He remembered an amusing Englishman he had seen in a show in New York, and phoning his partners in New York he asked them to find the man, whose name was "something like Chapman or Champion." The studio was a strange world to the new comedian, and at first things went poorly. One day, when Chaplin had finished a picture and was waiting to be assigned to the next Sennett turned to him from a set of a hotel lobby and asked him to get ready for the role of a comedian of whatever type he might choose. Intent on developing a costume with comic appeal, the actor decided to put on mismatching clothes. Fatty Arbuckle's trousers were spread on a chair in a dressing room, and Chaplin asked if he could put them on. Then he found a tight coat as contrast, and a small bowler hat.

Charlie Chaplin and Jackie Coogan in a scene from *The Kid*. (—*Academy of Motion Picture Arts and Sciences*)

He put on large shoes, but with the right shoe on his left foot. In order to look older than his 24 years, he added a mustache which he trimmed to suit his character. He found a cane. Sennett liked the new identity and sent him onto the lobby set to improvise as he went along. Chaplin stumbled over a woman's foot and lifted his hat in apology; then, turning away, he stumbled over a cuspidor and again lifted his hat. Actors and stagehands gathered to watch and laugh. The Tramp was an instantaneous success.

Later Chaplin became his own writer-producer-director. In his autobiography he describes the evening in 1917 when, disconsolate because he had no satisfactory ideas for his next picture, he wandered into a theater. A man doing a dance number brought on his four-year-old boy at the end of the performance to take a bow with him. All the boy did was bow, do a few steps, look archly at the audience and run off, but he was wildly applauded. Chaplin began thinking of the endless possibilities a story would have which revolved around that engaging boy and the Tramp. The boy, Jackie Coogan, was signed to do a picture. Eventually he made $4,000,000, but somehow the money disappeared. When he reached 21 he sued his mother and stepfather for an accounting. Although the court found that he had no redress, the case resulted in enactment of the "Jackie Coogan Law" protecting the earnings of child actors.

In 1918 Chaplin built a studio at 1414 N. La Brea Avenue, at Sunset Boulevard, in Hollywood. There he made *The Kid, The Gold Rush, The Circus, City Lights, The Great Dictator* and *Modern Times.* Although the buildings have had many owners since then, their appearance remains almost unchanged.

During the early days of moving pictures the Alexandria Hotel, downtown at Fifth and Spring Streets, was a favorite meeting place of all those who wanted to see or be seen. The elegant lobby had ten marble columns, walls with a marble decor and underfoot a huge oriental rug, the "Million-Dollar Rug." In the ceiling of the ballroom was a long skylight made of stained glass.* It was the custom that, while meeting informally at the Alexandria, producers, directors and stars arranged many of their contracts. The luxurious hotel drew not only people from the studios; presidents and statesmen stayed there, and such visitors as Paderewski, Caruso and Sarah Bernhardt.

With the start of World War I in 1914, Europe became involved in more serious things than the making of movies. At the same time the public became increasingly avid for the new type of entertainment and by the end of the war Hollywood — or rather, Los Angeles — was entrenched as the center of film making. Here were most of the leading actors and actresses, as well as screenwriters, directors and producers. Hollywood's stars were world famous. The production and distribution of motion pictures involved so much wealth that they were called America's fifth industry.

In 1914 Carl Laemmle bought 230 acres of hillside and canyon property in Cahuenga Pass where it spreads into the San Fernando Valley. When Universal City opened its gates the next year, the opening was itself a "spectacular." From New York City a special train arrived for the ceremony, after picking up Buffalo Bill and other invited guests en route. Thousands of spectators were on hand for the excitement. In a burst of showmanship Laemmle had erected a "city" complete with residents and mayor — a position usually held by one of the stars. The first citizens were 75 Indians who lived in tepees at the foot of a hillside while horsemen who filled the roles of cowboys and cavalrymen lived in bunkhouses. Throughout the years since then families have always been living on the lot, holding jobs there as well. The exterior of their homes, like everything else there, performs double

---

*Because of the blackouts required during World War II, the skylight was given a thick coat of black paint. When the hotel was restored in 1970, it took three months of painstaking labor to clean the stained glass.

duty as background for sets — for instance, in a porch or garden scene. Later the post office of Universal City was created, with boundaries the same as those of the studio. No mail carriers operate from the station, however, since everything incoming is sorted into post office boxes along the wall. In 1917, soon after the lot opened, 42 companies worked there simultaneously. This created a scarcity of stages, and at times filming was done by three or four companies on a single stage. Sound was no problem, of course, that being the day of silent pictures. Along certain stages bleachers were built so that paying visitors could watch in the same spirit that now, through studio tours, a million people each year buy tickets to enter the gates of cinemaland.

In small companies the men who financed the films would themselves often become extras in order to save added hiring. Other, larger, companies put advertisements in the newspapers telling the need for "500 extras in evening dress" or "1000 extras in western clothes." Enterprising men who answered the advertisements sometimes found themselves launched into exciting careers. W. S. Van Dyke II, future director of the *Thin Man* series and *Marie Antoinette*, is an example. He answered an ad to work in the filming of *Intolerance*, D. W. Griffith's spectacular story. In the picture, Van Dyke took the part of a king, a captain of Babylonian soldiers, a Christian soldier, a high priest, a charioteer, a bareback rider, a groomsman at the wedding when Jesus turned water into wine, a make-up man (the only one who satisfied Griffith, because he made extras look authentically Babylonian) and a second-assistant director.

Tom Mix and his horse jump Beale's Cut in the movie *Three Jumps Ahead*, directed by John Ford in 1923. (*—Robert S. Birchard Collection*)

Mary Pickford and Douglas Fairbanks on their honeymoon. (—*Robert Cushman Collection*)

Some cowboy stars and extras in movies were real cowboys. Tom Mix and Hoot Gibson both had won the top prize in the Pendleton Roundup in Oregon, where to win meant being all-around best performer in roping, bulldogging and bronco busting.

One star, Mary Pickford (real name Gladys Smith), was loved by the public above all others. It was in 1909, when she was 15 years old, that she entered motion pictures at the Biograph studio. After one day's work, director D. W. Griffith offered her the lead in *The Violin Maker of Cremona* playing opposite Owen Moore, whom she later married. With the leading role her salary jumped from $5 a day to $40 per week. In theater lobbies, while names were not mentioned, she was first billed as The Biograph Girl or The Girl with the Curls. As she grew older she was still cast in teenage roles, and such an affection for her developed among moviegoers that when someone called her "America's Sweetheart" the name became permanent.

Her marriage in 1920 to the popular star Douglas Fairbanks was a national event. It occurred soon after her divorce from Moore, and because she had become a familiar and beloved person to families throughout the country everyone assumed a right to have a strong opinion about the impropriety of her new marriage. Fairbanks, too, was divorced and it seemed likely that both their careers, or at least Mary's, had ended. Newspapers reflected the tumult which raged in every community. She was in the midst of filming a picture when they were married, and by the time the newlyweds started on their honeymoon the furor had died down. They were to go to Europe, and because Mary had never been outside the United States she studied history during the transatlantic crossing so that their visits to cities could be spent in sightseeing. What they planned was not to be. To their amazement, at the first stop, London, thousands gathered below their window hoping for a glimpse of the glamorous pair. The mobs became so huge that friends offered them a refuge in their country estate on the Isle of Wight, where there would be absolute isolation. The offer was immediately accepted. The first morning in that secluded place Mary awoke at 6:30 and opened the shutter to see the countryside. Beyond some flowers a ten-foot wall had been built to ensure privacy. It was covered with people who had arrived before dawn to greet Mary and Doug the instant their shutters were opened. And so it went. In Amsterdam, Paris, Rome, Venice, always the crowds were tremendous. It was an example of a fact now commonly realized, that the screen knows no international boundaries and its stars belong to the world.

David Wark Griffith was one of the greatest directors of all time. He made the first use of the closeup, a picture of Mary Pickford from the waist up. It infuriated the executives of his company, who reminded him indignantly, "We're paying this girl the large sum of one hundred dollars a week, and we want to see all of her, including her feet — not just half of her." He also was the first to use a fadeout when it happened by accident, although opportunely, at the end of a kiss. His earliest feature, *The Birth of a Nation,* filmed in 1914, had unparalleled success. It was the first film ever shown in the White House, and President Wilson is quoted as saying, "It is like writing history with lightning." Two decades later Griffith's career ended after a series of financial failures. From then on no one offered him work of any kind, and the industry he had done so much to build ignored him. Most of his friends ceased to call. In 1948 he died at the Knickerbocker Hotel in Hollywood, where he lived alone. The enormous crowd at his funeral, and the number of stars who attended, made an ironic postscript to the loneliness of his last years.

One day in 1916 Thomas Ince was filming a picture in which Indians paddled down Ballona Creek. Cameras onshore were trained on the swift-moving canoes, and a crowd of spectators watched the creation of a moving picture. Among them was Harry Culver, owner and subdivider of neighboring land. His Culver City was too far from town, and he found few buyers, but if a studio were there it might cause people to build homes and stores nearby. Pointing out to Ince that all types of locations were right in that area — plains, hills, farmlands, the river, beaches — he offered to give him land at no cost whatever

The chariot race was filled with exciting and realistic accidents that, fortunately, injured no one. (*—From the M-G-M release* BEN HUR © *1927 Metro-Goldwyn-Mayer Distributing Corp. Copyright renewed 1955 by Loew's Inc.*)

if he would put up a studio there. The offer was accepted, and Ince built a studio (Washington Boulevard at Goldwyn Terrace). By the time it was finished his company had become part of a new one called the Triangle Film Corporation, whose three partners were D. W. Griffith, Mack Sennett and Thomas Ince.

In 1918 Irving Thalberg, private secretary of Carl Laemmle in his New York office, came to the Universal City studio in California. His responsibilities were vague, and the studio operations were chaotic. One day Thalberg told Laemmle that there should be a studio manager to watch day-to-day operations, to which Laemmle replied, "All right. You're it." Thalberg was then twenty years old. Under his influence Universal's pictures improved in quality; the studio's income soared, but Thalberg's salary remained low. In 1923 he moved to Louis B. Mayer's studio, and the next year a merger resulted in the formation of Metro-Goldwyn-Mayer. The company moved into the Goldwyn studio in Culver City, originally owned by Triangle. At 24, Thalberg was made supervisor of production. During his years with M-G-M he showed himself to be the most inspired man in motion picture history.

His first production was *Ben Hur*, starring Ramon Navarro and Francis X. Bushman. One of the film industry's most exciting experiences was the chariot race, held in a coliseum built on a large lot at La Cienega and Venice Boulevards. The race was to be filmed on a Saturday, and a majority of the stars, directors and producers of Hollywood came to watch. Three thousand extras were hired to be the coliseum audience (at $3.50 for the day, plus lunch), and when Thalberg decided there were too few, 300 more were hired from the crowd outside which was watching with fascination. The Roman horse guard scheduled to precede the chariot race was made up of a cavalry troop from the Presidio at Monterey. Forty-two cameras at various locations covered all views. The stuntmen driving the 12 chariots were told that the one coming in first would be given $150 extra pay. Then director Fred Niblo signaled from his place on a high tower that the race should begin. The buglers blew, the chariots raced into the coliseum, the crowd roared. Rounding a turn, one of the vehicles had a wheel come loose. The chariot lurched into another, and then two more crashed into them headlong. The cameras recorded the real accident and the real horror of the spectators. Most amazing of all, however, was the fact that not one man or animal was hurt in the smashup which seemed, and easily could have been, as disastrous as any race held in the Circus Maximus.

Although Hollywood was a center of glamor, it found in 1921 that it was nevertheless subject to the nation's ideas of moral behavior. In that year Roscoe Arbuckle — known on the screen as Fatty because he weighed 300 pounds — gave a party in his suite at the St. Francis Hotel in San Francisco. Immediately afterward one of the women died, and Arbuckle was accused of manslaughter. Sensational exposés reported that during an orgy he attacked the woman who later died. There were hints of perversion. Arbuckle was tried before a jury three times — the first two were hung juries, but the third returned a verdict of acquittal within seconds after retiring for a decision. Though he was cleared, he was never on-screen again.

Dozens of magazines had emerged, devoted to gossip about people in the motion picture industry. With relish, all of them seized any slight piece of news as the basis for a lurid article. In the public mind the Hollywood movie colony was as depraved as Biblical accounts of Sodom and Gomorrah. The Arbuckle scandal seemed to verify even the worst accounts. In the face of public attacks on Hollywood from pulpits, women's clubs and newspaper columnists, the studios formed the Motion-Picture Producers and Distributors of America in 1922, and at a salary of $100,000 a year Will Hays was hired to lead censorship control. Hays had been postmaster general in President Harding's cabinet and was a man the public respected.

Two weeks after his appointment a new scandal broke in the headlines. On February 3, 1922, William Desmond Taylor, a director, was found murdered. Mabel Normand, Sennett's leading comedienne, had been at his home the evening before and was the last person who had been seen with him.

A beautiful young actress, Mary Miles Minter, hurried to Taylor's house as soon as she heard of his death. She pushed her way through the police lines, sobbing words about her intense love for him, and later told the police she was to have married him as soon as she was of age and could leave her mother.

Mabel Normand's chauffeur told police investigators that at 7 p.m. he had driven the car to Taylor's house, where she went in for about half an hour and then came out accompanied by Taylor, who was murdered half an hour later. Unexpected information was disclosed: William Desmond Taylor was really William Cunningham Deane-Tanner, who at one time owned an antique shop on Fifth Avenue in New York City and had suddenly disappeared, abandoning his wife and daughter. Eventually he arrived in Hollywood and found work in motion pictures using his new name. Four years after he left New York his brother also disappeared, leaving a wife and two children. Later Taylor had a butler known as Edward Sands, who forged several checks in his employer's name and also stole and pawned his clothes and valuables. He seemed to feel safe from punishment — was he the brother? Two weeks before the murder, Sands disappeared. In the victim's home, police found a nightgown on which were embroidered the initials M M M, and love letters from Mary Miles Minter were found hidden in the toe of a boot. A neighbor had seen a man coming out of Taylor's house right after the time of the shooting, but his appearance was strange. Not only did he wear a hat pulled far down and a muffler which further concealed his face, but the man's suit was poorly fitted: it looked as though the person wearing the clothes was in reality a woman. Suspicion then focused upon Mary's mother, who was known to have been intensely jealous of Taylor. The case was complicated by the fact that the police received an average of ten "confessions" each day. Speculation about the mystery and the persons involved continued endlessly, yet no trial was ever held, apparently for lack of sufficient evidence to indict anyone for murder. At first it seemed that Mabel Normand's career had been ruined by the scandal, but her producer, Mack Sennett, stood by her. Mary Miles Minter never appeared in another film.

Soon afterward Wallace Reid, a leading actor, died from drug addiction at the age of thirty.

Faced with a nationwide outcry over the scandals, the studios turned humbly to Will Hays, accepting him as their absolute authority. He wasted no time. Studio contracts soon included "morality clauses" stating that a contract could be nullified if an actor were accused of immorality (proof was not necessary). Reforms suggested by the Hays office regarding the subject matter of films were accepted by every studio.

Hollywood as the world knew it was a name, not a place. It was thought to be the location of all the studios, whereas although several important companies started in the small suburb, others operated in quite different areas of Los Angeles. Inceville was in Santa Monica until the studio moved to Culver City; M-G-M and Hal Roach were in Culver City; Universal was in San Fernando Valley; Warners (originally First National) moved from Hollywood to Burbank; Disney was in the Silver Lake District and then Burbank; and Mack Sennett started in Edendale and moved to Studio City. Yet in distant countries Hollywood became far better known than Los Angeles.

Theatrical producers usually developed from a stage career, but motion picture producers were a new breed of men. Many of them came from walks of life unrelated to show business: Adolph Zukor was a furrier, Sam Goldwyn a glove salesman, William Fox a cloth sponger, Carl Laemmle a clothing salesman and Louis B. Mayer a junk dealer.

To the upper society of Los Angeles the film colony was not acceptable. The Los Angeles Country Club and other clubs turned a cold shoulder toward such people, however important they might be, when they applied to become members. But to foreign visitors Pickfair — the hilltop home of Mary Pickford and Douglas Fairbanks in Beverly Hills — was the home of royalty. Among its guests were Alfonso XIII (former King of Spain), the King and Queen of Siam and Crown Prince Hirohito (later Emperor of Japan). When the Duke and Duchess of Alba arrived in California their first request was to visit Pickfair, and when Lord and Lady Mountbatten arrived on their honeymoon they refused invitations from the local leaders of society and instead gave their full time to the "stars."

By the 1920s the production of motion pictures was the largest industry in Los Angeles. Crowds thronged to *The Thief of Bagdad*, *The Ten Commandments*, *Orphans of the Storm*, *The Sheik*, *The Covered Wagon*, *The Big Parade*, *The Hunchback of Notre Dame*. Moviegoers watched for films starring Mary Pickford, Douglas Fairbanks, Charlie Chaplin, Lillian and Dorothy Gish, Gloria Swanson, Norma Talmadge, Rudolph Valentino, Wallace Reid, William S. Hart,

Tom Mix, Clara Bow, Jack Gilbert, Colleen Moore, Vilma Banky, Ronald Colman, Lon Chaney, Ramon Navarro and countless others. Hollywood was followed by many as an arbiter of fashion and ideal living. At first most of the stars lived in Hollywood, but as soon as the neighboring residential suburb of Beverly Hills was founded it became a glamorous community of stars, producers and directors. Salaries of the stars climbed ever higher, and income taxes were very low. Tastes became extravagant. The stars vied with each other regarding homes, clothes, cars, jewelry and investments in real estate. Some acquired stables of thoroughbred horses.

Late in 1921, advertisements of *The Sheik* urged moviegoers to see:

The auction of beautiful girls to the lords of Algerian harems.

The heroine, disguised, invade the Bedouins' secret slave rites.

Sheik Ahmed raid her caravan and carry her off to his tent.

Her captured by bandit tribesmen and enslaved by their chief in his stronghold.

The Sheik's vengeance, the storm in the desert, a proud woman's heart surrendered.

The words heralded a flaming love story starring one of the great screen lovers, Rudolph Valentino.

He had already appeared in *The Four Horsemen of the Apocalypse* playing the role of a gaucho from the Argentine. His sensual magnetism and the lithe grace with which he danced the tango made him an immediate hit. In *The Sheik* he epitomized the conquering male, and across the nation women thronged to see the movie. Today the melodramatic scenes are laughable, but not then: women by the thousands became infatuated with him. After making *Blood and Sand* he married Natacha Rambova (real name Winifred O'Shaughnessy, stepdaughter of Richard Hudnut). Later they were divorced, and his name was next linked with that of Pola Negri, a sultry actress. His last film was *The Son of the Sheik*, after which he went to New York. There in 1925, at the age of 31, he was stricken with appendicitis and died.

His death let loose an orgy of mourning. It was reported that two women committed suicide over his loss. Thousands of women gathered outside the building in New York City where Valentino's body lay in state. Mounted policemen tried to keep order, but windows were broken and those who were able to enter the funeral home left it a shambles after they stripped it of souvenirs. From Hollywood, Pola

Rudolph Valentino as a gauch
(—*From the M-G-M release* TH
Four Horsemen of the Apoc.
lypse © *1921 Metro Pictures Cor*
Copyright renewed 1948 by Loew
Inc.)

Negri hurried to attend the funeral. When she arrived at the mortuary and was taken in through a side door, she collapsed beside the bier. In an hysterical tumult, 100,000 people crowded into the street near the church on the day of the funeral. Valentino's body was brought to Los Angeles for burial at the Hollywood Cemetery. There a woman, heavily veiled, brought flowers to his crypt. In excitement, movie magazines speculated who the solitary, mysterious mourner might be — she was too tall to be Pola Negri. Whether or not she reappeared on the anniversary of Valentino's death no one knows, for at that time 11 heavily veiled women appeared with offerings of flowers.

The next romantic male star to be an outstanding favorite was John Gilbert. In the early twenties he starred at M-G-M in *The Merry Widow* and *The Big Parade*. In 1925, the year of Valentino's death, a Swedish actress named Greta Garbo (real name Greta Gustafson) arrived in Culver City. While talent scouting in Berlin, Louis B. Mayer had engaged Maurice Stiller, a director, and the actress who was his protégée. Her first screen test was a disappointment, but Stiller directed her in the second and her skill in acting was made plain. Thalberg was preparing *The Torrent* and placed her in the leading role opposite Ricardo Cortez, but because she understood very little English an interpreter was kept on the set to explain instructions to her. When the picture was released, critics responded favorably. The understanding with Mayer had been that Stiller would direct Garbo's films; so he was assigned to her next, *The Temptress*, co-starring Antonio Moreno. However, to the M-G-M executives, Stiller was arbitrary and extravagant: after ordering 100 extras, he used none; he reshot scenes endlessly. Thalberg quickly replaced him with Fred Niblo. Garbo's next film assignment was one that made history — she was to play in *Flesh and the Devil,* and John Gilbert was to be her leading man.

Because Thalberg assigned Clarence Brown instead of Maurice Stiller to direct, Greta Garbo remained away from the set until the day filming was to begin. The time came for the stars' first scene together. The director started them in a flirtatious episode, and immediately a real-life flirtation began, as each became intrigued by the other. Throughout the picture the love scenes were genuine, and the studio publicity department allowed the press to follow their romance avidly. When the film was released it was a smash hit. Their next picture together was *Love.*

The day of the silent film was coming to a close. In 1927 *The Jazz Singer* led the way for sound when Al Jolson spoke a few words and sang. The public's reaction was so enthusiastic that all the studios realized sound was inevitable. They engaged voice and singing teachers, and all actors and actresses who needed the training reported daily for classes.

Unsure about Greta Garbo's strong Swedish accent and low, husky tones, M-G-M executives kept her in silent pictures as long as possible. Finally the moment could be postponed no longer. She was assigned to *Anna Christie* in 1929, and to the studio's delight her voice recorded as attractive and eloquent. A short time later theater marquees blazed with "GARBO TALKS."

For John Gilbert the advent of sound was a tragedy. The first picture he made with a sound track was *His Glorious Night.* The mediocre script itself was unfortunate, and Gilbert's voice was naturally high pitched; when he spoke the flowery dialogue the script called for, the audience began to laugh. Even his dramatic manner

Greta Garbo and John Gilbert. (*—From the M-G-M release* FLESH AND THE DEVIL © *1927 Metro-Goldwyn-Mayer Corp. Copyright renewed 1954 by Loew's Inc.*)

of love-making seemed out of place when accompanied by sound instead of silence. Humiliated by the laughter, he lost his self-confidence and became bitter and depressed. In spite of efforts to learn, he had no knack for using his voice expertly. Although he made several more pictures, they were inadequate. Formerly Gilbert had been an extrovert, but he began to avoid people and even to enter the studio by a back gate in order to escape notice. In 1933 Greta Garbo insisted that he play the male lead in *Queen Christina* instead of Laurence Olivier, who had been promised the part. In spite of a fine performance, it failed to change the tide of failure for him. In his hillside home alcohol became a steady companion, while his moroseness and bitterness drove friends away. In January 1935 he died.

With sound, a new kind of star was born. Walt Disney had his idea for Mickey Mouse cartoons just as sound tracks came into use. He added sound to animation, and the comic skill with which it was handled made the Disney cartoons outstanding. They lasted only five minutes, but they put the audience into a completely receptive mood. It was a tribute to Disney's genius that soon after the Mickey Mouse cartoons appeared theaters were giving them billing on the marquees. A famous cartoon in *The New Yorker* magazine showed the entrance to a theater on whose marquee glowed the names of glamorous stars. A gloomy audience straggled out, heads sunk in dejection. Below the cartoon, the caption was "No Mickey Mouse."

Walt Disney had first presented his idea to M-G-M. At a private screening executives were shown a sample reel, and Frances Marion, an M-G-M scriptwriter who was there, describes the scene in her book *Off with Their Heads*. The executives were impressed with the film's cleverness and called Mr. Mayer to see it. "Damndest best cartoon I've ever seen!" one of them said. The picture was started, and soon Mickey Mouse appeared. "Stop that film! Stop it at once!" Mayer shouted. Angrily he told his aides to think of "the poor frightened women in the audience" and added, "All over this country pregnant women go into our theaters to see our pictures and to rest themselves before their dear little babies are born," but "every woman is scared of a mouse." He was already on his way out the door, and it slammed behind him.

(—© *Walt Disney Produc*

The crime wave which arose during Prohibition gave a theme to gangster films starring Paul Muni, George Raft, James Cagney, Edward G. Robinson, Humphrey Bogart and many others. Popular, ornate theaters such as Grauman's Egyptian and Chinese gave spectacular premieres. In 1930, when *Hell's Angels* opened, 250 searchlights filled the sky with brilliance, and ten blocks of Hollywood Boulevard were roped off, sacred to the proceedings.

The gala premiere marked a crest, a high point, because with the beginning of the thirties new aspects of life in the Southland were due to appear. But on that evening no person in the crowd thought beyond that moment as, under myriad searchlights interweaving their beams overhead, he watched the limousines drive up to the theater's entrance and the stars emerge. From the days when horsemen tended their cattle on this same land, it has been easy to accept each change which "progress" has brought, but no metamorphosis can have been less expected than the rise of the industry of make-believe.

2. *Water by Aqueduct*

At the turn of the century the Southland was in the middle of a ten-year drought. Starting in 1895, each rainy season brought disappointment, and though Los Angeles doggedly tried to keep life on a normal basis, the water level in the few reservoirs steadily dropped. Artesian wells could not by themselves take care of a population of almost 300,000. The city was forced to look clearly at the fact that its existence did not depend on a growing industry, fine weather or dazzling scenery.

Its existence depended upon water.

In the midst of the drought one man stepped into leadership, a man who more than anyone else was to shape the future of the Southland.

In 1877 Bill Mulholland, 21 years old, had ridden into Los Angeles on his horse. The young man looked around at the gardens, the hills, the orange groves and vineyards, the river banked with willow trees, and he knew that he was home. With the exception of a few months, he lived in Los Angeles the rest of his life.

Mulholland's first job was in the Compton area, digging artesian wells with a hand drill. When he found fossils several hundred feet belowground he wanted to understand their significance, and so he began to study geology. When later he became interested in the storage of water, he took up the study of hydraulic engineering. Later yet, wanting to beautify reservoirs and dams, he studied botany. And

Water pours down The Cascades in Sylmar celebrating completion of the Los Angeles Owens River Aqueduct, November 5, 1913. At the top of the same hill a Second Los Angeles Aqueduct began operation on June 26, 1970. Its waters now cascade down to mingle with those shown here. (—*Los Angeles Department of Water & Power*)

in his imaginative mind the information was turned to uses never thought of before.

A year after his arrival he was zanjero for the Los Angeles City Water Company, in charge of the Buena Vista Reservoir and its open ditches. The water came from the Los Angeles River at a point not far from today's Los Feliz Boulevard and Riverside Drive; Mulholland lived in an old house nearby. (At the intersection a large fountain now splashes, its waters commemorating the man who became one of the city's leading benefactors.) When the Los Angeles Water Works System was established in 1902 — a few months later it was renamed the Water Department — William Mulholland was appointed the first superintendent.*

The drought continued without a sign of ending. There was no question about it, more water had to be found. But where?

Fred Eaton, a former mayor of Los Angeles, owned a ranch in the Owens Valley, about 250 miles to the north. In 1904 he took Mulholland there and showed him the green, fertile valley overlooked by the Sierra — Mount Whitney and many other peaks which rise over 11,000 feet — where a thousand lakes catch the melting snow and countless mountain streams carry the water into the Owens River. At that time the river flowed into a strange lake, a volcanic bowl with no outlet: the water could only evaporate, leaving a great quantity of borax and soda in the lake which made it unfit for irrigation or drinking. However, canals took water from the river before it reached the lake. Standing on a high vantage spot, Fred Eaton pointed to the lush valley, evidence of the river's abundant supply. Mulholland was convinced at a glance.

For Los Angeles to use any of the water, it would be necessary to buy riparian water rights from the residents of Owens Valley and to obtain permission from Congress to build an aqueduct across intervening Federal lands on the way south. Without giving any exact reason, Eaton went throughout the Owens Valley buying options from willing farmers who thought that a government irrigation project was to be undertaken. In the meantime, few people in Los Angeles knew what was being done. To keep the price of options in the Owens Valley from soaring, everything had to be managed with extreme secrecy.

Los Angeles voted a $25,000,000 bond issue, and the Owens Valley options were taken up. Then the farmers realized that they themselves

---

*In each successive water company (eventually the Department of Water and Power) there was an official zanjero. Not until 1928 was the office discontinued.

had signed away their water rights, and angry meetings denounced the trick that had been played upon them. Speculators raced to buy land in the path of the proposed aqueduct, but President Theodore Roosevelt ordered the land to be declared a forest reserve. Then Los Angeles was granted a right of way across.

The aqueduct was a tremendous project. At one place a tunnel five miles long had to be bored through the Coast Range. In some areas of the Sierra foothills especially strong sections of steel pipe were needed. As no railroad went near, the heavy pipe was pulled by teams of 52 mules. Through boldly imaginative planning, water was brought the entire distance south by gravity flow — with no pumps used at any point, possible because the ultimate destination was lower in altitude than the source.

In his projects, Mulholland sometimes reached far into the past: cement for the aqueduct was made according to an ancient Roman system. At the same time he reached into the future: his ingenious system of hydraulic sluicing was adopted by the builders of the Panama Canal as they approached their most difficult work, Culebra Cut and the Gatun Dam.

Finally the day arrived when the Los Angeles Owens River Aqueduct was ready — November 5, 1913. In San Fernando Valley a crowd assembled for the great moment when the water would come through the aqueduct. On the hillside above, a crew waited for the signal from the platform to turn the wheels and unleash the water. The signal was the raising of the flag. As Old Glory rose, the water came in a splashing torrent, a symbol of the prosperous days that had burst upon Los Angeles.

William Mulholland gave the special address of the day, as short and memorable as any speech on record. In full, it was: "There it is — take it!"

Today from the Golden State Freeway where it passes Sylmar, the plunging terminus of the aqueduct can be seen. Fittingly, that section is called The Cascades.

Until then, Los Angeles had been subject to the hazards of undependable rainfall, but with water always available, the supply for irrigation could be regulated. The results were especially dramatic in the San Fernando Valley, as groves of avocado, orange and walnut trees spread across the plain, along with acres of truck gardens and burgeoning communities. Furthermore, it was found that the ground itself provided a natural storage basin relatively free from evaporation. Surface reservoirs in warm, dry climates lose a large proportion of their water through evaporation, but water distributed for irrigation seeps underground after use and later can be reused a number of times.

Of course the water was needed by all the Southland, yet Los Angeles had gone deeply into debt to acquire it. The upshot was that any community wanting to share the aqueduct would have to become annexed to the city, assuming a portion of the bonded indebtedness. That was the beginning of a long string of annexations. The city of Los Angeles, 114.92 square miles in area, more than doubled as it was joined by most of San Fernando Valley as well as other towns in the Los Angeles Basin. Eventually, due almost entirely to the wish to share water privileges, the city expanded to approximately four times its original size, or 457.92 square miles.*

---

*Los Angeles is no longer the largest city in the United States. During the early sixties Oklahoma City, Oklahoma, made annexations in five counties, and as a result reached a size of 647.6 square miles. In 1967 the city of Jacksonville, Florida, and Duval County consolidated their government and boundaries for economic reasons, and Jacksonville covered 827 square miles. In 1970 the cities of Juneau (capital of Alaska) and Douglas combined with the borough of Juneau to make a city-borough covering 3108 square miles (land 1476 square miles, ice cap 928, inland waterways 704).

William Mulholland.
(*—Los Angeles Department of Water & Power*)

The increasing number of communities, and enlarged population, caused water to become once more a problem. In 1923 Los Angeles decided to accept no more annexations because it could share the water supply no further. Actually, a great deal more was available from the Owens River than was brought by the aqueduct, but it was held by people who owned water rights and sluiced a proportion of the riverflow into their canals. When Los Angeles sent representatives north to buy additional rights, the farmers of Owens Valley declared all-out war against the powerful metropolis. Led by two local bankers, Wilfred and Mark Watterson of Bishop, the owners of canals far up the river drew off as much water as possible and left the stream below them comparatively dry.

In a desperate effort to get more water, Los Angeles sent workmen to build an illegal ditch connecting the aqueduct with the lowest canal, whose rights were owned by the town of Big Pine. A posse drove the workmen away. Finally Los Angeles was able to buy the Big Pine and some other rights for a very high price. Still the upper valley farmers continued to draw off as much of the river as possible. Resentful farmers dynamited the aqueduct leading south.

The Watterson brothers insisted that Los Angeles had to buy the entire Owens Valley, since not only farmers had suffered by the diverting of water but also business had suffered when people moved away. The battle reached newspaper headlines throughout the country, and most of the sympathy was against Los Angeles, with no comprehension of the Southland's particular need. Again and again the aqueduct was dynamited, although Los Angeles sent an armed guard north to give it protection.

The angry stalemate lasted until the State Corporation Commissioner, acting upon a suspicion, investigated a bank in Bishop which was controlled by the Watterson brothers. To the commissioner's surprise and that of everyone else, it was revealed that the Wattersons had embezzled two million dollars to cover bad investments. The brothers were sent to San Quentin Prison, and Owens Valley lost its leaders.

To end the problem, Los Angeles voted an indemnity of $12,000,000 to be paid to the areas affected by allotment of the water to the city. Also, at the head of the valley a dam was built forming Lake Crowley, and there water was stored for use in dry years.

More water was available than could be carried by the aqueduct, and several decades later the thirsty Southland built a second aqueduct from the same area. It starts farther north than the first, at the headwaters of Grant Lake. Above Sylmar the first aqueduct can be seen emerging into the San Fernando Valley halfway up a hill, from a passage bored through the earth. The second aqueduct ends on the crest of the same hill. The water from them both tumbles in separate cascades of rushing white foam, merging at the foot of the hill and flowing under the Golden State Freeway, to be routed to reservoirs as well as directly into watermains.

One of the dams built in connection with the Owens River system, the St. Francis Dam near Newhall, was considered by experts to be the "safest dam ever built," but on March 12, 1928, it was the scene of Southern California's greatest disaster. Less than two years after the dam went into use, and only a few hours after William Mulholland had himself made a tour of inspection, the dam broke in the middle of the night. A wall of water 125 feet high crashed down upon the concrete powerhouse, tossing the enormous generators around like toys. Ten-thousand-ton chunks of broken concrete were strewn by the fury of the waters. Below the dam the flood rushed into the dry bed of the Santa Clara River, killing about 400 people (the exact number was never known) and destroying over 600 homes as the waters raced to the sea 42 miles distant. However, when daylight came, only a narrow, harmless stream of water lay in the riverbed.

The city of Los Angeles immediately assumed all blame. A board of inquiry found that although the concrete dam was structurally faultless it was built upon inferior rock. One side of the dam stood on mica schist, the other side on a rock foundation which was defective in a strange way: although hard when dry, it became soft when saturated and could not hold against constant, heavy pressure. In court, before a coroner's jury, a devastated William Mulholland said, "If there is any responsibility here, it is mine alone. I envy the dead." He was absolved by the jury, the verdict stating, "The building of such a dam should never be left to the sole judgment of one man, no matter how eminent . . . for no one is free of error." Since then all dams built in California have been subject to approval by engineers of the State Department of Water Resources.

After that Mulholland and other engineers developed what are known as earth dams. On a foundation excavated into bedrock, very thin layers of moist dirt are laid down and compacted by heavy rollers, one layer after another, with continuous testing. This makes an impervious material, and for many years the method was considered the safest type of construction for dams.

After the tragedy of the St. Francis Dam, William Mulholland became a changed man. Perversely, one of his great achievements had been twisted into harm for others. The agony of this thought was reflected physically. Within a short time friends saw the buoyant step of "The Chief" become slow, reluctant. Seven months after the disaster he resigned the position of chief engineer and general manager of the Bureau of Water and Power, a post he had held for 26 years. Yet he remained with the organization as advisor until his death in 1935. For half a century he served the people of Los Angeles.

Mulholland's name was given to a road along the ridge of the mountains which separate the Los Angeles Basin on one side from the San Fernando Valley on the other, lands which owe their growth to water's lifegiving quality. Without it there would be few cities where many now stand; years of drought would have been cataclysmic. In 1900 there was barely enough water to take care of a population of less than 300,000. Now in the city of Los Angeles alone there are over 100 reservoirs, about one-fourth of them major. It is wholly appropriate that Mulholland Drive follows the crest of the hills, commanding a view of the immense acres which by their very prosperity are a memorial to the vision of William Mulholland.

3. *More Oil*

As the 20th century began, Los Angeles was a strange sight indeed. From Elysian Park to Vermont Avenue near today's Wilshire Boulevard, 1150 ungainly oil derricks stood in vacant fields and among houses along a belt two or more blocks wide. Through a pervasive odor of petroleum, grimy pumps steadily chugged away. Other important fields had been discovered in California, but the Los Angeles City Oil Field was one of the state's three largest producers.

Overproduction finally brought down the price of oil. It also depleted the oil pools belowground, and by 1904 many of the wells in the city field were dismantled. However, by then oil was discovered

in an area one mile square bounded by La Brea and Fairfax, Wilshire and Beverly Boulevard. Called the Salt Lake Oil Field from the name of a main producer there, it was the leading field in Southern California in 1905. (Today the Farmers' Market stands on the site of the discovery well.)

One day in 1914, in the hills of Rancho La Merced across the road from his home property, nine-year-old Tommy Temple (grandson of F. P. F. Temple) was trying to catch lizards. Beside a clump of wild oats he saw a pool of water which was varicolored on top and had an unpleasant odor. Thinking he might have found oil, he ran to get his father. The water was bubbling, and his father held a match near a large bubble, which sputtered. He decided it was natural gas. Three years later the father described the pool to a friend, who persuaded Standard Oil to sink an exploratory well. Black gold poured out. The well on Rancho La Merced was owned by heirs of Lucky Baldwin, but when the second well was dug on Temple's property, oil poured out there too. Soon the Montebello Oil Field sprouted a forest of derricks.

Three years after that Standard Oil found a rich field in Huntington Beach, and Union Oil's development of another in Santa Fe Springs followed within a few months. There wells were dug alongside dwellings, just as they had been two decades earlier in downtown Los Angeles.

Then Signal Hill in Long Beach became a headliner. Geologists of the Shell Oil Company were exploring in the neighborhood of Los Angeles, and one of the men remembered that as a boy playing on Signal Hill he saw marine fossils and tilted strata, which together might indicate that the hill was part of an oil-bearing anticline. Digging was begun near the crest for a wildcat (experimental) well. After two months, oil began to accumulate in the hole. As word

In this panorama of the Salt Lake Oil Field (Hollywood and Wilshire District) 164 oil derricks may be distinguished. (–G. Allan Hancock Collection)

A Union Oil Company gusher on Signal Hill, Long
Beach, about 1925. (—*Title Insurance & Trust Co.*)

spread, people began climbing the hill to watch whatever might happen. One night, working under two lights high on the derrick, the Shell drillers could hear what sounded like waves surging underground. Suddenly the noise got louder, until with a thunderous roar the oil gushed forth, leaping 114 feet in the air — far above the top of the derrick. The discovery on Signal Hill was the hottest news in the oil industry. Thousands of people came from all directions to join the excitement, and speculators raced to find the owners of the recently subdivided hill in order to buy their property. The well quickly choked up and the flow of oil stopped, but workers cleaned the hole and arranged to channel the oil to tanks. At the early hour of 4 a.m. on June 25, 1921, five hundred spectators crowded to watch as Alamitos No. 1, the discovery well, began to pump oil. (The well is at the corner of Temple and Hill Streets on Signal Hill.)

The next year General Petroleum brought in a gusher on the other side of the hill, but this one was uncontrollable. Oil rained over a thousand homes as the owners fled. With that promise of wealth, derricks rose on all sides, hundreds at a time. In terms of barrels produced per acre, the Signal Hill field was the world's richest oil deposit.

The success of those oil ventures led to one of the worst stock swindles in California's history. Investors of all types — businessmen, janitors, housewives, secretaries — had profited from the drilling on Signal Hill, and now the Julian Petroleum Corporation put out full-page advertisements in homey language — "You'll Never Make a Thin Dime Just Lookin' On!" — which appealed to people so much that they flocked to buy stock to the eventual amount of $100,000,000. The stock was heavily overissued, and the owners of the company were brought to trial. They were acquitted, after bribing District Attorney Asa Keyes. In later trials they, and Keyes also, were sentenced to prison.

After Signal Hill, fields were discovered in Torrance, the Baldwin Hills and in the coastal towns of Venice, El Segundo and Wilmington. Disorganized drilling of too many wells, whose operators frantically competed to drain as much as possible before others would get it, disrupted the oil industry. Once more prices fell because of overproduction. At the same time the heedless rush to draw oil out, with no organization to maintain underground pressure, left pools of oil forever lost.

4. *La Brea Pits*

Alongside Wilshire Boulevard at the southern limit of the huge Salt Lake Oil Field, Los Angeles archeologists made an important discovery. There, in the old La Brea Pits,* was found the world's largest collection of fossil remains of prehistoric animals.

In 1905, workmen drilling an oil well for George Allan Hancock (son of Henry Hancock, pioneer lawyer and surveyor) came upon layers of skeletal remains. Some of the bones were taken to Dr. John C. Merriam of the University of California, Southern Branch (forerunner of U.C.L.A.), and he found that they were of animals long extinct. As a result, Mrs. Hancock Ross gave scholars the right to excavate and make collections of whatever fossil remains were taken from the pits. This privilege was given to the University of California, Occidental College, the Southern California Academy of Sciences and Los Angeles High School.

---

*Although often called "La Brea Tar Pits," they really contain asphalt, a residue of petroleum. They are in Hancock Park on Wilshire Boulevard, two blocks east of Fairfax Avenue.

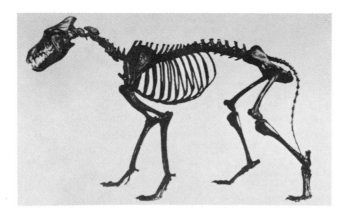

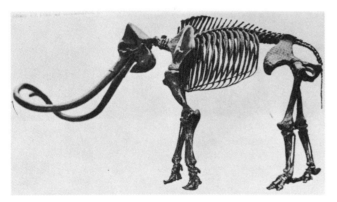

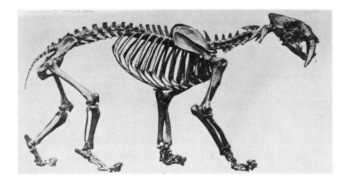

Fossil remains found in
La Brea Pits include
(from top to bottom)
skeletons of the dire wolf,
emperor mammoth,
sabre-tooth cat, ground
sloth and stork.
(—*Los Angeles County
Museum of Natural
History*)

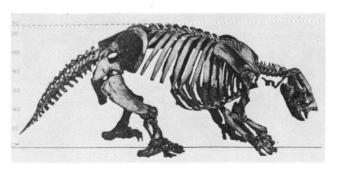

As time went on the discoveries became so fantastic that in 1913 Allan Hancock gave exclusive rights of excavation for two years to Los Angeles County, the work to be supervised by the Los Angeles County Museum. At the end of that time the 23 acres of fossil area were given outright to the county. On that land were twenty brea pits of different sizes, the largest about twenty feet across. A great part of the skeletal remains were of the Pleistocene era, also called the Ice Age. Hundreds of thousands of bones were gathered by the museum into its Hancock Collection.

The original pits were large and deep, but they looked exactly like the small pools which can be seen in Hancock Park today. Around the deep pools the trees and shrubs were similar to the present vegetation of Los Angeles; so it is not hard for the viewer to imagine himself as standing there in prehistoric ages. Bubbles of gas rise in the same manner, and the thin surface of water and oil still gives the deceptive lakelike appearance. Yet the black ooze remains a lethal trap. As protection, a high wire fence surrounds the pits, but any bird or insect touching the asphalt is drawn into its depths just as relentlessly as in ancient times.

Many of the animals who became mired were predatory, for the reason that any trapped victim became a lure. Thirsty animals drawn by the deadly mirage of an inviting lake, waded in and were held in the sluggish grip of the quagmire. Other animals leaped on the helpless prey to devour them, and irresistibly both attacker and attacked were drawn down into the black ooze. There, underground, the remains piled up, the bones to lie undisturbed through hundreds of centuries.

Among species now extinct were the dire wolf (also called the grim wolf, larger than today's timber wolf), the saber-toothed cat, the California lion (which weighed about a thousand pounds), a small antelope (less than 2 feet tall at the shoulders), the mammoth elephant (about 12 feet high with curving tusks as long as 13 feet), the mastodon (half the size of the mammoth), and the ground sloth (a huge animal with footprints almost 1½ feet long). There were also extinct types of horses and camels. Thousands of skeletons of birds were found — storks, vultures (some with a wingspread of 14 feet), hawks and eagles (carcasses of over 800 golden eagles were found in the pits). There was one ancient human skeleton, given the name La Brea Woman.

When the property was still "out in the country" and the pools were not guarded by fences, boys often stood at their edge tossing in stones which quickly disappeared. One day three boys chasing rabbits fell into the clinging depths at a place where the tar was hidden from view by an outcropping of weeds. They were pulled far in by the time their screams were heard. The fire department was called and a ladder thrown across the pool. One boy was pulled out when only his head and shoulders remained visible, another when the asphalt reached his neck. The third boy had already sunk up to his nose when the fireman trying desperately to save him fell into the tar himself. As he fell, however, he grabbed the ladder with one arm and held the boy up with the other until both were finally freed.

Today many structures in that area are built on "floating foundations" over the tar. The buildings include a bank at Wilshire and Curson, a department store at Wilshire and Fairfax, and the Los Angeles County Museum of Art. Dangerous? Quite the contrary. In the event of an earthquake, the fluid pool would absorb the tremors and leave the buildings serene.

5. The Big Red Cars

The real estate boom which ushered in the 20th century moved in the wake of Henry E. Huntington's electric "Red Cars."

Collis P. Huntington, president of the Southern Pacific Railroad, had a nephew, Henry. When the young man was still under 21 his uncle decided to test his ability. First he was put in charge of a sawmill which made railroad ties. The results were remarkably successful; so next he was made vice-president and general manager of a dilapidated railroad line which had gone into receivership. Again the results were extraordinary. He was made an official of one railroad after another until his uncle called him to San Francisco, headquarters of the Huntington railway interests. Collis died in 1900, having willed a large part of his ownership of the Southern Pacific to his nephew. But the next year, instead of trying to take his uncle's place as president, Henry sold the stock to E. H. Harriman and moved to Los Angeles. There he built up a railroad empire of a different sort, creating a network of trolley lines through the Southland. Wherever the tracks were laid suburbs arose. Because of the convenient Red Cars, Los Angeles County became a collection of far-flung suburbs.

In 1898 Collis and Henry Huntington, as part of a syndicate in San Francisco, had bought their first electric railways in Southern California — one small line which served Pasadena and another serving Santa Monica. Beyond that, practically no trolley lines existed in Los Angeles outside the downtown area. With formation of the Pacific Electric Railway Company by Henry Huntington in 1901, the picture totally changed.

An excursion to Mount Lowe on a Big Red Car. (*—Huntington Library*)

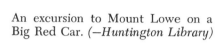

Scheduled for frequent departures, sturdy trolleys rolled across the countryside to Long Beach, Alhambra, Santa Monica, Monrovia, San Pedro. Until then travelers had had no choice but to ride on trains of the Southern Pacific Railroad, but as each community was included on a new route of the Pacific Electric, people chose the fast trolley whose comfortable cars (called the Big Red Cars) were extra long and wide.

In order to destroy the competition, Harriman of the Southern Pacific secretly bought 45% of the Pacific Electric stock, and suddenly Henry Huntington found that he might possibly lose control of his line. Cleverly outwitting Harriman, he incorporated a new line, the Los Angeles Inter-Urban Railroad, under his own complete control; then he suspended all new extensions of the Pacific Electric line and built them on the Inter-Urban instead. Trolleys sped to Santa Ana, Whittier, Riverside, Redlands, Newport Beach, Glendale; they rolled down the San Gabriel Valley, along the ocean, through Cahuenga Pass to San Fernando Valley. Arrival of the tracks at each destination set off land speculation as transportation opened up new places for settlement. An extreme was reached at Redondo Beach when Huntington bought land there as well as a small trolley line which went to the area. The news caused wild excitement as speculators raced to share the increased land values. Lots changed hands several times within

Duck hunting in the coastal marshes south of Santa Monica, about 1903. (—*Title Insurance & Trust Co.*)

two or three days; one building which sold for $4000 in the morning was resold for $20,000 the same evening.

In spite of the popularity and success of his carlines, Henry Huntington grew more and more interested in collecting books and paintings. By 1908 he began to withdraw from the field of transportation and leased the Inter-Urban to the Pacific Electric. The next year he sold other, subsidiary lines to the Southern Pacific. But the Red Cars continued to serve the Southland.

From 1928, continuing through most of the Depression, a Sunday pass offered "A Day for a Dollar." One rider who believed in getting his money's worth logged 127 miles during a day. Another man claimed that for the price of one pass he rode 334 miles.

What might a passenger have seen during such a day? The lines passed bright splashes of orange groves and the somber greens of walnut and olive groves; homes festooned with the semitropical trumpet vine or exotic Copa de Oro; streets lined with eucalyptus trees or palms; the tall silhouettes of oil derricks rising in unlikely places as well as clustering above wide oil fields; truck farms of celery, lettuce, beans and cauliflower; cattle and sheep and horses, still roaming on plains and hillsides in the same way as a century before. Driving through Hollywood the Red Cars passed an orange grove at Hollywood and Vine, passed pepper trees and dignified homes framed by deep lawns. The small amount of traffic along the boulevard often included horseback riders, for many people kept stables behind their homes. Motion picture cowboys swaggered by in fancy western clothes — or one would drive past in an auto with a saddle slung over the hood. A favorite destination for travelers was, at Hollywood and Cahuenga, the large rose garden of Paul de Longpré, the noted artist. Another favorite was Venice, on the coast just below Santa Monica; there Abbot Kinney had built a town modeled after its namesake in Italy. Over a network of canals which radiated from the Grand Canal, Italian singing gondoliers poled gondolas (imported from Italy) past high-arching footbridges, ornate arcades, the elegant St. Marks Hotel (an exact copy of a Renaissance-style hotel in Venice, Italy) and a restaurant designed like a Spanish galleon from which at sunset a trumpeter clad in armor sounded a salute to the close of day. The Red Cars followed the shore from Santa Monica to Balboa, skirting inland at Palos Verdes. The beaches, ocean and offshore islands glistened in the clear California air. On the route through San Gabriel Valley, the Red Cars wound through foothills to connect with a cable car which climbed Mount Lowe, above Altadena. Far out at San Bernardino the Red Cars ascended to Arrowhead Springs. Hikers rode to the mountain destinations, disembarked and followed trails already outlined for them by the electric railway system. Neither hills nor view were ever shrouded in smog, and although occasionally a haze hung in the air, it usually was burned away quickly by the morning sun. Through Cahuenga Pass to the San Fernando Valley, tracks were laid in 1910, and the Red Cars rolled through the pass alongside a narrow, seldom-traveled, winding dirt road. In every direction, the familiar

Venice, California. (−*Title Insurance & Trust Co.*)

voice of the Red Cars' air horn, deep and distinctive, all but spoke the words "Come ride with me."

The speed of the cars was an advantage for people going to distant places. Most of the trolleys averaged forty miles per hour, but on three special lines (to Long Beach, Santa Monica and San Bernardino) where the right of way was uninterrupted by crossroads, the cars were capable of reaching sixty. In general, the cars were made of wood, but on those three lines they were steel and built like trains. Due to speed, inexperienced motormen, carelessness of pedestrians and of people getting on and off the cars, and also due to other causes, both local and express cars were involved in many accidents. For instance, in 1915 there were 11 people killed and 659 injured. A newspaper crusade and public indignation brought about better training of motormen and improvements in safety equipment.

In time, more and more roads crossed the rights of way, and the Red Cars had to operate on a slower schedule. They became outmoded by automobiles and buses. By 1949 all the trolley lines were discontinued.

Yet old-timers still recall the delight of cruising companionably through the countryside, residents and sightseers, rich and poor in friendly fellowship. For many of the riders the fondest memory of those days was, beyond question, the simple joy of a daylong excursion in the Big Red Cars.

6. *Expansion Along Wilshire*

As the suburbs grew in every direction, Wilshire Boulevard showed signs of becoming the most important thoroughfare in Los Angeles. It was extended westward toward the ocean, and gradually residences arose along each side. Still, it went no nearer downtown than Westlake Park. It wasn't until 1934 that a roadway was carved through the park to join Orange Street, whose name was changed in order to form one continuous Wilshire Boulevard from the heart of Los Angeles to the Pacific.

Far out on the dirt road which was to become part of the boulevard, Rancho Rodeo de las Aguas was bought in 1906 by the Rodeo Land and Water Company with the idea of forming a subdivision, the name of which for a while remained in question. Burton E. Green, president of the land company, was fond of telling about how the real estate was christened. One day he happened to read in the paper that President Taft was vacationing at Beverly Farms, Massachusetts. The melodic "Beverly" caught Green's fancy, but instead of "Farms" it seemed more appropriate to mention the hills which dominate the former rancho. And so the subdivision was given the now-famous name of Beverly Hills.

Less than six square miles in size, it was designed to be a luxurious community. On a hillside, the elegant Beverly Hills Hotel, surrounded by 15 bungalows, led the way. Fields of barley and lima beans were replaced by wide, tree-lined streets and exceptionally large home lots. When Beverly Hills wanted to incorporate as a city in 1914 it found that a population of 500 was required, and therefore the boundaries were extended in order to include enough residents to qualify. Pickfair, the home of Mary Pickford and Douglas Fairbanks, overlooked the subdivision from its highest point. Charlie Chaplin, Harold Lloyd, Gloria Swanson, Tom Mix and other film stars flocked to buy land there. Will Rogers was made honorary mayor, and the city took on an immediate aura of glamor. Within a decade a bridle trail was installed down the middle of Sunset Boulevard. At the same time a nursery provided a final touch: westward from Hollywood, where Sunset Boulevard curves into Beverly Hills, a huge field of scarlet poinsettias bloomed at Christmastime each year.

The city of Beverly Hills, surrounded by Los Angeles, has its own police and fire departments, school system, city hall and municipal officers. Upon incorporation, no salary was paid to the mayor or councilmen, but the treasurer was allowed a salary of $1 a year. The picture changed slightly when in 1968 an ordinance was passed granting the mayor and councilmen $2400 annually. The treasurer was not so lucky – he is still enriched by just $1 a year.

At the end of World War I, the Ambassador Hotel was built on the site of a dairy farm near Gaylord Wilshire's subdivision. At first it was to be a hospital, but at the war's end the plans were changed to build a hotel instead. The acreage was large, and opulently furnished cottages were added around the hotel's grounds. (Cottages were a feature of luxury hotels in Southern California.) It was the golden era of moving pictures, and up the curving driveway to the Ambassador's entrance the celebrities of movieland arrived for an endless succession of glittering parties.

By the 1920s at least 100,000 people a year arrived in Los Angeles. Among real estate buyers, property along Wilshire was valued far more than elsewhere in the city. When a subdivision was laid out beyond Western Avenue, north and south of Wilshire, almost all the lots were sold within one day.

The architecture of downtown Los Angeles and the surrounding suburbs kept a low profile. There were few tall structures. But during the first decades of the 20th century, as thousands of buildings rose in the Southland, architecture ran wild. The adobes of the first settlers had been simple and integral with the surrounding landscape. Then a Victorian style common to the Midwest became the rule, followed by the "California bungalow" (designed especially for the strong sunlight of Southern California, with a wide porch in front and an overhanging roof to shelter the interior from too much glare), as well as buildings with tile roofs and Mediterranean design. In the twenties, other types of architecture arose — Moorish, Incan, New England and a multitude of nonrelated styles. Gas stations were ornamented with classic Greek columns, sprouted parapets and turrets, or took on the appearance of a Hopi Indian village. There were pink houses, orange houses, lavender houses, and restaurants in the natural shape of their names, such as the Brown Derby. For a few years Los Angeles reveled in a gay architectural carnival.

In 1920, Wilshire Boulevard was paved only for a short distance. For instance, in the area of Rancho La Brea (which lay between La Brea Avenue and Beverly Hills), both Wilshire Boulevard and La Brea Avenue were dirt roads along barley fields, scattered oil wells and barren acreage. One day A. V. Ross, a specialist in investments, had

At the intersection of Wilshire Boulevard and Fairfax Avenue, here looking north about 1920, was Syd Chaplin's airport. Haystacks dot the adjoining fields. (—*Title Insurance & Trust Co.*)

Hollywood Boulevard at Wilcox, looking west
about 1901. (*—Title Insurance & Trust Co.*)

a bright idea. Struck by the fact that with the use of automobiles customers could go to stores farther out of town than ever before, he tried to analyze a good location for a new business development. Figuring that anyone would be willing to drive four miles to a shopping center, he pinpointed a place within four miles of the wealthiest areas of Los Angeles — from Westlake Park at one end to Beverly Hills at the other, and from Hollywood on another side to the homes on West Adams. Centered between these points was Wilshire near La Brea. So, investing for himself and for friends, Ross bought land along Wilshire, subdivided it and sold the frontage for business.

This is one more story in which people say with a sigh, "If I had only bought, I would be a millionaire today!" The remark is an old refrain in Los Angeles, where in countless locations property has multiplied thousands of times in value within a few years. Along Wilshire the price of land soared to such an extreme that businessmen who refused to pay $3000 for certain corner lots would have later had to pay $600,000 for them.

For several years the development was known as the Wilshire Boulevard Center. One day as Ross was talking about it eloquently, a friend mentioned that it sounded like a miracle mile. The words were soon put up in lights along the boulevard. The name was well chosen, because companies moving there from older centers found their business increased as much as 700%.

Beyond Beverly Hills stretched huge fields of barley and lima beans * on Rancho San José de Buenos Ayres. There a new subdivision called Westwood was started in 1922. Six years later it was extended, as Westwood Village, into the foothills of the Santa Monica Mountains. At that same time the regents of the University of California were searching in Southern California for the best location of the Southern Branch to accommodate many thousands of students. (Its campus, then on Vermont Avenue on the site of today's Los Angeles City College, offered no opportunity for expansion.) From San Diego to Santa Barbara the regents looked at property, and in 1925 their choice was an area in the hills by Westwood. Four cities — Los Angeles, Venice, Beverly Hills and Santa Monica — decided to tax themselves in order to buy 384 acres and donate them to the regents. A California bond issue paid for the buildings. In 1927 the name was changed to the University of California at Los Angeles, and two years later, on September 20, 1929, the new school in Westwood opened its doors. The first year there were no sidewalks, and during the rainy season students and teachers struggled through mud. When the ground became dry enough, the students themselves built the sidewalks.

The land boom came to a halt with the Depression, for money was as scarce in California as it was everywhere else in the world. Men's thoughts turned to the problem of simply making a living, and enthusiasm over real estate had to wait for another day.

7. Philanthropists of the Arts

Millionaire philanthropists gave the first strong impetus to art and music in Los Angeles.

Henry E. Huntington, whose Big Red Cars made travel easy through the Southland, had other interests than those of business. When in 1903 he moved to Los Angeles after selling his Southern Pacific stock, he bought the San Marino Ranch where he had earlier been entertained by its owner, J. de Barth Shorb. There he built a Georgian mansion and with the help of a young landscape gardener began the development of spacious botanical gardens containing rare and exotic plants and trees. When the mansion was finished in 1910,

---

*Near the coast, lima beans flourished because of the heavy dew at night. In most cases the dew sufficed for irrigation. For this reason many farmers in the area between Pacific Palisades and Playa del Rey grew them. As an example, at Playa del Rey the land between the cliffs and the ocean was one long stretch of bean fields.

he turned his attention to collecting 18th-century art under the guidance of Joseph Duveen, the English art dealer. As a start he bought a portrait by George Romney and three by Thomas Gainsborough. One of the finest paintings in the gallery is Sir Joshua Reynolds' *Sarah Siddons As the Tragic Muse*, bought from the Duke of Westminster. Because Mrs. Siddons was an actress, it took much persuasion by Duveen before Henry and his wife Arabella would agree to buy the painting. (Arabella, widow of Collis P. Huntington, married Henry — divorced from his first wife — 13 years after his uncle died.)

At the same time that Huntington began his art collection, he started to buy books and manuscripts. Usually he did so by purchasing entire private libraries. Among the treasures he assembled are: a Gutenberg Bible; Shakespeare folios; the original manuscripts of Benjamin Franklin's *Autobiography*, Alfred Tennyson's *Idylls of the King*, Robert Louis Stevenson's *A Child's Garden of Verses* and *Kidnapped*, Mark Twain's *The Prince and the Pauper*, Henry David Thoreau's *Walden*, Edgar Allen Poe's "Annabel Lee"; the largest collection of Abraham Lincoln letters and manuscripts in existence; original signed documents of the Pizarros, and the royal decrees relating to the conquest of Peru; an order signed by John Hancock, president of the Colonial Assembly, appointing George Washington commander-in-chief of the Colonial Armies; letters — one from George

Henry E. Huntington's mansion is now an art gallery. (*—Huntington Library*)

III of England to the House of Commons authorizing it to give the American colonies their independence but saying he does so against his will, and one from Benedict Arnold to Lord North acknowledging receipt of money for betrayal of his country but objecting that it is too little. These and an infinite number besides.

Construction was begun on a library building which would be used partly as a museum for display of special items, partly as a research library for scholars. It would house hundreds of thousands of manuscripts and rare books.

Henry had chosen Los Angeles County as his home and played a vital role in its development. When in 1919 he and his wife made a will concerning their home, the gardens, the art treasures and the library, they jointly left everything in a magnificent bequest to Los Angeles.

During that same year, 1919, William Andrews Clark, Jr., founded the Philharmonic Orchestra of Los Angeles. For expenses he guaranteed $100,000 per year at first but soon increased his guarantee to $200,000. Only once before in the United States, in Boston, had a symphony orchestra been founded by a man who also undertook its support. The Los Angeles Philharmonic with 94 musicians took the place of the Los Angeles Symphony which had been founded in 1898 with 35 musicians. Tickets to the performances cost 25 cents to $1.

Clark, who had studied the violin in Paris, often took the place of the second violin during rehearsals, though never during a regular concert. For 15 years, until his death in 1934, he remained the orchestra's sole guarantor. After that the Southern California Symphony Association was established to manage the orchestra. Clark left his mansion to the University of California at Los Angeles to house the bequest of his collection of original music scores, autographed manuscripts and rare books.

Also in 1919 another venture began, one financed not by a millionaire but by the public. A play, Sir Edwin Arnold's *Light of Asia,* had been staged outdoors so successfully the year before that the Theater Arts Alliance was organized to present concerts and plays under the stars. H. Ellis Reed climbed through the hills near Cahuenga Pass, leading a search for a place with good acoustics. Looking down from a hilltop, he saw a bowl-shaped area. His father, helping in the search, went down to the valley's center and sang and called out while Ellis listened above. It was acoustical perfection. When a community sing was held there, Director Hugo Kirchhofer called it the Bowl, and the Hollywood Bowl became its permanent name.

At first there were no seats. People sat on the grass of the hillsides, and the platform was a barn door taken from an earlier build-

At the Hollywood Bowl, the first Easter Sunrise Service was held in 1921. (—*Title Insurance & Trust Co.*)

ing on the site. For the Bowl to become a permanent theater, money and organization were needed. Through the enthusiastic leadership of Mrs. Artie Mason Carter, a music teacher, equipment and labor were donated and "Penny Banks" put in stores, hotels and offices throughout the city. Tourists took Penny Banks along when they left California, collecting more money back home. Hollywood High School, for a performance of *Twelfth Night* it gave in the Bowl, installed lighting equipment which afterwards was donated. Also, the proceeds of the evening were given for the purchase of a permanent electrical system. In recognition, the Bowl has been the scene of Hollywood High School's June graduations ever since.

As the next season was about to begin, Mrs. Carter found out that Highland Avenue, by which the Bowl was entered, was to be torn up most of the summer for a public works project. The department would not change its plans, and a steam shovel was put in place to begin digging up the street. But in front of the shovel Mrs. Carter and an 86-year-old Bowl worker, Mrs. E. J. Wakeman, sat determinedly in rocking chairs. The city bowed to the "rocking chair" antagonists, and the shovel was removed. Los Angeles had experienced its first sit-in.

At the last concert of that same summer, with a large amount still due on the mortgage of the Hollywood Bowl property, Mrs. Carter went out on the stage during intermission. Holding up the mortgage, she asked what the audience would do about it, saying, "Anything can happen on this beautiful night." The people of Los Angeles had developed a personal feeling toward the Bowl. Starting with a donation of $100 from the conductor, donations came so fast that within twenty minutes the remaining amount was pledged. Thereupon she dramatically burned the mortgage on the stage as the orchestra played "The Star-spangled Banner."

8. *Griffith Park*

Colonel Griffith J. Griffith was among the principal landowners of the city, and his property included part of Rancho Los Féliz. At Christmastime in 1896 he astounded Los Angeles with a gift of 3000 acres of land, to be the largest city park in the United States. But the generous Christmas gift was given a bleak reception. Major Horace Bell, publisher of *The Porcupine* (and former writer of *Reminiscences of a Ranger*), was an antagonist of Griffith and reported that the land was given solely to avoid paying taxes. A bitter contest of words followed. Reflecting the general distrust, the City Fathers were slow in taking steps to make the land suitable as a park, and it remained mostly unused.

In 1903 Colonel Griffith was involved in a sensational trial for attempted murder. After an evening of drinking he accused his wife of conspiring with the Pope to have him poisoned so that she could give his money to the church. Then he leveled a revolver at her while she pleaded, "Don't kill me, darling. Don't kill me — please!" He shot her. Injured in one eye, she tried to escape by jumping from the window, and a porch roof saved her from being killed in the leap. The decision of the court was a two-year sentence for Griffith in San Quentin Prison.

After the prison term he resumed his place in local affairs. Then, to prove his civic spirit, he offered a new Christmas present to the city: $100,000 for the erection of an observatory atop Griffith Park. This time loud protests arose against acceptance of the money, on grounds that Griffith was trying to bribe his way to an honorable place in the community. On the front page of a newspaper a letter was published which insisted: "This community is neither so poor nor so lost to sense of public decency that it can afford to accept this money." The offer was refused.

The Big Parade,
directed by King Vidor,
was filmed in Griffith
Park. The director
quotes Abe Stearn's
movie dictum: "A rock
is a rock, a tree is a
tree. Shoot it in Griffith
Park." (*—Courtesy
King Vidor*)

Undeterred, the Colonel thought of a way by which he could circumvent the rejection and at the same time prove he was not bribing his way to community leadership. On his death in 1919 he willed $700,000 to the city for construction of the observatory and also a Greek theater. This time the gift was accepted. Eventually the city built a large zoo in the park, provided over 43 miles of bridle trails, set aside remote areas for camping and created golf courses, tennis courts, athletic fields and 35 picnic areas. The grounds now include over 4000 acres.

Griffith Park was used by the early motion picture studios as a setting for stories of the wild West, and certain areas of the park are still used by studios today.

On October 4, 1933, without warning, the park became a scene of disaster. Shortly after noon a small brush fire broke out deep in Mineral Wells Canyon. At that time a road system was under construction throughout the park, employing over 3000 workers who quickly brought shovels to put out the fire and make a firebreak. They were directed to a narrow cowpath leading them single file into the canyon from the San Fernando Valley side of the park. Neither the foremen nor the workers knew the danger of entering such a cul de sac. When a fire warden saw them and shouted, "Get out of here, you fellows — there may be some wind," a few turned to leave, but the line was long and they had little room to maneuver. Most of the men continued on. As those in front drew near the fire, a sudden breeze spread towering flames along the canyon. The men tried to claw their way up the canyon wall, but the flames climbed as fast, especially at one place. There 36 men burned to death on the steep slope. Each body was found in the same position of frantic effort, arms reaching upward.

The fire and police departments arrived, as did every ambulance in the city. A first aid station was set up in the park near the golf clubhouse, lit by hastily borrowed Hollywood studio floodlights. From there the ambulances took some victims to hospitals, others to the morgue. All entrances to the park were thronged with relatives of workmen who had not returned home for dinner. The flames had been so intense that identification was possible only by means of keys or rings. Of the 36 bodies, only 28 were identified with certainty. In loss of life, it was the most disastrous fire in the entire history of Los Angeles.

9. *Malibu, Last of the Ranchos*

Rancho Topanga, Malibu y Sequit, stretching in isolated beauty along the Pacific Ocean, was the last of the old ranchos to remain intact. Others still had a place on the map of Los Angeles County when the 20th century began, but they no longer had the huge private acreage of earlier days. Rancho Malibu was an exception.

In 1887 the property was bought by Frederick Hastings Rindge of Massachusetts, a wealthy man who found that the rancho embodied his dreams of the most perfect place for a home. Its boundaries were the ocean on one side, on the opposite side a line about a mile inland through the Santa Monica Mountains, Las Flores Canyon on the east and 16 miles to the west, Sequit Canyon near the southern border of Ventura County.

The rancho was separated from the rest of Los Angeles by mountains which descended directly to the sea, with no space along the shoreline for a road; so a makeshift road was arranged along the beach, usable only at low tide. Rindge and his bride May determined to make their inaccessible home self-sufficient. Orchards and vineyards were laid out, grain and vegetables planted, livestock and poultry brought in, dams built, blacksmith and carpenter shops equipped. Ranch operations eventually included a lumber mill, small railroad and a tile factory. It resembled a feudal, self-supporting duchy.

But time brought change. In 1903 a fire blazed across the rancho, destroying everything in its path including the ranchhouse. Two years later Rindge died; his wife had to take over all responsibilities. By then shrubbery and trees grew once more on the hills, and May with the help of her children — two sons and a daughter* — was able to re-establish the agricultural and livestock business. A large new home was begun.

Never again was the rancho a place of tranquil contentment. Homesteaders had moved into the mountains just outside the rancho boundary line, and several fires occurred on their lands. The strangers used roads through the rancho as though they were for public access and even camped on the ranch land. Sometimes thirty to fifty percent of the newborn among the rancho livestock disappeared (before they had been branded), and during a two-month period 400 pigs were taken from fields near Zuma Canyon. Annoyances multiplied, but worst of all was the danger that a fire might be set by careless intruders. Mrs. Rindge closed the roads to trespassers, securing the thoroughfares by gates. High fences were put up along boundary lines. Armed guards patrolled on horseback, and May Rindge herself drove along the roads, pistol in holster.

The situation was unique. Coastwise travel was possible only by way of the beach at low tide. Northbound traffic was forced to turn onto a route through the mountains to the San Fernando Valley and along an inland route to Ventura. The Southern Pacific Railroad was denied passage through the rancho on the basis that one railroad — the small one used by the rancho — was sufficient. State and local efforts to build a highway directly between Santa Monica and Ventura were without avail.

In the face of this stalemate, the government in 1908 began a series of court actions against the Rindge family, which incorporated as The Marblehead Land Company, named for the ancestral home town in Massachusetts. For 15 years the battle was waged through complicated litigation. Four times a court action went to the California Supreme Court, twice to the U.S. Supreme Court. In 1923 final judgment was given that California had the right of eminent domain. Still, armed guards prevented the entrance of surveyors and engineers. The matter of payment for the ranch land which had been condemned for the public highway was not yet decided. Mrs. Rindge

---

*The daughter's name was Rhoda. She married a dairyman who changed the name of his company to Adohr, which is Rhoda spelled backward.

A road along Malibu coastline in early 1900s. (*—Title Insurance & Trust Co.*)

asked for $9,180,000; in 1925 she was awarded damages of $107,289 for the coastal strip. The battle was over.

Surveyors moved onto the land, followed by bulldozers and an army of workmen. A wide highway was completed in 1928, and as automobiles rolled over the road the public was able for the first time to view the spectacular Malibu coastline. But along the new property line of the rancho, fences had been built and mounted guards patrolled as before.

It was not long before 132 squatters climbed the fences and attempted to homestead the land. They had been told that a Spanish rancho was public domain, but Mrs. Rindge brought suit and they were defeated.

The years of litigation, compounded by ranch expenses and the construction of a large mansion, created financial problems. Mrs. Rindge decided to utilize part of her land to bring an income, so she agreed to lease ocean frontage although not to sell any. One section appealed to movie stars, who hastened to lease land along the beach. Lots were small (forty-foot frontage); so each would-be resident leased several. Then, although the land was not owned and the lease would expire in ten years, expensive homes were built. That was the famous colony called Malibu. In 1927 Anna Q. Nilsson signed the first lease, followed by John Gilbert, Ronald Colman, Corinne Griffith and a long list of other film notables. At first the colony was extremely secluded, with only a narrow road to the entrance, where a gatekeeper barred all except residents and those visitors whose names had been left with him. No phones linked the colony to the outside world.

During the Depression the liabilities of the family firm, The Marblehead Land Company, exceeded its income, and in 1936 a petition of bankruptcy was filed. The company was reorganized, the ranch land divided into different categories — such as ocean-front lots, acreage for small ranches, land appropriate for hotels, etc. — and in 1940 the entire rancho went on sale. The uncompleted Rindge mansion was sold to the Franciscan Order and became the Serra Retreat. Since then it has been partially burned by a forest fire, but it still can be seen from the highway, on a quiet hillside far above.

The mountains no longer drop steeply into the ocean, and travelers driving north pass swiftly on roads instead of hurrying along the beach in an effort to outrace a rising tide. But Spanish names remind us of the rancho which once encompassed the land. And where streams poured down past Indian villages into the ocean, the names of those villages still mark the canyons today: Zuma, Trancas, Sequit, Topanga and Malibu.

10. *Bombing of the* TIMES

The 20th century began in the midst of industrial class warfare. As labor unions increased in power, labor and management confronted each other in Los Angeles in a melodramatic struggle. In 1910 the city's foundry workers, led by the International Iron Workers, went on strike engendering a violent contest between strikers and scabs.

Gen. Harrison Gray Otis, publisher of the Los Angeles *Times,* looked upon labor's tactics as evil. He felt that the open shop — employment of anyone, whether a union member or not — was necessary for true industrial freedom. Of the labor organizers he said, "Their instincts are criminal, and they are ready for arson, riot, robbery and murder." For this he became a target of the unions.

At the same time the Socialist Party was growing as an important factor in politics, with labor the party's main support. To General Otis, the future of Los Angeles was threatened by the power of labor and by the Socialists. Through his paper he expressed in vehement words his opinion that if their power grew in Los Angeles, industry would stay away and so would new residents.

The Los Angeles Times

For Liberty and Law, Equal Rights and Industrial Freedom

PER ANNUM, $9.00

SATURDAY MORNING, OCTOBER 1, 1910.

UNIONIST BOMBS WRECK THE TIMES; MANY SERIOUSLY INJURED

Terrific Explosion at 1 o'Clock This Morning Starts Fire Which Engulfs Score of Employes in Great Newspaper Plant---Many Victims ---Great Property Loss.

Many lives were jeopardized and half a million dollars' worth of property was sacrificed on the altar of hatred of the labor unions at 1 o'clock this morning, when the plant of the Los Angeles Times was blown up and burned, following numerous threats by the laborites.

Not quite as many of the employes were on duty as would have been the case earlier in the night, when all departments were working in full blast, but even so, the murderous cowards knew that fully 100 people were in the building at the time.

With the suddenness of an earthquake, an explosion, of which the dry, snappy sound left no room to doubt of its origin in dynamite, tore down the whole first floor wall of the building on Broadway, just back of the entrance to the business offices. In as many seconds, four or five other explosions of lesser volume were heard.

In the time it took to run at full speed from the police station to the corner of First and Broadway, a distance of less than half a block, the entire building was in flames on three floors. Almost in

INJURED

E. B. ASPINALL, linotype operator. Cut over left eye; nose cut; right wrist strained.

S. W. CRABILL, foreman composing room. Burned and cut with flying glass.

WILL LATTA, sterotyper. Burned arms and back.

U. S. G. PENTZ, linotype operator. Jumped from window; wrist broken.

G. RICHARD, cut.

M. WESTON, cut on shoulders.

RANDOLPH ROSS, lynotype operator. Jumped from second story window; abrasion left knee; ankle sprained.

CHARLES VON VELSEN, fireman. Cut on left hand.

MRS. J. B. ULRICH, fell down elevator.

CHARLES E. LOVELACE, editorial staff. Jumped from third floor window; injuries perhaps fatal.

AUGUST KOTSCH, compositor. Slightly burned.

J. F. LINK, glass cuts on head.

CHURCHILL HARVEY-ELDER, burned over body and head; broken right leg; will probably die.

RICHARD GOFF, slight burns and cuts.

MISSING

J. C. GALLIHER, 40, linotype operator, married and five children.

W. G. TUNSTALL, 45, linotype operator, married.

FRED LLEWELLYN, 36, operator, married.

JOHN HOWARD, 45, printer, married and one child.

GRANT MOORE, 42, machinist, married and three children.

ED. WASSON, 35, printer, married.

CHIEF'S STATEMENT

CHIEF GALLOWAY, AT 3 O'CLOCK THIS MORNING, SAID:

"THAT THE BUILDING WAS WRECKED BY DYNAMITE SEEMS CERTAIN FROM ALL MY MEN CAN LEARN. THERE ARE ABOUT 100 PATROLMEN ON DUTY AT THE FIRE NOW, AND MOST OF THE DETECTIVES. WE HAVE FOUND SOME THINGS THAT SEEM TO US TO POINT TO THE AUTHORS OF THIS CALAMITY. WHETHER THEY WILL END IN ANY REAL RESULT IS IMPOSSIBLE TO TELL NOW, BUT I DO KNOW THAT WHETHER THEY DO OR NOT THE POLICE WILL KEEP AT IT WITHOUT REST UNTIL THIS WHOLE MATTER IS LAID BARE."

was a way out for brave men, and they took the desperate chance.

The explosion caught the working force unawares and many were buried in the ruins, while others jumped from windows, fell through the elevator chutes or climbed down fire escapes after receiving terrible injuries from flying timbers and debris.

A few in the building escaped uninjured.

N. Y. DEMOCRATS SELECT DIX FO[R] STANDARD BEAR[ER]

State Chairman Finally Agree[s to] Run for Governor of the Empire State

FULL TICKET IS NOMINA[TED]

When Independence League [is] Mentioned It Is Greeted with a Storm of Hisses

Bombing of the Los Angeles *Times*, October 1, 1910. *(—both, Los Angeles* TIMES *photos)*

The above issues and the intense feelings involved set the stage for calamity.

On October 1, 1910, when Otis happened to be in Mexico, there was an explosion in the *Times* building. His son-in-law, Harry Chandler (editor of the paper), had just left the building seven minutes before the blast. In the explosion and resulting fire twenty people were killed, including the man sitting next to Chandler's desk.

Two months later, on Christmas Eve, the Llewellyn Iron Works foundry was dynamited, though this time there were no casualties.

William J. Burns, hired by Los Angeles County District Attorney John D. Fredericks to trace the source of the conspiracy against the *Times,* tracked down a union man in Detroit who gave him a 36-page confession about a dynamiting conspiracy of labor throughout the country, masterminded by John Joseph McNamara. He further stated that Joe's brother, James B. McNamara, had bombed the *Times* building. Burns' agents arrested Joe in Indianapolis and Jim in Detroit, and immediately they were brought to Los Angeles. The fact that no time had been allowed for a legal fight against extradition to California meant that the prisoners found themselves in the role of martyrs who had been "kidnapped." Flowers and gifts deluged the jail.

The trial then became involved with politics. It was an election year, and as victims of capitalist persecution the case was a campaign issue for the Socialists. The Socialist candidate for mayor of Los Angeles, Job Harriman, was attorney for the defense. The primary election took place as the court trial was being prepared, and Harriman beat the incumbent mayor by a majority of votes. With the final election a few months away, Los Angeles realized it soon might have a Socialist mayor.

Clarence Darrow, the eminent criminal lawyer, arrived to help Harriman defend the two men. U.S. Secretary of Labor Samuel Gompers announced his belief that the men had been framed by a pre-arranged plot. Money poured into a McNamara Defense Fund. On Labor Day demonstrations took place in large cities all over the United States, and the courtroom became a focus of interest even in Europe.

In advance of the trial, although witnesses as well as prisoners were closely guarded, there were accusations of attempts to bribe or intimidate witnesses. Both sides used spies to find out the other's information and plans. Both studied the labor attitude of each person on the list of prospective jurors, and accordingly one side or the other objected to practically every panelist brought forward. Going through almost 600 names, the lawyers tried for six weeks to impanel a jury.

Then out of the blue, while jurors were being questioned, spectators and reporters in the courtroom were electrified to hear it announced that the plea of not guilty was to be changed. Not only would Joe McNamara acknowledge guilt in the dynamiting of the Llewellyn Iron Works, but Jim would plead guilty to the charge of murder. Such confessions as these could not be the result of a frameup; they must be the truth. Those who had supported the two men were stunned to find that instead of heroes they had been vicious extremists, willing to use dynamite as a coldblooded tactic. With no further need for a jury trial, Jim McNamara was condemned to life imprisonment. Joe, who had not been directly involved in a bombing, was sentenced to 15 years (later shortened).

The events of the case had been dramatic but no more amazing than the political motivation which had brought matters to an abrupt end. Strong evidence against the accused had been found, but instead of using it in a long trial the district attorney made a bargain. Elections were only six days away, and if the trial were still in process on that date the Socialist candidate, Harriman, would possibly win because of public sympathy with the accused. If the city had a Socialist mayor, the fact could alienate financiers in New York who customarily sold the city's bonds, and might also alienate prospective midwestern immigrants. Therefore, in return for an immediate confession of guilt by Jim McNamara, the district attorney promised not to press for a death penalty, but instead for life imprisonment. At the same time Joe would immediately confess his own guilt in ordering, as an officer of the Iron Workers' Union, the bombing of the Llewellyn foundry. The confessions were made, and on election day Harriman was overwhelmingly defeated.

11. *America's First International Air Meet*

The Wright brothers flew their first airplane at Kitty Hawk, North Carolina, in 1903, yet for seven years no plane crossed the continent to the western part of the United States. The Rocky Mountains formed an insurmountable barrier. In spite of this, Los Angeles staged America's first international air meet in 1910, and since the competing planes were unable to fly over the mountains, they arrived in crates by train.

Two years earlier New York had held the world's first "public exhibition of flying machines," but none of the competing planes were able to get off the ground. At a small meet in Indianapolis aircraft

Airplanes at the Dominguez Air Meet, 1910. (*—Title Insurance & Trust Co.*)

This dirigible, at Dominguez Field, rose or descended as the flyer moved forward or back along the framework. (—Hatfield History of Aeronautics)

flew, but without competing seriously. It was in Europe, especially at Rheims, France, that leading fliers established world records.

In Los Angeles, on land that was once part of Don Manuel Dominguez' Rancho San Pedro, a beanfield near his ranchhouse was chosen for the big meet. The place was named Dominguez Field. (No street passes by the field, but a monument on Wilmington Avenue just south of Victoria Street points to its location.) A huge grandstand erected at one end would hold the audience; tents were set up for the competing airplanes, dirigibles and balloons; and the Big Red Cars prepared special trips to carry spectators. The date chosen for the meet was in midwinter, January 10 to 20, in order to advertise the fact that in California flying is unhampered at any time of the year.

The two leading contenders, Glen Curtiss and Louis Paulhan, a Frenchman, had both been served with injunctions by the Wright brothers, who claimed their patents had been infringed. However, the court hearings were to be after the meet was over, and both men continued with plans to fly.

The opening day of the meet finally arrived. Eager and curious, 20,000 spectators streamed toward Dominguez Field. Nowadays travel by air is taken for granted, but at that time Southern California had never seen the miracle of powered flight.* Children asked, "Do you really think we'll see someone fly?" Parents asked themselves the same question. While the throng filled the grandstand, fliers and mechanics within the tents made last-minute inspections of their aircraft. A band stood by to give spirit to the proceedings. Overhead a sparkling sky offered perfect flying weather.

At one o'clock in the afternoon a biplane with Glen Curtiss at the controls was rolled from its tent to an edge of the field. The crowd grew silent as a mechanic twirled the propeller and the plane started down the field. For a while it jounced over the ground, and then it lifted to about fifty feet in the air and swept into a turn. For over half a mile the craft flew and then returned to land near the spot where it rose. Glen Curtiss had made the first powered flight in the West. The band and the crowd joined in a wild ovation.

Next, Charles F. Willard took up a second Curtiss plane and thrilled the spectators by the ease with which his craft, too, became airborne. Later Willard became the first aviator to make a flight over downtown Los Angeles. (In reminiscences Willard has described his

---

*Gliders had flown in Southern California before 1910.

first flying lesson, given by Glen Curtiss. There was a place for only
one person on the plane, with no room for an instructor alongside.
Curtiss explained how the controls worked, pointed to spectators and
warned him not to hit them, then told him he was ready to fly. Somehow he did what he was supposed to do, and later was hired to
demonstrate Curtiss planes.)

The third pilot was the Frenchman, Paulhan, who made a spectacular appearance. Dirigibles were flying about 200 feet above the
crowd, and all eyes were upon them as they maneuvered. Unnoticed
Paulhan's assistants led his plane into a low gully, and with no announcement the motor was started. Suddenly the plane swooped up
in front of the grandstand, then went into a turn and landed in cen-
terfield. The crowd cheered with delight. It was only the beginning
of Paulhan's "grandstand plays."

Los Angeles became aviation mad: the air meet was the one topic
of conversation. Even with the threat of untimely rain the crowds
continued to flock to Dominguez Field, and the meet went on. On
a day when 50,000 people appeared, Paulhan made a long-distance
flight to Arcadia. The band played the *Marseillaise* and autoists
honked encouragement from the parking area as he started toward
the mountains. Along the route people stood on housetops to watch
the lone flyer; others gaped from the streets. In thirty minutes he
reached Arcadia and then turned back. The crowd watched a speck
in the distance grow clearer until Paulhan landed his plane in front
of the grandstand. Once more the *Marseillaise* blared forth, and this
time the crowd rushed onto the field. His cross-country flight was the
longest that had ever been made — 45 miles the round trip.

Balloons and dirigibles took part in the meet, although planes drew
the greatest interest. Below each dirigible an open framework dangled;
there the pilot stood. When wind swept the clumsy airship toward a
tree or building the airman had no protection against the danger
except his skill in maneuvering away.

During the air meet the prizes for speed were won by Glen Curtiss
(1½ miles in 2 minutes 12 seconds, 16 miles in 23 minutes 43 2/5
seconds, to break the world's speed record). The prizes for endurance and altitude went to Louis Paulhan (64 miles in 1 hour 49 minutes
40 seconds, and for altitude 4140 feet, both world records). Charles
Willard won the prize for precision landing when he was able to
take off and land at the same spot.

Curtiss and Willard believed in flying safely, but Paulhan preferred to be spectacular. He flew low over the ground directly toward
spectators and waited until the last instant before rising above them.

He cut off his engine until it seemed the plane was about to fall but then, with a gay wave to the crowd, started the engine and continued on his way. The stunts were received with such cheers that when pilots began barnstorming exhibitions they followed Paulhan's dramatic example.

Many years were to go by before smog would begin to trouble the Los Angeles Basin. The visiting aviators marveled that, except during short spells of rain, every day was clear and sparkling, and they left convinced that Southern California was the perfect place for all-year flying.

In September of the next year, 1911, Calbraith Perry Rodgers started on a flight from New York to California, hoping to win a $50,000 prize William Randolph Hearst had offered to the first flyer to make the trip coast-to-coast within thirty days, the offer to expire that October. Eight men signed up for the attempt, but five withdrew before the start. Of the remaining three, one flyer's plane was demolished, which left only two contestants — one flying from California to New York, and Rodgers flying from Long Island to Long Beach.

Rodgers' route paralleled a railroad track, because accompanying him was a special three-car train provided by the Armour Company of Chicago. (His plane, the *Vin Fiz*, would advertise a soft drink promoted by Armour.) The train carried a second plane and spare parts, and included a Pullman car where Rodgers and others involved in the trip could sleep each night; there was no nighttime flying. The flight was an odyssey of disaster. The second day out the plane crashed, but mechanics repaired it by working steadily for forty hours. Because he had to land in fields, there was no control over people drawn by curiosity, who climbed over the plane, worked its levers and then got dangerously in the way when it tried to take off. He reached Pasadena in 49 days (actual flying time of 3 days, 10 hours, 4 minutes, at an average speed of 51.5 m.p.h., covering a total of 4231 miles), but by that time his plane had crashed four times and undergone seven takeoff and landing accidents. Rodgers considered that his flight wouldn't end until he reached the ocean; so he started the last lap from Pasadena to Long Beach. However, that short distance was to take him over a month. En route he had to make an emergency landing on the rough surface of a plowed field. It was his fifth smashup and this time his ankle was broken grounding him for several weeks. At last, with crutches placed alongside him on the plane, he took off from an alfalfa field near Compton and landed on the sand in Long Beach where 50,000 people waited to cheer him. He was the first coast-to-coast flyer, because three more weeks would go by before his competitor in the race finished, but Rodgers was too late to qualify for Mr. Hearst's prize.

The aviation industry of Southern California began with a few men who designed and built their own planes. In Santa Ana, in an abandoned church used as a workshop, Glenn L. Martin worked with just one assistant, his mother. Both he and Curtiss, who was also constructing aircraft, made enough money performing as stunt pilots for Mack Sennett and other movie producers to finance their work on planes.

In a film starring Mary Pickford, the plot called for a supporting actor to play romantic scenes with the villainess, a vamp, but it was necessary for him to be able to fly a plane. In response to an advertisement in the newspaper, Glenn Martin appeared and was signed on. In her reminiscences, Mary Pickford described the arrival of the young aviator on the movie set. A shy man, he was totally unprepared for his role as an actor: first he had to take off his thick spectacles and allow a make-up man to put on lipstick and face powder; then he was led to the vamp and asked to begin making love to her. "Put your arms around me, Mr. Martin," she urged. "You must kiss me." He pulled away. "I refuse to kiss you. I'm going home." Adolph Zukor, the producer, explained in a diplomatic way that in the contract Martin had signed he agreed to act and to fly his plane, for which he would be paid $200. "But I didn't know I'd have to kiss strange girls!" Zukor overcame the problem, but Martin could not be persuaded to give the actress more than a cold peck. It was only when he flew that his performance had any value.

Although Curtiss built one of the first successful seaplanes, he grew embittered by lawsuits over patent rights and other legal complications, and soon left aviation for Florida real estate, but Martin never lost his enthusiasm. In 1912 he made the first oceanic flight, from Newport Bay to Catalina Island and return. Three years later, after establishing his company in Inglewood, he hired Donald W. Douglas and James A. "Dutch" Kindelberger, both destined to become presidents of leading aircraft companies in Los Angeles.

World War I had started in Europe, and in Washington the War Department needed designs for military aircraft. Douglas decided to start business on his own; so in the back room of a barber shop on Pico Boulevard he designed airplanes and took them east to show to the War Department. There he found that the Navy, too, wanted military planes, in particular one to carry torpedos. Douglas' design was the one chosen, and three were ordered. That left him with only one problem: where could he find $15,000 with which to start build-

Opening of the tenth Olympiad, Los Angeles, 1932.

ing them? Luckily he had a good friend, Bill Henry of the Los Angeles *Times*. This friend convinced Harry Chandler, owner of the newspaper, that Douglas' company would be a good investment. Chandler wrote a letter saying he would invest one-tenth of the amount if nine other people would do the same. Armed with the letter, Douglas went to a local financier, O. F. Brant, but Mr. Brant was too busy to see anyone. Then would he just look at the letter? The secretary returned, and on the letter was written "Me, too," with Brant's signature. After that there were no problems.

Searching for a large building, Douglas found an empty motion picture studio on Wilshire Boulevard in Santa Monica with vacant fields all around (now Douglas Park). There he began making planes for the Navy and later for the Army. After that he moved to Clover Field, also in Santa Monica, which provided a larger field and factory.

In 1916, the same year that Donald Douglas started his own company, Allan and Malcolm Loughead (pronounced Lockheed) began to make airplanes in the rear of a garage near the harbor in Santa Barbara. One of their first employees was John K. Northrop, who helped to design a plane which could carry ten persons. The Loughead Aircraft Manufacturing Company also built a plane which many studios chartered, because the specially installed camera in the front cockpit could photograph, during flight, actors inside the plane or walking on the wings. At the end of World War I hundreds of war-surplus planes were put on the market at low prices, and aircraft companies could find few buyers for their products. Malcolm Loughead had already left the field of aviation to manufacture hydraulic four-wheel brakes for automobiles, an invention of his, and in 1921 Allan closed his workshop and went into real estate. Still, his interest was only in planes, and after five years he started another company. The new venture was in Los Angeles and, with a phonetic spelling, was named the Lockheed Aircraft Company.

Northrop, who had been working with Douglas Aircraft, returned to Lockheed to become its chief engineer. He designed the Vega, a craft notable among early airplanes. With skis affixed to the plane in place of wheels, Capt. George Hubert Wilkins flew a Vega over the Arctic Ocean and the North Pole in 1928 and, in the same year, over the South Pole as well. Two of his discoveries in the antarctic he named Cape Northrop and the Lockheed Mountains. About that time a large holding company negotiated to buy Lockheed; Northrop left to form his own Avion Corporation (and later Northrop Aircraft, Inc.), and Allan Lockheed resigned in disapproval of the sale which had been agreed to by the company's board of directors. It was

1929, the year of the stock market crash, and the holding corporation carried its various companies into receivership, including Lockheed. When Robert E. Gross, an investment broker, and a group of associates offered $40,000 for the company in bankruptcy court, the judge who authorized the purchase said dubiously, "I hope you know what you're doing!" For a while there was reason for doubt, because problems seemed overwhelming, but when both Northwest and Pan American Airlines bought the Electra 10, the first all-metal airliner (before that they were made of wood and cloth), Lockheed started on its way to become the largest aircraft producer in the country.

In 1932 General Motors decided to enter the field of aviation and asked Dutch Kindelberger (then chief engineer at Douglas) to mastermind a company to build planes. With the nucleus of a small but expert company in Baltimore, Maryland, which moved with its entire staff and equipment to Los Angeles, North American Aviation was formed in 1934, and Kindelberger was made president. One of the company's first designs was the Texan, a training plane for pilots. By the time it appeared Europe was preparing for World War II, and Great Britain ordered hundreds of North American trainers and fighter planes.

So, by the 1930s, the four companies which were to lead the defense industry in Los Angeles during World War II were ready for their role. Lockheed, Douglas, North American and Northrop had already laid the foundation of successful design and craftsmanship. From the first day of the Dominguez meet it would have been easy to predict that aviation would someday become the most important industry in Los Angeles.

12. *The 1932 Olympic Games*

In the late twenties, plans were begun for Los Angeles to be host in 1932 to the tenth Olympiad. (The first modern Olympic games were held in Athens in 1896.) The Coliseum was enlarged to seat 105,000, which made it the largest sports arena in the world at that time. Enthusiastically the city built an Olympic Village, the first since the ancient games. (Now they are customary.) In the Baldwin Hills, along a high ridge with a 360° panoramic view, 600 bungalows were built to house the visiting athletes, trainers and coaches from forty nations, as well as a native cook for each team. The Post Office Department established a special office for the athletes, with the official address "Olympic Village, California, U.S.A." All over the city banners waved.

In the Coliseum crowds watched as twenty new Olympic or world records were established — four of them on the first day. Among the women Babe Didrickson tied for first place in the high jump and won a gold medal in both the javelin throw and the eighty-meter hurdles.

Yet all the excitement wasn't confined to the stadium. Contests of horsemanship were held on the Polo Grounds out on Sunset Boulevard, and near Sepulveda Boulevard riders gathered for the cross-country horserace. Among them was a Japanese, Lt. Colonel Kito, who had been training 12 years to race in the Olympics. On the course his horse was among the fleetest as it cleared obstacle after obstacle, including a 13-foot water jump, but increasingly it stumbled. At last only the final jump remained. As the animals raced toward it, Kito knew he would risk his horse's life if he urged him further. Pulling the reins, the Colonel dismounted and left the course, forfeiting a position in the race. The public showed itself less interested in who won or lost than in "how he played the game," and Colonel Kito discovered he was a hero. On top of Mount Roubidoux, near Riverside, a tablet was placed commemorating his sportsmanship. After his return to Japan the Mikado made him Master of Horse to the Emperor, which is the highest honor a Japanese horseman can receive.

The cottages of the Olympic Village were dismantled and sold; the banners were taken down. But high in the Baldwin Hills, Olympiad Drive and Athenian Way remind us of an exciting year when Los Angeles was host to distinguished athletes and with equal ardor cheered the heroes who won and those who lost.

13. *An Expansive Era Comes to an End*

With the Depression the expansive years halted. The Olympic games were the last surge of glamor for a long time in a Southland faced with grim realities. Because Hollywood was the motion picture capital, the area had a tinsel image. Because Los Angeles real estate advertisements featured bathing beauties under a perpetual sun, it seemed a frivolous lotus-land. Los Angeles itself knew better. Countless investors who had been caught in the rising tide of the real estate boom found themselves "land poor," with taxes to pay and little or no income. The studio industry felt the cold breath of hard times, as people stayed home in preference to spending money on movies. Thousands of people went on the rolls of the W.P.A. (the federal Works Progress Administration, designed to create work for the otherwise unemployed), and undertook a wide range of jobs such as development of parks and playgrounds, improvement of school buildings, projects in art, music, the theater, historical research and writing.

The next migration to California was to begin in the mid-thirties, but it would be one such as the state had never experienced before, wholly unlike those which had brought rollicking boom years. It would be born of the Depression and the Dust Bowl — a wave impelled by crisis and swelled by migrants forced from their homeland in the southern Midwest by the encroachment of relentless, life-choking dust. Close behind that wave would come the defense migration of World War II. Once more Los Angeles would be engulfed by change, tossed in its whirlpool and, this time, emerge in an altered world.

VIII

MODERN TIMES 1932 TO THE PRESENT

1. *Migration from the Dust Bowl*

Modern times in Los Angeles commenced with uncertain steps. As the Depression spread across the country, the boosterism which had for decades advertised Southern California as a carefree place caused the impoverished and despairing to look in that direction for the perfect paradise in which to make a new start. Handbills put out by certain large-scale agricultural operators advertised jobs for "pickers." Above all, there was a natural yearning for the Promised Land.

Along the highways 350,000 people streamed west, California-bound. They included not only jobless casualties of the Depression, but also unfortunate refugees from the Dust Bowl of the Great Plains (in particular Oklahoma and Texas) and from the agricultural depression in the South Central States (especially Arkansas, Missouri and Kansas). The Dust Bowl had developed with the plowing up of grazing land to allow for cultivation. Grasses, some with deep roots, had held the topsoil, and they were plowed under. Because the relatively few trees gave little protection, winds went unchecked across great expanses of tilled fields. The topsoil was literally blown off the land. Then, over all, thick layers of dust choked every growing thing, formed deep drifts and even piled up inside barns and homes.

In California the new arrivals found that their problems continued. Migrant work is seasonal; for several months out of the year no work was available anywhere. And, through automation, agriculture had already been employing steadily fewer workers. Unscrupulous employers took advantage of the heavy labor surplus to pay literally starvation wages, such as 2½ cents per box of peaches, and that amount only if no bruised fruit were included.

California, expected to be the land of milk and honey, found itself victimized by the situation. Nowhere were communities prepared for the sudden avalanche of migrants. It was frightening for everyone. In the San Joaquin Valley — destination of most of the migrant agricul-

Los Angeles police turn back a large Oklahoma family at the California-Arizona border in 1936. (*—Wide World Photos*)

tural workers — relief and school costs in many places went up 300%. Migrants could not afford normal housing; so shantytowns were built on the outskirts of cities.

As more and more families arrived without funds, Los Angeles sent a special corps of 130 policemen to the state border to check boxcars and stop Los Angeles-bound hitchhikers. The problem was real, but this solution was ludicrous in view of the fact that until then the city's chamber of commerce had been trying to lure people to the Southland. The corps of special policemen at the border was disbanded after two months.

California's labor market had been hurt by the Depression already; with the new arrivals it became chaos. Headlines announced that the state faced bankruptcy because of the migrants. In the farming areas, residents tried to ward off the newcomers in ways which sometimes included violence. John Steinbeck publicized this cruel situation in *The Grapes of Wrath*. The United States and the entire world were horrified, and in 1939 the La Follette Committee came to California to investigate.

The results of the committee's inquiry were a surprise to everyone. It found an unsuspected pyramid of control: the migratory worker was dependent upon the owners of farms and orchards, who were dominated by large-scale growers, who in turn were manipulated by the canning companies and financiers located throughout the country. Those at the top of the pyramid made regulations and quotas scaled down to the very lowest level. Large finance corporations and railroads made heavy donations toward frustrating the investigation, at the same time veiling in secrecy the source of the bribes.

Because of the committee's report, the country realized that the problem of nonresident migrant workers is national rather than local. Community welfare covered only residents of over one year, and therefore the United States established the Agricultural Workers Health and Medical Association for residents of less than a year. Another Federal agency gave them grants of food and clothing. California developed a state employment service and a mobile health unit especially to take care of migrants. These efforts brought the oversupply of labor into some kind of order, and then the rising defense industry in Southern California gave employment to much of the extra manpower. Before long not enough farm labor was available, and Mexican braceros (laborers) were imported to do most of the migrant farmwork, until the system was ended by Federal law in 1965.

The influx of new residents during Depression years was hardly over when the national defense migration began in 1938. Los Angeles was on its way to becoming one of the most populated areas in the country.

2. *Still More Water*

California faces an ironic paradox. The northern part of the state has an enormous surplus of water, most of which flows unused into the ocean. Southern California has only two percent of the state's supply, yet at the same time it has about four-fifths of the state's population.

In most places the ground below the earth's surface is, as a natural condition, soaked with water. In the days of the Southland's pioneers the ground water was practically unused and therefore was close to the surface and easily drawn up by artesian wells. Then gradually it was used up faster than it could be replaced by rainfall or underground springs. By the early 1940s the water table in most of Southern California was below reach of the pumps. Near the ocean this meant that the water table was lower than the sea level, and

salt water began to infiltrate to a distance of two miles inland at
some places. The salt and other minerals could ruin water storage
there for generations to come; so in 1944 a state "watermaster" was
appointed to ration the amount of ground water available for each
user, to ensure a water table of sufficient height. Experiments were
undertaken in methods to make a permanent barrier against the ocean.
As a result during the 1960s and early 1970s wells were placed in a
line along the coast in the region of danger, and through them fresh
water was injected. From the International Airport to the Palos Verdes
Hills and along San Pedro Bay, a fluid barrier of fresh water pro-
tects the underground reservoirs of Los Angeles from intrusion by
the sea.

It was early in the 20th century that William Mulholland knew
Los Angeles could not base its existence on the available ground water
or the local rivers, and just as certainly he knew within a few years
of the first arrival of water through the Owens River Aqueduct that
it would never be sufficient. In a way the aqueduct was self-defeating,
because the very growth which it made possible created in turn the
need for a much larger supply.

Mulholland and his engineers, confident from experience that construction of an aqueduct across hundreds of miles was feasible, decided that the next logical source would be the Colorado River. Along
the eastern border of California, at the far edge of the Mojave Desert,
the river flowed toward the Gulf of California with its waters unused.
In any case a dam would have to be built to control the river, for
in flood years it caused wild destruction along its banks. For instance,
in 1905 a tremendous flood created a new channel for the river, and
half the flow poured into Imperial Valley toward the Salton Sink, the
valley's lowest point. The next year during another flood the Colorado
left its regular channel, the entire flow of water streaming into Imperial Valley again to create the Salton Sea. Each time when it seemed
that levees and dams had gained control, another flood sent the river
on a rampage. Not until more than half a year later was the Colorado
forced permanently back into its true channel.

In 1922 what became the Hoover Dam project was introduced in
Congress, but not until the fourth time the bill was presented, in 1928,
did it pass both houses.

The Colorado River and its tributaries flow through or along the
borders of seven states — Colorado, Utah, Wyoming, New Mexico,
Arizona, Nevada, California. In addition, the Colorado runs through
Mexico for fifty miles before emptying into the gulf. When California
presented its idea of building an aqueduct to use the water, the other

states wanted to be sure their own rights were protected. A turbulent controversy began: what proportion of the river's flow should belong to each state and to Mexico? Also, should the flow of a tributary which lies entirely within one state (such as the Gila River in Arizona) be the property of others as well? The states generally aligned themselves against California. Finally, six of the seven involved made a compact agreeing to a certain ration. Arizona, however, balked on two points: she considered the Gila River to be exclusively hers, and she wanted California's share of the Colorado to be considerably lower than the original claim. Only after forty years of political moves and interstate lawsuits over division of the water was a final judgment made by the U.S. Supreme Court.

In 1935, before the issue was decided, Boulder (now Hoover) Dam was finished. Parker Dam, forming Havasu Lake, was then to be built farther south, where the river flowed between Arizona and California, and an aqueduct would cross the desert in the direction of Los Angeles. On the day in 1934 that work on this dam was due to begin, the governor of Arizona protested that Congress had never authorized its construction. He declared martial law and sent Arizona National Guardsmen to take possession of the Arizona side of the dam area. The U.S. Secretary of the Interior thereupon ordered work stopped, and not until Congress specifically authorized the construction did it begin again — almost a year later. The first water from the Colorado arrived in 1941.

Eleven cities including Los Angeles united to form the Metropolitan Water District of Southern California, which would pay for construction of the aqueduct and for most of Parker Dam. (By 1965 the district included 125 cities as well as large unincorporated areas; so the aqueduct served over half the population of California.) The 242-mile aqueduct led from the dam to Lake Mathews near Riverside, a few miles east of the Los Angeles County line. From the Imperial Dam, near Yuma, the All-American Canal took water to irrigate the Imperial and Coachella Valleys. On former desert land, across plains and hillsides, spread endless truck gardens as well as groves of trees bearing avocados, nuts, olives, dates, oranges, fruit of all kinds. Water, the magician, brought the earth to life.

But the controversy had not yet ended. Three times during the thirties Arizona went to the U.S. Supreme Court with a lawsuit to establish her water rights in the Colorado River, and each time she lost. Finally in 1952 she made a last, all-out effort, in which Arizona and California faced each other for a showdown. For four years each side prepared its case; then for two years hearings were held in a special court in San Francisco. In 1963 the Supreme Court announced its decision: Arizona had won at last. California's share of the Colorado River water was lessened, and Arizona was awarded the entire flow of the Gila River.

If California had been allotted a larger share, the water would still have been distributed throughout the Southland, where it was estimated that need would always outrun supply. Before the issue of the Colorado River was finally settled, the California Water Project (originally called the Feather River Project) was laid before the voters of the entire state. Near Mt. Lassen, the Feather River flows south to join the Sacramento River and continue in the direction of San Francisco Bay. The idea was to harness the waters of the Feather by constructing the Oroville Dam, which would then regulate the current and also prevent the frequent disastrous floods along the riverbed. (Before the dam was finished it saved the Feather River region from what might otherwise have been the worst flood in its history.) From the Delta — the area inland from San Francisco where several rivers empty into the Bay — a 444-mile network of canals, dams and pipelines would move river water southward for use in the arid central and southern parts of the state, the users to pay the cost of construction. The project, called Proposition One, was approved by California voters in 1960.

Because in several places the California Aqueduct would have to cross the San Andreas Fault, all construction was designed to withstand an earthquake. For instance, where the conduit crossed a danger area the joints were made of rubber so that the pipeline, instead of cracking, could move with the fault. Also, the pipelines in those areas were laid on the surface instead of underground, to make quick repairs easier. The earthquake of 1857 was centered near Fort Tejón, at the northern boundary of Los Angeles County; somewhere near there the California Aqueduct would have to cross the San Andreas Fault. Planners chose to cross at Quail Lake, where the lake itself would be the connection between the northern and southern portions of the pipeline; thus the aqueduct could not be endangered. Through modern improvements, control centers monitor the entire system for emergencies.

A decade after the project was approved, ecology had become a national issue, and questions were raised about the last phase of the project — questions which had been unforeseen when it was designed. Nevertheless, when the main system was completed in 1973 the project's basic premise remained unchanged. Based on the California Water Code, a state law, all unappropriated water in California belongs to all of her people, with no division into haves and have-nots.

In Southern California there are problems unknown in most other parts of the country. The hard, claylike adobe of hills and fields, baked through long months of the dry season, refuses to absorb the rain that comes in a sudden downpour. After a flood in 1914 washed away houses and left hundreds of people homeless, the State Legislature created the County Flood Control District. The New Year's Day flood of 1934 sped the project. At that time bridges were swept downstream and thousands of homes stood underwater. In Pasadena, where the annual Rose Parade and Rose Bowl Game were scheduled, over 12 inches of rain deluged the area. Now storm drains lie unsuspected beneath streets which have a heavy runoff. Some of the underground drains are wide enough to be driven through by two trucks abreast.

Allied to Southern California's need for water is its need for electric power. In the Pacific Northwest the Columbia River usually provides a surplus of hydroelectric energy. Through the U.S. Department of the Interior a plan was arranged whereby the Northwest and Southwest could be linked in a power interchange system, with sale of the energy which previously went to waste. In summer, when the need for power in the Southwest is highest because of the extra pumping for irrigation and the added load of air conditioning, power from the heavy runoff of northwestern rivers is sent south. In winter the runoff in the Northwest lessens but that area's need for power is greater; so then power can be returned along the same route by which it came. At Sylmar, across the Golden State Freeway from The Cascades, rises a huge skeleton. In 1970 it began operations as terminus of the Pacific Intertie. From a station near the Dalles Dam on the Columbia River to the station at Sylmar, the 846-mile transmission line is the longest in the world.

3. Still More Oil

Oil wells, refineries and storage tanks are prominent in the landscape of Los Angeles, and oil is obviously a leading source of the area's wealth. In the 1950s it became a source of calamity for Wilmington and Long Beach.

The substratum layers of the Wilmington Oil Field are unlike those of fields in general, because the oil pools of different levels are not separated by thick layers of shale, as is usually the case. Instead there are thin layers of shale and sand. Accordingly, when oil was pumped from the underground pools, the surface sank. Within

This is how oil rigs were camouflaged on one of four islands off-shore from Long Beach. (—*Long Beach Convention & News Bureau*)

27 years the Southern California Edison Company's steam generating plant sank 29 feet. In some places the land in Long Beach sank two feet or more within a year. Some buildings moved horizontally also; for instance, the Villa Riviera on East Ocean Boulevard moved three feet from its original land base. Steel rails, sewers and pipelines were snapped. The Long Beach Naval Shipyard on Terminal Island dropped 24 feet. Since much of Long Beach was built on filled-in tideland only a few feet above sea level, it became necessary to construct dikes, raise buildings when possible, raise and replace streets and bridges. The Navy announced it planned to abandon its base, which maintained half the Pacific Fleet. Geologists predicted that Long Beach could sink seventy feet deeper, literally dropping into the sea.

Experts were called in, and they decided that the depleted strata should be flooded with filtered sea water through "injector wells." In 1959 the project began; within four years it was certain that the battle would be won. Not only did the earth surface become stable, but more oil was recovered, because the water pushed residual oil ahead until it reached a well and was pumped to the surface instead of remaining lost.

Once again a new discovery of oil was made when, after many false starts earlier, the Mission Oil Field was developed in the mountains north of San Fernando Valley about 1953. Covering a region of 100 square miles, it included scattered fields near Newhall, Castaic Junction, Placerita Canyon and elsewhere.

Also in the fifties, offshore drilling began in the neighborhood of Los Angeles. Explorations showed that a coastal range of oil fields probably extends from about 25 miles above Santa Barbara to the same distance south of Wilmington.

In 1965 several oil companies combined to create four 10-acre islands offshore from Long Beach. On those islands, made of rock and sand, oil rigs were installed yet were unrecognizable as such because, in true Hollywood tradition, the derricks were built with false facades appearing to be apartment houses complete with balconies to overlook the view. Palm trees of different heights — some sixty feet tall — were planted to wave picturesquely in the ocean breeze. Waterfalls sparkled in the sun. The noise of drilling was subdued by soundproofing. Each "apartment house" rig was built on rails at ground level so that, when the well was finished and its underground pump connected to pipelines, the rig could move along the track to another site and recommence drilling. In a final dramatic touch, the lovely South Sea archipelago was illumined at night.

People familiar with the densely packed derricks on Signal Hill are today amazed when revisiting the area. Although over 800 wells are still active, most of the derricks have been taken down. The old pumps were replaced with smaller new ones, because today's techniques make unnecessary the black, oil-soaked apparatus which blemished the earlier landscape. A seven-acre park on top of the hill signals that the seamy, noisy era has ended.

Through the first half of the 20th century solitary skeletons rose in every part of Los Angeles. At the busy intersection of La Cienega and Beverly Boulevards traffic was routed around each side of a tall derrick in the street. Not until 1946 was the rig taken down and the well redrilled from the western side of La Cienega. Lately the oil industry has become skillful at covering its ugly features with make-up. Brick fences and shrubbery hide wells. Along West Pico Boulevard one building contains not only offices but also two derricks. Another "office building" has no occupants except 34 oil wells. And an attractive one-story building has a street number by the front door but no rooms inside: it houses 21 wells, and the roof is constructed to tilt open when space is needed for work on them. At Venice Beach a derrick is camouflaged as a lighthouse. In the most thorough disguise of all, 15 wells operate unnoticed beneath the feet of golfers on the Rancho Park Golf Course in Cheviot Hills; 32 more operate under the grass of the neighboring Hillcrest Country Club, and about 100 diligently pump oil below Century City.

4. Climaxes in the Motion Picture Industry

"Movies Are Your Best Entertainment" was the slogan with which the film industry fought the Depression. To lure customers, giveaway nights were advertised, when sets of china, radios and other prizes were offered. Some houses began showing double features to draw an audience, a change which spelled the end for vaudeville acts and short two-reelers. Instead an animated cartoon began each performance as the most likely way to put an audience in a mood for enjoyment.

The most popular pictures were frothy musicals with elaborate dance numbers, or Graustarkian romances — especially those directed by Ernst Lubitsch. Pretty girls were like melodies and sang in the rain with their boyfriends who were apt to ask if you could spare a dime. All Maurice Chevalier wanted was "A one-man girl, a two-pants suit, and three square meals a day." Paramount, on the verge of bankruptcy, was hoisted into the black by Mae West in *She Done Him Wrong*, a picture whose script she wrote herself. It included the famous invitation, "Come up and see me sometime."

M-G-M had the foremost galaxy of stars. Under Irving Thalberg's creative leadership the studio filmed *Dinner at Eight*, *The Guardsman*, *Smilin' Through*, *Rasputin and the Empress*, *Grand Hotel*, *The Barretts of Wimpole Street*, *The Good Earth*, *Mutiny on the Bounty*, *A Night at the Opera* and scores of other exceptional pictures.

Mae West and Cary Grant in *She Done Him Wrong*. (—*Academy of Motion Picture Arts & Sciences*)

The evening of December 14, 1939, crowds waited in Atlanta, Georgia, for the world premiere of *Gone with the Wind*. Atlanta was the home of Margaret Mitchell, author of the book, and also the main setting of the Civil War story. On Peachtree Lane the theater, its facade decorated to resemble the plantation home at Tara, stood in dazzling lights. The governor of Georgia had declared a statewide holiday, and from surrounding communities people streamed into Atlanta for the important event. Excited crowds filled the streets, windows and rooftops. Then the sirens of a motorcade shrilled the approach of the stars everyone had come to see.

Three years earlier, David O. Selznick had bought the film rights before the book's sensational leap to success. The entire country was engrossed in the story and the people whose lives it described. The producers of the film let it be known they were conducting a "talent hunt" for the different roles, and the public began an endless debate over which actors should be chosen. Publicity releases fed the national guessing game. Norma Shearer was the first actress decided upon to play the part of Scarlett O'Hara, but she dropped out of the running after being deluged with letters from fans begging her not to accept the role of such a "bad woman." Among other actresses considered were Bette Davis, Margaret Sullavan, Miriam Hopkins, Katherine Hepburn, Paulette Goddard, Claudette Colbert, Carole Lombard and Joan Crawford.

For the male lead, Rhett Butler, there was no question: Clark Gable was the unanimous choice. But he was under contract to M-G-M. To obtain Gable for the picture, Selznick agreed to release it through M-G-M, and as though a partner, M-G-M would pay half the production costs as well as share the profits equally with Selznick's company.

On the studio's huge backlot, sets which had been used in past motion pictures were to be torn down and removed so that in their place could be built sets for Tara and the city of Atlanta. William Cameron Menzies, art director of the film, suggested that false fronts could be added to the old sets, and then they could be set on fire to simulate the burning of Atlanta. The night chosen for the conflagration was six months before production would begin, to allow time to construct new sets afterward. The role of Scarlett was still to be cast, so in long shots a stuntman represented Scarlett in a wagon as it was driven frantically by Rhett (another stuntman) with the burning city as a background. Since there could be no retakes, seven cameras were set up to record the fire simultaneously from different angles. David Selznick gave an order to ignite the blaze, and as the flames began to spread, the director signaled to the wagon

Old movie sets are put to the torch to simulate the burning of Atlanta. (*—From the M-G-M release* Gone with the Wind © *1939 Selznick International Pictures, Inc. Copyright renewed 1967 by Metro-Goldwyn-Mayer Inc.*)

carrying the doubles to start past the burning scene. Just then Selznick's brother Myron, an actor's representative, approached with an English actress. As David turned, her eyes reflected the leaping fire and the intensity of excitement. "I want you to meet Scarlett O'Hara," his brother said. It was Vivien Leigh.

Audiences found most indelible the scene in the railroad yard, where after a closeup of a dying man the camera pulled back in a superlative revelation of tragedy, to show the yard filled with wounded and dying men. The day that scene was to be filmed, the first extras arrived at 5 a.m. In a steady stream they went through the make-up and wardrobe departments and onto the set until finally 1500 "wounded" Confederate soldiers were in place on the ground along with 500 "dead" dummies. The Central Casting Agency had sent its entire stock of male extras. With the years the studio changed hands several times, but the railroad yard stayed on the backlot. Across from the railroad station the false building fronts which once represented a street in Atlanta were no longer recognizable. Remodeled, they were a Chicago street used in the television series *The Untouchables.* The railroad station burned down in a studio fire in 1971.

At the end of *Gone with the Wind* a problem arose which would have no counterpart today. To Scarlett's pleading "What will I do now?" the contemptuous response by Rhett was "Frankly, my dear, I don't give a damn!" Only after lengthy arguments with the Hays office and payment of a $500 fine did Selznick win permission to use the word "damn."

During the forties and fifties a number of leading actors and actresses were involved in scandals that once would have ruined their careers, but times had changed. In 1942 Errol Flynn was accused by a 17-year-old girl of statutory rape. The handsome actor was brought before the grand jury, while crowds jammed the courtroom and the corridor outside. Columns written about the case pushed most other news off the front pages. After the grand jury weighed the circumstances and the provable fact that Flynn had considered the girl unattractive, it declared the accusation false, but the district attorney overrode the decision and insisted that the actor face a trial. Flynn hired Jerry Geisler as his attorney. The trial actually included two cases, because another woman had added her own charge of rape. Geisler, by assuming a confidential, fatherly manner, led the first girl into unwary statements which disproved her accusation. The second woman was 21; so for there to be "rape," she would have had to resist Flynn's advances. Through use of her own words, Geisler was

Errol Flynn on his yacht. (—*Museum of Modern Art, Film Stills Archive*)

able to prove that she had consented. As a result of the lawyer's skill-ful defense, Flynn was acquitted of all charges. During the trial and afterward he was bombarded with fan letters, and instead of being damned by the public his box office value soared.

A year later another actor faced a similar test, when Charlie Chap-lin went before a Federal grand jury on a paternity suit brought by Joan Barry, a young actress. Once more the tabloids reveled in scan-dal. Before the court met, Chaplin married another young actress, Oona O'Neill, daughter of playwright Eugene O'Neill. Like Flynn, Chaplin hired Jerry Geisler, and when the grand jury ended its de-liberations it found in his favor. Nevertheless, after the baby was born Chaplin was brought to trial. Although blood tests proved he couldn't have been the father, the jury decided against him, and he was ordered to pay $100 a month child support. The sensational trial had no adverse effect on Chaplin's career. Later, accusations that he was a Communist alienated the public, which refused to believe his denials and statements that he was an internationalist, a member of no political party. The actor had never become a U.S. citizen, and when in 1952 he sailed to England to make a picture, the State De-partment announced he would not be readmitted into the country.

There was a sequel. Two decades later, in 1971, Charlie Chaplin received a special invitation from the Academy of Motion Picture Arts and Sciences asking him to attend the Oscar presentations that year. He had some hesitation about accepting, uncertain what his recep-tion by the public might be, but huge crowds welcomed him in New York and Los Angeles. The ceremonies were held in the glamorous setting of the Dorothy Chandler Pavilion of the Music Center. There the high point of the evening was when, in an emotional scene viewed over television by millions across the nation, he was given an honor-ary award for the incalculable effect he had had in making movies an important art form of the 20th century.

Jerry Geisler continued to be the favorite lawyer for any actor who faced a court trial. He represented Robert Mitchum, who at first groaned, "This is the bitter end of everything," when he was arrested in Laurel Canyon while smoking a marijuana cigarette. Geisler de-fended Cheryl Crane, lovely 14-year-old daughter of Lana Turner, who in 1958 stabbed to death her mother's paramour, Johnny Stom-panato, when he threatened Lana with serious injury or death if she left him. In each case, instead of condemning, the public sympathized with the individuals in trouble.

In 1915 a movie gossip column had been started in the Chicago *Record-Herald* by Louella Parsons. Early in the twenties she was hired

Clark Gable and Vivien Leigh. (*—From the M-G-M release* Gone with the Wind © *1939 Selznick International Pictures, Inc. Copyright renewed 1967 by Metro-Goldwyn-Mayer Inc.*)

Mickey Rooney, Elizabeth Taylor and Butch Jenkins (below) as children on the M-G-M lot. (*—Metro-Goldwyn-Mayer Inc.*)

by William Randolph Hearst and her column was syndicated so that it appeared in newspapers across the country. Fifteen years afterward Hedda Hopper, a well-known actress, joined the staff of the Los Angeles *Times* to write a similar column. For many years these two women dominated the crowded field of writers devoted to news of personalities in the movies. Each fought to be the first to know intimate details in the lives of the famous — a wedding, a divorce, a pregnancy, an illness, an affair. Informants might be studio employees, friends, headwaiters, a cook or maid, a moving man, a debt collector, a salesclerk in some store, a press agent or a parking lot attendant. Most frequently the famous person involved gave the information himself in order to remain in the columnist's good graces.

Children working in studios must fulfill the same educational requirements that all children do across the country. Under California law, studio classes are provided for a daily minimum of three hours' study (four hours maximum) for each child. He must also be allowed one hour's recreation, and no more than four hours of work before the camera. Classes are held by authorized teachers, who must be prepared to instruct any grade, in subjects ranging from fingerpainting to languages to calculus. Most studios have a permanent class-

Shirley Temple, Jack Holt and John Boles in *The Littlest Rebel. (—Academy of Motion Picture Arts and Sciences)*

room, but during filming a portable dressing room beside the stage is used. School goes where the children go, and classes have been held on schooners at sea, in mountain cabins, on the beach, in a Chinese village, in a circus tent. There might be only one or two pupils or, overnight, more than a hundred because of a particular film. In that case there is usually one teacher for every ten children. If at the time of graduation they are enrolled at a studio school, the students receive their diplomas from University High School in Los Angeles. Many stars received schooling at a studio: Elizabeth Taylor, Mickey Rooney, Anne Shirley, Jean Parker, Jackie Cooper, Freddie Bartholomew, Judy Garland, Anne Blythe, Piper Laurie, Deanna Durbin, Lana Turner and numerous others.

During World War II, motion pictures were considered so important for propaganda and to maintain morale that their production was declared an essential industry, and a large number of workers were tied to their jobs until the war's end.

The Spanish Civil War of the late thirties, and afterward the alliance of the United States with Russia during World War II, created a sympathetic attitude toward Socialism and Communism among many idealists and liberal-minded people. With the growing estrangement of the two nations, the F.B.I. warned that there had been large-scale Communist infiltration and the establishment of party "cells." The House Committee on Un-American Activities singled out Hollywood as the region most threatened and on October 20, 1947, subpoenaed 41 members of the film industry. Nineteen refused to cooperate — they were named the "Unfriendly Witnesses" — and ten (eight screenwriters and two directors) were declared in contempt of Congress because they refused to state whether they were or ever had been members of the Communist Party. Most of their prepared legal briefs were refused by the committee and not heard. "The Hollywood Ten" were sentenced to six months to a year in a Federal penitentiary. A contagion of fear spread through the industry, and the Association of Motion Picture Producers assured the committee that the ten men would immediately be discharged by their employers. To clear themselves, witnesses were forced to name others known (or thought) by them to be Communist-influenced, including friends and associates. One man gave a hundred names. Guilt by association was the rule of the day and, with or without proof, growing numbers were on an unofficial blacklist held by studios and unions; many careers were ruined. This condition prevailed for almost a decade, until the public attitude changed and suspicions about Communist infiltrators gradually eased.

Most of the major movie companies not only produced films but also distributed them and owned theaters in which they were shown. For the studio this meant guaranteed booking for all the pictures it produced, but for small companies and independents it meant their films were automatically excluded from a large proportion of theaters. In the eyes of the Justice Department a monopoly had been created, and in 1938 suit was brought against Paramount under the Sherman Anti-Trust Act to force the studio to confine itself to production only. The case was carried to the Supreme Court. Major studios consented to abide by the results of the lawsuit against Paramount, and in 1948 the Supreme Court made its consent decree announcing that studios could function only as producers of films. That was the beginning of the end for the large studios.

At the same time, in the late forties, they faced a new threat, the rising competition of television. Former customers of movie houses stayed home, fascinated to have free entertainment brought right into the living room. In obstinate resistance, theater owners warned there would be reprisal against any studio which made films for the new medium. The major studios made no television pictures nor would they allow their contract players to appear in any. Independent companies seized this opportunity to move in and establish themselves in the field. No major studio accepted the inevitable until in 1952 Columbia formed a subsidiary, Screen Gems, to make pictures specifically for television. Columbia led the way again when it sold old features for TV release. As the number of stages needed for features dwindled, empty stages as well as sets on the backlots were rented to companies making television series. In fact, a large part of studio profits came from TV activities. By the mid-1960s most of the major studios were taken over by conglomerates, huge corporations which also owned, for example, companies handling music, recordings and cable TV as well as businesses totally unrelated to entertainment.

In early days actors and actresses were hired under long-term contracts, but under a new custom of hiring for individual pictures only, the star system collapsed.

By 1970 the film industry was in the process of total change. Instead of being censored, motion pictures were "rated" — marked with a letter to indicate their appropriateness for select age groups. With the discovery that most audiences were made up of young adults, a high proportion of movies were oriented toward their tastes. Pictures made on low budgets often succeeded while those with expensive budgets failed; so economy became a rule. Producers experimented with artistic, off-beat stories and camera work. With the added exposure given by television, local scenery grew overfamiliar and audiences more critical. Production units left Hollywood to work in the actual locations in which stories were set, or where scenery would look like the real thing. High wages and studio costs in Hollywood gave producers an added incentive to film elsewhere. Major studios frequently produced their entire year's schedule in distant places, in what was called runaway production. This was made even easier by development of specialized trucks which could carry all necessary equipment in a compact unit. Studio stages were mainly used for the production of television programs. The backlots, once valuable for storing scenery for reuse, had more value as real estate. Sale of the land helped feeble studio finances and also was a windfall for eager developers. On the Twentieth Century-Fox property at Olympic Boulevard and Motor Avenue oil wells brought in extra revenue, but the land reached its fullest value when, in an historic real estate transaction, Century City was built on the former backlot.

Meanwhile, economic pressures caused James Aubrey, newly installed as M-G-M's president, to turn a cold business eye on studio assets and liabilities. In huge wardrobe rooms over 150,000 costumes were carefully preserved. The property department stored furnishings large and small from decades of motion pictures; among them were treasures, including antiques collected from the palaces of Europe and Asia.* On enormous backlots, sets from old movies remained — staircases leading nowhere, houses, churches, castles, ships, medieval buildings, fountains, western streets, European streets, New England streets, Chinese streets, the surface of the moon. The time came to realize that most of these sets would never be used again and the land involved had greater value as a real estate subdivision. With a firm announcement that "M-G-M is not in the business of nostalgia," a half century's accumulation of film memorabilia went on the auction block in April 1970. To the moviegoer, that single event more than any other marked the end of an era.

For a week visitors were allowed on the stages and backlots where relics of over 2000 films were on display. A catalogue listed each item and gave a brief description, along with the name of a picture in which it had appeared, though most pieces of furniture had been used in many films. The scene was a phantasmagoria of memories — Roman

---

*Three crystal chandeliers now hanging in the Founders' Room of the Dorothy Chandler Pavilion of the Music Center had been used in *The Great Waltz* and were taken from storage in the warehouse a few years before the auction.

chariots used in *Ben Hur,* the square-rigged schooner from *Captains Courageous,* Mickey Rooney's 1931 Model A used during his role as Andy Hardy, the Pope's throne in *Shoes of the Fisherman.* . . . Through summerlike spring days and evenings visitors swarmed into the studio, not only the stage-struck and the curious, but also representatives of shops in foreign lands. When the auction began, a few of the stars themselves bought some memento from a favorite film. One after another the articles were auctioned off: Clark Gable's "lucky" trench coat which he wore in most of his pictures, a dress worn by Norma Shearer in *Marie Antoinette,* the cape worn by Greta Garbo in *Anna Karenina.* Most sought-after of all were Judy Garland's ruby slippers from *The Wizard of Oz;* they were sold to an anonymous buyer for $15,000. After the auction there was a general sale of less important things, such as clothes worn by extras in *Quo Vadis,* Civil War uniforms of Confederate and Union forces, army uniforms of all nationalities. By chance the sale coincided with the fad among young people for fancy dress, and to hippies it was a bonanza. One group of students from the University of California in Berkeley came in search of overcoats at low prices and found just the right thing. For three dollars, each of them bought a Russian soldier's overcoat from *Dr. Zhivago.* One dollar bought a pair of Roman centurion sandals which laced up the calf. Soon those costumes appeared on the Berkeley campus in the daily masquerade.

In spite of changes, Hollywood has remained a center for motion pictures made in the United States and headquarters of the Directors Guild, the Screen Actors Guild and other craft associations. And the magnetic pull of cinema glamor never seems to wane. Today on streets in Hollywood, especially those leading toward Beverly Hills, hawkers vend maps to the stars' homes. Sightseeing buses drive up and down streets where celebrities live, not only to point out their houses but also on the chance that sometime, somewhere, a star might appear in real life. And the entrance of Grauman's Chinese Theater is always filled with tourists eager to place their feet in the footprints of the stars.

5. *Defense and Space*

Los Angeles was launched toward a new destiny as center of the aircraft industry when in 1938 orders came from Washington for the construction of 10,000 airplanes. Hitler's victory at the Munich Conference had convinced President Roosevelt that airpower was an important weapon in international politics. Two years later, at the

During World War II the rooftops and streets of Lockheed Aircraft's plant in Burbank were camouflaged. (—*Lockheed Aircraft Corp.*)

At Rocketdyne's field laboratory in the Santa Susana Mountains, rocket engines held in giant stands are tested at night. (—*Rocketdyne Div. of Rockwell Int'l Corp.*)

fall of France, the President announced that 50,000 more planes were to be built, a large proportion of them in aircraft factories on the West Coast. The defense migration began as thousands of people streamed across the continent to work in the huge new plants. When the attack on Pearl Harbor brought the United States into World War II, over 34% of the factory workers in Los Angeles County were employed in the aircraft industry.

In Pasadena the California Institute of Technology held studies in aeronautical physics and, in a ravine north of town, built the Jet Propulsion Laboratory to conduct experiments with rockets. During the war the laboratory was taken over by the Army to make rocket projectiles, and later it came under the National Aeronautics and Space Administration (NASA) for use in probing outer space.

The emphasis of Los Angeles' industry by the late forties began to shift to electronics and the development of missiles, anti-missiles and spacecraft. Efforts for operational craft were stepped up after the launching of Sputnik by Russia in 1957, and technical staffs of colleges were used for expert advice. By 1958 a ring of six Hercules underground missile sites guarded Los Angeles.

Rocketdyne, a subsidiary of North American Aviation, developed rockets to propel spacecraft. When the engines were tested in the company's field propulsion laboratory in the Santa Susana Mountains above Canoga Park, San Fernando Valley residents could hear the mighty power being held in check, feel the ground shake and see light flare over the testing grounds.

By the late sixties about 12,000 firms in the Los Angeles area were connected with some aspect of the aerospace industry. Because of personal involvement with the Apollo space project on the part of thousands of contractors, subcontractors and suppliers, Los Angeles was swept with special elation when man successfully landed on the moon July 20, 1969.

6. Freeways

The freeways, which grew to dominate life in Los Angeles, started along the route of a bicycle track following the Arroyo Seco between Pasadena and downtown. When in 1940 the Pasadena Freeway opened, delighted motorists discovered they could make the entire trip within 12 minutes. Immediately plans were made for the Hollywood Freeway to link Los Angeles and the San Fernando Valley, but building restrictions due to World War II caused postponement for seven years. In those years superhighway designs improved, and the many curves and sharp, narrow exits of the Pasadena Freeway became obsolete. The expanding network of freeways built throughout California made the state a huge experimental laboratory for all the details of their construction.

Nowhere was a freeway more welcome than through the mountains between the San Fernando and San Joaquin Valleys. In a difficult engineering feat, the Ridge Route had been constructed in 1914. It snaked across hills and through ravines; north of Tejón Pass it made a steep, spiraling descent through La Cañada de las Uvas. ("Uvas" means grapes, and since the twisting road resembled a vine it was called The Grapevine.) Throughout its winding path a driver made more than 100 complete circles, and trucks' brakes failed so often that at strategic places ramps were built leading off the road on a sharp upgrade to enable runaway trucks to halt. Ice added a new danger during cold months. At first the highway consisted of only two lanes, one for each direction, but after about twenty years it was reconstructed along a slightly straighter course and with two full lanes on each side. From today's freeway, in its final miles of easy descent to the San Joaquin Valley, one can see The Grapevine nearby, still winding its tortuous pathway down the mountain.

During World War II, about 1943, an ugly phenomenon began to develop in the atmosphere above Los Angeles — smog — and with each year the problem became worse. It was the custom for residents throughout the county to use backyard incinerators to dispose of trash; so authorities decided that those burners were the probable cause of smog. In 1957 their use was banned, except at night, and instead trucks collected all trash as a regular service. The smog only increased. Industry was next pinpointed as the culprit; the government regulated industrial combustion, and at enormous expense many plants converted to oil-burning machinery. Still smog increased. Then scientists found that automobiles were intensifying the air pollution, because engine emissions react in sunlight to form new, harmful substances.

The basic cause of the problem is that the atmosphere of Los Angeles is prone to level out in what is called an inversion layer of warm air, and at the same time the surrounding mountains and the cold front of air from the ocean act as walls. Therefore polluted air is often unable to disperse. Experts devised a way to measure the degree of pollution so that when it reached too high a level a smog alert could be called and people would be asked to do only necessary driving. A more serious alert would cause industries contributing to air pollution to shut down temporarily, and in a most serious situation Air

Aerial view of the Music Center, showing the Dorothy Chandler Pavilion, Mark Taper Forum and Ahmanson Theatre. (*—Courtesy the Music Center; photograph by Otto Rothschild*)

Pollution Control could stop all traffic in the Los Angeles Basin except for emergency vehicles. For a long time it was thought that smog was confined to Southern California, but the problem became known in other parts of the world. By then the studies and regulations made in Los Angeles were used as models elsewhere.

7. New Centers for the Arts

Culture and Los Angeles have never been considered synonymous. In Northern California and among the older communities of the East, the lack of culture in Southern California has been a subject of derision. The shortcomings have been unquestionable, although not in the field of books. As a market for books, Los Angeles is second only to New York, and the public library system is the most-used in the United States.

But in 1960 the symphony orchestra still had no concert hall of its own and instead rented from the Temple Baptist Church an audi-

torium (used for Sunday services) on Pershing Square. Three times
a bond issue to construct a hall for concerts and opera failed when
presented to the voters.

In 1955 Dorothy Chandler, wife of Norman Chandler, publisher
of the Los Angeles *Times,* had been made chairman of the Citizens'
Advisory Committee to work out the location and financial details of
a music center. To forward the project she and a friend arranged a
benefit party at which $400,000 was donated. The large sum, offered
during just a few hours, made her certain of success even without a
bond issue, because obviously enough people cared. Even so, a business recession and multiplying problems forced postponement of the
costly plan. In 1958 she was named president of the Southern California Symphony Association. Two large donations given in December of the same year brought the fund up to $600,000. This gave
Mrs. Chandler the impetus she needed, and two months later she
was able to offer the amazed Board of Supervisors $4,000,000, pri-
vately subscribed, toward building the music center. She suggested
that the site be on land already owned by the county, at the summit
of the Civic Center, whose structures rose on a hillside downtown.
It was an ideal location. And so the unusual project was launched,
where private funds were to create a public building.

When structural work on the Dorothy Chandler Pavilion was finished, there was a dedication ceremony on the plaza in front. Mrs.
Chandler expressed a hope that there might still be small donations,
and from the spectators so many $1 and $5 bills were handed up
that two paper shopping bags were found and the money was stuffed
into them. That began a "Buck Bag" campaign throughout the city.
The new Music Center eventually included not only the Dorothy
Chandler Pavilion but also the Ahmanson Theater and Mark Taper
Forum for creative work in the theater. Donations large and small
reached a total of $35,000,000.

The center was inaugurated on December 6, 1964, with concerts
by the Los Angeles Philharmonic Orchestra under the direction of
Zubin Mehta (chosen permanent conductor two years earlier, when
he was 25). Instruments of especially fine workmanship — by Stradi-
vari, Guadagnini and others, dating as far back as 1550 — had been
donated to the orchestra or bought by the Southern California Symphony Association. Special construction had created perfect acoustics
in the concert hall. A Music Center for Los Angeles is wholly appropriate, as the city has been the chosen residence of great musicians, including Rachmaninoff, Heifetz, Piatigorsky, Stravinsky, Iturbi,
Rubinstein and Schoenberg.

The opening of the Music Center was an important landmark in modern Los Angeles history. The fact that rich and poor, young and old had contributed made people, who otherwise might well have been indifferent, feel involved. The event seemed to infuse a new self-respect into the community – a strong psychological effect not confined to the performing arts. It was a subtle but pervasive change caused by an extraordinary woman who cared about the quality of life in Los Angeles.

Until 1965, Los Angeles County's collection of art was housed in a minor wing of the Los Angeles County Museum of History, Science and Art in Exposition Park, a building erected in 1913. A few months after the Dorothy Chandler Pavilion was completed, a new Los Angeles County Museum of Art opened its doors in Hancock Park on Wilshire Boulevard. From the original meager group of paintings, the permanent collection has grown to represent all schools of European and American art, as well as ancient, medieval and modern sculpture and the art of the Orient. In addition, the museum is one of the nation's largest purchasers of works by living American artists.

The museum is composed of three buildings. The Ahmanson Gallery, largest of the structures, houses the permanent collection. Nearby, the Leo S. Bing Center contains a library, auditorium and other facilities, while the Frances and Armand Hammer Wing displays traveling collections.

Not long after the new museum opened, Norton Simon, a chief donor, bought Rembrandt's *Portrait of Titus* (the artist's son) for over two million dollars at an auction in London. A furor arose in England upon discovery that the painting was to be taken to America. The new owner offered England one week in which to equal the price he had paid, but it turned out to be an impossible goal, and the painting was relinquished. On the way to California it was first shown in a special exhibit at the National Gallery in Washington, but as time came for it to be taken west on loan to the Museum of Art in Los Angeles, there were fears that the painting, on a small canvas 21½x25¼ inches, might be stolen en route. By a clever trick, its safety was made certain before the treasure was carried onto the plane. How? With some simple magic words. The flight was made in December, and so the painting was Christmas gift-wrapped; on a card, with the words clearly readable, was:

Merry Christmas
to
MOTHER
With love from your Son

There are over a hundred art galleries in Los Angeles, and many centers for creative work. Among them, the most remarkable is the Watts Towers Community Art Center for painting, sculpture, ceramics, dancing and drama. Classes are held in a building near three highly individualistic steel towers (the tallest is 100 feet). Over a period of 33 years an Italian immigrant named Simon Rodia built the towers and covered them with cement in which he embedded seashells, metal and broken pieces of glass, china and tile in fanciful mosaics. Using discards collected wherever available, he melded a cheerful design, singing as he worked. When the spires were finished, he moved on. After the Watts riots the neighborhood banded together to rebuild itself, and Simon Rodia's imaginative creation, in which all types of materials were used, was made a symbol of the community.

At the Los Angeles County Museum of Art, the buildings are (from the left, clockwise) the Ahmanson Gallery, the Frances and Armand Hammer Wing and the Leo S. Bing Center. In the surrounding grounds of Hancock Park may be seen La Brea Pits. Inside the small, white observatory Pleistocene fossils lie in an asphalt pool, clearly visible. Alongside the Hammer Wing, where in this picture trees line a pathway, excavations began during 1969, and today the area is a large excavation site. The street in the foreground is Wilshire Boulevard. (—*Los Angeles Co. Museum of Art*)

8. *Archaeological Discoveries*

As summer began in 1969, a drama of prehistoric times was unearthed near busy Wilshire Boulevard beside the sleek, modern Los Angeles County Museum of Art when excavators began to dig in the asphalt pits of Hancock Park, once part of Rancho La Brea. The first probes, half a century earlier, had gone to a depth of 27 feet, but improved shoring techniques allowed renewed exploration to at least 50 feet. Because the museum had little available money, an unusual opportunity was given to the public: the people of Los Angeles were invited to join the undertaking as volunteers. Under the direction of a few professional scientists the volunteers — housewives, vacationers, retired businessmen, students, clerks on a Saturday off from work — at long tables sorted not only remains of animals, birds and insects but also of cones and pollen, leaves and grasses, even fragments of trees. The painstaking work would eventually make possible a complete reconstruction of the site as it existed in Pleistocene times.

Passersby gazed at a remarkable scene. The smooth white walls of the art museum formed a backdrop for what appeared to be primitive construction in a huge mud puddle. By some strange, anachronistic turn of events, the world's most valuable site for Ice Age fossils lies in the midst of a metropolis, emphasizing a contrast which spans millenia.

Man's history in California does not begin with the arrival of the Spaniards, nor with the Indians, but with the arrival of man in the Americas. Until recently it was thought that no human life existed on this continent until a relatively brief 10,000 years ago — certainly not during the Ice Ages. Also, there was a question about where man first arrived in the Western Hemisphere. Today the leading theory is that, as a hunter following a herd of animals, he came from Siberia across the Bering Strait by an early land bridge. During the Pleistocene or Ice Ages, glaciers advanced and receded over the northern part of the globe four times. As the glaciers changed, the climate changed, and it would have been during times when the Bering land bridge was above water that Siberian hunters crossed to the New World and then roamed south and east.

Scientists had trouble determining how long man has lived in the Los Angeles Basin, for when human bones were found it was usually difficult to measure their age with exactness, unless studies of the surrounding geological strata could fix the date with some certainty. In 1947 a sensational breakthrough in this field was made when Dr. Willard F. Libby at the University of Chicago discovered a dating method based on radiocarbon-14, often abbreviated to C-14. The process is complicated and, briefly, it relies on the fact that radioactive carbon dioxide, atomic weight 14, is present in known proportions in every living thing, including plants. After death, radioactive decay reduces the amount of C-14 at a fixed speed, so that by measuring the amount of radiation emanating from a fossil its age can be determined up to 50,000 years, by which time no C-14 remains. For many years the method was tested with remains whose age was exactly known — for instance, those from a tomb of known date in Egypt. The success of Dr. Libby's discovery brought him the Nobel prize in 1960.

During early excavations at the La Brea Pits in 1914, some human remains were found. Although surrounding asphalt held fossils of Pleistocene animals, circumstances made it seem likely that the human bones had entered that part of the asphalt at some fairly recent time. The bones were similar to those of Indians in Southern California and, analyzed as belonging to a woman in her mid-twenties, were named La Brea Woman. The skull had a large hole, suggesting that she had been killed by a severe blow on the head. Even using radiocarbon-14 dating years later, bones found in the pits were difficult to assess because they were petroleum-impregnated. That problem was solved with a special process developed in 1968. Analysis of La Brea Woman's bones then showed that she lived 9000 years ago, plus or minus 80 years.

Two teenage boys found another skull in 1933 while treasure hunting along an embankment in Laguna Beach, a short distance south of Los Angeles. One of the boys, 17-year-old Howard Wilson, took it home and showed it to his mother, who told him to throw it into the garbage can. Instead he kept it in a shoebox where it lay for two years. Then he brought it out for another look and sent a drawing to various museums and universities, but the consensus of opinion was that undoubtedly the skull was only that of an early Indian. Back it went into the shoebox, where it lay for 16 more years, until Wilson showed it to a man who was able to interest a scientist about to leave for the European center of anthropology, La Musée de l'Homme in Paris. For eight years the skull was carried along to various museums in Europe then once more returned to Wilson. In 1967 when the renowned archaeologist Dr. Louis S. B. Leakey was lecturing in California, the skull was brought out again and shown to him. On Leakey's advice Wilson took it to the University of California at Los Angeles where Dr. Rainer Berger, former assistant to the man who invented C-14 dating, was in charge. Early in 1969

Part of a mural showing the kinds of animals that succumbed to La Brea Pits, a re-creation of 40,000 years
ago. (—*Los Angeles Co. Museum of Natural History*)

Dr. Berger announced that carbon-14 dating showed the skull to be
17,150 years old, plus or minus 1470 years. Studies indicated that it
was probably a woman's skull; so it was named Laguna Woman.

In 1936 some W.P.A. workers on a storm drain project were digging
near Higuera Street on the northern edge of the Baldwin Hills. About
12 feet below the surface, in sandy clay beneath an old riverbed, the
men came upon a skull and other bones. Because they were heavily encrusted, the remains were obviously ancient. The University of Southern California was notified, and a representative of the Department
of Anthropology and Archaeology arrived at the excavation. A farci-
cal sequence with red tape followed when the university was not
allowed to take the bones for study because two zealous officers of

The earliest human remains found in the Los Angeles region are displayed at the Museum of Natural History. In the foreground, left to right, are Los Angeles Man, Laguna Woman and La Brea Woman; at the rear, a prehistoric Indian skull (about 1450 A.D.) is included for comparison. Note that a large portion of Los Angeles Man's skull was consumed in the process of radiocarbon dating; the others, except for the Indian, have been reconstructed. All are skulls of *Homo sapiens,* modern man. (*—Los Angeles Co. Museum of Natural History*)

the homicide squad seized them as property of the county coroner's office. Only after insistent efforts were they at last released to the university laboratory. Later the skull — by then called Los Angeles Man — was taken to U.C.L.A., as the other discoveries were, for carbon-14 dating. To establish an exact date, most of the bone would have had to be used and little would have remained. Therefore the scientists determined that the skull was at least 23,600 years old, but they stopped short of discovering exactly how much older. Other prehistoric human remains have been found in North and South America, but to judge by the carbon-14 dating Los Angeles Man is the earliest human inhabitant of the Western Hemisphere yet discovered.

The ancient remains have helped us to gain a perspective on man's existence in the New World. Thanks to the amazing discovery by which we can, with a large degree of certainty, measure the age of former living things, we now know that by the late Pleistocene era, when glaciers held the north in icy fingers, man had already crossed the land bridge from Asia and made his way far to the south in the Americas.

9. *Earthquakes*

Some of the largest earthquakes on record in the United States occurred in Missouri (1811), South Carolina (1886) and Alaska (1964).

It is recorded that during the quake centered in New Madrid, Missouri, hills sank, crevices appeared, new lakes formed and the shock was felt throughout an area of about 1,000,000 square miles. The South Carolina earthquake, centered about twenty miles north of Charleston, damaged ninety percent of the city's brick buildings and took 27 lives; the shock was felt and recorded as far north as Boston. The Alaskan quake, felt over an area of almost 500,000 square miles, triggered landslides and a tidal wave, and the sharpness of its jolts snapped off the tops of some trees. However, the earthquakes in Missouri and South Carolina probably totaled about magnitude 8.0 each, while, except for Alaska, California has had three known quakes of higher magnitude.

Gaspar de Portolá and the explorers of the first land expedition up the Pacific coast, in 1769, were greeted by an earthquake as they camped near the Santa Ana River. Other shocks — today called aftershocks — followed; so the river was named El Rio de Jesús de los Temblores. A half century after that, in 1812, the San Fernando and San Gabriel Missions were damaged in two different quakes. In 1857 one of the most severe earthquakes ever recorded in Southern California hit Fort Tejón.

Today the scientific study of the size of an earthquake is aided by two systems of measurement. In 1935 Charles F. Richter of the California Institute of Technology devised the Richter magnitude, a method of using seismographs to measure the total energy released in an earthquake. Because the scale is logarithmic, and because of the relationship between energy and magnitude, an earthquake of magnitude 8, for example, is about 32 times as strong in total energy released as one of magnitude 7. The C.I.T. Seismology Laboratory estimates that the Fort Tejón jolt reached about 8.3. The great earthquake of San Francisco in 1906 was of approximately the same strength, although there the damage was intensified by broken gas mains and water lines which led to uncontrollable fire. The Alaskan quake of 1964 reached a magnitude of 8.4. The other system, the modified Mercalli scale, ranges from I to XII and measures the intensity of the quake's effects based on eyewitness reports. Established in 1902 by the Italian seismologist Mercalli, the scale was modified by American scientists in 1931 to apply to such modern features as tall buildings, automobiles and underground pipes. On the modified Mercalli scale the San Francisco quake had an intensity of XI, and the Alaskan of X. In short, the Mercalli scale is concerned with the intensities of local ground shaking, while the Richter magnitude gives some measure of the total energy released.

As evening began on March 10, 1933, a heavy earthquake struck Long Beach, Compton and nearby communities south of Los Angeles. It was 5:54 p.m., Pacific time, when the ground started to rock, streets buckle and buildings fall. From the Pacific Fleet in the harbor, 4000 marines and sailors came ashore to help with rescue work, and Los Angeles dispatched its entire fire-fighting force. The quake, whose magnitude on the Richter scale measured 6.3, caused 120 fatalities as well as extensive damage because of the concentration of buildings, many of them poorly constructed. Especially horrifying was the news that 22 schools were badly damaged: only a few hours earlier those structures had been filled with children.

Immediately after the disaster Los Angeles established a new building code, ninety percent of it concerned with earthquake-resistance. The damage to schools turned a spotlight on the need for a strict building code in California. Assemblyman Don Field of Glendale presented a bill to the State Legislature, which passed it into law exactly a month after the catastrophe in Long Beach. Called the Field Act, it provided that construction of all school buildings in California should comply with a carefully formulated state (not local) building code, and the work should be closely supervised. The measure applied only to new construction; so in the sixties another bill was added which declared that by June 30, 1975, all schools built before the Field Act must meet the safety requirements or else close down. Later this was extended two years.

On February 9, 1971, another serious earthquake struck, this time in the northern area of Los Angeles. At 6:01 a.m. a supposedly inactive fault about six miles northeast of Sylmar, in the foothills of the San Gabriel Mountains, sprang violently to life. Throughout a large surrounding area everyone awoke at the same instant.

In the early morning the freeways were almost empty of traffic, but two men in a pickup truck happened to drive under a freeway overpass at the moment it collapsed. Both men were killed. Several other bridges and overpasses nearby were destroyed, but there were no more casualties. Above the sleeping San Fernando Valley the Lower Van Norman Reservoir lay quiet in the darkness as the quake struck. Intense shaking badly damaged this old earth-fill dam, and it was nearly topped by waters of the reservoir. Below, 80,000 residents were hastily evacuated to school buildings, and almost two-thirds of the reservoir's water was emptied into the Los Angeles River in case the dam, weakened further by aftershocks, gave way.

Both the Lower and Upper Van Norman Reservoirs had been built in 1914, when hydraulic earth-fill construction was common and

Freeway damage during the San Fernando Valley earthquake of February 9, 1971. (—*Los Angeles* Times *Photo*)

economical. Farther east, the Pacoima Dam lay five miles south of
the epicenter (the point on the surface directly above the quake's
point of origin). There the ground was shaken by the most severe
motion ever recorded during an earthquake, but the 370-foot-high
concrete arch remained structurally undamaged.

Hard hit were three hospitals in the area. In one of them, Olive
View, the entire first story of a psychiatric ward collapsed. Because
of the early hour no one was there, and although forty to sixty persons were sleeping above in the second story, there were no casualties when it fell. Of the three people who lost their lives in that
hospital, two were in iron lungs and succumbed when the power went
off. At a second badly damaged hospital everyone was evacuated
safely. The third, the San Fernando Veteran's Administration Hospital, about one mile from the Pacoima Dam, included 45 separate
buildings. Over half of them had been built before 1933 and they
received the heaviest damage; among them, two main buildings collapsed and claimed 46 lives. An hour went by before rescuers began
to arrive, because during the quake all telephone service was cut off
and the building which housed the hospital's emergency power for
communication was destroyed. It wasn't until a helicopter observed
the catastrophe from above that the need for help was known.

In all, 64 lives were lost as a result of the quake. Over 1300 buildings were badly damaged, but a large proportion of the structures in

the area most affected were not seriously harmed. A shortwave radio network, set up in disaster planning, coordinated the resources of 110 hospitals in Los Angeles County and dispatched doctors and nurses where they were needed.

The earthquake originated approximately seven miles underground, and there were hundreds of aftershocks. After months of painstaking study, the C.I.T. Seismology Laboratory reached an appraisal of the tremor's magnitude as 6.4 on the Richter scale at the epicenter. On the Mercalli scale, it had a maximum local intensity of IX to X. The quake took place along what is now called the San Fernando Fault, which is not directly a part of the San Andreas Fault system. No known active fault lies under downtown Los Angeles.

Scientists learn with each earthquake. California structural engineers have studied those in this country and also in Venezuela, Japan, Nicaragua and elsewhere. The San Fernando Valley quake provided an especial wealth of information, because earlier the area had been studied and mapped in detail and, in conformity with the Los Angeles building code, strong-motion seismographs had been placed in buildings over six stories high in the city. It is significant that all of the buildings which suffered damage in downtown Los Angeles, forty miles south of the epicenter, had been constructed prior to the strict building code that followed the Long Beach disaster. Structurally the new high-rise buildings performed well. Engineers found that internal fixtures which broke loose created the chief danger, and so appropriate new rules were added to the code, specifying what fixtures should be more firmly attached to the basic structure.

The rupture along the rim of the Lower Van Norman Reservoir posed a danger to homes below, and police officers were dispatched to give warning throughout a six-square-mile area. While driving up and down the streets the officers, over loudspeakers, advised all residents to leave immediately. Television and radio stations broadcast the same warning. Hastily the Red Cross set up emergency centers for the refugees in communities nearby, especially in the schools. Residents fled, some pausing only long enough to gather pets and maybe to grab coats on their way, others stopping longer to collect special valuables to take along for safekeeping. One confused woman in her haste to leave took along a plant but left her dog behind. A very few remained inside their homes, either doubting the dam would break or wanting to protect their belongings from looters.

Soon all the streets were empty, and the officers, risking their own lives in the line of duty, began their day and night patrol through an eerie, silent world. They drove past bicycles and toys in driveways and on lawns, cars parked at the curb and even, here and there, clothes hung on a line. But no people.

Then another kind of patrol entered the evacuation area. Before the first afternoon ended, humane societies arrived to take care of the animals left behind, and they were allowed passage. If it was necessary to enter a home, the owner made arrangements to give a driver the key. Only volunteers went into the danger area. Of the many humane societies, the S.P.C.A. was the largest. Driving trucks laden with dog and cat food, bird seed, duck mash and rabbit pellets, and a special truck which hauled hay for livestock, the drivers fed chickens, geese, ducks, dogs, cats, canaries, guinea pigs, rabbits, goats, horses and one man's aviary of 150 parakeets. All water had been turned off, and though large jugs could hold enough water for most of the animals, there were horses to care for, and one horse drinks between 12 and 18 gallons a day. The S.P.C.A. brought in a 500-gallon water tank and the problem was solved. In the quiet of early night hours, several trucks returned, pausing on the way down each street to listen for the sound of any animal in distress.

Steadily the water level behind the dam grew lower until the risk was over and residents were allowed to return. In time the reservoir was entirely drained, to be used no more.

With the realization that, if the earthquake had taken place two hours later, classrooms would have been filled with children, attention once more focused on schools. Inspectors meticulously surveyed each school building in Los Angeles — there were 9642 just in the city's Unified School District, or about 5 buildings to a school campus — and those which had been made unsafe by damages were closed. Los Angeles High School, the city's first high school, was among them. The large administration building, dating from long before anything was known about earthquake-resistant construction, had become a shambles and was torn down. A total of about 85 buildings were closed as potentially unsafe in case of a severe earthquake; they were to be strengthened or replaced.

The earthquake offered California engineers an opportunity to observe the success or failure of their efforts to make schools safe for children. In the area most affected, all the schools had been built to earthquake-resistant specifications. The results were impressive: damages were of such a nature that if the classrooms had been occupied, probably no child would have been seriously hurt. For instance, though the earth beneath part of a school building in San Fernando moved 3½ inches to one side, the structure held firmly together. In Little Tujunga Canyon near the Pacoima Dam, where extreme violence was recorded, the buildings of a probation camp had been constructed under the code. The ground wrenched and jerked, forcefully reshaping itself. When it was all over, inspectors found that under one of the buildings the site had moved four inches to one side; beneath a wall of another the ground had risen six inches. But both buildings remained securely intact.

The effects of the San Fernando earthquake show clearly that other factors than nearness to the underground fault determine a building's safety. The foundation material — bedrock rather than clay or sand — is important. And proper construction requires that the walls, roof and floor should be tied together strongly, so that during a quake all structural elements act as one.

10. *Minorities — Mexican Americans*

Los Angeles was never a melting pot in the manner of New York, which has assimilated large numbers of immigrants from many different countries. In Los Angeles, sizable immigrant colonies have been relatively few.

The Mexican-American minority has a basic place in the fabric of California. When this area was transferred from Mexican to U.S. sovereignty, there were a mere 300 Americans living in Los Angeles. Before long the Americans greatly outnumbered the original Californios, but nevertheless through the years there has been a constant stream of immigrants from Mexico. Except for Mexico City, Los Angeles has more residents of Mexican origin than any other city in the world.

Unexpectedly, serious trouble arose during World War II between the Mexican Americans and the servicemen stationed near Los Angeles — who naturally had no understanding of the close ties between California and the Spanish-speaking people. At that time many young Chicanos wore so-called "zoot suits" (clothes cut very loosely at the top, but with trousers tapering at the ankle). On June 3, 1943, a group of sailors walking through town was attacked by a gang. The assailants were never found, but the sailors described them as Mexican and a feud began. Bands of sailors, joined by soldiers and marines, roamed Los Angeles searching for zoot suiters and picking fights. Apparently due to the patriotism of wartime, the police cooperated with the servicemen to the point that usually the Chicanos were the ones arrested, however severely they had been beaten up. Often when victims were otherwise unhurt their zoot suits were ripped off. The

rioting continued for a week, but public indignation at the persecution of innocent people finally stopped it. Parts of Los Angeles
were made off limits to servicemen, and organizations were formed
for the purpose of protecting minorities. The police department was
reorganized, and police training henceforth included education regarding all minority groups.

According to the census of 1970, the residents of Los Angeles
County who were Spanish-speaking or had Spanish surnames numbered 1,289,311, or approximately 18% of the total population. Among
them were an estimated 100,000 illegal aliens: many had arrived as
"wetbacks" (a term derived from illegal crossing of the Rio Grande
into Texas); others entered legally on a 72-hour permit but then disappeared into a Spanish-speaking barrio (neighborhood).

When California joined the Union, English became the language
taught in schools, and the Mexican Americans suffered a disadvantage. This still happens today: Spanish-speaking children often begin
school without knowing a word of English. Over a period of time the
new language is learned, but those students who start behind the class,
understanding little that is said, often remain behind until eventually
they drop out of school. More than half of the Chicano students leave
high school before graduation.

In a unanimous ruling which referred particularly to San Francisco's Chinatown but applies also to other minority groups, the U.S.
Supreme Court on January 21, 1947, declared that school systems
receiving Federal funds (most public school systems in the nation do)
must give special instruction to students unable to speak English well
enough to comprehend classroom proceedings. Increased concern
about this problem led to innovations in schools, especially regarding use of the Spanish language, and to the election of Dr. Julian
Nava, professor of history at San Fernando Valley State College, to
the Board of Education in 1967 — the first Mexican American ever
elected to that body. In 1968 the U.S. Congress passed the Bilingual
Education Act under which Federal funds would be given to states
to subsidize the teaching of basic subjects in Spanish as well as
English. The move was essential for California, where during the
decade 1960-70 the Spanish-speaking population increased from 1.4
million to 3.1 million.

Until recently, citizens of California were eligible to vote in state
elections only if they could read English. This law, a constitutional
amendment passed by the California Assembly in 1871, was presented by A. J. Bledsoe, who earlier caused everyone of Chinese
ancestry to be expelled from Humboldt County on the basis of "cor-

rupting influences." In 1970, almost a century later, the California
Supreme Court unanimously declared the law to be in violation of
the 14th amendment to the U.S. Constitution.

Slowly and yet certainly, the tide has reversed the pattern of discrimination which began with the Gold Rush. The issues are basically
those of civil rights, but the Mexican Americans' ethnic heritage in
Los Angeles provides an additional source of pride and stimulus to
seek recognition.

11. Minorities — Japanese Americans

The largest Japanese-American community on the North American
Continent is in the city of Los Angeles, which in 1970 contained about
55,000 people of Japanese ancestry. The center of the enclave is Little
Tokyo, only two blocks from the Los Angeles City Hall.

It was 1869 before any Japanese came to Los Angeles. At that time
Japan lifted travel restrictions and allowed her citizens to go abroad.
Most of the Japanese who came to California settled in the north, but
after the San Francisco earthquake in 1906 several thousand left for
the Southland. They took work mainly in agriculture, and by 1916
eighty percent of the vegetables in Los Angeles markets were grown
by Japanese farmers.

A few days after the attack on Pearl Harbor in 1941, Secretary of
the Navy Frank Knox announced that the Japanese force had been
aided by a fifth column — a clandestine organization working within
Hawaii. Although a committee was immediately formed to investigate, and the report of a fifth column was proved untrue, by the time
the denial appeared it was too late to change the general belief. On
the West Coast the public's fears centered around the probability that
a fifth column already existed and would help Japan in a military invasion. To prevent sabotage or espionage, all alien Japanese, Germans
and Italians were removed from areas around military and naval in-
stallations, airports, dams and power plants.

Allied disasters in the Pacific quickly multiplied. The Japanese
conquered Guam, Wake Island, Malaya, Manila, Hong Kong, Singa-
pore. Shipping off the West Coast suffered three submarine attacks
during the month of December 1941. Reports circulated that the
Pacific coast was in imminent danger of attack, and Los Angeles went
on complete war status. Headquarters for the coastal defense was Fort
MacArthur, on the Palos Verdes Peninsula. The fort was strengthened
and additional gun batteries were hastily installed at several points
along the peninsula and at Pacific Palisades, Playa del Rey, Manhat-

tan Beach and Redondo Beach. Huge searchlights — one every five miles along the shore — scanned the ocean. The roofs of airplane and other defense plants were camouflaged to give the appearance of rural scenes, with fields, trees and homes.

Rumors spread that submarines had been seen prowling offshore. It was rumored among housewives that Japanese fruit vendors had suddenly begun to threaten their customers, announcing they were generals who would soon overcome America. The cliff land of the Palos Verdes Peninsula was one vast truck garden, and rumors claimed that not only had the land been chosen because from there signals could be sent to Japanese ships at sea, but also that the gardeners had been treating their vegetables with arsenic. Newspapers reported that in the Japanese community of Sawtelle (part of West Los Angeles) many homes had been found to have large supplies of water stored, which indicated there might be plans for sabotage of dams and reservoirs. Organizations known for prejudice against the Japanese claimed that all their accusations had been proved true — that the "yellow race" was intrinsically different from others, its people not to be trusted; that all Japanese, even those who had become American citizens, felt loyalty only to their emperor and the home of their ancestors. As a matter of fact, not a single case of sabotage or spying was ever proved.

For three months after Pearl Harbor, measures taken to control aliens from enemy countries remained under the supervision of the Justice Department. Throughout that time the constitutional rights of naturalized citizens were recognized. The Western Defense Command, under Lt. General John L. DeWitt, had responsibility for West Coast security against possible attack, and by the end of February 1942 he felt that because of "military necessity" all people of Japanese ancestry should be removed from Military Area No. 1 (stretching from the Canadian to the Mexican border and from the coast to about 100 miles inland). On February 19, President Franklin D. Roosevelt signed Executive Order 9066, authorizing the War Department to exclude any or all persons from designated military areas. The control of enemy aliens was transferred to the military authorities. Congress, not fully understanding that citizens as well as aliens would be involved, passed a measure providing for the enforcement of the executive order. Later a ruling of the U.S. Supreme Court upheld the right of the military to imprison arbitrarily in time of urgent need, in effect deciding that urgent public need is of greater importance than constitutionality, although without inquiring if the beliefs of the military authorities were justified.

On February 23 a Japanese submarine surfaced off the California coast at Goleta, a short distance north of Santa Barbara, and shelled an oil field. A derrick and a pier were damaged but other shells fell harmlessly; before long the submarine sank under the surface and went away.

In Los Angeles the next night at 2:25 a.m. air-raid sirens began to blare into the darkness, continuing for two minutes on a steady pitch. Hastily awakened residents made sure that all their outdoor lights were extinguished and their windows covered so that no light showed outside. Drivers caught by the alert pulled over to the curb and parked with lights out. Searchlights cast their beams into the cloudless sky, seeking enemy planes. Antiaircraft batteries sent up orange bursts of shrapnel.

The cause of the air raid was a report to the Army's Western Defense Command that unidentified aircraft had been sighted over the coast of the Southland. A number of practiced observers — soldiers, officers, newsmen — were certain they saw planes moving overhead slowly as if for reconnaissance, and Army Chief of Staff George Marshall reported, "As many as fifteen planes may have been involved." Some observers thought they saw a hundred or more during the antiaircraft barrage.

Ten thousand air-raid wardens in the Los Angeles area made their rounds, checking that every home was dark. To make certain there would be no fifth-column activities, twenty Japanese were arrested upon reports that they were trying to signal with automobile lights or flares. Only in emergencies could vehicles move on the streets — yet without headlights. During the blackout eight babies were born. Finally, at 7:21 a.m. the undulating wail of the all-clear sounded. "The Great Air Raid" had been a farce — there were no planes — but it was symptomatic of the fear and expectation among residents of the West Coast.

Under Executive Order 9066, the Western Defense Command urged all Japanese to leave the coastal area and settle elsewhere voluntarily. (European enemy aliens were not included, only those whose ancestry was Japanese.) Several thousand tried to comply and some succeeded, but most inland communities made it plain they were not welcome. Armed posses on the Nevada border barred their entry, and elsewhere they were threatened or jailed as a public danger. By the end of March the Western Command declared that, to ensure orderly evacuation and resettlement, the problem would be handled under military control. Plans were made to create hundreds of work camps across the country, where families could live and the able-bodied find employment in the local communities; also, the Japanese would be employed on public works projects in relocation areas. At a meeting of governors and other state officials to discuss the plans, Milton S. Eisenhower represented the Federal Government. When he asked for cooperation, they all expressed such strong opposition that it was obvious the small relocation centers would be impractical. Eisenhower reported to President Roosevelt that because of "the exceedingly hostile attitude demonstrated toward any resettlement," it would not be until the end of the war, when people again felt tolerance and understanding, that there could be "a genuinely satisfactory relocation of the evacuees into American life."

The Western Defense Command then divided Military Area No. 1 (the coastal strip) into 99 "exclusion areas." In a sequence based on the relative military importance of the sectors, the Japanese living in each were to be sent to an assembly center, usually within five days of receiving the order. During those five days they had to sell their homes, shops and furnishings and prepare to leave with only a few belongings. People who had built up their own places of business through thirty years of work saw those years end in futility and loss. A poignant sign, "I Am An American," stood mute in a store window below a notice that the property had been "Sold." Family

Evacuation of the Japanese from Los Angeles in 1942. (*—Los Angeles* TIMES)

treasures were left behind with sympathetic non-Japanese friends or with opportunists who exploited those forced to depart. Then the deadline came. Early in the morning buses lined up along the streets and the emigration began.

The evacuation from the West Coast of people with Japanese ancestry affected 112,000 persons, two-thirds of them United States citizens.

First they were taken to an assembly center; the racetrack at Santa Anita was one of the largest. On the huge parking lot 400 buildings had been erected and streets laid out, with a high wire fence surrounding the area. By April 20, 1942, the center contained 12,000 people; there were 19,000 by June 1. Three months later the relocation process began, and within two months the camp was empty.

The Japanese were transshipped to ten relocation centers — tar-paper cities — in different states. In several of them the buildings had not been completely finished because the evacuation had taken place so quickly, and this caused serious hardships. For instance, in some of the porous buildings no stoves had yet been installed even when temperatures dropped below freezing. In many centers there was no running water within the barracks, nor toilet facilities.

While living there the Japanese formed self-governing community groups and organized athletics and other activities. The U.S. Govern-

The Japanese relocation center was at Santa Anita Race Track; on the 127 acres of the north parking lot, 720 buildings similar to army barracks were erected. Movable interior partitions made rooms of varying size, usually accommodating two persons to a room. Stables were reconstructed into slightly larger apartments. The front of the grandstand appears in the background. The saddling barn and jockey room (out of picture to right) constituted a large hospital, about 260 x 80 feet, where many babies were born, sometimes nine in one day. (—Los Angeles Co. Museum of Natural History)

ment contracted with many of the Nisei (people born in America of parents who had immigrated from Japan) to undertake work that needed to be done — making camouflage nets or helping on sugar beet farms, for example. Several hundred students whose college education had been interrupted were relocated at certain colleges and universities. Some Nisei undertook work with the Office of Strategic Services, where they were greatly needed as interpreters. In 1943, Assistant Secretary of War John J. McCloy recruited an all-Japanese combat team to fight in Europe. The 442nd Infantry Regiment, composed mainly of Nisei troops from Hawaii and California, more than proved their patriotism. The regiment suffered 300% casualties in Italy (Nisei reinforcements were constantly added to bring the regiment back to combat strength) and became the most decorated unit in the military history of the United States. Eventually 33,000 Nisei joined the armed forces.

For two and a half years the relocation centers continued in operation. Not until January 20, 1945, did the program of mass exclusion end and a return to freedom begin. About 8000 people, including both aliens and former American citizens, left this country to live in Japan.

After the war ended, it became clear that the treatment of the Japanese was one of the most serious injustices in U.S. history. Over 100,000 persons were deprived of their legal rights, subjected to heavy financial loss and imprisoned without trial. The responsibility was a national one. When the military, concerned with protecting the West Coast against attack, judged that all Japanese were potential saboteurs and spies, that judgment was accepted by a large majority of people throughout the country, by the President, Congress and the Supreme Court. After the Battle of Midway on June 6, 1942, when the United States sank four Japanese aircraft carriers, American military leaders realized that from then on the Japanese Navy could not assemble enough strength for an invasion of North America. But Executive Order 9066 remained in force after that battle, and the thousands of men, women and children were interned in evacuation centers for the duration. Their civil rights were invaded long after there was a "military necessity."

When the relocation centers were closed, the evacuees returned to the West Coast at a time of severe housing shortage, especially in Los Angeles. But problems were eased by local cooperation and by lectures and other measures to ensure tolerance. Many of those returning resumed their former businesses; others took up positions they had never held before. Earlier their work had been primarily agricultural, but after the war increasing numbers entered the legal and medical professions, became architects, scientists, teachers.

Gradually new legislation righted past wrongs. The Oriental Exclusion Act of 1924, which had prohibited most Chinese and Japanese from entering the United States, was repealed in 1952. However, repayment to the Japanese of money and property lost at the beginning of the war was not as simple a matter. For instance, under the Evacuation Claims Act of 1948, Japanese were to be repaid for their lost property, but most families had no records of the cost of furniture they had owned, and former businessmen could show no inventory of merchandise lost. In the end, the United States paid back about ten percent of the losses. In 1959, 17 years after the Nisei were deprived of their rights of citizenship, those rights were restored.

Immediately after Pearl Harbor the American branches of the Japanese-controlled Yokohama Specie Bank, Ltd., were closed under the Trading With the Enemy Act, to prevent any deposits from reaching the Japanese Government. The United States never denied that the money belonged to the depositors, and it was held in a special account for them, but due to legal complications thirty years of litigation were required before the money was released. Twice the case was sent to the Supreme Court, which decided that the statute of limitations would not apply to repayments nor would any Japanese be penalized for not understanding the complicated recovery procedures. Finally in 1972 the House of Representatives unanimously passed a bill (later ratified by the Senate) which returned $4,500,000 to 2000 first-generation Japanese immigrants or their heirs.

The fate of the Japanese community, if there had been no relocation to camps, remains an open question. Would those people still have found themselves helpless victims of wartime? In the early days of World War II there were cases on the West Coast of innocent Japanese being shot solely because of their origin. The feeling against Japan increased with the publication of "The Death March of Bataan," which appeared in daily newspapers a chapter at a time and disclosed to horrified readers the brutal treatment of American prisoners in the Philippine Islands after the fall of Corregidor. Los Angeles, a center for defense industries, was also a staging center for servicemen in training or en route to the Pacific — men psychologically ready for battle. The mere wearing of a certain style of clothing had been enough to bring injury to Chicanos. Would some incident or rumor of an incident have set off a far greater tragedy for the people whose appearance was also that of the enemy? Fortunately, as Milton Eisenhower had foretold, with peacetime their situation completely changed.

Ondo dancers perform in the annual Nisei parade in Little Tokyo. The Los Angeles City Hall can be seen in the background, only two blocks from the large Japanese community. (*—Toyo Miyatake Studio*)

During the middle of August each year a Nisei Week Festival takes place in the area around First Street, east of the Los Angeles City Hall. Attention focuses on a life style that dates from long before the problems of World War II, and long before Japan opened her doors to foreigners. On the last evening of the festival the ondo dancers pass through the streets. In groups, dancers wearing ancient-style decorated headdresses, kimonos and zoris (sandals) slowly move through traditional steps in a routine created centuries ago. To spectators in the center of the busy western city, time is suspended for the procession of unhurried, graceful dancers representing the opposite shore of the Pacific Ocean.

12. *Minorities — Chinese Americans*

The Chinese community in Los Angeles was founded long before that of the Japanese, yet it numbers less than one-third the population. It is in San Francisco that the Chinese have their largest center.

The census of 1850 shows that there were only two Chinese in Los Angeles, although thousands were arriving in the north with the Gold Rush. A decade later there were only 14 Chinese, 2 of them women. Few women came with the early emigrants because of the accepted oriental rule that women should stay with their ancestral hearth.

In the 1860s, with the Six Companies as hiring agent, entire ship-loads of people crossed the Pacific to work on the Central Pacific Rail-road. After it was finished in 1869, some of the men came to Los Angeles in search of other work. At the same time a rabble rouser in San Francisco daily made inflammatory speeches appealing to fear and prejudice, telling his listeners that the Chinese were depriving them of work by accepting low wages. Northern newspapers head-lined his harangues, and his attitude spread to other parts of the country like a contagion. It was after this that the Chinese Massacre took place in Los Angeles.

Prejudice became involved with politics, and because anti-Chinese legislation was popular politically, both the Democrats and Republi-cans in Congress supported passage of the Chinese Exclusion Act of 1882. Immigration of Chinese laborers was suspended for ten years (later extended for several more decades), and the interpretation of "laborers" proved to include such men as physicians and priests. Other restrictions were added and then confirmed by the U.S. Supreme Court as constitutional. (This gave rise to the phrase "He doesn't have a Chinaman's chance.") Chinese were forbidden to own land along the West Coast.

Among the Chinese already in the United States there were so few women that if a man were to marry and have children it was generally necessary to go all the way to China. Then, in 1924, the Oriental Exclusion Act closed the door on most Chinese and Japa-nese: a naturalized citizen could no longer bring his wife and chil-dren into this country but was separated from them by an ocean. Most of the injustices ended when in 1952 this act was repealed. Later, under the Immigration and Nationality Act of 1965, all dif-ferentiation against the Chinese was discontinued.

The first Chinatown in Los Angeles included much of the old Plaza and the area surrounding it, especially along Alameda Street. By 1890 the Coronel adobe was torn down — the crumbling building where Chinese had listened, aghast, to the sounds of a lynch mob outside. Other buildings, too, were removed; Los Angeles Street was length-ened to extend to the Plaza, and Philippe Garnier built a large brick structure, the Garnier Block, for offices and shops. On the second floor the Chinese Free Masons made their headquarters, and all the tenants downstairs were Chinese. A tong had its headquarters in what once was the home of Don Vicente Lugo. A Chinese shop rented part of Pico House.

A Chinese procession moves through Chinatown toward the Plaza in the early 1900s. (—*Los Angeles Co. Museum of Natural History*)

Los Angeles' large Chinese community is seven blocks north of City Hall. (—*Chamber of Commerce, Chinatown*)

It was especially during the Chinese New Year that the Plaza, center of the early Spanish and Mexican Pueblo de Los Angeles, exemplified the change which time can bring. Apablasa, where the Union Station stands now, was the main street of Chinatown. At the sound of a gong the festival began, and men wearing the ancient, ceremonial black silk robes moved toward the Plaza behind the huge, tossing head of a dragon. Manchu banners bobbed over men in skull-caps, coolie hats, or with their queues wound tightly around their heads. In that same area Spanish and Mexican religious parades once moved slowly past adobe homes.

When Dr. Sun Yat-sen was preparing a revolt against the Manchu dynasty at the beginning of the 20th century, a young American of Los Angeles, Homer Lea, was a leading figure in the revolutionary group and became a genius of military strategy.* Sympathy with the rebellion spread through Chinatown and led to a dramatic scene when many of the young Chinese cut off their queues, which were a symbol of servitude to the dynasty. They formed an infantry regiment and drilled at night in Chinatown; quite a few of the men later became officers in the forces of the Republic of China.

To make room for the Union Station in the twenties, Chinatown buildings on Alameda and eastward were removed, and although old shops and residences clustering north of the Plaza remained, a large New Chinatown was built a few blocks away on Hill Street and on North Broadway.

Until a few decades ago the Chinese found little opportunity beyond what people considered their appropriate fields. They did truck farming, laundry work or followed occupations in Chinatown. Since World War II there has been an astonishing change. For instance, in percentage of minority peoples receiving advanced degrees in college, the Chinese Americans and Japanese Americans are the leaders. Their talents find recognition in every field.

In the 1960s a tide of refugees from Communist China made its way to Los Angeles, and most of the newcomers looked for lodging in or near Chinatown because of the familiar language and culture. In 1970, of the 27,000 Chinese residents in Los Angeles, about 6000 could speak no English. Although the young people, schooled in English, tend to be more assimilated into current urban ways, there are certain strong characteristics which have remained unchanged:

---

*A brilliant analysis in his *Valor of Ignorance* predicted a U.S.-Japanese war in which Hawaii would be a central focus and the Philippines would be conquered.

the community itself tries to help those in need; family ties are close. The minority which was once the victim of a massacre is now seen as a bastion of "old-fashioned" virtues increasingly lost to the modern world.

13. Minorities — Blacks

Los Angeles was already integrated at its founding in 1781. Of the 44 men, women and children who came from Sonora to establish El Pueblo de la Reyna de Los Angeles, over half had Negro blood.*

In Mexico, slaves had been brought from Africa on Portuguese and Spanish ships during the 16th and 17th centuries. Beginning as early as 1518, the importation of Blacks into the Americas was considered a significant part of colonization. Most of them worked on agricultural lands along the Atlantic coast, and it is probable that before 1575 the relatively few white settlers there were outnumbered by Blacks. Slavery in the Spanish empire was not like that which developed in the United States. The slaves could buy their own freedom and often were set free voluntarily by their owners. Anyone mistreated could appeal to the government, and if the complaint were proved true, he could be freed. Nor was there any social stigma in having once been a slave. Few Spanish women came to the New World, so Spaniards frequently married Indian or Negro women. As settlements pushed farther inland and to the Pacific coast, colonists, miners, cattlemen, missionaries and Indian and Negro slaves moved toward the outposts. In the development of mines throughout Mexico, slavery formed an important part. Near the Gulf of California the mining town of Los Alamos was the starting point for the colonists of Los Angeles; most of them were recruited in Rosario (south of Mazatlan), where approximately two-thirds of the inhabitants were mulattoes, a majority free.

Los Angeles' first American Negro, Tom Fisher, arrived in the settlement in 1818, captured from an invading privateer, but most of the American pioneers of the Black community arrived after 1850, and even then they came in small numbers.

In 1829 Vicente Guerrero, President of Mexico, announced, "I thus decree: Slavery is forever abolished in the Republic." (He was

---

*Specifically: Antonio Mesa (a Negro), his wife (a mulatto) and their six children; José Moreno and his wife (both mulattoes) and their five children; Manuel Cameron and his wife (both mulattoes); the mulatto wife of José Antonio Navarro (a mestizo) and their three children; the mulatto wife of Basil Rosas (an Indian) and their six children.

speaking of Negroes. A great many Indians continued in virtual en-slavement, although it was not recognized as such and was instead called peonage.) Eight years later a law was passed re-emphasizing Guerrero's decree.

California, preparing itself to become a state, took a bold stand in 1849. The East was riven with controversy over slavery, and the delegates who met to write the California constitution chose that issue as pre-eminent. Article 1, section 1 of the document declared: "Neither slavery nor involuntary servitude . . . shall ever be tolerated in this state." Under that law any slave brought into the state was auto-matically emancipated. However, if the former slave later voluntarily returned to his master's home in a slave state, the laws there would apply to him once more and he would be a slave again. As protection, the law added that anyone persuading a Negro by false promises or misrepresentations to leave the security of his freedom in California would be guilty of kidnapping. This law was the basis for an historic legal case in Los Angeles.

A leading player in that drama was Robert Smith, owner of a plantation in Mississippi. The southerner had become a Mormon con-vert, then sold his home and, with his wife and his household slaves, joined a wagon train bound for Utah. Two years later, in 1851, they continued to California with a wagon train from Salt Lake City to found San Bernardino. There Smith built a home and maintained a plantation style of living similar to the one he had known in Missis-sippi. In other words, his servants were his possessions to use as he might choose.

In the new settlement the colonists grew increasingly antagonistic toward Smith, while at the same time he felt ever more at odds with the church and colony. Late in 1855 he once again filled his wagons with family belongings and gathered his household, which consisted of two Black women, Biddy and Hannah, and their children. (Smith's wife, who had been an invalid, was no longer living.) This time he planned to go east to Texas. However, Smith first directed his small caravan of wagons westward so that supplies could be bought in Los Angeles. On arriving there, the travelers continued through town to camp in a canyon near what today is Santa Monica. The journey from San Bernardino had taken three days.

In the meantime a Mrs. Rowan back in the colony had been grow-ing more and more concerned about the Blacks because their desti-nation, Texas, was a slave state. She sent word to Frank Dewitt, sheriff of Los Angeles County, that apparently they were being re-turned to slavery and clearly they needed protection.

Within a short time the sheriff was on his way to Smith with a writ of habeas corpus, requiring him to appear in the court of the Southern District of California as defendant in an inquiry into the lawfulness of his detaining others in custody. At that time the city was small, with fewer than 4000 residents, and the unusual caravan with a dozen Blacks attracted so much attention that the sheriff had no difficulty in finding the travelers. He brought the Blacks into town in his own safekeeping, all except Hannah, who had a newborn baby, and a son who remained to take care of them both; another son was still in San Bernardino. Dewitt was aided by Robert Owens, also a Black, owner of a livery stable.

The case was to be heard before District Judge Benjamin Hayes, who held court not only in Los Angeles, but also in San Diego, Santa Barbara and San Luis Obispo. Fortunately he was in Los Angeles at the time, and the case could be handled immediately. News of what was happening spread through town, and for the next few days the judge's courtroom was the focus of attention for the entire community.

On the first day Robert Smith appeared with his attorney. Smith testified that he had brought his former slaves from Mississippi and had come to California with the intention of living there. Four years later he had decided to move to Texas, taking all the Blacks in his household with him. He insisted that the woman named Hannah and her children wanted to stay with him and had not known about the petition against him or agreed to it. He made no mention of Biddy's wishes.

One after another the Blacks gave their testimony. About their own rights — either in California or in Texas — they knew only what Smith had told them, since none could read or write. They agreed that Smith had treated them all kindly.

The next day began with startling news. Hartwell Cottrell, a partner of Smith's, had tried to induce two of the Blacks to leave the sheriff's custody. On top of that, their attorney stood up to announce that it was the wish of his clients, Biddy and Hannah, to drop the case. All in the courtroom, including those he represented, were taken by surprise. The ruse did not work. Judge Hayes issued a subpoena to the attorney, who was then ushered to the witness stand. Under questioning he admitted that he had tried to abandon the suit because of threats, by persons unnamed, and in addition he had been paid $100 for doing so. None of the Blacks had been informed of the plan, however, nor had their wishes been asked. Smith himself denied having any knowledge of the plot whatever. The court decided that no attorney could desert his clients at his own pleasure without good reason and fair notice to them, and thereupon the trial was resumed.

The judge needed to find out what Biddy and Hannah really wanted to do; so he arranged for private questioning. Except for the women, only Judge Hayes, Abel Stearns and James B. Winston, a physician, were present. Biddy frankly declared she had always been afraid of the trip to Texas but was accustomed to doing what she was told. Besides, Smith had said she would be as free in Texas as in California. Hannah said that she, too, had been told she and her children would be free in Texas. Her answers were given with great hesitancy, as though she were trying to foresee the consequences of what she might say.

The case did not take long. Before a crowded courtroom Judge Hayes declared Robert Smith guilty of misrepresentation, because the law in Texas forbade importation of free Negroes. Therefore the Blacks in Smith's household were traveling either as his slaves or else to be sold into slavery. All of them were taken from him. The court was especially concerned about protecting the children from possibly being persuaded to leave California for a slave state. Consequently, the sheriff of San Bernardino County was appointed guardian of Hannah's son who had remained there. The new sheriff of Los Angeles County was David W. Alexander, an important ranchero who had been president of the first Los Angeles City Council in 1850. He was made guardian of all the other children except the two oldest (the 17-year-old daughters of both Biddy and Hannah), those under 5 years old (left with their mother Hannah as guardian) and an older son who was of especial help to Hannah and so was left in her care. Court costs were paid by Robert Smith.

The court's decision concerning the 14 Blacks was hailed with cheers throughout Los Angeles. In its issue of February 2, 1856, the Los Angeles *Star* printed the full text of Judge Benjamin Hayes' opinion under the heading "Suit For Freedom"; it filled most of the editorial page.

Hannah and her family returned to San Bernardino, and there she married a Black named Toby Ember. In later years she told how terrified she had been when the wagon train reached California, where there were no slaves. Not knowing how she could make a living for herself and her family, Hannah had begged Smith to take them back to a slave state. Undoubtedly he counted on that attitude four years later when he decided to go to Texas.

Biddy, while traveling with the wagon train to California, was a shepherdess. On foot she guided a flock of sheep behind the caravan of 140 wagons on their slow journey across plains, mountain passes

Biddy Mason.
(*—Los Angeles Co.
Museum of
Natural History*)

and arid desert land. Undisturbed by the dust the wagons raised, she took care of the animals and also of the children, who played around her. After the trial she remained in Los Angeles.

Robert Owens, who had aided the families when they moved into town from Santa Monica, invited Biddy Mason and her daughters to stay in his home with his wife and children. Two years later his son Charles married Biddy's eldest daughter, Ellen. Among the people who had followed the trial closely was Dr. John Strother Griffin, who was engaged to Judge Hayes' sister Louisa. Griffin offered Biddy work as a midwife and nurse for his patients at the wages of $2.50 per day, which seems low now but was a splendid wage then. In fact, she was able to save and invest her money. Dr. Griffin was a shrewd investor in real estate (he owned part of Rancho San Pascual and sold his portion to the founders of Pasadena); it was probably on his advice that Biddy bought two downtown lots for $250. They were between Third and Fourth Streets, in the middle of the block, and stretched in a compact piece of land from Broadway to Fort Street, later named Hill Street. Her children, too, bought property in downtown Los Angeles, and it increased many times in value. In the early 1880s, during a long and heavy rain, the Los Angeles River overran its banks, leaving many families homeless. In a remarkable gesture to her community, Biddy placed a standing order with a grocery store on Spring Street to give free food to anyone, black or white, who needed it.

In her home at 331 Spring Street the First African Methodist Church, the first Negro congregation in Los Angeles, was organized in 1872. The building at Eighth Street and Towne Avenue, erected for that group thirty years later, was the first Black church in Los Angeles of any denomination. In May 1971 the building was declared an historic monument by the Los Angeles Cultural Heritage Board and named the Biddy Mason Cultural Center in honor of the former slave.

Her descendants still live in Los Angeles today. Biddy's copy of the court verdict, written in longhand and signed by Hayes, has been saved by the generations down to the present. It is a reminder of the stirring moment when the California court, five years before the outbreak of the Civil War and seven years before Abraham Lincoln's Emancipation Proclamation, used its authority to declare 14 Blacks "free forever."

The Black population in Los Angeles increased slowly until World War II, when the development of defense industries caused a sudden influx. By 1965 the number of Black residents totaled 650,000, two-thirds of whom lived in Watts and the nearby area. Since most came from the South and had an agricultural background, urban Los Angeles found that problems arose faster than they could be solved. This was an acute disappointment to the newcomers, who somehow expected to find that their lack of employable skills would be unimportant in California, Land of Promise.

August of 1965 began with a heat wave, and Los Angeles sweltered as temperatures remained in the nineties. Near Watts, at seven o'clock on the evening of the 11th, a Black was stopped for reckless driving and was given a sobriety test, which he failed. This simple event sparked a riot during which 34 persons lost their lives, over 1000 were wounded, almost 4000 were arrested and property damage amounted to $40,000,000.

On that evening almost everyone was outdoors seeking relief from the heat. Tempers were flammable. When an altercation began between police and the family of the arrested man, 300 spectators gathered within moments. The crowd grew hostile, and the officers radioed for reinforcements. When the police finally left, they were surrounded by about 1000 persons.

Instead of dispersing, the mob swarmed into the main streets, stoning autos, dragging motorists from their cars and beating them.

As leaders on both sides tried to restore order, many courageous Blacks as well as white men risked their own lives to save the lives of others.

The next day the rioting increased. In the business section of Watts a mob of 3000 gathered and looting became frenzied. Buildings were set on fire. Excited coverage in the news media seemed to feed the intensity of violence. All that night and the next day the madness continued, but finally the California National Guard arrived on the scene at ten o'clock the third evening. They found they had stepped into an insane asylum. Ambulance drivers and firemen were attacked as they answered emergency calls. At night, with police protection, 100 engine companies were fighting fires in the area. Police and National Guardsmen moved en masse along streets to clear them of rioters.

The looting, burning and shooting continued into the next day, but gradually a total of 14,000 guardsmen moved into the district. A curfew was declared. By the sixth day the riot was over, having covered 46 square miles.

As the smoke and flames had risen above Watts and spread along streets ever nearer to downtown, Los Angeles watched in disbelief. Only the year before, the Urban League had rated Los Angeles best among 68 cities examined for basic racial conditions in such categories as housing, employment and income. There was no ghetto like those in many eastern cities. Most of the Blacks lived in cottages with lawns and backyards; one-third of the residents owned their own homes. There were parks, public swimming pools and playgrounds, and wide, clean streets. No buses were segregated. Yet 10,000 Negroes had joined the rioting. Obviously there were serious problems which needed to be solved.

California's Governor Edmund G. Brown organized an investigation by the McCone Commission, under Judge John A. McCone, and the report was presented at the end of the year. It found that instead of a race riot, there had been in effect an explosion. The fundamental cause was a spiral of failure which included home life, the schools (a high school dropout rate of two-thirds in Watts and the surrounding neighborhoods), extensive unemployment, ineffective police-community relations and resentment at housing discrimination.

A City Human Relations Commission was appointed to develop constructive programs. Community projects were begun so that people who lived in the area would take an interest in their own neighborhood. Schools began Head Start programs and more remedial classes; an art center was created where talent could be developed. Plans were studied for job training among the unemployed. The police were given more extensive education in race relations. Black ownership of property was encouraged, to replace absentee ownership. Black-owned factories were established, and the Watts Labor Community Action Committee was formed.

Several years after the riot, its scars could still be seen. On main streets many of the shops which had been looted were still boarded up, unable to find tenants. Much of the land where buildings had been burned still stood as vacant lots.

Los Angeles, whose population by 1970 was 18% Black, has discovered that the problems of its racial minorities are similar to those in cities across the country, where lives have been caught up in the cruel complexities of the 20th century. However, new opportunities have been opening, and the life of Tom Bradley is an outstanding example. Son of a Texas sharecropper, he served on the Los Angeles police force for 21 years and on the City Council for 10. On July 1, 1973, he was inaugurated as mayor of Los Angeles, the first Black in history to reach the city's highest position.

14. *Minorities — Indians*

The Bureau of Indian Affairs is trustee for the Indians. When it was established in 1834, treaties were still being made with Indian tribes, and so the bureau came under the War Department. Fifteen years later it was transferred to the Department of the Interior.

In 1852, soon after California became a state, Edward F. Beale was appointed superintendent of Indian affairs for California and Nevada. He asked Benjamin D. Wilson, a longtime inhabitant of Los Angeles who knew the Indians well, to suggest a program under which a reservation might be of most value to them. Then a reservation was created, the first in California, on land between Tejón Pass and the San Joaquin Valley in an area at that time included within the boundaries of Los Angeles County. It was named the Sebastian Reservation, for William King Sebastian, chairman of the Senate Committee on Indian Affairs.

Beale formed seven rancherías (Indian villages), and each family was allowed land for its own personal cultivation. As the Indians plowed their fields, dug irrigation ditches and sowed wheat and barley, Beale and his men worked with them, demonstrating agricultural methods and teaching blacksmithing and other skills. The reservation was so successful that in two years about 2500 Indians were living within its boundaries. In some cases entire Indian villages had migrated there.

Then politics entered the picture. Accusations were made against Beale (which he later proved false), and another man was put in charge of the reservation, a man without Beale's dedication to the work. General neglect as well as misuse of funds earned from sale of the crops nullified any benefit for the Indians. Ten years after the reservation was started, it was abandoned by the government as no longer important.

On most of the reservations across the continent, life has been marked by poverty, disease and neglect. After World War II the Indians came home from military service in other parts of the world or from jobs held during the wartime labor shortage, where they had received fixed, regular salaries. Not all of them were willing to return to poverty and a primitive life; they wanted a share of the nation's economic opportunities. Also, many had become convinced of the importance of education as affecting a man's future. Until then the average extent of schooling on a reservation was the fifth grade, but attendance began to increase in grammar and high schools. Many young people decided to go to college.

Few reservations have opportunities for gainful employment; so in 1956 the Bureau of Indian Affairs began a Vocational Training Service, to which any Indian between 18 and 35 years of age might apply. Included in the offer was the provision that the government would assume the cost of one-way transportation to a city, would pay for living expenses and the training itself, and would help with job placement.

For Indians, the move to an urban life is not easy. Most of them have never been in a large city before. They have known only the simplicity of country living, of a quiet land, of open space and a community where each person knows his neighbors. Leaving behind the solitude of the reservation, they reach the "concrete prairie," a new world full of buildings, automobiles and strangers. To most of the newcomers the transition is frightening.

During the first few years after the Vocational Training Service — generally called the Relocation Policy — was established, most of the Indians returned to their reservations. If illness or a serious problem arose, or simply if the loneliness became too much to endure, it was natural to go where brothers, sisters and other relatives were, to go home. As the number of Indians in the cities increased, assimilation was easier. It meant that some relatives were nearby as well as on a faraway reservation. Also, their children, born in the city, felt less alien and could adapt more easily to the problems of urban life. Even so, few were able to rise above the level of poverty.

By January 1972, after more than 100,000 Indians had been moved from their reservations to cities, an estimated forty percent relocated had returned home. Criticism of the Relocation Policy was growing. So emphasis was shifted to the creation of industry on or near the reservations, where the Indians might find training and employment without having to move to a strange environment.

In Los Angeles, other minority groups center around closely knit communities in definite parts of town, but the Indians are scattered through different areas. To provide a place where they can meet and find advice and understanding, there is an Indian Center; in addition the Indians hold a powwow each week somewhere in Los Angeles so that they can dance in their own way and enjoy being with their own people.

The census of 1970 showed approximately 25,000 Indian residents in Los Angeles County. Statistics concerning Indians have never been exact, because until 1970 the official census counted only those on reservations. In that year it was allowable for the first time to ask a person living away from a reservation if he was of Indian ancestry: to be counted, he would need to be at least one-fourth Indian.

Today the groups of Indians which lived in Los Angeles are extinct as a cultural and linguistic entity. But Indians from tribes across the country — Sioux, Navajo, Apache, Hopi, Creek, Pawnee, Ute, Pueblo, Chickasaw, Cheyenne and others — form the largest concentration of Indians in any urban area of the United States.

Two centuries have gone by since the Spaniards first saw the village among the trees by the river. The huts were probably on the bluff out of reach of flooding waters, but long ago all trace of village and bluff disappeared. In today's city the site is marked by the trees and paths of the Los Angeles Mall, a quiet oasis in the shadow of City Hall.

Los Angeles in the 20th century took an integral place in the modern world, no longer separated from it by deserts and mountains, now so effortlessly crossed. Seemingly a permanent way of life had been established; then once again the focus changed and a new era began to evolve. Turning our eyes from the past, where we have watched history being made, we become more sharply aware that we ourselves are making the history of today.

IX

TODAY

1. *Buildings Rise Skyward*

Today the pattern of life in Los Angeles changes within a month, a week.

The low-profile central city, whose tallest building until the 1960s was the 28-story City Hall, is filled with skyscrapers, rising dramatically across the landscape like giant exclamation points. On Bunker Hill the forlorn remnants of Victorian grandeur have ceased to exist. The hill itself has been reshaped, and new roads, bridges, tall buildings have appeared on the totally remodeled scene.

To avoid chaos, the City Planning Department was asked in 1964 to formulate a Master Plan (a name later changed to General Plan) to guide and control growth in Los Angeles. This would prevent haphazard building of skyscrapers downtown and also find ways of keeping intact the individuality of communities within the huge urban area. Surveying the problems, *Los Angeles Magazine* in an imaginary interview quoted a director of the plan as saying, "Our job was relatively simple. We took a cold, hard look at Los Angeles, asked ourselves what was wrong, and the answer was obvious: *everything.*"

Before World War II the downtown area grew increasingly shabby and ugly, and business began to move into outlying communities to such a degree that Los Angeles was spoken of as "suburbs in search of a city." Then a number of important changes happened simultaneously. A network of freeways was completed which linked the downtown area with communities in all directions. The law which limited the height of buildings to 13 stories had been changed in 1959, because new techniques of engineering promised that even tall buildings could be earthquake-proof. Gradually builders gained confidence, although for a while the public ignored the new ruling through reluctance to follow a course that seemed dangerous.

In 1964 the Community Redevelopment Agency finally succeeded in launching its first project, Bunker Hill. After enduring 16 years of opposition the agency, helped by Federal funds, began a carefully designed renewal of 136 acres of land in the heart of the city. The tall, new buildings held not only business offices but also residential apartments. Nearby stood the Music Center. The new development touched off an explosion, a sudden revitalizing of the entire downtown area.

Yet Los Angeles needed far more than renewal. In common with other cities it had become involved in the endless complications of the urban crisis, with its problems of race relations, housing, crime, drugs, unemployment, education, rapid transit and a multitude of etceteras. In one particular field, ecology, developments illustrated more strikingly than in any other the unfolding of a new period in history. Until late in the sixties "ecology" was a word seldom used, its meaning unknown to most people, but within a short time the term became significant throughout the United States — and no place more so than in Southern California.

2. Pollution

The people of Los Angeles felt no danger from water pollution until a dramatic disaster occurred in nearby Santa Barbara. Along the coast of the Southland, oil lies just beneath the ocean floor, and title to the offshore land has been an important political issue. In 1953 Congress declared that state ownership of submerged land extends only to the three-mile limit, with Federal ownership beyond that point.

Geologists have long known that in the Santa Barbara Channel the ocean floor is extremely unstable. Numerous earthquake faults create a constant danger, and oil from reservoirs close to the surface frequently seeps through the porous ground. The California State Legislature established a sanctuary along 16 miles of the Santa Barbara coast within the three-mile limit to prohibit drilling for oil. Outside of that area, where drilling was allowed, strict state laws regulated the offshore construction of oil wells and pipelines.

But the Federal Government felt no such concern. In 1968 the United States, through the Department of the Interior, gave 71 leases to the oil industry for land on the Outer Continental Shelf in the Santa Barbara Channel. Oil was to be drilled from derricks on huge platforms, each one comparable in height to a twenty-story building and capable of supporting at least sixty wells. Eventually such platforms would cover the channel, while Federal regulations concerning the work were lenient. Platform A, five and one-half miles out on land leased by four oil companies, was one of the first erected. As its fifth well was completed, a malfunction developed in the pipeline. Beneath the platform only a thin (thirty foot) layer of easily fractured siltstone and claystone protected the channel from underground oil deposits – and gases under high pressure accompanied the subsurface oil. When the malfunction caused the counterpressure in the pipeline to decrease suddenly, mud shot upward through the well and then a heavy cloud of gas roared out. Workmen tried to seal off the hole, but already a chain reaction of explosions had been set in motion far below, rupturing the protective layer under the channel floor. During 11 frantic days, while every kind of effort was made to stop the flow of oil, over 200,000 gallons poured out, to be carried by the waves into harbors and onto beaches.

The harbor of Santa Barbara presented a strange sight. On the sand, bales of straw were stacked high and then were taken to a lighter offshore from which, through a huge blower, the straw was spread across the water. Later, the oil-soaked straw was raked into buckets by men in rowboats.

The disaster gave impetus to the study of ecology along the coast, and in 1969 California enacted the strongest water quality control laws of any state. As a further result, in 1970 the National Environmental Policy Act went into effect, ordering that before any project was undertaken which might affect the environment, a Federal agency must first study the probable results and report to both the Council on Environmental Quality and the public.

At first it seemed a simple solution. But in 1973, after Israel fought Egypt and Syria in a short, bitter war, Arabian countries cut off oil supplies to this country in retaliation for its support of Israel. Pressures grew to obtain fuel from any source available in North America and to disregard environmental quality. The geologic dangers in the Santa Barbara Channel were well understood, but Federal politicians suddenly found the offshore drillings no longer obnoxious. With explanations that engineering improvements had changed the situation, plans were made to resume exploration in the unstable channel bed. California followed suit in the channel area under its own control.

In the mid-1960s Los Angeles' worst pollution problem was the air, and the automobile was the chief offender in creating smog. For vehicles to be effectively regulated, Federal and state legislation was necessary, as well as local laws. The U.S. Senate's Public Works Committee prepared a law requiring emission controls, but since it was a Federal regulation, applying to all states equally, it would prevent California from enforcing her own stronger restrictions. Thus a committee member, Senator George Murphy of California, formulated an amendment whereby California could be granted a waiver, and automobiles sold to that market would have to satisfy higher standards. The Air Quality Act and the Murphy Amendment passed the Senate unanimously, 88 to 0. After that it still had to pass the House, and there a huge lobby waited, ready to oppose the amendment. Before the law could be debated it had to go to a House Committee — where the amendment was deleted. Next the law was taken to the floor of the House. The California delegation united in support of the Murphy Amendment, and an avalanche of letters reached representatives, urging them to include it. Large photos of Los Angeles on smoggy days were exhibited in the Capitol, and a glimpse of the city densely shrouded in murk was enough to convince anyone that in California the problem was desperate. As a result, when the law was passed in October 1967, it was a blanket ruling for all states, but California was able to apply for a waiver to enforce higher standards for emissions.

Even so, improvement of the urgent problem was constantly delayed. Smog, which began by polluting the air of the Los Angeles Basin, has over the years spread inland, killing trees and plants as it went and affecting the quality of life in helpless communities. An obvious remedy was the installation of a rapid-transit system whereby autos would be parked in outlying areas and passengers would then travel by public transportation. But plans and financing were controversial, and time continued to go by with no definite results.

When 1973 ended, and low-sulphur, nonpolluting oil was scarce, industry began seeking the right to use a poorer grade of fuel. Also, California postponed a ruling which would have required installation of anti-smog devices in older automobiles beginning in January 1974. Yet inadvertently anti-smog efforts received a boost from oil scarcity: rapid transit suddenly took high priority.

During the sixties the shrill whine of jets signaled another problem — noise pollution. Propeller planes, relatively quiet, were supplanted by faster craft which gave a high-decibel screech during takeoff and approach. Because of the jets, runways at the Los Angeles International Airport were made longer. Because of increased air traffic, land which formerly was a buffer zone against noise was used for more runways. The sound of huge planes, flying in ever-increasing numbers, enveloped nearby communities — Inglewood, Westchester and Playa del Rey — in an intolerable din.

Residents protested to the airport, the Planning Department, the City Council. Indignantly they pointed out that windows of homes and schools had to remain closed, that speakers in schools and churches lost twenty minutes out of every hour while the audience

(—Nelly Davison)

In removing homes at Playa del Rey, along the northern boundary of Los Angeles International Airport, in 1968, various problems were encountered. Wooden houses were moved without difficulty, while those of brick or stone were extremely expensive to relocate. Those that had been built on a concrete slab were impossible to move; bulldozing was the only answer.

(—Margaret Townsend)

(—Margaret Townsend)

was unable to hear, that because of the noise life was insufferable. Federal court rulings make the Federal Aviation Administration the final authority over aircraft operations, but appeals to that body were in vain. The planes continued their near-continuous takeoffs, sometimes only two minutes apart. In search of a solution, the City of Los Angeles purchased almost 1800 homes to create an uninhabited space where the noise was most serious. (Later a similar pattern was followed regarding other homes in the airport's vicinity.)

Early in 1972 a visitor driving by the ocean on Vista del Mar found himself passing a strange scene. Lovely palm-lined streets of Playa del Rey were closed off by high chain-link fences. Along those streets vacant lots marked sites where homes sold to the city had been bulldozed into rubble and then cleared. In front of beautiful residences with view windows and carefully tended gardens, large posters read "For Sale — To Be Moved." Other houses, odd silhouettes, perched on logs while in transit. A few months later the scene was transformed. With few exceptions, gone were the homes, lawns, swimming pools, trees, gardens, lampposts and even the streets. Their traces were buried deep under sand hills on which wild grasses grew — a desolate no-man's land, a community destroyed by noise.

3. *Geologic Patterns*

Los Angeles lies in a geologically active part of the world. Through millions of years the past has been a continuity of change, as seas have advanced over the land, retreated, advanced and retreated again, and as mountains have risen, eroded and risen once more. Southern California's mountains are still rising.

Fifteen million years ago the area which is now Los Angeles lay deep underwater — possibly at a depth of 5000 feet — far from a distant shore. Then slowly, very slowly, the land rose and the water receded. That was the last far-reaching invasion of the sea, but part of the Los Angeles Basin was to be underwater a final time. About 250,000 years ago, during the Ice Ages (geologically a recent time) a shallow bay with beaches of shining white quartz, whiter than today's beaches, spread in a wide arc from approximately Santa Monica to the place where now the Santa Ana River reaches the ocean north of Newport Bay. Small islands rose above the waters — Signal Hill, Dominguez Hill, the Baldwin Hills, the Coyote Hills — and farther offshore stood a larger island, now Palos Verdes Hills. The ocean was slow to recede: excavations alongside Wilshire Boulevard near Fair-

In this photograph of the Palos Verdes Peninsula, taken in 1953 before houses covered the hillsides, 13 marine terraces can be clearly discerned. Each was once a beach, formed as the land rose ever higher above the ocean level during succeeding ages.
(*—R. C. Frampton and J. S. Shelton photograph*)

fax Avenue have uncovered proof that as recently as 100,000 years ago a large part of the Los Angeles Basin still lay underwater.

Evidence left by successive ages can be clearly seen today. As the Palos Verdes Hills periodically rose higher above the water, beaches remained in the form of 13 distinct terraces on the hillsides. In 1971, in a field between Gaffey Street and the Harbor Freeway, the skeleton of a whale was found about fifty feet above sea level. Sandstone and shale from marine beds once deep under the seas are visible high in the San Gabriel Mountains north of Castaic as well as in Cajon Pass through the San Bernardino Mountains. In downtown Los Angeles, workmen excavating for the foundations of skyscrapers unearthed mudstone full of prehistoric snails, clams and other fossil seashells which had been there for millions of years. Petroleum, so important in modern times, is itself evidence of once-intruding seas: it originates in fine-grained marine sediments thousands of feet deep, in which marine organisms were embedded long ago.

Offshore, two groups of the Channel Islands rise above the ocean, some of them as far as fifty miles from the coast. They are really the

This skeleton of an Ice Age California gray whale was found on the Palos Verdes Peninsula in 1971 at approximately fifty feet above sea level. (—*Los Angeles County Museum of Natural History; photograph by Lawrence S. Reynolds*)

tips of two mountain ranges, peaks with canyons and valleys which, although submerged, are similar to those of inland mountains. The Transverse Ranges, which cross the northern part of Los Angeles County, include not only the Santa Monica and San Gabriel Mountains but also islands — San Miguel, Santa Rosa, Santa Cruz and the Anacapa islands. The Peninsular Ranges, which extend south into Baja California, include not only the Palos Verdes Hills but also the islands of Santa Catalina, San Nicolas, Santa Barbara and San Clemente.

Geologists have been long aware of a "mysterious" movement of land in California. West of the San Andreas Fault the ground appears to move northward about two inches per year relative to a comparable point on the opposite side of the fault. In 1962 two geologists, R. S. Dietz and H. H. Hess, presented new evidence bearing on the theory of continental drift, now accepted by many scientists. For example, it explains that through the East Pacific Rise, an underwater spreading mountain ridge in the Antarctic Ocean, molten rock has for millions of years issued from beneath the earth's crust into the Pacific Ocean. There it has solidified and spread out in what is called the Pacific Plate. That crustal plate extends from the Asian shoreline on the west to the San Andreas Fault on the east. Los Angeles is on the

The Los Angeles Basin, surrounded by mountains and ocean, was photo-graphed from 569 miles in space by the ERTS-1 satellite. Three separate negatives — in green, red and infrared — were combined at NASA's Goddard Space Flight Center in Maryland. (The full-color photograph appears on the jacket.) The brightest reds indicate healthy crops and trees, which are strong in the infrared but normally invisible at this altitude. Sparse vegetation makes suburban areas appear light gray, while cities and industrial lands are green or dark gray. Los Angeles' major streets and canals show as line patterns through the smog. The Pacific is black, covered by swaths of white cloud. In the upper center, the Mojave Desert shows scattered cultivation, while rich fields are clearly seen northwest of the Tehachapis. (—*Courtesy, National Aeronautics and Space Administration*)

Pacific Plate, for the San Andreas Fault passes 33 miles east of the Civic Center.

In mid-Atlantic another huge plate, the North American Plate, originates through a submarine ridge and extends as an underground landmass as far west as the San Andreas Fault. There the two plates meet obliquely. Geologic investigations suggest that during the last 135 million years the land west of the fault has moved northward more than 300 miles relative to the land opposite. In some places the movement is gradual, in the form of "creep," with slight shifts several times a year. Where there is no movement the tension builds until it is relieved by an earthquake somewhere along the fault, generally originating two to ten miles under the surface of the earth.

From the coast in Mendocino County, north of San Francisco, the San Andreas Fault extends toward the Gulf of California for a distance of over 600 miles. In addition there is a network of secondary faults. Because of the role which fracturing plays in mountain building, faults are a normal characteristic of regions where mountains are growing. For instance, after the San Fernando earthquake, geologists discovered that a surface area of about 100 square miles in the western San Gabriel Mountains moved outward and upward over the San Fernando Valley a maximum of about 7 feet. The mountain block moved westward a like amount relative to the valley. Results of that earthquake and its aftershocks gave proof of the continuing action of ageless forces within the earth.

4. Reminders

As we think of the steady current of history which flows through infinite ages as well as immediate years, we wonder at the cliché so often repeated, that Los Angeles is "a city without a past."

Today in unexpected ways there are still similarities to the pastoral life of early days in the pueblo. For instance, the cattle which then roamed over the wide, unbroken range formed the one real industry of the Southland. Today few herds can be seen — they would seem to have disappeared. On the contrary, cattle by the thousands throughout the county live in milking barns. In 1968 Los Angeles had more dairy cattle than any other county in the United States.

Nor has the horse been outmoded. Riding stables hold increasing numbers, and along the foothills of the San Gabriel Mountains thousands of saddle horses graze in the backyards of homes. In 1972 there were an estimated 50,000 horses in Los Angeles County. Griffith Park, in the middle of the city, has 43 miles of bridle trails and, nearby,

(—David Muench)

riders follow the Los Angeles River along its bank or in the riverbed, in the manner of years ago. Equestrian communities adopt a life style true to California: in Diamond Bar a development allows each homeowner to keep horses, and the municipality provides miles of bridle trails; in densely wooded Rolling Hills, on the Palos Verdes Peninsula, a stable adjoins every home and there are at least twice as many horses as people.

The current of history has even found its way back to the old Plaza, once surrounded by the homes of Californios. There the families met and children played, and around it processions slowly moved on religious feast days; it was the absolute center of life in Los Angeles. Then gradually people drifted southward — one block, three blocks, ten blocks. The Plaza became a sordid relic until Governor Pío Pico rejuvenated it temporarily with his hotel, the Pico House. But the trend away from the Plaza could not be reversed. It became a slum in disrepair. The turning point was reached, appropriately enough, with the oldest dwelling remaining in Los Angeles, the Avila House on Olvera Street adjoining the Plaza. In 1928 the city put up a notice that it was "Condemned," but a quick-thinking woman named Christine Sterling in turn put up a much larger sign, "Why Should This Be Condemned!" and underneath added the history of the house. Not only was the building saved, but it became a focus for restoration of other structures. When 25 years later the Plaza area was made a state historical monument, restoration of the entire area began.

Today the personality of the Plaza is composite. On adjoining streets a few Chinese shops remain where once they were legion. The name of an alley, Shanghai Street, is an echo. The Plaza itself is a quiet pedestrian walkway shaded by enormous trees planted long ago. In its center the bandstand with a decorative grille recalls days when concerts were played for promenaders on Sunday afternoons. Pico House, the Governor's pride, once more looks as it did when it was "The Finest Hotel South of San Francisco." And the old church still stands at the head of the Plaza. Most of the baptisms and weddings there are for people of Mexican origin, and at the melodic sound of occasional Spanish words it takes little stretching of the imagination to feel that one is watching the Carrillos, the Picos, the Lugos, the Avilas or indeed any family among the Californios.

---

5. *Conclusion*

Seen from the air, Los Angeles spreads like a kaleidoscope, swiftly changing, colorful and diverse. In one view the freeways intermingle in graceful curves, then swirl apart, writing a modern rubric over the land. The view changes to a cluster of oil rigs, stark skeletons like strange other-world phantoms. On the deep green and brown of hillsides, raw slashes carved by bulldozers mark slopes reshaped for homes. A myriad of swimming pools — some on the roofs of skyscrapers — shine like bright turquoise tiles in a gigantic mosaic. The scene shifts to orchards and groves, to rivers and reservoirs, then to remote mountains etched here and there by sharply-inclined strata, the dramatic signature of a prehistoric age. At last, with a twist of the kaleidoscope, it is night and we see the glow of millions of lights, like jewels tossed lavishly across the scene. Emeralds and sapphires form a tiara over a group of buildings. Along the freeways the headlights of end-less lines of cars throw a golden glow ahead and leave a ruby trail behind. The lights stream across the plains stemmed only by the dark spread of ocean and hills.

The metamorphosis of Los Angeles sends our thoughts reminiscently toward the settlers who in 1781 came from Mexico to found El Pueblo de la Reyna de Los Angeles. To the weary but hopeful band of 11 families looking curiously at the hills and plains which were to be their home, what indication could there have been that the pueblo honoring the Queen of the Angels would someday be among the largest cities in the world, what hint in the sere September landscape of the groves and gardens to come, what promise to these people who traveled slowly by carreta and horseback that someday men and women would speed along freeways soaring in arabesques over the landscape, what prospect from the four square leagues allotted to the pueblo that in less than 200 years it would become the nucleus of 78 cities? Yet the hills and far-reaching plains are the same; the river still winds through the valley on its way to the sea; and the families who first stood in the isolated valley are part of a heritage belonging forever to the Southland.

Bibliography

The material for this book has come from a multitude of sources — documents in the Spanish Archives, memoirs, government papers, books, articles, unpublished theses, newspapers and personal interviews. The following list includes sources which would be most useful to the general reader.

CHAPTER 1

Bancroft, Hubert Howe. *History of California*, Vol. 1. San Francisco: The History Company, Publishers, 1886.

Beilharz, Edwin A. *Felipe de Neve, First Governor of California*. San Francisco: California Historical Society, 1971.

Bolton, Herbert Eugene, ed. & tr. *Anza's California Expeditions*, Vols. 2-4. Berkeley: University of California Press, 1930.

———. *Fray Juan Crespi — Missionary Explorer on the Pacific Coast, 1769-1774*. Berkeley: University of California Press, 1927.

———. *Spanish Exploration in the Southwest, 1542-1706* (Original narratives). Scranton, Pa.: Barnes & Noble, Inc., 1963.

Cannon, Raymond. *The Sea of Cortez* (by Raymond Cannon and the Sunset editors). Menlo Park, Calif.: Lane Magazine & Book Co., 1966.

Caughey, John Walton. *California, A Remarkable State's Life History*. Englewood Cliffs, N.J.: Prentice-Hall, Inc., 1970.

Chapman, Charles E. *The Founding of Spanish California*. New York: The Macmillan Company, 1916.

———. *A History of California — The Spanish Period*. New York: The Macmillan Company, 1921.

Cleland, Robert Glass. *From Wilderness to Empire — A History of California*. New York: Alfred A. Knopf, 1959.

Costansó, Miguel. *The Costansó Narrative of the Portolá Expedition; First Chronicle of the Spanish Conquest of Alta California* (edited by Ray Brandes). Honolulu, Hawaii: Hogarth Press, 1970.

Eldredge, Zoeth Skinner. *History of California*, Vol. 2. New York: The Century History Co., 1915.

Geiger, Maynard J. *The Life and Times of Fray Junipero Serra, O.F.M.; or, The Man Who Never Turned Back, 1713-1784*. Washington: Academy of American Franciscan History, 1959.

Hittel, Theodore H. *History of California*, Vol. 1. San Francisco: N. J. Sloane & Co., 1898.

Landaeta, Martín de. *Noticias Acerca del Puerto de San Francisco* (annotated by José C. Valades). Mexico, 1949.

McWilliams, Carey. *North from Mexico: The Spanish Speaking People of the United States*. Westport, Conn.: Greenwood Press, Inc., 1949.

Maynard, Theodore. *The Long Road of Father Serra*. New York: Appleton-Century-Crofts, 1954.

Palóu, Fray Francisco. *Historical Memoirs of New California*, Vol. 2 (ed. and tr. by Herbert E. Bolton). New York: Russell & Russell, 1966.

Portolá, Gaspar de. *Diary of Gaspar de Portolá During the Expedition of 1769-1770* (edited by Smith and Teggart). Berkeley: University of California Press, 1909.

Putnam, Ruth. *California: The Name* (by Ruth Putnam with the collaboration of Herbert I. Priestley). Berkeley: University of California Press, 1917.

Reps, John William. *The Making of Urban America; a History of City Planning in the United States*. Princeton, N.J.: Princeton University Press, 1965.

Richman, Irving Berdine. *California Under Spain and Mexico, 1535-1847*. Boston and New York: Houghton Mifflin Co., 1911.

Robinson, William Wilcox. *Los Angeles from the Days of the Pueblo*. San Francisco: California Historical Society, 1959.

Serra, Father Junípero. *Diario, the Journal of Padre Serra* (translated by Ben F. Dixon). San Diego: Don Diego's Libreria, 1964.

Treutlein, Theodore E. *San Francisco Bay: Discovery and Colonization, 1769-1776*. San Francisco: California Historical Society, 1968.

Wagner, Henry Raup. *Spanish Voyages to the Northwest Coast of America in the Sixteenth Century*. San Francisco: California Historical Society, 1929.

––––––––––

Historical Society of Southern California, Annual Publication, Vol. XV, 1931, Part I. (150th Anniversary of the Founding of Los Angeles.)

Touring Topics (published by The Automobile Club of Southern California). September, 1931. "Our Lady in the Beginning," Phil Townsend Hanna.

CHAPTER 2

Bancroft, Hubert Howe. *California Pastoral, 1769-1848*. San Francisco: The History Company, 1888.

––––. *History of California*, Vols. 1-5. San Francisco: The History Company, 1886.

Blackmar, Frank Wilson. *Spanish Institutions of the Southwest*. Baltimore, Johns Hopkins Press, 1891.

Bolton, Herbert Eugene, ed. & tr. *Anza's California Expeditions*, Vol. 3. Berkeley: University of California Press, 1930.

––––. *Outpost of Empire – The Story of the Founding of San Francisco*. New York: Alfred A. Knopf, 1931.

Caughey, John Walton. *California, a Remarkable State's Life History*. Englewood Cliffs, N.J.: Prentice-Hall, Inc., 1970.

Caughey, John Walton and LaRee. *California Heritage: an Anthology of History and Literature*. Los Angeles: Ward Ritchie Press, 1962.

Chapman, Charles E. *A History of California – The Spanish Period*. New York: The Macmillan Company, 1921.

Cleland, Robert Glass. *From Wilderness to Empire — A History of California.* New York: Alfred A. Knopf, 1959.

———. *Pathfinders.* Los Angeles, San Francisco: Powell Publishing Co., 1929.

Corney, Capt. Peter. *Voyages in the Northern Pacific.* Honolulu, Hawaii: Thom. G. Thrum, 1896.

Dakin, Susanna Bryant. *A Scotch Paisano; Hugo Reid's Life in California, 1832-1852, Derived from His Correspondence.* Berkeley: University of California Press, 1939.

———. *The Lives of William Hartnell.* Stanford: Stanford University Press, 1949.

Dana, Richard Henry, Jr. *Two Years Before the Mast: A Personal Narrative.* Boston: Houghton Mifflin Co., 1911.

Eldredge, Zoeth Skinner. *History of California,* Vol. 2. New York: The Century History Co., 1915.

Guinn, John Miller. *A History of California and an Extended History of Los Angeles and Environs,* Vol. 1. Los Angeles: Historic Record Co., 1915.

Heizer, Robert F., ed. *The Indians of Los Angeles County: Hugo Reid's Letters of 1852.* Los Angeles: Southwest Museum, 1968.

Hittell, Theodore H. *History of California,* Vol. 2. San Francisco: N. J. Sloane & Co., 1898.

Johnston, Bernice Eastman. *California's Gabrielino Indians.* Los Angeles: Southwest Museum, 1964.

Kirsch, Robert, and Murphy, William S. *West of the West.* New York: E. P. Dutton & Co., Inc., 1967.

Kroeber, Alfred L. *Handbook of the Indians of California.* Washington: Government Printing Office, 1925.

Massey, Joseph Earl. *America's Money; The Story of Our Coins and Currency.* New York: Crowell, 1968.

Palóu, Fray Francisco. *Historical Memoirs of New California,* Vols. 1 & 2 (ed. & tr. by Herbert E. Bolton). New York: Russell & Russell, 1966.

Packman, Ana Begue. *Leather Dollars; Short Stories of Pueblo Los Angeles.* Los Angeles: The Times-Mirror Press, 1932.

Pattie, James Ohio. *The Personal Narrative of James Ohio Pattie* (edited by Timothy Flint). Cincinnati: 1833.

Robinson, Alfred. *Life in California; During a Residence of Several Years in That Territory.* Santa Barbara: Peregrine Publishers, Inc., 1970.

Robinson, William Wilcox. *Los Angeles from the Days of the Pueblo.* San Francisco: California Historical Society, 1959.

———. *The Indians of Los Angeles.* Los Angeles: Glen Dawson, 1952.

Sanchez, Mrs. Nellie (Van de Grift). *Spanish Arcadia.* Los Angeles, San Francisco: Powell Publishing Co., 1929.

Smith, Sarah (Bixby). *Adobe Days.* Los Angeles: J. Zeitlin, 1931.

Thompson and West. *History of Los Angeles County.* Berkeley: Howell-North Books, 1959.

Warner, Jonathan T.; Hayes, Benjamin; Widney, Joseph P. *An Historical Sketch of Los Angeles County, California.* Original edition published by Louis Lewin & Co., 1886. Reprinted by O. W. Smith, 1936.

———————

Los Angeles County Natural History Museum, History Division *Bulletin*. No. 1, 1964. "A Guide and Catalogue of the California Hall at the Los Angeles County Museum." Los Angeles: Ward Ritchie Press.

Pacific Historical Review. Vol. 4, No. 4, December, 1935. "Bouchard in the Islands of the Pacific," Lewis Baker.

The Capital. March 8, 1902. "Noted Marriage Feasts of Spanish California," Mary M. Bowman.

CHAPTER 3

Bancroft, Hubert Howe. *History of California*, Vols. 2-5. San Francisco: The History Company, 1886.

Bonsal, Stephen. *Edward Fitzgerald Beale, a Pioneer in the Path of Empire*. New York & London: G. P. Putnam's Sons, 1912.

Bryant, Edwin. *What I Saw in California*. Minneapolis: Ross & Haines, 1967.

Caughey, John Walton. *California, a Remarkable State's Life History*. Englewood Cliffs, N.J.: Prentice-Hall, Inc., 1970.

———. *History of the Pacific Coast*. Los Angeles: private publication by author, 1933.

Chapman, Charles E. *A History of California — The Spanish Period*. New York: The Macmillan Company, 1921.

Clarke, Dwight L. *Stephen Watts Kearny — Soldier of the West*. Norman, Okla.: University of Oklahoma Press, 1961.

Cleland, Robert Glass. *A History of California: The American Period*. New York: The Macmillan Company, 1939.

Emory, William H. *Lt. Emory Reports: A Reprint of Lt. W. H. Emory's Notes of a Military Reconnaisance* (introd. and notes by Ross Calvin). Albuquerque: University of New Mexico Press, 1951.

Frémont, John Charles. *Memoirs of My Life*. Chicago & New York: Belford, Clarke & Co., 1887.

Griffin, John S. *A Doctor Comes to California, the Diary of John S. Griffin, Asst. Surgeon with Kearny's Dragoons, 1846-1847* (introd. & notes by George W. Ames, Jr.). San Francisco: California Historical Society, 1943.

Hill, Charles Edw. *Leading American Treaties*. New York: The Macmillan Co., 1922.

Kirsch, Robert, and Murphy, William S. *West of the West*. New York: E. P. Dutton & Co. Inc., 1967.

Nadeau, Remi. *Los Angeles: From Mission to Modern City*. New York: Longmans, Green, 1960.

Nevins, Allan. *Frémont, Pathmarker of the West*, Vol. 1. New York: D. Appleton-Century Co., 1939.

Revere, Joseph Warren. *A Tour of Duty in California*. New York: C. S. Francis and Co.; Boston: J. H. Francis, 1849.

Robinson, William Wilcox. *Los Angeles from the Days of the Pueblo*. San Francisco: California Historical Society, 1959.

Wiltsee, Ernest Abram. *The Truth about Frémont*. San Francisco: L. H. Nash, 1936.

Woodward, Arthur. *Lances at San Pascual.* San Francisco: California Historical Society, 1948.

Historical Society of Southern California Publications. Vol. XVIII, No. 1, March 1936 (reprinted from *Southern Vineyard,* May 22 and 29, June 5 and 12, 1858). "A Visit to Los Angeles in 1843 — Commodore Thomas ap Catesby Jones' Narrative of His Visit to Governor Micheltorena," Thomas ap Catesby Jones.

CHAPTER 4

Bancroft, Hubert Howe. *History of California,* Vols. 2-5. San Francisco: The History Company, 1886.
Becker, Robert H. *Diseños of California Ranchos: Maps of 37 Land Grants 1822-1846 from the Records of the United States District Court, San Francisco.* San Francisco: Book Club of California, 1964.
———. *Designs on the Land: Diseños of California Ranchos and Their Makers.* San Francisco: Book Club of California, 1969.
Cameron, Janet Scott. *Simí Grows Up; the Story of Simí, Ventura County, California.* Los Angeles: designed by Ward Ritchie, printed at Anderson, Ritchie and Simon, 1963.
Cleland, Robert Glass. *Cattle on a Thousand Hills; Southern California, 1850-1880.* San Marino, Calif.: Huntington Library, 1941.
Conner, Palmer. *The Romance of the Ranchos.* Los Angeles: Title Insurance & Trust Co., 1939.
Dakin, Susanna Bryant. *A Scotch Paisano; Hugo Reid's Life in California, 1832-1852, Derived from His Correspondence.* Berkeley: University of California Press, 1939.
Davis, William Heath. *75 Years in California* (edited by Harold A. Small). San Francisco: J. Howell Books, 1967.
Doran, Adelaide L. *The Ranch that was Robbins' — Santa Catalina Island.* Glendale, Calif.: The Arthur H. Clark Co., 1963.
Fink, Augusta. *Time and the Terraced Land.* Berkeley, Calif.: Howell-North Books, 1966.
Garner, Bess (Adams). *Windows in an Old Adobe.* Pomona, Calif.: printed by Progress-Bulletin in collaboration with Saunders Press, Claremont, Calif., 1939.
Gillingham, R. C. *The Rancho San Pedro; the Story of a Famous Rancho in Los Angeles County and of its Owners the Dominguez Family.* Los Angeles: 1961.
Gudde, Erwin G. *California Place Names.* Berkeley: University of California Press, 1969.
Guinn, John Miller. *A History of California and an Extended History of Los Angeles and Environs,* Vol. 1. Los Angeles: Historic Record Co., 1915.
Hoover, Mildred Brooke; Rensch, Hero Eugene; Rensch, Ethel Grace. *Historic Spots in California* (revised by William N. Abeloe). Stanford, Calif.: Stanford University Press, 1966.

Hotchkiss, Katharine (Bixby). *Christmas at Rancho Los Alamitos.* San Francisco: California Historical Society, 1971.

Manly, William Lewis. *Death Valley in '49.* New York, Santa Barbara: W. Hebberd, 1929.

Robinson, William Wilcox. *Land in California.* Berkeley: University of California Press, 1948.

————. *Ranchos Become Cities.* Pasadena, Calif.: San Pasqual Press, 1939.

Robinson, Wm. Wilcox, and Powell, Lawrence Clark. *The Malibu.* Los Angeles: Dawson's Book Shop, 1958.

Rowland, Leonore. *The Romance of La Puente Rancho* (including excerpts from "La Puente Valley, Past and Present," by Janet and Dan N. Powell). Covina, Calif.: Neilson Press, 1958.

Temple, Thomas Workman, II. *The Founding of San Gabriel Mission.* Los Angeles: Southwest Museum, 1971.

Warner, Jonathan T.; Hayes, Benjamin; Widney, Joseph P. *An Historical Sketch of Los Angeles County, California.* Original edition published by Louis Lewin & Co., 1886. Reprinted by O. W. Smith, 1936.

Weber, Francis J. *Mission San Fernando.* Los Angeles: Westernlore Press, 1968.

————

Bowman, Jacob N. *California Private Land Grant Records in the National Archives.* Manuscript at the Bancroft Library, Berkeley, and California State Archives, Sacramento, 1956.

Historical Society of Southern California Publications, Vol. VIII, 1909-1911. "The Passing of the Cattle Barons of California," John Miller Guinn, pp. 51-60.

CHAPTER 5

Bancroft, Hubert Howe. *History of California*, Vols. 6 and 7. San Francisco: The History Company, 1886.

Bell, Horace. *On the Old West Coast; Being Further Reminiscences of a Ranger* (edited by Lanier Bartlett). New York: W. Morrow & Co., 1930.

————. *Reminiscences of a Ranger, or Early Times in Southern California.* Los Angeles: Advertisers Composition Co., 1965-67.

Block, Eugene B. *Above the Civil War.* Berkeley: Howell-North Books, 1966.

Brent, Joseph Lancaster. *The Lugo Case, a Personal Experience.* New Orleans: Searcy & Pfaff, 1926.

Caughey, John Walton. *Hubert Howe Bancroft, Historian of the West.* Berkeley and Los Angeles: University of California Press, 1946.

Cleland, Robert Glass. *A History of California: The American Period.* New York: Macmillan, 1939.

————. *Cattle on a Thousand Hills; Southern California, 1850-1880.* San Marino, Calif.: Huntington Library, 1941.

Cowan, Robert G. *The Admission of the 31st State by the 31st Congress.* Los Angeles, 1962.

Coy, Owen Cochran. *California County Boundaries: A Study of the Division of the State into Counties and the Subsequent Changes in Their Boundaries.* Berkeley: publication of the California Historical Survey Commission, 1923.

Crowe, Earle. *Men of El Tejon: Empire in the Tehachapis.* Los Angeles: Ward Ritchie Press, 1957.

Fowler, Harlan D. *Camels to California; a Chapter in Western Transportation.* Stanford, Calif.: Stanford University Press, 1950.

Giffen, Helen S., and Woodward, Arthur. *Story of El Tejon.* Los Angeles: Dawson's Book Shop, 1942.

Gilmore, Raymond M. *The Story of the Gray Whale.* San Diego: 1961.

Guinn, John M. *A History of California and an Extended History of Los Angeles and Environs,* Vol. 1. Los Angeles: Historic Record Co., 1915.

Hill, Laurance L. *La Reina, Los Angeles in Three Centuries.* Los Angeles: Security Trust & Savings Bank, 1929.

Kirsch, Robert, and Murphy, William S. *West of the West.* New York: E. P. Dutton & Co. Inc., 1967.

Krythe, Maymie. *Port Admiral: Phineas Banning 1830-1885.* San Francisco: California Historical Society, 1957.

Nadeau, Remi. *Los Angeles: From Mission to Modern City.* New York: Longmans, Green, 1960.

Nevins, Allan. *Frémont, Pathmarker of the West,* Vol. 2. New York: D. Appleton-Century Co., 1939.

Newmark, Harris. *Sixty Years in Southern California, 1853-1913* (edited by Maurice H. and Marco R. Newmark, revised by W. W. Robinson). Los Angeles: Zeitlin & Ver Brugge, 1970.

Newmark, Marco Ross and Maurice H. *Census of the City and County of Los Angeles, California, for the Year 1850.* Los Angeles: Times-Mirror, 1929.

Pitt, Leonard. *The Decline of the Californios: A Social History of the Spanish-Speaking Californians, 1846-1890.* Berkeley and Los Angeles: University of California Press, 1966.

Ridge, John Rollin. *The Life and Adventures of Joaquin Murieta, by Yellow Bird* (pseud. for J. R. Ridge). Norman, Okla.: University of Oklahoma Press, 1962.

Robinson, Wm. Wilcox. *Land in California.* Berkeley: University of California Press, 1948.

——. *Lawyers of Los Angeles; A History of the Los Angeles Bar Association and of the Bar of Los Angeles County.* Los Angeles: Los Angeles Bar Association, 1959.

——. *Los Angeles from the Days of the Pueblo.* San Francisco: California Historical Society, 1959.

——. *Maps of Los Angeles, from Ord's Survey of 1849 to the End of the Boom of the Eighties.* Los Angeles: Dawson's Book Shop, 1966.

——. *People Versus Lugo.* Los Angeles: Dawson's Book Shop, 1962.

——. *San Fernando Valley, a Calendar of Events.* Los Angeles: Title Insurance & Trust Co., 1951.

Smith, Sarah (Bixby). *Adobe Days.* Los Angeles: J. Zeitlin, 1931.

Thomas, Lately (pseud. of Robert V. P. Steele). *Between Two Empires: The Life Story of California's 1st Senator, William McKendree Gwin.* Boston: Houghton Mifflin, 1969.

Warner, Jonathan T.; Hayes, Benjamin; Widney, Joseph P. *An Historical Sketch of Los Angeles County, California.* Original edition published by Louis Lewin & Co., 1886. Reprinted by O. W. Smith, 1936.

Workman, Boyle. *The City that Grew: 1840-1936.* Los Angeles: The South-land Publishing Co., 1936.

Bowman, Jacob N. *History of The Provincial Archives of California.* Manu-script at the Bancroft Library, Berkeley, 1946.

CHAPTER 6

Bancroft, Hubert Howe. *History of California,* Vol. 7. San Francisco: The History Company, Publishers, 1886.

Bingham, Edwin Ralph. *Charles F. Lummis, Editor of the Southwest.* San Marino, Calif.: Huntington Library, 1955.

Caughey, John Walton and LaRee. *California Heritage; an Anthology of History and Literature.* Los Angeles: Ward Ritchie Press, 1962.

Beebe, Lucius M. *The Central Pacific & the Southern Pacific Railroads.* Berkeley: Howell-North Books, 1963.

Cleland, Robert Glass. *A History of California: The American Period.* New York: The Macmillan Co., 1922.

Dumke, Glenn S. *The Boom of the Eighties in Southern California.* San Marino, Calif.: Huntington Library, 1944.

First Federal Savings & Loan Association of Hollywood. *History of Holly-wood.* Hollywood: 1969.

Glasscock, Carl Burgess. *Lucky Baldwin, the Story of an Unconventional Success.* Indianapolis: Bobbs-Merrill, 1933.

Graves, Jackson A. *My Seventy Years in California, 1857-1927.* Los Angeles: Times-Mirror Press, 1927.

Gudde, Erwin G. *California Place Names.* Berkeley: University of California Press, 1969.

Guinn, John Miller. *A History of California and an Extended History of Los Angeles and Environs,* Vol. 1. Los Angeles: Historic Record Co., 1915.

Hendrickson, Joe (in collaboration with Maxwell Stiles). *The Tournament of Roses, A Pictorial History.* Los Angeles: Brooke House, 1971.

Jackson, Helen Hunt. *A Century of Dishonor — A Sketch of the United States Government's Dealings with Some of the Indian Tribes.* Boston: Roberts Bros., 1885.

———. *Ramona.* Boston: Little Brown, 1939.

Nadeau, Remi. *City Makers, the Story of Southern California's First Boom, 1868-1876.* Los Angeles: Trans-Anglo Books, 1965.

———. *Los Angeles: From Mission to Modern City.* New York: Longmans, Green, 1960.

Newmark, Harris. *Sixty Years in Southern California, 1853-1913* (edited by Maurice H. and Marco R. Newmark, revised by W. W. Robinson). Los Angeles: Zeitlin & Ver Brugge, 1970.

Nordhoff, Charles. *California: For Health, Pleasure and Residence.* New York: Harper & Brothers, 1872.

Odell, Ruth. *Helen Hunt Jackson.* New York: D. Appleton-Century Co., 1939.

Palmer, Edwin Obadiah. *History of Hollywood.* Hollywood: A. H. Cawston, 1937. Los Angeles: privately printed by L. L. Morrison, 1964.

Page, Henry Markham. *Pasadena — Its Early Years.* Los Angeles: L. L. Morrison, 1964.

Robinson, Wm. Wilcox. *Los Angeles from the Days of the Pueblo.* San Francisco: California Historical Society, 1959.

Wood, John Windell. *Pasadena, California, Historical and Personal.* Pasadena: published by the author, 1917.

Workman, Boyle. *The City that Grew; 1840-1936.* Los Angeles: The Southland Publishing Co., 1936.

———

California Herald. Vol. 9, Nos. 9, 10, May and July, 1963. "The Case of Pico vs. Cohn," Leo J. Friis.

State of California, Division of Oil & Gas. *Oil and Gas in California, a Primer.* "History of Production in California."

CHAPTER 7

Carr, Harry. *Los Angeles, City of Dreams.* New York: Appleton-Century Co., 1935.

Chaplin, Charles. *My Autobiography.* New York: Simon & Schuster, 1964.

Cooper, Erwin. *Aqueduct Empire.* Glendale, Calif.: The Arthur H. Clark Co., 1968.

Crowther, Bosley. *The Lion's Share.* New York: Dutton, 1957.

Crump, Spencer. *Ride the Big Red Cars; How Trolleys Helped Build Southern California.* Los Angeles: Trans-Anglo Books, 1965.

Hancock, Ralph. *Fabulous Boulevard.* New York: Funk, 1949.

Harris, Sherwood. *The First to Fly; Aviation's Pioneer Days.* New York: Simon & Schuster, 1970.

Jones, Isabel Morse. *Hollywood Bowl.* New York: C. Schirmer, 1936.

Kieran, John, and Daley, Arthur. *The Story of the Olympic Games, 776 B.C. to 1972* (revised ed.). Philadelphia: Lippincott, 1973.

Knight, Arthur. *The Liveliest Art, A Panoramic History of the Movies.* New York: New American Library, 1957.

Lasky, Jesse L. (with Don Weldon). *I Blow My Own Horn.* Garden City, N.Y.: Doubleday, 1957.

McWilliams, Carey. *Ill Fares the Land; Migrants and Migratory Labor in the United States.* Boston: Little Brown & Co., 1942.

Nadeau, Remi. *Los Angeles: From Mission to Modern City.* New York: Longmans, Green, 1960.

———. *The Water Seekers.* Garden City, N.Y.: Doubleday, 1950.

Northcutt, John Orlando. *Magic Valley, The Story of Hollywood Bowl.* Los Angeles: Osherenko, 1967.

Palmer, Edwin Obadiah. *History of Hollywood.* Hollywood: A. H. Cawston, 1937. Los Angeles: privately printed by L. L. Morrison, 1964.

Pickford, Mary. *Sunshine and Shadow.* London: Heinemann, 1956.

Ramsaye, Terry. *A Million and One Nights; A History of the Motion Picture.* New York: Simon & Schuster, 1964.

Robinson, Wm. Wilcox, and Powell, Lawrence Clark. *The Malibu*. Los Angeles: Ward Ritchie Press, 1970.

St. Johns, Adela Rogers. *Final Verdict*. New York: Bantam, 1964.

Sennett, Mack. *King of Comedy*. Garden City, N.Y.: Doubleday, 1954.

Sibley, Gretchen. *La Brea Story*. Los Angeles: L. A. County Museum of Natural History, 1969.

Smith, Caroline Estes. *The Philharmonic Orchestra of Los Angeles*. Los Angeles: Press of the United Printing Co., 1930.

Stock, Chester. *Rancho La Brea: A Record of Pleistocene Life in California*. Los Angeles: L. A. County Museum of Natural History, 1956.

Swann, Howard. *Music in the Southwest*. San Marino, Calif.: Huntington Library, 1952.

Thomas, Bob. *Thalberg; Life and Legend*. Garden City, N.Y.: Doubleday, 1969.

Vidor, King. *A Tree is a Tree*. New York: Harcourt, 1953.

Zukor, Adolph. *The Public is Never Wrong*. New York: Putnam, 1953.

Hatfield, David D. *Ten Days in January: The Dominguez Air Meet*. Manuscript, to be published by Hatfield History of Aeronautics, 1974.

Lockheed Aircraft Corporation. *Of Men and Stars; A History of Lockheed Aircraft Corporation*. Burbank, Calif.: Lockheed, 1957.

State of California, Division of Oil & Gas. *History of Production in California*, Vol. 47, No. 1, Jan.-June 1961. "Los Angeles City Oil Field," Robert E. Crowder.

CHAPTER 8

Beasley, Delilah L. *The Negro Trail Blazers of California*. Los Angeles: Times-Mirror Printing and Binding House, 1919.

Ceram, C. W. (pseud. of Kurt W. Marek). *The First American: A Story of North American Archaeology* (tr. from the German by Richard and Clara Winston). New York: Harcourt Brace, 1971.

Chapman, Charles Edward. *Colonial Hispanic America: A History*. New York: Macmillan, 1949.

Chu, Daniel. *Passage to the Golden Gate*. Garden City, N.Y.: Zenith, Doubleday, 1967.

Citizens' Advocate Center. *Our Brother's Keeper: The Indian in White America*. New York and Cleveland: A New Community Press Book, distributed by The World Publishing Co., 1969.

Cooper, Erwin. *Aqueduct Empire*. Glendale, Calif.: The Arthur H. Clark Co., 1968.

Crowther, Bosley. *The Lion's Share*. New York: Dutton, 1957.

Deloria, Vine. *Custer Died for Your Sins: An Indian Manifesto*. New York: Macmillan, 1969.

Gridner, Audrie, and Loftis, Anne. *The Great Betrayal: The Evacuation of the Japanese-Americans During World War II*. London: Macmillan, 1967.

Griffith, Richard, and Mayer, Arthur. *The Movies*. New York: Simon & Schuster, 1970.

Iacopi, Robert. *Earthquake Country*. Menlo Park: Lane Book Co., 1969.

Kanfer, Stefan. *A Journal of The Plague Years*. New York: Atheneum Press, 1973.

McWilliams, Carey. *North from Mexico: The Spanish Speaking People of the United States*. Westport, Conn.: Greenwood Press, Inc., 1949.

Nadeau, Remi. *The Water Seekers*. Garden City, N.Y.: Doubleday, 1950.

Rand, Christopher. *The Ultimate City*. New York: Oxford University Press, 1967.

Stein, Walter J. *California and the Dust Bowl Migration*. Westport, Conn.: Greenwood Press, Inc., 1973.

Steinbeck, John. *The Grapes of Wrath*. New York: Viking Press, 1939.

Sung, Betty Lee. *Mountain of Gold; The Story of the Chinese in America*. New York: Macmillan, 1967.

TenBroek, Jacobus. *Prejudice, War and the Constitution*. Berkeley: University of California Press, 1968.

Thomas, Bob. *Selznick*. Garden City, N.Y.: Doubleday, 1970.

Thomas, Dorothy S., and Nishimoto, Richard S. *The Spoilage*. Berkeley: University of California Press, 1946.

Wilson, Benjamin Davis. *The Indians of Southern California in 1852: the Benjamin D. Wilson Report and a Selection of Contemporary Comment* (edited by John Walton Caughey). San Marino, Calif.: Huntington Library, 1952.

————

California Geology, Vol. 24, No. 4-5, Apr.-May 1971. California Division of Mines and Geology. Special San Fernando Earthquake Edition.

Los Angeles County Museum of Natural History. *America's Black Heritage*. "The Los Angeles Black Community, 1781-1940," William M. Mason and James Anderson.

Proceedings 6th Pacific Science Congress 4:177-181 (1940). "Fossil Man in the Vicinity of Los Angeles, California," I. A. Lopatin.

Time. December 18, 1964. Cover Story — "Los Angeles' Buff Chandler."

U. S. Dept. of Commerce, National Bureau of Standards, Building Science Series 40. *Engineering Aspects of the 1971 San Fernando Earthquake*. Lew, H. S.; Leyendecker, E. V.; Dikkers, R. D. December 1971.

CHAPTER 9

Bronson, William. *How to Kill a Golden State*. Garden City, N.Y.: Doubleday, 1968.

Camp, Charles Lewis. *Earth Song: a Prologue to History*. Berkeley and Los Angeles: University of California Press, 1952.

Dye, Lee. *Blowout at Platform A: The Crisis That Awakened a Nation*. Garden City, N.Y.: Doubleday, 1971.

Oakeshott, Gordon B. *California's Changing Landscapes — A Guide to the Geology of the State*. New York: McGraw-Hill Book Co., 1971.

Shelton, John S. *Geology Illustrated*. San Francisco: W. H. Freeman Co., 1966.

West Magazine, Los Angeles Times, September 29, 1968. "The High and the Noisy," Victor Boesen.

West Magazine, Los Angeles Times, April 18, 1971. "The Miracle of Sixth and Flower," John D. Weaver.

MOTION PICTURE STUDIO PRODUCTIONS FROM WHICH ILLUSTRATIONS ARE SHOWN IN THIS BOOK

Stella Maris: Paramount-Artcraft

Comedy scene: Keystone

The Kid: First National

Three Jumps Ahead: Fox

Ben Hur: Metro-Goldwyn-Mayer

The Four Horsemen of the Apocalypse: Metro

The Flesh and the Devil: Metro-Goldwyn-Mayer

Gone with the Wind: Selznick International, Metro-Goldwyn-Mayer

She Done Him Wrong: Paramount

The Littlest Rebel: Twentieth Century Fox

Appendices

THE COLONISTS OF EL PUEBLO LA REYNA
DE LOS ANGELES

1. Antonio Clemente Féliz Villavicencio (30) Spaniard
    The first settler to enlist, May 30, 1780.
    María de ols Santos Seferina (26), wife, Indian
    María Antonia Josefa Piñuelas (8) adopted daughter
2. Antonio Mesa (38) Negro
    María Ana Gertrudis Lopez (27) wife, mulatto
    María Paula (10) daughter
    Antonio María (8) son
3. Joséf Fernando de Velasco y Lara (50) Spaniard
    María Antonia Campos (23) wife, Indian
    María Juana de Jesus (6) daughter
    Joséf Julián (4) son
    María Faustina (2) daughter
4. Joséf Vanegas (28) Indian
    The first alcalde of the pueblo, 1786-88 and 1796.
    María Bonifacia Máxima Aguilar (20) wife, Indian
    Cosme Damien (1) son
5. Pablo Rodriguez (25) Indian
    María Rosalia Noriega (26) wife, Indian
    María Antonia (1) daughter
6. Manuel Camero (30) mulatto
    María Tomasa García (24) wife, mulatto
7. Joséf Antonio Navarro (42) mestizo
    María Regina Dorotea Gloria de Soto y Rodriguez (47) wife, mulatto
    Joséf María Eduardo (10) son
    Joséf Clemente (9) son
    Mariana Josefa (4) daughter
8. Joséf Moreno (22) mulatto
    María Guadalupe Gertrudis (19) wife, no race recorded
9. Joséf Antonio Basilio Rosas (67), Indian
    María Manuela Calistra Hernandez (43) wife, mulatto
    Joséf Máximo (15) son
    Joséf Carlos (12) son
    María Josefa (8) daughter
    Antonio Rosalino (7) son
    Joséf Marcelino (4) son
    Juan Esteban (2) son

10. Alejandro Rosas (19) Indian
        Son of Joséf Antonio Basilio Rosas.
        Juana María Rodriguez (20) wife, Indian
11. Luís Quintero (55) Negro
        The last colonist to enlist, February 3, 1781.
        María Petra Rubio (40) wife, mulatto
        María Gertrudis Castelo (16), adopted daughter
        María Concepción (9) daughter
        María Tomasa (7) daughter
        María Rafaela (6) daughter
        Joséf Clemente (3) son
Antonio Miranda Rodriguez (50) widower, and his daughter Juana María
(11) accompanied the colonists as far as Loreto.

APPENDIX B

Letter from Don Teodoro de Croix, Commandant General, to Capt. Fernando de Rivera y Moncada, which accompanied instructions for recruiting the expedition of 1781.

With the due aims of defense, conservation and development of the Province of Californias, toward which the service of God and King is especially directed, I have resolved upon Occupation of the Channel of Santa Barbara with a Presidio of this name, and three Missions; the erection of a Pueblo with the title of la Reyna de los Angeles on the River of la Porciúncula, and His Majesty has approved the one named San Joseph which I ordered founded on the margins of the river of Guadalupe.

In order to bring to happy success these important new establishments, the Señor Gobernador of that Province, Don Phelipe Neve, has deemed it expedient and requested of me in various communications, that you join this party of Troops, and I having heartily consented, the time is now come for your zealous performance of the duties enunciated in the attached Instructions.

They refer to the advantageous Recruital of Families and Soldiers for Californias, so that this Province [Sonora] will not be laid open to risk by serious diminution of its already small population; and to useful increase and requisite remount of Mules, Horses, Mares, etc., needed by both old and new establishments of the Peninsula.

Giving precedence to and with due reflection upon all things imposed by my instructions, you must inform me before your departure from this Capital, and during the time subsequently employed in your Commission, of the doubts and difficulties which confront you, in order that I may clarify and surmount them.

In Article 14 of the *Instruccion* I say to you that recruits must not be deceived with offers of more than can be fulfilled, and realizing that this delicate Point requires the greatest clearness I advise you that the Poblador recruit is to receive the monthly stipend of ten pesos and daily rations with the understanding that the payments will terminate at the close of three years exactly, which must be counted from the day of enlistment. That to each one will be given two Cows, two Oxen, two Mares, two Horses, one Mule, two Ewes, two Goats, and the tools and utensils necessary for the Labors of the Field: And that for all these supplies and those of clothing and riding equipment which they now receive, they will reimburse the Real Hacienda, (with exception of the amount of the monthly stipend and the rations) with part of the crops and increase of the Herds, making allowance so that they shall not lack in whatever is requisite for their own subsistence and yet carry out reintegration as indicated.

As the Soldier Recruits enjoy a fixed position and better wages, and are governed by distinct regulations, they will, by means of prudent discounts, satisfy out of their income the expenses incurred in supplying them and their families with clothing, accoutrements, armaments, provisions and remount.

The false interpretation which the people have given to the Reglamento de Californias, persuading them of greatest detriments in the surcharges or discounts there made against the Salaries of Officers, troops and Pobladores, may prevent many from taking advantage of the opportunity which now is presented to them for gaining an honorable and happy berth and of performing a loyal service to the King which will merit in all times his sovereign pleasure and just remuneration.

In order to dispel these harmful impressions it is imperative that you strive to exercise prudence and skill, not lacking in the slightest degree the truth and probity which are the Northstar of my disposals, in the understanding that I am endeavoring seriously and efficaciously to find the remedy for the imagined detriments, which I am sure, partake more of appearance than of reality; for all those (detriments) which thus are experienced here on these frontiers, as on that of California, do not result actually from the provisions of the Ordinance but rather from the vicious mode in which it is being enforced, which difficulty is most easy of remedy through methodizing the rules, clarifying those which time and experience show to need some alteration, and zealously working for its exact and proper fulfillment.

I am certain that you will be scrupulously faithful to the important Commissions which I confide to you, as you need be in order that I may recommend to His Majesty this new special service so that he will deign to extend to you the favors of his Royal pleasure, and in this understanding advising you that I will arrange for the supplies of clothing, accoutrement, remount, etc., for the recruits and families, of which Article 22 of the *Instruccion* treats, and as your first march must be to Los Alamos, I enclose the attached Passport so that you will not delay your journey.

God and Country, Arispe, December 27, 1779.
Sr. Dn. Fernando de Rivera y Moncada.
(—Translation by Marion Parks, The Bancroft Library)

Padrón and Confirmation of titles to Pueblo Lands

DISTRIBUTION OF TOWN LOTS AND TRACTS OF LAND FOR IRRIGATION AND DRY PLANTING

Monterey, August 14, 1786.   Pedro Fages.

Inasmuch as, in Article 14 of the Royal Regulations, which rule in this peninsula, provision is made for the arrangement, method, and order in which the town lots and tracts of land for irrigation and dry planting are to be distributed, with everything else pertaining to the cultivation of farms, raising of cattle, and the encouragement of the pueblos of white people situated in the territories adjacent to the presidios of these new establishments, and since it is necessary for the formalities required to give possession to the citizens of the Pueblo de la Reyna de los Angeles shall be put into effect, in order that they may live in quiet and peaceful harmony: I therefore commission the Alférez of the City of Santa Barbara, Don José Argüello, to go to the said Pueblo and, in accordance with the cited Royal Regulations, give possession in the name of his Majesty (whom God preserve) to each one of the settlers to the tracts of land and town lots which are assigned to them, by means of legal writs, which will follow at the end of this order, preparing for each interested person a warrant, including a copy of this *expediente* and the measures respecting each one. These papers he will send to be ratified (so that they may serve as titles) to this governor, so that, after examining them, he may decide what is best. Care must be taken to make it clear that the citizens understand what pertains to the royal government and what is held in common, such as crops, water, pastures, and wood, which must be stated in each warrant or act of possession, which they accept, under the conditions and penalties provided in the above-mentioned Instruction, as well as the privileges, exceptions, and favors with which the sovereign gives them this grant. They, or some other person at their request, will sign these papers before the commissioner and witnesses. Finally, record shall be made in the administration book of each of these acts of possession, as well as of the branding-irons which are given to them for marking their cattle; and there shall be a copy made of everything, to be placed in the archives of the aforesaid Presidio of Santa Barbara.

Auto of Obedience

In the Pueblo of La Reyna de los Angeles, on the 4th day of the month of September, 1786, I, Don José Argüello, Alférez of the Company of the Royal Presidio of Santa Barbara, in consequence of the preceding order from Señor Lieutenant-Colonel Don Pedro Fages, Governor of the Peninsula, declared that proceedings should be started for the exact fulfillment of giving possession to the citizens of the aforesaid Pueblo of la Reyna de los Angeles, in the name of his Majesty (whom God preserve), of the town lots and sections of land which are assigned to them in accordance with the orders in the Instruction which is inserted in the Royal Regulation of this province for the Pueblos of white people. And, after they had been informed of its articles, with the rest pertaining to the literal contest of the cited *expediente*, I ordered that as soon as these measures were completed, with the necessary formalities and requisites, in the presence of two witnesses, the papers should be sent (conformable with orders) to the said Señor Governor for his validation, or whatever may seem best to his superior judgment; and that a copy should be made of them to be placed in the archives at the Royal Presidio of Santa Barbara. I so directed, ordered, and signed, to which I make oath.

José Argüello.

_____

Nomination and acceptance of two witnesses. In the said Pueblo, on the aforesaid day, month and year, I, the above-mentioned Alférez-commissioner, in view of the *auto* which precedes, it being necessary to appoint two witnesses to be present at the subsequent proceedings, for this purpose ordered to appear before me Corporal Vicente Felix, and the soldier Roque de Cota (of the Presidio of San Diego) who, when the nomination was made known to them replied that they accepted it, and promised to be present punctually whenever they were required during these proceedings. And they signed it with me, to which I make oath.

José Argüello, Vicente Felix, Roque de Cota.

_____

Act of giving possession to the first settler, Felix Villavicencio, of his respective lot. In the aforesaid Pueblo, on the day, month, and year mentioned, I, the above-mentioned Alférez-commissioner, in continuation of these proceedings, ordered to appear before me and the witnesses, the nine settlers, including the son of Antonio Navarro, who represents his father during the latter's absence. All being present, I gave possession of his respective lot, twenty varas wide and forty long, to the settler, Felix Antonio Villavicencio. I explained to him, and he replied that he understood the privileges, exceptions, and favors with which the sovereign makes him this grant, under the penalties imposed upon the disobedient. Being asked if he accepts his act of possession, he replies that he accepts it, obligates himself, and promises to fulfill the obligations pertaining to his establishment. Not knowing how to write, he made the sign of the cross. I signed it with my witnesses, to which I make oath.

José Argüello, Vicente Felix, Roque de Cota.

_____

Act of possession of four tracts of land belonging to the said Villavicencio:

In the said Pueblo, the day, month, and year cited, I the aforesaid Alférez, accompanied by the witnesses and settlers, went to the farm lands, where, after making the necessary measurement of 200 varas square for each lot of land, I gave possession to the said Felix Antonio Villavicencio of the four lots pertaining to him, all irrigated, in view of the fact that there were sufficient of this kind. The said possession having been effected with the same formalities and proceedings as are described in the preceding measure, and the settler having been satisfied and informed of everything, not knowing how to write, he made the sign of the Holy Cross, and I signed it with my witnesses, to which I make oath.

José Argüello, Vicente Felix, Roque de Cota.

_____

Measure to confirm the branding-iron of the aforesaid Villavicencio. In the said Pueblo, the same day, month, and year, I, the said Alférez, having the settlers and my witnesses before me, delivered to the above-mentioned Villavicencio his corresponding branding-iron (the design of which is shown in the margin), he having been informed that it was the same with which he would have to brand his cattle. The iron was registered without any charge, according to the provision of article 8 of the aforesaid Instruction. Not knowing how to write, he made the sign of the Holy Cross. I signed it with my witnesses, to which I make oath.

José Argüello, Vicente Felix, Roque de Cota.

(Note. Then follow autos of lots and branding irons, with slight variation of language, to the following settlers: José Vanegas, Pablo Rodriguez, Manuel Camero, Antonio Clemente, José Antonio Navarro, José Moreno, Basilio Rosas, Alejandro Rosas, and José Sinova. None was able to write and all had to sign with their mark.)

Autos to assign lands to individuals and the royal government for irrigation, pasture, etc.

In the Pueblo of la Reyna de los Angeles, on the 5th day of the month of September, 1786, I, Don José Argüello, Alférez of the company of the Royal Presidio of Santa Barbara, commissioned for these measures, declared the acts of possession of the town lots and tracts of land corresponding to each one of these settlers concluded. I then went with them and the witnesses to the lands that were not yet assigned. Having made the necessary measurement from near the dam as far as the dividing boundary of the lands already partitioned, the measurement resulted in a length of 2200 varas from north to south for those which has been assigned to individuals of the Pueblo; leaving for the government all the land on the opposite side of this river and Pueblo, over 2000 varas long. Those which are not comprised in the aforesaid lots of possession, nor of individuals, I assigned to them, together with sufficient pasture land for their cattle. I caused them to be informed of all of this, and also that they were to enjoy the right to maintain their cattle from the community supply of water and pasture, wood and timber, with everything else pertaining to the spirit of the aforesaid Instruction for Pueblos of white people, to all of which they replied that they understood and agreed. Not knowing how to write, they made the sign of the Holy Cross, and I signed it with my witnesses, to which I make oath.

José Argüello, Vicente Felix, Roque de Cota.

At the Royal Presidio of Santa Barbara, on the 18th day of the month of September, 1786, I, Don José Argüello, Alférez de la Compañía of the said Presidio and commissioner in the present proceedings, in view of their conclusion, and having made a record of each of the respective possession and their lands in the book of settlements in charge of the Comandante of that presidio, Don Felipe de Gycoechea, for whom a copy was made of everything to remain in the archive, I directed that the originals should be sent to the Superior governor of this province, as is required in their heading. I so provided, ordered, and signed, to which I made oath.

José Argüello

(—Translation by Phil Townsend Hanna, The Bancroft Library)

———◄•►———

APPENDIX C

SPANISH AND MEXICAN RANCHO LAND GRANTS
CONFIRMED BY THE UNITED STATES

Rancho	*Patentee*
Aguaje de la Centinela 2,219.26 acres	Bruno Abila
Azusa de Dalton 4,431.47 acres	Henry Dalton
Azusa de Duarte 6,595.62 acres	Andrés Duarte
Boca de Santa Monica 6,656.93 acres	Ysidro Reyes et al.
Cahuenga 388.34 acres	David W. Alexander, Francis Mellus
El Conejo 48,671.56 acres	José de la Guerra y Noriega
El Encino 4,460.73 acres	Vicente de la Osa et al.
El Escorpión 1,109.65 acres	Odon, Manuel and Urbano (Indians) and Joaquin Romero
Ex-Mission San Fernando 116,858.46 acres	Eulogio de Célis
Huerta de Cuati 128.26 acres	Victoria Reid
Isla de Santa Catalina 45,820.43 acres	José María Covarrubias
La Ballona 13,919.90 acres	Agustin Machado et al.
La Brea 4,439.07 acres	Antonio José Rocha et al.
La Cañada 5,832.10 acres	Jonathan Scott and Benj. Hayes
La Ciénega ó Paso de la Tijera 4,481.05 acres	Tomás Sanchez et al.

La Habra 6,698.57 acres	Andrés Pico et al.
La Liebre 48,799.59 acres	José María Flores
La Merced 2,363.75 acres	F. P. F. Temple and J. M. Sanchez
La Puente 48,790.55 acres	John Rowland, Julian Workman
Las Ciénegas 4,439.05 acres	Januario Abila and 3 sisters
Las Virgenes 8,885.04 acres	María Antonio Machado
Los Alamitos 28,027.17 acres	Abel Stearns
Los Alamos y Agua Caliente 26,626.23 acres	Agustín Olvera et al.
Los Cerritos 27,054.36 acres	Juan Temple
Los Coyotes 48,806.17 acres	Andrés Pico et al.
Los Félis 6,647.46 acres	María Ygnacio Verdugo
Los Nogales 1,003.67 acres	María de Jesús Garcia et al.
Los Palos Verdes 31,629.43 acres	José Loreto Sepúlveda et al.
Paso de Bartolo (Guirado) 875.99 acres	Bernardino Guirado
Paso de Bartolo (Pico) 8,991.22 acres	Pío Pico, Juan Perez
Potrero Chico 83.46 acres	Antonio Valenzuela, Juan Alvitre
Potrero de Felipe Lugo 2,042.81 acres	George Morrillo, María V. Romero
Potrero Grande 4,431.95 acres	Juan Matías Sanchez
Providencia 4,064.33 acres	David W. Alexander, Francis Mellus
Rincón de La Brea 4,452.59 acres	Gil Ybarra
Rincón de los Bueyes 3,127.09 acres	Francisco and Secundino Higuera
Rodeo de las Aguas 4,449.31 acres	María Rita Valdez

San Antonio 29,513.35 acres	Antonio María Lugo
San Fernando Mission (Church property) 76.94 acres	Joseph S. Alemany, Bishop of Monterey
San Francisco 48,611.88 acres	Jacoba Félis, Ygnacio del Valle et al.
San Francisquito 8,893.62 acres	Henry Dalton
San Gabriel Mission (Church property) 190.69 acres	Joseph S. Alemany, Bishop of Monterey
San José 22,340.41 acres	Y. Palomares, R. Vejar, H. Dalton
San José Addition 4,430.64 acres	Y. Palomares, R. Vejar, H. Dalton
San José de Buenos Ayres 4,438.69 acres	Benj. D. Wilson, Wm. T. B. Sanford
San Pascual 14,402.50 acres	Manuel Garfias, Benj. D. Wilson
San Pedro 43,119.13 acres	Manuel Dominguez et al.
San Rafael 36,403.32 acres	Julio and Catalina Verdugo
San Vicente y Santa Monica 30,259.65 acres	Ramona Sepúlveda, widow of Francisco Sepúlveda
Santa Anita 13,319.06 acres	Henry Dalton
Santa Gertrudes (Colima) 3,696.23 acres	Tomás Sanchez Colima
Santa Gertrudes (McFarland and Downey) 17,602.01 acres	J. P. McFarland, J. G. Downey
Sausal Redondo 22,458.94 acres	Antonio Ygnacio Abila
Simí 113,009.21 acres	José de la Guerra y Noriega
Tajauta 3,559.86 acres	Enrique Abila, executor for Anastacio Abila, deceased
Temescal 13,339.07 acres	Ramon de la Cuesta et al.
Topanga Malibu y Sequit 13,315.70 acres	Matthew Keller
Tujunga 6,660.71 acres	D. W. Alexander, F. Mellus, A. Olvera

APPENDIX D

RANCHO LAND GRANTS WHICH TODAY LIE ONLY PARTIALLY IN LOS ANGELES COUNTY

Rancho	County	Acres
El Conejo	Los Angeles	3,966.76
	Ventura	44,704.80
La Habra	Los Angeles	4,550.37
	Orange	2,148.20
La Liebre	Los Angeles	17,341.93
	Kern	31,457.66
La Puente	Los Angeles	48,741.73
	Orange	48.82
Los Alamitos	Los Angeles	10,910.35
	Orange	17,116.82
Los Alamos y Agua Caliente	Los Angeles	234.35
	Kern	26,391.88
Los Coyotes	Los Angeles	20,860.02
	Orange	27,946.15
Rincón de la Brea	Los Angeles	3,562.08
	Orange	890.51
San Francisco	Los Angeles	37,870.32
	Ventura	10,741.56
Simí	Los Angeles	4,334.28
	Ventura	108,674.93
Temescal	Los Angeles	5,937.35
	Ventura	7,401.72

GROWTH OF THE CITY OF LOS ANGELES

Year	Area in Square Miles	Population	Year	Area in Square Miles	Population
1781	28.01	44	1880	29.21	11,183
1790	28.01	141	1890	30.62	50,395
1800	28.01	315	1900	43.26	102,479
1810	28.01	415	1910	89.61	319,198
1820	28.01	650	1920	363.92	576,673
1830	28.01	770	1930	441.70	1,238,048
1840	28.01	1,250	1940	450.83	1,504,277
1850	28.01	1,610	1950	453.42	1,970,358
1860	29.21	4,399	1960	457.95	2,479,015
1870	29.21	5,728	1970	463.64	2,811,801

CITIES IN LOS ANGELES COUNTY

1. Alhambra
2. Arcadia
3. Artesia
4. Avalon
5. Azusa
6. Baldwin Park
7. Bell
8. Bellflower
9. Bell Gardens
10. Beverly Hills
11. Bradbury
12. Burbank
13. Carson
14. Cerritos
15. Claremont
16. Commerce
17. Compton
18. Covina
19. Cudahy
20. Culver City
21. Downey
22. Duarte
23. El Monte
24. El Segundo
25. Gardena
26. Glendale
27. Glendora
28. Hawaiian Gardens
29. Hawthorne
30. Hermosa Beach
31. Hidden Hills
32. Huntington Park
33. Industry
34. Inglewood
35. Irwindale
36. Lakewood
37. La Mirada
38. La Puente
39. La Verne
40. Lawndale
41. Lomita
42. Long Beach
43. Los Angeles
44. Lynwood
45. Manhattan Beach
46. Maywood
47. Monrovia
48. Montebello
49. Monterey Park
50. Norwalk
51. Palmdale
52. Palos Verdes Estates
53. Paramount
54. Pasadena
55. Pico Rivera
56. Pomona
57. Rancho Palos Verdes
58. Redondo Beach
59. Rolling Hills
60. Rolling Hills Estates
61. Rosemead
62. San Dimas
63. San Fernando
64. San Gabriel
65. San Marino
66. Santa Fe Springs
67. Santa Monica
68. Sierra Madre
69. Signal Hill
70. South El Monte
71. South Gate
72. South Pasadena
73. Temple City
74. Torrance
75. Vernon
76. Walnut
77. West Covina
78. Whittier

Index

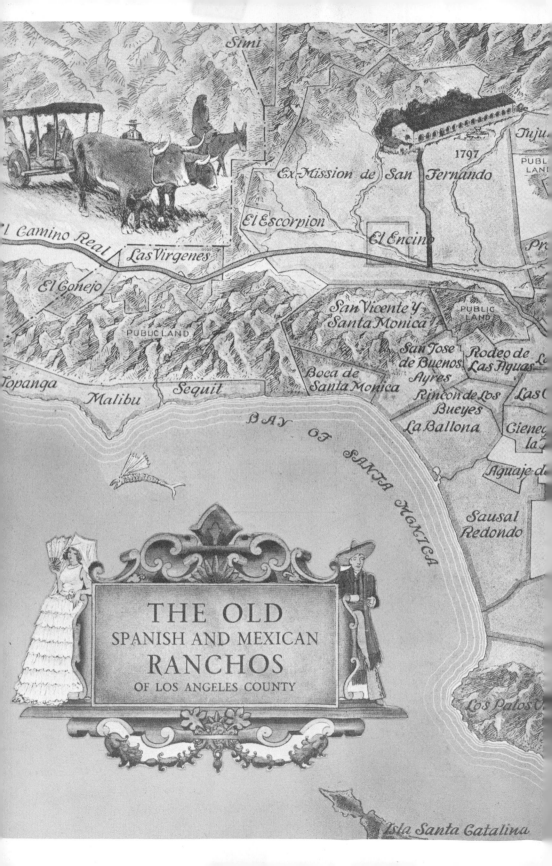

Simi

Ex-Mission de San Fernando

1797

Tuju

PUBL
LANI

El Escorpion

El Encino

Pr

'l Camino Real

Las Virgenes

El Conejo

PUBLIC LAND

San Vicente y
Santa Monica

PUBLIC
LAND

San Jose
de Buenos
Ayres

Rodeo de
Las Aguas

Le

Boca de
Santa Monica

Topanga

Malibu

Sequit

Rincon de Los
Bueyes

La Ballona

Las C

Cieneg
la

BAY OF SANTA MONICA

Aguaje d

Sausal
Redondo

THE OLD
SPANISH AND MEXICAN
RANCHOS
OF LOS ANGELES COUNTY

Los Palos V

Isla Santa Catalina

Santa Clara County Free Library

REFERENCE

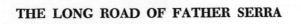

THE LONG ROAD OF FATHER SERRA

JUNÍPERO SERRA

)AD OF
ГАＴНЕК ЅЕRRA

By

THEODORE MAYNARD, *1890-*

APPLETON-CENTURY-CROFTS, INC.

NEW YORK

NIHIL OBSTAT: THOMAS W. SMIDDY, S.T.L.
Censor Librorum

IMPRIMATUR: EDUARDUS P. HOAR, LL.D., P.A.
Vicarius Generalis

Brooklyni, die XVIII Ianuarii 1954

To *Alfred Noyes*

Introduction

THERE are people who will never read an introduction, being anxious to come at once to the core of the book, even if the author is not. And indeed many introductions are mere "prolusion and display." So it is possible that there may be those who will not get even so far in what I have just written as to have my assurance that some preliminary observations are, in this case, not superfluous.

First of all, there are preliminary difficulties to overcome in writing the life of a man like Junípero Serra. He has his important place in history as the man who secured the destinies of California, for without him they would have been vastly different. Yet this, in so far as he surmised it at all, was quite secondary in his own mind. We must therefore present a missionary who was also, in the secular field, a Founding Father. Nevertheless, to present him merely in this role (were it possible) would be misleading. Then, too, it is unfortunate that in many eyes a missionary is a comic character fit only for a cannibal stew-pot or the reverend gentleman who at Timbucktoo for our entertainment got eaten by a cassawary, he and his hymnbucktoo.

However, I suppose that some of those who acknowledge that missionaries may have been heroic also consider them misguided, when they addressed themselves to one of the ancient and elaborate religions of the Orient, and will only grant that missionaries have served a useful purpose when they helped to civilize savages. Even here, though, the critic of missionaries may complain that soldiers and

vii

the settlers who pressed close behind them counterbalanced other benefits by introducing the white man's vices and diseases. To which one can only say that Junípero Serra was so fully aware of this that he did his utmost to keep colonists (and even soldiers) apart from the Indians, even when such segregation increased his own physical danger.

The Indians of California were quite different from those of the forests of Canada and our own Northwest or those of the great plains. Alexander von Humboldt, one of the greatest experts in his field, after a prolonged visit to the Spanish dominions of the New World, said that the Californians could be matched in the low grade of their mentality only by the aborigines of Tasmania, a race now extinct. This judgment may have been extreme but it derives further force from the fact that Humboldt saw the California Indians only after thirty years' work on the part of the missionaries had considerably raised them from their original degraded condition. When Serra arrived among them they were hardly to be distinguished from animals. Even so, from the first instant Serra's love for them flowed out, and it is touching how he always thought the best of them and how they showed themselves responsive to his affection. Where common Spanish opinion distinguished them from the *gente de razon,* Serra, while he missed nothing of what others saw, also perceived in these wretched savages souls of infinite value; and so they were who have been redeemed by Christ at such a price.

This must be stressed at the outset because to many Americans today the Indians mean something like that chief of the Dakotas on our five-cent piece. Little as the early Jesuits in Canada and upper New York State were given to idealization, they fully recognized the Indians' noble qualities and their intelligence; and the Indians of the South and Southeast encountered by the Spaniards set in such strong motion that myth of the savage as an unspoiled child of nature, as contrasted with so-called civilized man, that the eighteenth century was able to concoct those absurd theories of perfectibility which plagued Europe for a long time to come. On the other hand the Indians of California might almost be called Yahoos, even if of a docile and amiable sort.

In Mexico and Peru the *Conquistadores* came in contact with a high civilization. Even the nomadic tribes farther north had elements of political order. But California was a good deal of a shock, for though the Spaniards for the sake of convenience talked about tribes, these Indians really had no organization of any kind, which was one of the main reasons that it was so easy to penetrate into their country. They had no towns—at most a cluster of verminous huts. And the very abundance of their opulent lands made them disinclined to cultivate fields. In other parts of the world, where an even greater opulence prevailed, as in some of the islands of the South Pacific, the natives lived a life in which great dignity was not at all incompatible with ease. Not so in California. Though it might be possible to exaggerate their poor quality as human beings, it is at least true that these Indians were content with a disgustingly low standard of existence.

It is to these people that Serra joyfully went. And it is by this standard that the Franciscan effort in California must be judged. There was no other possible way of handling them at the outset except as mental defectives or as very small children. The mission system, while vesting all ownership in the neophytes themselves, was obliged to have the Padres, who owned nothing, act as trustees and guardians for those who placed themselves in the mission in the status of wards. The system was never thought of as something that would last forever, but merely as a temporary arrangement that would eventually bring the Indian to the responsibilities of ordinary civilized life. Until then he had to be guarded against the premature exercise of rights he was as yet incapable of assuming. Whatever troubles arose later were caused by doctrinaire officials who in their impatience wished to speed up a process which the Fathers came to recognize would require even more time than anybody had supposed. In this it is surely likely that the missionaries were more correct in their judgment than outsiders could be. At least there has never been any question, even among the severest critics of the mission system, but that the Fathers were entirely devoted and disinterested men.

A pragmatic test may be applied. In other parts of the United States the Indians were ejected, swindled and, if resistance was put up, killed by frontiersmen who were not to be denied. In California the secularization of the missions meant that the Indians were (at first) made to leave the lands they held communally, on the ground that they would never make any progress until they held private property. The result was precisely what the Fathers foretold; the Indians were hardly capable of imagining such a thing as private property. It perhaps did not greatly matter that they got nothing like their full share of the valuable mission lands, for they soon sold them for a song, or rather for a bottle, and when new settlers arrived, peonage became general. The few survivors were finally put into reservations which, in the case of California, was land that could be used for no other purpose.

Furthermore it should be remembered that California, largely because of its climate, had a much larger Indian population than any other part of the country. Yet the California Indians are the ones who now are nearest to being extinct. They were also, in the time of the Franciscan fathers, the ones who were most prosperous (with large communal holdings) and they lived a more civilized life than Indians had ever known. They were undone by ideas that had slight relation to reality, ideas that were applied by unscrupulous and venal politicians.

The notion is still current that the Spaniard was a monster of cruelty. It can hardly be denied that during the initial stages of the conquest—that is, the sixteenth century and even beyond—some, but only some, of the *Conquistadores* were ruthless. This could scarcely be otherwise because of the desperate straits in which a handful of men found themselves in a savage new country. It may also be explained by Spanish history, in which the long struggle against the Moor had welded a frame of mind that made them both prompt to accept and to inflict death. And, as Señor Madaríaga points out in one of his historical works, if the Spaniard was sometimes cruel to the Indian he could also be cruel to men of his own breed. But leaving such a tangle of considerations to one side, what will probably surprise many of the readers of this story is the almost excessive kindness showed by the Spaniards we encounter. One might have expected this in their missionaries; one finds it exemplified also by the soldier and the civil administrator.

Again, the Spaniard is imagined to have been the haughtiest of human beings. But though pride is one of the keys to the Spanish character, the student of Spanish affairs is struck over and over again with things that we would look for anywhere but among Spaniards. For instance, though one finds that Serra and his most intimate friend used an elaborate and ceremonious style of address in their correspondence, Spanish officials of even the highest rank, while on due occasion preserving all the punctilio of their position, could at other times divest themselves of it completely. Thus, as we shall see, the most exalted personage in Mexico at that time, José de Gálvez, stripped off his gold-laced coat and rolled up his shirt sleeves to help calk ships or to pack goods for the California expedition. It was taken so much for granted that nobody thought of making any comment. And officers rose from the ranks— at any rate in the provinces overseas—in a way that would have been inconceivable in England and France.

Another point to bear in mind is the fact that the constant crossing of blood streams in the Spanish colonies between whites and Indians and Negroes was creating in many a breast a private war which was before long to erupt into the age of revolutions. Most of the highest positions in Church and State went to the "Europeans," as the American-born creoles rather bitterly called them, though to a great extent this was true because those who came from Spain, being near at court, could obtain such positions more easily than those at a distance. Yet there was a definite policy at work: the avoidance of putting too much power in the hands of the American-born, lest that power be used for the benefit of relatives or friends. To that extent the policy was wise; in other respects it was a further irritant. In addition one must note the practicality of the Spanish temperament, as shown at this time. It appears in nearly all the many reports made to administrative superiors, or in the directives issued by the high officials, this though the practicality was often deflected by a curious pedantry. The soldier, the friar and the lawyer all have to be reckoned with.

It must always be remembered that during this period the official mind of Spain began more and more to be exercised over the possibility that Russia might attempt to annex the whole Pacific coast. This has been cheerfully discounted by some historians, who say that the real danger—if any existed—lay in England. But though I am not among those given to gasping with terror at the thought that a Bolshevik may be lurking under the bed, it is only a matter of history that Russia had long been full of imperialistic dreams. The Communist plan of world conquest was inherited from the Czars. In forestalling the Russian efforts that were tentatively being made, from the time of the discovery of the Bering Strait, Serra played a great part. Even if this was subsidiary to his main concerns, he understood quite clearly that Russia in California would spell an end to his plans for bringing the Indians into the Church and at the same time making them Spanish subjects.

What we shall witness is, as D. W. Brogan has said, the last spasm of Spanish imperial energy. Though Serra did not himself initiate the California scheme, and may never have heard of the Russian plans until after he was playing his decisive part in holding California for Spain, it was at his urging that Spanish ships were kept on the scene to keep a watch over the Russians—this just at the moment when the administration was on the point of abandoning the use of ships for the furnishing of the mission needs, as too expensive a method. In doing so he may have deliberately played on Spanish fears for his own purposes, though there is no indication of this. He had a strong patriotism, and he was the shrewd kind of a man who saw that the evangelization of the heathen would be all the more effectively brought about by linking it to a political object.

Nobody understood better than Serra how feebly California was held by the little garrisons stationed there. But though these would not have sufficed to repel an invasion in force by any European power, their presence in the country was notice to all the world that this was Spanish land. The consequences were prodigious. Californians of every shade of religious belief, or none, have rightly recognized that Serra was the true father of their great state. He wished to hold the land for Christ; that meant holding it also for Spain. Had Spain not been there in later years there were several occasions when Russia could easily have moved down the coast and taken possession, possibly not only of California itself but of the whole Pacific coast. Had that happened the Russians would have been very hard to eject. We might ponder what it would mean for us now if we had the red dictatorship at our very doors.

Instead of giving a formal bibliography, I will content myself with a bibliographical note. Twenty-five years ago I had just signed a contract to write a life of Junípero Serra when Michael Williams told me that he was working on such a book. At once I said, "Well, in that event I will write on something else; I am sure that my publishers will be glad to assign the Serra job to you." So they were, but Williams, being quite busy at the time, never got very far with the task he had accepted. After his death his widow generously made over to me all that he had written—some first drafts of chapters and a large number of notes. My first indebtedness is here.

Though a good many books have been written about Serra and his missions, nothing like a definitive biography has been produced. This, however, may now be confidently looked for when the Franciscan Father Maynard Geiger completes the labors upon which he has long been engaged. But as he tells me that his work will not be ready for publication for several years, I have decided to write my own book, utilizing what material is now available.

A small biography may have some use, especially as I am able to draw upon recently published sources and because I have tried to give a more ample picture than has anybody else of Serra's early life.

Another Franciscan, the late Charles J. G. Maximim Piette, in his *Evocation of Junípero Serra* (1946) followed by his two-volume *Le Secret de Junípero Serra* (1948) has presented some new data and the old data fully. Nothing recently written has much value except some periodical articles, which I will cite in the proper place. Though Piette ventures to say of his *Secret* that it is the only real life of Serra that has been produced, it seems more a collection of documents, interspersed with running comments. Yet though, like the *Evocation,* it is very valuable, it by no means precludes his confrere's work. In this last-named book he gives an excellent bibliography, but makes no attempt to evaluate the books and articles he lists, except sometimes in his text itself. These volumes have been published by the Academy of American Franciscan History in Washington, D. C., which is also to publish the definitive edition of Serra's letters and the new translation of Palóu's *Vida.* In 1944 this Academy began issuing an admirable quarterly, *The Americas,* which contains a certain amount of the fruit of Father Geiger's researches, an earnest of what we may eventually expect.

Palóu's *Vida,* first published in Mexico City in 1787, and since then many times republished, remains indispensable, though, no doubt because of Palóu's haste to get it out, it lacks the solidity of his *Historical Memoirs of New California,* translated and edited by Professor Herbert E. Bolton in 1926. The same scholar has also produced the five volumes of Anza's diaries (1930) and Font's diary, which appeared the following year. Of peripheral importance is the diary of Father Garcés, edited in two volumes by

Elliott Coues and issued under the title of *On the Trail of a Spanish Pioneer.*

Of great weight, because it draws so constantly and directly from archival sources, are the four volumes of Father Zephyrin Engelhardt, *Missions and Missionaries of California* (1908), and his earlier and slighter sketch in one volume, *Franciscans in California* (1897), should not be forgotten. One must link with these works Hubert Howe Bancroft's *History of California,* despite its weakness in dealing with archival material and its frequent rashness of judgment and occasional prejudice. A more accurate assessment is made by Bryan J. Clinch's two volumes, *California and Its Missions.* The general histories of California are many; among the best dealing with Serra's period are those by Charles E. Chapman (1936), I. B. Richman (1911) and Alberta Johnston Denis (1927), though some of their conclusions have to be taken with a little reserve.

In my opinion, the best of the popular biographies of Serra in English are those by Abigail H. Fitch (1904) and Agnes Repplier (1933), the second being at once written with great literary skill and with a special Catholic insight. Of monographs there are too many to mention, though I do not think one should pass over in silence A. L. Kroeber's *Handbook of the Indians of California,* Father P. M. Dunne's studies, Father Culleton's *Indians and Pioneers of Old Monterey,* or Father Gerald J. Geary's doctoral dissertation, *The Secularization of the California Missions.* Of books consulted for the general background, I have found most useful Salvador de Madaríaga's *The Rise of the Spanish American Empire* and *The Fall of the Spanish American Empire* and C. H. Haring's *The Spanish Empire in America.*

Books on the missions of California have been many, and if.few of them have been of much service to me this is not because they all lack value but rather because I wished to avoid anything resembling a guidebook plan. The best of these are George Wharton James's *The Old Franciscan Missions of California* (1915) and John A. Berger's *The Franciscan Missions of California* (1941). However, I was obliged to consult what might perhaps be described as travel books to obtain what I needed for my Mallorcan background in describing Serra's early life. But I had for my account of Serra as a student and professor there some of the articles in *The Americas* as well as a series of articles in which the *Provincial Annals* of Santa Barbara published in mimeographed form the late Father LeRoy Callahan's doctoral dissertation at the University of Fribourg, Switzerland.

Finally I have to thank the librarians of Fordham University, St. Bonaventure University, Manhattan College, the New York State Library and St. Mary's Abbey, Newark, N. J., for the loan of books, lacking which I could not have undertaken this work.

Contents

THE LONG ROAD OF FATHER SERRA

CHAPTER ONE

The Enchanted Isle

ISLANDS—that is, islands small enough to make one conscious that this is what they are—always shine in a romantic and magical light. This would be true, I have always fancied, even of Alcatraz, were it set where nothing is to be seen but waters around, the sky overhead, instead of in the middle of San Francisco Bay with a tall skyline in the background and ships passing day and night. The whole fascination of *Robinson Crusoe* is that a shipwrecked sailor built his life on an island of what he could salvage from the sea, with goats and parrots his only companions until most wonderfully he encountered his Man Friday.

If the charm associated with an island is not recognized by everybody, at least it will be admitted that the Balearics, where Junípero Serra was born on November 24, 1713, at Petra, one of Mallorca's little inland towns, are among the most entrancing places to be found in the world. The ancients must have thought so to have located there the Garden of the Hesperides, and if tourists have fortunately not yet quite overrun the place, this is because the Ballearics are hard to reach. Those who do go there all lie under a spell for the rest of their lives. It is perhaps significant that the man who was to spend the most important period of his life at the rim of the world should have begun where he did.

The wonder is that he should have been able to tear

himself away from Mallorca, for few who are born there can bear to do so. But even in his time California must have been a very pleasant place, though that of course was not why he went there. Junípero Serra was not given to commenting upon the charm, or lack of it, of any of the spots to which he was assigned, but it seems a little strange that—not in a spirit of complaint but merely as one casually mentioning a fact—he found California cold, as no doubt it was to one accustomed to the Hesperidean climate. Even so, he never expressed the faintest wish to leave.

Mallorca, by far the largest of the Ballearics, is in size only a little over a hundred and thirty square miles. None of its inland towns lies more than a dozen miles from the sea, but no people can be more insular than its inhabitants, most of whom have no desire to see more than they have always known. Even if some family event should take them on a visit to their sister islands, Minorca or Iviza, the Spanish mainland hardly exists for them, and still less of course North Africa, hardly farther away, this though at every turn are to be seen the traces left by the Moors. As for Spain, the people of the islands say that they are not Spanish and feel rather insulted if taken as such, even while, like the Basques, they find it hard to explain just what they are. They have their own language, Mallorquin, even if this is no more than a dialect of Catalan. Yet in spite of insisting upon their uniqueness, they were ready to act with the Spain in which they were incorporated toward the end of the fifteenth century. A Mallorcan of Mallorcans though Serra was, he acted like a good Spaniard.

The climate of the islands is unrivaled, except perhaps by Hawaii. Yet although Serra and the fellow Mallorcans who accompanied him may have thought California cold, the Ballearics themselves can get chilly. On some days braziers of charcoal are needed to warm the rooms. But frost never comes, and all the year round flowers bloom. The physical features of the islands seem to comprise not only those of California and Bermuda but Capri, the Maine coast, Nova Scotia and the Riviera. But the great rocky gorges, caves in the cliffs (about two hundred of them, many inaccessible except by boat) and steep winding roads are characteristics of their own. At the fishing village of Arta, the path that follows the overhanging cliffs reaches little bays of green, purple or turquoise, where one can see deep down the translucent water to the little rose-colored fish moving among the rocks on the floor of the Mediterranean. Then there are the windmills on the road to Randa, and at Cap Formenter red dolomites rising out of a purple sea. Everywhere there are olive orchards and vineyards and melon patches that are less dramatic but equally lovely.

"From an ornithological point of view," writes Captain P. W. Munn in the chapter he contributes to Frederic Chamberlin's *The Balearics,* "Majorca and Minorca are disappointing." Nevertheless, he lists two hundred and sixty varieties of birds, while adding that some of the varieties are not very numerous. That is the technical view of the specialist; the ordinary visitor notes that while the eagle floats slowly overhead, flocks of wild canaries fly about the orchards and woods. These orchards stretch on every hand, almonds and olives, oranges and lemons, apples, cherries, quinces, grapes, figs and plums—and on either side of the roads leading to the sea are fields ripening to gold in the sun. Some of the villages are tucked so close to the mountains that it would seem that at any moment the rocks above would fall with a crash. Yet the land is filled with peace. Indeed, contentment is its chief characteristic. Its people never think of wanting more than they have; to those who visit them they seem the happiest people on earth, always smiling in their joy, bearing themselves with quiet dignity.

Some ancient families still survive from the feudalism of the past. The splendor of that time may also be seen in the majestic mass of Bellever Castle and in Lonja Palace, as it also endures in the Vivot, one of whose bedrooms matches in its brocaded hangings anything in Spain or Italy, and in the staircase in the gardens at Raxa and their pool. But lest I be suspected of deliberately splashing on the colors, I mildly protest that this cannot be avoided if the Balearics are to be described at all, and described they must be, if only by way of providing a contrasting background for what will follow. Among much else that might have been brought in are the mountains clad in smilax, the maidenhair fern, the *Sylvestris montana* creeper with its creamy blossoms, the wild lavender and periwinkles with blooms as large as pansies.

So much for the natural beauty of the islands. One must also mention their extraordinary prehistoric remains. England's Stonehenge is still a puzzle, but in Mallorca are relics of a similar sort that are far more numerous, better preserved, and still less to be explained. These have to be classified as *talayots*—buildings which clearly were never used as forts, or as memorials to chiefs, or as tombs, or dwellings. Some of these are quadrilateral and with more than one chamber, and in at least one instance there is a second story. One archaeologist, despairing of accounting for them in any other way, has suggested that they were erected merely with the object of clearing the fields of stones! The *taula* are somewhat like the enormous tables or altars of Stonehenge, except that the stones have rarely fallen and that each *taula* stands apart from the others. The *naus* are rather like *talayots,* but are shaped like ships where the *talayots* are mostly circular. Some purpose must have been served, and that was undoubtedly ceremonial if not religious. There they stand to tease, stimulate and baffle the imagination.

Of history proper much goes back so far into antiquity as to have largely dissolved in myth. But we know, without possessing all the details, of invasions or settlements of Phoenicians, Carthaginians, Greeks, Romans, and Vandals, but never of Goths. Still more is known of the long Moorish rule, of which there are vestiges on every side. It lasted until Jaime I, brought up in Carcassonne by Simon IV de Montfort in the thirteenth century, gave the islands a Christian king. They became part of the kingdom of Aragon in 1349, and were merged with Castille in 1479 during the reign of Ferdinand and Isabella, and thus passed to their Flemish grandson, the Emperor Charles V. He visited the islands in person in 1549, being charmed with their beauty and greatly impressed by Bellever Castle which, standing at the summit of a hill of pines, is one of the most splendid structures of its kind in the world.

The peasantry in many parts of Europe continues to wear a distinctive dress. Nowhere is this more true than in the Balearics. The women wear today what they wore two centuries ago. It may be as Frederic Chamberlin says, ugly and ridiculous, but it has the merit of being Mallorcan. A sleeveless garment, whose waistline is about six inches below the armpits, bells out into a huge skirt that reaches to the toes. Under this are layers upon layers of petticoats, "rounded out into a circular tube, as if a balloon tire were put on," all the petticoats of strongly varying colors that flare out at the bottom into an immense diameter. Mr. Chamberlin's description is not very gallant; he refuses to admire even the rows of gold buttons on the cloak from wrist to elbow, or the bright kerchief over the head. Nor is religion ever forgotten, as a cross of gold, with chains and pendants, hangs from the shoulders to the waist. But while the dress is cumbersome, it is a noble protest against the stereotyped, all the more valiant because so unabashed and, one fears, so unavailing.

Men and women walk separately, and even Mr. Chamberlin thinks that "No sight could be more delightful than to see four Ivizian maids of differing heights, from the very tall to the very short, walking arm in arm after church, each costume the replica of the others, the tallest invariably on the left and so down the line." The inevitable apron is merely conventional, hardly ornamental, nor is the fan of much obvious use. It has nevertheless to be carried, and in the prescribed manner in the right hand, the left being gloved in embroidered white, with a ring for every finger. Mr. Chamberlin might reflect that the Elizabethan age in England, about which he has written with such vivacity, was one in which both men and women dressed whenever they could in a style which cold consideration would oblige him to think as absurd as the peasant costume of the Balearics, and outdone only by the still greater fantasticality flaunted by the rich in seventeenth-century England. The Mallorcan men do not go much further than to wear baggy trousers, somewhat suggesting those of the women of old Turkey, but as brightly colored as the dresses of the women. For dancing they have white damask knee breeches, striped blue and white blouses, and plumed hats. When the music begins, the men and boys move in liquid grace, never leaping but gliding, and posing with an occasional pirouette. Every movement of most Mallorcan dances has a religious symbolic meaning, the chief device being the "S" for the *Santísimo Sacramento,* encircled with an "O" expressive of wonder and awe.

Most of the merrymaking in Mallorca has a religious significance. On the Feast of *Los Reyes,* Epiphany, every child puts his shoes on the window sill at night filled with grain for the horses of the Three Kings, and in the morning looks for something in those shoes. At midnight Mass on Christmas an altar boy dresses in white to play the part of the Angel Gabriel, wearing a red cap and carrying a sword. Often the fun is a bit rough and rowdy, as when on the Assumption men or boys dressed as girls go in procession, in which there are gigantic figures made of hemp. Havelock Ellis in his book on Spain tells us something of such doings, and Chamberlin writes: "The costume [of the devils] is faced with very bright colors. These devils wear masks, and on their heads is a hood with the ears and horns of an ox, a long tail with bells on its end wagging behind." One of them carries a pole eight feet long made from the flower stem of an aloe, and with this he clears his path, for behind follow the fifes and drums and dancers of both sexes. In this way they go to church for Vespers, the devils leading another procession afterwards. Even when the symbolism grows a bit confused, it still is entwined with religion. And so it was in Serra's day.

Matters of this sort were left untouched by Palóu in his contemporary *Vida,* along with others that one might have thought him likely to bring in. Perhaps this is because he had little of the modern biographer's feeling for background, but even more because he was writing for a Mallorcan audience and so did not wish to weary his readers by telling them about what they already knew. Although this may have been a sensible line to take with the merely picturesque, he left out facts relating to Serra's university studies and his professorship on the supposition that those who wanted the details could easily look them up. He was naturally unaware that the university was eventually to be suppressed and its records lost or scattered. If they are ever found now it will only be by dint of some hard digging which Palóu might have spared scholars making later researches. But the main reason for the meager attention Palóu paid to his hero's early years is that he was primarily interested in the missions of Alta California, the California we know, and so skimmed hurriedly over all that went before, the quicker to arrive at his main theme.

In many, indeed most, of the Mallorcan documents of the time the name Serra was spelled "Serre," the final "e" being pronounced very lightly. It is in this form in his baptismal record and in some of the documents of the Franciscan novitiate and the university. On at least two occasions Serra himself inserted an "i" just after the "S," *Sierra* being the Castillian form, *Serra* the Catalonian, and *Serre* the Mallorquin. The variants all mean the same thing, a saw. Indeed the saw is part of the coat of arms of the Serras, whose lineage entitles them to this emblem.

The parents of the child were pious, as is indicated by the fact that he was baptized on the day of his birth as Miguel José (for some reason this appears as Joseph, doubtless because that is the Biblical spelling, which makes one wonder why Michael was not also used). The name of Junípero was taken later when he entered religion. The officiant was the parish priest of Petra, Bartolomeo Lledo, the godfather Bartolomeo Fiol, and the godmother an aunt, Sebastiana Serre. The names of the parents were Antonio Serre and his wife Margarita, she being a Ferrer. Her namesake, the canonized Vincent Ferrer, was no forebear, although he had once visited the island three centuries earlier.

Confirmation seems to have been administered in the Balearics at a very early age, for the parish church records that Don Atanasio de Estarripa y Tranjauregui, the Bishop of Mallorca, confirmed little Miguel on May 26, 1715, when he was about a year and a half old. This has a special interest in the case of Junípero Serra because in 1774 he received special permission, covering a period of ten years, to administer confirmation in California, though he was not a bishop.

The Serra house was typical of that peasant community, for it was bunched with others in the narrow village street for the sake of sociability. Only rather well-to-do farmers, who were obliged to do so, lived apart in the middle of their acres. The rest of the people tilled the land they held nearby, walking the short distance to and fro but keeping (as did the Serras) what livestock they possessed virtually as members of the family. For years a house on Calle Botellas was pointed out as the Serra home, and in 1913 a plaque was put there marking it as his birthplace, but further investigation proved this identification incorrect and settled on what is now No. 6 Calle Barracas. When this was verified, the cottage was bought by the Rotary Club of Mallorca and presented to the city of San Francisco.[1] The whole street remains just as it was in Serra's time. Even the rather surprising formation of a Rotary Club on the island has not made any noticeable alteration in the life of Mallorcans.

The calle is hardly wide enough for a car but is just the right width for the family washing that stretches from side to side all down the street. The house, which is without the tiniest scrap of sidewalk, is of stone covered with cement, with an arched doorway and a side entrance to the stable. Above the entrance is a single small window, and the inside would be very dark were it not for the light that streams down the wide chimney. The roof is tiled, the floors are of stone and left bare. The beams are no more than untrimmed trunks of trees, which the smoke of cen-

[1] The cottage has now been taken over by General Franco, and claimed as Spanish property.

turies has blackened. On the ground floor the half of the room used for cooking is slightly raised and off this opens what was the bedroom for Miguel's father and mother, with a cubbyhole for the boy. One goes half a story up to a loft where the baby Juana María slept, after she was old enough to sleep alone. In this loft were stored the cheeses, hams, and strings of the red sausages in which Mallorcans delight. Here, too, was kept the crockery that was used only for very special occasions—ordinarily wooden platters sufficed—when there was a visitor, or when a member of the family was ill.

As among many peasant people, the animals were not much separated from those who cared for them, giving a very intimate sense of the kinship of all God's creatures, something of deep value for a young boy and girl. One recalls Padraic Colum's poem about "the peering of things across the half-door." The goats and the donkey and the cow were all within reach; even the chickens in idiotic cheerfulness ran across the floor. Above the stalls there was an open gallery which served as the barn loft, and this abutted upon the storeroom.

Everybody went to bed early. Except for lighting the way to Mass on dark mornings or for the hunting of snails at the right season, there was no lantern, only an earthenware open lamp whose wick was fed by olive oil. There was therefore no opportunity for reading at night—and what did a peasant need with books anyhow? they would have said—and the stirring of the animals at dawn demanded that they be cared for at once. It was a life very close to nature.

Everything was simple. Though the women put on a prodigious number of petticoats, these garments were reserved for Mass on Sundays or festivals. Much of their clothing was woven on hand looms at home, and virtually everything was made by women brought up in a tradition of delicately skilled needlework. The fantasticality of their dress was an opportunity to display their dexterity as seamstresses, but of course for work around the house everybody wore what was more suitable. Fashions did not change, unless perhaps this or that color had a temporary vogue, though every imaginable color was utilized.

The women were too busy with their household duties to have leisure for afternoon calls; these were for the well-to-do on their country estates. The rest had all the opportunity needed for sociability by simply sitting beside their front door and gossiping with the women on the other side of the street. Men could get their gossip by going to the tavern and drinking the local brandy served (as it is still served) in minute glasses at an incredibly low cost. A thimbleful lasted a whole evening, for it was soon time for them all to go to bed. One never hears of even the mildest intoxication among a people of habits so abstemious.

The food was cheap and abundant, though ordinarily somewhat monotonous. The standard dish for the peasantry was *abbas* or beans. It was the foundation of every bread soup, into which were also thrown any available vegetables, after they had been boiled in olive oil to make them richer and more tender. Every housewife made her own vermicelli, but the bread came from a community oven. There, very early in the morning, the baker in the glow of his fire looked like a benign demon as he pushed into the oven on the end of a long shovel the dough that each woman had kneaded herself, while the women talked pleasantly among themselves, waiting their turn. This bread, with the *sobradas,* the sausages, or the *butifarras,* the blood sausages, and washed down with a little wine, made a hearty and sustaining meal. For water one had to go to the pump near the Franciscan church. Its main use was for cooking, for a few leaves scraped around the wooden platters got them clean. What was left was carried to the pigs; nothing was wasted.

The autumn pig killing was an exciting event before which few hands failed to give an unconscious anticipatory pat to the stomach. Most of the villagers raised a few pigs in their back yards; those who did not could buy what they wanted at the fair. The actual execution, with all that went with it, was usually relegated to experts. They did what had to be done with the utmost dispatch, saving every particle of the flesh, which was separated into heaps according to the use to be made of it, and even reserving the blood for puddings and sausages. The main parts were set aside for curing in the enormous fireplaces of the houses, but some smaller bits were eaten with rich gusto the following week, during which time other bits were minced with the bright red peppers and the blood and made into the sausages which afterwards festooned every attic. It called for precise calculation to know just how fast they could be eaten, for they had to last until the next pig-sticking time. For the rest of the year there was only an occasional chicken or rabbit or the fish which abound in the waters of the Balearics. Those who did not have a boat of their own could buy fish from a neighbor at ridiculously cheap prices, if the neighbor did not insist upon giving what was so easy to obtain.

It was the cooking that lit up the whole house, cooking at an open fireplace, mostly in an iron pot hung on a hook. But when the crackling brushwood and the almond shells that were thrown on afterwards had died down, one could look up the great tunnel of the chimney. During the day it cast a wide pool of light on the floor and was obscured only by the rising smoke. At night a small child, bending his head down and looking upwards, could see the stars.

The furniture of the house was as bare as the house itself, simple, solid, unpretentious, of little value or comfort. The tables were low, the chairs merely stools. A plain heavy chest for the feminine finery—such of it as was too good to hang on hooks upstairs in the loft—the beds and a closet for such little treasures as they possessed, about completed the scene. It never occurred to anyone to lock a door. Who would steal, everybody having the same things themselves? Besides, to steal would be a sin, and though not all Mallorcans were so pious as the Serras, a social crime was hardly thinkable among so neighborly a people.

It was in such a peasant commune—friendly and happy and industrious and desiring nothing that it did not already have—that Miguel José Serra grew up, he and a sister two or three years younger than himself. At first a sister who was hardly more than a baby could not have been much of a companion for a growing boy, so presumably he found playfellows among the boys of the village. (Later we hear of a Franciscan at Petra as Fray Francesh Serra, according to the familiar Mallorcan mode, though the official records have him down as Francisco. He is styled a nephew, but apparently was the son of his father's sister-in-law, perhaps the one who had been Miguel's godmother.) But there was not a great deal of time for play; even children had their little tasks, leading the animals out to pasturage and carrying water from the village pump. And soon there was also school, for the Franciscans interested themselves in the clever and charming boy who served Mass, and may already have been thinking that he might have a vocation for their Order.

That Miguel went to school at all probably suggested to everybody that he would probably enter the priesthood. It was the one profession a peasant boy could enter because his family lacked the means to provide the training needed by a doctor or lawyer, slight as were the formal requirements at that time and place. Therefore we may conclude that Miguel's completely unlettered parents were from the outset presented with a demand which they thoroughly understood and which they accepted. This involved a sacrifice, for Antonio then had no son to carry on his little farm after he was gone; two elder sons had long since been buried, and of course Juana María would marry a farmer, to whom Antonio's few acres and his livestock would pass. Yet though it must have been a sacrifice for him, he knew, too, that his son might find a career in the Church. Nevertheless, however much ambition may have operated, it would be very unfair to Antonio not to say that, at this stage, the piety of the father may well have been greater than that of the son.

Piety is in fact apparent in everything we know about the Serras, so much so that it has been surmised that the father and mother may have been tertiaries. Although this is a mere guess, it is probably not far from the mark. In a Franciscan parish a tertiary group is usually set up, and it would be hardly surprising if Antonio and Margarita had belonged to it. We may take it as certain that the school the boy attended was conducted by the Franciscan Fathers, for what need would a place like Petra have of a second school? A private venture would have been foolhardy, and the parish church would have been most unlikely to burden itself with giving secular instruction. A school conducted by the state was something as yet quite unthought of.

How large a school this was we do not know, but probably it took in hand only a small group of the more promising boys. A girl, it need hardly be said, was believed to have no need of anything except a knowledge of housecraft, unless wealthy parents sought further education as a grace that would make their daughter more acceptable to a rich husband. As to just what such a school taught we have no definite information, but it may be surmised that (as with all schools of the period) Latin was basic, even for little boys, and that later there were some mathematics for the sharpening of the wits and also some music, as this would have been useful in the choir. And of course Christian doctrine was heavily stressed. Perhaps some scraps of geography were now and then thrown in, but hardly in the form of a regular course; and the same may be said of history. Probably the dominant idea was to teach what the good Father felt like teaching, or what he thought his boys showed aptitude for. Certainly anything like the curriculum of today could not have been followed.

But let us stop guessing, even though our guesses are in all likelihood correct. We know that a great deal of attention was paid to handwriting. This is an inescapable inference after one has looked at the exquisite script of some of the documents that have come down to us. Serra's own handwriting, though good and showing the care given to this matter in his youth, is, however, less cause for astonishment than the script written by some of the soldiers he was to meet in the Spanish dominions overseas. In this respect, as in all others, they felt obliged to display style; in Serra's case, as I fancy I have perceived in other priests, style mattered less than utility; and he was a busy man, writing under difficulties. But, I repeat, his script is very well formed, and this I credit to the Franciscans of Petra.

The Franciscan church of San Bernardino is architecturally more striking than admirable. By the beginning of the eighteenth century Spanish taste had turned unabashed to rococo, the endless elaboration of detail for its own sweet sake, with all but total disregard for structural values. The ingenuity displayed is often astonishing, the working over and over again of old or new motifs, more often in plaster or cement than in stone. So enamored were the builders with what they were doing, so eager to hurry into still more profuse opulence, that they rarely had the patience to carve, as formerly, in stone, nor would those with the skill to work directly upon stone have been willing to debase their craft. Yet at its best rococo has a certain innocent gaiety in proclaiming its freedom from regular rhythm, adopting instead the curve of the shell and the broken line. This gives it a charm that differentiates it from the grave pomposity of the baroque. We shall find it again in most of the churches in Mexico, including those which Serra, full of memories of home, built there. If it does not appear in the mission churches of California this was only because simplicity was forced upon the missionaries in the absence of Spanish masons and plasterers.

The friary of Petra follows the usual plan of the quadrangle with its three arched colonnades, the fourth side being the church itself. Here there was a slender tower, topped with a balcony of salmon color and a cupola of the same shade. All this is very effective against the brilliant Mallorcan sky, and though some of the splendors of Palma, the capital, forbid one to say that rococo is the best-fitting style for that many-hued land and its glowing sea, one must admit that it has what seems to be a unique appropriateness there. The ocher stone of the church has in the course of time taken on much of the aspect of a rich tapestry—green and blue and yellow and citron fading into one another, as though woven on a loom. The velvet moss and the dark ivy on the walls have acquired a beauty more to be applauded than the somewhat grim outline of the structure itself—this in spite of its rococo adornments and the luxuriance of the blue-green shadows within the church.

The vault is impressive in its gloom, a gloom one soon perceives to be fallacious, so playful are the details. Yet it does not quite measure up to the parish church, which is older. Whereas the Franciscans let their fancy have its rein, the parish church depicts in bas-relief scenes in the life of St. Anne. There we see her newborn daughter Mary in her arms, the bed exactly what Mallorcan craftsmen made, correct down to the detail of having a brazier of charcoal against the cold. It is all homely and intimate, bringing heaven very close to earth, the saints to sinful man. The total impression left by the interior of the friars' church is one of austerity, the extravagance being incidental. But it must be said that the parish church, as it is now, has permitted additions that do not improve what they sought to adorn.

But to return to San Bernardino; from the moment one crosses the heavy door, all studded with the wide heads of nails, one finds walls covered with fuchsia brocade, and velvets and laces and tiles whose hues, mellowed by age, melt and flow into one another. The poverty of a primitive Franciscanism was to be Junípero Serra's in the New World; but perhaps he was drawn to St. Francis by the splendor and alternating light and shade in a San Bernardino enriched by the piety of a people whose hope of heaven had been fostered there.

There must have been many opportunities, even in the life of a boy who had tasks on his father's farm and studies at his school, to ramble through a countryside full of beauty at every step. The beauty of the Mallorcan scene has been touched on earlier in this chapter, not only to indicate the background of what must have been an entranced childhood but to show how strong must have been the impulse that eventually drew him, for the love of souls, into a land so distant from his own. Yet the adjoining sanctuary of Bonany should be mentioned, and not merely because there is a tradition that Serra preached his last sermon in Mallorca there. Bonany was a small chapel built in honor of Our Lady at the top of a rocky hill. It got its name in a year of rare drouth when prayers to the Blessed Virgin had brought rain. Afterwards people had gone to this shrine with special confidence that their petitions would be granted. A group of hermits acted as custodians. The devotion was a purely popular one and for a while received so little approval from ecclesiastical authorities that the triennial Easter procession there was nearly discarded. It nevertheless continued, and to round out the story, when the old church, the one Serra knew, fell down in 1919, it was rebuilt by the rector of the parish church, though he was not very enthusiastic about it. Yielding to his parishioners he allowed a new shrine to be erected, one whose ugliness gives it a kind of impressiveness. It was always the main center of devotion to the Blessed Virgin on the island. If Junípero Serra really did kneel there just before he left for his new life as a missionary to the Indians, he must have intoned the traditional litany:

Send good crops,
Virgin of Bonany.

CHAPTER TWO

The University

IT NEED hardly be said that the university system of Serra's time was in many respects different from our own. But it might be remembered that Spain in Salamanca had a university as illustrious as those of Paris and Bologna, of Oxford and Cambridge. Furthermore, the New World had universities in Mexico and Peru long before the foundation of the colleges—at that time only colleges, mind—of Harvard, Yale, Princeton, and William and Mary. What is rather surprising is the fact that the little island of Mallorca also had a university.

In England the two universities had been since the Reformation the preserves of the rich, and only within recent memory have an abundance of scholarships modified that situation. In Spain, however, as in all Catholic countries, the older concept of a university prevailed. Though a student met fewer difficulties if he could draw upon private means, or the support of a patron, a university education was a possibility to any youth of parts—especially if, as with Junípero Serra, he had a religious order to look after his material requirements.

The university was at Palma, where there was not only a majestic castle but a cathedral which such a competent judge as Ralph Adams Cram rates among the four finest in the world. Whether this is so or not, there can be no question but that it occupies the finest site of any, for it lies along a water front of stone where only small sailing boats harbor. This gives it a dramatic effect that is almost overpowering.

Miguel's move from Petra to Palma was not one of great distance, and no doubt the youth must have often seen the capital. What he saw must have confirmed what he had already heard: that the Mallorcans were a race apart. But primarily Palma was to him the third (and also the fourth) stage in his education. Ultimately his goal was admission into the Franciscan Order, for which certain educational requirements were demanded.

For these he had to prepare himself by private study, supplementing the instruction received at the school in Petra. One hears of his studying with a canon of the cathedral—one would probably not be far wrong in thinking of him as a tutor. Presumably this gentleman asked a fee, and even if he did not, Miguel had to rent a room and buy food, but all this might not have been beyond his father's means, or he may have had some backer in Petra who paid the bills. Palóu did not supply the canon's name; nor has Father Geiger, who has been investigating all possible sources of information, been able to make the identification.[1] It does not matter a great deal.

Possibly the studies were conducted for a secondary reason: Miguel Serra was still young, and though there was at that time no absolute rule about the matter (such as would have debarred St. Benedict's boy monks), ordinary prudence required that a candidate be reasonably mature. It was therefore not until he was sixteen that the youth applied to Antonio Perelló, the local provincial, for admission to the novitiate. But Perelló, though he was from Petra and must have had some knowledge of the Serra

[1] See his articles in *The Americas,* Vol. IV, No. 1, p. 68 and Vol. VI, No. 3, p. 293.

family, declined the applicant as too young, for Miguel was one of those daintily formed persons whose looks belie their years. However, it would seem that the Provincial made inquiries that satisfied him, for we find that he clothed Serra with the Franciscan habit on September 14, 1730, at the house of his Order, which was just outside the walls of Petra—the Convento de Jesús.

In those days a protracted postulancy was not required, so it is probable that Miguel became Brother Junípero immediately. As such he was handed over to the charge of Father Antonio Carrío, the novice master, and under his care he remained for the prescribed year of preliminary training. His head was shaved, except for a "corona" circling his pate, and he took part in all the religious exercises of the friars, in addition to those which the novices had to perform. We hear that he was so diminutive in stature at this time (he suddenly shot up in height after admission, but still remained rather small) that when he had to take his turn at the lectern during the choral Office, he could hardly reach the book—no doubt much to the amusement of his fellow novices and perhaps even of some of the professed friars.

He spent this year, and all the rest of the years he was to spend in Mallorca, at the main house of the friars, that of San Francisco, in Palma. The church itself, though it does not approach the cathedral's splendor, is, after it, the most impressive ecclesiastical building in the city. It stands in a plaza and dates from the thirteenth century. The façade is severe except for the central door, which is considered one of the finest in Spain. Inside it is too dark for the visitor to see details very clearly, though on close examination these turn out to be rich. The friary cloisters are a hundred and fifty feet long, the quadrangle enclosing a garth of flowering shrubs, and though there are cloisters elsewhere that are grander, there are none more beautiful. Brother Junípero must have thought that the lines had certainly fallen to him in a pleasant place; there, should his luck be good, he might spend the rest of his life.

His novitiate need not be described, except to say that it was a testing of his vocation and no doubt had things in it that were hard to endure, the hardest possibly being the most trivial, the maddening ringing of the bell that summoned to the performance of a small duty. But of course there were also great spiritual consolations, especially those of chanting the Office in choir. I suppose that in a spot so "conservative" as Palma, Matins and Lauds were still said at midnight, which nobody—even after many years—accepts without a midnight groan. But it was taken for granted that this was the lot of the monk and therefore it needs no further comment.

We hear of no close friendships formed by Junípero Serra in the novitiate. Perhaps this is because such friendships are there systematically discouraged in favor of a friendship for the whole group. It was not until later, while a professor at the university, that he was drawn into intimacy with two men who were his students. We might never have heard even of these had they not decided to throw in their lot with him and go as missionaries to the New World.

Of the two the dearest was perhaps Juan Crespí, who lies buried side by side with him at Carmel, California. But Francisco Palóu was, at least in the initial stages, a more decisive influence. Indeed, had it not been for Palóu, who lived to close Serra's eyes, we might not have a very definite picture of him, for though no doubt his letters would have eventually been gathered and have provided the formal substance for a biography, they are all about his work and tell us little about himself. What appears clearly is that his friendships were based upon an object held in common.

The seeds of Junípero Serra's holiness were sown at this time, for he was later on to tell Palóu that he wished to be a missionary as a means of regaining a fervor that he felt he had lost. It was obvious throughout his life that he was not of the contemplative but of the active type. One may find in his letters indications of his spirituality, but these are to be extracted only as inferences; hardly ever does he touch upon anything save practical considerations.

It has already been remarked that Palóu refrained from telling his audience what he supposed they already knew. Though by the time he wrote there were new men in control of the friary and the university, he was aware that his readers could easily check details should they wish to do so. Moreover in Mexico—where he wrote his book— his memory might have grown somewhat hazy. It is more likely, however, that he took too much for granted, as assuredly he had a somewhat different concept of biography than the one that now prevails.

The university at Palma, which was in the charge of the Franciscans, was named after that very remarkable man Ramón Lull. We have a portrait of him, bearded and handsome, and there are some who pronounce him the greatest figure of the Middle Ages—which seems ridiculous when we recall Thomas Aquinas, Dante and Francis of Assisi. However, it is safe to say that Lull was a great man frequently overlooked. In Mallorca he was a national hero and received the kind of local beatification not unusual at that time but which would be quite impossible now. He was not a priest but a Franciscan tertiary, as such married and the father of six or seven children.

This circumstance, however, did not prevent him, prior to his conversion, from prodigious extramarital excursions.

These generally had all the success he wished until an event occurred which proved decisive in his life. This was when he was so enamored of a beautiful lady as to pursue her on horseback into the cathedral. Upon this the lady assigned a meeting in her own house, like a bit out of Boccaccio. When Ramón Lull arrived at the appointed hour, she took him to her room and bared her breasts—cancerous! The remarks she is supposed to have made are probably only an embroidery upon what happened; if she had had any dramatic sense, she would have said nothing. Nor could Lull have known what to say. He left her house, if not converted, at least with a terrible vision of reality.

To say that he immediately turned to preaching Christ among the Moors of Mallorca and North Africa would give a wrong impression. His own life first had to be built anew. But preach he did, though as a layman, and he also wrote voluminously—novels, poems (including epics), and treatises on philosophy. His writings are still held in high enough esteem to warrant a definitive edition which is now in preparation.

All that need concern us is Ramón Lull's philosophy. The Dominicans attacked him but he found defenders among the Jesuits, and of course also among the Franciscans of whose Third Order he had become a member. For a while his system, while less well known than theirs, was put on much the same plane by professional philosophers as those of Duns Scotus and Thomas Aquinas. So far as I can make out he took a position not far from that of Scotus, one in which Plato rather than Aristotle was given the dominant place.

In Mallorca he won esteem on the grounds of his varied writings, but had, among philosophers, what was a unique distinction, in that he was also a martyr. The Moors in Mallorca itself were almost unbelievably tolerant and allowed him to preach freely. It was not so, however, in North Africa. There he received the martyr's palm in 1315 and his body was brought back to Mallorca for burial, where it lies in their great church in the capital.

Ramón Lull obtained local veneration of the kind which at the time of his death carried the title of "Blessed." He was proclaimed *doctor illuminans* in Mallorca, Catalonia and other parts of Spain, but his doctrines were condemned in 1376 in a papal bull which his devotees declared spurious and which was annulled by Martin V in 1417. The controversy was several times renewed but today his speculations receive little serious attention outside of Mallorca. Fantastic though he may have been, in any age he would have been regarded as an extraordinary man.

By way of producing an opinion that comes from a very surprising source, Havelock Ellis's book *The Soul of Spain* [2] may be cited: "We can well understand the enthusiastic verdict of those who declare that he is the most remarkable figure of the Middle Ages. For the philologist he is the first of Catalan poets. In philosophy he is the great Spanish schoolman, a daring and remarkable thinker. In religion he is on the spiritual side the founder of Spanish mysticism, the father of all the Spanish and many of the later European mystics, and on the practical side the finest type of modern missionary, admiring the learning of those he seeks to convert, even though he dies for his own faith." Although much of this is perhaps an exaggeration, at least what it says about Lull as missionary is true, for he adumbrated the methods of those seventeenth-century Jesuits in India who assimilated, whenever possible, the fine and true elements of the paganism to which they preached, showing how these found their fulfilment in Christianity. Lull could do this more easily, for he addressed himself to

[2] Houghton Mifflin Company, Boston, 1931.

Islam, which from some aspects may be viewed as a kind of Christian heresy, though the dangers he ran from its fanatical adherents were greater than could have been encountered elsewhere. Affable as he was in his presence, affable as his reception often was, he paid in the end for his fervor with his life, though not until he was eighty.

It would be hard to say to what extent Junípero Serra was affected by the Lullian philosophy at the Lullian University, but we know that system received great respect there and was taught in regular courses, alongside other courses which expounded Aquinas, Scotus and Suarez. The personal example of the great missionary—a layman with a wife and family to whom, after he became a tertiary, he made over his considerable fortune—might well have helped to inspire Serra. Be this as it may, there was a wide difference: Where Lull made his appeal to the men who were often as highly cultivated as any Christian they were likely to encounter, Serra, when his time came, went out to people who were among the most degraded of the human race.

The Lullian University had been placed in 1673 by Clement X on the same standing as those of Paris, Bologna, Salamanca and Rome. At the same time its name was officially altered to that of the Pontifical, Imperial, Royal and Literary University of Mallorca. New chairs were founded in Law, Medicine and Surgery that conferred further prestige, though it could not have been possible for a relatively small institution on a remote island to have operated with all the brilliance, or for the same throngs of students, as those universities to whose privileges it was technically raised. Conditions in the modern world were to doom it to decline and suppression; yet in Serra's time it was by no means negligible.

Naturally enough it gave preference to the philosophical

system of Ramón Lull, which was to some extent bound up with the controversies about the doctrine of the Immaculate Conception. Against this doctrine the great Aquinas had delivered an unfavorable opinion—as was within his rights before the Church had spoken definitively—but the Franciscans were its ardent protagonists. Serra, when he was appointed to the faculty, was given the Scotist chair, though his mind must have been deeply colored by Lull. If the charge brought against the *doctor illuminans* was that his special brand of mystical rationalism tended to obliterate the distinction between faith and reason, Serra no doubt was not much affected, if at all, by the alleged Lullian errors but drew from the philosophy only its helpful insights. From all that we see of Serra's mind in operation—at any rate after it had been brought up against the practicalities of the missions—he could not have been greatly interested in merely speculative considerations.

While the Lullians had most of the chairs of the university courses at Palma, Serra's chief professor was Fray Bernardino Castelo, and he was a Scotist. In all the courses in philosophy, Franciscans constituted the majority of the students, although candidates for the secular priesthood were also admitted, together with a sprinkling of laymen. Students from all over Spain were attracted to this main center of Lullism—the Basque Palóu among them.

The records of Serra's philosophical and theological studies have been lost so that his performance can only be inferred from other facts. One of these facts—a very surprising one—is that, according to Palóu, the young friar was elected to a professorship in 1744, two years before his ordination. In January, 1744, he was elected to one of the two chairs of Scotist philosophy at the university, that known as the *Prima,* because the lectures were delivered in the morning, to distinguish it from the course held in the late afternoon, the *Vespertina,* which it was regarded as a less signal honor to conduct.

However, Palóu's statement has been corrected by Father Geiger, a later investigator, who pronounces without hesitation: "Serra was definitely a priest by February 21, 1739, if not by the earlier date of March 19, 1738. On the former date he received faculties of the diocese from the Bishop of Mallorca as a confessor, and on the latter those of a preacher." This would seem to be decisive—in fact it makes the earlier of these two dates certain—so one must suppose a lapse of memory on Palóu's part, and he could hardly have had access in Mexico, where he was when he wrote, to official records in Palma. The explanation may be the simple one that Serra received a professorship before being ordained and that this rather than the later doctorate was in Palóu's mind. Father Geiger gives it as his opinion that Serra taught philosophy from 1737 to 1743 at the friary of San Francisco. He establishes that Serra as a deacon entered a competitive examination for the lectorship on November 29, 1737, and that therefore Palóu must have confused this with the appointment as *lector de primus* at the university. We also know that Fray Junípero was the librarian at the friary up to the autumn of 1740, and from 1740 to 1743 conducted a three-year course of lectures in Scotist philosophy. It was then that Palóu and Crespí became his students as what we would describe as freshmen. They were only a few years younger than he, and probably looked older; yet he formed their minds, scholastically speaking. Even more important was his part in their spiritual development; to them as to him there was a vista more radiant than any to be found in moldy books. If Palóu in the end retired to scholarship, this was only after Serra's death and in order to glean the gold of Serra's life.

What his students had to say of Serra by way of formal praise is less important than what several of them did, by going out under his influence as missionaries to the New World. One of them, Francisco Palóu, as we have noted, wrote his biography as well as what is, historically speaking, a still more valuable work, the voluminous history of New California. A second of his friends at the university, one not so intimate because he was himself later to be at a distance working as a missionary in Mexico City, where several times he served as superior of the San Fernando College that directed Serra's work, was Rafael Verger, who eventually was made a bishop. A third was the most beloved of all; this was Juan Crespí. Such devotion proves beyond all question what they thought of their professor and must have meant far more to him than honorary degrees or any other form of the world's vapid acclaim.

During the years 1744–1749 when he held the *Prima* chair at the university, the young professor found a certain amount of time for general preaching in Mallorca—for the most part during vacation periods. We hear of at least twenty-seven engagements of this sort in the island, which probably means that there were a good many others of which no record exists. Father Geiger shows that there were few of the principal towns where he did not appear, or few of the convents of Sisters, sometimes being rewarded by an alms paid to the syndic or business manager of his house. On at least one occasion he was invited to preach on Corpus Christi at the cathedral, that superb building which Sacheverell Sitwell describes as like "some golden trireme or galleon about to raise anchor and move off into the bay." He says it is a conqueror's church, and was built by James II of Aragon after his great naval victory over the Moors. Its nave is nearly twice as wide as that of any cathedral in England and it is higher than any French cathedral except that of Beauvais.

The pulpit from which Serra preached may still be seen. Massive, it rests on a towering base with eight legs, then spreads out to a width of at least twelve feet, with every inch ornately carved. The whole setting was so grand as to make any man eloquent—or strike him dumb with awe.

Just how Junípero Serra acquitted himself on that occasion we do not know. But we do know that he had a very resonant voice, something rarely found in so frail a man, and this always helps. Indeed if that voice be golden in tone it is the main part of an orator's equipment. One would gather that Serra's power was not so much due to the artifices of oratory as to the appeal of fervor, and for my money that is always best. But we do have a somewhat detailed account of one special occasion which would seem to indicate that he was held in high esteem as a preacher (or at least as a scholar), and this occasion had best be mentioned, though we have no record as to just what it was he said. This may have been the time when he gave his best performance; more likely it was merely the time when he had his finest opportunity. Yet it may well be that he preached best when he was least studied. The occasion in question was when he was elected by the faculty to deliver the sermon on the feast day of Blessed Ramón Lull, January 25, 1749, in the friars' church where repose the martyr's remains. On that day and before such an audience he would have been obliged to be more formal than was his wont.

The English enjoy the reputation of being past masters at staging ceremonial affairs, but the Spaniards also have a great sense of dramatic dignity, and Palma was able to prove that it could put on a magnificent display when necessary. At ten in the morning the faculties of Theology,

Jurisprudence, Medicine, and Arts and Letters assembled, each member richly capped and gowned according to the faculty to which he belonged. The theologian flaunted his white tassel, the philosopher his blue. In America today the cap of a doctor is betasseled in gold, but in Europe then as now there were hats and hoods and capes of great variety and richness.

Before the Rector went a beadle with a mace, and the beadle's gown was so elaborate that its train was supported by a page. Then the faculties followed, each as a group, all going in procession to the Bishop's palace, where he joined them. Now drums and minstrels went ahead, playing without ceasing; then came a standard on which was shown the seal of the university, bordered with red and held high by a Licentiate in Theology, with the students, arranged according to their department of study, bringing up the rear.

In the cathedral the Viceroy occupied the place of honor, with the Bishop by his side, and the mayor and aldermen of Palma grouped around. The professors and students of the university filled most of the seats, but there were some for the more distinguished people of the city, and it may be presumed that the preacher's father and mother and his sister had come from Petra to hear him. The whole church was decorated with magnificent banners and flowers. After Mass had been sung Junípero Serra went up into the pulpit to pronounce the eulogy on Ramón Lull.

Though not a word of the sermon has been recorded, Palóu tells of a comment made afterwards by a member of the faculty who was not usually very favorably inclined to the preacher of the day. He said the sermon deserved to be inscribed in letters of gold. That the orator carried himself nobly I do not doubt; but I suspect that he was laboring under the handicap that bedevils every commencement speaker, and said what he was expected to say. It seems likely, after all the backing and filing on the subject of Ramón Lull that had gone on in Mallorca for four centuries, that Serra on a ceremonial occasion would have expounded no very novel view. Let us be honest: we have here a very good mind but not a mind that ever shows itself as particularly original. While I would very much like to have a report on that sermon, its lack is probably no great loss.

If that sermon on Ramón Lull be taken as the high point in Junípero Serra's professorial career, it in no way deflected him from a determination he had reached, one infers after turning it over in his mind for several years. This was to toss up all that he had attained, and the strong likelihood of attaining a good deal more, and to go out to the New World to preach Christ to the heathen. Just what led to the decision does not seem to have been known even to Palóu, his student and confidant, though he has something to say that bears on the subject, so in part we can only guess. What Serra told Palóu may have been the sole motive, though that does not seem altogether likely, as all such fundamental decisions are reached after the weighing of a number of factors. At any rate, Serra told Palóu that he wished to recapture the fervor he had known in the novitiate. He did not say it could be done only through some heroic and self-sacrificial act, but it is patent that this was precisely what he meant.

He did not need to tell Palóu that the life of a professor in Palma, even though the professor lived in a Franciscan friary under the Franciscan rule, ran the danger of degenerating into a comfortable routine performance, for Palóu must already have discovered this for himself. Had Serra remained, he might in course of time have become the

Rector of the University—perhaps even the Bishop of Mallorca. He wished to avoid such a temptation, though ecclesiastical advancement need not necessarily have militated against the deeper spiritual life he sought.

There were arguments that could be used against what he proposed doing. In the first place he knew his aging father and mother would feel the pang of his loss keenly, so keenly that he could not bring himself to give them any inkling of his plans. They probably did not need any material assistance from him, as their wants were few. In any event a Franciscan friar would have nothing to give, except of himself. He had to trust in their trust in God. But he may also have wondered whether it was right to waste an equipment painfully acquired. He *was* a professor, and as such doing useful work. In hours of weakness he may have asked himself whether some man less well trained would not serve equally well in the Indies. To what grade of Indians he was finally to go he could not have guessed. Probably after the stories that had reached Spain of the civilization of the Aztecs—in spite of its incidental abominations—at the time of the conquest of Mexico, he pictured a rather superior people among whom his intellectual gifts would have some outlet, even if he was never called upon to lecture to them on the fine shades of difference between Duns Scotus and Thomas Aquinas and Ramón Lull. Yet he was well aware that to go so far from home, with virtually no chance of returning, involved a great sacrifice. It was through that sacrifice that he wished to regain the first fervor of his Franciscanism.

Serra may have been inspired by reading of missionary work among the Indians. Presumably the fascinating account given by the *Jesuit Relations,* that wonderful series of reports of missionary work in Canada, would have reached him, if only in a condensed and generalized form. If so, Palóu does not mention it. But we do know that he had read a life of St. Francis Solano, who early in the seventeenth century had labored among the Indians of Peru, at a period when there was a wonderful efflorescence of religious fervor in Lima exemplified by Rose of Lima, St. Turribius (or Torribio) and Martin de Porres, though the beatification of the last of these was as yet only talked about. Serra was fired by Solano and took him as a model for imitation.

Moreover, it is impossible that he was not also stimulated by the life of St. Francis Xavier, the best known and the greatest of all missionaries since the days of St. Paul. Even during Xavier's life an unauthorized collection of some of his letters had been published, and a passage in one of them must have seemed to Serra to apply closely to his own case. In it the Jesuit missionary had written: "How I should like to go through the universities of Europe shouting like a madman about the souls that are being lost. How many there are in such places who are thinking only of getting a high position in the Church through their reputation for learning, instead of using their acquirements for the common good. If only they would leave their miserable ambitions and say, 'Lord, here am I. Send me wherever Thou wilt!' ... How much better their own case would be when they come to die." Serra must have been familiar with this outburst, and it must have struck home with irresistible force. He was thirty-six and at the apex of his professorial achievements; the time had come when it had to be now or never.

Palóu tells us in a general way that Serra told him his decision had been reached through the reading of the lives of the saints, these having had the same effect upon him that such a reading had had upon Ignatius Loyola. We also hear from Palóu that, after Serra had made up his mind, he hoped that God would supply him with a companion, and that he also hoped it would be Palóu himself. But instead of making any direct appeal to his disciple, Serra left everything to God's guidance, being moved to tears when Palóu revealed his own resolve. Such an answer to prayer was the confirmation of everything. He therefore said: "I am the one who is anxious to make this long journey, and my grief has been that there was nobody to go with me as a companion... though, for that reason I had not given up my purpose.... I had just come here determined to speak to you... because from the moment that I myself reached a decision I have felt in my heart the greatest desire to speak to you, and this has made me think that you might be persuaded to go. But in view of the fact that though I had kept the matter a secret in my heart the news came to you in the way which you tell me it did, without your knowing who it was who planned to go... there can be no doubt but that this is the will of God." What had happened was that another of the professors, Rafael Verger, soon himself to be a missionary in Mexico, had mentioned to Palóu that one of the friars wished to offer himself, without mentioning Serra's name. It all seemed very wonderful; the two men now pressed forward with their plans.

Palóu, writing nearly forty years after this event, could not be expected to remember all the details of the conversation that took place between himself and Serra and therefore reports it in the "set-speech" form which no doubt gives the substance with accuracy but does not attempt to convey the conversational exchanges. Father J. G. Maximim Piette, in the first volume of his *Secret de Junipero Serra*, is no doubt doing what is perfectly permissible, in spite of his insistence that documents alone are history, when he permits himself an exercise of imagination which I shall avoid. After all, it will be very easy for anybody to translate with fair accuracy the bare condensed statement that here, as elsewhere, was provided by Palóu into the lively talk that no doubt occurred.

It was one thing to wish to be a missionary and quite another to be able to put the wish into execution. Leaving to one side for the moment the question of the need for obtaining the approval of secular authorities, in Mallorca there was something like a prejudice against foreign missions. While it is not surprising that Serra encountered among the naval officers on the Pacific coast a high proportion of Mallorcans—for they, being an island people, were attracted by a seafaring life—the Mallorcans generally were stay-at-home bodies. Even among the Franciscans there it would seem that missionary ardor came into being because Serra lighted the flame. In 1688 there had been the incident of Fray Llinas, the Apostle to Texas, when he appealed in the Balearics for recruits, only to be met with a blank refusal. The reason given by the Provincial of the time was that the volatile temperament of the island race made them totally unfit for such work, as though Francis Xavier had not been as vivacious a character as one could meet. The Provincial felt so strongly on the subject that he threatened to appeal to the Holy See if the subject were pressed.

After that occurrence those commissioned to look for missionary recruits among the Franciscans had never gone to Mallorca, thinking it a waste of time to do so. When the applications of Serra and Palóu reached the proper authorities, an anti-Mallorcan frame of mind had been built up, as far as the missions were concerned. The reply therefore came from the Spanish mainland that the two commissioners who had been there asking for volunteers had just completed their work in Andalusia and were about to depart with their complement filled. The most that was promised was that Padre Mathias Velasco, the Commissioner of the Indies, would bear the applications in mind when a vacancy occurred. There was also a reminder that Franciscan work in New Spain was under the direction of the two colleges of the Holy Cross at Quarétano and of San Fernando in Mexico City. The chances of Serra and Palóu did not look very hopeful.

But in human life unforeseen circumstances are always liable to arise. Francis Xavier went to India in the six-teenth century only because he was asked at the last minute to take the place of a Jesuit who had been assigned to this work and had fallen sick. So now of the thirty-five Francis-can friars collected for Mexico and waiting at Cadiz for a ship, three of them, beholding for the first time the awe-inspiring glory of the sea, were suddenly afraid of such a long and dangerous voyage. It was only because they asked to be excused that Serra and Palóu were hurriedly sent for.

The other difficulty that might have arisen proved, in this case, to be no difficulty at all. In Spain and its dominions, under what was known as the *Patronato Real,* royal confirmation had to be given to every ecclesiastical appointment. But though there was a common saying that not even a sacristan could be given his post without the approbation of the King and his Council, of course if a close examination had been conducted into every applica-tion the wheels of secular administration would soon have ground to a complete halt; therefore, except where a dis-pute arose, the *Patronato Real* was a mere formality; it was so this time.

Yet difficulties remained. The head of the delegation wrote by ordinary mail to Palóu announcing his and Serra's appointment, but about this Palóu makes the acid comment: "These did not reach us and if we may believe what a certain religious of . . . Palma said to me, the patents were lost between the doorway and my cell," which can only mean that one of their brethren who did not want the two friars to leave Mallorca quietly abstracted the official documents. Only by writing again did Palóu obtain— this time by a special envoy so that they might not again be "lost"—the indispensable patents. Palóu said that he received them on March 30, 1749, just as he was going to the Blessing of the Palms on Palm Sunday. At once he carried the news to Serra, who was in Petra making a visit to his parents. Great as was Serra's joy, he was careful to conceal that anything unusual had happened. He was well aware that he would never see his father and mother again, and he wished to spare them the bitter pang of a face-to-face parting, something that he also would have found it hard to bear.

Not much time was allowed for preparation. Palóu tells us that on April 13th the farewells were said to the community, on the Sunday variously known as Low Sunday, *Quasimodo*, and *Dominica in Albis*. As this too was a final parting, though several of the friars before long joined Serra and Palóu in Mexico, Serra's good-by was made in tears rather than in words. Palóu adds that the "austere community," as he calls them, were affected with deep emotion when Serra insisted upon going the rounds of the assembly, kissing each man's bare feet, "down to the most humble novice," asking pardon for any fault he might have committed. Then, having received the blessing of the Superior, he and Palóu went straight down to the dock and embarked on the packet boat for Malaga, from where they would have to take another boat to Cadiz. It was the first stage in their long journey to the New World.

CHAPTER THREE

To the New World

IT WAS for Junípero Serra the end of much else. Though he had for some time feared the effect upon his spirit of the comfortable kind of life that he had been leading as a university professor, with at least a local reputation as a scholar and orator, he must have formed close attachments to a place in which he had spent close on to twenty years. He did not depart feeling in the least aggrieved against the institution or any individual there—he broke his bonds only because they were too pleasant; he felt an inner impulse to the heroic and the self-sacrificial.

However, let there be no exaggeration. Though the ripest scholars are always humble, knowing in proportion to what they know how much there is that they do not know, the lesser men are eaten up with a strange sort of vanity, that which attaches an undue importance to the mere apparatus of scholarship, which they all too easily come to regard as scholarship's only valid proof. Still worse is the case of the orator; of all men he is in the gravest danger of being intoxicated with a sense of his power over the applauding crowd. But Serra probably was never much of a scholar, never much of an orator. He taught well and formed minds, but his was a temperament for which mere scholarship had little interest. He was a man of action, and in becoming a missionary fulfilled not only the will of God but his own nature. As for his oratory, in all likelihood he was an acceptable rather than an irresistible speaker. His power here sprang rather from his earnestness than any conscious exercise of what is always a dangerous art. Even so, it called for great courage for him to wrench himself away from a professorship in which he had proved himself a success and to launch, at a time he was approaching middle age, a completely new sort of life.

It may be that his departure hastened a process of decline that had already begun at the university, and that this was the reason the rather shabby trick was resorted to of trying to hold him back by suppressing the patent appointing him a missionary to the Indies. As to this, though, we cannot be sure; it may have been only an attempt to keep a useful man from wasting himself on benighted savages. The decline of the university may not even have been noticed at this time, except perhaps by a few who had a gloomy insight into conditions. But looking back we can see that the Lullian University did not have the resources to cope with the demands that were soon to be made by the new kind of society that developed at the end of the century. It struggled on as best it could until at last on September 2, 1829, it was suppressed.

Had Serra remained he could not have saved it. Nor could he have divined in 1749 what was to happen eighty years later. He had no standard of comparison by which he could measure his own alma mater against other universities, which probably to his dying day he regarded through rose-tinted glasses, though his break with it was clean and complete. Even had he been so extraordinarily acute as to guess at the decline that was to come, it must be presumed that he had it within his power to obtain an appointment to a professorship on the mainland. The sole reason he left was that he wished to go to the New World to do work that was more immediately conducive to the salvation of souls.

His second cousin (referred to as his nephew), Francisco Serra, had become a priest. His sister Juana had married a small farmer named Miguel Robot y Botellas, and they now had three children. It was to the nephew that Junípero Serra addressed the letters that the other members of the family were unable to read themselves. Two of these letters have come down to us, and will be introduced soon, and in all likelihood there were others, though at no period of his life was Serra accustomed to write letters unless about the business of the missions, and in their case he was so careful not to leave anything untouched as to become occasionally prolix.

It is a bit odd that Serra did not say anything in either of these letters—one of them written at Cadiz, the other just after his arrival at Vera Cruz in Mexico—about a matter which Palóu, his fellow traveler, deals with at considerable length. This may be because he did not want to alarm his family. But it may also be that Palóu touched up the incident, perhaps after having heard it often related in a humorous style, and with some embroidery. Written down, it might well have seemed more frightening than it would have appeared in a conversation where a smile or a wink would have indicated that it was not intended to be taken quite literally.

Before coming to the incident itself, a little further discussion might be advisable lest one draw the inference that Palóu records something that never happened or made a great deal out of a trifle. This must be said at the outset because all of Serra's biographers necessarily turn to him as a main source, and the question comes up as to how reliable he is. So I give my strong belief that Palóu was a most truthful man, that his matter-of-fact style itself

carries conviction, and that he is in general supported not
only by his much longer *Historical Memoirs of New California* (for who would expect him not to back up his own
veracity?) but by the vast amount that other people wrote
about Serra and his times. One does not get of course a
perfect tallying of all that the witnesses relate, and too
close a corroboration would in itself appear rather suspiciously like collusion, since something must be allowed
for the personal point of view.

A charge has fairly recently been brought against Palóu
that he invented a story which he records of 1770, and
this will be dealt with when the time comes. But though
in that matter I express my conviction that the critic has
misunderstood the situation, and that Palóu was a very
honest man, I think I can see that there were tracts of
intelligence in which now and then he was somewhat gul-
lible. For instance, there is a chapter in which he scoops
together a number of incidents that may be described as
having a supernatural coloring (the only chapter of its
kind in his book), in which I cannot resist the impression
that he did so under pressure and against his own better
judgment, and that these are mentioned in case his biography should ever be used as one of the exhibits for Serra's
beatification. If I very slightly demur at that point, it is
only because Palóu seemed to be writing a bit out of character, being elsewhere so very matter-of-fact and businesslike in his approach. This is not, I hope it will be
understood, because I adopt any *a priori* attitude against
the miraculous or murmur in a supercilious tone with
Matthew Arnold, "Oh, yes, to be sure miracles are very
wonderful—only they do not happen." But while myself
certain that they do happen, one should be most cautious
in dealing with them. Palóu's very lack of literary skill
helps to give us confidence in him. That he is so plain and

blunt leads us to take his word for what he tells us, but about things which look as though they had been dragged in willy-nilly we are inclined to have some reservations.

In what I am about to relate—which is not, I repeat, alluded to in Serra's letters written at the time—there is a doubt in my mind created by another set of possibilities. The man in the story may have been drunk; he may have been insane; even the wildest and most ferocious of religious fanatics can hardly be imagined behaving in the way that Palóu describes. While some such incident doubtless happened, I am left with a feeling that Palóu, as he was telling what he considered to be a funny story, felt that a certain amount of embroidery was permissible. He did not have much sense of humor, though he is now and then very effective in his quiet use of the sardonic.

But the reader shall be the judge. According to Palóu the coastal vessel in which he and Serra traveled from Palma to Malaga was under the command of an Englishman. This man was raised to such a pitch of frenzy at the sight of two Popish friars that he could hardly leave them in peace long enough to say their Office but kept thrusting himself upon his passengers insisting on arguing about religion. That he knew no other language than English (with a smattering of Portuguese) did not deter him; he came before them armed with an English version of the Scriptures, and these he would quote from, in his halting Portuguese, interpreting everything according to his own pleasure, but always to prove how the Bible contradicted the Church. Serra, however, was so well grounded—as well he might have been as a doctor of theology challenged by this sea-dog theologian—that when it came to chopping texts, he could always cite another passage, for which he had the exact reference. Then the captain would turn over the pages of the volume and, seeing that he had been confuted, would declare that the page on which the particular passage appeared must have been torn out. This happened every time that Serra brought up a text that told against the Englishman's position—which probably was one of the more eccentric forms of Protestantism. Yet the poor man would never give up pestering the two friars, hoping to confute them though himself invariably confuted.

Even this would be a little hard to swallow, but Palóu went on to say that the captain in his frenzy threatened to throw them both into the sea and to sail to London. There Palóu overlooks the circumstance that had the captain done this, he would have had to answer to the ship's owners for changing the vessel's course. However, it seems that he was brought to some degree of reason by being reminded that, if he committed murder, England would have to pay Spain a heavy indemnity and that his own head would pay for an act so outrageous. Upon this he threw himself upon his bed to find oblivion in sleep, but Serra, still afraid that the threats would be carried out, asked Palóu to awaken him in good time. Not long before, the enraged fanatic had put a dagger against Serra's throat. Yet Serra was not really afraid, for he had remarked to Palóu with a light jest (no doubt quoting one of the captain's sentences): "Yes, it may be that even before we reach Malaga we shall find the gold and silver in search of which we are going to the Indies!" For the rest of the voyage, which Palóu says took two weeks, the captain left them unmolested. Serra's summation of the affair was: "I can comfort myself by the thought that I have never provoked him in conversation or to dispute, as it seemed to me that time was wasted, but that in conscience it was my duty to make a reply for the credit of our Catholic religion."

As it stands the story seems incredible. But there may have been a very ignorant English captain, inflamed equally by religion and rum, and he may on one occasion have produced a Bible and then pleaded that the page wanted was missing. He may have growled something to the effect that such people ought to be thrown overboard, or even have flourished a dagger for dramatic effect. But that he had any real intention of doing bodily harm to his passengers is simply not to be believed. Finally, it might be noted that Palóu did not claim to have been present at the interviews but was merely reporting what Serra had told him. Serra's own account of what took place was probably facetious and taken much too seriously by Palóu.

None of this must be taken as casting doubts upon Palóu's trustworthiness as a biographer. But as everybody knows, few people are "of a piece" throughout, and Palóu, ordinarily so very conscientious about keeping notes and preserving letters, had occasional lapses, whether in memory or taste or judgment. While I usually rely with perfect confidence upon him, I propose at all times to exercise a certain amount of caution (if only in the form of common sense) with regard to all those who have details to contribute to Serra's story, and I fully admit that my readers should also turn upon me a critical eye.

At Cadiz Serra wrote on August 20, 1749, a long letter to his nephew Francisco, the Franciscan, asking that it be read to the family, from whom he had departed without giving any precise particulars about what he proposed to do. He had sailed from Palma on April 13th, and by that time his relatives had surely received word of his departure for the New World, but naturally they wanted to hear about it from him. "Tell them," one passage reads in a letter that need not be quoted in its entirety, "that I feel deeply that I cannot be nearer to them, but that thinking the first is always the first, and the first thing is to do the will of God, I have left them for no other reason than the love of God. And if I, for the love of God and His grace, have been forced to leave them, it will be very fitting that they also, for the love of God, be content to remain without my company. Let them hear what their confessor has to say on this point, and they will see that verily God is present in their house now." No considerations could be more fitting to Christians, as we may be sure all the Serras at once recognized.

To condense a little: They should be happy to have a priest, "although unworthy and a sinner," who will remember them every day of his life at Mass and in his private prayers. They are urged to make the appropriate reflections regarding patience in work, resignation to the Divine Will, resistance to the temptations of the Devil, and so prepare for a holy death. "If," he adds, "I by the grace of God come to be a good religious, my prayers will be more efficacious." He reminds his father that once, when he believed himself close to death, he said with what he expected to be his last words, "My son, what I charge you with is that you be a good Franciscan." As for his mother, he expresses his belief that it was her prayers that led him to this path—not merely to be a friar but a missionary. He offers to his sister Juana the suggestion that, when she recovered from a sickness which seemed to be her last, it was no doubt so she might be a consolation to their parents now that he has gone away. He urges constant love between her and her husband Miguel, and to both of them care for the education of their children, frequent confession and Holy Communion, and especially the following of the Way of the Cross, a typically Franciscan devotion. It is clear from all this that the whole family was exemplary. The nephews receive words of loving advice, especially Francisco, who has already been ordained in the Friars Minor.

There is a long list of personal salutations to friends in Petra, two of them doctors and two of them Sisters. But the letter enjoins that the priests he names—the vicar of the parish church and the Guardian of the local Franciscans—they and they alone, except for the family, be present at the reading of the letter. "And if anyone else must hear it, let it be my cousin Juana, the neighbor, for whom I add my cordial remembrance." That leads him to say, "Salute Ruig, his wife and also Aunt Apolinia Bornado, Xurxa and the other relatives." Even after all these, and many not mentioned in these extracts, he writes, "To make it short [regards] to all the friends." Then on the last page of the letter, as he has just sent the affectionate regards of Father Palóu, Serra is reminded of still one more name: "Salute from both of us Señor Guillen Roca and all his family." If we had nothing else we should know from this that Junípero Serra was a warmhearted man of strong family attachments and many friends. That he completely severed himself from them is the measure of his sacrifice. Even his method of taking farewell, by not announcing his intention of sailing for the Indies until he knew that by the time his letter reached Mallorca he would be well on his way across the Atlantic, reveals his tender and considerate solicitude for feelings which would inevitably be lacerated.

The ship finally sailed from Cadiz on August 30th, loaded to the gunwales with missionary friars, for in addition to the large Franciscan contingent, there was a group of Dominicans bound for Mexico. To crowd them all in must have meant that they did not get anything better than we hear of in the steerage quarters of a hundred years ago. The food provided was poor—as it was for the sailors, too—being mostly dried meat, salt pork, and ship's biscuit which soon became hard, crumbly and full of maggots. The water supply was limited and the ration doled out each day was yellow and slimy, but even so eagerly taken. However, word had reached the friars from others who had made the crossing to take some stores of fruit and wine—the fruit as a preventative against the dreaded scurvy. That the friars suffered from thirst is plain from one little fact that Palóu records. A fellow passenger asked Serra about this and got the reply: "It does not bother me at all." When asked further how this could be, the explanation came: "I have discovered an excellent remedy against thirst, and that is to eat less and talk less, and so save my saliva." Despite which Serra was to confess at the end of the voyage, "Sometimes I would have drunk from the dirtiest puddle in the street; for a sip of water I would have done anything." His answer to the thirsty friar suggests that Serra was not without pawky or owlish humor. In all probability the man was a bit too concerned about his comfort and had wearied everybody with complaints. A suggestion that has been made by some of his biographers that Serra did not have much humor may be due rather to Palóu's own deficiencies in this respect. Yet that both men had more of this commodity than might appear seems to be indicated by the patience and tolerance they later showed in their handling of several of the self-important officials encountered in California. Some of the incidents there had a decidedly comical aspect, even if Palóu rarely stressed that side of the matter.

The long voyage was uneventful. During it Palóu noticed that Serra never took his crucifix from his breast, even while he was asleep. He was to notice the same of him during Serra's last days, when Serra happened to be with him, so we must suppose it was a settled custom. As he was not seasick he was able to say Mass every morning, unless the sea was too rough. Almost every evening he gave himself to hearing confessions, winning a great respect for his saintliness and patience from all on board. He was lucky in finding a Mallorcan among the sailors; this man was of very practical help to them, as he was sometimes able to bring them little extra rations of the precious if evil-smelling water. While most of the passengers on the ship made the voyage the opportunity for getting a long rest—there was not much else to do but sleep—Serra showed that he looked upon his missionary labors as having already begun, even if they were directed to fellow Christians instead of the pagan Indians whose souls he would save.

The same was true during their stay at Puerto Rico, where they arrived on the Feast of St. Luke, October 18th. This meant a quick crossing for those days. Even so, everybody disembarked for a stay on dry land, and for the obtaining of the fresh water of which they were in sore need. Apparently the captain announced that the passengers during this stop would have to fend for themselves, which probably indicated that his supplies were about exhausted but also, perhaps, that he knew they would get on much better in this way. Why, things had been so hard that they had not been able to get so much as a cup of chocolate, so parsimonious had the captain been with water! Though the friars were without any money worth mentioning, they had to do their own foraging during a stay in the port that lasted fifteen days.

They did fare very well, as it happened, for the Puerto Ricans vied with one another in bringing them things to eat and drink and even forty dollars in money. Palóu tells a little about this but more comes from a letter that Serra wrote to his Franciscan nephew in mid-December from Vera Cruz, when they had landed on the mainland. One notes with a little amusement that the presents Serra most appreciated were those of tobacco and chocolate. We shall often hear of how much the missionaries suffered when they could not get what was, for Spaniards, an indispensable drink. Often the measure of their hardship was that they were obliged to drink coffee instead of chocolate! It is pleasant to observe that Serra was glad to take small creature comforts (including tobacco) when they came his way, though without complaint when they did not, as was usually the case. Some Mallorcan inhabitants of the island came forward, too, with offerings of meat, fruit and cakes and candles, for they had no oil for lamps. They were all housed, not uncomfortably, in the Hermitage of the Immaculate Conception, which was just outside the city. This was, one would gather, the kind of caravanserai for travelers still provided in some parts of the Orient.

If the friars were so well looked after, it was largely because Serra—misunderstanding something said by the friar in charge of the party—announced a mission at the cathedral, with the use of the Hermitage as an annex, necessitated by the crowds that came. Yet Serra deprecates his own eloquence, as compared with that of some of the other priests. "My preaching was as different from that of the other two Fathers as straw from gold, snow from fire, night from day." His measuring rod seems to have been that when the Father President preached one could hear the sighs and sobs of the whole congregation, and that many of the people returned home still in tears. But as for himself, though he shouted as loudly as he could (and he had, remember, a stentorian voice for one so diminutive), he did not hear even so much as a single sigh. From this he concluded that he was "the only one who did not have that interior fire which inflames the speech and moves the hearts of those who listen."

It could be, however, that Serra failed (if he really failed at all) because he was trying to adopt an oratorical style not natural to him. More likely he was too modest about his own performance. Whatever his lack of success in the pulpit, he showed an exemplary zeal in the confessional, entering it at three or four in the morning and remaining there until midnight—something that challenges comparison with the Curé of Ars. The mission was of great benefit to everybody. The Puerto Ricans who, so one would infer, had been rather neglected spiritually, now profited from this visit from a shipload of priests. Serra was glad of what could be done for them but also records with satisfaction that, because of the generosity of the people, the priests were better fed during their stay than they would have been in any convent.

The stay was so long, presumably, because some repairs had to be made to the vessel by which they had come. But on the 31st of the month they all embarked for what was to be the last lap of the journey to Vera Cruz. No sooner had they spread sail than they found themselves in danger of running aground, which meant that they all had to get off again and spend another day in Puerto Rico. This gave them an opportunity of saying Mass on All Saints' Day. And the saints did come to their help. When almost within landfall of the Mexican coast a storm of such violence suddenly raged down that many of the friars gave themselves up as dead men. In that predicament somebody suggested that each person on board write the name of his favorite saint on a scrap of paper and that the one whose name was drawn from a hat should be the saint to whom they should all commend themselves. Serra tells his nephew that he wrote the name of St. Francis Solano and Palóu that of St. Michael. Neither was drawn but instead the bit of paper on which was written St. Barbara. Upon this the whole group with one voice shouted, *"Viva Santa Barbara!"* That there was something more than mere chance in all this is suggested by the fact that the so narrowly averted shipwreck occurred on December 4th, the day on which the Church commemorates St. Barbara. Though the name of St. Francis Xavier did not appear (though his name was probably one of those dropped into the hat), it is worth remarking that on December 4, 1552, he was buried, on the day following his death, for the first time, on Sancian Island within sight of the China he was never able to enter. That great missionary's protection may be presumed to have been extended to this shipload of fire-bright missionaries for the Indies of the West.

However this may be, the salvation really did appear to have been miraculous, for at once a great calm descended, so that by the 6th they crept, crippled, into the roadstead of Vera Cruz. Not until the 10th, the day on which they landed, were the unnautical eyes of the friars able to see how close they had all come to death. The ship was leaking and without a mainmast, and the officers assured them that they could not have kept at sea a single day longer in that condition. When they all assembled in the Franciscan church at Vera Cruz for their Mass of thanksgiving, the sermon was entrusted to Junípero Serra, though again in his letter to his nephew he deprecates his "poor talents." He gave, he says in this letter, a complete account of everything that had happened during the voyage; which, if taken literally, would have meant that he would have delivered an inordinately long discourse. Presumably he confined himself mainly to an account of the perils they had survived the previous week. At that time a journey across the Atlantic was always full of danger. He wrote home at length as he did to reassure his family as to his safe arrival.

CHAPTER FOUR

Mexico

VERA CRUZ was then, as it still is, the most important port of Mexico. The harbor into which Cortes had sailed in 1520 was hardly more than a narrow channel running in from a flat, barren, torrid coast, protected against the seasonal hurricanes—through one of which Serra had just come—only by a line of reefs and small islands. But as such it had to serve until engineering skill in the nineteenth century could build the needed breakwater. It was the line of Cortes' march to Mexico City that Serra and the friars who had come with him were now going to take.

Already the descendants of the *Conquistadores* had effected many changes. While the harbor itself had not as yet been greatly improved, its defenses had been strengthened by the erection of the fortress San Juan de Ulua on one of the islands guarding the approach. This had been a matter of necessity, for twice, in 1653 and 1712, it had been pillaged by pirates; once by a band of eight hundred men led by a blond ruffian of whom an admirer had said, "His only fault was his impatience and a habit of swearing a little too frequently." To prevent such a thing from happening again, San Juan de Ulua mounted about a hundred and twenty-five guns and therefore was quite strong enough to drive off any marauders.

The city itself, though now secure and prosperous, remained very unhealthy because of its swamps, which brought on a peculiarly nasty type of malaria whose

symptoms are described by its name, *vomito,* and also
yellow fever. The miasmas were more dangerous to life
but not more unpleasant than the sands which during the
winter (and it was winter when Serra arrived) blew in
on the northwest winds and made breathing itself difficult.
For these reasons nobody lived at Vera Cruz except those
who had to, though its position as a port made it indispensable. It was filled not only with soldiers and sailors
but merchants engaged in a lucrative trade. Serra and
Palóu cut short their stay in so unhealthy a place, but
it was long enough to bring Palóu close to death, while
Serra suffered a mishap which, without ever being particularly dangerous, was to hamper him for the rest of
his life.

The Franciscan rule, when strictly observed, demands
that the friars go everywhere on foot. Only after the pain
caused by his stigmata made him unable to hobble more
than a few steps did St. Francis permit himself the luxury
of an ass. Franciscans of our own time of course very
sensibly recognize that they cover distances far more
quickly by train and car than by trudging along in sandals.
And many Franciscans of the eighteenth century accepted
the nearest equivalent to a train or automobile for the
same reason. It was suggested to Serra that he ride on
horseback along the hundred miles to Mexico City, especially as the authorities had provided this form of transportation, but he refused. Possibly this was because he
was a poor rider; more likely it was because he wanted
to be completely Franciscan. Though he did not suspect
just what was involved in a terrain so difficult as the one
he proposed to subdue on foot, one must add that in later
life, while fully aware of the hardship involved, he always
walked, even when he had, in the company of soldiers, a
good mount available.

To be as unpractical as this may seem to verge on the pedantic. But there is (or may be) after all something to be said for the unpractical point of view; in Serra's case he got to his destination slowly but it is at least possible that the merit he acquired by sacrifice made the work done more fruitful. Palóu was allowed, on account of the sickness through which he had just come, to travel on one of the horses provided by the Viceroy, but Serra asked permission of the friar in charge of the group that he and another Padre be allowed to go on foot. "So," says Palóu, "they both set out without other guide or provisions than the Breviary and a firm confidence in divine providence." Franciscans indeed!

Just how they managed we do not know, for though Palóu learned something about their journey later, and tells us some fascinating stories about what he had heard, he was necessarily vague about many details. We hear of the two friars once being lost at night and being guided by a well-dressed Spanish stranger to his own house, where he provided them with food and beds. In the morning, when they left the house for the church to say Mass, they found the roads all coated with ice and realized that they would have perished if the stranger's help had not come. Later, when all wearied from the heat of the sun and the roughness of the way—evidently they encountered varied weather as they climbed up towards the central plateau from the coastal plain—a man offered them a pomegranate, promising that it would refresh them. That it did is hardly to be wondered at; what made the two friars wonder was at the complete and instantaneous removal of their fatigue. So Palóu continued: "Having noticed the effect of the fruit they began to talk about the person who had given it to them, for from his aspect and mode of speech, he seemed to be the same person who the night before had showed them the ford in the river and given them the hospitality of his house." That is charming but, as will be seen at once, very naïve; had this really been the same man of course they would have recognized him instantly. One cannot help but suspect that this is a variant of another story which Palóu relates further on in his book—a much more astonishing story but one which I am more disposed to believe, if only because of its greater artistic verisimilitude. However, I do not wish to be captious. Both incidents could have happened, but as Palóu tells them only at second hand, he may not have got all the details quite correctly. It would not be extraordinary if he should sometimes be hazy about matters that had not come under his personal observation and that could not be checked by any document he (or we) possessed.

Now there comes a matter about which there can be no question, and it was of greater consequence in the long run than the sickness which nearly carried off Palóu at Vera Cruz. During the journey Serra's lameness started. He was only thirty-six and of wiry build, but of all things in the world a mosquito bite nearly robbed him of his usefulness. Miss Repplier finds it so hard to believe that she turns it into a snake bite, which is a mere improvisation on her part and one which she introduces without a word of apology or explanation. I am afraid that in this matter—as in most—we shall have to stick to Palóu.

Yet it was not the bite itself that caused the damage but apparently an infection, which eventually spread as far as Serra's knee. One feels that if only he had been willing to get competent medical treatment in Mexico City, the trouble would soon have been cleared up. But all men have their little oddities; Serra's was a disbelief in doctors, in spite of which he lived to a good old age—to that extent justifying himself. In this instance one supposes that he simply dismissed the matter as of no consequence, for what real harm could be caused by a mosquito bite? However, his partial lameness is what everybody noticed about him, in spite of which they also noticed that he never let it bother him but covered more ground than most people do on two sound legs.

Mosquitoes are not unknown in Mallorca, but I am told that those of the Mexican Gulf are of a huge and terrible species. Even so, it was scratching at the sore place that did the real harm. And the absurd little accident could of course have occurred had Serra traveled on horseback or even in one of the great coaches of Mexico, as years later he did, though rather against his will.

The road—in many places it was a trail or a series of trails—was fairly well defined because of the constant stream of traffic, but sometimes it was almost lost as they pushed through rocky and shaggily overhung defiles to mountains that rose about 7,500 feet above the sea from which they had started. They felt they had done well when on the afternoon of the last day of December, 1749, they reached the celebrated sanctuary of Our Lady of Guadalupe. It was eminently fitting that they should approach their goal in this way, for here was the shrine of the poor, especially of the poor Indians. It was there that they passed the night before continuing the further league or so to the College of San Fernando, the Franciscan organization with which they were to be associated and which was to direct their work.

The story of the devotion to Our Lady of Guadalupe has often been told, but a few facts about its origin should be given here. It was in 1531, only ten years after Cortes had taken possession of the Aztec capital, that an Indian, baptized now as Juan Diego, upon reaching the brow of a rugged hill known as Tepeacac, heard the most wonder-

ful music and saw above him a brilliant light. A Voice
called him by name, and when he answered the Lady appeared. She announced herself as the Mother of God and
told him to go to the bishop saying that it was her will
that a temple be raised on that spot to her honor. The
Indian pleaded his lowliness and begged that somebody
more illustrious be sent, but at last he went to the Franciscan Bishop Zumárraga, who, naturally supposing that
the poor fellow was suffering from a delusion, dismissed
him with a few noncommital words. It was no use; the
Blessed Virgin sent him back again, a second and third
time, finally with the sign the Bishop had demanded. She
told Juan Diego to carry in his mantle some of the flowers
he saw growing around. When the mantle was opened in
the Bishop's presence, it showed a painting of Our Lady
herself, depicted as a beautiful Indian maid.

At this point the prudent, the cultured and the skeptical
have a right to ask a question. Who painted that picture?
If its origin was heavenly would one not expect a better
work of art than it is, though it is not negligible as such
and definitely is not to be called a "primitive"? Though
I am not prepared to give any positive answer, there are
a few considerations to bear in mind. No Indian of that
time can be imagined to have had the skill for such a
painting. Moreover it is equally beyond any style that a
Spaniard could have produced, which makes it impossible
to believe that it could have been fabricated. Even a very
gifted Spanish painter—and where could such have been
found in Mexico?—would not have understood the Indian mentality well enough to produce something that
so strongly appealed to Indian taste. But heaven—only
heaven—would have understood. As a subject for art criticism the painting must surely be one of the most curious
in the world.

Even so, the possibility that there was a hoax was investigated then, and many times since. When the not only permissible but imperative archaeological tests are applied, we are confronted with the facts that Hubert Howe Bancroft—no friend to Catholicism or much of a believer in anything beyond the historian's weights and measures, but an honest man—was rather bewilderedly obliged to set out in his *History of Mexico:* "In 1835 a formal investigation was made with regard to the genuineness of the existing painting, from which it was discovered that its identity with the one miraculously depicted on the mantle of Juan Diego, was not proven until its removal from its place on the old altar on account of repairs, when attention was attracted to its extraordinary weight. Examination revealed the fact that it was attached to the top of Zumárraga's table, on which was an inscription by the bishop, certifying this the true and original picture. The painting had been stretched upon five boards, solidly jointed together by tree-nails. The carpenter, who accompanied the committee, testified to the antiquity of the boards, while the wooden nails were like those used by the Indian carpenters in the bishop's time."

That the evidence shows the picture goes back to Zumárraga's time must be taken as irrefutable. However, it might still be said that the Bishop had made himself a party to a hoax. It is inconceivable that anybody—whether Indian or Spaniard—in the Mexico of the Conquest could have produced a painting of just this sort. So a later historian, H. I. Priestley, in his *Mexican Nation,* while gratuitously suggesting that the cult was a "clever device" to give impetus to the campaign of conversion, is obliged to add that "frequent investigations of the alleged miraculous painting have failed to establish any other than the mysterious origin claimed by the early ecclesiastics." I mildly submit that the circumstance that the conversion of the Indians was furthered by the cult in no way points to the cult having been a "clever device" and that Professor Priestley surrenders all the objections he might have raised as a philosophical skeptic by the admissions which, as a historian, he is compelled to make. One might more reasonably suggest that the Mexican revolutionaries who, since the time of Hidalgo in 1810, have fought under the banner of Our Lady of Guadalupe, did some contriving. But that too would be silly: They naturally took advantage of any kind of popular appeal, and in Mexico there has never been an appeal so popular as this.

The fame of this shrine had rung throughout Spain. It was to have been expected of Junípero Serra that he would go first to that sacred spot, just as many other missionaries and failures and discouraged sinners have done before and since. Not until that duty was done did the two friars complete their journey to the College of San Fernando near the Alaméda, just outside Mexico City.

There was a university there, one founded soon after the conquest, and also about forty colleges and seminaries in the country, though of these only half prepared their students for the taking of degrees. The university had a great dignity, however, as is attested by the fact that its Rector had the privilege of being attended by Negro lackeys who carried sidearms, something resented by the Viceroy and Archbishop, as they did not rate such a bodyguard. But the University of Lima once petitioned (unsuccessfully) that their doctors also have the privilege, as the prestige that would result would induce more men to seek postgraduate degrees!

San Fernando was primarily a seminary for the training of missionaries, though most of the men it obtained were priests ordained abroad; but since 1734 it had also been a center from which operations were directed, bishops not always being able to exercise their jurisdiction in the remote parts into which the friars went. It was with San Fernando men and under the direction of the San Fernando Guardian that Junípero Serra worked for the rest of his life.

There Palóu was anxiously awaiting his arrival, and because he was there he was able to give the exact date, something that he always did when it was within his power. As this was a seminary, which accepted novices in Mexico as well as those who came from overseas, there was a more than usually strict discipline. The rules laid it down that "indispensably every day they shall devote two hours to mental prayer, one in the morning and one in the evening," in addition to the ordinary community exercises. All the friars were withdrawn as far as possible from outside contacts so that their energies should not be frittered away before the time came when each man was assigned a task to which he was expected to devote the full force of his being. Lest the community grow too unwieldy for management, it was limited to thirty, of whom four could be lay brothers. San Fernando was small and compact and all the more important for that reason.

Palóu probably was one of a crowd of friars who greeted Serra fairly early in the morning of New Year's Day, 1750, when the Guardian said, "I wish I had a forest of such Junipers!" It was a pleasant but rather obvious jest, and of course was a quotation from the *Fioretti,* St. Francis himself having tossed this out about the Brother Juniper who has been too often represented as a sanctified clown who was not far from being a half-wit. The allusion was one which of course every Franciscan would have instantly caught. Though no doubt the Guardian at San Fernando had already heard Palóu sing his former professor's praises, he did not necessarily believe all that he had been told. Being a prudent man, he meant to keep his eye on Serra before deciding upon his assignment.

Fray Junípero made a good impression from the start by asking that he be admitted to the novitiate, to live exactly like the novices. But there was evidently some doubt as to the advisability of allowing a man in his thirty-seventh year to do so, for the youths under training would be more malleable if they were kept as a group apart. However, a compromise was made: Serra was to have his cell in the main part of the friary but might attend the special exercises of the novitiate; for he might have been a somewhat alien element if he had slept in the novices' dormitory and taken part in their prescribed recreation. Under the method hit upon he would give edification and at the same time strengthen his own spiritual life, or, as he had put it to Palóu in Mallorca, regain the fervor he had had while a novice. Perhaps it was partly because of this zeal, but no doubt also because missionaries were urgently needed for the Sierra Gorda that the period of preparation was in his case reduced from the usual year to five months.

For the rest of Serra's life, even when he went to Lower and then Upper California, Mexico City was the point from which his operations were directed, though for the most part he was, of necessity, allowed a fairly free hand. Some account of the situation there is necessary to understand his subsequent career. The city conquered by Cortes must always be one of the wonders of the world, a kind of inland Venice, being largely built along the shores of its lakes, connected by causeways and canals, so that parts of it seem to be floating on the water. Most of the ancient Aztec monuments had long since been obliterated—all of them without exception that had been associated with the hideous pagan religion whose main feature had been the offering of human sacrifices on a scale never approached before. But the Spaniards had substituted many magnificent works of their own—aqueducts, roads, wide and shady squares and splendid palaces. The spot was still pointed out where Alvarado is said to have made his famous leap, and the oak under which Cortes sat and wept on the *Noche Triste*. Indians of course were everywhere, for they were relied on for most of the manual work, and there were also a good many Negroes. Yet in spite of the fantastically glaring contrasts that existed side by side, Mexico City was, or seemed to be, as Spanish as Spain itself.

Few suspected, or weighed accurately, the many subtle changes that were occurring—least of all the explosion that was to come when it became manifest that the Spanish empire was in decline. Behind the superb and rather too ornate façade even the granite and marble had begun to crumble, for all human institutions are built upon men, and in this case there were elements that were seething with secret and, so far, inarticulate animosities.

Salvador de Madaríaga has provided a brilliant study of the causes of the decline. It was not merely that the *mestizo,* with his mixed Spanish and Indian blood, was already at war with the *Conquistadores;* he was also at war within himself, as was true of the mulatto and the octoroon and of all the other racial shades that had come into being as a result of an unchecked miscegenation. It was much to the credit of the Spaniards, both as men and as Christians, that all the subjects of the Crown were theoretically and legally equal. The seething that went on would probably have been quite ineffectual had it not been for the numerical predominance of the Creole, by which must be understood those of pure white stock born in the Spanish overseas dominions. They tended to look down upon the

"Europeans" (as they were called) as effete—for that is the way of colonials—and to resent it bitterly that the Europeans got nearly all the best appointments in the civil and ecclesiastical administrations. They had a real grievance against this policy of the Crown, which was designed to prevent power passing to men who might favor relatives and friends; and it must be added that those who came from Spain, having been near the source that dispensed offices, naturally were in the best position for securing them.

The rank and file of Indians had, in the past, often been roughly used, and the *encomienda* system, which had been supposedly introduced for their protection, was in practice often used for their exploitation, and of the most rapacious sort. On the other hand, many Indians had become more or less assimilated by the Spaniards. The hereditary chiefs were exempt from the payment of tribute, were addressed as *Don,* were permitted to ride horses and bear arms, and were little if at all socially below the descendants of the *Conquistadores.* In Mexico and Peru some of them headed rebellions. One of them, the Inca José Gabriel Condorcanquim, *curaca* of Tungascua and Marquis of Oropesa, just before Serra's death, headed a widespread revolt under the name of Tupac Amaru II. In short, when one bears in mind the attempt to weld so many diverse elements one can only say that while it is true that the imperial dream eventually faded, its failure does no more to discredit Spain than the Declaration of Independence on the part of the English Colonies to the North does discredit to England. Indeed, Professor Herbert E. Bolton says truly in his *Outpost of Empire:* "Spain's loss of her colonies was the best evidence of her success in transplanting people and civilization." [1]

[1] P. 9.

By the time that Serra arrived in the New World the period of military conquest was considered over, except for occasional flurries, and the conquest had passed to a new agency, that of the missionaries. The missionaries of course had always accompanied every Spanish army, which looked upon itself as engaged in a crusade, but peace was now normal, and what remained to be done could be brought about more effectively (not to say more economically, an important consideration) by the cross than the sword. The object was by civilizing and Christianizing the pagans—those who remained unconverted—to bring them into the Spanish scheme of society. Especially was this true of the as yet unreduced tribes, for so it was that their submission was termed. The civil administrator and the soldier in this had come to be looked upon as mere auxiliaries of the friars.

Though Spain's Bourbon King, Charles III, was a poor specimen of a human being in many ways—the portrait of him by Goya suggests that he was close to being half-witted, which, however, he was not—he was, despite a foreign policy almost uniformly disastrous, well served at home, and still more in the colonial dependencies, by a succession of able and devoted officials. We shall see that although Serra often had occasion to complain of the official underling in immediate contact with his work, he was usually befriended by those above. He would have been even more fortunately situated were it not that the central administration in Spain, while supposed to be tyrannical, was, if only because of the vast distances, obliged to leave the day-by-day decisions to the Viceroy and his Council, and they often ignored the wishes of the Crown and its advisers. Though in the matter of the expulsion of the Jesuits from the Spanish dominions in 1767 the King acted ruthlessly (as he did on a few other occasions), ordinarily the Indies were allowed to do pretty much as they liked.

The Crown, however, was jealous of the right given it by the Holy See to a jurisdiction over the administration of the Church that was quasi-pontifical. The King named bishops and sent them to their dioceses without even bothering to wait for the Papal confirmation. "Had writers on the Spanish Inquisition," remarks Father Zephyrin Engelhardt in one of the appendices to the first volume of his *Missions and Missionaries in California,* "considered this position of the Church in Spain, they would have avoided making themselves guilty of most unjust and ridiculous accusations." Yet had there not been very solid advantages to the Church in the *Patronato Real* it would not have been permitted; because of this the Crown, in working out for the missionaries a large and important part in its program of colonization, gave the missionaries protection and support. Serra benefited as well as suffered from it; without bearing this constantly in mind, his story cannot be properly understood.

Nevertheless a certain degree of skepticism was already at work in some of the highest circles. Though it is possible to exaggerate this—and it seems to me that Fathers Engelhardt and Piette, especially the latter, have used bright colors where only a faint tinge is justified—Spain, in spite of the enthusiasm of its masses for Catholicism, and the official Catholicism of everybody, was not unaffected by some of the ideas of the "Enlightenment." The minister of the Crown, Count Aranda, was more than suspected of what it is convenient though not quite accurate to call Voltairianism, and another minister, Count de Florida-blanca, derived some support for his ideas from the Encyclopaedists. Measured by this standard one would have to say that Charles III, while formally devout, found it desirable to circumscribe the influence of the Church though using it to further his designs.

One thinks of the Spaniards as a proud and inflexible people. What will seem surprising is their elasticity, as it will appear in these pages. Upon the whole they were extremely mild in their rule, sometimes forbearing even from the reprisals that one would have imagined prudence demanded. That they had so often been accused of cruelty in the past may have made them now all the more careful to give their foreign enemies no handle against them. The great official or military officer—at any rate when encountered abroad—rarely corresponded very closely to our picture of the grandee. The style of address even between intimate friends was almost ludicrous in its ceremoniousness, yet for usual purposes a shirt-sleeve informality was adopted when it was useful.

This adaptability was further exemplified in the way that important posts were found for foreigners of ability. Many of these were of course Irish, as the Gaels of that time could not often find an outlet for their gifts at home, and many of them had become naturalized and had modified the spelling of their names. Most of them were to be found in the army, but Lacy was the Spanish Ambassador to Stockholm, Mahoni the Spanish Ambassador to Vienna. O'Reilly was the Minister of State who reformed the infantry, and in Mexico we find a General Oconor, his name a bit transmogrified, as was that of the Mexican President of recent years, Obregon. In Serra's time a Felipe Barri (sometimes it appears as Barry) was briefly a Governor of the two Californias. But Italians were also taken into service, and we shall find Serra dealing with a Belgian Marquis de Croix as Viceroy and later very unhappily with a nephew of the same name. It is clear that, whatever else was true of the Spaniards, they were not encased in their own dignities but willing to give large opportunities to men of almost any nationality. Perhaps it is also significant that more than half of the Jesuits soon to be expelled from Lower California were not of Spanish blood.

"Above all," remarks Madaríaga of the Spaniards of that period, "they had style." Their prototypes were the *Conquistador* and the friar. Though the age of the Conquerors had passed, their epic greatness was not forgotten. Honor was the quality prized above all others, not least when it took the form of Balboa falling on his knees at the sight of the Pacific or Pizarro, dying from a sword thrust in his throat, making the sign of the cross in his own blood. Juan Bautista de Anza, whom we shall meet later, was cast in the mold of the Conquerors, even if he was mainly an explorer. And Serra was of the same breed, though it was for him to lead a peaceful conquest.

There is another and less noble aspect of the matter. Although one cannot but note how mild and moderate was the Spanish colonial rule at this time, how free from venality, how much more edifying these administrators were in their private lives than some of their predecessors, it was inevitable that luxury springing from wealth sapped the fiber of many people. We do not find any of that barefaced rapacity which Francis Xavier in the sixteenth century so fiercely denounced among the Portuguese of the East Indies—though no doubt it could have been found, especially among the lesser men—but Mexico City was famous for its opulent living. The Spanish Crown was constantly pressed for funds; the untold wealth of Peru had vanished, nobody could say just where, except that as the supply of bullion increased prices rose accordingly. Yet the Spanish dependencies were still great places for making quick fortunes. The gorgeous palaces of Mexico City told the tale; so did the great caparisoned coaches, which were far more numerous than those of Madrid. One little detail is in some respects more revealing—and here we have an exact parallel with Xavier's Goa—the way over-fed and overdressed women, lolling on their cushions at church, had to be fortified, even there, for their devotions with cups of chocolate. Oh yes, they went to Mass, even if their menfolk were sometimes remiss. But they demanded luxury, even at Calvary. This they considered their in-alienable right. And when a bishop of Chiapas attempted to stop this practice he was poisoned—as was fitting, in a cup of chocolate! On this account there came into vogue the proverb, "Beware the chocolate of Chiapas!"

Those gentlemen who had not yet attained splendid coaches rode on saddles encrusted with gold and silver. Many a hatband was completely made of diamonds, and even the tradesmen in their shops, so we are told, possibly with some exaggeration, sported their strings of pearls. Meanwhile lounging in the sun were Indians in their rags, often a scrap of greasy blanket their only garment. It might have been a harder task to convert Spaniards of this type than to go into the desert in search of savages who had never heard the name of Christ. Or it might have been so, were it not that where the loathsome luxury of the new rich was flaunted, there were also many who showed an honest attention to duty and a highly efficient handling of public business. This was especially true of officials who might have given themselves to amassing fortunes, as will be illustrated by some of the carefully prepared documents relating to mission affairs which we shall see.

During this period Serra—though it would seem at a time when he was visiting another place, and not because there is any record of his denouncing chocolate-drinking women—came near to being poisoned. Somebody had put

venom into the communion wine with the result that he
was taken very sick at Mass. Palóu said he had been poisoned, which may be the case, though it might have been
merely that Serra had an upset stomach from some other
cause. At any rate he was carried to his room and an antidote brought him. This he refused, as he could see
through the glass of what horrible compounds it was made.
His explanation was that under other circumstances he
would have swallowed the nauseous mixture, but not after
having just received the Sacred Species. This was not an
instance of his habit of refusing all medical aid—though
here was one time when it might have been justified—but
of his piety. Without the antidote he recovered. It was
this quality which pulled him through many a tight spot
where a more prudent man would possibly not have fared
so well.

But though Serra was not much addicted to denuncia-
tions, he had a terrifyingly effective way of making his point.
It must be remembered that he was of an Iberian race
that has always been drastic in its methods. Sometimes, in
public penance for his sins, he would beat his breast with
a heavy stone in the pulpit, or scourge himself with a chain.
At least once a man ran to him and seized the chain to
scourge himself, crying that it was he and not the Padre
who deserved it. And we hear that upon at least one occasion he opened out his tunic and put a lighted candle
against his flesh, so that those nearby could smell the burning. In this he took a leaf out of the book of Francis of
Solano, though he never, like Francis, threw himself upon
a bed of live coals and stayed there a moment or two, while
his Indians gazed in horror. Then he told them that what
it would have been impossible to endure longer, those in
hell must endure forever—and a fire compared to which
this earthly fire was nothing. With Serra, as with Solano,

this was done not as a mortification but to bring home to the dull minds of Indians what they might not learn except by such violent means. It might have done the overfed, overdressed Spanish women some good, too.

Junípero Serra was not an ascetic as we ordinarily understand the term; indeed, the days of old-style maceration had passed in favor of an internal conquest of the will. St. Francis de Sales, and in fact almost every writer since his time, has deprecated a merely physical asceticism, so that probably only in Spain or its dominions could one have found even as much as Serra performed. What he did should be considered nothing more than part of the work to which he had dedicated himself. Similarly, if he was never known to pay a merely social call while in Mexico City, this was not because he considered all such calls a waste of time (though a very large proportion of them are) but because he wished to remain undistracted, to canalize all his thoughts and energies to the missions. A social life could have had no possible relation to what he was preparing to do among the Indians.

As he lived under the rule of obedience, he left to those who were in charge of San Fernando's College the choosing of the time and place for him. Had it been decided to retain him there in some capacity, he would have acquiesced, though he would have been disappointed. In fact later he came close to being elected Guardian and did serve a term as novice master. In either capacity he would have been doing missionary work, even if at one or two removes, in the training and directing of others for the missions. But though without impatience, he rejoiced when at last word came that he was now to go out to preach to the savages. His time had arrived.

CHAPTER FIVE

Work Before Lifework

THE WORK to which Junípero Serra was sent in June, 1750, was not the work for which he is mainly remembered. It was not so much as thought of then that he was to be a missionary in the California peninsula, for the Jesuits had been given that field. The idea that he should eventually be selected to head the missionaries who moved into an Upper California which at that point was still completely unoccupied would have staggered his imagination. Before that venture was attempted political considerations had to arise which so far had not even shown themselves. He did not guess that his lifework would not start until he had reached late middle age; he was quite satisfied with his commission to go to the Indians of the Sierra Gorda, over two hundred miles northeast of the capital.

About this period we know a good deal less than about Serra's California years, though Palóu was with him at the time. This is because Palóu centered his narrative upon Serra's last and most important period, passing over everything else lightly. And though reports were made about this first phase of work, they do not have any great importance because they were of a routine sort involving no special problems. In fact, until Father Piette's studies of Serra, this aspect of his life had been somewhat neglected, and no doubt still further information will appear with the publication of the exhaustive biography on which

73

Father Maynard Geiger is now at work. Inadequate though my account of the matter is bound to be, I hope it will at least show that the experience he garnered in the Sierra Gorda prepared him for what he was eventually called upon to do.

Junípero Serra, accompanied by Francisco Palóu, left the quiet regularity of San Fernando's College and, on a journey requiring nearly a month, walked to what was to be his headquarters at Jalpán in Querétaro. Although he was relatively young and a newcomer, he had already won a reputation, as is indicated by the fact that he was immediately elected as head or president of this group of missions. But distrusting his lack of experience, he contrived to evade the responsibility until, when Bernardo Pumeda was elected Guardian of San Fernando in May, 1751, Serra was put under obedience to accept it. Pumeda showed that he had been greatly impressed by Serra during his five months in Mexico City, and presumably reports had since then reached him from those working in the Sierra Gorda as to Serra's qualifications. Even so, Serra resigned three years later, saying, according to Palóu, "If this office is an honor, then let others share the honor also—likewise if it is a burden."

We have records of Serra's only twice leaving this district, first in the late summer of 1752 and then in March, 1758. It was characteristic of him that when a matter of especially important business had to be dealt with he found it more advisable to consult in person those at the head of things than to write, though this involved a long journey on foot each way. In 1752 he journeyed to Mexico City to urge the appointment of a commissary of the Inquisition for the Sierra Gorda, stating his reasons first by word of mouth and then formally in writing. This request we know to have been made on September 1st, with the result that the office was given to Serra himself three days later. His powers, however, were not limited to the Sierra Gorda but extended to the whole of New Spain. Serra's reasons for asking that a commissary be appointed will appear very soon. I note now only that his second visit occurred because he had been summoned to give evidence regarding a legal case bearing upon precedence within the college. He no doubt found this an annoying interruption to his work, but of course he obeyed cheerfully; after all, the efficient operation of the directing agency at San Fernando depended upon all such questions being decisively settled.

The district of the Sierra Gorda was an ellipse of five churches grouped in the rugged mountains. This great range has sometimes been called the Switzerland of Mexico, though except for its height it is not very like the Alps. The loftiest of the summits lie somewhat nearer the coast than Serra was, rising in one instance to over 18,000 feet, in two others to not much less; towards the east the section of the mountainous backbone that runs from north to south of Mexico drops somewhat, but still has a giant of 14,220 feet. Most of them are extinct volcanoes, and all are thickly covered with forests that make them beautiful and nearly impassible. Some paths, however, are to be found, although they often lie along the edge of stupendous chasms. Now and then everything opens out to offer a sight that calls to mind the Grand Canyon. Father Piette says that the traveler there often has the impression of beholding the creation of the world. Whatever the majesty of the scenery, Palóu was not at all enthusiastic about the climate, which he found hot and humid and detrimental to health. It must have been trying to men from the island paradise of Mallorca.

The Pame Indians whom they had come to convert

seemed to like to do nothing but "prowl the mountains like wild beasts," in which respect they were not unlike the Indians later encountered in California. Like them, too, they were not at all inclined to establish settlements and to cultivate fields, though this would, after the preliminary work, have given them food and comfort without much expenditure of effort. This was all the worse in their case because they had no sea from which they could obtain fish. A real problem lay before the missionaries in how best to Christianize and civilize them. The two operations had to be pursued simultaneously, for a veneer of social order would soon have been stripped off unless it were also a manifestation of the religion they professed. But though they were savages they seem to have had a fairly high degree of natural intelligence. By working among them Serra gained invaluable knowledge and experience.

The mission in the Sierra Gorda had been begun in 1744 by friars sent there from San Fernando's College, and they had selected five points not too far from one another, so that at least within the ring so formed there would be some chance of effecting the objects at which the missionaries aimed. Two priests were assigned to each station and at each a wooden church with a thatched roof was built with the aid of those Pames who would help, but with more reliable assistance from the Christian Indians brought from Mexico as colonists. A military governor was located at Jalpán, with a captain, lieutenant and ensign under him and a force of soldiers sufficient to overawe the Pames, should any of them prove fractious. A few men were spared as a guard for each of the dependent missions and as an escort for the priests when they had occasion to move from one base to another. There were no troubles that we hear of, probably because the Pames had heard of the decisive-

WORK BEFORE LIFEWORK 77

ness with which the Aztecs had been subdued and therefore did not dare be other than submissive.

The management of the temporal affairs of the missions
remained in the hands of the Padres, and the civil and
military authorities understood that only by holding out
material benefits could the Indians be induced to make
settlements near the missions. Yet these were not missions
in the Californian sense; the Indians simply lived in their
huts nearby but they owned (if they ever really understood
the term) the lands they cultivated, planting seed as it was
supplied them and using implements whose purpose they
had been taught. Everything, including the livestock they
raised, had to be sent them from the outside; and nothing
so supplied would have been much use to them without the
direction of the friars.

It should be noted that the secularization of the missions
was the plan envisaged from the start by both State and
Church. This should be borne in mind in relation to what
happened in California. As John Tate Laming writes in
his *Academic Culture in the Spanish Colonies:* "The idea
was that the religious orders should serve parishes only as
long as secular priests were not available. But this yielded
to harsh facts—the worldliness of the secular clergy and
the poor material of the neophytes." Pope Innocent XI
had directed that as soon as the Indian missions were
sufficiently advanced they were to be turned over to the
local ordinary, who was to put a secular priest in charge.
We find the Franciscans in June or July of 1770 offering
their Sierra Gorda territory to the Archbishop of Mexico
City, and when he declined, the Viceroy, Marquis de
Croix, having been appealed to, put pressure on the Archbishop to accept these churches for his diocese. Indeed, in
their own way, the Franciscans themselves applied pressure—though it was to the Viceroy—when they promised

thirty missionaries for California only on the condition that they be relieved of missions that had been in their care for twenty-six years.

The rules and regulations regarding spiritual affairs were somewhat rigid, so one would think, for savages; but here Serra took over a system already existing. All had to gather at sunrise in the church, "both men and women, those who have been baptized and those who have not, as well as the neophytes without a single exception." Later experience made it evident that this rule could be applied only to those who had accepted baptism. The Christian doctrines were explained to them in classes held three times a day—the adults, the adolescents and the smaller fry in separate groups. It may seem surprising that these doctrines should have been taught in Spanish, of which few of the Pames could have known much, but according to the legal code, they were subjects of the King of Spain and could satisfactorily become so only through assimilation, in which language was the main instrument.

At Mass on Sundays and holy days everybody had to be present, and to make sure that they were, each member at the close of the service had to answer a roll call. Moreover, to prevent any kind of subterfuge—for instance, getting one person to answer for another—all present had to go up in turn and kiss the missionary's hand. Attendance at Mass was encouraged even on days when it was not compulsory, and those capable of spiritual development were exhorted to receive the sacraments. Much of this strikes us as rather impracticable, but it was all aimed, whether advisedly or not, at these untutored Indians' good. One of the things enjoined upon the Fathers was that they "carefully try to do away with enmities and quarrels among the people, teaching them to live in peace and Christian love and be careful to see that there be no scandal or evil example in the missions." Yet how little was being accomplished is indicated by Palóu when he notes that on account of the Indians' lack of knowledge of Spanish, and the friars' lack of knowledge of Pame, "there was not a single one who fulfilled his obligations to the Church by coming every year to confession and Communion." He also tells us that when the census was taken, those settled near the missions numbered 3,840, from which it must be inferred that they visited the missions more for the food they hoped to obtain than out of any desire for Christianity. As to what was eventually accomplished we shall hear in a moment.

But first a glance must be given to the kind of paganism in vogue among the Pames, since this was the main obstacle to the work of the missions. The Sierra Gorda was quite unlike California, where there was no idolatry and the very vaguest religious ideas of any kind. In 1752, as we have seen, Serra sought the appointment of a commissary of the Inquisition, an office given to himself. This gave him authority to eradicate any pagan worship by positive suppression. Here on one of the highest mountains there was a temple, rough in structure, in which was housed what Palóu describes as "the well wrought face of a woman, sculptured on a block of marble." It was that of Cachum, the Mother of the Sun, tended by an aged Indian who performed the duties of a priest. Though in all probability Palóu's account of the matter is rather incomplete—if only because he could not bring himself to take much interest in such things—there was in this instance what must have seemed to pious Spaniards a blasphemous parody of the veneration of the Blessed Virgin, which was all the more reason for stamping it out. Serra managed to destroy Cachum's temple, for Palóu mentions that when he left the Sierra Gorda he bore off that idol as a trophy.

To reach Cachum one climbed to the summit of the mountain by a stairway cut in the solid rock, along the sides of which, as on the summit itself, were the tombs of Pame chieftains. For whatever reasons the Indians first visited the missions, it was apparently to Cachum that they repaired when they needed something really badly, such as rain for their crops, or the cessation of a pestilence, or a safe journey, or success in war, or the obtaining of a wife. In fact it was there that they went to be married, the custom being to carry a scrap of paper on which nothing was written—for they did not know how to write—but which was received by the priest as a token of marriage. (One surmises that the Indians had seen the Padres make mysterious signs on paper and knew that these had something to do with religion; they now quite literally stole a leaf out of the Christians' book.) Whole basketfuls of these bits of paper were found by the Spaniards, together with the images of a number of minor deities, all of which were destroyed, with the exception of the massive idol of Cachum. This had been regarded by the Indians as so extremely sacred that their priest kept it covered up, allowing it to be seen only by pilgrims from a distance and those who brought him adequate offerings.

Such is the account given by Palóu of the matter, which may not be too reliable. But it would seem that this idolatry was of a very primitive sort and had few if any general theological ideas, such as we understand them, connected with it. It may have been a secret vestige of what was customary before the Conquest, though without any of the abominations of human sacrifice; gory rites which the dominant Aztecs reserved to themselves. Palóu gives an astonishing detail which he says he received firsthand from the sergeant sent with a platoon of infantrymen to burn the hut that housed the chief idol. Three or four times they set fire to it, but it would not burn—though only constructed of dry branches and thatch—until the sergeant used the conjuration: "Put fire to it in the name of God and our Most Holy Mother!" whereupon it immediately went up in flames. A thick disgusting stench came out, and this they attributed to the Devil's having been driven away. The soldiers took that opportunity to burn the huts of the Indians living on the mountains so as to drive them down to the settlement prepared for them, which it is to be hoped was done on the initiative of the sergeant and not of the missionaries. Though Palóu advances no opinion about this, he says that Serra, after he had learned the Pame language better, obtained some further information from the neophytes, and that it was they who brought him the image of Cachum. The idol, he says, was placed in the archives of San Fernando, but presumably must now be somewhere else in Mexico City as the college itself no longer exists. At all events the practice of idolatry in the Sierra Gorda was put down with a strong hand. That was something not to be tolerated by the Commissary of the Inquisition, though no compulsion was exercised to make the natives Christians.

Gradually the work progressed, though it was laborious, necessitating the formation of a completely new mode of life for the Pames. Under the instructions of the missionaries, and with one of them always working beside the Indians, each year more abundant crops were obtained, those of corn, chili, beans and pumpkins being specially mentioned. Moreover, as the Indians became accustomed to the notion of work and private property, they were assigned as individuals what they had been holding communally, so that they cultivated their own strips of land, and tended their own cattle. They were also encouraged to sell whatever they could make and with the money obtained to buy horses, mules, and clothing, though apparently they were not permitted to sell their holdings, which was a wise provision when one considers the improvident character of these particular Indians.

Nor was this all. Artisans were imported from Mexico City and these, while plying their trades, taught them to the Pames, so that a considerable degree of skill was attained in masonry, carpentry, blacksmithing, painting and the like, while the women learned to spin, to weave and to sew. They were able to sell their products at Zimapán and Huasteca, mostly grain and ropes twisted from palm leaves. The plan worked not only for the benefit of the imported colonists but for the erection of some fine churches, the wages for the skilled artisans coming out of the profits. It was all accomplished without running into debt, a real achievement. Yet this had been brought about among a people only recently sunk in gross savagery.

By degrees the makeshift mission churches were replaced by structures which may still be seen. Probably some technical advice was given by the artisans brought from Mexico City, but Serra himself, if not the actual architect of the fine if somewhat florid church built at Jalpán, at least inspired it. It was at his urging that the Indians brought stone for the masonry and sand for the lime and mortar. The work, says Palóu, was steadily carried out through all seasons free from rains, except when it was necessary to sow grain or harvest it. At the end of seven years they had a church measuring fifty-three yards long and eleven wide, with a vaulted ceiling over the altar and a smaller vaulted ceiling over the adjoining sacristy. Not only that; there was a gilded communion rail and side altars and altarpieces. Even an organ had been brought from the capital, as well as a man who could play it and teach the Indians how to sing the Masses. If that is not sufficiently remarkable, Palóu tells us how at Christmas some of the Indian children "dramatized in a devout colloquy the birth of the Infant Jesus"—a miniature miracle play!

Serra was nine years in the Sierra Gorda, part of which time he acted as President, in which capacity he had to make the rounds of the five churches, not confining himself to Jalpán. All this should be borne in mind in relation to charges that have been made (they are much less frequently heard today) that his methods, though nobly intentioned, had the effect of reducing the Indian neophytes to perpetual dependence upon their missionaries, thus destroying their initiative. Here is the proof that his purpose was to raise up the savages until they were capable of standing on their own feet. If in California the goal aimed at was not reached, this was because the Indians there were of a still lower grade than the Pames. Moreover, in California it was impossible to secure any stonemasons—at best only a few carpenters and blacksmiths—so that the mission churches had to be built in the simplest possible way and by the Indians themselves under the direction of the Fathers. And there communal ownership of the mission property proved to be under the circumstances the only feasible plan—that and work in which each of the neophytes had his designated role.

Reports must have gone to Mexico City and from San Fernando have reached the Viceroy that Serra was just the man to head a new mission field he hoped to open. This was on the San Sabá River in what is now Texas, a district about four hundred miles away from the capital. Its conversion was to be a joint undertaking on the part of the Franciscan colleges of San Fernando and Querétaro, and to Serra it had the attractiveness of the great danger already thoroughly demonstrated. For the Comanche Indians, a tribe like the fierce Apaches and long a byword as thievish marauders, had wiped out most of the friars sent them. Nothing could have been more seductive than the prospect of martyrdom.

The upshot was that Fray Junípero returned to San Fernando on September 26, 1758, quite expecting to go to San Sabá but finding upon his arrival that the expedition had been countermanded; therefore he had to hold himself in readiness for another appointment, though with lingering hopes that the road to the Comanches would open before long. It was a delay that, as events were to show, was to last for nine years, and it seemed for a while as though it would permanently hold him at the college, but it was a delay that helped further prepare him for the great task ahead.

We know that two months after his return from the Sierra Gorda he received twenty-five votes for the office of Guardian in the Chapter held on November 25th, but his election was not confirmed by the Visitor General, probably because Serra was considered too valuable a man to spare from the active life of the missions. However, he was elected (and confirmed) as a "discreet" or councilor, serving until the end of 1761, the confirmation probably being given because it was not an office which would have prevented transference to some other field. On November 28, 1761, at the triennial Chapter, when again he was chosen as Guardian, the Visitor General once more intervened against confirmation. But he was permitted to become master of novices, holding this position for three years.

He now was charged with the delicate task of developing the inner life of those who were, in their turn, to become missionaries. Nevertheless he seems to have combined this with a good deal of preaching, mostly near the city, as long absences would have prevented his keeping in close touch with the young men whom it was his duty to form. And he also continued as Commissary of the Inquisition, though this does not seem to have been a very heavy burden. It had been useful to him mainly for the uprooting of idolatry in the Sierra Gorda.

As to Serra's own piety Palóu tells us that whenever he was at the college he was most faithful in the saying of the choral Office and that this filled up six hours of every day. (One concludes from this that the Franciscans there maintained the midnight saying of Matins and Lauds and that everything was given a Carthusian solemnity.) Not content with what was prescribed, he was always found present at voluntary devotions, such as the recitation of the rosary or the making of the Way of the Cross. One would almost get the impression of a man who was devout in a somewhat formal fashion, were it not that Palóu, when they were on some journey and staying for the night in a hut, would be awakened by hearing him say, *"Gloria Patri, et Filio, et Spiritui Sancto,"* and would ask anxiously, "Father, is there anything the matter?" only to find that Serra was praying in his sleep. Yet from Serra's own letters he appears as a good, hard-working, practical man, engrossed in external concerns, and not what one would call a mystic. Had he been constituted otherwise, it might have seriously interfered with the labors he was called upon to perform.

Another office he undertook, at the special request of the Guardian, was that of vicar of the choir. Palóu says somewhat quaintly that he accepted it "because he was not called upon to sing so very much." It has been noted that for so small a man he had a very resonant voice, but one would have to infer from Palóu's comment that it was not a particularly tuneful voice. When one remembers St. Francis Solano and the violin to which he was so much attached, it would seem that Junípero Serra was not much like him in musical gifts, closely though they resembled each other in some respects. As vicar of the choir he probably had to arrange for those who took individual parts in the chanting of the Office, without having to do much more himself than join in the communal chant.

It is perhaps not necessary, or even advisable, to burden the reader with names of places in Mexico which he might find hard to identify on a modern map. The important thing is that—except during his period as novice master, when he had to remain near the city—Serra traveled back and forth to the great mining camps of Zimapán and similar spots, where nearly all the laborers were Indians, at least nominally Christian and in many instances devout in their own fashion. About seven months in the year were spent in preaching and hearing confessions in these stations, another two in traveling (invariably on foot) and the rest of the time in that very essential spiritual recollection with which he strengthened his soul for another such excursion. It is to be feared that the lot of those to whom he ministered was hard and that, whatever their legal rights may have been, they were so often exploited as to have been reduced to virtual peonage. They lived in squalor, huddled together in shacks, eating poor food, with a blanket their most serviceable garment. Yet the Padre did not live in a comfort greatly superior to theirs, for when he had had the dignified title of the President of the Missions of the Sierra Gorda, his habit was usually in tatters, his bed merely a board, and for mantle he was himself content with an Indian's blanket.

During these missions Serra repeated his customary observance of Good Friday. Then at the Veneration of the Cross Palóu used to observe that Serra supplemented this by carrying on his own shoulders to the Chapel of Calvary he had erected on a little hill nearby a cross so heavy that

Palóu, a younger and more robust man, could scarcely lift it. The Thursday before, after having washed the feet of twelve old Indians and eaten a sparse meal with them, he delivered a sermon on Christ's washing of His disciples' feet in the Upper Room. On Good Friday in the church edifice he used to preach in the morning on the Passion; in the afternoon the Descent from the Cross was represented in most lifelike style by means of a figure which had limbs movable with hinges. It was not strictly liturgical, though as much of the prescribed liturgy was used as was practicable; the important thing was to bring home to the Indians mysteries that were difficult for them to comprehend unless presented in some dramatic way.

Although as Commissary of the Inquisition Serra's powers were extensive, we hear of his being directly concerned, during these years, in only a single case; it was that of a mulatto woman who in 1766 was charged with sorcery. He signed the initial document but, as he was summoned to preach a mission, he arranged for the appointment of a secular priest to act as his substitute. Yet Palóu may be correct in saying that in discharge of his office he was called upon to labor in many different places and to travel a great many leagues, fulfilling every one of the duties he was called upon to perform to the satisfaction of the Inquisitors, who regarded him not only as a wise minister but as a most zealous one in his defense of the Catholic faith and religion. However, as Palóu did not see Serra very often, he had only a general idea about his doings and may have imagined that he was occupied with matters connected with the Inquisition when he may in fact have been engaged in something quite different. Though we may be sure that Serra was conscientious, the truth is that in Spain, and still more the Spanish dominions, the Inquisition was by this time no more than a shadow of its former self.

In these missionary journeys on foot Serra covered what would have been considerable distances for any man, but were doubly hard for one who was lame. In addition he always ran dangers from dark-browed men living in the woods and ravines as outlaws, and suffered the extremes of heat and cold in that rugged country, with its multitude of noxious flies and reptiles. But one fears that Palóu was drawing a bit upon his own imagination when telling about the "tigers and lions" that Serra often encountered, unless under these terms he was thinking of animals which, while ferocious enough, are not quite the same. These wild creatures he would have us believe made it unsafe for Serra to disembark from the canoe he used on some of the rivers, but, if so, were not the alligators an equal menace? Serra was never a man to say much about any dangers he ran, and though these were often very real, he usually dismissed them with a smile and a deprecatory wave of the hand. Palóu, however, was always available with a little embroidery, being on one side of him very exact and precise and on another inclined to relish marvels.

In the eleventh chapter of his *Vida* he scoops together a handful of what he calls "minor incidents," some of which are rather startling. We hear of one mission during which an epidemic broke out; it was found that of the sixty who died, every single one of them had neglected to go to confession to Fray Junípero. Then he has the story of Serra's inducing a woman who had been living with a man as his mistress to leave him, upon which the man, unable to persuade her to return, hanged himself from the iron bars of a window of his house. This in itself, though distressing, would be a common enough tragedy were it not that Palóu says an earthquake occurred at the very moment when the body was discovered in the morning. But it should be noted that Palóu, while relating the sort of "minor incidents" calculated to foment piety (and perhaps also be useful in an eventual process for beatification, were this ever started), never tells us that Serra performed any miracles but only about a kind of supernatural "fringe" surrounding some of these happenings.

The most charming of all these stories, and the one I find easiest to accept, is the story that Willa Cather tells so beautifully and with some embellishments in her *Death Comes for the Archbishop* (legitimately, I think, since she was writing a novel and not a life of Archbishop Lamy). Palóu relates how Serra and his companion, on a lonely road in the desert at nightfall, saw a small house nearby, whose only vegetation besides cactus and thornbushes was three cottonwood trees. Going there to ask for lodgings, they found a venerable man with his young wife and child, by whom they were given most kind welcome. In the morning they thanked their hosts and continued their journey until they met some muleteers who asked them where they had spent the night. Upon being told, they exclaimed, "There is no house anywhere within leagues of here!" Serra and his companion returned to have another look at this humble house, and found the three cottonwood trees easily enough but no habitation of any kind. Then the two friars, remembering the cordiality with which they had been received into so poor—but so clean and neat—a place, could only believe that they had been entertained by Jesus, Mary and Joseph.

CHAPTER SIX

The Fabled Land

THE NAME California is first to be found in a work of fantastic fiction. This was *Las Sergas de Esplandian* by Ordonez de Montalva, which was published in 1510, long before any European foot had been set on it and without the slightest relation to geographical facts. It was one of the books listed by Cervantes as among the favorite reading of Don Quixote. There California is described as a land east of the Indies where dwelled a race of black Amazons. "Their island was the strongest in all the world, with its steep cliffs and rocky shores. Their arms were of gold, and so was the harness of the wild beasts they tamed to ride; for in the whole island there was no metal but gold." When not long after the conquest of Mexico the "island" was discovered—it was not positively known to be a peninsula until two hundred years later—the name California was reserved to the lower part. What we now think of as California was then so remote as hardly to enter into anybody's consideration. And when it was settled at last, it was at first often called Monterey, after its main center, to distinguish it from what continued to be thought of as California proper.

Cortes was the first to go to the Peninsula, sending an expedition there in 1533 and going in person two years later. His soldiers and their officers were so disappointed with what they found that they wanted him to waste no more time on such a desolate region. Charles V meanwhile, now that the existence of a real California had been established, tried to prohibit the exportation of Montalva's book to the Indies lest it give too romantic a *Conquistador* wrong ideas on the subject. Their heads were receptive to almost any tale, especially where lands of fabulous riches were concerned. Even after the sea expedition sent out under Francisco de Ulloa in 1539 ascertained that this was a peninsula, earlier concepts prevailed and the majority of people thought it an island, and of course incredibly rich.

As we shall see, the Pacific coast further north was more often visited by adventurous seamen in search of the Northwest Passage. Then it was discovered that there was fairly good harborage at San Diego, Monterey and what is now called Drake's Bay, just north of San Francisco Bay (which was consistently missed), whereas the Peninsula did not offer more than a roadstead of little or no value. Now and then a privateer dropped in there for a day or two to refit or for water—something not at all easy to find on that barren coast. Among those who came early in the eighteenth century was Alexander Selkirk, the prototype of Robinson Crusoe, after he had been rescued from Juan Fernandez Island off Valparaiso. That detail is more amusing than important; for practical purposes it may be said that only the shore facing New Spain was generally familiar. Monterey's existence, however, was known, and from what Viscaíno had said of it after his visit there early in the seventeenth century it was supposed to be a magnificent harbor.

Yet the west coast of the Peninsula, though offering nothing worth calling a port, has a delightful climate (of which promoters of health resorts are now beginning to take advantage), handicapped only by its inaccessibility. Except immediately after the season of torrential rains, when it comes out in sudden brief bloom, the rest of the Peninsula is arid, treeless, sultry and unhealthy. It drops from the central chain of rugged hills to a bare, sandy shore. Cactus, rattlesnakes, scorpions and tarantulas complete the dreary picture. The only reason that the Spaniards held on to it was that it possessed a port not too far from the mainland and that the Peninsula, even after its mines of gold and silver were shown to be mythical, was supposed to be opulently productive of pearls. Moreover it protected the Spanish flank as a bastion and was useful because of trade with the Philippines.

The pearls did exist and there were a few enterprising people who fished for them successfully. Yet in general that source of wealth was meager simply because the Indians brought up the oysters and devoured them before really good pearls had had a chance to develop. Nevertheless, rumors about these fabulous pearls were so widespread as to contribute a good deal to the ejection of the Jesuit missionaries. These rumors were more readily believed because it was a fact that Père Lavalette, their Superior in Martinique, had gone in for trading and banking operations on a large scale and had ended in bankruptcy. Though (or because) Lorenzo Ricci, the General of the Society, repudiated the debts, on the ground that Lavalette had acted in contravention of the Jesuit constitutions, great indignation was aroused. In 1760 it was reported—quite falsely—that a Venetian merchantman had arrived at Cadiz with a cargo of Californian pearls, and it was believed that vast treasures had been hidden away. Some even professed to have information as to their value—$4,000,000. It was obviously necessary to get rid of these Jesuit Fathers so that the Spanish Crown should obtain what rightfully belonged to it.

All this fitted in with a new attitude towards religion

found in some of the highest Spanish official circles. No Spaniard would have admitted to being anything but a good Catholic, but many were disposed to be suspicious of priests. In California the Jesuits were imagined not only to be gathering a great hoard for the furtherance of their world-wide designs but to be living in luxury with their neophytes reduced virtually to the status of slaves. Concerning this, one of their number, the Belgian Jacob Baegert, scornfully commented: "Kings indeed! . . . kings that drank with the horses, ate corn with the chickens, and often slept on the ground with the dogs. A great honor, really!" But as so often the important thing is not what is true but what is believed to be true, the Jesuits were summarily ejected in 1767. Had it not been for this, in the ordinary course of events they would have expanded into Upper California when that region was annexed by Spain.

The consequences of this drastic action were many, not all of which were even faintly foreseen. Salvador de Madaríaga, a writer who cannot be considered to have clerical sympathies, says, "The King of Spain with his own hands cut the most solid link between his Crown and his subjects overseas"—this not because the Jesuits were invariably supporters of monarchy but because the popularity they enjoyed would have been a powerful brake on all revolutionary tendencies. It is worth noting that in Spain and its dominions the ejection of the Jesuits preceded the Papal suppression of the Society by six years, an end to which several of the monarchies were working but which nobody could be sure would ever be achieved. When on February 3, 1768, the Fathers of the Peninsula assembled for their last High Mass, they embarked on the waiting ship to the tears of their neophytes.

Only half of the Jesuits working there were Spanish, even if we include the Mexican-born. The rest were Alsatians, Germans, Croatians and Italians. Even one Scot, William Gordon, was sent there in 1730. The most celebrated of the Jesuits was the Tyrolese Eusebius Kino, who died in 1711. This great explorer—though it had been known before—at last brought home to the world the realization that Lower California was quite certainly not an island. His story has been brilliantly related by Professor Herbert E. Bolton in *The Rim of Christendom*, a book whose only flaw is that, while its author is uniformly friendly towards the Catholic Church, he hardly seems to be aware that a priest says Mass and recites his Office, a curious blindness side by side with a charming affability.

Although the Jesuits had no treasure, they provided for their work in California by means of the famous Pious Fund, which still exists and about which we shall hear more. So far from drawing upon the King for support, they actually relieved him of the major part of the expense he would have incurred, since provision for missionaries was rightly looked upon as part of the process of civilizing the savages and bringing them within the Spanish order. The most lavish of all the contributors to this fund was the Marquis de Villa Puente, who gave away the whole of his immense fortune (though only part of it for this purpose) before entering the Society of Jesus in his old age. The very first donation was staggering, that of $20,000 from Juan Caballero y Oziom, but on the same munificent scale was the generosity of the Duchess of Gandia. Her letters to Father Kino (or rather the correspondence between them) are now in the Huntington Library in California, purchased at the advice of Professor Bolton for $18,000. In an article in *The Americas* (Vol. VI, No. 3, p. 359) he makes the pleasant jest: "Bigger sums have been paid for letters written to a lady, but seldom for letters written to a lady by a Jesuit priest." The Duchess had expressed a wish to contribute to missionary work in the most distant and forlorn place that could be suggested, and Father Kino could think of none that more exactly coresponded to her specifications than Lower California.[1] The total sum available was very large for those days but was doled out with a niggardly hand. Yet without it Spain might have been a good deal more hesitant about embarking upon its venture in Upper California than it was. Surely no ecclesiastical fund paid higher dividends in the material order, and what it made possible spiritually cannot be measured.

Palóu tells us that the government at first intended to put secular priests into four of the old Jesuit missions of the Peninsula, doubtless with the intention of using none but seculars as soon as these could be obtained. On such terms San Fernando was not at all eager to accept the charge and may have agreed to supply missionaries only because, as Father Piette thinks, the Franciscans were afraid after what had happened to the Jesuits of annoying the Viceroy by a refusal. This is far more probable than Mrs. Abigail H. Fitch's flat assertion (which does not have a scrap of evidence to support it) that the Franciscans connived at the expulsion, of which they were informed in advance. The truth is that not even Croix, the Viceroy, had any inkling of what was afoot until he opened and read the decree, hidden under several wrappers, which ordered that "at the pain of death" he was not to read it until the

---

[1] The Fund, first administered under the direction of the Spanish Crown, was in 1842 abrogated by Santa Ana, the President of the Republic of Mexico, who, however, pretended that he was only borrowing it. A partial restoration occurred later, but it was not until 1902, after the settlement of the question of the ownership of the Fund that had been before the Hague Tribunal for arbitration since 1869, that Mexico was condemned to pay $1,460,682 in cash and $43,050 to the Church in California every year in perpetuity. The state of this fund at the time that Palóu wrote is indicated in detail on pp. 222-224 of the first volume of his *Historical Memoirs of New California*.

appointed day. It ordered him to carry out the royal will to the letter, sparing not even the old or the ill or the dying. All were to go at once, taking with them nothing except the clothes they wore and a Breviary.

To Serra the news that he was to go as President of the missions in Lower California brought joy, whatever may have been the views of those in charge at San Fernando's College, though it is to be supposed that all of them deplored the rough handling their Jesuit confreres had received. He had worked patiently and very hard during the past nine years, since his recall from the Sierra Gorda, but all this, though fruitful in itself, was not quite the same thing as having a settled center, where he could know every soul intimately and guide them all to their destined place in heaven. Yet he had shown no impatience, obeying cheerfully the decisions of his Guardian, taking it as the will of God. Now even though San Fernando may have acted under some constraint, Serra was at last given what he would have chosen for himself.

Or so he thought. He did not realize that crosscurrents were at work—that sending the Franciscans to the Peninsula was hardly more than an interim arrangement, that the Dominicans were very anxious to have this field allotted to them, and that even after the Franciscans had obtained it, it would be proposed that they share it with Dominicans. He may have been informed that the Order of Preachers had powerful friends in Spain, and that these included the King himself. Even so he could hardly have foreseen that the Franciscans would have to withdraw before long in favor of the rival order of friars, though under an amicable agreement and not by suffering a rude expulsion like the Jesuits.

He could not have guessed that he was to be commissioned for the field further north, for while Spanish expansion into what we now think of as California was already being talked of in Spain, no decision about this was reached until Serra had settled in the Peninsula, quite expecting to remain there, and being caught with surprise when the new instructions came. He supposed he was to take over the fifteen missions from which the Jesuits had been forced, and for the rest of his life operate from the ramshackle little settlement of Loreto, trudging up and down the seven hundred miles of the arid tongue of mountainous land on his tours of inspection.

Even so, there was an unexpected delay before the Franciscans got to their work at all. The ships built on the Pacific coast were all rather poor and unseaworthy, for the reason that, while shipwrights could be sent to the naval station of San Blas, hardly anything except the wood they needed was obtainable locally. Therefore all the metal, the sailcloth, the caulking and the nautical instruments had to be sent by mule train from the capital. Consequently, so much economy had to be exercised that it was not possible to build good boats under such conditions. With what they had they were, in later years when greater efforts were made, to perform prodigies, but largely because of stout hearts and skillful seamanship. At this stage even to cross the Gulf of California from San Blas to Loreto was a hazardous undertaking, though in a straight line (could this ever be followed) it was only a journey of four hundred miles. Therefore the order commanding the Jesuits to leave took some time in reaching them, and it took still longer to round them all up. Serra and his friars had to wait from August 21, 1767, until March 14th of the following year before they were at last able to embark.

Serra had, however, already discovered that the missionary field is a school of patience; he had also discovered that delays did not necessarily mean idleness. As during the much shorter stay in Puerto Rico eighteen years previously—when after the buffeting of the long voyage across the Atlantic the friars would have been well justified in taking several weeks' rest—he at once found something to do by sending out those under him to preach to whatever Spanish settlers or Indians they could find. But at last, after taking six weeks to cross the Gulf, they made landfall at Loreto on April 1st, Good Friday, in time for the celebration of Easter, an auspicious day.

The mission at Loreto had only recently been completed. It contained by far the best house in the place, which Gaspar de Portolá, the Governor, had already appropriated as his official residence, and Serra and his companion had to take lodgings with him, having no house of their own. Portolá was a Catalan of good family and a captain of dragoons, forty-six years old, who had been sent to the Peninsula to eject the Jesuits. Though the bluff captain was a likable person and friendly to the newly arrived Franciscans, he had arrived with instructions from the Viceroy that soldiers were now to be stationed at each mission to administer the temporalities which had hitherto been under the care of the Jesuits. It was a very awkward situation, but neither Serra nor Portolá could do anything about it, and it speaks volumes for them both that then and afterwards they managed to get along so well together.

Fortunately that situation was rectified soon afterwards with the arrival at Loreto of José de Gálvez, the *Visitador General* recently sent over from Spain. He had come armed with powers superior even to those of the Viceroy, and his title, as Father Engelhardt suggests in his *Missions and Missionaries in California,* might be best translated as "Inspector General." Though he did not intend to stay long in the Peninsula, his presence being needed in the rather thickly settled province of Sonora to the northeast of the Gulf, he recognized at once that the new arrangement would be very hampering to the Franciscans, if only because of lowering them in the eyes of the Indians. He instantly ordered that the administration of temporalities be restored to the missionaries and in every way showed himself their true friend.

He had come to Loreto with a new plan; it was to send Portolá with a column of soldiers to the unexplored district to the north—what constitutes the present State of California. There they were to establish presidios at several points, and also three missions (as a start) for the conversion of the Indians, the easy and economical way of bringing them into the Spanish system. But before we come to that scheme, only now at last decided upon, it would be as well to say something about Gálvez, especially as Father Piette several times goes out of his way to sneer at his "altar-boy" piety, though allowing that it was sincere if somewhat limited in its manifestations. Even if Gálvez was antagonistic to the Jesuits and not very favorable to the Dominicans, the Franciscans certainly had no reason to complain.

José de Gálvez was of the new school of Spanish officials. So far from being of noble stock, his father had been a farmer (though of fairly good birth) and young Gálvez in his youth had done his full share of hard manual work. But he was able and ambitious and energetic, so that after a bishop had become his patron and had sent him to an ecclesiastical seminary, he finally managed to study law, to enter the civil service where he made a mark, and now had become invested with large authority. Though not long afterwards this somewhat saturnine, horse-faced man had a violent spell of insanity, he recovered and for the services he had performed was created a marquis and, upon returning to Spain, was made a minister of state, dying in office well advanced in years. His biography has been written by H. I. Priestley.

What he did in the way of suppressing the Indian rising in Sonora, in introducing new fiscal methods to New Spain and laying a heavy hand on any form of "graft" when it was discovered need not concern us, though these themselves were things of major importance. What is much more significant to us is the farsightedness he displayed in taking possession of the lands to the north before Russia was able to push down there from the Aleutians. While it would be too much to say that this policy was initiated solely by him, at least he had advocated it and was the man selected for carrying it into effect. Fortunately he found in the Viceroy, the Marquis de Croix, a man who for the sake of the common good laid aside the jealousy that one of baser metal might have felt; Croix might have hampered his plans but instead strongly backed them. It is evident that Spain was well served by the officials of the time, and though King Charles III made blunder after blunder in his European policy, thereby weakening his country and earning for it the reputation of decadence, Spain was by no means exhausted in its imperial role, even though its military and naval forces were weaker than formerly. In fact, we find it now about to demonstrate that along the Pacific coast it was prepared to dispute possession with any rival power, but in particular with Russia, whose aims were known and feared.

The bearing of all this upon our country needs no argument. But it might be worth pointing out that European statesmen were well aware that the Czars, like their successors the Bolsheviks, set no limits to the imperial expansion for which they thirsted. Nor did Spain, so far

as the Pacific coast was concerned, set—at least not in theory
—any limits to its own expansion. We know from the paper
of instructions from Spain sent on by the Viceroy to
Gálvez, that a definite if limited order had been given
that, on account of the Russians, he must at least try to
establish settlements at San Diego and Monterey. It was
a venture he was most eager to direct.

The ships he had at his disposal were two newly constructed packets known as the *San Carlos* and the *San
Antonio,* which had the alias of *El Principe,* together with
the boat upon which Serra had crossed the Gulf and a
fourth, still abuilding, named the *San José.* It was little
enough but it had to serve. But so as not to put all the
Spanish eggs in one basket, and also because an escort of
soldiers would be needed for the mule train and some
cattle, two expeditions by land were planned along the
rugged mountain range that ran the length of the Peninsula.

Before we come to Spain's new venture, it should be
looked at in its historical perspective. Peter the Great, who
died in 1725, conceived the idea of finding a passage from
the Pacific to the Atlantic by driving east. It was therefore
due to him that Bering made his expeditions of 1725–1730
and 1733–1741, in the second of these discovering the
strait that bears his name, coasting the American mainland
and investigating the possibilities of the fur trade. In the
years that followed there was a rush of traders to the
Aleutians and ships were built on Kodiak Island, the chief
market being China. All this made Spain very uneasy,
especially in view of a growing friendship between Russia
and England, Spain's traditional enemy. No action was
taken for a long while but at last in January, 1768, Grim-
aldi, the royal Minister in charge of such matters, sent
Croix orders to resist any move on the part of the Russians.

It was in furtherance of these orders that Gálvez acted as he did.

It should be noted that though Russia was nothing to Spain in its general foreign policy, whereas England was of immense importance, so far as California was concerned Russia was regarded as by all odds the main threat. Of course had England had any designs on the Pacific coast it might have found means of carrying them out, though its hands were full of other concerns. But it was considered that, the world situation being what it was, England would hardly have men and ships to spare for a new enterprise on a large scale, whereas Russia could without much difficulty push down from Siberia and its possessions east of the Bering Strait. If Spain had few men to spare for California, so need Russia have sent only a few; what mattered was a force not large and strong enough to resist a large-scale invasion—for that was hardly feasible—but large enough to maintain military and civil establishments in the country. It was not necessary to sink a lot of money in the venture, but merely enough to get a firm foothold, though, as subsequent events were to show, Spain later made excursions as far as the Arctic Circle to forestall any Muscovite machinations. What swifter, easier, cheaper and more praiseworthy effort could be made than to send out missionaries to effect a peaceful conquest for Christ and the Spanish Crown? The soldiers who accompanied them need only be numerous enough to offer them protection from the savages and to prove, in case the Russians put in an appearance, that this was Spanish land.

If Spain had not extended itself into Upper California, it may be taken as certain that the Russians would have claimed the territory, all the more so because they would have calculated that England would do nothing. As it was, the Russians were soon made aware that any movements they made were being closely watched. Spain not only intended to hold what it had but to expand still further. Gálvez, then, arrived in Loreto to put in motion the first stage of the new colonization project—the digging in at Monterey. Portolá was put in charge. Having been sent to Loreto to eject the Jesuits, he was on the spot, available for a task that had to be performed without delay. An honest soldier, he was without any notable capacity, and it may well have been that Gálvez would have picked somebody else had there been sufficient time. Portolá's instructions were that, though he had been given the title of Governor, he was to hand over his command to a younger man as soon as Monterey had been located and a presidio set up there; and that he himself should then return to Mexico.

Portolá acquitted himself well, yet probably nothing would have been accomplished had it not been for the fact that Gálvez found in Serra the man of genius and spiritual passion he needed. Portolá, while perhaps no more easily discouraged than most people, lacked the grim determination called for by his assignment. But as for Serra, even from the secular and political point of view, it was, as Father Piette puts it, "an inestimable windfall for Gálvez to come upon in the Peninsula a collaborator of this quality." As we shall see, after Portolá's fumbling attempt to locate Monterey had failed, he would have withdrawn disheartened, had it not been that Serra refused to give up.

Serra remained for over a year at the mission of Loreto. The Peninsula in itself seemed hardly worth occupying. The land was poor and the Indians there of a lower grade than those of the Sierra Gorda. Palóu, who gives a fairly full account of them in the first volume of his *Historical Memoirs of New California,* for he remained after Serra had departed, says that when the Franciscans arrived they found that all the former Jesuit missions together contained only a total of 7,149 Indians, "counting even infants at the breast," and that when the Franciscans handed over the missions to the Dominicans only three years later, the number had declined to 5,094, and "if it goes on at this rate in a short time Old California will come to an end." The main reasons for this were the constant epidemics and the prevalence of syphilis, for the records kept by the individual missions, and cited by Palóu, show a considerable preponderance of deaths over births and baptisms. But he also complains of the action of the local officials who in spite of the fact that Gálvez had put the missionaries in charge of temporalities, in practice often ignored the instructions. Palóu says that the royal Commissary, Antonio José López de Toledo, announced that he had come with the understanding that everything in the missions was at his disposal, while another officer said that "if the Fathers did not send what he asked he would go with soldiers, unlock the granaries, and take it by force." Though this of course happened after the departure of Gálvez, it reveals a good deal about the attitude of the officials and military officers towards the missionaries. It was not at all helpful, for the more the soldiers demanded, the less there would be for the Indians, and unless there was food to give them, there was no chance of making headway in the missions.

One wonders how, in view of their lack of water, their inertia, the difficulties they had in raising crops, the Indians of the Peninsula had managed to survive as long as they had. In the north (in what is now California) the climate was so good, game and berries and roots so abundant, that little effort had to be made. But to the south, says Herbert Ingram Priestley in his *Mexican Nation*,[2] "at

2 The Macmillan Co., 1923.

all times, except during the pitahaya [prickly pear] season, hunger seemed to be the normal condition. They tracked the flight of buzzards with eager eyes, and followed them to share in the bodies of the dead animals that might have perished by accident or by the jaws of the pumas that infested the land. Even carrion was a treat of the highest value in their famished lives." Add to that, tuberculosis and smallpox and what the Elizabethans called the "great pox," and it is not to be wondered at that the Indians were a dying race. Though Serra had accepted his commission to them with joy, even his energy and efficiency would hardly have been able to accomplish much. One cannot but see that, happy though he had been when sent to the Peninsula, he was glad to get out.

Though Serra was in charge of the mission a little over a year, and left friars behind, the greater part of that time was spent in preparing for the expansion northwards. In this Gálvez showed his characteristic drive. The form that it took was often surprising, for though he was the Viceroy's superior, it was not at all beneath his dignity to assist in person at the repairing of the ships, taking off his grand coat and, with sleeves rolled up, pitching in with the workmen. Can this be imagined of any Lord of the Admiralty in England? The very fact that he had risen upwards from somewhat lowly origins would in itself, one might think, have made him all the more insistent on all the outward signs of the exalted position he had reached. Quite the contrary in Gálvez's case. And the help he gave was of a very practical sort, for when it was discovered that the supplies of caulking were exhausted, he suggested that a substitute could be extracted from the local cactus, and though the experienced shipwrights told him that this would be of no use, it was found to be perfectly adequate. By his resource he saved several months of delay, as by his resolute verve he urged everybody to the further exertions needed. All this was noted down with no flattering gush of enthusiasm about the Inspector General's "democracy"; that much was taken for granted, the only surprise expressed was over his capacity to get things done with dispatch.

He exhibited this same drive in helping to pack ecclesiastical supplies for the missions that were to be founded. These were gathered from such missions in the Peninsula as could spare them, because there was no time to send to Mexico City for new vestments and church plate and furnishings. A careful list, which we still have, was made of everything that was taken, but no indication is given that much of the altar plate was tarnished and dinted, many of the vestments old and soiled and even tattered. This fact emerged later, though one might have guessed as much, since these articles were taken from the old Jesuit missions, where they had had long service; and we may suppose that the best of them were left behind with the missions.

The point to be made at the moment is that the packing of these church supplies by Gálvez gives Father Piette the opportunity to make another slighting reference to the piety of the former altar boy. Well, it is probably true that the altar boy's experience may have come in handy on this occasion, but it is much to the credit of Gálvez that he displayed the expedition so characteristic of him. The long-faced, tight-lipped man even challenged Father Serra to a kind of contest. Each of them would pack for a separate mission—and Gálvez beat Serra, and humorously boasted of it. Neither Gálvez nor anyone else could foresee that "his" mission of San Buenaventura, though one of the three first projected, was, because of the dilatoriness of minor officials in California, the ninth and last mission that Serra was to found. Until then the crate of ecclesiastical goods that the efficient Gálvez had packed remained unused.

The alarming mental breakdown that the Inspector General was to suffer before long was due, one suspects, to the way he remorselessly drove himself. One rejoices to record a marvellous recovery, and a long, honorable life afterwards in the service of Spain.

José de Gálvez, in short, deserves the highest praise for the part he played in the venture into "New" California, for though he was only carrying out orders received from Spain, other officials might have executed them in a perfunctory style, whereas he threw his whole heart and soul into the project, thinking everything out, taking all possible measures to insure its success, and never sparing himself. He was very fortunate in finding in Junípero Serra, a man he had never met until this time, one who, while somewhat small and not very commanding in presence, had that quietly smoldering fire which is always so much better than sudden incalculable spurts which are only too apt to fade away.

Gálvez and Serra had many consultations, and at least at one of these Palóu, who was to remain in the Peninsula in charge of its missions, was present. He tells us about the plan that was formed: There were to be three missions, as a start, each with its presidio or garrison. The first was to be at San Diego, the nearest point in the new territory; the second at Monterey, the best harbor they knew of; the third midway between these, at the strategic point of what we now know as the Santa Barbara Channel. It was there that the mission for which Gálvez had packed was to be established. Even its name was decided upon—that of San Buenaventura, the only Franciscan who at that time had been honored with the title of Doctor of the Church.

In compliment to Gálvez, St. Joseph was taken as the patron of the whole enterprise.

One thing came up in a jesting tone. After the three first missions had received their names, Serra asked, "And isn't our Father St. Francis to have a mission?" Gálvez threw the ball back adroitly with, "If St. Francis wants a mission, let him find it for himself." So the two men folded their legs comfortably under the table, sipping their wine (or was it merely Serra's adored chocolate, of which Gálvez had seen to it that a good supply should be taken along?), and, their humor blending with piety, proved themselves to be true prophets.

CHAPTER SEVEN

The Virgin Field

GASPAR DE PORTOLÁ had been sent to the Peninsula with fifty soldiers—far more, one would think, than were needed for ejecting less than thirty Jesuits—but that force was rightly considered too small for the reduction of Northern California, even if this was to be a project mainly entrusted to missionaries. Therefore a newly arrived officer, about whom we shall hear a good deal, Pedro Fages, young, energetic, able, but more than a bit consequential, was summoned into service.

Gálvez took a liking to him at once, or if "liking" is not quite the word, at least he recognized his capacity and picked him as the man who should succeed Portolá as soon as the establishment had been made at Monterey. Fages no doubt was sufficiently subdued in the presence of the Inspector General and showed only his more amiable qualities; at any rate, Gálvez perceived (or thought he perceived) in him the right man for the important task that lay ahead. Yet Fages was only the lieutenant in command of a company of twenty-six soldiers described as "Catalan volunteers," a term we should probably not be far wrong in translating as "yeomen" or "militia." Everything we hear about them suggests that they were not a very well-trained or very well-disciplined body, but they were Spaniards and, of course, valiant—perhaps a bit too much so. Officially they were infantry, which did not prevent them from riding horses when horses were obtainable.

The men under Portolá on the other hand were mounted, though they may not have been included in the cavalry arm. But they were more carefully selected and well equipped. From the Aztecs they had borrowed an idea very useful in that climate; wearing a kind of breastplate made not of steel but of six or seven layers of white doeskin, from which they derived their name of leatherjackets. This breastplate could stop an arrow shaft, though we are told that on De Soto's expedition two hundred and more years earlier the Seminole warriors could shoot with such force as to pierce metal armor. In addition the leatherjackets carried a small round shield of two thicknesses of rawhide known as the *adarga,* and their horses had an apron of leather fastened to the pommel and falling over the chest of the horse and the thighs of his rider. That so large and well-equipped a force had been sent to the Peninsula to bundle out the Jesuit Fathers suggests that the authorities in Mexico City must have had minds so inflamed about treasures as to think it not impossible that the Black-robes and their neophytes might offer some resistance and were therefore taking no chances.

Although reports had often enough been received as to how poor a land this was—Portolá in disgust was to find the right phrase for it, a lot of sand strewn with thorns and thistles—people persisted in believing in the non-existent mines, and that the waters of the Gulf were rich in pearls. The truth is that even the crops were raised with great difficulty by painfully carrying soil in baskets down to the few places that were irrigable, and then trying to induce the laziest of people to do enough work to insure them a regular sufficiency of food. The Franciscans in their turn had the same problem. When they tried to plan settlements for the neophytes, many of the Indians slipped away to the hills, and there it was hard to know what they

found to live on except rabbits and rodents and snakes
and the prickly pear. This last was a staple crop even for
the missions.

The Jesuits had never been able to accomplish much,
nor did the Franciscans succeed a great deal better, though
they had the advantage of dealing with Indians to whom
a veneer of civilization had with vast trouble been im-
parted. Their flocks were always more or less discontented,
never losing a hankering for their former savagery and,
while tractable to the extent of not offering violence, were
almost to a man thievish and unreliable. Yet these people
they not only had to Christianize, in so far as this was
possible, but also to give them some agricultural and
manual training and to see to it that they wore some
clothes. The savages preferred their native nakedness, and
the Fathers—since they insisted on a modicum of decency
—were obliged to purchase the stuffs necessary from the
royal warehouse, paying for them with the oil and fruit
and grain which they, coming after the Jesuits, were able
to raise in small quantities. One hears also of some wine
and even of brandy, one must suppose of a rather poor
quality.

The Crown, though theoretically under the obligation
of supporting the missionaries—and at one time doing so
at an expense that is said to have exceeded that of its
colonial military establishments—actually did very little.
As far as California was concerned, the money needed for
the erection of a new mission and the stipends for the
Fathers was not contributed by the civil authorities but
merely controlled by them—everything coming out of the
Pious Fund. But because this remained under the administration of the King he seems to have brought himself
to believe that he was generous. Actually the Crown was
not merely doing everything upon the most economical

scale, but was often parsimonious. Father Zephyrin Engelhardt has written: "The King, indeed, desired the conversion of the Indians to Christianity, and frequently declared this to be the chief aim of the conquest; nevertheless, the object for which alone expenses were incurred was political." The missionaries in general—at any rate in California —paid their own way, immensely benefiting Spain while receiving not much more than protection and the prestige conferred by the royal name.

This aspect of the matter should be clearly understood, though it need not be denied that the civil authorities had some Christian charity, even if not quite so much as they credited to themselves. We do not find the Padres, even during moments of severest tension, ever accusing the officials with whom they came into conflict of being hypocritical. It was merely that two different points of view have to be allowed for. The friars recognized that their work usually could not have opened up at all without official backing, and for this they were duly grateful. They also recognized that the soldier and the civil administrator, however well disposed towards religion, had to promote secular objects. It should also be said that the officials and officers were always Christians, if not in every instance exemplary as such, and the missionary, when not a Spaniard, as most of them were, thought of Spain as the most Christian of countries, with a splendid mission of bringing the New World to Christ. Any clash that occurred between friar and *conquistador* was due not to any fundamental disagreement over aims but only about ways and means.

In all this we have in Serra and Gálvez as good exemplars as might be found. Gálvez had, it is true, a dislike for Jesuits, a feeling common among Catholics at that time and found even now. But he was a strong supporter

of the missionaries—at all events of the Franciscans—and
not merely because they were useful instruments for effecting his political designs. Serra was a man consumed by a
spiritual idea—the salvation of souls—but he took the
suzerainty of Spain for granted and saw that only under
the royal aegis could he do his work. The two men worked
together in close harmony regarding California, and while
their motives may not have been identical in all respects,
they accorded sufficiently well for the carrying out of a
great idea. Had either man stood alone it is virtually certain that the whole project would have failed, and probably would not have been so much as attempted except
in some halfhearted fashion that would have been worse
than no attempt at all. A fiasco would have simply informed the Russians that they had nothing to fear, but
that if they acted promptly and with decision they might
seize the whole Pacific coast north of the Gulf.

If anybody imagines that Spain was already listless he
should take a look at Gálvez. The Inspector General, according to Palóu in his first volume of his *Historical
Memoirs of New California,* saw at once what was needed.
Accordingly he established at San Blas a marine college,
in which he proposed to train young Indians as sailors,
setting the number at forty. He provided for their maintenance, and though he reduced the wages of those at San
Blas—for he had an eye to economy—he prevented any
discontent by simultaneously reducing prices at the royal
warehouse, both for food and clothing. If he did not at
this time think of sending the ships from San Blas on
explorations far north, but merely of their use by the
missions, he laid down the foundations which before long
made it possible to send out ships to the sixtieth and
even the seventieth parallel so that they might find out
what the Russians were doing. All this could not have

been done at once but took time. That it could eventually be done was due to the plans of Gálvez, plus, as we shall see, some vigorous prodding at a crucial moment from Serra.

Apart from the friars the human material at the disposal of Gálvez was of questionable value. Portolá, a good soldier of the routine type, had his limitations; Fages, in whom Gálvez reposed more hope, was able and energetic, and though it could hardly have escaped the observation of the Inspector General that the young man was irascible and a martinet, he counted upon his mellowing and developing. But the soldiers were not of the best; the sailors were mostly riffraff; the artisans who had drifted there were men for whom the capital had little use; the muleteers, indispensable though they were, were *mestizos*, or Indians not far removed from savagery. One might seriously blame Gálvez for entrusting so important an enterprise to such people, if one did not remember what Cortes and Pizarro had accomplished. At least he could be sure of the indomitable heart of Junípero Serra.

To those who sailed in the first boat to San Diego—where all the parties were to gather before going on to their ultimate goal of Monterey—the Inspector General made a stirring speech, after they had all gone to confession and attended Mass and received Holy Communion. For this was a crusade. After the speech everybody knelt down and Father Serra blessed them. He himself did not plan to go by this boat, or the one that followed just a little later, but with the main column that Portolá was to lead by land. But Gálvez, who was unable to go (and never in fact set foot in California) because pressing matters in Sonora called him there, had so keen an interest in the expedition that he followed the ship in a sloop until it reached the cape of the Peninsula. From there he waved them on, standing in the sloop until the larger vessel had faded from view.

The odd fact is that already the Dominicans in Spain were trying to get Lower California alloted to them. One wonders a little why. Perhaps they wanted to show that they could succeed where their traditional rivals the Jesuits had failed. Perhaps they thought that the Franciscans should be content with the Sierra Gorda and not request to be allowed to withdraw from that field. But of course they may have been filled with the purest apostolic zeal and have wished to dedicate themselves to the forlorn deserts of California. Serra himself had rejoiced at being sent there, though San Fernando consented with reluctance in accepting what they feared would be an unrewarding task, and though Palóu, the man he left in charge, was frankly relieved when he was summoned north. He is not usually very eloquent, but his words "That exile!" speak volumes.

Junípero Serra, who went ahead a year in advance of the majority of his contingent, was himself probably glad to get away. In his case it does not seem to have been because he had found the Peninsula desolate and the work there hardly capable of producing much fruit, but because he wished to go to a virgin field in which he could preach Christ to those who had never heard His name. He always saw possibilities of good in even the most degraded of human beings, and where soldiers delivered their scathing views bluntly (and even some of his fellow missionaries more gently expressed opinions that were not greatly different), he was invariably hopeful about the Indians. This means of course that he had the perfect make-up of a missionary, one more perfect than even that of the great Francis Xavier, who frequently showed impatience, not with the stupidity of many of the ignorant Malabar fishermen but with what he considered Brahmin craftiness and arrogance. We have, however, no means of comparing the two men; Serra had to deal only with mental obtuseness, and because of this he habitually condoned the thievish and lying disposition of the poor savages he had come to save. When he felt obliged sometimes to use punishment as a corrective, it was in the same way as a father deals with the child he chastises; punishment was always light— never more than was just sufficient to make them perceive the error of their ways.

Of the two boats that departed, each bearing friars and some soldiers, the second to leave reached San Diego first. A third, the *San José*, was also dispatched, and in this had been packed a good deal of the church furnishings for the three missions that were to be founded. Its captain had the Irish name of Callegan. But whether because it was even less well built than the rest of the San Blas flotilla, or because it ran into an exceptionally bad storm, it was never heard of again. Of the two that did arrive it might be said that they not merely limped but crawled into port, with half their crews dead and some of the survivors almost dying of scurvy.

One wonders at this, as it indicates a lack of elementary foresight. Gálvez himself can hardly be held responsible; he had no knowledge of seamanship, and in any case even a man who paid such close attention to details could not look into everything. But the officers should have been aware that scurvy is a disease due to dietary deficiencies, particularly a lack of fruit and vegetables. The lime juice carried by all English ships since 1795 has given Englishmen the name of "limey," an unconscious testimonial to their practical good sense and the experience gained by a seafaring people in their long voyages. The three Spanish ships had hitherto gone no further distance than across the Gulf of California; now they failed to provide what was indispensable in a long voyage—and therefore had to suffer the consequences. Fortunately the matter subsequently came to be rectified, for though scurvy continued to take its toll on those whose staple fare was salt pork and maggoty hardtack, it never again worked the havoc of a plague.

It is not necessary to trace the fortunes of these ships, except to remark that the state of their crews would have brought the enterprise to frustration, had the whole issue depended on them. Even making all possible allowances for the officers of the *San Carlos* and *San Antonio,* one cannot acquit them of all blame, as one would suppose that they had occasionally met the captain of one of the ships that put in at San Blas after a journey from the Philippines. But it would seem that they only provided for the officers' mess, for none who dined with the captains (and this includes the Padres) suffered. But for the ordinary seamen it is evident that little, if any, of the necessary provision was made.

The first of the land expeditions was put in charge of Captain Fernando Rivera y Moncada, a name to be borne in mind since we shall come across it many times again. At this stage it will be enough to remark that he was a middle-aged officer who for more than twenty years had been commandant at the presidio at Loreto. His was the somewhat unromantic duty of stopping at every mission as he went northwards to take from it all the cattle and food and mules that could be spared. He seems to have appropriated whatever he wished—and he gathered a hundred and forty horses, forty-six mules and two burros—yet Serra's mild comment was, "Although it was done with a somewhat heavy hand, it was undergone for God and the King." In the absence of Gálvez, who had already crossed to the mainland, Rivera interpreted his instructions pretty much as he pleased. Yet it must be granted that had he not ridden north with his lowing cattle and his big bales of grain, the missions would not have been able to support themselves nor would the expedition itself have had enough food.

Portolá had been given the title of Governor, though it was not intended that his authority should be permanent. But as Governor he was the superior officer of both Rivera and Fages, with the duty of locating Monterey, after which he was to return to Mexico at once. He had already received precise indications of the limits of his commission, but about this neither of the other officers had received any intimation, as Gálvez was sure that heartburning would result. Gálvez meant to give Fages, the younger man and the officer of lower rank, a position more important than the one he had in mind for Rivera. Serra himself apparently was kept in the dark about what was a purely military matter, one that, so it was supposed, would never affect the missionaries.

Serra was to go with the second land expedition under Portolá, and we have a diary he kept, covering his long journey over the sterile rocks of the Peninsula. It was the admirable custom of Spanish soldiers and explorers to make a written account of any special duty to which they were assigned. Because of this we have a wealth of material of the most factual sort, practically all of which bearing on California has been carefully edited, mostly by Professor Bolton. The best of these are the diaries relating to the Anza land journeys that opened up a new route across the Colorado and Gila rivers, which were made by Colonel Anza himself, though even more useful is that kept by the priest Pedro Font, who once accompanied him; and the most disappointing was that kept by another priest, Francisco Garcés, magnificent man though he was personally.

Hubert Howe Bancroft pronounces Serra's letters "long, verbose, rambling, but [leaving] no detail of the subject untouched. The loss of a sheep from a mission flock evoked a communication of the same style and length, with the same expressions of trust in heaven, as the conversion or destruction of a whole tribe; and it is to be noted that in his writing to friars, especially about his political quarrels, he adopted a style wholly unintelligible, as it was doubtless intended to be, to all but the initiated." That is a little unfair, but it was hardly necessary for Father Piette to point out indignantly that never once did Serra mention the loss of a sheep, for that is brought in by Bancroft merely by way of illustrating his meaning. It is true, however, that Serra has a habit of dealing fully with details. But he did not expatiate about his "political quarrels," except in the sense that he was obliged to explain his difficulties with some of the officials, though always very temperately. Nor is Serra really verbose, except for leaving no matter untouched. On the other hand Piette claims too much in saying that "the style of Serra is always natural, positive, simple, clear, lapidary"—at any rate not the last. He wrote in a clear and sometimes lively way, without any attention to literary graces, but with an eye for character, painting it without malice, and with occasionally a knack of recording conversations instead of rendering everything in broad general statements. Never can he be detected in the slightest untruth, or even exaggeration, and he wins our confidence and affection by the courtesy and forbearance he never failed to show to people who must have sometimes seemed beyond endurance. Finally, he never exalts his own achievements, but sets down modestly what really happened. A little more humor (he does show some now and then but not so much as to seem a humorist) might have enlivened his narrative but also have brought it under suspicion, as the humorist is always under the temptation to touch up what he has to tell.

About Serra's diary Father Piette is very enthusiastic, praising extravagantly both Serra's literary style and his calligraphy. I believe I have more accurately estimated his style; as for his script, though it is clear and well formed, no comparison can be endured between it and the exquisite penmanship of Colonel Anza, a man who spent his entire life on the Mexican frontier. One may subscribe without reservation, however, to Piette's admiration of the moral qualities of his hero: "A great joy sang in his soul. In it he forgot the tedium and the weariness of the great roads scaling the mountains, and the pain racking his hurt foot."

It was the condition of Serra's foot (actually of the whole leg beneath his knee) which made Palóu beg him not to attempt so arduous a journey but to allow him to go instead. Serra would not hear of this, even though Portolá added his plea. He who was so little given to complaints records that he had to pass some days at Velicatá, the northernmost mission of the Peninsula, lying down. He was beginning to fear that, if he went, it could only be on a stretcher, for one day he was unable to say Mass simply through being unable to stand, much less walk. What seems to have revived him was the news that forty-four Indians—men, women and children—had asked for baptism in a body. If that awaited him, he would find a way to go.

Palóu adds a charming story. He says that Serra sent for one of the muleteers, a man named Juan Antonio Coronel, and asked, "My son, don't you know how to find a remedy for my foot and leg?" What could the man answer but, "Father, what do I know about remedies? Am

I a surgeon? I am only a muleteer and only know how to cure the galls on the backs of the pack animals."

Serra persisted; very well, the muleteer was to treat him as one of his mules, for, he added, "The pains I feel are so great that I cannot sleep."

Coronel laughed at the idea that one of his salves could be of any use to a human being, but to humor Fray Juniper he undertook what was asked. Accordingly he mashed some tallow between two stones and, mixing in it some of the herbs of the fields which he knew sometimes helped his beasts, he spread this over Serra's sore leg like a poultice. The very next morning Serra, after having slept soundly, woke at daybreak to say the Office of Matins and Lauds and was able to offer Mass as though free of any malady. This was not, as events were to show, a complete cure, for that sore leg troubled Serra for the rest of his life, but the salve worked at a time when it really looked as though Serra would be hopelessly crippled. The improvement was so sudden and astonishing as almost to seem miraculous, for Palóu does not seem disposed to give much credit to Juan Antonio. We do not hear of Serra's ever calling upon the services of a horse doctor again, though he may have done so whenever his leg got specially troublesome. As for doctors of medicine, though there was one in the party, Serra never asked for his help at any time, his faith in the profession being slight, and because he was willing to accept his ailments, and whatever alleviation that might come, as from God.

Portolá had by this time ridden off, Serra undertaking to catch up with him when he felt a bit better. The captain probably thought there was no use to wait any longer for one who was in no condition to travel—least of all on foot. Therefore he was much surprised when a day or two later Serra limped into camp accompanied only by an Indian boy. He made the rest of the journey with them, protesting that if he fell by the wayside and died, he would be quite content to be buried in Californian soil, even if he had not reached his goal. The Governor saw that he would have to let this intrepid friar do as he wished, foolhardy though he may have considered him.

When Serra set out for the North, he carried so little food—merely a loaf of bread and some cheese—that when Palóu insisted on supplying him with things to eat and some clothing and a few comforts, he grumbled, "For my sins I do not cease to be fond of my convenience." Yet Palóu knew what he gave would prove to be indispensable before the journey's end. The time was to come when the Indian porters and muleteers had to be sent to the hills to forage for themselves. And before he had left the Peninsula, Serra met some women and children crying with hunger. He made them a meal of *atole,* the porridge which was to be the staple diet in the missions he founded. He was consoled by hearing them sing in their happiness, though the other Spaniards considered this a hideous caterwauling.

The Indian boy—one whom Serra had taught how to serve Mass—went on muleback, wearing new clothes and even riding boots, of which he was very proud, while Serra limped beside him on foot. At night they slept on the ground but the next day, when they caught up with the main body under Portolá, they were somewhat better cared for. They had committed themselves to the care of St. Raphael, who since the days of Tobias has been the patron of travelers.

At the various missions they passed en route, strung along the Peninsula, they were met with manifestations of joy—songs again and the dances of which the Indians were so fond. But the urgency was such that when on May 1st

Serra received some mail, and was unable to sit down and write a reply, he simply returned the letters by the bearer as a sign—which he could be sure would be understood—that he had safely received them and had read the contents. On the 12th of the month they saw, it would seem for the first time, some of the huts of the "Gentile" Indians, but not one man would let himself be seen, except from a distance. The country was so bare that it had not even a pitahayas tree, but only now and then a cactus and a garambullo. The cactus was what Serra called of the "candle" variety, "a tree useless for everything, even for fire."

When Serra celebrated Mass at the last mission, San Fernando, the only one he himself had founded in the Peninsula, the muskets of the leatherjackets were fired at the elevation, their fumes taking the place of incense. But still no Gentiles appeared, Serra imagined because "perhaps they were scared of so many thunders." However, some prowlers attempted to steal stray cattle, whereupon Serra told them that if they needed anything they would get it, for the soldiers and the Fathers only wished their good. On the 21st, the Feast of the Holy Trinity, Serra preached after Mass, telling the soldiers that they were on an expedition for the greater honor and glory of God and should comport themselves accordingly. And it must be said that though later some of the soldiers misbehaved with Indian women, it is really remarkable, when everything is considered, how orderly nearly all these soldiers were.

At last the desolate country began to look more "smiling and gladsome," for there were tall and tufted trees and some that were a species of cypress. Soon afterwards they came upon many wild flowers, especially what Serra lovingly described as the "rose of Castille." He said he was writing while a branch on which there were three buds lay before him. It reminds one of the joy felt long before in the swamps of Florida by Ranjel, the secretary of De Soto, who wrote an account of the expedition. At that sight they stood, like Ruth, "in tears amid the alien corn"; though Serra rejoiced that he was at the rim of the world in the service of Christ.

An Indian was finally brought into camp, bound because he was so frightened of the strangers that they could get him there in no other way. But after Serra had laid his hands on his head and blessed him, the poor terrified savage calmed down. Like all the Indian men, he went naked, wearing only a fillet of some blue-stained fiber around his temples. Other Indians showed some truculence at first and threatened fight but scampered away when a few shots were fired over their heads. Some of them had well-made bows that shot arrows tipped with obsidian or flint, but they laid these down when they wished to show that they had no warlike designs, whereupon the Spaniards found that they had better do the same with their muskets. Upon the whole the savages were friendly, and some of the men were even prevailed upon to exhibit in dumb show how they fought.

So far Serra had not seen an Indian woman, and he was apprehensive about the first encounter, lest they should be as naked as the men. His fears were groundless, for throughout California the women, and even small girls, sported a fiber apron before and behind and usually had a cloak of deer or rabbit skin over their shoulders. The very fact that the women were so decently clad made the men regard dress for themselves as effeminate. When they wanted any protection against the cold they bedaubed themselves with mud, rubbing this off as soon as the sun warmed the air. Somewhat naïvely the Spaniards wondered that these men never showed the faintest sense of shame in not having a stitch on. Indeed, with the first neophytes one of the main difficulties was that they were expected to wear at least a loincloth; this they thought ludicrous in the extreme, and eventually did what was asked of them mainly out of good nature, or perhaps thinking that this was one of the Christians' magical rites, to be accepted as such, without inquiring whether it made much sense.

When at last Serra saw his first Californian women he was not only vastly relieved that they were not naked but permitted himself the little jest that they were talking away just as those of their sex are everywhere accustomed to do. One of the women yelled rather than talked, but this may have been because her companion bore on her head some substance of the consistency of dough brought to Serra as a present. When he put his hand upon it to bless her, he drew away his fingers all sticky. He had probably thought the dough was some kind of feminine adornment.

Friends were now being made, and the country grew better at every mile, showing many trees and an abundance of flowers and wild grapes. Clearly it was all going to be very different from the stony and sterile Peninsula they had left. Even so, the finding of good water was sometimes a problem, and sleeping on the ground left them covered with fleas and ticks. But Serra's judgment always was, "Such good people!" Never once did he permit himself to think that they were as dirty and lazy and degraded a lot as could have been encountered anywhere on the earth. On the purely natural side he stressed only what was true, the gentleness of these Indians; supernaturally he saw them as souls for whom Christ had died and who were therefore, at least potentially, heirs of the Kingdom.

Serra was called upon for a miracle of patience. Even

of the Christian Indians brought from the Peninsula as porters, muleteers and in the hope that they might be useful as interpreters, eighteen out of forty-four deserted along the way. Those remaining had to be constantly watched and urged on. The story in this matter, as in most others, is much the same in Serra's own diary and in that kept by Fray Juan Crespí, his former student in Palma, who had gone with Rivera. Of the two, Serra's is by far the more informative. One of the most interesting facts—the significance we shall see later—is that with Portolá rode Sergeant Ortega, a man who so greatly impressed Serra at this time that he was to make in his regard an astonishing suggestion.

One of the things that Serra had enjoined upon Juan Crespí was that he give names to all the places they passed that stood out in the landscape. Crespí did so, and of course Serra was careful to observe his own injunction. It is hardly surprising, though somewhat amusing, that where the friars used the names of saints, the soldiers bestowed names of a somewhat different sort, those of some little incident connected with the spot. Thus we get the Lake of the Lean Bear, the Crows, and the like, and in the majority of cases these are the names that came to be attached to the places and in some instances are still used, whereas those that sprang from the Padres' piety have faded from recollection. Thus an Indian afflicted with goiter is commemorated in Point Buchon; another Indian who was lame has come down to us as El Cojo; and a seagull shot by one of the soldiers gave Gaviota Pass its name, though Serra had called it after San Luis, having in mind King Louis IX, the most notable of Franciscan tertiaries. The soldiers, however, were not without piety of their own, so that though one of the other Fathers used the name of San Jorje, Serra changed this to San Antenógenes, because Sergeant Ortega had a special devotion to that bishop and martyr.

As for the ships, though it took the *San Antonio* only fifty-five days to sail from Loreto to San Diego, the *San Carlos* took just double that time, because it had been blown by contrary winds as far south as Panama before it managed to go northwards again. It was not until April 29th that it made landfall. Of its ninety soldiers, sailors and artisans only one-third were alive, and most of these were half-dead. They could do no more than lie there miserably and would have died had they not found the *San Antonio* in the harbor. Though that ship too had suffered greatly from scurvy, only seven of its crew being left, the *San Carlos* was in worse plight with only five. Somehow they managed to carry the sick ashore, and of these some were too far gone to survive, though they were put under sailcloth awnings on the beach. Fortunately Rivera's land expedition reached San Diego on May 14th, and Portolá's (with Serra) on July 1st. The following day, the survivors of all four groups, now gathered together, assisted at a Mass of thanksgiving to St. Joseph. It was the Feast of the Visitation.

Those who had come by land were all in good health, and they and the officers of the ships and the priests who had come with them had escaped the scurvy. Therefore they were able to do something for the sick—those for whom anything could be done. And Dr. Prat, the Frenchman serving as physician with the Spanish force, used what skill he had, which one fears was not very great. One gathers that scurvy was looked upon as a kind of pestilence, an infection which needed good air. But though this no doubt helped, a much more efficacious remedy was better food and fresh water.

Rough palisades were run up around the camp, a bulwark that would have been a slight obstacle to foes who made a determined attack, such as did occur while Portolá was away. He had gone on July 14th by land in search of Monterey, the finding of which was considered so urgent a matter that the Governor could not wait even for the founding of the San Diego mission, on July 16th. In the interval a few wooden houses had been put up, thatched with *tule*, the bulrushes the Indians used to cover their huts.

Yet the attack was made rather to plunder than to kill. The Spaniards had quickly become familiar with the thievish propensity of these San Diego Indians, for even while they were talking to somebody (if it could be called talking when communications had mostly to be by signs) their bare feet would be quietly picking up anything lying on the floor. They also came out in their canoes at night to the ships to steal any sails or ropes they could lay hands on, until a guard was placed on board to prevent it. The effrontery of these savages was such that they even descended upon the sick in their sailcloth tents and dragged away the sheets on which they lay. They too were protected by a guard, but very inadequately.

The Indians, about a month after Portolá's departure, began to count upon his being away long enough for them to seize all that the Spaniards who remained at San Diego possessed. Those remaining were few and most of them still weak from disease. On August 12th and 13th the savages descended, evidently with the idea of killing the missionaries and those with them. Resistance, however, was made, and it sufficed to beat off the savages without any casualties on the Spanish side. Nor apparently had any Indian been killed because the muskets were fired mainly with the idea of frightening the attackers. It was hoped in this way to quiet down these thievish people.

Those hopes were deceived. On the 15th a more serious attack was made, one that must have succeeded had the Indians been resolute and well organized. Luckily, they were cowardly, marauders rather than warriors. Even so, for a while it was touch and go. Just after Mass the Indians with their clubs and bows made a real rush at the little encampment, if it deserved the name. But the corporal in charge at once gave the alarm and the handful of men under him, helped by the carpenter and blacksmith, leaped up to do battle, the blacksmith distinguishing himself by his valor, Palóu thinks, on account of the Holy Communion he had just received. He kept shouting, "Long live the faith of our Lord Jesus Christ, and may these dogs of enemies die the death!" firing meanwhile at any Indian he could see, while exposing himself fearlessly though he had no leather jacket for breastplate.

The blacksmith's attitude was not quite the same as Serra's. The priest remained in the little house in which he had just offered Mass, commending all to God, praying that there might be no fatality among the defenders but also praying that none of the Indians be killed before receiving baptism. It was just then that Father Vizcaíno, wishing to see if the Indians had retired, as they had done before, raised the thick mat which served as a door for the chapel and received an arrow wound in the hand, one that left him always slightly disabled. The shouting and the firing went on, and then an Indian servant who had come from the Peninsula rushed into the chapel and fell at the feet of Serra, crying, "Father, absolve me, for the Indians have killed me." It was so, for his throat had been pierced by a shaft, but he died receiving Serra's absolution.

How many Indians were killed or wounded in this scuffle was not exactly known, as their casualties were quickly borne away. But it came out that the number of wounded was fairly large, for a few days later the Indians returned, this time seeking peace and bringing with them their injured to be treated by Dr. Prat. They did not show any inclination to apologize or even explain, but merely took it for granted that things could go on as though no incident had happened. Palóu expresses the opinion that their quietness after this was due to the charity they had been shown, which may be the case; one is nevertheless left wondering whether it was not mainly due to the proof that had been offered that even a small group of Spaniards with muskets were more than a match for a much larger number of naked savages. But proof positive had been given that it was absolutely necessary to station a small guard of soldiers at each of the missions.

CHAPTER EIGHT

The Search for Monterey

A FAIR amount had long been known about the Pacific coast, though not all of the information was very accurate. As early as 1542 Cortes had sent out Juan Rodríguez Cabrillo to explore and in particular to try to discover the entirely mythical Strait of Anian; Francisco de Galli also went on this mission in 1584. Five years later came Francis Drake, going further north than either of these, but also failing to find any sign of a northwest passage. It is interesting that this famous seaman completely missed the entrance to San Francisco Bay, no doubt because of fog, though he anchored only a few miles to the north of it. Had that magnificent harbor been known to exist, Portolá would have aimed for it. Instead he sought to locate the Monterey about which Sebastián Vizcaíno had left what seemed to be an exact account after he visited the place in 1603.

He had named it in honor of the Viceroy of New Spain in his day, Gaspár de Zúñiga y Acevedo, Conde de Monte Rey, a spelling which was still in use in Serra's time, the two words only gradually merging into one as their origin was forgotten. For that matter, the whole of this northern territory was sometimes referred to as Monterey, the term Upper as distinguishing it from Lower California also being a gradual development. In Palóu's great history it appears as "New" California. Its possession was imagined to depend upon the holding of Vizcaíno's Monterey, supposedly the only first-rate harbor on that coast.

The account of Monterey left by the diarist of that time described it as "the best port that could be desired." It was sheltered from all winds and abounded in tall pines suitable for masts, with a good many oaks and much water, all near the shore. "The land is fertile, with a climate and soil like those of Castille; there is much wild game, such as harts like young bulls [evidently elk], deer, buffalo [!], very large bears, rabbits, hares, and many animals and many game birds." Though the buffalo were a figment of the imagination or, more probably, elk seen at a distance, we do know that California then had some grizzlies and not merely the small bears that seem so harmless and friendly today. The picture was a bit highly colored, and certainly the harbor—now merely an anchorage for fishing boats—was far from being as described, for though it takes in a wide arch, it is only a fairly good roadstead. But this was what Portolá set out to find.

It should have been easy to locate merely by riding north, as Portolá did along the coast. For not only had the harbor been described but Father Torquemada, one of the Carmelite friars who had gone with Vizcaíno, had reported that they had landed on December 17th, the day after their arrival, to say Mass. "The chapel," he says, "was placed in the shadow of a large oak-tree, some of whose branches reached the water"—a tree standing in Portolá's time, and whose huge bole may still be seen at Monterey. In addition, at the estuary of the Carmel River, only about four miles away, there had been erected a large cross on which the inscription had been placed, "Dig at the foot and you will find a writing."

Portolá, riding along the rolling lands beside the sea, came to Monterey without much trouble. But when he reached it, he concluded that it could not be the place he was looking for, so little did it correspond to Vizcaíno's description of a magnificent harbor. Some of those with him suggested that the calculation of latitude made in 1603 must be wrong—something that happened often enough on the ships of those days—and that Monterey must lie farther north. Others were of the opinion that the harbor had filled in with the sands that had drifted down from the many dunes. It was a charming spot, with its lupins and a beach where sandpipers raced down towards each wave as it retreated; only it was not Monterey.

The Feast of St. Francis (October 4th) was celebrated, Mass being sung in a rustic arbor of boughs. But Father Crespí records that Portolá held a council of war, asking those present to give their opinion freely, whereupon "the officers voted unanimously to continue the journey, as it seemed the only thing to do, in the hope of finding, through the favor of God, the desired harbor of Monterey, and in it the packet San José, which would relieve the suffering. And if it should be God's will that we should all perish in looking for Monterey, we should have done our duty to God and to all men by cooperating unto death to bring success to the undertaking that we had been commanded to carry out." With Portolá were not only Rivera and Fages, his second and third in command, but also Sergeant Ortega and, perhaps most important of all, Miguel Costansó, an engineer and surveyor, an expert who had come along to make the identification, after which he was at once to return to New Spain.

About seventy miles farther on the expedition struck much more than they had dared to hope for, although its significance escaped them. This was San Francisco Bay. It was an expanse of water so vast that it did not seem so much like a harbor as a sea, one perhaps lying between them and another continent, though the opinion was that it was the estuary of an immense river. From a height they were able to see the Golden Gate, with Point Reyes beyond, and below it what we now call Drake's Bay, but which was at the time styled San Francisco Bay. But they had no means of crossing those waters anywhere. And in any event they were not explorers at large but men with a definite commission, that of finding Monterey. That they had failed to do. There was nothing for it but to go back to San Diego and try again with a ship.

Considerably discouraged, Portolá and his men retraced their steps, reaching San Diego on January 24, 1770. There they were not made any happier by hearing of the Indian rising the previous August and of how near it had come to wiping out the little group they had left behind. In the harbor the *San Carlos* lay at anchor, but even before the departure of Portolá the *San Antonio* had been dispatched to San Blas with the convalescents, who formed what might almost literally be called a skeleton crew. They were to bring back supplies and replacements for both ships, after which they would sail to search again for Monterey.

But it was now January and more than six months had passed since the *San Antonio* had sailed for San Blas; she was so long overdue that it began to be feared that she had suffered the same fate as the *San José*. Portolá, though a stouthearted man, had begun to give up hope. An indication of what was already in his mind, the abandoning of the whole enterprise, appeared when on February 11, 1770, Captain Rivera departed with the wounded Father Vizcaíno and a company of soldiers towards the Peninsula. Only at Serra's entreaty did Portolá decide to remain a little longer himself, for after all the *San Antonio* might have been delayed and would still arrive. But he made it clear that he did not propose to stay indefinitely; indeed, it was impossible for him to do so.

Serra and Crespí nevertheless announced that, come what may, they intended to remain—something said not in mere foolhardiness but in a confidence that help would arrive. But Portolá finally set a definite date, that of March 20th, when he would return to Lower California. From there he would have to go on to Mexico City to make his inglorious report. He had done all that was possible, and though he would fail to achieve glory, he could not fairly be blamed. It might sound a lame story to say that the harbor of Monterey had filled in with sand, but everybody who had been with him could testify as to the facts.

On February 10th Serra wrote Palóu a letter which Rivera was to carry. In it he enclosed a letter to Gálvez, explaining the situation, which he was to read before sending it on. He expressed sorrow that even his one little mission of San Diego was to be deserted and the whole project given up, yet he writes in a calm and cheerful tone. "What I most desire," he says, "is some help, although our physical necessities are not a few, yet while we have a tortilla and some herbs from the field, what more do we need?... Through the mercy of God I am quiet at heart and willing to accept what He may send." There are no dramatics of any kind, unless this be considered such: "Four of us remain here, Fathers Juan Crespí, Fernando Parrón, Francisco Gómez and myself, to see, if in case the ships should arrive, we may be able to found a second mission. If we see that our provisions are exhausted and also our hopes, then I shall remain with only Father Juan to endure up to the very last. May God give us of His holy grace. Please commend us to God that so it may be." Palóu was strictly enjoined not to come north, as he could be of more use where he was. All that was asked of him was that he try to get the cattle left at Velicatá driven to San Diego, and "please have them bring a little incense, for while we remembered to load the censers we forgot the incense."

That is not the tone used by a man who has resigned himself to death, though death would certainly have come quickly had Portolá and the leatherjackets ridden away. He asked for incense, clearly indicating that he wished to carry out the church services fittingly—and also that he counted upon founding at least one more mission of the other two that had been planned. The cattle were not for their food, but for the stocking of these missions. He and Crespí, he felt, would be able to exist somehow on a pancake a day. One is continually struck by the frugality of these Spaniards—soldiers as well as priests—who always seem to have been able, if necessary, to sustain an arduous life on extremely meager fare.

Although it might be said that what he had discovered would serve well enough as a port—whether it was the real Monterey choked with sand, or whether that lay beyond the "great Estuary," and as such should have been hung on to—that was not Portolá's view. He had been unable to carry out his orders and there was no use in remaining. The fate of everything now seemed to hang by a hair. Portolá acted as a soldier should in making a careful calculation of the provisions left and deciding that, in face of imminent starvation, he should withdraw his men. He was aware that retreat would end all chance of Spain's occupation of Upper California, for the last attempt, which was no more than a formal gesture, had taken place a hundred and sixty-seven years previously. But sadly, grimly, he recognized harsh facts. He had gone north as far as he could in the absence of available ships. Without them he could merely repeat what he had already done—go as far as the impassable "estuary." Beyond it he might of course still locate Monterey, but as the *San Antonio* had not arrived, he fixed on March 20th as the date for his departure.

At this crisis Serra proposed that they all make a novena to St. Joseph, a nine-days prayer that must have begun on the 10th of the month. It was characteristic of Portolá that, though he could see no possibility of help arriving, he agreed to join in this novena. Only a miracle could now extricate the expedition. Let St. Joseph, whom they had taken as the patron of the enterprise, come to their aid; otherwise he would adhere to the date set for their march southwards.

Non-Catholics may put this down as one of those superstitions to which Catholics are notoriously addicted, but there are few if any Catholics who are unable to testify to the efficacy of a novena. This, it need hardly be said, is not because there is any magical power in the number nine, for a single prayer may bring the desired result, but there is a pious attachment to this devotion in memory of the first novena, the nine days of prayer that preceded the coming of the Holy Ghost at Pentecost. At any rate, on the afternoon of the 19th, the Feast of St. Joseph, a sail was descried, and though later it was lost to view, on the 24th the *San Antonio* came safely into the roadstead of San Diego. Just in the nick of time the California enterprise was saved.

The fact of the ship's arrival at this time is not questioned. But Dr. Charles E. Chapman makes the gratuitous suggestion that the story about the novena was an invention of Palóu's intended to exalt Serra at Portolá's expense. His argument is that there is no documentary evidence, except Palóu's statement, that a novena was made at all. To this one must say that Palóu indicates that his information came from Serra and that a letter written by Crespí at least implies that the arrival of the ship was in answer to prayer. Furthermore, nobody intimately acquainted with Catholics would be able to imagine them *not* praying very hard in such desperate straits. And a novena is precisely the form of prayer that would spontaneously suggest itself. Finally, though novenas are of many different varieties, the saying of the rosary is the kind of novena that would commend itself to soldiers. Few of them could read, and those able to do so would probably not have carried a prayer book into the wilderness. Even if all of these men had not taken their beads with them, they could have counted the Hail Marys on their ten fingers. All probabilities tell in favor of the story that Chapman would dismiss as an invention.

We have here, too, another instance of the misunderstanding of Catholic things all too common among otherwise well-informed and well-disposed people. The glory would not go to Serra but to St. Joseph, for it was his miracle, if it was a miracle at all. I myself have occasionally questioned Palóu's perfect reliability in minor matters, but any reader of his books knows that he was very matter-of-fact and of transparent honesty. Though he did sometimes express a little annoyance with some of the other officers, he has nothing but good to say of Portolá, who even in this story figures as a good Christian.

Of course, the incident may be set down to mere coincidence—and admittedly a positive answer to prayer cannot be proved, though it looks like one. But if it was a coincidence it was, to say the least, very strange that the ship was sighted on St. Joseph's day. It would seem to be sensible to perceive here the power of God as exercised through the saint's being invoked. A denial would wear all the appearances of being merely on *a priori* grounds.

Moreover, had Palóu been making things up, he could easily have wrapped the whole affair in additional mystery.

He could, for instance, have suggested that the appearance of a sail on the horizon was simply a miraculous phantom, provided to hold Portolá there a few days longer, until the ship, which was beating its way up the coast, had time to arrive. Instead, Palóu provides this explanation: The *San Antonio* was making for Monterey, not San Diego, taking it for granted that the main port would have been occupied. For this reason it passed by the assembled group and bore north, but had to put in for water at the Santa Barbara Channel, where the commander heard that Portolá had twice been there (going and returning), which almost decided the commander to turn back to San Diego. In this state of hesitation he lost one of his anchors (was this an act of St. Joseph?) so that he had no choice in the matter but to try to get another from the *San Carlos*. Had it not been for this, he would have gone on to Monterey only to find nobody there; then on retracing his course he would have discovered that San Diego had been abandoned and that Serra and Crespí, the two friars who were determined to remain, had been murdered by the local Indians.

A final point might be raised so as to dispose of this question. Palóu in his *Vida* quotes in extenso several letters he received from Serra about this time. But since he quotes only a few, we may reasonably assume that there were others that were not preserved. Under the circumstances in which he was placed, it was not easy to keep a careful file of documents; Palóu could have had no idea at this time that it would fall to him to write Serra's life, and there was no special reason why he should have put all of Serra's letters in a safe storage. Dr. Chapman's reputation as a scholar is deservedly high, but one fears that in this case he has been hampered by a habit of skepticism and also by his lack of knowledge as to how a Catholic mind operates. Imponderables of this sort, not to be learned out of books, are often as weighty as any document. It is not necessary to believe that a miracle actually occurred; on the other hand, it is not necessary to demonstrate the integrity of one's disbelief by calling Palóu a liar.

We have an account of what happened afterwards in a letter written by Serra on board the *San Antonio* on April 16th, as it lay in the roadstead of San Diego preparing to sail to Monterey. Though Palóu was the younger man and a subject of Serra's, as he had earlier been his student in Mallorca, Serra ceremoniously addresses him as "Dearly beloved friend, companion and esteemed sir," and the letter ends with "I kiss the hand of your reverence." Many years before, when they were about to leave Mallorca for the missions, he had asked Palóu to lay aside all formal titles and precedence when dealing with him, but the habit of politeness was too deeply engrained to permit this. There were still greater flourishes of course when it was a matter of writing to some exalted official, but that was natural; the customary forms were always kept up between the friars and minor military officers, even when relations between them were somewhat strained, and this was the case also between intimate friends.

In the letter Serra tells of the arrival of the *San Antonio*. Though he says nothing about the novena, Palóu would have taken it for granted that one was made. What he does say is that the *San Antonio* had been sighted on St. Joseph's Day, March 19th, but had not come into San Diego until the 24th. As Serra does not say how this happened, one must suppose that there was a subsequent letter that gave a fuller account of events and that it was upon this that Palóu drew when writing the *Vida*.

It is clear that Serra was writing in considerable haste, for he had not expected, he says, to embark so soon and had done so only because their fellow Mallorcan, Juan Pérez, the captain of the ship, had suddenly decided to leave that day. Serra therefore had said Mass on board, and even while he was writing, the sailors of the *San Antonio* were busy setting the sails.

Fathers Parrón and Gómez were to stay at San Diego to look after the mission there, while Crespí, who was to be placed in charge of San Buenaventura as soon as it was founded, was to accompany Serra to Monterey. He says he cannot write much, as he is doing so under difficulties, seated upon the deck. Mostly he is concerned with affairs in the Peninsula, which was still under his direction, though Palóu had been left in charge there. Regards are sent to various Fathers, who are always in his mind. But the great item of general news, something of which Palóu may himself have already heard,[1] is that Pope Clement XIII had died and that Ganganelli, a Franciscan, had been elected in his place. The news was so recent that word had not yet come as to what name the new Pope had chosen. He became Clement XIV, and it was he who in 1773 suppressed the Jesuits, who had already been expelled from the Spanish dominions and other parts of the world.

Serra wrote again to Palóu on June 13th, which was the Feast of St. Anthony of Padua, giving an account of what had happened since he last wrote. The voyage from San Diego to Monterey had taken a month and a half of hard sailing in bad weather, so that Crespí and the party that had gone by land had long before this arrived. On June 3rd, which was Pentecost that year, all the officers and men had gathered by the side of the little ravine under the oak where the friars with Vizcaíno had sung Mass in 1603. Bells were hung and a large cross set up, with the royal stand-

[1] Palóu might not have heard this because the *San Antonio* sailed from San Blas without touching at Loreto.

ard beside it. After Mass the *Veni Creator* was sung and also the "Hail, Holy Queen" before the image of the Blessed Virgin on the altar. It was the same prayer that Pizarro's expedition, at a moment when it seemed unlikely that they would ever be able to land in Peru, had said. Nothing could have been more appropriate than its close, "After this our exile show unto us the blessed fruit of Thy womb Jesus." In this case, however, it was not so much an exile from their earthly country, but from their heavenly *Patria,* the home to which they had come to lead the poor savages of California.

Then came the *Te Deum* and the formal taking possession of the land by Portolá and his officers. Everything ended with a dinner—poor enough but as good as they could make it under the circumstances—taken under the same ancient oak beneath whose boughs Mass had been said. Everything had been accompanied by much firing of muskets by the leatherjackets, answered by the guns from the ship riding in the bay. Serra concluded: "As regards the fact that this port could not be found by the members of the other expedition and that they had given it out that it no longer existed, I have nothing to say, nor is it incumbent upon me to judge in the matter. Let it be sufficient to know that it has been found and that, although tardily, the wishes of His Excellency, the Inspector-General, have been carried out, as we all desire with him the success of this Spiritual Conquest." That was a charitable way of covering over what we now see was an almost incredible blunder committed the year before.

Not only was the oak identified as the one under which Mass had been said in 1603, but the large cross erected at that time was also found. On it were hanging all kinds of oddments of half-decayed sardines, showing that the Indians, though they understood nothing of its significance,

at least divined that it was some kind of a sacred object.
As such they thought it advisable to propitiate whatever
powers were connected with it. But the eyes of Portolá
and his officers—and perhaps still more of the engineer or
surveyor they had brought with them—had apparently been
blind to everything except the harbor itself. And that harbor, so they decided—to this extent correctly—did not correspond to the "magnificent port of Monterey" described by
the diarist of the Vizcaíno expedition.

Junípero Serra rarely permitted himself any expression
of pathos, but in this letter he did mention a little wistfully
that it had now been just over a year since he had received
any letter from Christian people—which meant even from
Palóu—so they were all hungry for news. What he now
asked for was to be informed as to the name taken by the
new Pope, so that it might be introduced into the appropriate place at Mass. Also, he asked, had Joseph of Cuper-
tino, a Franciscan whose cause had been pending, been
canonized yet? How slowly news traveled is indicated by
the fact that this saint had been canonized in 1767. The
day on which he is celebrated, which Serra wanted to
know to introduce it into the Ordo, was September 18th.
He also asked whether any other canonizations had recently
occurred.

Serra was already making plans for equipping all three
missions that he had been commissioned to found as a start.
Since two of the friars had left for the Peninsula in February, when it was thought that California would have to be
abandoned, he noted that he would like to have them (or
two others) sent back, as he now had only four missionaries,
himself among them, available. He was thinking especially
of San Buenaventura by the Santa Barbara Channel. "Provisions," he reminded Palóu, "have already been twice
sent for this mission and now, since the failure to establish

it could not be blamed in any way on the friars, I do not want the blame to fall upon us when the proper military protection is at hand for its inauguration." Serra had endured delay without impatience; but once the road was at last clear he intended to proceed at once with what he had come to do.

Now that Monterey had been identified beyond question and a presidio established there, Portolá handed over his command (but not the office of Governor) to Lieutenant Fages. This ambitious young man has been described as a protégé of Gálvez, but the truth would seem to be that Gálvez, having to choose between him and Rivera, preferred the more energetic of the two; it does not follow that he considered Fages the best possible man for the job. There were, however, other considerations that might have been weighed: Captain Rivera was very bitter at being passed over in favor of a junior officer, and to a great extent this explains his behavior when at last in 1774 he came to have the command at Monterey. He himself was appointed to the presidio at San Diego.

The consequential Pedro Fages was accordingly given the more important post. As Father Piette says in the first volume of his *Secret de Junipero Serra,* he did not lack literary culture, for his letters and journals display a clear, lively and observant spirit. He seemed to be the incarnation of the career soldier, but he kept his natural faults to the end, though he modified them to some extent. "Servile to his superiors, he found a compensation to this humble obsequence in an extreme harshness to his subordinates." That judgment of Piette's is no doubt correct upon the whole, but there is no evidence for his assertion that Rivera was disqualified in the opinion of Gálvez because he had been too friendly towards the Jesuits during the years when he had been stationed at Loreto.

Portolá had been appointed Governor of the two Californias but, as I have pointed out, mainly to give him standing while he ejected the Jesuits, and because he was on hand, he had been sent north to find Monterey. Now Matías de Armona was given the position of governor—but only as a stopgap, remaining at Loreto for less than a year. In any event it was the commandant at Monterey, the man on the spot, who really mattered.

So on July 9, 1770, Gaspar de Portolá, accompanied by Costansó the engineer, sailed from Monterey, their work having been completed. In Mexico City, where Portolá arrived a month or two later, he was received in audience by Gálvez and the Viceroy and treated as a hero, with a High Mass of Thanksgiving at the cathedral. The official announcement was perhaps a shade too "official," for it declared that the Spaniards in Monterey (meaning Upper California) were living as quietly as in the heart of the capital. So also was it stretching things a bit to say that "the new presidio is abundantly furnished with artillery, troops and munitions of war." But though Portolá is not very impressive in the role of a hero, it may be granted that he had done what had been required of him. He was rewarded by being promoted to a lieutenant colonelcy and a few years later was appointed Governor of Pueblo, New Spain. When he retired in 1784, in which year he returned to Spain, he was created a full colonel. One may regret that he was not left at Monterey and that the governor's seat was not transferred there, as was done in 1776, for Portolá was at least sufficiently able for the post and had always got along well with the friars. But of course in 1770 it was still a little doubtful as to whether the California venture would justify itself; that being the case, it was considered that Portolá was too good a man to spare.

CHAPTER NINE

Carmel

DESPITE the official report of how well California was garrisoned, actually only a small body of men were stationed there, most of them being at Monterey but with a contingent at the southern presidio. Excluding some artisans (and it will be remembered how valiantly the blacksmith had fought in the Indian attack on San Diego), and a few muleteers and servants, who were of little if any use apart from their employments, the whole country could not have had more than a hundred men. And while the leatherjackets were excellent soldiers and among the best horsemen in the world, others—particularly Fages' own company of Catalan volunteers—were not of the best quality, even if they were better than their tatterdemalion aspect might suggest. These men had to hold the coast of California against thousands of Indians who, had they ever been belligerent and found a capable leader, would have made short work of the invaders.

Fortunately the Indians had been persuaded that the Spaniards did not intend to exploit them in any way but that instead might be expected to confer much material benefit. Even in San Diego things had quieted down, and after all the Indians there had been thieves rather than warriors. At every established mission five soldiers were put under the command of a corporal for the protection of the friars, but Serra found, more and more as time went on, that these men were sometimes more of a detriment than a help to the missions because of the bad example a few of them set. While upon the whole the soldiers were remarkably well behaved, it was only to be expected that disorderly elements should appear among them and that their officers would take a lighter view of their offenses than did the Fathers. In any event it was hard to inflict severe punishment under the circumstances, and Fages, martinet though he was where military matters were concerned, was inclined to wink at everything else, if only because he thought that things of which the friars disapproved were no business of his

It was for this reason that Junípero Serra saw the desirability of separating mission and presidio. He felt that a small guard at the mission would suffice, as the presidio was not far away and could be called upon in case of real trouble. But that guard, he came to feel, should be made up of picked men, and any soldier among them who, in his opinion, was not the kind of person he wanted should be recalled to the presidio and another of a better type sent to replace him. It was an attitude that Fages resented, because he considered that this was something for him and not the Fathers to decide. Moreover, the Commandant did not much like it that the guard at the missions was used to bring back runaway neophytes who had put themselves under the charge of the missionaries; that too he thought was giving the friars an authority which belonged to himself.

Finally, both Monterey and San Diego were ports, where the coming and going of ships was a distraction, seldom though it occurred. At these ports part of the duty of the soldiers was to keep order among the sailors on shore leave, as they were men of a somewhat low grade. Such being the case, Serra undertook to send a priest on Sundays and holy days to the presidio; at Monterey he lost little time in transferring his mission to the mouth of the Carmel River, about four miles away.

This move called for some tact on Serra's part. But he could argue that the river, small though it was, would provide the water needed for the farming operations that formed an essential part of his plan. The soil was better, too, being less sandy and with level stretches suitable for agriculture. Although the name of San Carlos was selected for the little church built there, chosen at once in honor of "our beloved Sovereign, the Prince of the Asturias, and of the viceroy of New Spain," before long the mission came to be referred to simply as Carmel. As such it forms today a little town, the restored church of San Carlos still bearing that name.

Carmel (or Carmelo) first appears as the name given to the river by the three Carmelite friars who went on Vizcaíno's expedition of 1603, but the Franciscans took it over willingly enough. Today some of the local inhabitants claim—I cannot believe that it can have a shred of justification—that the twisted cypresses found in their locality, which they also say exist nowhere else in California, are of the same species as those on Mount Carmel in the Holy Land. For the rest there are a number of live oaks, funereally draped with Spanish moss, and firs, with blue lupins and shrubs on the sand dunes. The beauty of the spot charmed Serra, and there were places nearby, such as what is now Pebble Beach and the rugged Point Lobos, which may have reminded him somewhat of his native Mallorca.

Even before the Carmel mission formally opened, which was not until December, 1771—for it took time to build its stockade—Serra had founded another mission not very far away, one dedicated to San Antonio, on July 14, 1771. It was there that Serra very characteristically hung up the church bells on the bough of a tree, there not being as yet even a little shack of a church, and started to ring them. As he did so he called out, "Come, Gentiles, come to Holy Church! Come and receive the faith of Jesus Christ!" One of the priests assigned to this mission, Miguel Pieras, was a bit amused, as there was not so much as a single Indian in sight. To his expostulation Serra merely answered, "I can hear them coming." In this Fray Junípero was being very Franciscan, for whether he remembered the incident or not, it was recorded of St. Francis of Assisi that when he was living with his first followers in a shack, he saw in a vision the thousands of all nations—Frenchmen, Germans, Spaniards and Englishmen—who would soon be flocking to join him.

The Indians did come but a good deal more slowly than had been hoped, largely because not all the missions that had been projected could be established. While those of San Gabriel and San Luis Obispo soon followed, that of San Buenaventura had to wait a long time. Though it had been projected, and its name chosen in consultation between Serra and Gálvez, Fages and his successors always pleaded that it would necessitate the establishment of a third presidio, and there simply were no soldiers to spare. This they could say even when, after Felipe Barri became governor in 1771, he sent twenty recruits from the Peninsula and at the same time the Viceroy, Croix, had sent a dozen others. The channel area was more thickly populated than any other part of the California coast, and the sentiments of the Indians there were unknown. That there were so many souls to save was a powerful motive with Serra; to the military officers it was a reason for proceeding with great caution. They managed, like many of the officials in the Spanish dependencies, to give great lip service to their superiors but to ignore their instructions, or to put on them an interpretation of their own which was virtual nullification.

The Indians around Monterey seem in our eyes to be like the rest of the natives of California. Here, as elsewhere on the continent, there was an inexplicable medley of tongues, so that little groups living within a few miles of one another could have slight communication—a circumstance that added immeasurably to the difficulties of the Fathers. As Serra wrote to Palóu: "If all are not Christians already, it is in my opinion only owing to our want of understanding the language. This is a trouble not new to me, and I have always imagined that my sins have not permitted me to possess the faculty of learning strange tongues, which is a great misfortune in a country like this, where there is no interpreter or teacher of languages to be had." The solution attempted was that of getting the Indians to learn Spanish. At first it was merely a question of imparting a few stock phrases and the greeting *Amar a Dios,* or Love God. But by degrees Spanish became the language of the missions, and in it most of the religious instructions (all, of course, extremely elementary) were eventually given.

Some observers thought that the California Indians were more like Europeans in appearance than Indians elsewhere. But this probably means that they did not much correspond to the Indians of the great plains. These were a tall, vigorous race, haughty in bearing. The California Indians on the other hand were rather under medium size, chunky in build, with short necks, which made them look as though their round heads had been sewn on like bulbous buttons. Their noses were flat, their eyebrows bushy, their mouths large with thick lips. They walked pigeon-toed and listlessly, except during their games and dances, or when they went hunting, which was much less

often than they danced. It was really mainly in the contour
of their ears and chins that they suggested Europeans. They
were far from being prepossessing.

Even the highly intelligent Iroquois found it hard to
grasp abstract ideas, but the California Indians found it
hard to grasp even the concrete, if it was in any respect
new. It was so doubtful whether most of them understood
the difference between a consecrated Host and ordinary
bread, that this at first made the Fathers reluctant to administer Holy Communion, even to those who had long
been under instruction, except when they were dying.
Their memory was so poor that the same thing had to be
painfully repeated a hundred times, and even then with no
assurance that it would be retained.

In one sense their conversion was relatively easy. Their
religious concepts, if they existed at all as we understand
them, were hazy. They were not idolators and though
they had their magicians, these had less authority than
the medicine men elsewhere. The famous couplet of Pope
about "Lo! the poor Indian" did not apply very much
anywhere, in the sense of seeing God in every cloud and
hearing Him in the wind, but it applied less here than
perhaps to any people one could find. They did have some
notion of a future state, but it was exceedingly vague. The
Spaniards were at once helped and hampered by the fact
that they encountered almost nothing similar to the tribes
with whom they had any acquaintance. The Indians did
not make what could be described as wars, for though they
fought now and then, it was over issues so trifling as to fade
quickly away. They were not bloodthirsty and attached no
great prestige to prowess in battle. All of which, added up,
meant that the Fathers could write on a *tabula rasa,* but
a tablet which, alas, could receive impressions only at the
cost of most patient training.

The Indians were not obliged to organize any hunting expeditions, for during all seasons of the year food of a sort was readily procurable. Small animals abounded on the hills and the sea was full of fish. Only in the Santa Barbara Channel were there well-constructed canoes, but the rest of the savages could scoop up what they wanted in inlets when the tide went out or venture for a short distance on rafts of bulrushes tied together. Wild fruits and berries and roots mainly sufficed. By pounding in a stone pestle the seeds they gathered, the women made a not unpalatable paste. The samples of these pestles that survive show them to have been so well constructed, despite the lack of metal tools, that one wonders why the Indians did not bother to make other articles. They had no cooking utensils of clay but instead used baskets, woven so closely that they would hold water, and into these baskets heated stones were placed. Like lazy people everywhere they did a lot of work merely to avoid work.

Music, if what the Spaniards considered a horrible noise could be called music, was a passion with them. They had a drum, and a flute or pipe of wood, and rattled stones in a shell. To this accompaniment they sang—they would sing all night, if they were permitted to do so. Several times the soldiers had forcibly to make them desist. Similarly, though they loathed anything like work, they would put any amount of energy into dances which were devoid of all grace in Spanish eyes.

Their houses were mere huts, with the ground scooped out a little, and in a single hut a number of savages would huddle together for warmth. When these huts became too verminous even for them, they were simply burned down and new huts constructed. This only called for a few poles covered with branches or bulrushes, the *tule*. Like the In-

dians around San Diego, all except the women and girls
went naked.

One of the features of their way of life was their fre-
quentation of sweathouses. These were a strictly masculine
institution, and one may imagine that they had been established as a device for the men to get away by themselves
into a species of club. In these houses the men would
gather, completely naked as always, and sit or loll in a kind
of turkish bath, chatting comfortably, until one of them,
feeling that he had by then sweated enough, ran down to
the river or the sea. They claimed that this restored them
when they were tired—though it is not easy to know what
made them tired, unless it was their dances—and also that
the sweathouses had curative properties. This was likely
enough in the case of some ailments, even if it had a fatal
effect in others. But if it was good for the men, why did not
women have their own sweathouses? Perhaps it would not
do for them because of the final act of running out naked,
something the women never did. There may have been an
answer behind that answer: that the modesty so strictly enjoined upon the female sex was by way of preventing them
from having sweathouses, a mere means of preserving a
masculine prerogative. None of the women were in the
slightest degree disturbed by seeing stark naked men
around all the time. As their modesty was not affronted
on this score, one questions whether it could have existed
in any sense comprehensible to us. One must surmise that
nothing but a taboo was involved, whose origin nobody
knew. All that we can find is that men had their club—a
means of escape—and that women had to do their gossiping
wherever they happened to be.

Marriage was a very simple affair, demanding no ceremony of any kind; a man and woman went to live together;
that was all. Usually they were faithful in these unions,

and polygamy was not general, though it existed. We do hear of a case where a man had married not only three sisters but their mother as well. It would seem that a man assumed responsibility for all his "in-laws," though of course such a term would have been beyond his comprehension. The only way he could protect them was by being their husband. It did not make much difference to him; he had more women to work for him and he himself did no additional work, other than perhaps killing another rabbit and bringing home another basket of acorns. The idea of marriage, in our sense, hardly existed. Yet the unions were usually affectionate, for these people, however stupid and lazy they may have been, however poorly equipped for dealing with the ordinary affairs of life, had a sweetness of disposition that is always of immense advantage in the relations between the sexes.

If their children did not get much care, this was because they did not know how to give it, not because they were deliberately neglectful. The mortality among the young was enormous, but it was also high among adults. Epidemics of smallpox were frequent and tuberculosis and syphilis were rampant. A few medical missionaries would have done a world of good, yet there was only one medical man in all California, the Dr. Prat who had arrived with the Portolá expedition. About this time he went insane and had to be sent home, so nothing whatever was done for the health of the savages except for those few simple remedies the Fathers knew how to administer.

From the start the mission operated on carefully thought-out principles, in so far as this was practicable. The system in its more developed form will be described in a subsequent chapter; at this stage it was necessarily rudimentary. It consisted of little more than grouping around the mis-

sion station the huts of such Indians as professed themselves willing to receive religious instruction and who
might be persuaded to do a little work. Since the majority
of these were adults, and very dense in mind, baptism was
not administered until the Fathers were satisfied that certain minimum requirements had been met. But as that
situation was at best rather unsatisfactory, the aim was to
get the young to live within the mission enclosure, bound
to what might be called a kind of apprenticeship. This
meant that they were committed to a Christian upbringing
and were no longer free to wander at large, lest all their
training should be wasted by a relapse into savagery. At
first, however, such arrangements were of a makeshift character, as makeshift as were the mission buildings themselves.

The initial inducements were kind words and a few
presents. A handful of glass beads worked wonders. And
when it became apparent that a good deal more might be
looked for—in particular a regular supply of food—many
neophytes were glad to remain. Yet in the beginning the
Fathers had very little to offer, for until they had sown
what grain they had with them and had reached the time
of harvest, they had to be careful not to give away too
much of the seed upon whose multiplication so much
depended. The Indians had never cultivated any fields, but
had got all they needed in the woods; they had to be taught
agriculture. The Fathers, assisted by the guard at the mission, planted a few vegetables and a little grain, getting
some of the neophytes to work with them. But because
their minds could hardly grasp the idea that this was making provision for the future, and because the stores available at the moment were meager, everybody lived sparsely.
In fact the Fathers were often obliged to encourage the
Indians to go out to the hills and bring back whatever

they could find, which was not much of an inducement to get them to stay at the missions.

The time came in the summer of 1772 when famine stared them all in the face. They might, of course, have sent a few mules to San Diego, hoping to find something there that could be spared. But as likely as not the muleteers would have had to go on down the Peninsula, which was a barren land, though under some cultivation. If that were done, however, by the time the men who had gone for help returned, most of the people in the mission and the presidio might be dead. It was rightly decided not to slaughter any of the cattle; they were needed for breeding and the replenishment of the missions. Daily the Fathers hoped for the arrival of a ship and daily they were disappointed. Even a pancake a day was now hard to manage; vegetables and milk had to suffice.

Yet one wonders a little that the Spaniards themselves did not show themselves more resourceful. If the Indians could survive on their roots and berries, so, one would imagine, could other people. And the sea gave plentiful supplies of fish, especially sardines, though of course the only means available for fishing were the rudimentary ones of the savages. Moreover, some of them were fairly good hunters, going disguised in deerskins right into a herd and then shooting with their stone-tipped arrows. But only the more expert could do this; most of the Indians could do no more than use a kind of boomerang to bring down rabbits. In any event the starvation could not have been so extreme as we have sometimes been led to suppose.

In this emergency Lieutenant, now Captain, Fages hit upon a happy idea, though one so obvious it is remarkable that it had not occurred to anybody before. In a certain valley not too far away there were a number of bears, and though probably most of them were not grizzlies but the smaller and harmless animals of the same species, Fages determined to organize a bear hunt. The Indians themselves never went after these creatures, for the simple reason that their shafts could not penetrate a hide so thickly covered with fur. It would be a different matter with firearms.

The first explorers of 1769, of whom Fages had been one, when searching for Monterey had come upon a deep ravine, which they had named *Cañada de los Osos,* the Valley of the Bears, not thinking to what use it would be put. Doubtless they now weighed the consideration that by hunting the bears they would drive them out, and then that source of food would be lost. But everything yielded to the crisis. If they could tide themselves over until the autumn harvest, scanty though it might be, they could manage. Besides, a ship would sooner or later arrive. Serra had been teaching prayers to his neophytes and then kneeling most of the night in prayer, asking divine succor. He became so worn down that his guard of soldiers begged him to take a little rest. Instead he continued to do violence to heaven. Now Fages' idea seemed the answer they needed.

With a file of a dozen men, all picked shots, Fages went off to bag his bears, and with his soldiers went a number of Indians to act as bearers. It may be that Fages, while he was ordinarily very considerate of the Indians, did not forget the fracas in San Diego and thought it just as well that some of them be witnesses to the execution of which Spanish muskets were capable. If an Indian was charged by a bear—for even a small bear could be dangerous when angry—he climbed up the nearest tree, while the white men stood their ground and let the bear have it between the eyes or down the throat. For a full six months Fages and his men beat the coverts of the Valley of the Bears, sending ample supplies to all the missions every day. If the meat was a bit tough, it was still very welcome to men who had not tasted beef for a long while, and like the beef carried on the ships, it could be salted or dried in the sun so that it would last a good while. Fages gained immense prestige among the natives, and while his men took the bear hunting as a matter of course, they gave him credit for his resourcefulness.

Even so, the men of his command continued to dislike him as a martinet. He irritated them, as he also irritated the Fathers, by losing no opportunity for exercising his authority, usually in rather trivial ways. Everybody sighed for the bluff and genial Portolá, and even the easygoing Rivera. That he had been appointed to San Diego instead of to Monterey was a kind of grievance to the soldiers. The result was that—partly owing to the manner Fages had of comporting himself, but partly owing to the short rations he had been obliged to dole out—some of them began to desert, a party of nine once going off into the hills and at another time a party of five with a corporal.

In some way or other Fages got it into his head that these desertions were the fault of the Fathers. It was actually a kind of strike, a demonstration to obtain better treatment. It was of course in no way instigated by any of the friars, though one may suppose that when the soldiers had grumbled about their hard lot, the friars listened with some sympathy. After Fages marched against these men and found them behind a barricade, apparently ready to give battle, he prudently withdrew, not being able to afford casualties among his small force. He therefore asked Serra to go to them and offer full pardon if they would return. These persuasions had their effect, for Serra pointed out that what little supplies of food they had would soon be exhausted, after which they would have no choice except that of accepting the degraded manner of life of the savages. Even were they able to make their way back to the Peninsula, they would be sure to be severely punished by the Governor at Loreto. Fages could have offered the deserters terms in person but was too proud and irascible a man for that. The fact that these men showed themselves willing to listen to Serra only confirmed the Commandant in his warped idea that the desertions must have been due to Serra's influence.

Now and then Serra had occasion to lodge complaints against one or other of the soldiers on very valid grounds, grounds that Fages, otherwise so strict, took too lightly. It sometimes happened that an Indian woman was maltreated. On one occasion we hear of a group of soldiers riding out and, possibly at the outset merely in fun, lassoing a few Indians. The men, being nimble, usually dodged the thrown noose, but in the case of women so captured—or at least one case—the rider, dismounting, proceeded to gross indecency. In another, a wife of a chief—or a man who came closest to being a chief among a people so unorganized—was raped. When her husband tried to come to her rescue, the soldier shot him dead. Then, to make matters worse, he cut off the chief's head and set it on a pole as a warning of what might be expected by anybody who attacked a Spaniard. It was no use complaining to Fages. He took the line that he could not be everywhere at once, and that even if the soldier had done wrong, it was upon the whole a good thing that the Indians were taught a lesson.

Although such incidents occurred so seldom that one marvels at the good behavior of the Spanish soldiers, a few licentious soldiers were capable of undoing all the principles enunciated by the Fathers. Serra was realist enough to know that unfortunate incidents were only to be expected; he was also an idealist who expected that Fages would punish those who were guilty.

Nor did matters rest at that point. When mail arrived for the Fathers Fages opened it, and if he disapproved of the contents did not hand out the letter. It was the same with the letters they wrote; he suspected, not without cause, that he was being reported to the authorities in San Fernando College and that the Viceroy would hear of it. So he took it upon himself to censor letters, or even to withhold them. It need hardly be said that this was utterly impermissible. Though one may have some liking for Fages, he was the perfect example of one heady with a little brief authority.

Serra had received the reinforcement by now of ten additional friars. Some of them were put to work in the new missions he founded, and he was able to allow two missionaries in California who were not in good health to retire. Even so, he found himself with a number of supernumeraries, men at loose ends until their missions were founded. They helped, of course, in the work being done, but until the missions for which they had been sent came into existence they were officially *non est,* unable to draw upon the stipend allotted by the Pious Fund. This did no special harm to them personally, because the $275 a year paid at this time to the account of each friar was expended in Mexico City on goods needed by the missions. But their support was a further drain on the missionary work, already very inadequately sustained.

Nevertheless Serra, as was his way, gave the most hopeful interpretation of the situation. Without deluding himself, he was able to report that San Diego, Monterey and San Antonio could all show a fair number of converts, though at San Gabriel—probably because of the incident of the raped woman and her murdered husband—the Indians were distrustful. Serra did not blame the Indians, but he remarked, "There are those who say that though they seem as harmless as lambs, they will yet turn into lions and tigers." As for Monterey and San Antonio, he goes on: "The natives have grown more reliable every season." He begs that the new missionaries who are sent "come well provided with patience, charity and good temper, for they may find themselves rich in tribulations. But where can the laboring ox go that the plough will not be heavy to drag? And unless he drag it, how shall the seed be sown?" That was written only for the private ear of Palóu, and it will be seen that even to this confidant his complaints were very mild. It could be said that they were not complaints at all but merely an explanation of some of the difficulties with which he was contending.

CHAPTER TEN

Clash With the Commandant

SUCH A clash was perhaps inevitable because of the existence of a divided authority. Dr. Charles E. Chapman has said, "Disputes between the religious and military were a chronic feature of Spanish colonial administration everywhere. Neither element can justly be charged with fault for this situation; it was inherent in the dual system of government, employed where powers were either too loosely defined, or else too specifically stated in some instances which did not fit actual circumstances." [1] But if that is true —and it is—one wonders at his view of Serra as a man who could get along with none of the officers who served at Monterey. We have seen that he accused Palóu of exalting Serra (in the matter of the novena in March, 1770) at the expense of Portolá. He himself is rather consistent at disparaging Serra in favor of his successor Firmín Lasuén.

It is clear enough from the instructions issued by the Viceroy in November, 1770, that he regarded the position of the military commander as subordinate to that of the President of the Missions. The main idea was that in California there was to be a spiritual conquest, with the soldiers there to protect the friars, though the presence of both soldiers and friars was to establish a claim against any intruding European power, with Russia specifically in mind.

[1] "A Great Franciscan in California: Fermín Francisco de Lasuén." *Catholic Historical Review*, V (July–October, 1919), p. 146.

However, it was only natural that the military officers should feel that, circumstances being what they were, they and not the missionaries would have to answer for anything that went wrong. Their tendency was to regard whatever assurances had been given to the missionaries as not always feasible, and to think of the Padres themselves as well-meaning men without much practicality.

There was also an idea that appeared more definitely after the time of Fages, but which may have been incipient in his mind too, that the mission methods introduced were somewhat out-of-date. He wanted the savages civilized and made good subjects of the King of Spain, Charles III, and he recognized that their Christianization was part of this process. But what he and his successors looked upon as a means to an end, the Padres regarded as the end itself; in fact ends and means were in this case more or less transposed, the missionaries being primarily concerned with the salvation of souls, but fully acknowledging that civilization (in the sense of the civil and military authorities) was a method of bringing about the spiritual object.

Father Piette explains this on the ground of what he calls the "Voltairianism" of the officials. That the spirit of what is called the Enlightenment had touched some of the highly placed people in Spain is no doubt true; there is not the slightest indication that it actuated the stiff, stubborn but stouthearted commandant at Monterey. Fages was merely exhibiting arrogance, innate with him but possibly increased by his having been put in command over his senior, Rivera, who was eating his heart out in discontent at San Diego.

Meanwhile Felipe Barri had been sent to Loreto on the Peninsula as governor to replace Matías de Armona. He was too far away to count for much, and most of the decisions had to be made by Fages, the man in charge of

Monterey. Furthermore, Barri was no help to Serra. He consistently backed up Fages, and he probably was (despite his Irish origin) somewhat anticlerical. The general situation had become very difficult.

Serra was a mild man, but he felt that official forces were now working against him in the highest circles. For instance, the Dominicans had been given the Peninsula as their missionary field, and they complained at once that the Franciscans had stripped all the missions there of the articles necessary to their work. No doubt the Dominicans did find the missions of which they had been put in charge rather bare. But what had been there during the regime of the Jesuits, until 1768, was much the worse for wear by the time the Franciscans were ordered to replace them. Serra had had carried to the north whatever he felt the missions could spare, but he and his colleagues had been reasonable. They had left enough behind them to justify Palóu's indignant repudiation, in the third volume of his *Historical Memoirs of New California,* of the Dominicans' complaints.

These complaints, justified or not, did Serra no good in Mexico City. Much more serious were the relations that had come to exist between himself and Fages. Matters had reached such a pass that Serra felt he had to write the Commandant letters, of which he kept copies, because conversations got him nowhere. These letters were politely phrased, all ending with the ceremonious "kissing of the hand," and for good measure an assurance that he was the Commandant's affectionate servant, friend and chaplain. But as early as September 22, 1772, Serra demanded a plain answer to his question: "Yes or no, are you able, are you willing to accord the things asked?" Fages, also kissing Serra's hand as his "very devoted, affectionate and loyal servant," does give a plain answer. His view is that the

CLASH WITH THE COMMANDANT 165

charge of the missions appertains to the friars, but that "the administration civil and military belongs to me." That stand would be unexceptionable, but Fages went on, with regard to the soldiers: "All remain subject to my pleasure at all times. They should recognize me as the chief of military justice and captain of infantry, me Don Pedro Fages." The last phrase gives him away. After that it was a little silly to say, as he did, that he had been nominated in his functions and confirmed by the new Viceroy, Antonio Bucareli.

In spite of its arrogance that letter of Fages might have seemed reasonable were it not that Serra had been given a rather different intimation of the intentions of the authorities in Mexico City. Therefore, on the evening of September 30th, when he received it, he took the precaution of having it witnessed by Fray Tomas Peña, his assistant at that time, appending his own name. When he replied on October 3rd, he took a careful copy of his letter, saying that he had sent it that morning to Captain Fages, but adding later the notation, "Up to today, the 17th of the month, he has not replied."

Fages did reply, however, writing from San Diego on October 11th, telling Serra that on November 30th of the previous year the new Viceroy, Don Antonio Bucareli, had written: "You shall make known to the Reverend Father Fray Junípero Serra, President of the Missions, and the other religious, that you recommend the important obligation of preaching by example and word of mouth, that they all ought to obey and carry out your orders." To this Serra replied asserting that he had always exhorted the Commandant's subjects to obey his orders, but adding, "I wish you would accord me the favor of seeing the original text of his Excellency." He also asked that the original of his own letter be sent on to the Viceroy.

The letter Fages quoted was authentic enough and seemed decisive. But a new and very important factor was that Bucareli might not be well informed about California. Gálvez had by this time gone back to Spain, recovered from his attack of insanity, but (though he held cabinet office) was no longer concerned with affairs in the new territory. And Serra knew that there would be no use in appealing to the Governor, Felipe Barri, at Loreto. He had already spread calumnious stories of the way the Franciscans had stripped the missions there.

There was only one thing to do: to take the next boat to San Blas, and from there make his way overland to the capital so that he might explain the whole situation to the Viceroy face to face. Writing would be of little if any use in view of the habit Fages had of suppressing any letters of complaint. And so much had to be told that to have written it out would have called for a small book. Even if he reached Bucareli, Serra was aware that his statements might be discounted; but he had to discover for himself what kind of a man the new Viceroy was.

At the end of 1772, when he arrived at San Blas, he got from the officer in charge of the shipyard the disturbing information that it was doubtful whether the new ship then on the stocks would ever be completed; he had received intimations that San Diego and Monterey were from then on to be supplied only by mule trains from the Peninsula. But as this was not yet an official decision, Serra, sustained only by hope in God, limped all the way from the coast to Mexico City.

Fages must have been apprehensive at Serra's departure, but he was not able to prevent it. Yet he knew that he could say that as a soldier he had only carried out written orders, even if he had interpreted them in his own way. If it crossed his mind that Serra's journey would result in his recall from Monterey, that probably did not worry him much. His little presidio, where the commandant's quarters at that time consisted of an adobe house of two rooms, could not have made Monterey seem very desirable. If he lost his position it would not be any tremendous loss.

Bucareli was a man not only personally unknown to Serra but one whose attitude to the missions was unknown. As we shall see, he was not only completely won over but proved himself an even better supporter than Gálvez. Yet Serra could only hope that he would receive a favorable hearing; he might have been given a rebuff that would have made his position more difficult than before, by increasing the arrogance of Fages. Nevertheless it was upon this stranger that Serra had to pin all his hopes. The situation he had left behind him was so very difficult that he was compelled to trust everything to this doubtful expedient.

Antonio Bucareli y Ursúa, unlike Gálvez, was an aristocrat. Among the members of his Florentine forbears had been three popes and six cardinals, not to mention many less highly placed people. His list of titles was about a yard long and his salary as Viceroy was $60,000, which was later raised to $80,000. When for some reason he wished to raise a loan of $2,500,000, the bankers gave it without security, such was his reputation for probity. When he died there was no *residencia* or examination into his official acts, such as was invariable when an administrator of his standing completed his term of office. Bancroft rightly says that it was unprecedented in the history of Spanish royal representation. Dr. Chapman remarks of him that he "seems to have been one of those rare individuals who can throw themselves wholeheartedly into an enterprise, merely out of a sense of duty, without a thought of self." Though a cynic may say that many people could do so on a salary of $80,000 a year (whose purchasing power was then three or four times what it is now), perhaps the answer is found in that enormous loan that Bucareli had to obtain, as it suggests that the maintenance of his office in fitting style did not even begin to be covered by his salary. I. B. Richman calls him "a master of urbanity and a connoisseur of vintages," a rather nasty dig. Bucareli was obliged to have a good table; there is no indication whatever that he unduly indulged himself with wine.

Serra's way had been prepared by the fact that the previous Christmas Father Verger, once a fellow professor with Serra at Mallorca and now the Guardian at San Fernando, had received a long report on affairs in California and had shown it to the Viceroy. Verger had suggested to Serra that he should "somewhat moderate his ardent zeal," but of course he knew that only the zealous get things done and he was waiting for Serra's arrival with some impatience. The zealous man arrived at Mexico City early in 1773, and on February 5th and 13th had interviews with Bucareli, finding him very willing to listen to his story but asking for a written statement.

Bucareli may have been somewhat discouraged. On February 24, 1773, Julián de Arriaga, the Minister of State in Spain, had written indicating the possibility of giving up Upper California, or at least all attempt to supply by sea the troops and missionaries there. Though this letter had not as yet reached the Viceroy, he was aware of how the wind lay. It is therefore much to Bucareli's credit that he was willing to receive Serra's representations at all. Arriaga as Minister of State was Bucareli's superior, yet Bucareli showed that he preferred Serra's opinion on this point, even if it would be going altogether too far to suggest that it determined his policy.

The Viceroy felt the questions now being laid before him were of too great importance to be settled by one man alone, or by anybody only on the basis of word of mouth. He therefore asked Serra to prepare a full written statement which he and his Council could consider together. Five statements were eventually presented, dated March 15th, April 22nd, May 21st, and the 4th and 12th of June. Not all of them had the same weight, those coming later being somewhat in the nature of postscripts. The group that gathered to discuss Californian affairs in the *palacio,* on the main plaza of Mexico City, were of such a standing that no less than thirty-six lines were needed for all their honorifics.

The presentation of the documents in extenso is outside the scope of this book. A summary of the main point will have to suffice. Naturally enough, as Serra now had an opportunity that would hardly occur again, he brought up everything that he could think of. For his pains in doing so he is described by Bryan J. Clinch as a "Sancho Panza," one cannot quite see why. Yet Clinch cites as illustration: "I think it would be well if Your Excellency would caution the storekeeper at San Blas to pay more attention to the packing of provisions. No meat at all came last year, and what came this year, besides being little in quantity was so dry and wormy that people said it was the remnant of the year before." That Clinch calls a "quaint remark," though it goes without saying that the people who had to eat the food were glad to have attention called to the matter. So also Serra's kindness was appreciated by the soldiers for whom he asked that they might be recalled, as it was a long time since they had seen their wives and families.

But though this last item may have been important only to the soldiers whom Serra took it upon himself to befriend, the documents as cited by Piette and Engelhardt

are very thoroughgoing. Indeed one gets the impression
that most of the official Spanish papers of this time show
that those who drew them up were very businesslike and
efficient. That the cogency of Serra's representations was
admitted is shown by the fact that, with only a couple of
exceptions, they were all acted upon favorably, or at least
held over for some further discussion.

One of the main things effected by Serra was that the
Fathers were to have a free hand in the missions, and that
at least some of the soldiers attached to them as a guard
were to be at the special disposition of the missionaries,
for reasons which will appear later. There was, in fine, to
be no pleading of conflicting orders on the part of the
commandant. And if any man's conduct was detrimental
to the mission work, that man should be recalled to the
presidio, if not discharged from the military force.

A new order was given for the establishment of the long-
projected and often deferred mission of San Buenaventura.
And two new missions were to be established on or near
San Francisco Bay. Fages had been somewhat negligent
regarding this matter (with some excuse); the new commandant had the founding of these missions pressed upon
him. Our Holy Father St. Francis was to get his mission
at last; so also was one to be named for Santa Clara, the
first of the Saint's women disciples.

The question of the ships was gone into at considerable
length. The continuance of the whole California project
was at stake, for official opinion was inclined to abandon
the naval yard at San Blas and the ship-building program
and to trust to supplying California by mule trains from
the Peninsula, using the existing ships to carry goods and
recruits across the Gulf to Loreto. Serra gave ample demonstration that such a method was impracticable. He
produced precise figures about the number of mules and

muleteers needed, showing that their cost would be pro-
hibitive. He also laid emphasis upon the need for conducting explorations up the coast. Beyond San Francisco,
where they had not established any stations, there stretched
a coastline of two thousand miles to the north. Apparently
the old fear of the Russians, if not entirely laid aside, was
not being given sufficient attention. That coastline could
become a possible field for Spanish expansion only if the
Spaniards kept a careful watch.

Briefly Serra's argument was this: If mules alone were
used, from eleven to fifteen hundred of these animals
would be required, as well as many drivers. He was able
to prove that the cost of maintaining San Blas would be
considerably less, and that counted a good deal at a time
when the administration was trying to effect economies.
Spain after its recent wars was in no position to disregard
the simple facts of bookkeeping. After San Francisco had
been founded, ships would be needed more than ever;
still more so, if they were to guard the coast. The statement
was incontrovertible.

The stipends of the friars were now raised—to $400 a
year—for what they received was not in the form of money
but in the form of supplies for the missions and the expenses of carrying these ate up a third of the stipends.
The friars never minded receiving so little; they had not
become missionaries for their material profit. It might
be added, however, that parsimonious as was the Spanish
government in many ways, it paid its soldiers well as compared with England and France, the leatherjackets being
given four times the amount given to a British redcoat.
Not only that; the difference in pay of men and officers
was surprisingly small. Where a private received three
hundred and seventy-five dollars a year, a corporal obtained only twenty-five and a sergeant seventy-five dollars

more. Even a lieutenant's salary was only five hundred dollars a year, which might seem to give little inducement for an enlisted man to strive for promotion. On the other hand, all this is indicative of a democratic spirit, which one hardly expects to find in the Spanish service.

Though Serra may not have gone to Mexico to promote the project of a new and quicker land route from Sonora, the province at the northeast of the Gulf, he was asked his opinion about it. A route across the Colorado and Gila rivers had several times been suggested by Juan Bautista de Anza, a very capable and courageous man who, like his father, had spent his whole life on the frontier. Regarding this Bucareli wrote on September 26, 1773, to Arriaga in Spain, reporting that he had questioned the missionary, "and he considered the project not only possible but very useful, as a preliminary to other explorations, if, communication by land to Monterey having been opened, use might be made of the troops who should effect it, in order that the coast might be followed and a more careful examination made from the port of San Francisco and beyond it, at the same time that an effort is being made to effect the same investigation by sea." Bucareli adds of Serra that "his suggestion may forward the desire of his Majesty that efforts be made to investigate the new explorations of the Russians."

In his report Bucareli, though he had not borrowed the idea of a land route from Serra (but had merely asked his opinion), held strongly to an idea which, it may be said, was Serra's—that of maintaining ships. If in this the Padre with perhaps a spice of guile stressed the Russian menace —which could only be effectually met by using ships—he was no doubt primarily thinking of the ships for maintaining the missions and, indeed, the presidios in California. He rather cleverly played upon the considerations in the

Viceroy's mind in establishing his point. Though Palóu is not correct in writing that the Anza expeditions were undertaken at Serra's urging, he is only a little wide of the mark. Had Serra not given his hearty approval, it is very likely that Anza would have failed to obtain official backing. Professor Bolton, in the volume which is his preliminary to the Anza diaries, does not hesitate to say that Serra's advice in the case was decisive.

The point upon which Serra was most insistent was that Fages be removed as an officer who would always be a hindrance to the missions. He recommended that Fages should not be disgraced or humiliated in any way, but he was clear that Fages was not wanted. Yet Serra—at least not in his written statements—brought no very serious charges against the commandant. Without much hesitation it was decided to recall him to Mexico.

At the same time they asked whom Serra would suggest to take his place. In answer Serra said a rather curious and perhaps a rather unfortunate thing. He was strongly in favor of Sergeant Ortega, on the ground that he had had many opportunities to observe his abilities; saying much more for him than he had said against Fages. That a sergeant should be promoted to captain and commandant at Monterey was not quite so strange as it may seem at first glance; such promotions were made in the Spanish army, though usually more slowly, and indeed Ortega was later made a lieutenant and commandant at San Diego. But at that time the Council, after thinking things over, decided that if they passed over Captain Rivera they would give him a serious affront. Accordingly the middle-aged captain obtained the position.

One suspects that a good deal of the obnoxiousness that Fages had shown was because of having been made somewhat "chesty" by being preferred to Rivera by Gálvez.

This made it all the more necessary for the Viceroy now to act with caution. One wonders whether Serra did not blunder by advocating Ortega's claims so strenuously, and whether it might not have been possible to have brought Fages to heel with a simple reprimand. Rivera turned out to have a dilatoriness which, during his time of office, was more of a hindrance than the arrogance of Fages had been. Possibly even Serra, had he been obliged to choose between the two men, would have concurred with the Viceroy and his Council. But when the *reglamento* for the two Californias and San Blas was issued in July, 1773, Serra won nearly all that he had asked for—particularly the retention of the naval yard and permission for Anza to seek the land route.

Serra waited until everything had been settled; then on September 20, 1773, just a year after he left California, he set out on the return journey, accompanied by Father Pablo Mugártegui, a recruit for work that was now expected to expand more rapidly. By way of farewell, he asked the Guardian in Mexico City to permit him to kiss the feet of every member of the community. This parting would be final, for he was now past sixty and in not very good health.

Until recently it had been supposed that Serra traveled to the coast on foot, though Palóu does not actually say so. Piette throws out a hint that this time Serra may have ridden on the back of an ass, in imitation of St. Francis of Assisi during his last years. But Father Geiger has shown in an article in *The Americas* (Vol. VI, 1950, p. 313) that Serra went by coach, and it is safe to infer that the Viceroy insisted upon it. Even so, it was not until January 18th that Serra reached San Blas.

From there he took the boat, the *Santiago,* which he had seen on the stocks the previous year, when he was told by the master of the shipyard that it would never be completed. However, orders had been received, probably in the spring, that its completion be expedited. Like all boats constructed on the Gulf, it was a rather poor piece of work, for the shipwrights had to use ironwork and sails sparingly. Nevertheless Serra, when writing to Melchor de Permas, the Viceroy's secretary, off the Isabels on January 27th, tells him that the new frigate was performing very well. This was written after they had been only two days at sea; the *Santiago* took forty days to reach San Diego, which was not bad for those days. That Serra had been able to sail in it at all was considered rather wonderful; those at San Blas remembered as a prophecy his saying that it was in this boat that he would return to California.

With him he took a number of recruits in addition to Fray Mugártegui. Of these the most valuable perhaps was Dr. Davila, the physician who was to replace poor Dr. Prat, who had gone insane. But very valuable in another way were the three blacksmiths and the three carpenters with their families whom he carried back. As these artisans would have been of little use without a supply of iron, Serra wrote from Tepic to the Guardian on January 16th to say that he had gathered "a quantity considerable enough." Even so, the carpenters often had to use wooden pins instead of nails.

Captain Rivera arrived at Monterey to replace Fages under the terms of the new *reglamento*. But Fages showed no anger against Rivera, nor against Serra. It may be that he recognized that it would be better to withdraw, in view of a difficult situation. And haughty man though he was, he asked Serra to write him a letter of recommendation which could be exhibited in Mexico City. This Serra very willingly did, for there was much good in the man; but his praise was a little less wholehearted than that given to Ortega.

Had Fages heard that Serra had advised the appointment of a mere sergeant as commandant at Monterey, he might have been even angrier than Rivera had been at being passed over in favor of a lieutenant. Later it is possible that Fages did get some wind of this; if so, he showed no resentment against Serra when at the end of his life he himself returned to California as its governor. Fages must have had a generous spirit. All the resentment was on the part of Rivera, whose somewhat childish behavior revealed that he had long nursed a grudge.

The absurdity of the incident has some comic aspects. In May, 1774, Fages took his dismissal as a soldier should, but asked Rivera's permission to go first to San Diego, because he had some affairs to clear up there. Rivera, standing on the letter of the Viceroy's orders, informed Fages that he must sail by the first boat. He added, "His Excellency was well aware that Monterey was your headquarters; it is therefore from Monterey that you must leave." Fages now produced an order from Bucareli giving him permission to sail from any port of his choosing. Although, faced with that, Rivera had to yield, he made trouble when Fages was saddling some mules to take his effects to San Diego. Rivera promptly stopped him, saying that the mules were military property. Again Fages was able to block Rivera's maneuver by being able to prove that the mules belonged to him. One gets the impression that, though Fages bore Serra no ill will, he took some pleasure in annoying his supplanter. But in the end Fages did take the *Santiago* back to San Blas. He probably had not needed to go in person to San Diego, where his accounts could be made up by a clerk, thus saving him a good deal of trouble.

The mules could follow at leisure. Having scored his point, he was content.

Nobody was sorry to see Fages go, least of all the soldiers of his command, for he was fussy about trifles yet too lenient where larger issues were concerned. It is certain that this had some bearing upon his removal, for though Serra was restrained in his complaints, he was obliged to meet the charge that desertions were due to the disrupting influence of the friars. But the main factor was that Fages had failed to further the work of the missions, and as this was in contravention to the general spirit of the instructions he had received from Gálvez and Croix, it had to be considered, if not precisely insubordination, at least as incapacity. The administration held to the principle that the military officers had to be more co-operative if the California venture was to succeed. Under an older and more experienced officer, it was hoped that everything would make more headway. That is why the Viceroy and his Council appointed Rivera as commandant at Monterey.

CHAPTER ELEVEN

The Land Route

FERNANDO RIVERA Y MONCADA, as a man in his mid-forties, should have shown more sense than he did and proved himself an abler officer when in command at Monterey. But though inclined to take things in much too easy a style, he was to prove himself—possibly as a result of the bitterness previously engendered in having young Fages, his inferior in rank, advanced over his head—a very rude and dictatorial person. This was not so much towards the friars, for now they were protected to some extent by the newly devised regulations, but he was astoundingly discourteous towards a man who was soon to arrive on the scene, with no direct authority over him but whom it was taken for granted he would help. This man was Captain Juan Bautista de Anza, the opener of the land route from Sonora. Rivera's animosity towards him had an obscure root, but probably stemmed from his fear that the San Francisco Bay settlements that Anza was commissioned to make would add to his responsibilities as commandant at Monterey.

Anza was a remarkable person, as one would divine merely by looking at the only portrait of him that exists. It is no great work of art, but Anza was too grand a subject for even a not very competent artist to spoil. There he stands before us magnificently bearded, and with still more magnificent mustachios, with long hair and a long melancholy face set off with a felt hat that seems to have been the forerunner of the sombrero. His force of character appears in a large, but not too large nose, and his intelligence in his deep-set eyes, which have something brooding and gentle about them. Altogether he was a man who, if not precisely handsome (although doubtless many did account him so), was of obvious distinction.

He was to prove himself a man of vision and action; indeed, from the way he managed to get a large body of soldiers and settlers (most of them women and children) so quickly over a difficult terrain, he became known as the "hard-riding captain." He was encumbered also with a large number of cattle and pack animals, yet he managed what had to be done without creating any complaints that he was driving those under him too hard. Professor Bolton says very justly: "As an explorer Anza stands beside Lewis and Clark. As a colony leader it is difficult to find anyone in Anglo-American annals with whom to compare him."

He had been born in 1735, so was still a little short of forty. He had served almost continuously in Indian wars, or in remote outposts where a rising against the Spaniards was always a danger. But though he could be severe when occasion demanded, he was never cruel but rather characterized by a vast patience. In these expeditions of his across the Colorado and Gila rivers one of his most useful assets was his ability to make friends with Indians known to be potentially dangerous and who, in fact, shortly after his time showed themselves to be formidable.

The worst things ever said about him—and clearly they are not to be taken very seriously—were written by Father Font, one of the priests who accompanied him. But really it is Father Font who places himself in not too good a light in his diary, for he was endlessly grumbling about the differences that he and the captain had over the taking of observations with the quadrant. One may suppose that an experienced officer understood this instrument better than a priest, but Font is apt to say: "I note this down that one may know the confidence with which such persons and lords are in the habit of speaking, who wish everybody to believe everything they say and not contradict them." One is obliged to believe that when he describes Anza as "arbitrary, cocksure and certain in manner" Font is really describing himself, excellent man though he undoubtedly was. Touchy he showed himself when he refused to accept the key to the quadrant merely because it had not been delivered to him sooner, and he goes on: "The commander tried to mollify me as best he could," so Font in the end accepted the key that was almost forced upon him, but only, he says, so as not to seem "stubborn and ill-natured." Anza, he wound up, "concluded by several times begging my pardon for whatever offense he might have given me, excusing himself by saying that it was inadvertency on his part."

Father Font also showed himself a bit strait-laced, as when he made a fuss about the pint of brandy that Anza served to each member of the party to celebrate Christmas. Now nobody can get very drunk on a pint, though of course it is not unlikely that some of those in the column (especially the women) may have taken only a glass and handed the rest to a tosspot friend. Anza did not hold with drunkenness and had not supposed that it would occur; he made the mild comment, "Well, Father, it is better that they should get drunk than do some other things."

Moreover, Font expressed his disapproval of a widow—the only widow—in the group. She sang a song some verses of which he says were "not at all nice," though just how indecent they were does not appear. One would imagine that they were spicy rather than obscene. Perhaps she had the notion that this gaiety would win her a husband, for she would hardly have gone to California unless a second husband was part of her purpose. Father Font observed with distaste that she was "applauded and cheered by all the crowd." Not even the censorious Font blames Anza for her conduct.

The first expedition of Anza was made mainly to test the possibilities of the route. Afterwards he intended to bring in colonists, people of a kind that had so far been lacking, except in so far as the handful of artisans at the missions could be considered colonists. Serra recognized that settlers would benefit the country, but he wished to keep them entirely apart from the Indian neophytes, even though they were to be chosen from married men who would take their wives and children with them. A very few unmarried women were permitted to go, since they would have no difficulty in securing husbands; which was the case with our boisterous friend with the song that so scandalized Father Font. The first time, however, Anza traveled light, with very few who were not soldiers; and he took along only a few cattle, in order to discover just how they would fare on the journey, to provide food in emergencies, and also to replenish the livestock in the existing missions.

Already it was known that there was a way of getting across the rivers without too much difficulty by means of fords and by rafts which the obliging Indians propelled by swimming alongside. As the friendliness of the Indians was assured, Bucareli authorized what Gálvez previously had blocked, so in January, 1774, Anza left Tubac, and after negotiating the Gila River, sent a scouting party ahead through the San Gorgónio Pass, reaching San Gabriel on March 22nd. From there he sent most of his men back by the route they had come, while he himself visited

Monterey; then, accompanied by Father Garcés, the chaplain, he made the return trip from San Gabriel to Tubac in three weeks. The rapidity of his movements astonished everybody, demonstrating that this way was not only feasible but in every respect to be preferred to the arduous journey up the rocky and torrid Peninsula.

Before giving an account of Anza's second expedition, the one that brought the colonists, it should be said that on September 5, 1772, Costansó, the engineer who had accompanied Portolá, told Bucareli: "The distance from Tubac to the port of San Diego is not excessive . . . and by opening the communication which Captain Juan de Anza proposes, San Diego and Monterey will be able to get supplies more promptly and families will be able to settle in those new establishments, giving them another basis and greater stability than they now have." This had been Serra's view as well, when he had been consulted. Now Anza had demonstrated that the idea was sound. Indeed, Anza was able to write to Bucareli during the course of his first expedition that if the horses and mules and cattle were not so prostrated—for the main obstacle was the finding of good water in sufficient quantities—"it would be a march of only fifteen days or less."

Events were to show that almost everything depended upon the good will of the Yuma Indians settled around the junction of the rivers. They were akin to the marauding Apaches who, while the first expedition was assembling, swept down and drove off a number of its horses. But though the Yumas demonstrated that they were not despicable as warriors, they lived a sedentary life in the main, to the extent of cultivating large fields of maize, beans and melons.

The Yumas had horses, which Anza noted in his diary were fat, probably because they were given little to do;

the natives, who went completely naked and used no saddles, found that the bodily heat that came from their mounts was unendurable for long. They were an intelligent people, picking up a few Spanish phrases readily, both sexes adopting the salutation, *"Ave María, Viva Dios y el Rey."* They also learned to make the sign of the cross. All this could be taken as a fair start, though Anza admitted that the expedition did not get very far in teaching them Christian doctrine. He set down what he called their affection to curiosity and the fact that the Spaniards distributed such trifles as glass beads and tobacco. On December 8, 1775, he wrote to Bucareli of the affection and docility of the tribes but attributed a good deal to the example of Salvador Palma, their chief.

They called him Palma because his real name of Ollyquotquiebe was unpronounceable, and Palma was the name of a major domo of the mission of Caborca with whom he had been friendly. Salvador was what he had been called by an Indian from Lower California. In 1776, when he went with Anza to Mexico City he and some other Indians were baptized, Palma then receiving the name of Sebastian. About this we have several letters written by Bucareli to Gálvez (who had not lost his interest in New Spain). In fact during that visit Anza wrote in his beautiful script to Bucareli in Palma's name, the chief protesting his horror of polygamy, saying, whether truly or not, "On account of finding it generally accepted, I did not condemn it in others," but claimed that he himself had had only one wife by whom he had had six children. He even said that he had now suppressed the practice among the Yumas, not even excepting his own brother but taking from him seven of the wives he had. All of which sounded very impressive but it also meant, it is to be feared, that the Indians wished to have a presidio because of the protection it would afford, and a mission because of the material benefits they hoped to obtain. The matter was handled badly and led to the tragic events which will be recorded in a subsequent chapter.

We have a very exact account both from Father Font and Anza himself of the second expedition. The march began on September 29, 1775, from the presidio of San Miguel de Orcasítas, with a hundred and seventy-seven people, men, women and children; in this number there were twenty muleteers and a few other men who were not to remain. The settlers were of a relatively high grade, certainly much superior to the mulattos, *mestizos* and convicts who had made up almost the whole of the first settlement at Los Angeles. Twenty soldiers under Lieutenant José Joaquín Moraga were to be left as the garrison for San Francisco and ten other soldiers went as an escort during the journey. A hundred and twenty mules carried provisions, munitions of war and the baggage of the colonists, in addition to which there were twenty mules for the baggage of Anza, the officers and the chaplain, and four hundred and fifty saddle animals besides, some of which belonged to members of the party. At Tubac, which was left on October 22nd, two priests were picked up, Francisco Garcés and Thomas Eixarch, who were to remain at the Colorado River, some more women and children, eight more soldiers for San Francisco, some cowboys and servants and three Indian interpreters, bringing the number to two hundred and forty. The cattle now totaled three hundred and fifty-five, and the horses, mules, burros and a few colts came to just under seven hundred. It was certainly a trek on a large scale. For the first time a real effort to colonize California was being made.

This Fray Garcés was a very exceptional man, of whom Governor Sastre of Sonora was to write, "With no other

provisions than a little *pinole,* a little chocolate and a few
strips of jerked beef, and with no other escort than his
guardian angel," he made many missionary journeys to
the adjoining tribes, winning from them the affectionate
title of the "Old Man," though he was not yet thirty. Font
gives a vivid picture of him: [1] "Father Garcés is so well
fitted to get along with the Indians and to go among them
that he appears to be an Indian himself. Like the Indians
he is phlegmatic in everything. He sits with them in the
circle, or at night around the fire, with his legs crossed,
and there he will sit musing for two or three hours or
more, oblivious to everything else, talking with them with
much serenity and deliberation. And although the foods
of the Indians are as nasty and dirty as those outlandish
people themselves, the Father eats them with gusto and
says they are good for the stomach and very fine. In short,
God has created him, as I see it, for the sole purpose of
seeking out those unhappy, ignorant and rustic people."

However, Garcés and his connection with events still
veiled by the future do not concern us at the moment.
Nor does what happened on the two expeditions headed
by Anza, except that it was established beyond all question
that a large body of human beings and a still larger one of
animals—over a thousand head—could make the land passage without serious difficulty. What is equally to our
purpose is the cost of outfitting the colonists, a charge
borne by the government. Chapman seems to have made
some miscalculation here, for he says in his *History of
California* that the total bill for the settlers' outfits came
to $1,957, whereas the food for the officers and the chaplain
amounted to $2,232.50. Palóu, on the other hand, in his
Historical Memoirs of New California says that the royal

[1] *Father Font, A Complete Diary,* ed. by Herbert E. Bolton. University
of California Press, 1933.

treasury spent about eight hundred pesos for each settler and his family, and Anza in a memorandum of December 5, 1774, estimates, in a most detailed manner, the clothing and the food needed for the colonists as coming to about 13,000 pesos. While the rest of his estimate totals nearly 22,000 pesos, it included the pack train, the provisioning of the soldiers and muleteers and food for the missions to be established and gifts for the Indians. I can see what happened to Chapman: His eye fell on the wrong line— while the rations for the people were indeed 1,957 pesos (a peso being about equal to a dollar), those for the officers' mess came only to $333.60. Though a few little luxuries were included in their case—the most expensive being six boxes of biscuits, a box of fine chocolate and a barrel of wine—even these items were pressed upon Anza and not asked for. There was none of the disproportion that Chapman asserts. As I find no item for brandy—which so aroused Father Font—it must be concluded that this was Anza's personal Christmas gift to the people with him.

It was noted that the Yumas still knew a few Christian prayers, and had adopted loincloths and "the slight touch of good manners which we instilled into them when we passed, and all, generally speaking, urge us now that we remain to reside among them." But as they lived in pueblos, instead of roaming the hills like the Indians of California, the kind of mission system that Serra had organized was not suitable to them, only a house for the two missionaries whom Anza left behind. As an earnest of more to come the commander delighted Palma and another chief by presenting each with a suit of fine clothes and a silver-headed baton as emblems of the authority they enjoyed. The Spaniards were much too tactful to show any amusement at the way Palma strutted about in this finery. After

the soldiers had built a cottage for the two priests they
continued their journey.

Anza's excellent ordering of affairs is attested by the
fact that his colonists remained in good health, despite
some privations. One woman died in childbirth, but her
baby was at once adopted by another, and as a second and
third woman successfully bore children, the company arrived in California with their number increased by two.
Presumably the new mothers were carried in litters for a
while, but they were of sturdy stock and were soon on
horseback again. The march was slowed down not so much
by incidents like these as by the need for sending out
scouts to locate water holes for the animals; in spite of
which some perished on the road. All in all Anza performed a most brilliant exploit.

He had met Serra at Monterey during his first visit,
and now he met him again under very different circumstances. Just prior to his arrival something that was close
to a disaster had occurred at San Diego. The Indians there
had always been somewhat intractable, though thievish
rather than bloodthirsty. But on the night of December
4th a well-concerted attack on both mission and presidio
was made with the object of exterminating all Spaniards.
Sixty Indians had been baptized as a group on the Feast
of St. Francis, October 4th, and this caused a rumor that
the Fathers proposed making all the Indians Christians by
force. Two neophytes had decamped, as happened every
now and then, and the sergeant sent to look for them
could not find them. But he had no suspicion as to what
was afoot, because no warlike attitude had appeared, which
went to show with what secrecy the rising had been
planned. When it broke everybody was caught completely
unprepared.

About five hundred Indians descended on the mission,

some of them standing guard at the houses where the neophytes lived (or so the neophytes said afterwards) to prevent their giving any help to the Fathers and their small guard of soldiers. Three soldiers and their corporal were asleep; so also were the two Padres, Vincente Fuster and Luis Jayme, the second of these a Mallorcan. Everybody woke to find the mission in flames and the savages seizing anything on which they could lay their hands.

The soldiers quickly rallied and were joined by the blacksmith Diego Romero, and the carpenter, a man named José Urselino. Another blacksmith, who had come there sick from the presidio, was killed in his bed, but the others fought off the Indians, though not without suffering casualties. Father Jayme had been so imprudent as to go towards the attackers with the usual salutation of "Love God, my children!" and was at once dragged into a gulley where he was stripped and his body so hacked with wooden sabers as to be all but unrecognizable afterwards. Urselino the carpenter also died five days later of his wounds, leaving a will bequeathing the whole of his savings to the mission for the Indians who had killed him; "an action," comments Palóu, "which was heroic and also worthy of a true disciple of Jesus Christ." The slain man's last words had been, "Ah, Indian, you have killed me! May God forgive you."

Two of the soldiers had been put out of action by severe wounds, so the corporal—a man named Rocha, or could it have been Roche?—had to continue the fight almost singlehanded. Being an expert marksman, he told the uninjured soldier and the blacksmith to do nothing but load the guns for him. With these he did great execution, meanwhile shouting out orders to make the Indians believe that he had his little force intact. His valor was great but that of Father Fuster was even greater, for as the thatched roof was smouldering, he spread himself and his habit over the gunpowder, to ward off any falling spark. The remaining soldier was at last wounded by an arrow, and so was the corporal, though this he would not admit. Almost alone he had won a battle against a horde estimated at about five hundred.

The plan of the Indians had been to make an attack simultaneously upon the mission and the presidio, which was about four miles distant. But while the affair had been managed with some degree of skill, the Indians' lack of power to organize was shown by their falling back from the mission too disheartened to direct an assault at the more strongly held presidio. The force there peacefully slept through the battle, quite unaware of what had happened until it was all over.

As soon as the news reached Monterey on December 13th, Rivera rode over to Carmel to tell Serra. His response was characteristic: "Thanks be to God that that soil has now been watered with blood! We shall soon see the complete subjugation of the Indians of San Diego." He intended to have a requiem for Father Jayme the next morning and invited Rivera and all the garrison to attend. But Rivera answered that this would be impossible, since he would have to leave at once for San Diego. When Serra proposed accompanying him, he was told that this could not be, for it would only result in delay. But another company of soldiers would leave Monterey in a few days, and the Father President could go with them to San Diego more slowly and easily.

On his way south Rivera stopped at the missions of San Antonio and San Luis Obispo, and though everything was quiet there, he took the precaution of leaving an additional soldier in each place. He reached San Gabriel on January 3, 1776. By the best of good fortune, Anza's expedition arrived the very next day. This meant that Anza and a lieutenant and forty men could go with Rivera to round up the ringleaders of the rising. The party of colonists and the animals, with a small guard of soldiers, were left at San Gabriel until this had been done.

The rounding up proved no easy matter, for though there were strong reasons to suspect that the neophytes' story about being forcibly kept from coming to the help of the Spaniards was bogus, and that some of them were among the attackers, except in the case of the two Indians who had decamped before the occurrence it was almost impossible to pin anything on anybody. In the darkness no face had been seen, nobody recognized. And the two men they were looking for had vanished into the hills. Later several arrests were made and the two chief culprits were sentenced to death, though the sentence was never carried out. But as this properly belongs to the time of stress between Serra and Rivera, it had better be held over until the next chapter.

The body of colonists had been left waiting while Anza himself and most of his soldiers gave aid to Rivera. However, when things subsided as quickly as they had erupted, it became evident that nothing more could be done for the moment. Accordingly Anza rejoined his colonists, and with them reached Monterey on March 10, 1776. From there the captain and Father Font—the priest who so prided himself upon his skill with the quadrant—went to San Francisco, where they selected sites for a mission and presidio within the present limits of the city, and the site for another mission at Santa Clara nearby. Close to it, but separated from it, was the settlement of the colonists, to which was given the name of San José, for St. Joseph was the patron of the whole enterprise.

Anza was present at the preliminaries to the founding

of San Francisco, though as he was needed elsewhere, he left most of these matters to his second-in-command José Joaquín Moraga, the commandant of the presidio. He records that when he said good-by to those whom he was leaving in San Francisco, most of them, "especially the feminine sex, came to me sobbing with tears, which they declared they were shedding more because of my departure than their exile, filling me with compassion." He declared that he was not worthy of this but also spoke of "the affection which I have had for them, ever since I recruited them . . . for up to now I have not seen a single sign of desertion in any one of those whom I brought to remain in this exile." He continued in a strain of high praise of a people who, he was sure, would be very useful to the monarchy. They had accomplished much together; on both sides the affection was well earned.

The rest of Anza's stay was marked by a disagreeable falling out with Rivera. The finder of the land route sets down his reason for the quarrel, which he believed was due to Rivera's idea that the troops at San Francisco were not sufficient for the enterprise. Quite forgotten by Rivera was the help Anza had given him in pacifying the Indians after the rising at San Diego, and all that appears is Rivera's resentfulness. As he could not prevent what Anza was doing, which was by order of the Viceroy, he went out of his way to vent his spite in most unmannerly style. Serra records that when Anza came to Monterey Rivera would not even extend him the courtesy of the key to his rooms. Since he could not be lodged at the presidio, the Fathers had to take him in at the mission. And Font, who had now and then grumbled a little at what he considered Anza's haughtiness, was asked to sign a paper on April 15, 1776, testifying to Rivera's behavior. When the two officers met afterwards, the Commandant of Monterey was extremely curt, and on at least one occasion passed him without a word or a salute. On the 28th, Anza said he would remain in his tent rather than expose himself to being insulted again. Font at first tried to dissuade him but later wrote in his journal that he had reached the conclusion that Anza was right. On the 30th the entry in Font's diary is: "We remained at this mission and the two commanders communicated in writing, discussing their affairs officially and wasting paper, one from his room and the other from his tent, each one with a soldier postman, maintaining themselves thus without showing their faces."

Anza had received much provocation, but Palóu in the fourth volume of his *Historical Memoirs of New California* expresses the opinion that both men behaved rather badly; that the Fathers tried to patch up the quarrel between these officers, but without much success. On May 2nd, Anza told Rivera that if he wanted to send any letters to His Excellency, he would take them, only to be told—apparently very rudely—that he had not finished writing as yet but would send the package by a rider who would overtake him. When the man drew up, Palóu says, "Señor Anza's reply was to return the letter to him, with the answer that he was no messenger, and that he had already warned him in an official paper that he would not carry any letters except those that contained matter concerning the settlement of San Francisco, which was the commission he had brought." That was his final and not too laudable word.

Although Serra himself did not see the great bay of San Francisco—a whole pocket of harbors was how Font described it—until October, 1777, he had long been thinking of foundations north of Monterey, and it was the decisive encouragement he had given to the project of Anza's overland route that had made possible the settlements there. Also, it was at his insistence that the naval yard at San Blas had been saved, for the use of the existing missions, true, but also for those to be established on the immense bay. The immediate result was that while one ship went very far north another, the *San Carlos* under Ayala, sailed around those landlocked waters, giving to our San Francisco at last the name it now bears. Formerly the name had been associated with the little harbor under Point Reyes where Drake had landed in the late sixteenth century. There Drake had built a little temporary fort of stone, and had received some sort of Indian headdress, which he represented to be the crown of what he was pleased to call New Albion, and he had left there a brass plate and a sixpence nailed to a post as a token of having taken the land for Queen Elizabeth. Yet all that was no more than a romantic memory; it was the Spaniards who at last exploited the country.

Palóu relates how after the site of the San Francisco mission had been selected, a little chapel was constructed quickly, and a tiny house for the priests who had been assigned there. The soldiers had meanwhile built their presidio. All was in order by September, but it was formally opened only on the 17th, the day on which the Church commemorates the reception of the stigmata by St. Francis, the opening of the mission to follow on the saint's Feast Day, October 4th. Solemn High Mass was sung, and although the Fathers had bells, there was a free use of muskets, the ship in the harbor joining in with its swivel guns. The firing terrified the heathen so much that they would not allow themselves to be seen for several days. After this there was the chanting of the *Te Deum* and on the 8th there was a great banquet, for which two beeves were killed. A more wonderful achievement had come about than probably any of those present realized.

All this, however, happened in 1776, a year before Serra's arrival. As for the Santa Clara mission, at first things did not go very well there. Early in 1777, a foundation was made but on a site which proved to be poor, being subject to floods, and higher ground was not selected until November 19, 1781. Built by Father Murguía, it was the finest of all the missions architecturally, but Murguía did not live to see it dedicated, for he was buried by Palóu on May 11, 1784. The mission flourished and found a ready market for its products, as was true also of the settlement of San José nearby, which one of the Fathers visited to say Mass on the prescribed days. It was for Serra happiness enough to hear of what was being done.

Anza, in recognition of his services, performed with such clean dispatch, was rewarded with a colonelcy and was made Governor of New Mexico, his soldiers on the expedition being given extra pay. But the land route he had developed and from which so much had been hoped did not last long, for, as we shall see, his friend Salvador Palma, the Yuma chief, turned against the Spaniards, probably because there was nobody at hand with Anza's ability to win the Indians to Spain. That disaster should have come in the end in no way detracts from Anza's exploit; he had made colonization possible. And although Serra feared that the presence of settlers in the country might offer drawbacks to missionary work, he nevertheless recognized that they greatly strengthened the hold of Spain and therefore furthered the missionary cause.

CHAPTER TWELVE

Dead Weight

THE SITUATION at the end of 1773, a time when there was cause to believe that all the hampering influences against the missions would be removed, was roughly this: There were nineteen Franciscan Fathers at work in California, though some of them were still waiting for the founding of the missions for which they were intended. Nearly five hundred Indians had been baptized, of whom about thirty had died, and over sixty couples had been united in Christian marriage. Most of these marriages were between Indians but in a few cases Spanish soldiers had taken Indian brides, a practice encouraged by the Padres and also by the government as a means of assimilating the natives to civilization. Only at San Diego had there been any trouble, as it remained the least easy spot in California.

There was always some difficulty in inducing the neophytes to do any work, yet this was a point upon which the Fathers laid great stress, since regular habits were essential to civilization and even to the practice of religion. Although in agriculture only slight progress had so far been made, there was in every mission at least a vegetable garden with a few patches of beans and corn. From the first the cattle had flourished, the pasturage being excellent, and the care of the animals called for little effort. But the only missions were those of San Diego, San Gabriel, San Luis Obispo, San Antonio de Padua, and San Carlos

Borromeo, already becoming known as Carmel because of its location on the Rio Carmelo. After the founding of the two San Francisco missions, there was a decided leap forward, though this was brought about in the face of Rivera's opposition.

Running like a refrain throughout all Serra's letters and reports was his dissatisfaction that the mission of San Buenaventura had not been established, though its establishment had been definitely decided upon before Portolá led his men to the north in 1770. In making his report to the Viceroy Serra stresses the fact that it had been ordered by Gálvez and Croix. This caused him all the more grief because on the coast of the Santa Barbara Channel the Indians were more numerous and intelligent than anywhere else. As things stood at the close of 1773, nearly half of the neophytes were at Carmel and San Antonio, with Carmel supplying more than half of the marriages. San Diego, disappointing in the number of its neophytes, which at that date numbered only seventy-six, was, however, the best stocked with animals. There too were most of the horses and mules and donkeys, as it was from this point that supplies from the Peninsula were distributed.

Serra reported that every mission was enclosed with a stockade, but in no case was this very sound protection. For want of nails the posts could not be securely fastened at the top. That of San Carlos was seventy yards long by forty-three wide—only a fair-sized lot. Adobe, large bricks dried only by the sun, had begun to be used, but instead of tiles they preferred wood covered with clay for roofing or even thatch. When tiles were introduced, at first they were only slabs of adobe.

The presidios were distinct from the mission buildings and were also enclosed with a stockade. Around both kinds of establishment there were clusters of Indian huts, but already an effort was being made to persuade the neophytes to take up their abode within the mission enclosure, the life of which will be described in the next chapter. Though the missions from the outset had a clear plan of procedure, this could be put into operation only by degrees. How well the work proceeded on its material side is shown by the fact that at the end of 1784 the missions possessed 5,384 head of cattle, 5,529 sheep, and 4,294 goats, as compared with a total for eleven years earlier of 205, 94, and 67 respectively. There were also a number of pigs, and the grain raised came to be sufficient to support not only the neophytes but the garrisons. The spiritual progress will appear later.

In what has to be related of the period when Fernando Xavier de Rivera y Moncada was in charge, we should in justice remember certain facts of the man's career. He had entered the army in 1742 while still in his teens and had worked his way up through the ranks to his captaincy. When young Fages was put over him at the time of Portolá's withdrawal, Rivera applied to the Viceroy for permission to resign his commission, ostensibly on the grounds of poor health but actually in disgust. This being granted, he worked a farm in Mexico for a short while, but so unsuccessfully that he was obliged to re-enter the army, being assigned to San Diego. His men there and at Monterey liked him, which seems a bit strange, as he was inclined to be rather stingy in the matter of rations; but at least he was preferable to the martinet Fages. Even so, they had moments when they wondered whether he was quite sane.

It is perhaps understandable that he should have been cautious in action. No Spanish conquest had been effected with fewer men than that of California, and only because the Indians, except for the unreliable natives around San

Diego, were mild and lethargic. Rivera was haunted by visions of his bones whitening in the desert, and in the end, a fate of this kind did overtake him, though not in California. Rivera was personally brave, but after what had happened to Fages he was all the more concerned to make his administration a success. As he was not the kind of man to bring this about by driving energy, he tried to avoid mistakes by sitting tight—the worst mistake he could have made. Father Font records that Fray Mugártegui confided to him, "As between Captain Fages and Señor Rivera, Fages was the better, and we should be glad to have him back. The friars requested that he be removed and we are now paying for it."

Father Piette suggests that Rivera could not forgive Serra for having failed to recommend him to take the place of Fages, and on the face of it this would not seem unlikely—except that Rivera did not know of the lack of recommendation. Moreover, he did not actively oppose Serra, nor would he have dared to do so in face of the new *reglamento;* all that he did was to move slowly, if at all. This was more probably due to a disposition to which any unusual exercise of energy was distasteful rather than to positive malice. Rivera, in short, was the kind of man who serves excellently under a chief but is too passive by nature to initiate anything himself.

Serra had judged his man correctly in not advising his promotion to Monterey. But there was one thing for which he—always ready to say the best that he could of others—could praise Rivera, so when writing to Bucareli on January 8, 1775, he told him, "The Captain does all that is possible to exterminate public immorality." Although there had never been much of this, when it had occurred Fages was inclined to shrug his shoulders, on the principle embodied in the *Barrack Room Ballads* that single men in barracks are not plaster saints. Serra had similarly written with satisfaction to Bucareli on August 24, 1774, about three soldiers who had married Indian girls; this, he said, would reduce the likelihood of scandals, adding, a little surprisingly, that these families would form the nucleus of a pueblo. Yet though he did not want large settlements close to the missions, he had asked in Mexico City the previous year that soldiers when married be permitted to retire from the service and be given the salary of a sailor for two years and rations for five. As they were assigned land near the presidio, they would always be available for defense should a serious emergency arise.

Rivera himself suffered from the impermissible action taken by the new Governor at Loreto, Felipe Barri, when that official retained in the Peninsula the majority of the hundred mules that had been sent there for service further north. Indeed, the captain was pressed in many ways, and because of his worries felt himself unable to do all that the missionaries expected of him.

Yet when all due allowances have been made, Rivera must still be considered negligent of his duties. It was not only that he—like Fages before him—could not be induced to establish a mission and presidio by the strategic Channel, he also did nothing about rebuilding the mission of San Diego after it had been destroyed; for him it was apparently enough that the presidio there remained intact to guard the harbor. Therefore the three Fathers destined for the mission had to live among the soldiers until, in the end, Serra proceeded to do what needed to be done without any help from the Commandant.

Serra's chance came when the *San Antonio* arrived in the harbor under the command of Diego Choquet. Then the Father President asked him if he would allow his sailors to assist in rebuilding "the mission of the saint of his own name"—a highly diplomatic line to take. Choquet agreed and when Rivera was asked if he would provide a guard for the sailors while they were at work, he could hardly refuse, though he did not like the way his hand had been forced. He liked it so little, in fact, that two weeks later he found means of stopping the work that was in progress. He rode over to the mission and told Choquet that reports had reached him saying the Indians were planning a new rising, which of course may have had some basis in solid fact, but which his constitutional nervousness probably exaggerated. Choquet was disgusted and, according to Palóu, told him bluntly, "With all the armed force which is here, there is no danger. You would be more respected, if imagining danger, you increased the guard, instead of withdrawing it and bringing shame to Spanish arms." In spite of Rivera the work was completed.

The San Juan Capistrano mission also waited for its founding. It had been left before its completion with its bells buried after the rising at San Diego, and those who had expected to be sent there began to ask permission to return to Mexico, as evidently there was no use in remaining in California. Fortunately just at that time word arrived that an additional twenty-five soldiers were on their way up the Peninsula, and the Viceroy wrote in such terms about the San Francisco missions that Rivera considered it inadvisable to create any further obstacle to the missions in the south. Accordingly San Diego was reopened on October 17, 1776, and on the following November 1st, the Feast of All Saints, Serra said the first Mass at the reopened San Juan Capistrano.

At the same time Bucareli expressed himself in accord with Serra's policy of treating with leniency the ringleaders of the San Diego affair, who had now been rounded up. It was not surprising that a priest should recommend mercy even towards men who had, after all, committed murder—taking the line that they hardly realized the guilt of what they had done—but one is astonished that a secular official should concur in this view. Two of the criminals had been sentenced to death and others to serve as long-shoremen at the naval station at San Blas; yet all this was countermanded, naturally to Rivera's disgust, by the high-est authority.

The departed Anza had taken the soldier's attitude that condign punishment be meted out to the most culpable, and the rest pardoned. He had shown that he did not be-lieve the professions of the neophytes that they had been forcibly held back from coming to the assistance of those whom the Indians had sought to kill. He had had con-siderable experience of Indians, and he was aware that their faith was seldom to be trusted or their word believed. But Rivera went beyond this, and wished to punish every-body caught, though in varying degrees. But of course the matter was one that did not primarily concern Anza. Prob-ably Rivera resented his expressing even so much as an opinion, and was all the more stubborn in consequence.

Rivera was about to carry things too far, and the instru-ment of his undoing was Father Fermín Francisco de Lasuén, a friar who had been serving as his chaplain against Serra's wishes. Serra had not positively forbidden this only because he hoped that the arrangement would make Rivera more sympathetic towards the missions; though it is to be feared that the result was to make Rivera all the more inclined to act as he pleased, on the ground that he had some ecclesiastical backing. Even so, Serra tolerated Lasuén's being Rivera's chaplain, for this Padre had shown that he was dissatisfied and had expressed a wish to leave. Serra wanted to keep him, knowing his ability. As events turned out, it was Lasuén who succeeded Serra as President, and Professor Chapman even exalts him above Serra; and undoubtedly the golden age of the missions was during his administration, though he accomplished what he did by being able to build upon the foundations that Serra had laid.

In view of Lasuén's personal association with Rivera it is what people incorrectly describe as "ironical" that he should be the priest to pronounce Rivera's excommunication. The fact is that in the incident which placed him under the Church's ban, Rivera undoubtedly failed to realize the gravity of his actions. Or he may have had some idea that, as he and Lasuén were such friends, extenuation would be made, not understanding that it was not within Lasuén's power to do so, the offense being against the Church.

The incident was this: One of the offenders in the San Diego rising, a neophyte baptized under the name of Carlos, had crept down to the Fathers, sure that they would forgive him and hide him until the storm had blown over. Although Carlos could not have comprehended the idea of sanctuary, that was in effect what he sought, and sanctuary, though abrogated in most countries, still prevailed in Spain and its dominions. Rivera was aware of this but as the man was kept in a storage room that was only being temporarily used for Mass, he argued that the rights of sanctuary did not apply. When the Fathers refused to give Carlos up, Rivera strode in with a guard of soldiers and arrested him.

In the first stage of the affair Lasuén himself was not immediately concerned but Father Fuster, the priest in charge of the San Diego mission. He at once protested, giving Rivera notice that he had better not attempt what he threatened, but must proceed in a quiet way, according to canon law. The Commandant replied that he would take this under consideration, but nevertheless came at night, with a candle in one hand and a drawn sword in the other, and ordered his soldiers to drag out the cowering Carlos and put him in the stocks.

Even after that Fuster did not proceed precipitously but, while declaring that all concerned had by their own action put themselves outside the Church, he twice sent a formal notice to Rivera asking that Carlos be returned to sanctuary; otherwise he would be obliged to have the excommunication published. These notices Rivera would not so much as read. Accordingly two days later Lasuén, when he was about to start Mass, first addressed the assembled congregation, saying: "All those who had any part in taking the Indian whom they now hold in the guardhouse are excommunicated and therefore cannot assist at Mass. If any of them are in the church they will leave; if they do not, I cannot celebrate holy Mass." Thereupon Rivera and those implicated with him left the building and High Mass was sung.

The report of the excommunication was signed by Lasuén and the two friars who had acted as deacon and subdeacon and sent to San Fernando. The Guardian there expressed regret at Lasuén's action, which, not knowing all the circumstances, he considered rather drastic. Nevertheless Rivera had worked himself into a thoroughly bad situation. Not only had he failed to establish missions (or re-establish them) but he had sent orders to Moraga, the officer in charge of the presidio of San Francisco, about what he might and might not do, just as though he were the Governor. However, Moraga decided that, as he had received Bucareli's instructions, he could ignore Rivera and act on his own responsibility. Finally, when Fray Garcés visited California from the Colorado River on one of his journeys of exploration, Rivera had rudely refused him provisions or an escort to Monterey. As Engelhardt says of this last incident: "It lends color to the opinion of his associates that the California commander, upon whom then rested the ban of excommunication, might not be in his right mind."

The Commandant returned in a somewhat distraught state to Monterey, carrying with him the account signed by the three priests about his own excommunication, along with some other letters. As Rivera must have had a good idea about what at least one of the letters contained, he undoubtedly read them, though when he gave the letters to Serra he declared himself willing to take an oath that the breaking of the seals had been an accident and that he had not read what was inside. Serra, while he must have suspected Rivera of lying, nevertheless courteously assured him that he need not take any oath but that his word was sufficient. Yet with regard to the excommunication he was obliged to tell Rivera that it could be removed in only one way, by the return of Carlos to the sanctuary from which he had been dragged, which was eventually done.

By this time the Viceroy had had quite enough. In 1775 he had appointed Felipe de Neve as Governor of the Californias in place of Barri; he now decided that the capital should be moved from Loreto to Monterey, where of course Neve would replace Rivera. As an attempt to pour oil on troubled waters the arrangement, as will be seen before long, was not very successful, but at least it meant getting rid of Rivera. Yet Rivera was let off lightly by being transferred to Loreto, a post which, as it involved less work, was more to his liking. Gálvez, after the decision of 1773, when Rivera was given the post that Fages had held, had thrown up his hands, saying that now the missionaries had fallen from the frying pan into the fire. Bancroft

thought that "Had Rivera's peculiar conduct been known
in Spain it is not likely that he would have been retained
in office; but the Viceroy hoped that in a new field he
might do better." Perhaps so, but it must be remembered
that it was no easy matter to find the right man to place
in control in California.

It is probable that Anza would have been the best governor, for he had proved that he was able to get along with
people—with everybody, that is, except Rivera. But the
administration in Mexico considered that his special talents
would find their fullest scope in New Mexico, where there
were warlike Apaches to deal with, rather than in California where the Indians, though now and then a little
restive, were upon the whole too supine to give much
trouble. At least Neve was an abler and more energetic
man than Rivera, and with Monterey now the capital and
nearby Carmel the headquarters of the President of the
Missions, it was expected that the change would be bene-
ficial all round.

It has been charged by Chapman, in order to magnify
Lasuén, that Serra was never able to get along with any of
the commandants with whom he had to deal. That there
was frequent friction cannot be denied, yet it would seem
that in every instance it was due to the overbearing attitude of the soldier towards the friar. Also, Serra had been
sustained in his view that the objective was a peaceful
conquest, and that in this the function of the military
was subordinate to that of the missionaries. Since the commandants found it hard to grasp such an idea, conflict was
almost inevitable. These men meant well, but their minds
worked in a different groove from the friars'.

Furthermore it should be said that although the officers
were kindly in their treatment of the Indians, they were
sometimes exasperated that Serra was willing to pardon

and condone where they themselves believed a little severity was advisable. And they felt that the Fathers were a
kind of demoralizing influence on military discipline, especially as they had obtained a couple of men of each mission guard to perform services for them of a kind not usually assigned to soldiers, and had the right to ask that any
member of the guard who misbehaved himself be withdrawn. All this a succession of commandants looked upon
as priestly meddling with military matters.

Serra acted as he did, however, with the concurrence of
the Viceroy. It is evident from his voluminous correspondence that, though he was sometimes obliged to make
complaints, he never did so in acrimonious terms. But
he was quietly determined to fight for the good of the
Indians, those whose souls he had come to save. His fatherly
attitude towards the neophytes endeared him to them and
so paid large spiritual (and even political) dividends. He
was aware that some of the missionaries occasionally
thought him too indulgent. But his attitude was: Poor
ignorant people, they should not be judged by ordinary
standards! He granted that they had to be corrected at
times, but he believed it should always be in a gentle
paternal way. More often he was disposed to overlook the
faults of the Indians in his love for them.

Palóu gives an instance of this that occurred towards the
end of Serra's life. When a bent old crone of eighty went to
see him, he gave her as a parting gift the blanket from the
wooden plank that served him as bed. After she had gone
Palóu asked Serra, "Are you paying her for the chickens?"
Serra had forgotten about that incident, but now it came
back: At San Diego, at a time when Serra had been trying
with difficulty to raise a few chickens, she and her son had
raided the coop and had had a grand feast. Well yes, he was
paying her for the chickens she had stolen.

One matter should be touched on though it never had anything to do with Rivera or his successors but was under the direction of the Viceroy. This was the frequent voyages of exploration up the coast, where formal possession (in the sense of formal claims) was made as far up as Puget Sound. Between 1774 and 1779 there were three such expeditions by sea and they were conducted in order to guard against the Russian threat. They were possible at all only because Serra's representations in 1773 had prevented the abandonment of the shipbuilding program at San Blas.

Some of the reports about the Russians that reached Spanish ears were rather fantastic; for instance, that the Russians were claiming that, since the North American Indians were descended from people from Siberia, all the North American continent by rights belonged to Russia. Another rumor had it that Russia was on the point of forcing the Great Wall of China with an army of 25,000 men, and that it meant to attack Japan via Kamchatka, with the Pacific coast as the ultimate goal. Yet while such reports may be dismissed as nonsense, it remains true that Russia did have American designs then and for a good many years afterwards. Palóu, who refers to the Spanish expeditions, tells how the ships sent out got as far north as the sixtieth parallel, and though he admits that those on board found no evidence of the Russians, he adds that several of them "thought that the Gentile who showed no surprise at the sight of the frigate might have been some Russian, in the guise of an Indian who had been sent thither to explore and observe." Absurd though that is, by 1788 Russians were establishing themselves at Kodiak and Unalaska and other places in those regions.

Still later there was the famous incident of the arrival of Count Rezanov, mainly remembered now because of his whirlwind courtship of Concepción Argüello, the young daughter of the commandant at San Francisco, who was determined to marry him in spite of the arguments of the Padres. On his way to Russia to obtain the necessary dispensations from the Tzar and the ecclesiastical authorities Rezanov died; and when, some years later, this news reached California, Concepción became a Dominican Sister. Her story has been the subject of a rather bad poem by Bret Harte and a not very good novel by Gertrude Atherton. More to our purpose is that Rezanov had the idea of being sent to Madrid as Russian envoy, and of effecting a treaty of commerce. Long before, he had written to his government: "Our American possessions will know no more of famine; Kamchatka and Okhotsk will be supplied with bread.... When our trade with California is fully organized we can settle Chinese laborers there." Already he had established a rich trade in otter skins.

Later still, with Spanish consent (given with suspicion) the Russians were permitted to set up a trading post, sixty-five miles north of San Francisco, known as Port Ross. A river in that locality (it is hardly more than a shallow stream babbling over the rocks in its bed) is still known as Russian River. Although all this does not add up to Russian aggression, there is no doubt that the Russians would have made an attempt to seize California had the Spanish not got there first.

It seems highly unlikely that the Fathers (or the Spanish officials, as has been suggested) tried to conceal the fact that there were colonists there. The French traveler La Pérouse received this impression, to be sure, but that may have been because the Padres supposed that he was interested only in their neophytes and their way of life. Indeed, La Pérouse must have become so fascinated as to have been blind to everything else, because only a short distance away from San Francisco was the flourishing town of

San José, not to mention smaller settlements elsewhere. But one consideration should be final: There was simply no point in the Spaniards' wishing to keep their colonial undertakings a dark secret (even if this had been possible), for it was obviously all to their interest to have made known the existence of their settlements as a further substantiation to Spanish claims to the province.

How economically California was run in its early days appears from the figures that Serra presented to the Viceroy and his Council when he visited Mexico City in 1773. (He was merely summing up facts with which they were already acquainted.) The commandant at Monterey, being also a kind of deputy governor, was paid the salary of $3,000 a year, the two next best-paid men being the storekeepers there and at San Diego, with $1,000 apiece. There were two sergeants who received (together) $900, and four corporals who received (again together) $1,600. The forty-four soldiers at the two presidios were paid a total of $18,060. A corporal and five soldiers for all the missions together received $11,125. If we add the pay for the blacksmiths, carpenters and muleteers, the whole military establishment cost a sum just short of $39,000. Lower California cost only $16,450, though the Governor was stationed there at that time at a salary of $4,000. The marine department called for $34,038, though of course later, when there were more ships and a naval school, it needed perhaps $100,000, irrespective of the cost of building ships. The Fathers themselves cost the government nothing, being paid out of the Pious Fund, though the guard at the missions, as we have seen, at that time cost a little over $11,000. For later years of course all these figures have to be substantially increased.

Had the cost of the California enterprise been great, it would never have been undertaken, so low was the Spanish treasury, or so parsimonious its administration. Moreover, few as were the soldiers sent to Upper California, still fewer of them had anything like adequate equipment. Nearly all were bedraggled-looking, not in the least like those mustered on parade, even if they could acquit themselves well when called upon to do so. So great a conquest at so small a cost was achieved only because all conflict with the Indians was avoided, in so far as this was possible, and because the Padres brought them not only into the Church but made them subjects of Spain. This was the wise and humane policy of the mother country, and was loyally carried out by the Viceroy in Mexico. Unfortunately it was a point that few of the local officers could ever quite appreciate.

CHAPTER THIRTEEN

Life at the Missions

MAJOR FELIPE DE NEVE, the governor appointed at Loreto in 1775 for the two Californias, arrived at the end of November of the following year to set up the new center of administration in Monterey. He carried with him a letter dated August 16th in which Bucareli recommended him to Serra, praising him as an officer "who by his prudence, his love, his zeal, has always merited all my affection, since the time I knew him well in Spain. He will be able to engage the affection of your Reverence and of the other Fathers by his justice and moderation. Thanks to him, your Reverence will also find more easily the necessary help . . . following my orders." It was a splendid report, but almost entirely belied by events, some of them due to administrative changes, some to Neve's revelation of his true character.

An account of these changes, however, may be deferred in order to give an account of the general plan of work at the missions, since without this Neve's mode of procedure would hardly be intelligible. The Fathers had started work with a program so clear as to be called a blueprint, and one that was not merely drawn upon paper but that represented years of actual experience. It must always be borne in mind that Serra had worked about twenty years among the Indians of New Spain before being sent to open the field of California.

The first thing to remember of the missions during their very first phase was that, except in the case of the dying, there was some reluctance to baptize. This was because merely nominal Christians would in all probability revert to their godless form of life. The basic idea therefore was to make all the Christians, when this was possible, members of the missions. Boys and girls were preferred, as they yielded the best results under the training that was supplied. Infants were baptized, but a promise was usually extracted from their parents that they would bring them to the missions when they had grown a little.

Once anybody had been admitted as a neophyte, he was not free to leave. By their own act, or that of their parents, the neophytes had become wards of the Fathers, who exercised full authority over them. To put it in another way, they could be regarded legally as having the status of apprentices. As such they were not bound for any set term of years but for as long as their case required. This was because their dull intellectual faculties, their lack of will power and self-reliance and an indolence all but incurable, made it well-nigh impossible for many of them to reach the stage of development where they could stand on their own feet.

No Indian was ever forced to accept baptism, though strong inducements were held out to them to cast in their lot with the missions. There is no truth to the fancy picture that would have it that the foolish people who had been persuaded to help erect the mission stockade discovered, when the work was completed, that they had built their own jail. The stockade was more for protection than anything else. And they had plenty of freedom to go beyond the mission bounds. In any event about the most that any of the Indians ever did was to carry logs for the soldiers and carpenters who were constructing, rather flimsily, the enclosure.

When as every now and then happened, a neophyte ran away, a couple of soldiers were sent out to bring him back. They knew in what cluster of huts he would be, and no force was ever needed to bring about his return. After a day or two of Indian life, the comforts that had been enjoyed at the mission were sufficient inducement. Only for a day or two did the squalid indolence of Indian life seem attractive. Obviously, had resistance been put up, a couple of soldiers could have done nothing against a horde of savages.

But this is by no means all. The Fathers allowed their neophytes extended holidays, for they did not want them to get the idea that they were being held against their will. Those who went home used to tell about the missions in such a way that it was very common for them to be accompanied back by acquaintances who asked to be admitted. The neophytes were, in modern terms, highly effective publicity agents.

At the mission feast days were frequent, for in addition to those enjoined by the Church, the Franciscan saints were usually celebrated. On such days no work was done, and the Fathers welcomed these holidays as much as anybody else. Moreover whenever a youth and his friends asked permission to have a day off to go hunting or fishing, this was always allowed—unless there was some special pressure of work, as at harvest time.

Never, or virtually never, was everybody at the mission at work, even on ordinary days. And the working hours were no more than four or six, for that much time sufficed. It was well understood that it would not do to overwork the Indians. The old socialist contention that all the necessary work could be accomplished with little effort if everybody worked was amply justified. The neophytes worked even those short hours a day only because they were almost always slack, never exerting themselves over what had to be done, and often trying to get out of the lightest task.

The important thing in the eyes of the Fathers was not how much work was done but that it should be done regularly. Only by this means could orderly habits be acquired. To get them to work, the Fathers, or the Father assigned to the material side of things, worked with the neophytes, both by way of encouragement and to give necessary instruction. Needless to say, the Fathers worked at least twice as hard as their wards. These poor savages were completely ignorant of even the most elementary form of agriculture.

It has been suggested that the Spaniards were so welcome in California because, until their arrival, the natives had lived in perpetual boredom. Now they had something interesting to talk about, something interesting to do. Until then they had been accustomed to sleep about sixteen hours a day, and after the fall of darkness made it impossible for them to play their games or dance, they had merely sat and talked about nothing. It was a most empty existence.

The Fathers saw to it that their neophytes were provided with amusements. Cards were disapproved of, for fear they might lead to gambling. Although the Indians had no money to stake, there were other things that might have been gambled for—a little liquor on one side and, on the other, a wife who could pay a debt by prostitution. In these matters the Fathers were extremely watchful, which was why in the dances at the mission (and even the games) the sexes were kept carefully apart. At all times there was strict supervision. A young man might be allowed to work in his spare time at the presidio, a girl never.

The Indians were extremely fond of dancing and music,

though, as has been mentioned, to most Spanish ears the tunes and musical instruments—a kind of flute or reed, and a gourd or a shell in which stones were rattled—sounded horrible. The soldiers (and even some of the Fathers) when they could stand this no longer had to make them stop, for there were occasions when the Indians seemed ready to keep it up all night. Dancing was the only exercise they willingly undertook. As for music, their gift was by degrees trained, so that they learned a few Christian hymns. Some were even able to chant the responses at High Mass. Eventually little plays—performed in church, as in the days of the miracle plays—were introduced, for it was found that these people had a gift for mimicry.

Alexander Forbes in his *California,* written in the mid-thirties and published in 1839, while fully admitting the devotedness of the Fathers, is sometimes critical of their methods. Thus he says: "It is well known that savages are prone to be filthy in their habitations; but in their normal state, their living so much in the open air, their exertions in hunting and other diversions, counteract the causes of disease; but at the missions, the Indians being still allowed to live in all their filthiness and their lives being comparatively sedentary, with little purpose and less mental exertion, they inevitably grow up debilitated in body as well as mind." But Forbes should have seen the original state of the Indians. By his time they had been provided with decent houses, even if they were negligent in keeping them as clean as they should; and they had as much hunting and fishing as ever, if not more, to which should be added work in the fields, something they had never known until then. While much remained to be done about their intellectual development, at the lowest estimate a great deal had been done, as we shall soon see.

The games the Indians played were those of their own

invention. The one called *takersia* consisted in spinning straw rings three inches wide in the air and throwing a five-foot rod through the opening. In it two players competed in a cleared space. If the rod went through, two points were scored; if it merely brought the ring down, only one point. The player who first reached three points won. *Toussi* was played by two against two, all with their hands under a mat. Each player in turn had a small piece of wood hidden in one of his hands, and the object of the game was for the opposing side to guess which hand it was in, the youth who held it making all kinds of grimaces and motions of his body designed to mislead the other side. The point was won or lost according to whether the guess proved right or wrong. When the guess was right, the other side got the bit of wood. And the side that first obtained five points won.

These Indians did not have much idea of moral restraint, and with them, as with all human beings, after baptism's cleansing from original sin (or mortal sins, if these could be said to be committed by a people who had so vague a sense of right and wrong) concupiscence remained. Yet their passions were not particularly violent; it was rather that they were indulged without compunction. For this reason the unmarried girls in the mission (or the married women when their husbands were away) were kept at night under lock and key in what was called the nunnery. Their guard was the wife of one of the soldiers, and it was also her duty to teach the girls to sew and cook and to keep clean.

If the "nunnery" sounds a bit drastic, it should be remembered that in the Spain of that day young men and women were never allowed to meet alone until after marriage. A daring glance up at a latticed window or balcony, or perhaps a serenade from the street, was about as far as they could go. The Fathers were taking no chances with the girls they were trying to make good Christian wives and mothers, and, being realists, they knew that the nunnery was quite as much a protection against soldiers of a certain type as against other Indians.

Early marriages were the rule, but the choice was left quite free. However, the Fathers would often suggest marriage and a suitable partner. It was recognized that celibacy was incomprehensible to the Indian mind, so the safest course was for their neophytes to marry as soon as they were capable of marriage and then settle down—something that they were always delighted to do. By now the aprons (before and behind) and shoulder cloaks worn by the women and girls had been replaced by skirts and blouses, though it was something of a problem at first to secure enough cloth for these garments. Serra made himself into a tailor, taking pleasure in that work, and while it is probable that the clothes of his fashioning were far from stylish, they served his purpose.

As we have seen, the soldiers were encouraged by bonuses of various kinds to marry Indian girls; so were the colonists, when any of them became widowed. Indeed, soldiers were by such marriages turned into colonists, settling near the presidio from which they had withdrawn. And it must be said that these marriages were usually very happy, for the Indian girls were of an affectionate and gentle disposition. A few of the unmarried Spaniards were always liable to behave in a way detrimental to the work of the missions, which was why the Fathers were always glad to see any soldier marry.

No alcohol was permitted to the Indians, for it had long been known that they could not be trusted with strong drink. Yet this was not much of a problem in California. At first even the Mass wine had to be imported from Mexico, as was also a little brandy for special occasions. They were kept under lock and key. The Spaniards being the most abstemious of peoples, there was no free use of liquor. Later there was a fair amount of viticulture at the missions, but the actual making of wine (or even a knowledge as to how wine was made) was for good reason kept from the natives.

When Lasuén became President of the missions, he used to say: "Patience is the first, second, third and everlasting rule in dealing with the Indians." Again he declared, "The mildest and sweetest means must preferably be employed. Before severity one must first have carried gentleness to its extreme limits." George Vancouver, in the account he published in 1801 of his voyage along the Pacific coast during the years 1790–95, was to say that although some of the Indians imposed on the Fathers by going to the missions solely to obtain "a stock of food and clothing, with which they decamped," the Fathers always forgave them, and "uniformly supplied their wants on a second visit." Incidents of this sort were all the more aggravating because the missions were always understaffed, so that it was wonderful that such impostors did not get a sound box on the ear.

Some punishment, nevertheless, had to be used, though it was used so sparingly and mildly that the soldiers were continually complaining that the Fathers were much too lenient. It was no use at all to put the Indians in the guardroom, for then they escaped work and could sleep all day. Nor did it seem advisable to deprive them of food, unless perhaps the little delicacies they relished, as a naughty child is deprived of jam or ice cream. The only thing that did any good was a beating, and though the Indians—always incorrigible liars—sometimes said that they received unmerciful thrashings, actually not much more than the equivalent of a hairbrush on the backside was admin-

istered. This in mild cases was done in a paternal fashion
by one of the Fathers, in those that were more serious by
the corporal. Even then the lash was never laid on so as to
draw blood. Only as a last resort was this punishment
used at all, and never more than twenty-five strokes given,
"with a leather thong upon that part of the human frame
most susceptible of insult."

The girls, when they needed it, got a beating too, administered in private by the woman who had charge of
them at night, the one known as the *maestra*. In the case
of the young men the execution was public, for the sake
of its moral effect upon those who witnessed it. They were
made to *feel* the gravity of their offense, even when they
did not comprehend it. So far from resenting this punishment, they were generally made more tractable, as a slap
sometimes works wonders with a fractious child.

Food and other comforts were used as a bait to attract
the Indians to enter the missions. For this they came with
outstretched hands. And when anything good they did
received some sort of a reward, they concluded, as Engelhardt puts it, "that after all it was better to live with the
kind missionaries, and have plenty to eat, than to have to
be everlastingly on the look out for something eatable in
the mountains and valleys." That the inducement was
really attractive may be measured by the fact that in California some sort of food was always obtainable, whereas
other kinds of American Indians had to bestir themselves
merely to survive. It was for this reason that in California,
while the Indians multiplied far more than anywhere else,
they also grew lazy and their minds besotted and dull.

The food supplied at the missions was, according to our
standards, very monotonous, but it was what the Indians
liked. Until then their greatest delicacy had been a dead
whale washed ashore. Father Font tells us how the Indians

would gather like flies and devour it until it was all gone, eating it even when it was rotting. Moreover they used to besmear themselves with the whale's blubber, so that they stank to high heaven, perhaps to their own satisfaction but to the veritable torment of the Spaniards. Breakfast invariably consisted of *atole,* a mush of ground barley. The midday meal was *atole* again with the addition of bits of beef or mutton. During hot afternoons a mule carried buckets of what was considered a delightful drink to those in the fields—vinegar and sweetened water mixed together! In the evening *pinole* was served, but this does not seem to have differed very much from *atole,* except that to it were added nuts and wild berries. There were also various fruits. Palóu especially mentioned the peaches, apricots and pomegranates introduced from Spain. And beans also were eaten a good deal. Any of the mission Indians were free to cultivate gardens of their own.

The Fathers regarded the missions as belonging to the Indians; the missionaries were merely the guardians of those in the status of wards, preparing for the day when they would live, each man with his own house and piece of land. In the meanwhile efforts were made not to have Spanish settlers come too close lest—under one pretext or another—they annex what belonged to the neophytes. The charge has been made that this system kept the Indians in a state of dependence, but it was made by writers who knew little or nothing of the make-up of the Californian Indians. That the system had flaws is not unlikely, but it is to be noted that not even its severest critics have ever insinuated maladministration or that the Fathers were other than completely selfless men.

The day began with the Angelus summoning the neophytes to Mass, at which very few were permitted to receive Holy Communion; then came breakfast. The day ended with the Angelus at sundown, when the neophytes gathered in the church for the saying of the rosary and the singing of the litany. The law prescribed Spanish as the language to be used, and this was often a great convenience in view of the many different Indian languages. Eventually most of the natives living in the mission area accepted it as their mother tongue. Some of the Fathers refused to speak anything but Spanish and it soon came to be the custom that, when the Indians addressed the Padres, especially when making any requests, Spanish was used. In 1801 Lasuén reported that "it is customary to deny their requests if these are not put in Castilian," and that rewards and reprimands were given for the same purpose. Even so, despite official regulations, instructions sometimes were in the native languages, into which the familiar hymns also were translated. Engelhardt in his second volume (p. 257) gives a specimen of a musical score for a Spanish hymn. In this some notes were in yellow, others in red, white or black, indicating the part that the respective singer had to take.

Just how much the Indians comprehended of the Christian mysteries is a question. It is not to be answered by the rejoinder that the loftiest intellect cannot take in their full significance. Even on the basis of what children understand today, it seems likely that the Indians as a rule did not grasp very much. Not only were they dull in intelligence but they had wretched memories, so that things only said by rote had to be gone over and over again, and very often it must all have looked hopeless. Though progress was made, it was exceedingly slow.

If hardly any academic education was attempted, even of the most elementary sort, how could it have been otherwise? How could two fathers at a mission, looking after as many as a thousand neophytes (though many of them were adults and that large figure was not reached until later), conduct regular classes? Moreover one Father was always needed for the manual work. Yet some of the neophytes did learn to read and write, though we may be sure that their Latin singing was a mere enunciation of words which they understood only in general significance. The main thing had to be the teaching of agriculture and handicrafts.

This was a real apostolate, for by means of it the Indians were prepared for life—to contribute to the communal life first and eventually, it was always hoped, to be made self-reliant. Even here there were many handicaps. Because of the lack of iron the cart wheels were nothing but a slice out of the center of a redwood tree or, at best, of three pieces jointed together without nails. A plough was merely a forked branch tipped with a bit of metal. Despite these difficulties, the soil yielded abundant crops, though the raising of grain was not the strongest feature of the missions. Everything connected with this work was necessarily primitive, the threshing being done by spreading the wheat on a piece of hard ground and having cattle or the more swiftly moving mules and horses stamp out the grain. The method served well enough when there were plenty of hands for the work and no great pressure on their time.

We find also that the Indians learned to make oven-baked bricks as well as adobe, tiles and pottery, and that they became reasonably good carpenters, blacksmiths and even masons. They took to tanning quickly and were good workers in leather, their saddles being much admired. So too they produced soap, tallow and candles, and learned to comb sheep wool properly. The women were taught how to spin and sew and grind corn and look after household duties. Even small children were given a job within their powers—and one that they considered fun—that of scaring away the birds from the orchards and vineyards. But the main thing was the raising of what in due course came to be an immense amount of livestock of every kind. Yet as Father Font recorded in 1776, "as a beginning only nine cows and a bull were sent to each mission."

After a while the first makeshift mission buildings were replaced by structures which, whether in ruins or restored, have been much praised as specimens of architecture. As we know from the churches that Serra built during his years at the Sierra Gorda, his taste (the taste of the time) was for the baroque. It was possible to put up such churches there because skilled masons and plasterers could be summoned from Mexico City. As no people of that type came to California, the new series of missions were obliged to adopt a style of utmost simplicity. Though no two are patterned alike, all have a family resemblance, the general feature being a long colonnade with low blunt rounded arches, with no flamboyant façade. A tower on the church itself (sometimes two), heavy buttresses, and a wall pierced with spaces for bells, made up a structure of considerable dignity which possessed the beauty that always flows from a simple and honest use of available materials.

The remarkable fact is that they were put up under the direction of missionaries of whom only one or two knew anything about architecture, and that those working under them were Indians whose immediate forebears never went further than the construction of huts, a mere slanting of poles covered with branches and tule and mud and anything else that came easily to hand.

This much can be said in praise, though it is not unfair to add that the Fathers were compelled to act against their own taste, which was for something much more elaborate— for what would, in fact, have been much too elaborate. Yet, as the California mission churches stand, they have, in my estimation, been a good deal overpraised, quite apart from the fact that their merits are to a great extent accidental. However, when we consider that they were the productions of amateur architects and amateur builders, they deserve all the admiration they receive.

It is the same with the interior decorations, in so far as we can judge what they probably were from the few specimens that have survived to our own time. Here it was not a question of the taste of the Fathers but of their wisdom; they gave their neophytes a free hand, for these were their churches, not buildings designed for exhibition to future critics. Some of the Indians seem to have showed a certain skill as painters. Their pigments had to be made from the juices of various fruits and berries, so they were always under the handicap of lacking the materials ordinarily necessary for mural decorations. Yet gaudily bright though their work was, a rich effect was often attained, even by their artistic crudity. Unfortunately most of this painting faded, or was effaced as the missions fell into ruins. Even when the murals remained, later worshipers could see only their crudity and went in for the kind of restoration which, over and over again in the history of the world, has been disastrous—the removal of what was unique and the substitution for it of the commonplace.

Until the arrival of the Fathers it had never occurred to the Indians to paint anything at all. That is a means of measuring their development. Though the instruction of the neophytes in the Faith was the primary object, it went hand in hand with their elevation in the human scale, and revealed what might eventually have been accomplished had sufficient time been allowed. The Fathers would have been able to do even more for their converts culturally and artistically had most of their energies not gone into irrigation projects, in which they had to be their own engineers, or in teaching agriculture with the exceedingly primitive implements at their disposal, or in branding cattle, or even in acting as tailors.

In spite of all this the Fathers have been accused of having administered to their neophytes the "kiss of death." It has even been suggested that the Fathers were aware that their methods would bring about the eventual extinction of the Indians. That is something that can be disposed of in short order: While the Indians in California, as everywhere else, were an easy prey for epidemics, those of the missions were not only happy and good Christians but flourished materially and physically until events occurred which were deliberately aimed at undoing the Padres' work, a development which we shall hear about later.

While it may be arguable that the Fathers should have made the Indians independent sooner than they did, the neophytes in the missions were incomparably better fed than any other Indians, and were provided with living quarters more weatherproof than any they had known. The regular work they did—almost all of it in the open air—must have been much better for them than sleeping away two-thirds of the day in fetid and verminous huts, though some of these huts were allowed to remain, because the Fathers did not wish to interfere too much. The only point that there can be to accusations such as those of Alexander Forbes is that when an epidemic did break out, the contagion spread rapidly because the mission Indians were living together in close quarters instead of being scattered over the hills. The Fathers may be presumed to have had a few simple remedies they could apply, but in all California there was only one doctor. Finally it must be remembered that, even at the peak of the mission prosperity, the Fathers never had more than thirty thousand Indians under their charge (if that many) and in what is now the state of California there were three times as many Indians whom they never reached at all. According to the argument presented, at least these pagan Indians should have survived. But they did not; all, or virtually all, perished, wiped out by the incoming whites as soon as the protection the Fathers had given was removed.

While the missions lasted the Indians were prosperous—prosperous even though they held property communally and not as individuals. This much was attested by a number of visitors from the time of Vancouver and La Pérouse down to Dana in his *Two Years Before the Mast,* and that in spite of Dana's anti-Catholicism. They, like stray Russians, were hospitably received by the Padres, who produced good beef and mutton and pork and chickens for their guests, with wine from their own vineyards, and fruit from orchards which in some places were reserved for guests, the neophytes having their own. Though much of this was not possible in Serra's time, it was inherent in the system he established. The California missions deserve the title Cunninghame Graham gave to his account of the Jesuit reductions in Paraguay—a Vanished Arcadia.

CHAPTER FOURTEEN

The New System

ON APRIL 9, 1779, Bucareli died. He was the best friend the California missions ever had, even though Gálvez was the man mainly responsible for starting them. Gálvez himself lived on until a couple of years after Serra's own death, always interested in everything relating to New Spain but having no direct concern with it, as he held a cabinet post that dealt with other matters. In Spain he had fought hard for his Franciscans when the Dominicans wished to secure the peninsula of Lower California for themselves, and though he lost to the King, who backed the Dominicans, the Franciscans were not sorry to give up that mission field to concentrate upon the lands further north.

Under Bucareli's successor, Martín de Mayorga, who was Viceroy from 1779 to 1784, the missions were faced with increasing difficulties. The bad situation was caused mainly by an unsympathetic secular administration, and to some degree by the ecclesiastical instruments they were able to use. It exemplifies the worst aspects of the *Patronato Real.* Matters were made worse by administrative changes under which General Teodoro de Croix, a nephew of the former Viceroy of the same name, was put in charge of what were called the Interior Provinces. As a means of counteracting the depredations of the Apaches, the new arrangement was excellent. It gave the General a free hand, while it relieved the Viceroy from bothering

227

himself with matters that were becoming too complicated for him. But California fell under the General's jurisdiction, and as Father Piette writes: "[Croix] knew none of the missionaries. He comprehended nothing of their high civilizing ideals. Habituated to manage soldiers, he commanded the apostles of California as though they were common troopers." Yet as a matter of fact the worst element in the troubles that arose was that he did not bother himself about such matters. As Chapman says, "Croix's one merit in the management of California lay in the fact that he approved anything that the governor actually got done."

That governor was Felipe de Neve, and Croix had a way of putting what may be called his rubber stamp on everything proposed by Neve, often without reading his reports. He did not pretend to know much about Californian affairs and left them to be dealt with by the man on the spot whose capital, it will be remembered, had been transferred from Loreto to Monterey, in 1775, when he replaced the lethargic Rivera. Piette goes so far as to assert that "more even than Fages, Rivera and Neve, de Croix showed himself incapable of understanding the nobility of the soul of Serra." However, it seems to me that the man who counted most was Neve; certainly between him and Serra there ensued a long struggle.

Father Piette is perhaps a little too ready to accuse of what he calls Voltarianism anybody who did not completely support every plan that any missionary promoted. Even poor Gálvez, since this cannot be said of him, is charged with a bitter animosity towards the Jesuits because it fell to him to carry out the royal order of 1767 for their expulsion. But Neve, though it must be doubtful whether he was influenced by the ideas of the Encyclopaedists, unless perhaps in the sense that he was susceptible to what was in the air, did have certain notions not calculated to spell harmony between himself and the friars of his province. Irving Berdine Richman, however, is probably not far from the right explanation when he says in his *California Under Spain and Mexico:* "Neve and Fages remain each a man of character, but, strange to say, only one (Fages) a man of personality. Neve, indeed, possessed so much character, was so imperturbable, kept so well his temper, wrought with an inexorability so final, as to be personally of scant account. Neve was the Reglamento and the Reglamento was Neve—little besides." This is another way of saying that he was cold and went his way so calmly because he was sure he was unassailable; he was swaddled in red tape.

Yet what he did was possible only because Croix in 1777 became the man under whom he was to work. When Neve was first appointed, Bucareli (a man of very different views) wrote to Serra: "Señor Neve is charged to consult you, and to propose whatever means he may think necessary and expedient for the success of [the mission] establishments. He is also directed to act at all times in accord with your Reverence." Though there was no formal abrogation of the old *reglamento* (which may be described as a set of bylaws) as Serra had discovered during the regime of Rivera, an interpretation could be given that was virtual nullification, and this was followed by a new *reglamento* drawn up by Neve himself. When Neve wished further directives to justify what he wanted, all he needed to do was to make his suggestions to General de Croix, sure of being told in effect, "Quite so, quite so!" whereupon the General would turn to matters that interested him more.

Neve seems to have been a very decent sort of a person in his own way, one who carried out his duty as he saw it, even though making many serious mistakes and displaying a cold finality that must have been infuriating. But there is no reason to suppose that he was irreligious or antagonistic towards the missions; it was merely that he did not understand Serra's problems, and had a mind closed to all argument. In his justification it must be said that the colonial policy of Spain was to keep the Indians in a state of tutelage only as an interim measure—ten years was envisaged as the period that would be necessary, though there was no positive law about this, even if it was generally imagined to exist. After that ten years the Indians were supposed to be ripe for leaving the protection of the mission and for establishing pueblos, or village life, in which each individual would have his own holding of land and be able to manage for himself.

Nevertheless there were ideological factors at work at this time that were detrimental to the missions. Charles III, though Serra always referred to him as though he were the model of a Christian, was in fact far from that, as was true of many of the most influential people in Spain. Yet the Spanish were the most Catholic nation on earth, and their governing classes, even those personally negligent of religious practice, protested a strong belief in the Christian mysteries. This can go, and often did go, with a low opinion of the priesthood, which, as it actually existed, must be admitted to have been infected with worldliness. It was, however, a fixed point of policy to support missionary activities, if only as an economical and expeditious means of extending the secular power. It was in that light that Neve regarded the Franciscans in the province under his jurisdiction. He was ready enough to support them, but it had to be on his own terms.

Like his predecessor, he would do nothing about founding the mission of San Buenaventura, which itself was a great disappointment to Serra, as he had hoped that with a more energetic man at the head of affairs, something would be done in that matter. Yet that question during Neve's regime was completely dwarfed by two others, each of which was quite unexpected: The new Governor attempted an interdict in ecclesiastical affairs, and he insisted that at each mission Indians be elected with minor jurisdictional rights over the others. For the sake of simplifying the story of his administration it might best be confined to these two main considerations.

In 1774 the Pope had issued special permission to Serra to administer confirmation for a period of ten years. The document authorizing this did not reach California until June, 1778, because it had to be passed upon by the King and then the Viceroy in New Spain, another instance of the *Patronato Real*. But when it finally got into Serra's hands, he saw that all the requirements had been met and joyfully proceeded to exercise the powers conferred upon him.

Perhaps it should be explained that ordinarily the sacrament of confirmation is conferred only by a bishop. But it is not something that always exclusively belongs to the episcopal office, for in the Eastern Church that is in communion with Rome, confirmation is given by the priest who baptizes, and immediately after baptism. Now, I understand, Canon Law permits any pastor of the Latin Rite to administer confirmation, though only under special circumstances that are precisely defined. But the general rule remains that confirmation appertains to a bishop.

Serra, of course, promptly set to work. We hear of his confirming upwards of six hundred souls at San Diego in 1778, and on his return journey to Carmel he confirmed another hundred and forty-seven at San Juan Capistrano, three hundred and sixty-two at San Gabriel, two hundred and sixty-five at San Luis Obispo, and three hundred and thirty-two at San Antonio. We may be sure that many of those confirmed were not very clear about just what they believed, and could not have answered the kind of questions that a bishop usually puts to a child he is about to confirm; but the strengthening grace would flow from the sacrament, whatever might be the knowledge of the Indian mind.

Just when it was that Neve intervened is not certain, but intervene he did, though after Serra had made his chief confirming tour. He was well within his rights in asking Serra upon what authority he was acting, and perhaps it was permissible to demand to be shown the written authorization, so as to make sure that all legal requirements had been met. It was nevertheless very boorish, for obviously Serra would not have acted in this way unless the right to do so had been given. To Neve's demand he was obliged to say that the original brief of the Pope was in the possession of the Commissary in Mexico City. He had never received anything himself but an attestation from the Commissary that the document had reached him and had been countersigned by the proper authorities in Spain and New Spain. Even that he had sent for safekeeping to the Guardian at San Fernando.

A lot of wrangling ensued, Neve persisting and Serra having to reply each time that what he asked was an impossibility. The state of the Governor's mind is indicated in what he wrote to Teodoro de Croix on March 26, 1781: "Father Junípero Serra says that he sent his patents etc. to the Father Guardian. I shall not proceed to take possession of his papers, because, it not being certain that he has sent them away, he will with his unspeakable artifice and cunning have hid them, and the result will be delay in the Channel foundations, since these Fathers will not furnish the supplies which they have to contribute." The foundations at the Channel had absolutely nothing to do

with the matter. Neve was merely inventing a pretext for
delay and a means for bringing pressure to bear. He continued in the same vein: "There is no vexation which these
religious men will not attempt in their boundless and incredible pride, since on more than one occasion my policy
and moderation were not enough to turn them from the
opposition with which they surreptitiously conspired
against the government and its ordinances."

Just what he had in mind will appear in a moment.
Neve went on to say: "At a more opportune time certain
measures may be taken which for the present it has been
judged necessary to postpone, in order to bring this Father
President to a proper acknowledgment of the authority
which he eludes while he pretends to obey it." The man's
suspicious disposition and his lack of elementary good
manners are patent. In describing Serra he is really describing himself. His letter shows to what a pass things
had come between Serra and the dictatorial Governor.

The upshot was that Neve forbade Serra to do any more
confirming. Some writers on the subject, however, have
attempted to show that it was rather that Neve warned
and admonished Serra against continuing, without inter-
dicting it. Though it perhaps may be interpreted in that
way—as Neve could not claim that his permission was necessary but only that the formalities had not been complied
with—his whole tone was nevertheless peremptory and
rude.

Neve had been told where the documents were, and if
he felt that he should see them, the ordinary method of
proceeding was to write to Mexico City and in the meanwhile not to interfere with Serra. Instead Neve took a line
that charged Serra in effect with being a liar and impostor.
It was the easiest, and also the unfairest thing in the world
to say that he did not search Serra's papers (as though this

fell within his province!) only because he knew that such a search would be useless, because Serra could hide anything. It was also a rather stupid thing to say—though Neve was of good intelligence when not crazed with anger —for obviously Serra, so far from wanting to hide the document Neve was sure was in his keeping, would at once have produced it to his complete justification.

Serra was a mild man, mild even after what he had had to put up with from Fages and Rivera, and though Neve was far more arrogant than either—both because of his make-up and because he had a wider authority than his predecessors—Serra still kept his temper, good humor being one of his most marked characteristics. But this time he thought that the Governor was merely trying to be as unpleasant as possible. Therefore he was disposed to leave Neve to stew in his own juice, and so made no special effort to obtain posthaste from Mexico City the proof that he was authorized to act as he had done.

It should be noted that Serra was not contesting the principle of the *Patronato Real,* for this privilege had been granted to Spain by the Holy See. But frequently the Spanish Crown had stretched its rights further than was ever intended, the most glaring instance of which was the Inquisition in Spain, where that institution during the late Middle Ages had often been used as a means for breaking those of whom the King disapproved, or even as a pretext for confiscating the property of the condemned. And it was in vain that the Holy See protested. Now the Inquisition, while it still existed, was only a shadow of what it formerly had been, which was all the more reason for the Crown's attempting to exercise ecclesiastical control more rigorously in other ways. Truly the *Patronato Real* was a very mixed blessing.

Yet even this was not really involved in this case, though

it was on such grounds that Neve was proceeding. Every legal requirement regarding the Pope's brief had been complied with; Serra had sent back the document he had received to Mexico City for safekeeping. Serra can hardly be blamed if he took a little mischievous pleasure in the thought of the discomfiture of an obnoxiously bumptious official which he knew was sure to come.

However, he did intend to get the document asked for, but in his own good time. There was no hurry, for he had already confirmed nearly all the Indians who were ready for the sacrament. Meanwhile he did not stop administering confirmation, except in a public way to a large number of people, since that would only have further infuriated Neve to no useful purpose. But he continued quietly to confirm small groups, something that must have been well known to Neve, even if he found it advisable to pretend to be in ignorance. About all this there was no secret; had the Governor dared to seize Serra's papers he would have found the official record of these confirmations —of the time, place and number. The fact that Neve did not stalk in with an armed guard to carry off what he wanted to know would seem to indicate that he knew it already, if only in a general way. Also such action might have resulted in an appeal to the highest authority—and Neve's removal from office. Serra therefore went on with what he was doing, but in a manner that would give no offense.

Moreover, Serra did two things that he hoped would satisfy Neve. On October 30, 1779, he wrote to Croix asking for his permission to continue administering confirmation. But as he surmised what the reply of Croix would be, he wrote to Father Verger, the Guardian at San Fernando, asking him to show all the papers to the Viceroy and requesting him to provide officially attested duplicates.

As he had done all he could, he did not think it necessary to inform Neve further when the man began to talk about seizing papers.

As might have been expected, Croix consulted his lawyer, who gave it as his opinion that, the King being patron, the Viceroy was vice-patron (about which there was no question) adding a little surprisingly that General de Croix was equally so. This opinion, delivered on April 17, 1780, said that the Governor "could proceed to collect the said documents." Upon this Croix wrote to Neve three days later ordering him to take possession of the patent, as this must still be in Serra's possession, and to forward it to him, so that he might communicate with the Viceroy and settle the question. It is not hard to imagine what "stalling" would have followed had the paper ever come into the hands of Neve or Croix. Neve was instructed "under no pretext whatever to permit the President to go on administering the sacrament till new orders should be given."

Neve's answer to this, dated March 26, 1781, was to accuse Serra of having hidden the patent. But despite his bluster and his charges of deceit, he hesitated to proceed to extreme measures, or, as Bancroft puts it, of being the cat's-paw for taking "the chestnuts out of the fire," if indeed there were any to take. Therefore it was that he drew a red herring across the trail by trying to make the affair of the confirmations the reason why he could not found San Buenaventura.

On the same date as that on which Croix wrote to Neve (April 20, 1780) he also wrote to Serra, sending him the opinion of his legal advisor, and ordering him to deliver the documents to the Governor. On July 20th Serra replied to Croix, telling him that he had already sent the papers to San Fernando so that they might be put in the

form demanded by the Governor. When on October 6,
1780, the patent was transmitted to Serra from Mexico
City, along with a letter dated February 15, 1780, from
Father Verger the Guardian, telling him that duplicates
had been forwarded to Croix, Serra, instead of keeping
them to show Neve, sent them straight back to Verger by
the ship that had brought them, asking that they be passed
on to General Croix. Neve at that moment was absent in
Lower California, but Serra by this time had no intention
of treating with a man who had made himself so offensive,
and so merely told Neve, when he returned to Monterey,
that the papers were in Mexico City. Nor was he going to
explain further to Croix, knowing that he would soon
receive all the documents, but wrote to him on March 23,
1781, swearing "upon the honor of a priest" that, as the
papers were not in his possession, he was unable to show
them to the Governor.

In all this it must be remembered how long a time it
took for letters to reach those to whom they were addressed. But in due course Croix received the elusive
papers and so wrote on December 24, 1780, to Serra giving
him "permission" to confer confirmation. In his letter
Croix informed Serra that he had now been assured that
the papal brief had received the confirmation of the Council of the Indies and of the Viceroy of New Spain, so he
was that day instructing Governor Neve "not to prevent
your Reverence from using said faculty, and that for its
exercise he furnish your Reverence with the escort which
you ask of him and which you need." There was never
a word of apology from either Croix or Neve, but probably
both felt that Serra had set out to make fools of them,
which may indeed have been the case, though the two
men had got only what they had invited.

What the motive in all this could have been is hard to

say. It would seem that the object was not solely that of irritating Serra but rather that they had been afraid lest he should obtain further prestige from exercising quasi-episcopal powers. They wished to make him completely subservient to themselves but had only succeeded in making themselves look foolish. They should have understood that from the beginning Serra must have been perfectly sure of his position.

Serra, as we know, even after the attempted interdict had continued to administer confirmation. Palóu seems not to have been aware of this, so quietly had everything been done. But Serra's own register shows that between November, 1779, and September, 1781, he confirmed on twelve distinct occasions, conferring the sacrament on a total of thirty-one persons. However, on seven of these occasions only one person was confirmed, and we may be sure that this was because that person was on the point of death. To the end of 1778 the confirmation book contains the names of 1,897 people, almost all of them Indians. By July 16, 1784, when Serra's faculty lapsed, he had confirmed a total of 5,307 men, women and children. The number would in any event be impressive; it is doubly so in view of the difficulties created by Neve and the fact that it was a lame old man in poor health who made these tours on foot. But nothing daunted Junípero Serra when it was a question of saving souls.

A second main cause of friction between Serra and Neve arose from the Governor's insistence that the missions be organized as pueblos or villages. With this also went the idea that under this new system one priest for each church would suffice, for the Father who had hitherto given instruction in agriculture and handicrafts would no longer be needed. Yet even supposing that the mission were transformed into a parish—which was what Neve was driving at—two priests would still have found plenty to do. The prospect of living alone appalled them, though not long after this time many a Catholic priest on the frontier of the United States accepted such loneliness for the love of God. Thus we find that Jean François Rivet, the priest at Vincennes, Indiana, when dying there in 1804, had to write out the confession he was unable to make orally, and it was not found until the priest he had sent for arrived three days after Rivet's death. But there was no reason for such isolation in California; there were more than enough men available to supply two to each mission; in fact there were several supernumeraries who were waiting for the founding of the mission for which they had been designated.

It is hard not to believe that, at least in this matter, Neve was not exhibiting petty spite. The government did not have to pay the clerical stipends, as these came out of the Pious Fund, so that nothing was saved by the administration. But Neve may have calculated that some of the Fathers, if compelled to live in isolation, would ask to return home, which in fact several of them did. Then as there would not be two priests to spare for each place, the missions, as such, would collapse—two being the very minimum necessary for a mission, one priest for spiritualities, the other for temporalities. It was that method Neve was trying to destroy.

Neve refused to use the term "mission," though everybody else went on using it. He substituted the term *doctrina,* since that connoted only spiritual activities. He could not at a stroke of the pen and on his sole authority transform the missions into parishes, but he proceeded to introduce regulations which belong only to a pueblo, indirectly removing the Padres' control of their neophytes in temporal matters. Again it was the destruction of the mission system that he aimed at.

Neve—refusing to take no for an answer—demanded that the neophytes at each mission elect one of their number as *alcalde*, or mayor, and others as *regidores*, or prefects of police. They were to have special uniforms and batons and were to be exempt from the punishment of the stocks or the lash, though they might mete out these punishments to others. The Fathers were horrified and warned the doctrinaire Neve what the result would be: As soon as these Indians saw themselves invested with a little authority and exempt from all punishment, they would become unmanageable themselves and make the rest of the neophytes unmanageable. So it proved. At Carmel an Indian named Baltazar, who had been chosen as *alcalde*, proceeded to seduce his sister-in-law, neglected all his duties, and in the end ran off to the mountains with a gang of followers and lived in concubinage. Nor would Neve provide any soldiers to bring the fugitives back; in this case, however, the Fathers were relieved to be rid of Baltazar. Similarly a report came from San Luis Obispo that its *alcalde* Nicholas provided women for as many soldiers as wanted them, thus demoralizing the Spaniards as well as the Indians. When the Fathers turned him over to the corporal for a whipping, they were reproved by the Governor on the ground that only in the case of revolt or murder was the corporal empowered to arrest anybody, much less administer punishment.

There was no Spanish law that prescribed any kind of election for missions, so the whole thing must be called a whim on the part of Neve and Croix. There was no use to appeal to the General because he invariably backed up the Governor; nor was there any use in appealing to the Viceroy, who would only have said that this was a

matter to be dealt with by the official in charge of the
Interior Provinces. And an appeal to Madrid would have
taken so long a time that the missions would have been
wrecked before an answer arrived.

Serra in great distress wrote to Lasuén on March 29,
1779, about what was going on. He said that the day before, which was Palm Sunday, he had gone to the presidio
to say Mass, and that before he began he had a conversation with Neve which left him so agitated that he could
hardly compose himself for the altar. Yet, he added, "I
celebrated holy Mass, and after a short talk on indifferent
matters, came here to sing the Passion with my companions
as they expected me." Not until night did the solution
come to him. Then, as he was preparing himself for the
sleep he badly needed, it seemed that he heard an interior
Voice saying: "As wise as serpents, as simple as doves."
Much relieved, he sat up in bed crying, "Yes, Lord, so it
shall be with Thy grace," whereupon he fell asleep at once.

The method he devised was this. Among the neophytes
at Carmel was one named Francisco, who already had a
baton and coat, though none of the authority that Neve
had in mind, or only so much as marked him as a factotum
of the Fathers. Very well, let him be one of the *alcaldes;*
there would be nothing more than a change in name. Let
the other *alcalde* be a chief living in a nearby *rancheria.*
It was to be kept back from these men that they were
exempt from punishment; Neve would see them invested
with the tokens of authority but would be unaware that
authority itself had not really been conferred.

Neve soon began to perceive that his plan had only
brought confusion. Serra then seized the initiative by asking for his directives, thus making him the man responsible.
Serra was also careful to make sure that the Governor's
instructions were put in writing, so that there could be

no attempt to deny what had been said or to twist into it a new meaning. Neve, by this time seeing how awry things had gone, answered that he placed his confidence in the Fathers rather than the Indians, presuming that neophytes would be trained for the positions they were to occupy. "The tenor of my answer to him," wrote Serra to Lasuén on April 25, 1780, "was that if we were so good, and if we were to be trusted with the election of the *alcaldes,* as we had desired, then he could also trust us to rear them, correct them, chastise them."

To this letter Neve made no reply, which meant that he would not formally abandon his theory of Indian self-government. But it had so broken down in the face of actualities that after this no effort was made to enforce the plan as the Governor had envisaged it. A few neophytes were permitted a shadowy authority, while the effective control remained, as formerly, in the hands of the Fathers. Had it not been so, they might as well have closed shop and gone back to Mexico—an eventuality which even Neve would have looked upon as a disaster.

A year later—on July 17, 1781—there was a very real disaster, and one that showed that even the best-disposed Indians were not to be trusted, though it also proved that Spanish officials and soldiers had blundered badly. It resulted in the closing of the land route that Anza had so brilliantly opened in 1776 and which promised so much for the future. A rising of the Indians exterminated all those at both the mission and presidio on the Colorado River, together with a party of new colonists for California. The only people allowed to live were the women and children.

This affair had a number of remarkable features. As Elliott Coues, the editor of the diary of Father Garcés, writes: "The victims were all, or nearly all, [merely] clubbed to death; and . . . all the women and children were spared—captured and enslaved, but not outraged. I do not know where to find the exact parallel of this in the annals of Indian massacre." Palma, the chief, even tried to save the life of Father Garcés, but the fact is that he had never possessed the degree of authority with which the Spaniards credited him, so he was powerless in face of the general Yuma resentment.

The truth is that these Indians had looked for a good deal more than was done for them under a plan which was neither a presidio nor a mission nor a pueblo, but combined in a niggardly and inefficient fashion something of all three systems. One of the establishments had a corporal and nine soldiers, ten colonists, and six artisans; the other contained one soldier less than that—an altogether inadequate staffing at a point of such strategic importance. The friars had sent warnings of the mounting distrust but they were ignored, so rather despairingly they stayed at their posts.

General Croix was the man mainly responsible. These Indians came under his jurisdiction, and he had made them lavish promises of material benefits which he failed to carry out. It would seem that he was attempting an experiment, an improvement upon the missions of California, about which he was hearing nothing but criticism from Governor Neve. He too was something of a doctrinaire and as such out of touch with realities.

The local soldiers also were far from being without blame. They treated the Yumas in a highhanded style, putting a chief in the stocks on some trivial charge and flogging freely. Then our old friend Rivera arrived to make matters worse by bringing a body of colonists. Some of these were ill-conditioned fellows who exercised none of the care that Anza had shown in respecting the corn and melon fields of the natives. They simply appropriated what they wanted and allowed their cattle to wander at large, trampling down the communal Yuma farms. Rivera sent on to San Gabriel the main body of the settlers he was escorting, intending to follow in a few days, but meanwhile those with him (and their beasts) caused further depredations. It was too much to be borne. Suddenly the Indians rose and though Rivera and the forty-two Spanish soldiers there made a stout resistance, they were all killed. Rivera had long been haunted by the idea that his bones would lie bleaching in the desert, and that is what happened. Though Garcés, who was personally very popular, was hidden away for several days, in the end he too was dragged out and clubbed to death. As Bolton and Marshall remark in their *Colonization of North America:* "The experience of the Yuma missions is a pointed commentary on the need of soldiers to control mission Indians, and on the usual Spanish custom of separating the neophytes from the settlers." But though it was a justification of the methods Serra had employed, it came too late to help him with Neve, who was retired soon after this event.

One wonders a little that the Spaniards so easily gave up this invaluable land route, for although the Yumas were warlike as compared with the Indians of California, they were not, after all, so very formidable. Spaniards of earlier days would have soon restored their position, or if the use of main force was now considered undesirable, a man like Anza, who had won the friendship of the Yumas in 1774, would have regained it, because he knew how to deal with Indians.

One outcome of the massacre was that, when it was not followed by a rising of the Indians in California, as some feared would happen, Neve notified Serra that he might now proceed with the founding of San Buenaventura. He was brought to recognize that, as a strategic point, it should be held, of course with a presidio as well as a mission. Hitherto, as has been said, he had sought to make Serra's attitude about conferring confirmation an excuse for not doing what he was well aware he should himself have done.

Another event that followed the massacre (though not as a consequence) was the departure of Neve. He was promoted to the position that had been occupied by General de Croix as *Commandante Inspector* of the Interior Provinces. He was after all a rather able man. He was marching, accompanied by Fages, who was now a Lieutenant Colonel, to start retaliatory operations against the Yumas when the news reached them. Fages was to be the new governor of California but subordinate, of course, to Neve.

Two expeditions were sent against the Yumas but accomplished little except obtaining the release of the captured women and children. The Indians faded away, refusing to give battle. Since they had horses, they were not to be caught, except in isolated instances. It was therefore easier to come to an arrangement with them than to punish them. As for the departing Governor, Alberta Johnston Denis writes: "Felipe de Neve . . . leaves one cold. He has struck no responsive chord; not a single note vibrates in unison; while Pedro Fages—who in all probability could not have framed the famous *reglamento*—comes to us a glowing personality."

That Neve remained over Fages may have caused some apprehensions, but the fact is that Neve had by now learned that it was simply not possible to carry out his ideas to the letter, and the Yuma disaster had chastened him. Moreover his main interests were now engaged by his new office, and as he was henceforth far away, his existence could usually be forgotten.

CHAPTER FIFTEEN

The Shadow of Secularization

As HAS already been seen, there were a number of signs that pointed to the eventual secularization of the missions that was to occur, though only after Mexico had thrown off the rule of Spain. A drift in that direction appeared under the governorship of Neve, as described in the preceding chapter. But Neve's plans for the most part had to be abandoned when they resulted in a fiasco. Another indication, however, was the appeal published in New Spain on August 13, 1779, that "for once, and in the nature of a donation," contributions be made towards the expenses of the war that had broken out between Spain and England. It was "suggested" that each Spaniard contribute two dollars and each Indian half that amount—which of course assumed that such Indians had property of their own, or were paid for their work, an assumption that should have exempted all the mission Indians of California.

Although ostensibly the money was a free contribution, actually it was a head tax, for it was very hard for anybody to avoid paying. Yet what could any of Serra's neophytes pay? Money never came into their hands, for even the odd jobs that a few of them did at the presidio in their spare time were rewarded in goods, the soldiers themselves having little cash available. The result was that the Padres paid—not the full amount, as that was quite beyond their power, but what they could. Father Engelhardt lists the

246

sums raised, showing that the missions averaged a little over a hundred dollars each, and the presidios a good deal more—in the case of Monterey $833, the larger part of which undoubtedly came out of Neve's pocket. There appears to be some discrepancy here, for no mention is made of San Francisco (either its presidio or its two missions), or of the settlers at San José, who should have been able to make up a fairly good purse. Perhaps this is resolved by the difference between the total of $2,693 accounted for by Engelhardt and that of $4,216 acknowledged by General de Croix on December 7, 1782. Hubert Howe Bancroft says that Neve personally contributed $2,000, which seems excessive in view of the fact that his official salary was only $4,000 a year. If he really did pay as much, it may partly explain, as Engelhardt rather cynically hints, the honors he subsequently received.

Serra did not protest against this tax, heavy burden though it was on the missions, for he was a patriot. Moreover, he announced that the war should be regarded as one in defense of the Catholic religion against the enemies of the Church, for Spaniards considered all Englishmen heretics, just as most Englishmen imagined that the favorite occupation of Spaniards was burning Protestants at the stake. The Litany of All Saints was ordered by Serra to be said after Mass on Sundays, and after this the *Credo* was to be three times recited aloud by the congregation.

Yet Serra might have objected with reason. For the tax indicated an increasingly laical point of view. Even in this regard it was unjust, because the mission Indians were wards of the Crown. From the spiritual standpoint it was still more unjust, for these Indians were also wards of the Church. It was quite a different matter in the case of Indians organized in pueblos, as they were in many parts of the Spanish dominions, for they were subject to the obligations of ordinary citizens. However, the Fathers seem to have missed these implications, or to have been willing to overlook them for the sake of doing something towards the military success they hoped for. They were loyal patriots, and they counted upon national victory to strengthen the position of the missionaries.

The general situation, taking the end of 1783 as a convenient culminating point, was that there were nine missions, for at last San Buenaventura with its presidio had been founded. About six thousand Indians had been baptized, of whom three quarters were still at the missions, the rest having died. The livestock in round figures consisted of six thousand head of cattle, about the same of sheep, three thousand goats, nine hundred horses, two hundred mules, and three hundred pigs, not to mention donkeys and chickens. The neophytes were now harvesting each year eight thousand bushels of wheat, seven thousand of corn, fifteen hundred of barley, and a thousand of beans, and in addition smaller quantities of peas, chickpeas and lentils. The work was being directed by twenty Franciscans under Serra.

There were two settlements of colonists in California, San José and Los Angeles. Together they contained something over two hundred men, women and children. There would have been the expectation of a good many more settlers had it not been for the Yuma massacre. These settlers possessed about seven hundred head of cattle and horses and a thousand sheep and goats. Of various field products they raised about three thousand, seven hundred and fifty bushels. The military force at the four presidios, even counting the guard at each of the missions, amounted to almost three hundred men, for recruits came by sea as well as up the Peninsula. It was a great improvement on the past.

When Pedro Fages returned, this time not merely as commandant but with the ampler powers of governor, Serra may have felt some apprehensions. Fages knew perfectly well that he had been dismissed nine years earlier at Serra's request. However, any fears proved to be unnecessary. Serra's letter of recommendation may have helped when it was presented in Mexico; be that as it may, Fages had risen to be a lieutenant colonel, and was now Governor, so it was evident that Serra had not damaged his career. And while Fages would not have been Fages if he had not been short of temper and a martinet, he was the kind of man who, after exploding, quickly subsides. Experience had mellowed him somewhat, and his nature was not without generosity. Serra got along with him personally, recognizing that most of the difficulties that arose during his tenure of office were not so much of his creating as due to the fact that the new Governor was under the general supervision of the unlamented Neve.

The government in Spain had always taken it for granted that, after a period of tutelage in some form of mission system, the Indians would be organized in pueblos, with parishes that were under diocesan priests. And such was the policy of the Church as well. This did not mean that friars would not sometimes—at any rate as an interim measure—staff these parishes, but the function of the religious order was conceived as spearheading the process of conversion and then, when it had reached a stage of reasonably good development, handing over their work to seculars, while they themselves passed on to fields that were as yet unevangelized. Ten years was considered the period needed for this, and perhaps in some cases such a period sufficed. In Mexico itself, for example, many of the Indians had a native culture upon which to build and were fairly (occasionally very) intelligent. But despite the prevailing impression, there was no Spanish law limiting the period, which experience found to need wide latitude.

At this time there were elements in the government, both at home and in the overseas dominions, that were to some extent infected with what are called liberal ideas. Such ideas are not to be condemned wholesale, for many were admirable, though they were naturally suspect to those of a conservative cast of mind. And it must be said that even when they were good in theory, they were not always practicable in a particular time and place. Also some acute observers were aware that a leaven was working that might be dangerous; it was to culminate in the age of revolutions. Miguel Hidalgo, who was to lead the revolution in Mexico in 1810, had been a priest since 1779. Though he and another priest, Morelos, both failed after some initial successes, by May 22, 1822, Mexico had the first of its short-lived empires, to be followed a year later by the establishment of its first republic.

Not all of this was derived, as Father Piette would have us believe, from the French Encyclopaedists. A lesson was learned from the English colonies to the north who had formed themselves into the United States of America, and the much more drastic example of the French Revolution inflamed many a demagogue. The governing classes themselves were being permeated by ideas that would eventually wreck their own position. In general it might be said that conservative elements tended to protect themselves by liberalizing their regime. Properly controlled this would have been all to the good.

Only one aspect of this concerns us here—the process of secularization as it first appeared in California. About this there was no difference in principle between Church and State. The ultimate aim of the Fathers in California

was secularization, for the mission system, as established
by Serra, was thought of only as the soundest and most
solid means—though admittedly not the quickest—for
bringing their neophytes to the position where they could
stand on their own feet. Communal ownership, in which
the Padres acted as guardians, was no more than a stage
towards the responsibilities of private ownership. The only
points about which argument was possible referred to the
advisability of some of the mission methods, and most of
all as to how soon the end desired by all could be attained.

On the one hand there were those who thought that
the friars proceeded too slowly, and that in some ways
they even retarded matters. To this the friars' answer was
in effect the adage, more haste, less speed. They were convinced by experience that it was useless to toss the neophytes
before they were prepared for it into a life of which they
had no conception. If that were done, these Indians with
their natural disinclination for work, without regular
habits sufficiently developed, and without much notion
as to how to proceed except under direction, would inevitably revert to their former degraded state. All the devoted labor of the missionaries would then have gone for
nothing—except of course that some baptized children
had gained heaven and that a few of the adults might possibly retain enough of what they had been taught for
their salvation.

A criticism brought against the Fathers—not so much
by the soldiers and officials who came in contact with the
Indians as by later critics theorizing about matters of
which they knew little or nothing—was that the dependence of the neophytes upon the Padres was so great as to
prevent independence ever being obtained. Even the local
administrators of the Neve type, who daily saw the Indians,
did not have to try to teach them anything and could not

have had a clear conception of the difficulties involved. But the Fathers knew the Indians inside out, and what they did was dictated by their understanding of what the case required.

The emphasis of the times, however, was towards rapid secularization. At the instance of the bishop-elect of Guiana, the Cortes in Spain had recently legislated that all the missions in the New World were to be turned over to episcopal jurisdiction as soon as possible; that they were to be turned into parishes under secular priests, though the religious might remain as temporary curates, and that for the time being one or two missions might continue in each district; and finally that the government of the Indians and the administration of mission temporalities were to be surrendered to Indian officials, under the direction of the civil governor; and that the mission lands should be divided among individual owners. This was what Neve had tried to bring about, even before the passage of the law. It must in fairness be said that the program was not in itself irreligious but merely injudicious. It was also impracticable as it stood, though rapacious politicians of a later generation, when they appeared upon the scene, found it very practicable for feathering their own nests.

It has been complained that the friars did not institute academic education for the Indians. In answer, it has been pointed out that it was quite impossible that they should have done so, even had the Indians been far more intelligent than they were, for the simple reason that the missions were all understaffed. Furthermore, these critics overlook the fact that the vast majority of Spaniards of the lower orders—here one would have to include the soldiers and the artisans and the settlers in California—were illiterate; not unintelligent, but illiterate. It is to be doubted whether more than one in ten could so much as sign his own name.

Serra's own family, which was of the prosperous peasant sort, had to have somebody read his letters to them.

No doubt some education is very desirable, though modern America has grown superstitious on the subject. All that can be safely affirmed is that education tends to improve naturally good parts, but one should never lose sight of the sober truth that many a good mechanic has been hopelessly spoiled by getting it into his head that nothing less than a "white-collar" job will do for him, and even that education is liable to make the viciously inclined all the more dangerous. The worst thing of all is that we seem to be on our way to producing a generation of morons by means of an education which is hardly aware of its true ends. What the Franciscan missionaries wanted to do was to make their neophytes into useful members of society by training them to be at once good Christians and good farmers or artisans.

However, without going into an abstract discussion of the question, let the facts that the Fathers had before them be considered. They had to deal with a race that hated mental exertion even more than physical work. The forebears of the neophytes had lived little better than the beasts; they now had to be taught their dignity as human beings, and that by far the most important thing man can learn is a right attitude towards God and His laws. To them book learning was, except perhaps in a very few exceptional instances, completely irrelevant, and to have attempted to impart it would have been a waste of time, even had it been feasible. It might even be said that it would probably have been a crime to distract the Indian's attention from the useful things he was capable of acquiring, even these very slowly and as a result of unfailing patience on the part of those who had them in charge.

Even such teaching as was possible was made difficult

by the attitude of the secular authorities. Thus Viceroy Mayorga declined to furnish either church goods or farm implements when requested, on the ground that the Governor (at that time it was Neve) had indicated no need for them. Without proper equipment there could have been no missions, and though the Fathers spent their stipends for the purpose, the missions were so handicapped that Father Pangua (the Guardian at San Fernando from 1780–1783) had to inform the Viceroy that the six friars who had just been assigned to California refused to go there under such hampering conditions, thereby forcing Mayorga's hand.

This followed Neve's attempt to have only one priest at each station to look after the spiritualities, in the belief that the Indians could look after their worldly affairs; which, had it been successful, would have meant the destruction of the missions. We learn how essential two priests were from a report made after Serra's death by Father Salazar to the Viceroy on May 11, 1796: "The missionary who stays home is occupied morning to night, praying with the neophytes, teaching the gentiles, visiting the sick ... burying the dead. ... The other will be seen occupied in planting, managing gangs engaged in digging ditches, cutting out rock, hewing wood, irrigating, supervising the care of the livestock, the operation of the looms, and an infinity of such matters." He might have added that this Father did not merely tell the neophytes what to do but took an active part in it himself. It had been the same in Father Serra's time.

The establishment of settlements of colonists—made possible by Anza's expedition of 1776—should be touched on here. San José adjoined the mission of Santa Clara but was quite distinct from it and was founded in November, 1777, by Moraga, the officer whom Anza left in charge of the

San Francisco presidio. Each settler was allowed ten dollars a month and rations according to the needs of his family; he was also supplied (though as a loan to be repaid to the government) with two horses, a mule, two cows, two oxen for the plough, two sheep and two goats, together with seed for planting and the necessary implements. Taking 1790 as a date when comparison may fairly be made because of the progress effected, in that year San José had about eighty inhabitants, who owned about a thousand head of cattle and raised roughly two thousand bushels of grain; whereas the mission nearby had about nine hundred inhabitants, who owned about three thousand head of cattle and harvested the same number of bushels. From this it is evident that by then, prosperous though the mission was, the adjoining pueblo was relatively still more prosperous, a fact to be accounted for by the considerable difference between the industry of the Spaniard and the Indian. Horses about this time cost from $3 to $9; saddles, on the other hand, were costly, fetching $12 to $16. A sheep was worth seventy-five cents to $2, but mules were worth from $14 to $20, because of being in such demand as beasts of burden. Jerked beef was worth three cents a pound and fresh beef one cent. But eggs were high—twenty-five cents a dozen—the reason being that chickens had to be carried by boat.

In the south there was a rather larger settlement at Los Angeles. At first it consisted almost entirely of mulattos and *mestizos*, and these mixed strains still made up about half of the people. The mission of San Gabriel nearby had about a thousand neophytes, yet it owned only four thousand head of cattle and six thousand sheep, as against the three thousand cattle and five hundred sheep owned by somewhat over a hundred people. The expenditures of the pueblo were, however, vastly greater than the more economically managed mission, and it was less useful than the mission as a source of supplies for the presidio.

These settlements were somewhat detrimental to the missions, however much they may have contributed to the building up of California. The heathen Indians employed in them, like those employed at the presidios, largely neutralized the work of the friars. San José was a gambling center and as such had to be shunned by the neophytes, who might have got into other troubles there. Upon the whole, as Bryan J. Clinch remarks, "This showing indicates the practical difficulties of settling California at the time, except by the Franciscan method of converting and civilizing the original inhabitants. The comparative cost of pueblos and missions also throws a comic light on the urgency with which Neve called on the Franciscans for accounts."

Neve's demand for accounts might have been reasonable enough were it not for two facts. One was that the internal affairs of the missions were no business of the Governor; the other was that there was virtually no money in the missions. Serra, however, kept not only a careful record of such things as baptisms, confirmations, marriages and deaths but also tabulated at the end of every year the livestock at every mission and the amount of grain that had been raised. But to put things down as Neve expected would have involved cooking the accounts. This Neve must have understood perfectly well, but his pedantic mind was probably indifferent as to how the figures were arrived at so long as figures appeared. Even conducting farms and giving instruction in the trades was something that did not give the Fathers any pleasure except for the results achieved. They had no aptitude as accountants, and it may be that Neve, who grew more antagonistic towards the end of his term of office, hoped to be able to level a charge of mismanagement against the Fathers.

In the end San Fernando College had to present a memorial to the Viceroy dated April 19, 1781, setting out Serra's objections to Neve's methods. Plainly he said that experience had shown that the Indians were to be retained in the missions only by giving them tangible benefits; otherwise they would run away "to paganism and unhappy apostacy," and there would be no means of preventing it. Unless the Father had control of the missions he would not be able to give what they wanted. "When they perceive that he has it not, they will not obey, nor respect, nor even care to listen, no matter how much he may labor and tire himself for their sake." He goes on to say that, just as the soldiers have to be furnished with weapons of war, in the same way the missionaries are not to be looked on as "inferior to military men, and therefore must not be regarded as of lower quality or standing," since they are engaged in "the spiritual conquest which our Catholic monarch desires so much." The case was so unanswerable that the Viceroy, finding that he had been put in the position where, if he supported General de Croix and Neve, he would be in conflict with the royal policy, referred the whole matter to Madrid. The upshot was that the Neve *reglamento* was repealed by royal decree, though word of this did not arrive until after Serra's death.

One result of that *reglamento* had been that the influence of the Fathers was to a considerable extent undermined. The haughty attitude of the Governor towards the missionaries was not lost upon the neophytes, and with this their own respect diminished. Moreover, the Governor had often refused necessary military escort when Serra had to visit one of the other missions. This was done under the plea that men could not be spared. Similarly the guards stationed at the missions were ordered not to send out any men to bring home neophytes who had decamped. There was a day when Serra was obliged to go to San Gabriel for some cattle and was returning with them, accompanied only by a couple of *vaqueros,* and was set upon by a band of strange Indians who were decidedly threatening. Nothing but the unruffled courage of the friar saved him; he went towards the savages offering them little presents of beads, whereupon they laid down their bows and he blessed them and went on his way unharmed. But he confessed afterwards that there was a moment when he quite expected to receive an arrow through the heart.

These Indians of the south were always restive and fickle, as the two outbreaks at San Diego had shown. Even after the Indians of that region had accepted baptism, the majority of them, because of their dislike of the regular work of the missions, preferred to live in their own *rancherias,* which meant that they remained at least half savage. Rumors of a new rising reached Lieutenant Ortega, now commandant at San Diego, so he sent the Indians a warning message, receiving the truculent answer that he might bring on his soldiers and the Indians would kill them all. Ortega was not the man to let that sort of thing pass; he therefore marched against the disaffected *rancherias* and, after a fight, captured their chiefs. Then, believing that a lesson should be taught, he tried these men by court-martial and sentenced them to death. The Franciscans did not know of this development until they were told that they had better prepare the Indians for death. Tersely Ortega said: "If they are not baptized by Saturday, they will have to die, and if they are they will still have to die." It was in vain that the Fathers pleaded for mercy; the sentence was carried out, and one must say that there was peace in the neighborhood for a long time afterwards.

Moraga, using somewhat similar methods in the north, had been rather less successful. When some Indians near Santa Clara mission carried off a couple of cows, which they slaughtered and ate, the Commandant came from San Francisco as soon as he heard the news, so promptly that he found some of the savages enjoying a hearty beefsteak breakfast. He arrested several of them, and in the skirmish that ensued several Indians were killed. Those whom he had arrested were flogged, despite which the thieving continued. Yet when shortly afterwards an epidemic broke out, the Fathers were able to baptize some of the dying and induce others to enter the mission—its first real start. But it was the epidemic rather than Moraga's severity that brought this about.

The Santa Clara incident occurred during Rivera's time, and that at San Gabriel during Neve's, in each case the local officer acting on his own responsibility. One cannot but feel sympathy for the soldier's view that punishment should be prompt. In the case of Rivera's handling of the San Diego rising, there was hesitation and a disinclination to accept responsibility, than which nothing can be worse. The attitude of the Fathers was that while some punishment was necessary—and occasionally they inflicted this, in its milder form, themselves—they deplored the death penalty, even in a case that could be considered murder, because they felt that the Indians never fully realized the gravity of their crime. They believed that a whipping, followed by forgiveness, would be more just, more effective.

Neve, though he was given the position held by General de Croix as Commandant of the Interior Provinces, and as such might have been expected to do some Indian fighting, was never much of a warrior, and there were even those who questioned his personal courage. In this respect there could be no doubt with regard to his successor as Governor, Pedro Fages, for the Indians had known him since 1769 and were well aware that, whatever his faults, he was a man who would stand no nonsense. His famous bear hunt had become a legend throughout California, seeming in the eyes of the Indians an act of incredible bravery. Moreover, stupid as they were in many respects, they were able to reach a not inaccurate judgment of character. Here was a man less slothful and temporizing than Rivera, less pedantic than Neve. To them the explosions of temper to which Fages was addicted were terrifying; so they, even on the rare occasions when they were murderously inclined, took pains to appear to be their ordinary good-natured selves.

This time when Fages—now considerably mellowed—had outbursts of temper, the poor man had some excuse. He had married a wife in New Spain and a year after he had taken office at Monterey he at last managed to persuade her to join him with their two-year-old son. But she went unwillingly and largely at the prompting of Colonel Neve. When she reached California she did not at all like the hardships of the frontier where, though her husband had a handsome salary, she had no means of spending it. With it all she was so charitable in giving away so many of her clothes to the Indians that she had to be warned to desist, for no means existed of replenishing her wardrobe there. She was also rather crafty; after she had failed to pester Don Pedro into asking to be allowed to resign on a purely fictitious plea of poor health, she herself wrote to the Viceroy asking this on his behalf. Fortunately the Governor saw Doña Eulalia's letter and, guessing what it contained, stopped it.

After the birth of a daughter on August 3, 1784, she used the device of refusing her husband her bed to try to get her way. After three months of this his patience was exhausted, so he broke down the door of her room. Undisturbed by her screaming as though she were having her throat cut, he threatened to tie her up and carry her to the Fathers at Carmel so that they might instruct her in a wife's duties. Upon this she agreed to go quietly, and was of course told that her behavior was impermissible.

But she was by no means finished. She spread charges that her husband was misconducting himself with her Indian maid, and *la Señora Gobernadora* took to making scene after scene, even in church. In the end that fiction was disproved and she apologized, though without becoming reconciled to her fate. Finally poor Fages, worn down by her tantrums and constant complaints, allowed her to retire to Mexico with their children—one, or perhaps two, of whom were born in California—while he himself stayed on until 1791, long after Serra's death. One cannot but feel sorry for Don Pedro, and one must admit that as Governor he was, in spite of his domestic troubles, a more amiable man than he had been as Commandant.

Though the abrogation of Neve's *reglamento* by the King did not come through while Serra was alive, to a great extent it was a dead letter from the time of the arrival of Fages as Governor. It was known that the matter had been referred to Madrid for decision, and that put many of the clauses of the *reglamento* in suspense. Meanwhile Fages exercised a wide degree of interpretation and was willing to stretch a point when he could. So far from bearing a grudge against Serra for having been instrumental in getting him dismissed in 1773, he may even have been grateful; otherwise he would never have met and married Doña Eulalia. Termagant though she was, he seems to have loved her deeply. Besides, he was a reasonable man in spite of his quick temper, and he may well have recognized that Monterey was no place for a delicately nurtured woman. Being also an obstinate man, he was not going to resign a well-paid and honorable position merely because his wife demanded it. This time he was resolved to make a good record for himself and not get at loggerheads with the Fathers.

The worst worries that Serra had during his last years came not from the secular administration but from the threat that the friars would be removed from the control of the College of San Fernando and placed under that of a bishop. Father Antonio de Reyes, whom Piette describes as having an idealistic zeal but unhappily enthusiasm of the kind that made him lose contact with the world of realities, was appointed Bishop of Sonora and the Californias. Though himself a Franciscan, of the other Franciscan apostolic college of New Spain, he proposed to Neve on December 13, 1783, that Serra and his group of friars be replaced by Dominicans. He had some idea that the reorganization would make for efficiency, why it is hard to see, as new men in California, making a completely new start, would be likely to lose much ground before regaining it—if there ever was any eventual gain.

It was hardly feasible for Bishop Reyes to visit California in person, but he thought that difficulty might be circumvented by a plan that had worked well enough elsewhere, however unsuitable it was for the chain of missions strung along the *Camino Real* from San Diego to San Francisco. It was to divide his jurisdiction into a number of what were called custodies, each of them of course responsible to himself and not to any apostolic college. This plan was brought forward when it was seen that the Dominican project was not very feasible. The

Bishop claimed that the custody system had the support of the King and even of the Pope, though of this no proof was ever produced.

Father Zephyrin Engelhardt's explanation of the system may here be quoted. In a footnote to page 13 of his first volume of *Missions and Missionaries in California* he writes: "A custody is a small province. The head of a custody is called 'custos': the head of a province bears the title 'provincial'; the superior of a [Franciscan] monastery is styled 'guardian'; 'presidente' in Spanish countries is the superior of a small convent or hospice. The superior of all the Franciscans in California was also called 'presidente,' which is equivalent to 'commissary.'" But though custodies were for a short while set up in Bishop Reyes's diocese, the plan ultimately proved unworkable and so was abandoned. Serra's last years, however, were clouded by the strong possibility that the Bishop would have his way. In the eyes of the California missionaries the scheme was the less acceptable because it seemed to fit in with the ideas of Commandant-General Neve. It was all the harder to endure because a bishop was trying to assert an authority he did not really possess; nor did he improve the situation by working, doubtless with the best intentions in the world, with officials who had already done much harm to the missions.

Bishop Reyes, when a guest for a long period at the College of San Fernando just before his ordination, took great pains never to mention what was in his mind. Later, however, he did speak of the matter when at the other Franciscan College of Santa Cruz de Quarétaro. As soon as he did so the discretory, or council, told him plainly that the papal bull he produced as his authorization was fraudulent, and drew his attention to letters that he had himself written when a simple missionary priest opposing what he was now seeking to obtain. The Bishop was very angry and departed in dudgeon, having obtained only one backer, who accompanied him to his diocese. As Palóu acidly remarks in the fourth volume of his history: "It is not known whether he went there as confessor or consultor, or whether it was with the object of taking the appointment of apostolic commissary for the custodias, or as *Custos Custodium.*" It was another way of asking *Quis custodiet custodes?* In the face of the opposition of both the Franciscan colleges in New Spain the plan broke down. But it was heart-rending that a man so old and worn with cares as was Junípero Serra after his long struggle with Neve should have his last days overcast with the fear that his life's work was to be undone by an inexperienced bishop with a bee in his bonnet.

CHAPTER SIXTEEN

Serra's Last Days

ALTHOUGH conditions decidedly improved during the administration of Fages as Governor, the anxieties indicated in the previous chapter remained for Junípero Serra. Nevertheless he could be grateful to Fages, who was glad enough to do him small favors, all of which were in accord with the royal wishes as conveyed by Bucareli several years previously. For instance, where Neve had usually refused an escort of soldiers when Serra had occasion to travel from one mission to another, thus forcing him to wait until he could accompany a military group that was on the Governor's business, Fages was obliging whenever possible. The delay had never actually mattered much, as time was so cheap a commodity in California, but Neve's rather brusque refusals always hurt and were intended to hamper Serra in his work.

So also with regard to Neve's orders that none of the small guard stationed at each mission—a corporal and five privates— should be sent to bring back any neophytes who had run away. To this must be added his abrogation of the clause of Bucareli's *reglamento* of 1773 ordering that a couple of soldiers of this group should be placed at the disposition of the Fathers. We have seen that even during Neve's time his plan of having Indian *alcaldes* and *regidores* soon came to have no force except on paper. As previously, the punishment of the neophytes was administered (though rarely and reluctantly) by one of the Fathers or by the corporal at the Fathers' orders. It meant a restoration of the discipline without which the missions could not operate.

There was considerable advantage in now having as Governor a man who was primarily a soldier rather than an official. Fages so well grasped what was required that immediately upon going to California to take up his duties he went the rounds of the missions, warning the neophytes not to run away, for if they did they would be punished, and ordering them to spread word among the runaways, of whom there had been a good many while Neve was in charge, that they had better return without delay. If they did, he promised pardon without further inquiry; if they did not, he said he would himself round them up and give them a good flogging. Such words worked wonders, for the Indians had a great respect for Fages, whom they knew of old. Even though he soon had to leave in order to bring his wife and child up from the Peninsula, the runaway neophytes came back in a steady stream, and were received by the Fathers with open arms and no questions asked.

Some of the prices that prevailed at the time have already been given; to these may be added some items as taken from the price list issued by Neve on January 1, 1781. A two-year-old bull cost $4, when taken from the rodeo, that is, the roundup of cattle and not what we mean today. A calf was worth $2, and though beef was astonishingly cheap, tallow and lard were ten times as costly. All animals flourished in California, despite the somewhat negligent attention they received from the neophytes. The crops raised were so abundant as to bring low prices, though these were high in relation to meat of any kind. Wheat fetched two cents a pound, corn less, barley seventy-five cents a hundredweight. Beans, lentils and chick-peas were worth about three cents a pound. The missions profited by being able to dispose of their surplus to the presidios, though at rates fixed by the Governor, and while no money passed, the missions obtained a book-keeping balance which they could utilize for obtaining supplies from Mexico.

Although the missions that Serra himself had established had not as yet reached the peak of their prosperity—and were only nine as against the twenty-one that California eventually saw—seven or eight thousand people had been baptized, of whom about a quarter had died. Over five thousand people had been confirmed—probably almost all who up to 1783 were ready for that sacrament.

Every journey Serra made was on foot, an ordeal for an old man whose sore leg had given him a permanent limp. Some fanciful pictures have been drawn as to the number of these journeys. Father Geiger in an article in *The Americas* (Vol. VI, No. 3, pp. 323-6) makes careful esti-mates based on the known facts. He reaches the conclu-sion that Serra traveled 5,420 miles while in Mexico (at least 550 miles of this was not on foot, for, as Father Geiger has proved, the journey from Mexico City to San Blas in 1773 was made by coach); in Lower California there was something over 2,000 miles covered; but in Upper California Father Geiger reduces the land mileage to 4,285 miles.

Never had Serra been a man much attached to doctors, and in California at no time had there been more than one medical man, and he, it is probably safe to presume, not of the highest rating, even according to the standards of those days. Actually the only time we hear of Serra's seeking medicinal relief was when he asked the muleteer in the Peninsula to put on his painful leg some of the same salve that he used for the galls of his beasts. If he had pain in his breast as well, this is hardly to be wondered at, in view of the way he once used to beat himself with a heavy stone in the pulpit to bring home to his congregation their need for penance. On his visit to San Francisco in 1779 the captain of the ship that was in the harbor, Ignacio Arteaga, had begged him to submit to surgery (we are not told for what), but Serra refused. He did not have the time to spare, so he excused himself on the ground that he had grown used to his ailments and felt that it was best to leave everything in God's hands.

Old he was and frail, but he was the kind of slender little man who never looks very strong and yet is often much stronger than he looks. Such men do not seem to grow much older with the years. And though Serra was bothered with asthma, I can testify from my own experience that this disease, which is practically never curable nor can even be much alleviated, while it may make one die daily (if not in the Pauline sense) hardly ever kills directly. It may be endured—and for most of the time ignored—for a life's span. Serra himself never thought it worth mentioning.

It has often been noticed that much of the best work in the world has been done by invalids, or by those who might have regarded themselves as such. Serra was anything but a valetudinarian or hypochondriac. Palóu tells us that, even now, after sleeping on a board at night, Serra rose at daybreak to pray at the mission cross and to say some of his Office. After Mass and breakfast he often went into the fields to toil with Indians, none of whom worked half so hard as he did.

Work of this sort, however, Serra ordinarily left to his younger companion, Father Juan Crespí, his former student at Mallorca and his most intimate friend. Perhaps it was only when Crespí could not prevent it that the old man went into the fields to work. His real function was the instruction of the neophytes, and all the spiritual chores that had to be done—advising, consoling, and conducting a correspondence which, as its extant portion is so voluminous, must have occupied a great deal of his time. Yet as the Indians might not understand that such things were work, and hard work, he labored by their side as often as he could. In spare moments he used to sit on the floor sewing skirts and blouses for the girls or sit at a table cutting out these garments. By this time Indian women had been trained as seamstresses, and even taught to weave cloth, but Serra liked to help. It was hard for him to be without something to do.

There was another reason why Crespí used to give most of his time to physical work: He had so poor a memory, Palóu tells us, that he was not able to preach the doctrinal sermon on the Gospel of the Mass on Sundays and feast days; which reveals that these sermons were memorized, instead of being spontaneously delivered. Though not ordinarily a good method, it may be that because untutored minds were to be addressed, an exceptionally careful arrangement of the sermon was called for.

Crespí was a cheerful and gay companion. Yet he, like others, complained of the cold climate of Carmel. Father Piette says that "a modern medical diagnosis would perhaps have discovered that he suffered from sinus trouble," though two sentences further on he declares that "Juan had become a neurasthenic." At any rate he died of some unspecified disease when he was only sixty. He was the first Franciscan missionary to tread Californian soil, for he had gone with the advance division by land in 1769, and he had worked steadily, most of the time by Serra's side, since then. He was distinguished for his piety and simplicity, and some people gave him the name of "the Mystic," rather because of his unpretentious goodness than because of any special graces. He died on New Year's Day, 1782, after receiving the last sacraments from his friend, and was buried in Carmel Church, on the Gospel side of the altar, where Serra himself was to be buried before long.

Crespí's death was a natural grief but one of a kind that a Christian does not find it very hard to accept, when he is sure that the dear departed has gone to an eternal reward. There were disappointments that were harder to bear. A number of Fathers, especially during Neve's regime, grew so discouraged that they begged to be sent back to Mexico, pleading that it was obvious that they could be of no use in California. Now Palóu, who probably never had much of the missionary's temperament and who had gone out to the New World mainly out of devotion to Serra, wrote to Gálvez, pleading what he called his "advanced age" of sixty-one! Another who wanted to give up was Lasuén, the very able man who was to be Serra's successor as President of the missions. Serra managed to persuade them to change their minds, but several other men were given permission to withdraw.

It was disturbing that so many of the missionaries showed that they lacked the necessary stamina, though nobody knew better than Serra what their difficulties were. To one of these faint hearts, Father Juan Figuer, he wrote: "Whither will the ox go that does not plough, if not to the slaughter-house?" To him he recommended patience and the reading of what the Franciscan Doctor of the Church, St. Bonaventure, called his "library"—his crucifix. Serra told him the story of a friar of Valencia who asked his Guardian's permission to retire to his cell during Matins, as he was not in the right mood for prayer. The reply came, "Remain in your place. I assure you that if all of us who are not in the proper frame of mind should leave the chapel, there would be no Matins recited, and I would be the first to go." To another of the missionaries who gave reasons why he should retire Serra replied, saying that, on the basis of the arguments advanced, he himself should have retired long ago. The truth of that had to be acknowledged; everybody knew that the cares and burdens and frustrations had come more to him than to anybody else.

We have little knowledge of Junípero Serra's interior life, except that we now and then hear of his spending an entire night in prayer, when heaven had to be stormed for some particular object. No doubt there were many more occasions than those about which Palóu informs us. His letters, if we except some spiritual admonitions of a rather general sort, are almost all filled with what might be called business details, though these are concerned with his Father's business, the missions entrusted to him, nothing about which he ever overlooked. The active life completely absorbed him, as it also largely absorbed St. Bernard, though he is also among the greatest of contemplatives. Serra too may have been a contemplative in that sense. After all, there were a number of saints—among whom one might include St. Catherine of Siena and St. Philip Neri—who while living in the world's hurly-burly maintained an unbroken communion with God.

Yet if Serra had anything corresponding to this it does not appear very often in the accounts left of him or in his own letters. Palóu tells of some remarkable happenings during the years in Mexico, but has absolutely nothing to offer of the same sort about the California period. Nothing like a miracle is reported; the closest we get to the supernormal is the account of the novena to St. Joseph that a ship should come to California before March 20, 1770, the date Portolá had set for abandoning California. Even that was not Serra's miracle, but St. Joseph's—supposing that it was a miracle at all.

Nor did Serra go in much for austerities. It is true that he slept on a board for bed (when he did not sleep on the bare ground), but that is something anybody can get accustomed to. He had now and then beaten his breast with a stone, and at least on one occasion he had taken the discipline in the pulpit, using a chain, as he had also (again it seems to have been on only one occasion) bared his breast and put a burning candle to it—all of this apparently during the time he was in Mexico. But this was not so much by way of mortifying himself as a means of bringing dull lethargic minds to a sense of the enormity of sin and the frightfulness of hell.

Indeed, we must find that Junípero Serra was devoid of fanaticism or excess. His correspondence shows him to be eminently calm, good-tempered and practical—so much so that Clinch, otherwise an excellent commentator, describes him as being, in parts of his long memorials to Bucareli in 1773, something of a Sancho Panza, on account of the minute way he went into details. In short, we may say that Serra had zeal without being in the slightest degree a zealot. His devotion to his work was of the quiet, steady kind in which one cannot discover explosions of either energy or emotion. In California he followed the Franciscan custom of eating and drinking whatever was set before him. The only time he permitted himself a mild complaint was about the hardship of having to do without chocolate!

It is very seldom that a man's biographer is with him when he dies, but so it was with Serra. For Palóu was at that time at Carmel and witnessed everything that happened during the last days, recording it all both in the *Vida* and also in the fourth volume of his *Historical*

Memoirs of New California. He does so in the straight-forward, matter-of-fact tone characteristic of him, with no marvels of the supernatural sort but introducing one macabre detail—that, while Serra was nearing his end, the carpenter attached to the mission was so *gauche* as to come into his cell to measure him for the coffin he was about to make. It is perhaps as well that no other account but Palóu's was left, for different observers observe different details, and because of what may seem to be discrepancies the accuracy of all the witnesses may be questioned. But this time everything is simple; there does not seem to be any possibility of challenging Palóu, which makes at least the close of Serra's life very easy for subsequent biographers to handle.

It is well when the adage *Finis coronat opus* can be used of a man, if an exemplary end redeems a life that has not been unstained. But in Serra's case we have a life all of a piece, never anything but exemplary, even when he was at least locally famous as a preacher and professor in the university at Mallorca, sighing for the fervor he feared he had lost, and deciding to regain it by going to the New World as a missionary. Throughout he showed a steady glow rather than a leaping flame, and it was fortunate that this was so, for his quiet and cheerful persistence was what the situation required.

Serra was not so very old—only seventy-one—and the year before, he had gone on foot to visit San Buenaventura, at the same time visiting what Palóu described as "twenty Indian towns" stretching along the Santa Barbara Channel. "In each one of them," Palóu says, "his heart melted and his tears flowed as he thought how he had not been allowed to water that field with his blood in order to bring about their subjugation." On his way back to Monterey he stopped at San Luis Obispo and San Antonio, reaching

Carmel in January, 1784. Palóu records that it was a special joy to him to see Christians where only the previous year all had been pagans, and he seemed relieved of his maladies, in particular of the choking sensation of his chest. This chest trouble has often been attributed to the way he used to beat himself with a heavy stone, and that may indeed have had something to do with it. But what Palóu says points rather to asthma, for which I have heard that the clear dry air of Southern California is wonderfully good. However, as asthma is at least in part a psychic matter, the happiness that Serra felt at this time may have been what made him feel so well.

On the other hand, Palóu believed that the lack of missionary recruits shortened Serra's life, for he had received word that for the time being no more men were to be sent. Probably they were withheld by San Fernando College pending the outcome of the project of Bishop Reyes. There was not much use in sending additional men to California if they were all to be soon replaced by Dominicans, and it was very much of a question as to whether they would be willing (or permitted) to continue there under the custody system. When Serra was back at his own mission of San Carlos, though he did not cease celebrating Mass or saying the Office, it was with visible difficulty. When he was at San Gabriel one of the missionaries had written to Palóu that Serra "was so very bad of his chest that they thought he would die." Indeed, an asthmatic paroxysm makes the beholders think that, and the sufferer wish for death to bring relief. The little Indian altar boys who served Mass used to say to the other priests with much sympathy and sorrow and with tears in their eyes, "Fathers, the old Father wants to die." When he left San Gabriel those who took leave of him quite expected that he would perish on the road. The conflicting reports about his health while in the south indicate a rapid succession of ups and downs.

Serra's arrival at Carmel was not a signal to take even a short rest for his poor old weary body, but with greater fervor than ever he went on with his work, in so far as he was now able to do it. During the Lent of 1784 he did not give himself any alleviating dispensations, and after going through the exhausting ceremonies of Holy Week he at once took off for the north to make what he knew would be his last visit there.

He arrived at Santa Clara in the company of Governor Fages, who had been invited to sponsor the dedication of the new church there. On this occasion Serra sang the Mass and preached to a congregation which included the escort of soldiers who had come with Fages and the colonists of San José. After this he spent some time preparing himself for death and made a general confession to Palóu. Each man expected that he would never see the other again, as Palóu intended to return to his mission in San Francisco. However, in the end Serra persuaded him to follow him later to Carmel. The Father President administered confirmation, which he knew would be for the last time, for whether or not he lived a little longer, his patent for conferring the sacrament would expire on July 16th.

Serra got back to Carmel in June and Palóu arrived there in the middle of August. Everybody noticed that the old man was very weak, yet when he sang the hymn that one of the Fathers had composed in honor of the Assumption of Our Lady it was with so resonant a voice that Palóu said to one of the soldiers that the Father President did not seem so very ill. The soldier—a man who had known Serra since 1769—replied, "Father, we must not be too confident; he is ill, but this saintly Father, when it comes to praying and singing, is always well; but he is almost finished."

The soldier was right. Though Serra continued to take his place in the choir and to say prayers with the neophytes, he was usually very quiet, and the priest stationed at Carmel with him said that this quietness had descended on him when his faculty to confirm had expired. On August 23rd a ship anchored at Monterey and its doctor came out to the mission in the hope of giving him some relief. He applied plasters to Serra's chest without any result except that of adding to the pain. Yet as the ship had brought a supply of cloth, the dying man occupied himself at odd moments with cutting out garments for the neophytes. It was perhaps as well that he did not know that on the 21st of that month his old enemy Felipe Neve had died; the news would have been too agitating, for he would have felt obliged to offer specially fervent prayers for the repose of his soul.

Serra had written to the Fathers at San Antonio and San Luis Obispo asking them to come and see him, but when he inquired about this at the presidio he was told that the letters had been forgotten and so never sent. Thereupon Palóu dispatched messengers at once, adding that the Fathers had better not delay if they wished to see their President alive. But it was too late; not even the priests from nearby San Antonio reached Carmel in time.

On August 26th Serra arose very exhausted after a bad night, so passed the day in retirement. At night he repeated to Palóu the general confession made at Santa Clara, "but with complete knowledge of himself, as if he had been entirely well." When this was finished he spent some time in meditation, after which he took a cup of broth and lay down, saying that he did not wish anybody to remain with him. The next morning, when Palóu looked in, he found

him with the breviary in his hand saying his Office in bed.
He announced that after Mass he would go to the church
to receive Viaticum. Palóu of course wanted him to remain where he was, but Serra insisted that he was able to
walk to the church, though it was a hundred yards away
from the house where the Fathers lived. And this is just
what he did, accompanied by Governor Fages and some of
the soldiers from the presidio as well as by all the Indians
of the mission.

On arriving at the sanctuary steps the dying man knelt
at a little table that had been prepared for the ceremony,
such as would have been set up in his cell. Palóu came
robed out of the sacristy and approached the altar. While
he was preparing the incense he was astonished that the old
man chanted the *Tantum Ergo* in his usual sonorous voice,
and Palóu could see what was his emotion from the tears
in his eyes. Kneeling, he received the Body of Christ,
and afterwards, accompanied again by all those who had
brought him to the church, he returned to his own room.
There he sat in an abstraction so deep that Palóu would
not allow anybody to see him. Thus he remained all day.

At night he asked to be anointed. Sitting on a stool with
a rush seat, he repeated the Litany and the Seven Peniten-
tial Psalms. That whole night he passed without sleeping,
most of the time kneeling with his chest pressed against
the boards of his bed. He said he felt a little easier in that
position. But at other times he sat on the floor, leaning
against one of his neophytes, some of whom remained in
his cell, drawn by the great love they had for him. When
Palóu asked the doctor how the patient was, the reply
came that it appeared to him that Father Serra wished to
die on the floor.

Soon after this Palóu went in again and asked if he
would like to have the plenary indulgence of the Francis-

can Order. Serra said yes, so it was given. The next day, the 28th, the Feast of St. Augustine, Serra seemed a little better, with less suffocation in his chest. He spent the morning on his rush stool, leaning against the bed. It consisted only of a few roughly hewn boards covered with a blanket; there he always slept with a crucifix upon his breast. It was the one he had had since his novitiate days at Palma and it went with him on all his journeys.

At ten in the morning the officers from the frigate anchored in Monterey Bay arrived to see him. Their captain was José Cañizares, whom he had known since 1769. They were accompanied by the ship's chaplain, Crisóbal Díaz, also an old friend. Serra stood up to receive them and held them in his embrace. In their honor he ordered the mission bells to be rung. After this they all sat down, Serra again occupying the little stool, and an account was given of a voyage they had made to Peru since he last saw them. At the close of the recital the dying man said he was glad that they had come to throw a little earth upon his body at burial. They answered with the usual sort of thing—confident hopes that he would recover—but Serra knew that he was now very near death. It was then that he asked that he might be buried by the side of Father Crespí.

Palóu also expressed the hope that Serra would get better but promised that if it was God's will to take him his wishes about the burial would be carried out. He begged in his turn that when Serra arrived in God's presence he would pray for the missions and especially for those present on that occasion. To this Serra answered: "I promise that if the Lord in His infinite mercy shall grant me everlasting felicity, which I in no wise deserve on account of my sins, that I will pray for all of you and that He will grant the conversion of all the pagan people whom I am leaving unconverted." The whole scene was a wonderful blending of hope and humility, calm matter-of-fact and tenderness. It was a most Catholic death.

Not long afterwards Serra asked to have his cell sprinkled with holy water. He added that he asked this so that he might have no pain, though he felt none just then. Suddenly he said a very surprising thing: "I have come under the shadow of a great fear; I am very much afraid. Read to me the Recommendation for a Passing Soul, and say it loudly so that I may hear it." This Palóu did, assisted by all the officers from the ship, the doctor and Father Matías Noriega, the priest at Carmel, as well as some of the sailors and neophytes, as many of them as could squeeze into the little room. The dying man made all the responses to the Recommendation, sitting on the little stool, and moving the heart of everybody present. At the end he burst out in joy, "Thanks be to God! Thanks be to God! He has quite taken away my fear." He then gave a sign that he would be left alone, but before he departed the captain of the frigate said, "Father President, you know what my patron saint, St. Anthony, can do. I have asked him to make you well." To this Serra made no answer, but his smile made all understand that he expected no such thing.

Sitting in his chair by the table, he began to say his Office. When he had finished Palóu reminded him that it was now afternoon and suggested that he take a little broth. Serra consented, and then said, "Now let us go to rest," so, taking off his mantle, he lay upon his bed to compose himself for sleep. The officers were to dine at the mission but Palóu returned afterwards to see how Serra was. He found him lying exactly as he was before, apparently asleep, but dead. There was no sign of any agony, so Palóu concluded that he had died in his sleep, about two in the afternoon. It was St. Augustine's Day, August 28, 1784.

The double tolling of the bells announced the news and, hearing that doleful sound, the neophytes flocked in, all lamenting. To prepare Serra's body for burial nothing more was necessary than to remove his sandals, of which the captain and the ship's chaplain were each allowed to keep one as a memento. In the habit he wore when he died Junípero Serra was laid out. When the neophytes were allowed to come in, they had large bunches of wild flowers to strew over him. Not until night was his body carried into the church, where a guard was set lest any soldier or sailor attempt a pious theft, for all of them were anxious to have something as a relic of a man they considered a saint. Even so, some people managed to snip away a bit of the habit or some of the scanty hairs of the corona, and Palóu suspected that this was done with the connivance of the sentinel posted to prevent just such things.

The next day, a Sunday, Junípero Serra was buried. Governor Fages happened to be away, but the commandant of the presidio and all the soldiers went to the funeral, except for the few keeping guard. They, like the sailors left on the frigate for the same reason, kept firing their guns every half hour, and all day long the bells tolled.

In the afternoon there was a procession around the mission enclosure, the pallbearers changing at intervals, as all the officers of the army and navy wished to have the honor of bearing Father Serra on their shoulders. Then after Matins and Lauds had been said in the church, the body was buried by the side of Father Crespí on the Gospel side of the altar, where it still is. When some thirty years ago a mortuary chapel was built beside the church, with a sarcophagus in bronze, it actually contained nothing, and is no more than a monument, the most handsome one to Serra that exists.

Palóu says of the sobbing neophytes: "His children were

mourning the death of their Father, who had left his own
father and mother in his native land and who had come
this long distance for no other purpose than to make these
his children and the children of God through holy baptism.
The flock was lamenting the death of its Shepherd who
had labored so assiduously to provide them with spiritual
food and who had delivered them from the claws of the
infernal wolf. His faithful subjects were mourning the loss
of their Prelate, the wise, the prudent, the courteous, the
diligent, and the model leader, as they all recognized how
greatly he would be missed in the development of these
spiritual conquests." At the end of the ceremonies the
people crowded around Palóu, asking for some little thing
they might keep as a relic, but it was not easy to satisfy
them, as Serra had had so very few possessions of his own.
But the captain of the frigate received an undertunic which
he could cut up into scapulars, which would be blessed
on September 4th, when a memorial service was to be held.
The only other things that Palóu could find were two sets
of underclothing and a couple of handkerchiefs; these were
to be shredded into tiny particles for distribution.

Palóu's honesty (but also his discretion) is proved by his
recording two incidents which he is careful to say he is
not instancing as miracles, because they might have come
about by natural causes or mere coincidence. But the ship's
doctor came to him saying, "Father, I expect to cure more
people with that handkerchief you gave me than with my
medicines," and he told of a sick sailor around whose head
he had tied it, with the result that the pain he had been
suffering left him. And a priest who had hurried to
Monterey suddenly became so ill that it was quite expected
that he would follow Serra to the grave. But when they put
Serra's hair shirt on him—this, by the way, is the first time
we hear of any hair shirt—he quickly recovered. Palóu com-

ments: "It is not my duty to investigate or make any scrutiny" of such matters. In other words, he does not propose acting as a consultor of the Congregation of the Congregation of Rites examining a cause for beatification. So he scrupulously guards himself against any infringement of the decrees of Urban VIII in 1631 and of subsequent Popes about anticipating the decisions of the Holy See.

CHAPTER SEVENTEEN

What Happened Afterwards

THE INTRODUCTION of Junípero Serra's cause for beatification did not occur for a long while, as is usually true of such matters, and when it was actually introduced nothing much happened at first, mainly one must suppose because nobody was very actively interested. But just now it is being pressed by a very able and energetic vice-postulator, and coincidentally with this a definitive biography is in preparation. Furthermore, though the Institute of Franciscan Studies at Washington and its excellent quarterly, *The Americas*, by no means restrict themselves to the study of questions relating to Serra, there is no doubt that Serra is one of their main beneficiaries. While it would be rash and presumptuous to make any predictions, it would seem that it is probable that Junípero Serra will eventually be declared a saint.

In view of these developments General Franco has seized ownership of Serra's birthplace in Petra from the city of San Francisco, which received it as a gift in 1934 from the Rotary Club of Mallorca. It has been suggested (in an unsigned article in a paper entitled *Politics in California*) that General Franco's motive was one of political expediency, by way of putting political pressure on the United States. However, one readily understands that the people and Church in Spain should wish to keep Serra's birthplace as a national monument to a man of their own country

283

considered by many a saint. One may interpret Franco's action as evidence of the enthusiasm felt not only on the part of the people and the Church, but also on the part of the government for the cause of his canonization.

Such matters, however, are not those I wish to discuss in this brief concluding chapter, but rather devote it to a survey of what happened to the missions after Serra's time. First there came what has often been called their golden age, when Firmín Francisco de Lasuén, Serra's immediate successor, was President. Living on until 1803, when he died at the age of eighty-three, he benefited by the royal abrogation of the Neve *reglamento* that came just after Serra was dead. Furthermore the custody plan proposed by Bishop Reyes was finally abandoned, largely as a result of vigorous representations made by Gálvez, a minister of the Crown, and Palóu, who had retired to Mexico City, where he became the Franciscan Guardian. The road was now clear, though the tired old pioneer was no longer there to limp along its dusty way.

When revolutions broke out in Mexico they did not affect distant California to any great extent. A stray incendiary document or two that found their way across the border only caused the commandant at San Diego to strengthen his defenses, and in 1818, when a couple of privateers from Buenos Aires, upon failing to win Monterey to their cause, sacked the settlement and a few of the missions, that proved merely a passing flurry. California not only remained loyal to the Crown but was almost somnolent in its quiet. However, after the revolution of 1823, Lucas Alamán made an emphatic declaration in favor of secularization, saying: "If the mission system is that best suited to draw savages from barbarism, it can do no more than establish the first principles of society; it cannot lead men to their highest perfection. Nothing is better to accomplish this than to bind individuals to society by the powerful bond of [personal] property."

The principle itself was not disputed by the Fathers, but they knew that the Indians were still not ready for this, and they had reason enough to suspect the sincerity of such words. Agnes Repplier has pithily written in her book on Serra: "Two things bring ecclesiastical institutions into disfavor. If they are poor, they become a burden and a nuisance. If they are rich, they incite cupidity." This was the case with the new politicians. Santa Ana (President of Mexico off and on between 1833 and 1855) was typical of them when he "borrowed" the Pious Fund, thus depriving the missionaries of their stipends, and it was decided to break up the mission holdings and to distribute the land among the Indians. They were to be given their chance to develop as self-reliant owners of their own farms. At least that was the fine theory.

It was put into operation by a new class of officials, cynical and rapacious, yet always with unctuous phrases in their mouths, who got a fat salary for directing this process, and still fatter pickings when the Indians proved themselves unfit for what was so prematurely forced upon them. When it is recalled that in 1834 the records indicate that the missions had, besides their lands and buildings, 140,000 head of cattle, 130,000 sheep and 12,000 horses and mules, not to mention other livestock, and were producing annually 38,000 *fanegas* of grain, to which must be added vineyards and orchards, it will be seen what a prize the secularizers had found. The mission Indians at the time were close on to 30,000, and the value of the improvements at San Luis Rey alone was estimated at $203,000. After a brief respite, secularization may be said to have been completely effected by 1837.

As an illustration of how the process was worked, at San

Juan Capistrano the agent appointed by the Mexican government, out of $150,000 received, distributed $8,500 to the Indians as their share, nobody quite knowing where the balance went, though of course in one way or another it was taken by the politicians who were going to do so much for the poor Indians who had been so much retarded by the Padres. It was a sickening story, one that got uglier at every turn. As usual venality was a kind of rathole: the politicians exploited so inefficiently as to get relatively little for themselves.

The California Indians after receiving their pittance of property, not only would not work but (though there was supposed to be a law prohibiting it) sold their livestock and then their land for anything that was offered. Then they were obliged to hire themselves out in a state of virtual slavery to anybody who would employ them. Indeed, often the slavery was quite unqualified. To this must be added that when in 1838 a conspiracy was discovered among the Indians of San Diego, torture was resorted to to extract information, the method used being to cut off one ear, and then the other, with the assurance that general mutilation would follow little by little. It was all very unlike the methods in vogue in the time of the Padres. In a country now in a state of utter disorder, many Indians from the missions joined their pagan fellows in horse stealing, and were usually hanged when caught. All sank into a state of utter degradation; they had sold all that they had, having no idea of the value of money except that it would buy a little firewater.

The situation became such that at Los Angeles the Indians regularly got so drunk on Saturdays (when they received their pay) that late on Sunday afternoon they would be dragged by the heels in an insensible condition to the pound to sleep it off. For this purpose the sheriff kept a few Indian deputies safe under lock and key, so that they would not get into the same condition. Then on Monday morning the "drunks" would be fined *en masse* and the fines at once paid by employers who were waiting for that purpose. But it was on condition that those whose fines had been paid repaid the kind friends who had come to the rescue by working for them that week. During the week, the employers saw to it that the Indians got nothing to drink, for drunken Indians would have been of no use, but food and shelter of a kind were provided. Then on Saturday the whole of their miserable wages went for a supply of cheap *aguardiente* or they were paid directly in that commodity, and the whole process was repeated.

These Indians, when sober, were good workers, after the training the Fathers had given them, and were especially skilled as horsebreakers and herdsmen. But their weekly spree undermined their vitality, making them all the more subject to disease. This was of little consequence to the employers, the number of Indians at first available being seemingly inexhaustible.

It must be sadly confessed that the Indians fared worst of all after California passed into American hands, but this was only because they had already been completely despoiled and demoralized by the secularization of the missions. The "Anglo-Saxon" newcomers in many instances regarded these degraded Indians as vermin to be exterminated. At all events, exterminated they were, and in very short order, except for the remnants for whom reservations were belatedly provided. The nature of these may be gathered from the stock joke in California about any utterly worthless tract of land, "That must be an Indian reservation!" While there was some exaggeration in this, there was also much grim truth in it.

Bryan J. Clinch in the second volume of his *California*

and Its Missions puts up a powerful defense against the criticism that had earlier been made of the missions by such writers as Alexander Forbes, writing: "If there is in human history any more pitiful chapter of oppression and cowardly wrong than the steps by which the mission Indians, who once owned Southern California, have been crowded into the waste places, a student of twenty years' study has failed to find it, and hopes never to find it. In all the Spanish occupation of California I could not discover that it ever happened that an Indian was driven off his land. Under our own regime it has seldom happened that he escaped being driven off." It need hardly be added that in the course of the ugly process most of the Indians quickly forgot all the religion the Fathers had taught them.

Some crafty politicians suggested that the friars must have accumulated vast wealth. Wealth, indeed, there was, in land and improvements and livestock, but it was all held in trust for the neophytes. There was no possibility of the friars' hoarding anything, even had they wished it. The only sales the missions could make were to the presidios, and this merely meant that the military paymasters gave a bookkeeping credit upon which the Fathers could draw in the form of goods purchased in Mexico. Even the friars' own small stipends were almost wholly devoted to the same purpose. Money rarely if ever passed.

It is therefore idle to reproach the friars—though it must be said that no reproach is now heard, because our knowledge of the facts has grown. From the start the Padres had wished to make the Indians eventually independent, but they knew better than anybody else how very slow the process would be. Had they only been left alone for another generation undoubtedly they would have devised a system by which their neophytes—not as entire groups but as individuals who showed that they had become ready for it—

would have "graduated" to private ownership, and have been as safely protected as though still in the missions. But the mission plan was roughly broken by the external action of the State midway in its course. Even so, we can say that at the very least the plan, at the stage reached, had made the Indians happy and well cared for in body and soul, and had already done wonders for the development of the neophytes.

As soon as lay administrators were appointed for the missions, the neophytes, assured that they were now free, left refusing to do any more work. With that as their excuse the administrators proceeded to a wholesale slaughter of cattle, thinking only of selling their tallow and hides to the many trading vessels that now visited California to purchase these commodities. The carcasses were usually left to rot, for only a very few of them could be eaten. Theodore Hittell in his *History of California* (4 vols., 1898) says that some of the valleys were entirely covered with putrescent masses, and for years the country was white with the skeletons of the massacred animals. "In some places the skulls and large bones were so plentiful that long fences were built of them."

As for the American attitude towards the California Indians, attention might be drawn to two happenings in 1852. Two settlers having been killed in Humboldt County, it was assumed without any proof that the crime had been perpetrated by Indians, whereupon a posse went out and shot without any investigation the first fifteen or twenty they encountered. In the same month an Indian boy was murdered by a settler at Happy Camp on the Klammath River. As the boy's family charged the murderer with the crime, he gathered a band who burned an Indian village to the ground, killing every one of its male and some of its female inhabitants. Yet when McKee, the Indian agent for Northern California, asked Governor Bigler to do something to uphold the law, he was severely rebuked for his "imputation on the character of American citizens," the Governor adding that as between them and their savage enemies, he would always be in favor of his fellow countrymen. He therefore could not yield his approbation "to any imputations on their intelligence or patriotism."

Fortunately that is not all that there is to the picture. In 1850 the Dominican Joseph Sadoc Alemany became Bishop of Monterey and in 1853 Archbishop of San Francisco, which see he held for over thirty years. But he arrived upon the scene too late to do much for the Indians, though he succeeded in obtaining from the Mexican government part of the interest derived from the forced sale of the missions. Eventually, too, the Hague Tribunal decreed that Mexico disgorge the expropriated Pious Fund. But while all this helped the work of the Catholic Church in California, the fate of the Indians had long been sealed.

The secularization of the missions, and the abuses that inevitably followed, meant the ruin of all that Junípero Serra and his successors had worked for. It must be remembered that this was the part of the Northern continent (with the exception of parts of Mexico) most thickly populated by the natives. In Mexico the lot of the Indians leaves very much to be desired, but at least they have managed to survive; in California they have almost completely disappeared. Only some of the mission churches, the majority in ruins but a few in good condition after having been restored, remain as a memorial to the Padres.

The honor given to Junípero Serra in California is by no means confined to Catholics, for by far the largest amount of historical investigation—working in an almost uniquely rich documentary field—has been carried out by those not of the Faith. Chief among these great scholars must be placed Professor Herbert E. Bolton, who has edited about a dozen large volumes of contemporary histories and diaries. All Californians recognize that Junípero Serra was the true father of their golden land. In his case the prophet has for once received in his own country the full meed of honor due.

The contemporary portrait of Serra and the near-contemporary painting of him receiving Viaticum in church are not very good, but neither are most of the many statues that have more recently been erected to him in California. Probably the best is the one erected by the state of California in the Capitol, Washington, D.C., which is reproduced as the frontispiece of this book. Yet while it catches Serra's spirit, it is not much like him physically, in that it suggests that he was slim and rather tall, whereas he was decidedly undersized and, in his later years, one would gather from the contemporary print, inclined to plumpness. We have here an extraordinary man whose work seems to have failed but which still bears fruit though the missions he founded have long since gone. Whether or not Junípero Serra is ever canonized as a saint, the fame is quite secure of a man who probably never in his whole life gave it a thought. That itself is one means of measuring his greatness.

Index

293

(1)